THE SEVEN SOLDIERS OF VICTORY

ARCHIVES ▾ VOLUME 3

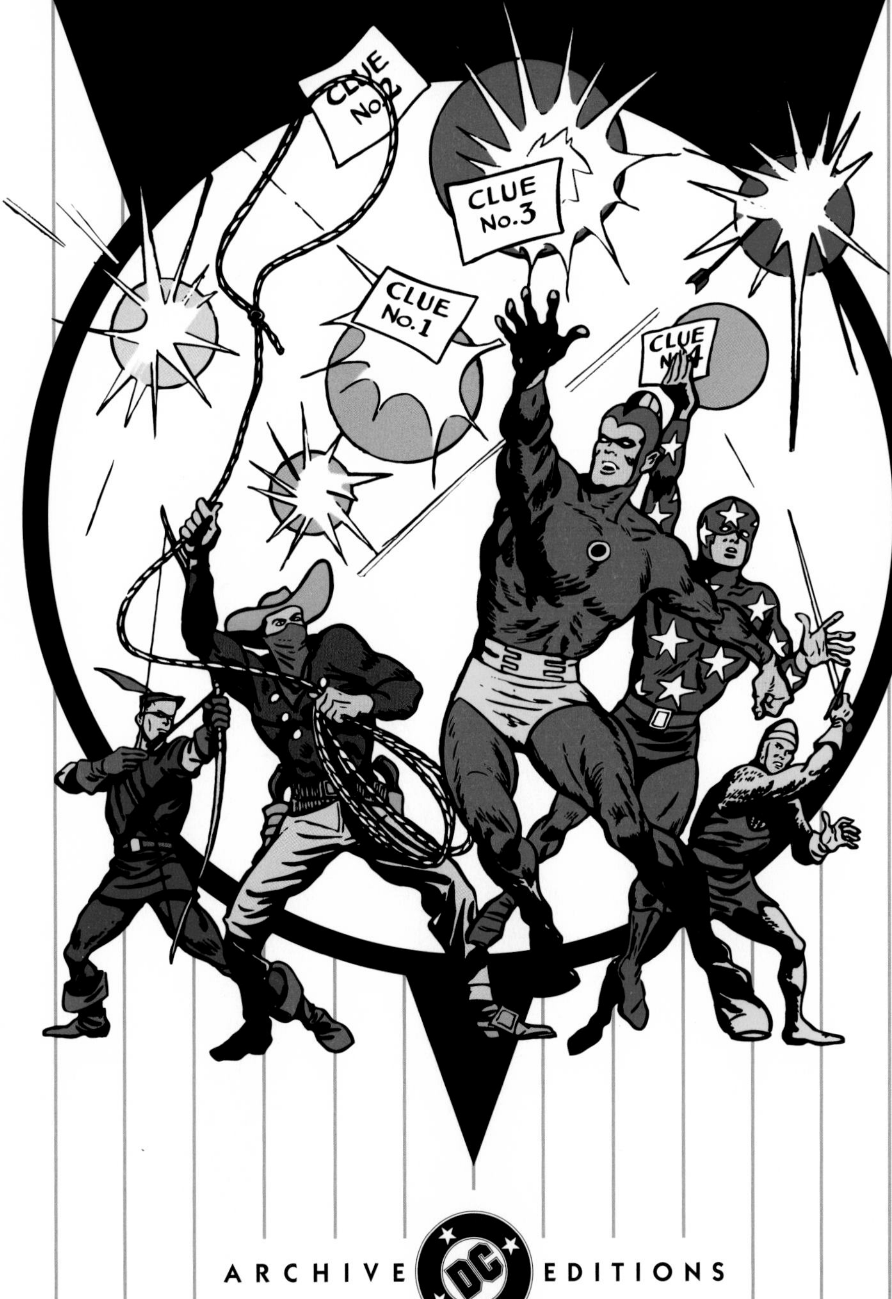
CLUE No.2
CLUE No.3
CLUE No.1
CLUE

ARCHIVE EDITIONS

DC COMICS

MORT WEISINGER
EDITOR-ORIGINAL SERIES

SCOTT NYBAKKEN
EDITOR-COLLECTED EDITION

ROBBIN BROSTERMAN
SENIOR ART DIRECTOR

PAUL LEVITZ
PRESIDENT & PUBLISHER

GEORG BREWER
VP-DESIGN & DC DIRECT CREATIVE

RICHARD BRUNING
SENIOR VP-CREATIVE DIRECTOR

PATRICK CALDON
EXECUTIVE VP-FINANCE &
OPERATIONS

CHRIS CARAMALIS
VP-FINANCE

JOHN CUNNINGHAM
VP-MARKETING

TERRI CUNNINGHAM
VP-MANAGING EDITOR

DAN DIDIO
SENIOR VP-EXECUTIVE EDITOR

ALISON GILL
VP-MANUFACTURING

DAVID HYDE
VP-PUBLICITY

HANK KANALZ
VP-GENERAL MANAGER,
WILDSTORM

JIM LEE
EDITORIAL DIRECTOR-WILDSTORM

PAULA LOWITT
SENIOR VP-BUSINESS &
LEGAL AFFAIRS

MARYELLEN MCLAUGHLIN
VP-ADVERTISING &
CUSTOM PUBLISHING

JOHN NEE
SENIOR VP-BUSINESS
DEVELOPMENT

GREGORY NOVECK
SENIOR VP-CREATIVE AFFAIRS

SUE POHJA
VP-BOOK TRADE SALES

STEVE ROTTERDAM
SENIOR VP-SALES & MARKETING

CHERYL RUBIN
SENIOR VP-BRAND MANAGEMENT

JEFF TROJAN
VP-BUSINESS DEVELOPMENT,
DC DIRECT

BOB WAYNE
VP-SALES

THE SEVEN SOLDIERS OF VICTORY ARCHIVES
VOLUME THREE

ISBN: 978-1-4012-1694-8

PUBLISHED BY DC COMICS.
COVER, FOREWORD AND COMPILATION
COPYRIGHT © 2008 DC COMICS.

ORIGINALLY PUBLISHED IN SINGLE
MAGAZINE FORM IN LEADING COMICS 9-14.
COPYRIGHT 1943, 1944, 1945 DC COMICS.
ALL RIGHTS RESERVED.

THE SEVEN SOLDIERS OF VICTORY AND
ALL RELATED CHARACTERS, THE DISTINCTIVE
LIKENESSES THEREOF AND RELATED ELEMENTS
ARE TRADEMARKS OF DC COMICS. THE STORIES,
CHARACTERS AND INCIDENTS FEATURED IN
THIS PUBLICATION ARE ENTIRELY FICTIONAL.
DC COMICS DOES NOT READ OR ACCEPT
UNSOLICITED SUBMISSIONS OF IDEAS,
STORIES OR ARTWORK.

DC COMICS
1700 BROADWAY
NEW YORK, NY 10019

A WARNER BROS. ENTERTAINMENT COMPANY

PRINTED IN HONG KONG.
FIRST PRINTING.

THE DC ARCHIVE EDITIONS

COVER ILLUSTRATION BY JON SMALL.

BLACK AND WHITE
RECONSTRUCTION BY RICK KEENE.

COLOR RECONSTRUCTION BY JAMISON.

SERIES DESIGN BY ALEX JAY/STUDIO J.

PUBLICATION DESIGN BY TERNARD SOLOMON.

TABLE OF CONTENTS

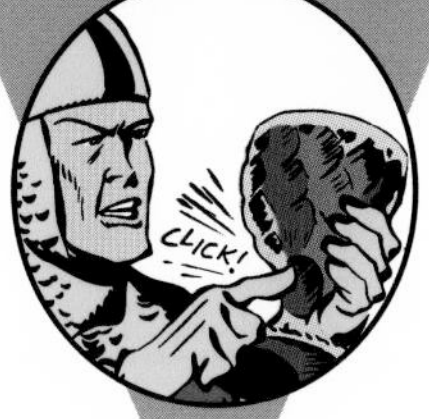
CLICK!

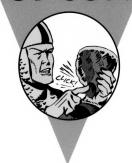

ALL STORIES WRITTEN BY JOE SAMACHSON AND ILLUSTRATED BY ARTURO CAZENEUVE.

TABLE OF CONTENTS

*THESE STORIES WERE ORIGINALLY UNTITLED AND ARE TITLED HERE FOR READER CONVENIENCE.

ASSISTANCE ON CREDITS PROVIDED BY CRAIG DELICH.

DC COMICS STRIVES TO BE AS THOROUGH AS POSSIBLE IN ITS EFFORT TO DETERMINE CREATORS' IDENTITIES FROM ALL AVAILABLE SOURCES. THIS PROCESS IS NOT PERFECT, AND AS A RESULT THERE MAY BE SOME ATTRIBUTIONS ARE THAT ARE INCOMPLETE OR WRONGLY ASSIGNED. PLEASE GO TO WWW.DCCOMICS.COM/ERRATA TO SEE A PERMANENT ARCHIVE OF CORRECTIONS FOR DC COMICS' COLLECTED EDITIONS.

THE COMICS REPRINTED IN THIS VOLUME WERE PRODUCED IN A TIME WHEN RACISM PLAYED A LARGER ROLE IN SOCIETY AND POPULAR CULTURE, BOTH CONSCIOUSLY AND UNCONSCIOUSLY. THEY ARE REPRINTED HERE WITHOUT ALTERATION FOR HISTORICAL ACCURACY.

FOREWORD

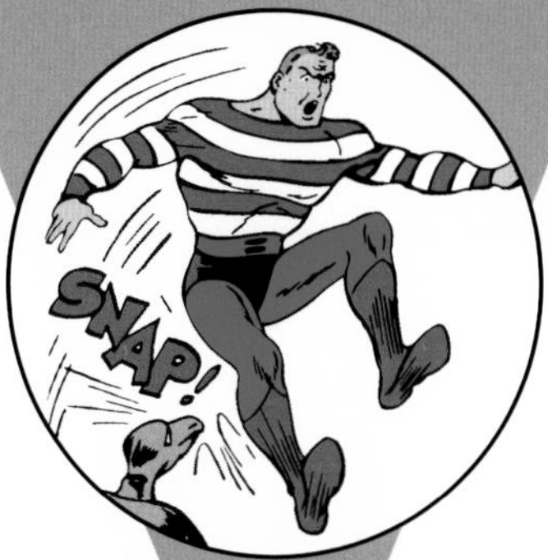
SNAP!

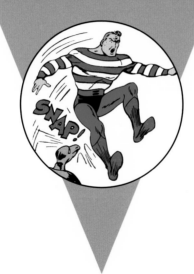

As a child of the 1940s — born in late 1940, in fact — I first learned about the Seven Soldiers of Victory around the end of that decade. By then they were already mere specks in the dustbin of comics history, and doomed, it seemed, always to remain so.

SUPERMAN #19 was my portal to the Seven Soldiers. One day, at my grandparents' farmhouse in Old Appleton, Missouri, I stumbled across an old comic book. I was ten years old at the most, and the comic was dated Nov.-Dec. 1942, so it was at least six years old. A real chunk of history — clearly thicker at 68 pages (counting covers) than the 52-pagers that I assumed would forever be the standard size of comics.

SUPERMAN #19 was a real prize, which my grandparents let me keep. Two of the four Superman stories inside were true classics: one had Clark and Lois watching a Superman movie cartoon (I had no idea, of course, such things had ever truly existed), and another featured villains from newspaper comic strips coming to life to battle the Man of Tomorrow (huh? in my day, they called him the Man of Steel!).

But even *more* thrilling to me were the *house ads* in the issue — up to eight covers shown on a single page. I beheld, wide-eyed, the cover to ALL STAR COMICS #13, with the Justice Society of America (including a couple of members I'd never heard of before) being "Shanghaied into Space." It was the earliest JSA picture I would see until late 1960. From time to time I'd squint at that smallish cover reproduction and try to imagine the wonders that my favorite heroes had found in the far reaches of the cosmos during 1942.

And then there was that ad for LEADING COMICS #4!

This was, if anything, even more of a mind-blower. At age ten or less, I had no idea there'd ever even *been* another DC super-hero group, let alone that it had contained several characters whose adventures I could still follow in current comics — Green Arrow & Speedy, the Shining Knight, Vigilante, and the Star-Spangled Kid & Stripesy. The only guy I didn't recognize was the one in the red-and-yellow costume. The line above the comic's title said "Five Favorite Features!" (though don't look for that phrase on the cover as reproduced in Vol. 2 of this series; somehow it got dropped) — while the smaller blurb about the story itself called them "The Law's Legionnaires." Boy, was that a sinister cover, with that fierce-looking (green!) face peering out of a giant glass tube at our heroes! It looked pretty well-drawn, too.

Again, it wasn't until the turn of 1961 that I learned that the "official" name of that group of heroes was "The Seven Soldiers of Victory" — although the term

"Law's Legionnaires" was used almost as often to describe them — or that that wonderful cover had been drawn by Mort Meskin, whose work I had admired on the Black Terror and other features.

In the 1960s, and for years, nay, decades after, it was an article of faith to all of us dyed-in-the-wool 1940s fans of the fabled JSA that DC's competing group over in LEADING COMICS couldn't hold a costumed candle to the colorful companions who held court in ALL STAR COMICS every two months. The evidence was plain and irrefutable:

1) The first 30-plus JSA stories were scripted by Gardner Fox (who had co-created the Flash, Hawkman, Dr. Fate and possibly Sandman) and edited by Sheldon Mayer (whom we knew as the writer/artist of the revered SCRIBBLY and SUGAR AND SPIKE), and the rest of the run was scribed by Robert Kanigher and John Broome. Who could compete with talent like that?

2) ALL STAR's artists included, among other capable journeymen, the likes of Joe Simon and Jack Kirby, Joe Kubert, Sheldon Moldoff, Jack Burnley, Bernard Baily, Alex Toth, Carmine Infantino, Lee Elias, Irwin Hasen, Arthur Peddy, Frank Giacoia, H.G. Peter — a reasonably impressive list, utilizing many of DC's best. So who was left over to scribble the Soldiers?

3) Those JSA stories: two Brain Wave battles; two *Injustice Societies*; two powerful morality plays (albeit with a Disney-derived fairy); a tale about handicapped people I remember being mentioned in the 1950 *World Book Encyclopedia*; another about juvenile delinquency, done at governmental request; Superman and Batman as guest-stars; John Broome's imaginative theory of "time ledges"; "The Man Who Conquered the Solar System," with its echoes of Burroughs and Lovecraft —

what could LEADING put up against *that*?

4) The Seven Soldiers didn't even sport a single member — except the Shining Knight's winged horse — with anything resembling super-powers.

5) ALL STAR started earlier (1940 as opposed to 1941) and lasted longer (1951 vs. 1944), and was published bimonthly except during the paper-deprived World War II years, while the Soldiers came out quarterly and didn't last long enough to see *how* they'd have fared postwar. The numbers told the tale: 55 JSA stories, 14 Soldier stories.

6) The LEADING team never even had their own title logo — nor, for that matter, could they ever quite decide if their group's name was "The Seven Soldiers of Victory" or "The Law's Legionnaires" — or maybe even just "Five Favorite Features," or "The Leading Heroes," as displayed on #9 in this volume.

Nope, ALL STAR COMICS and the JSA clearly had it all over LEADING COMICS and the Seven Soldiers of Victory — all eight of them!

This Rodney Dangerfield-esque, "I don't get no respect" attitude of Golden Age fans began, perhaps, with Richard Lupoff's cleverly titled article "The Several Soldiers of Victory" in the early '60s science fiction/comics fanzine *Xero* — and continued through my own magazine *Alter Ego* and the rest of Golden Age fandom.

But guess what?

Turns out we were wrong.

When we finally took a closer, unjaundiced look, we realized that the Soldiers had a lot more going for them than we'd long given them credit for.

Writers? Original scripter Mort Weisinger was the co-creator of Aquaman, Green Arrow, Johnny Quick, and Vigilante — all four of which would outlast any JSAer except for Wonder Woman, Superman and Batman. A few chapters were written by Jerry Siegel (co-creator of Superman and the Spectre) and by Bill Finger (co-creator of Batman and Green Lantern), and Joe Samachson had a reasonably imposing set of credits as well.

Art? Covers and some chapters were drawn in the early days by Mort Meskin, a man who truly deserves that overused title "Golden Age great." Was any ALL STAR cover really better than the one he drew for LEADING #4? Legendary Superman cover artist Fred Ray did one or two as well, and Jon Small's cover for #14 was a moody masterpiece. As for interior artists, Creig Flessel had made a name for himself drawing great early DC covers and would go on to succeed in the highly competitive field of advertising; Jack Lehti would eventually draw his own newspaper comic strip, *Tales of the Great Book*, for years; and George Papp was the artistic originator of Green Arrow and would later help make SUPERBOY a top seller.

And the stories? At least the Soldiers had an origin (and a fairly good one at that), which, until 1977, was more than the JSA ever had. What's more, that origin boasted a league of super-villains, half a dozen years before the Justice Society faced one. LEADING #3 had a heavy named Dr. Doome, a name that's proven to have a bit of resonance down through the decades. In #6, the heroes actually fought each other — and they weren't faking it; this let kids root for their favorite. (The JSAers never even argued. Never.) The eighth issue, like the third, made good use of time travel. And in #10, reprinted herein, the heroes get split into separate pairs by a shipwreck, resulting in some inventive combinations, something that wouldn't happen to the JSA until their stories' page count shrank in 1948 and forced them to double up. Even in its final Seven Soldiers issue, LEADING introduced readers to such towering characters of classical fiction as Long John Silver

(Stevenson), Falstaff (Shakespeare), Uriah Heep (Dickens) and the Lilliputians from Swift's *Gulliver's Travels*.

Yeah, we finally had to admit it: the Seven Soldiers may not have had the mass appeal and longevity of what baseball fans refer to as the "senior circuit," but they were definitely a lot more than just colorful also-rans. Hey, they outlasted every other ongoing super-hero group *except* the JSA and the Marvel Family (the latter was basically the same character cloned into a trio, anyway) — though come to think of it, there *were* almost no other super-groups in the 1940s.

From here on, in any case, we'll let the stories speak for themselves — after we toss in a final quartet of not-quite-random facts that I think should be preserved in the Archives:

1) Although the foreword in the first volume of this series lovingly recounts the origin of the Crimson Avenger, that hero never actually had one in the Golden Age itself. The tale referred to was actually scripted in the 1980s by my wife Dann and myself and drawn by Gene Colan for an issue of SECRET ORIGINS.

2) That same foreword erroneously adds that the 20th century name of the Shining Knight was Justin Arthur. In point of fact, amazingly, Sir Justin never *had* a last name in any Golden Age comics story; "Justin Arthur" was first used in ALL-STAR SQUADRON, the 1980s comic I developed for DC. ("Justin Arthur" = "just an author" — get it?)

3) While we'll probably never know for sure, it seems likely that that unwieldy moniker "The Seven Soldiers of Victory" was inspired by a once-popular novel titled *The Seven Champions of Christendom*, written around the end of the 16th century by one Richard Johnson and still in print today. It related the exploits of a septet of sainted knights, each from a different nation: St. George of England, St. Denis of

France, St. Patrick of Ireland, etc., fighting both solo and as a group against wizards and infidels. (This connection was first noted by a comics fan named Jeff Fruen in 1985.)

4) Finally, a 15th issue of LEADING COMICS starring the Seven Soldiers was in preparation in 1944-45 but was never published. Joe Samachson's script for this issue survived, however, and was found thirty years after it had been written (no art from it has ever turned up, and chances are the Seven Soldiers feature was canceled before the tale was drawn). In 1975 it was belatedly illustrated by such talents as Dick Dillin, Howard Chaykin, Mike Grell, Lee Elias and José Luis García-López in a half-dozen issues of ADVENTURE COMICS.

Although the art for the modern version is not included in this volume, as a special bonus feature, Samachson's complete script *is*. Read it — savor it — and perhaps you'll be able to picture it in your mind, drawn as it might have appeared in print had LEADING not been hijacked in 1945 by a bunch of funny-animal types. DC Comics should be commended for including it in this edition so that the saga of the Seven Soldiers is complete — as complete as the epic of the Justice Society is in the ALL STAR ARCHIVES.

The Seven Soldiers of Victory always deserved it.

It just took some of us a while to realize it.

— **Roy Thomas**
2008

Roy Thomas has written and often edited comics, primarily for DC and Marvel, since 1965. At DC in the early 1980s he conceived the World War II-era ALL-STAR SQUADRON, a super-hero group large enough to encompass both the JSA and the Seven Soldiers — with enough room left over for a bunch of additional heroes who'd never previously been "pledged" to any particular four-color fraternity. He currently edits the comics history magazine Alter Ego *and writes two or three new comic books a month as well.*

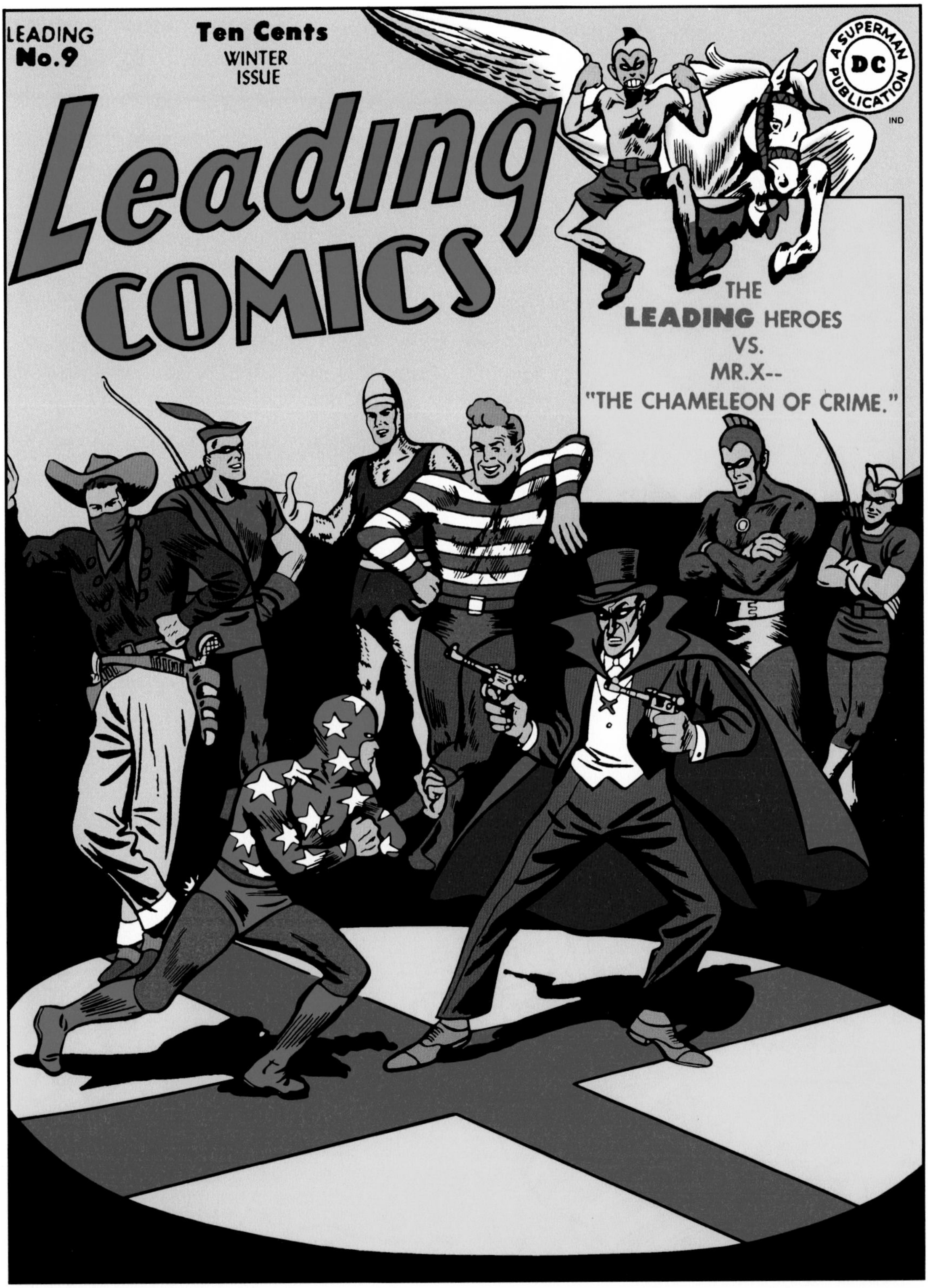
LEADING No.9
Ten Cents
WINTER ISSUE
Leading COMICS
A SUPERMAN PUBLICATION DC
IND
THE LEADING HEROES VS. MR.X-- "THE CHAMELEON OF CRIME."

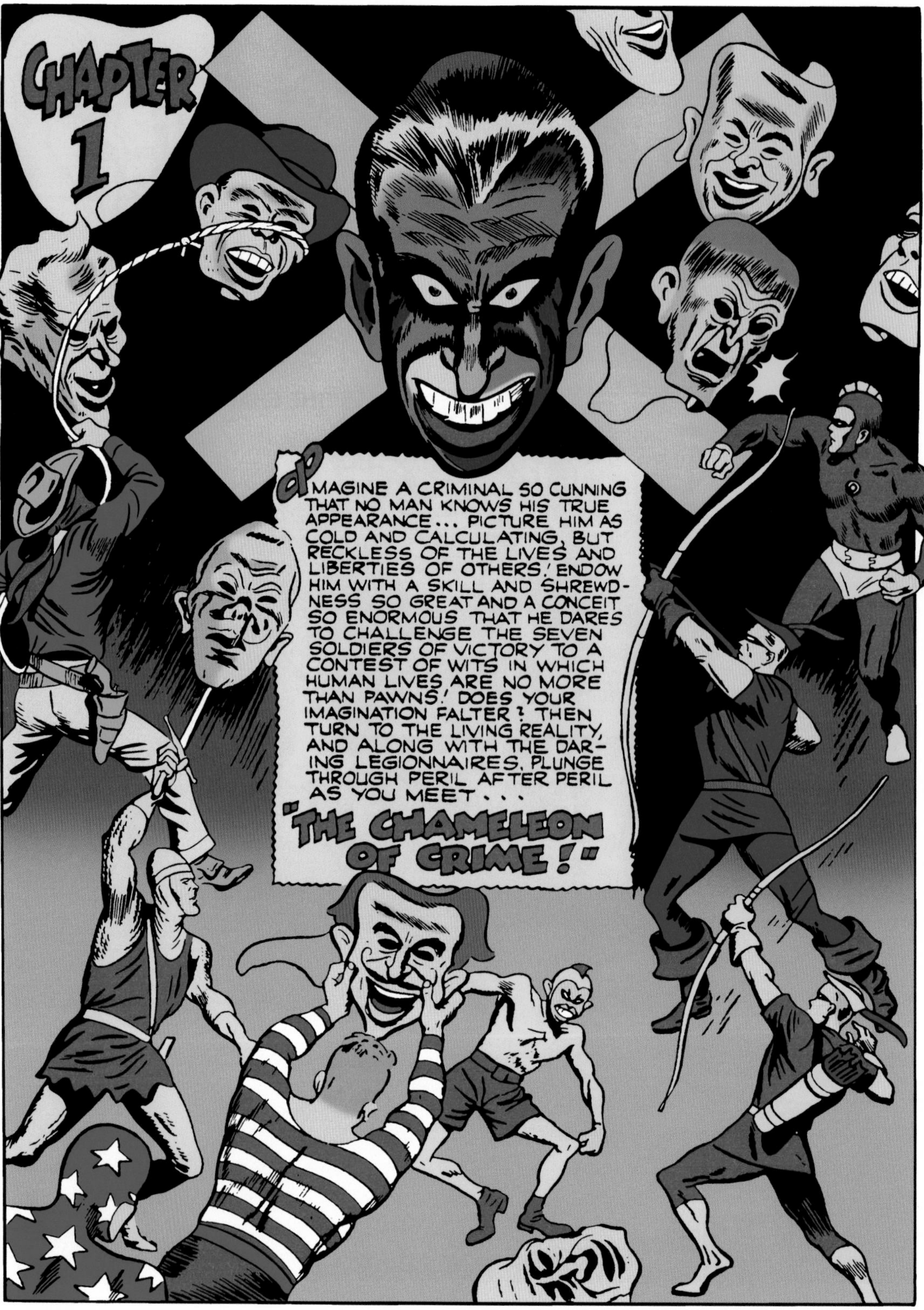
CHAPTER 1
IMAGINE A CRIMINAL SO CUNNING THAT NO MAN KNOWS HIS TRUE APPEARANCE... PICTURE HIM AS COLD AND CALCULATING, BUT RECKLESS OF THE LIVES AND LIBERTIES OF OTHERS! ENDOW HIM WITH A SKILL AND SHREWDNESS SO GREAT AND A CONCEIT SO ENORMOUS THAT HE DARES TO CHALLENGE THE SEVEN SOLDIERS OF VICTORY TO A CONTEST OF WITS IN WHICH HUMAN LIVES ARE NO MORE THAN PAWNS! DOES YOUR IMAGINATION FALTER? THEN TURN TO THE LIVING REALITY, AND ALONG WITH THE DARING LEGIONNAIRES, PLUNGE THROUGH PERIL AFTER PERIL AS YOU MEET . . .
"THE CHAMELEON OF CRIME!"

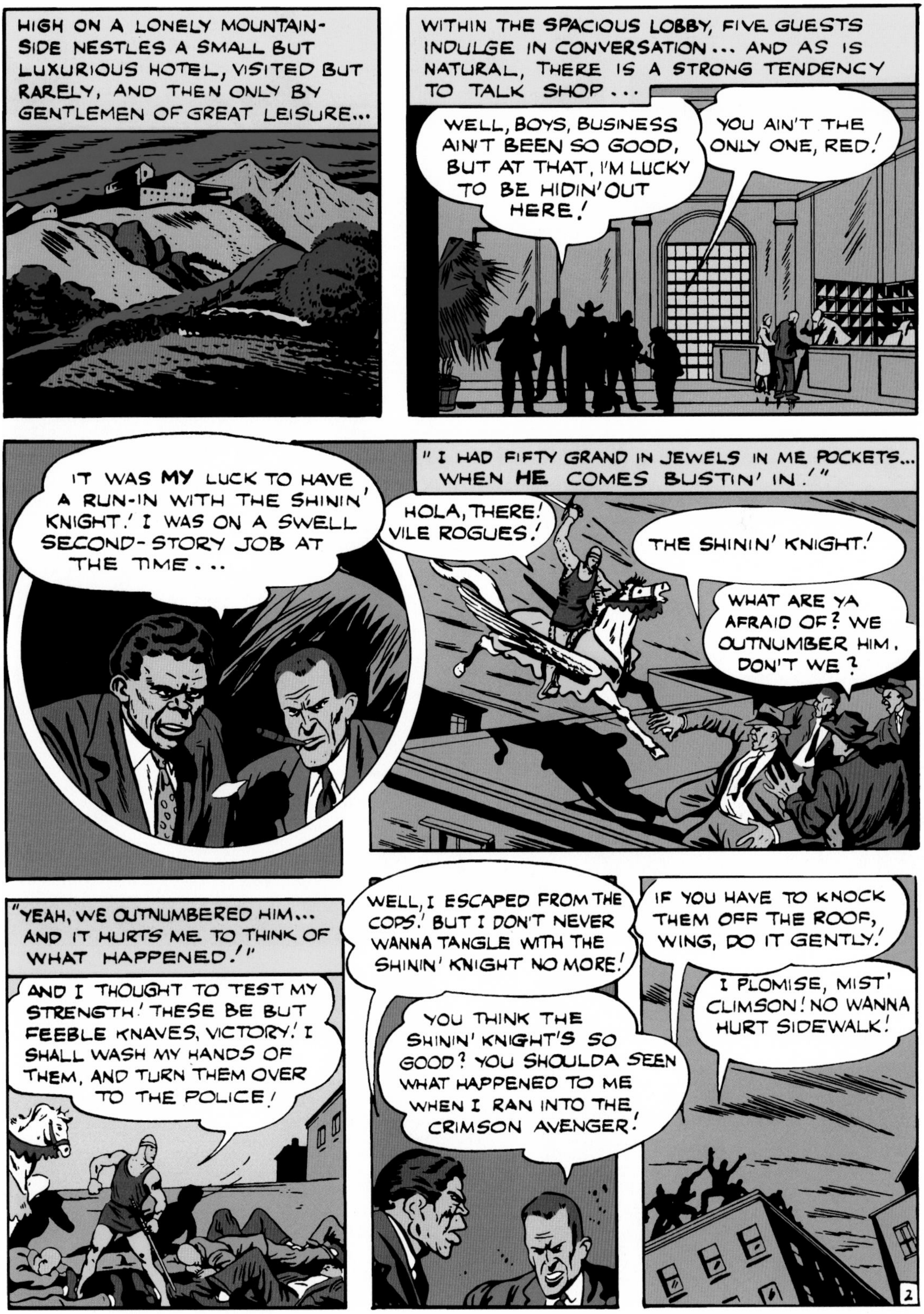
HIGH ON A LONELY MOUNTAIN-SIDE NESTLES A SMALL BUT LUXURIOUS HOTEL, VISITED BUT RARELY, AND THEN ONLY BY GENTLEMEN OF GREAT LEISURE...
WITHIN THE SPACIOUS LOBBY, FIVE GUESTS INDULGE IN CONVERSATION... AND AS IS NATURAL, THERE IS A STRONG TENDENCY TO TALK SHOP...
WELL, BOYS, BUSINESS AIN'T BEEN SO GOOD, BUT AT THAT, I'M LUCKY TO BE HIDIN' OUT HERE!
YOU AIN'T THE ONLY ONE, RED!
IT WAS MY LUCK TO HAVE A RUN-IN WITH THE SHININ' KNIGHT! I WAS ON A SWELL SECOND-STORY JOB AT THE TIME...
"I HAD FIFTY GRAND IN JEWELS IN ME POCKETS... WHEN HE COMES BUSTIN' IN!"
HOLA, THERE! VILE ROGUES!
THE SHININ' KNIGHT!
WHAT ARE YA AFRAID OF? WE OUTNUMBER HIM, DON'T WE?
"YEAH, WE OUTNUMBERED HIM... AND IT HURTS ME TO THINK OF WHAT HAPPENED!"
AND I THOUGHT TO TEST MY STRENGTH! THESE BE BUT FEEBLE KNAVES, VICTORY! I SHALL WASH MY HANDS OF THEM, AND TURN THEM OVER TO THE POLICE!
WELL, I ESCAPED FROM THE COPS! BUT I DON'T NEVER WANNA TANGLE WITH THE SHININ' KNIGHT NO MORE!
YOU THINK THE SHININ' KNIGHT'S SO GOOD? YOU SHOULDA SEEN WHAT HAPPENED TO ME WHEN I RAN INTO THE CRIMSON AVENGER!
IF YOU HAVE TO KNOCK THEM OFF THE ROOF, WING, DO IT GENTLY!
I PLOMISE, MIST' CLIMSON! NO WANNA HURT SIDEWALK!
2

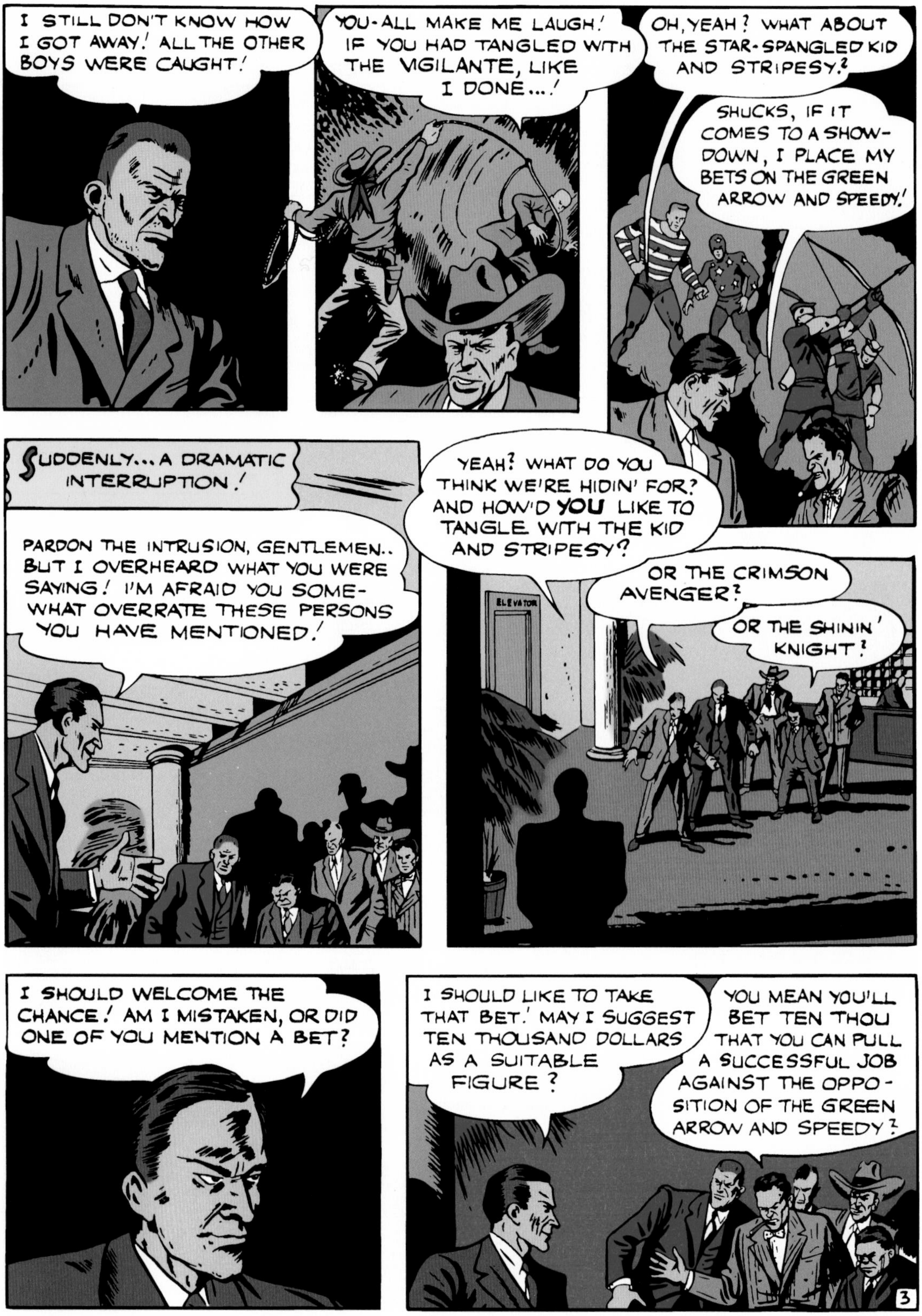
I STILL DON'T KNOW HOW I GOT AWAY! ALL THE OTHER BOYS WERE CAUGHT!
YOU-ALL MAKE ME LAUGH! IF YOU HAD TANGLED WITH THE VIGILANTE, LIKE I DONE...!
OH, YEAH? WHAT ABOUT THE STAR-SPANGLED KID AND STRIPESY?
SHUCKS, IF IT COMES TO A SHOW-DOWN, I PLACE MY BETS ON THE GREEN ARROW AND SPEEDY!
SUDDENLY... A DRAMATIC INTERRUPTION!
PARDON THE INTRUSION, GENTLEMEN.. BUT I OVERHEARD WHAT YOU WERE SAYING! I'M AFRAID YOU SOMEWHAT OVERRATE THESE PERSONS YOU HAVE MENTIONED!
YEAH? WHAT DO YOU THINK WE'RE HIDIN' FOR? AND HOW'D YOU LIKE TO TANGLE WITH THE KID AND STRIPESY?
OR THE CRIMSON AVENGER?
OR THE SHININ' KNIGHT?
ELEVATOR
I SHOULD WELCOME THE CHANCE! AM I MISTAKEN, OR DID ONE OF YOU MENTION A BET?
I SHOULD LIKE TO TAKE THAT BET! MAY I SUGGEST TEN THOUSAND DOLLARS AS A SUITABLE FIGURE?
YOU MEAN YOU'LL BET TEN THOU THAT YOU CAN PULL A SUCCESSFUL JOB AGAINST THE OPPOSITION OF THE GREEN ARROW AND SPEEDY?
3

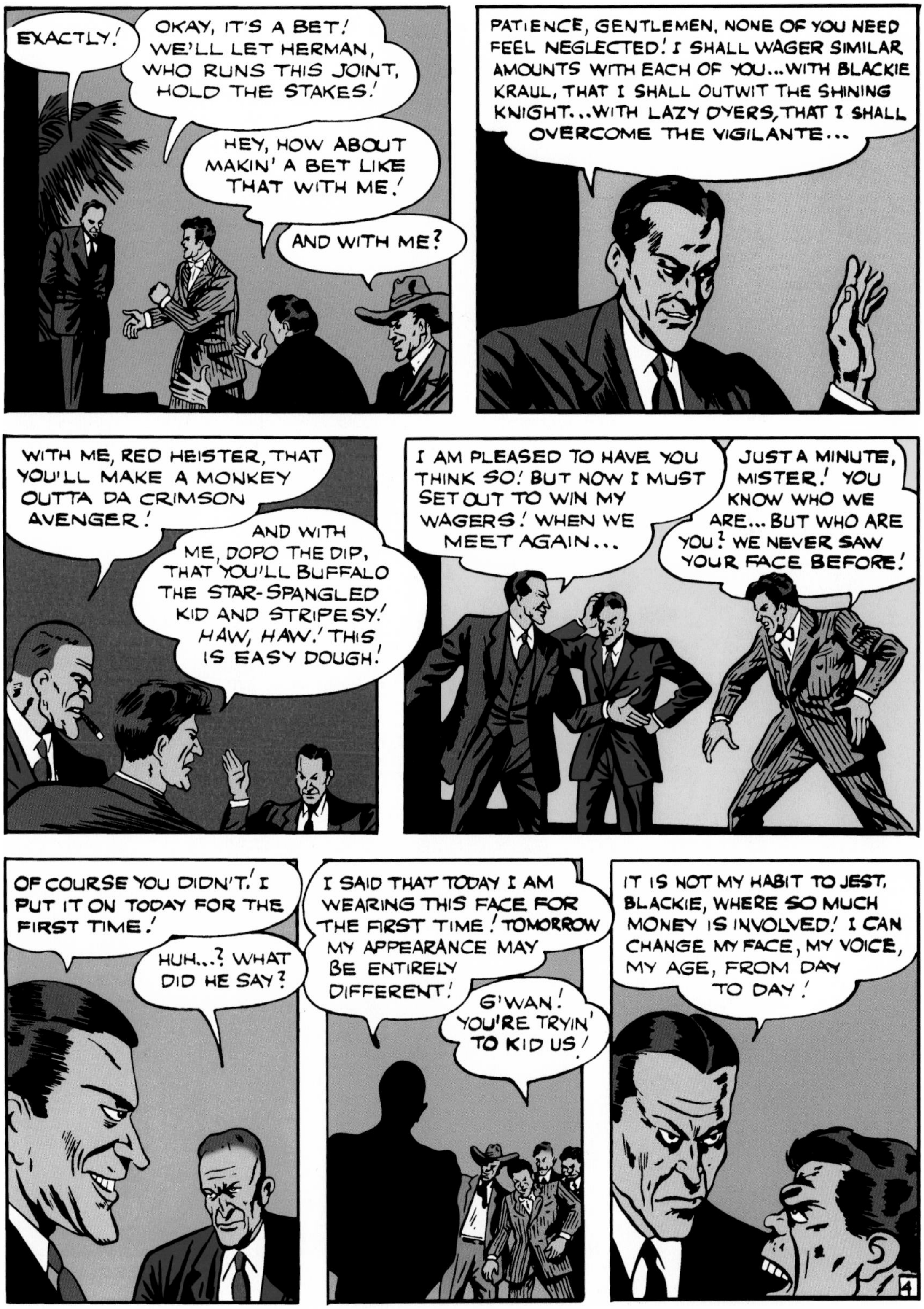
EXACTLY!
OKAY, IT'S A BET! WE'LL LET HERMAN, WHO RUNS THIS JOINT, HOLD THE STAKES!
HEY, HOW ABOUT MAKIN' A BET LIKE THAT WITH ME!
AND WITH ME?
PATIENCE, GENTLEMEN. NONE OF YOU NEED FEEL NEGLECTED! I SHALL WAGER SIMILAR AMOUNTS WITH EACH OF YOU...WITH BLACKIE KRAUL, THAT I SHALL OUTWIT THE SHINING KNIGHT...WITH LAZY DYERS, THAT I SHALL OVERCOME THE VIGILANTE...
WITH ME, RED HEISTER, THAT YOU'LL MAKE A MONKEY OUTTA DA CRIMSON AVENGER!
AND WITH ME, DOPO THE DIP, THAT YOU'LL BUFFALO THE STAR-SPANGLED KID AND STRIPESY! HAW, HAW! THIS IS EASY DOUGH!
I AM PLEASED TO HAVE YOU THINK SO! BUT NOW I MUST SET OUT TO WIN MY WAGERS! WHEN WE MEET AGAIN...
JUST A MINUTE, MISTER! YOU KNOW WHO WE ARE... BUT WHO ARE YOU? WE NEVER SAW YOUR FACE BEFORE!
OF COURSE YOU DIDN'T! I PUT IT ON TODAY FOR THE FIRST TIME!
HUH...? WHAT DID HE SAY?
I SAID THAT TODAY I AM WEARING THIS FACE FOR THE FIRST TIME! TOMORROW MY APPEARANCE MAY BE ENTIRELY DIFFERENT!
G'WAN! YOU'RE TRYIN' TO KID US!
IT IS NOT MY HABIT TO JEST, BLACKIE, WHERE SO MUCH MONEY IS INVOLVED! I CAN CHANGE MY FACE, MY VOICE, MY AGE, FROM DAY TO DAY!
4

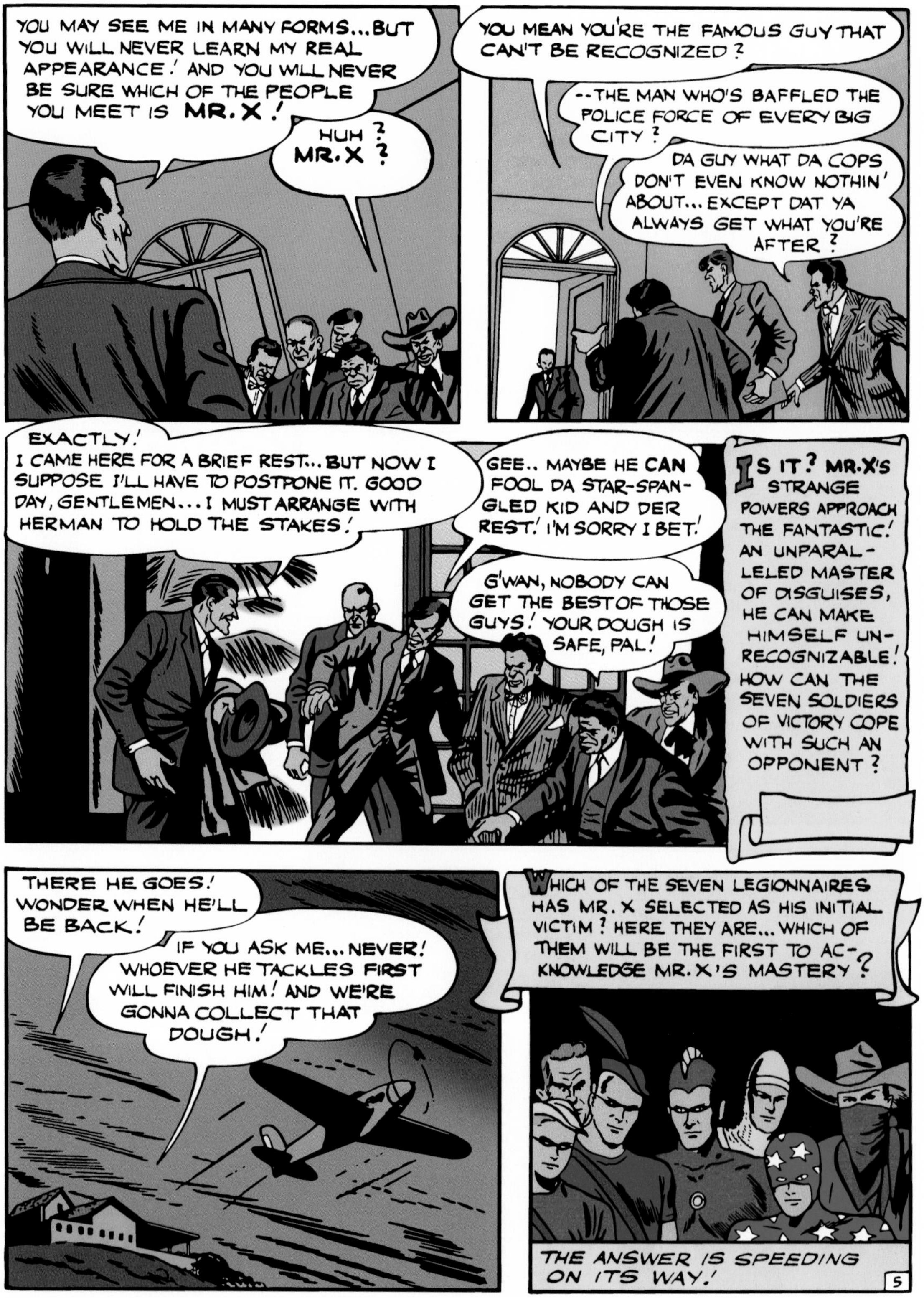
YOU MAY SEE ME IN MANY FORMS... BUT YOU WILL NEVER LEARN MY REAL APPEARANCE! AND YOU WILL NEVER BE SURE WHICH OF THE PEOPLE YOU MEET IS MR. X!
HUH? MR. X?
YOU MEAN YOU'RE THE FAMOUS GUY THAT CAN'T BE RECOGNIZED?
--THE MAN WHO'S BAFFLED THE POLICE FORCE OF EVERY BIG CITY?
DA GUY WHAT DA COPS DON'T EVEN KNOW NOTHIN' ABOUT... EXCEPT DAT YA ALWAYS GET WHAT YOU'RE AFTER?
EXACTLY! I CAME HERE FOR A BRIEF REST... BUT NOW I SUPPOSE I'LL HAVE TO POSTPONE IT. GOOD DAY, GENTLEMEN... I MUST ARRANGE WITH HERMAN TO HOLD THE STAKES!
GEE.. MAYBE HE CAN FOOL DA STAR-SPANGLED KID AND DER REST! I'M SORRY I BET!
G'WAN, NOBODY CAN GET THE BEST OF THOSE GUYS! YOUR DOUGH IS SAFE, PAL!
IS IT? MR. X'S STRANGE POWERS APPROACH THE FANTASTIC! AN UNPARALLELED MASTER OF DISGUISES, HE CAN MAKE HIMSELF UNRECOGNIZABLE! HOW CAN THE SEVEN SOLDIERS OF VICTORY COPE WITH SUCH AN OPPONENT?
THERE HE GOES! WONDER WHEN HE'LL BE BACK!
IF YOU ASK ME... NEVER! WHOEVER HE TACKLES FIRST WILL FINISH HIM! AND WE'RE GONNA COLLECT THAT DOUGH!
WHICH OF THE SEVEN LEGIONNAIRES HAS MR. X SELECTED AS HIS INITIAL VICTIM? HERE THEY ARE... WHICH OF THEM WILL BE THE FIRST TO ACKNOWLEDGE MR. X'S MASTERY?
THE ANSWER IS SPEEDING ON ITS WAY!
5

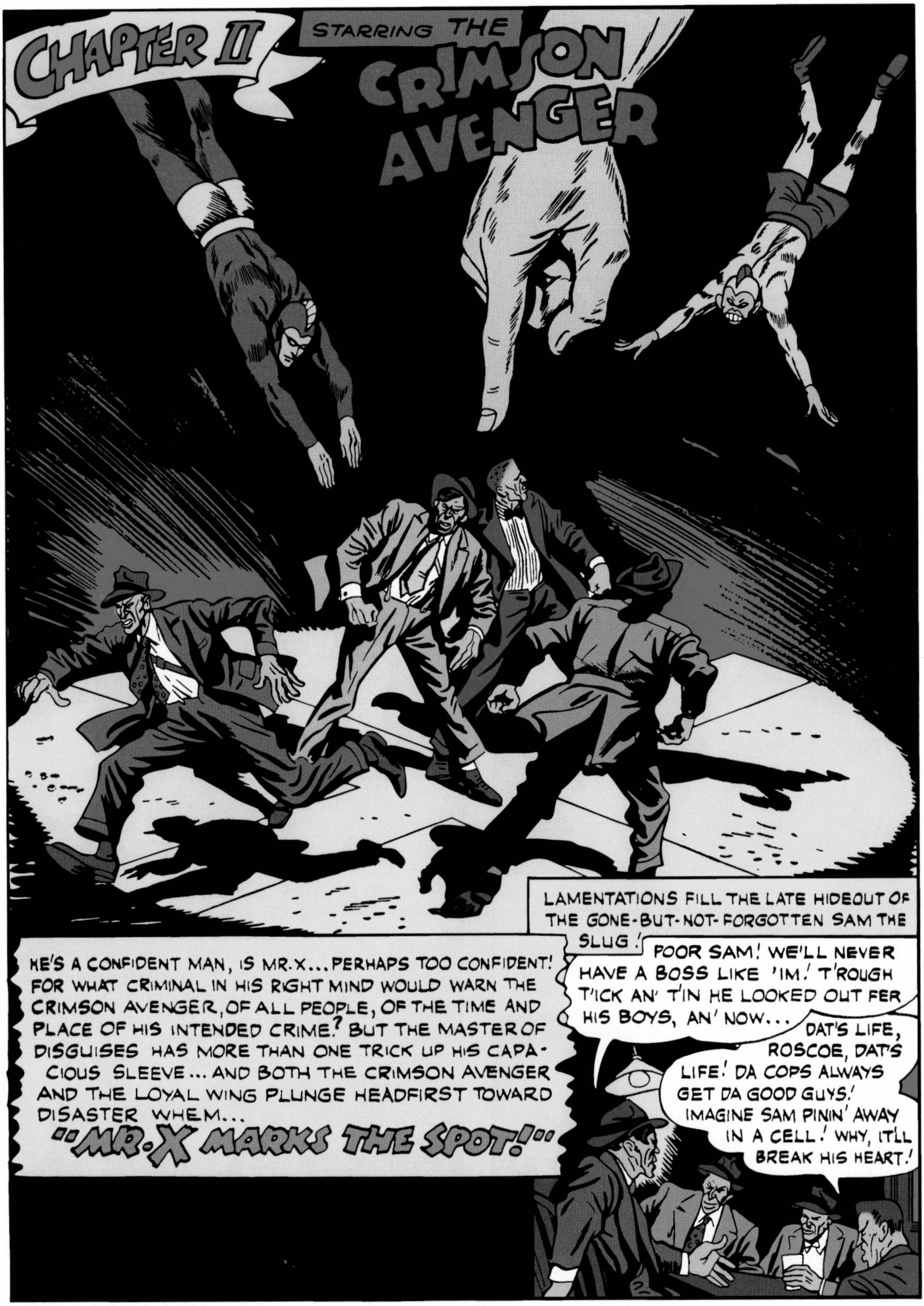
CHAPTER II
STARRING THE
CRIMSON AVENGER
LAMENTATIONS FILL THE LATE HIDEOUT OF THE GONE-BUT-NOT-FORGOTTEN SAM THE SLUG!
HE'S A CONFIDENT MAN, IS MR. X... PERHAPS TOO CONFIDENT! FOR WHAT CRIMINAL IN HIS RIGHT MIND WOULD WARN THE CRIMSON AVENGER, OF ALL PEOPLE, OF THE TIME AND PLACE OF HIS INTENDED CRIME? BUT THE MASTER OF DISGUISES HAS MORE THAN ONE TRICK UP HIS CAPACIOUS SLEEVE... AND BOTH THE CRIMSON AVENGER AND THE LOYAL WING PLUNGE HEADFIRST TOWARD DISASTER WHEM...
"MR. X MARKS THE SPOT!"
POOR SAM! WE'LL NEVER HAVE A BOSS LIKE 'IM! T'ROUGH T'ICK AN' T'IN HE LOOKED OUT FER HIS BOYS, AN' NOW...
DAT'S LIFE, ROSCOE, DAT'S LIFE! DA COPS ALWAYS GET DA GOOD GUYS! IMAGINE SAM PININ' AWAY IN A CELL! WHY, IT'LL BREAK HIS HEART!

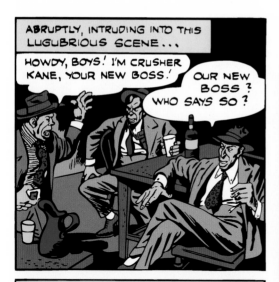

ABRUPTLY, INTRUDING INTO THIS LUGUBRIOUS SCENE...

HOWDY, BOYS! I'M CRUSHER KANE, YOUR NEW BOSS!

OUR NEW BOSS? WHO SAYS SO?

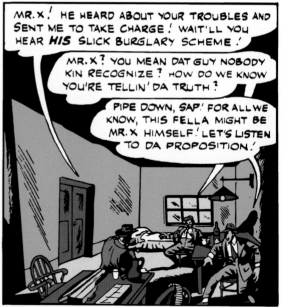

MR. X! HE HEARD ABOUT YOUR TROUBLES AND SENT ME TO TAKE CHARGE! WAIT'LL YOU HEAR *HIS* SLICK BURGLARY SCHEME!

MR. X? YOU MEAN DAT GUY NOBODY KIN RECOGNIZE? HOW DO WE KNOW YOU'RE TELLIN' DA TRUTH?

PIPE DOWN, SAP! FOR ALL WE KNOW, THIS FELLA MIGHT BE MR. X HIMSELF! LET'S LISTEN TO DA PROPOSITION!

MR. X'S SCHEME RECEIVES CAREFUL ATTEN-TION... AND SOON THE IRREPLACEABLE SAM THE LUG HAS BEEN REPLACED!

CRUSHER, ER...TELL ME...WHAT DOES DIS MR. X REALLY LOOK LIKE?

NOBODY KNOWS, PAL... KEEP YOUR MIND ON BUSINESS, AND DON'T ASK QUESTIONS!

HUH, WHAT'S THIS?

JUST AN AD FOR JOE'S JOINT! T'ROW IT AWAY, BOSS...YOUR TIME'S TOO VALUABLE TO WASTE!

JOE'S JOINT

BUT AS AN IMPATIENT HAND IS ABOUT TO FLIP THE CARD INTO THE STREET, A QUICK GLANCE SCANS THE MESSAGE... AND TWO CRIMINALS STAND PETRIFIED!

MR. X CORDIALLY INVITES THE CRIMSON AVENGER AND WING TO BE PRESENT AT A CRIME AT PAUL'S PAWNSHOP AT TWELVE MIDNIGHT. THE POLICE ARE REQUESTED TO ABSENT THEMSELVES.

DA NOIVE OF THIS GUY SQUEALIN' ON DA VERY T'ING WE'RE GONNA DO!

HOLD IT, ROSCOE... HE DON'T KNOW NOTHIN' ABOUT IT. REMEMBER, ONLY ONE GUY COULD GIVE EVERY-THING AWAY... MR. X HIMSELF! NOBODY ELSE KNOWS OUR PLANS! STOP WORRYIN' AN' COME ON!

2

WILL THE INSOLENT INVITATION GET INTO THE HANDS OF ITS INTENDED RECIPIENT?.. A MOMENT LATER, ANOTHER PASSERBY RECEIVES THE SUMMONS TO THE SCENE OF CRIME... NONE OTHER THAN LEE TRAVIS, THE CRIMSON AVENGER HIMSELF!

WHAT'S THIS...? AN INVITATION TO MEET THE FAMOUS MR.X? SOUNDS INCREDIBLE! I'D BETTER SPEAK TO THE POLICE ABOUT IT!

LATER, AFTER A TRANSFORMATION TO THE SCARLET SCOURGE OF CRIME...

YES, AVENGER, WE'VE HEARD OF MR.X TOO, BUT WE THINK HE'S OVERRATED! AND THIS WHOLE BUSINESS SEEMS TO US LIKE A HOAX! YOU'VE QUESTIONED THE SANDWICH MAN...

I HAVE, AND HIS DESCRIPTION OF THE MAN WHO PAID HIM TO PASS OUT THESE CARDS IS VERY VAGUE!

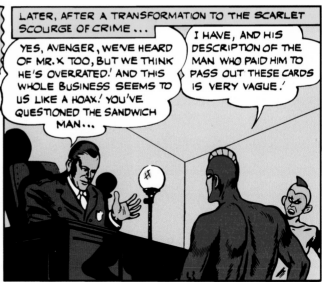

WELL, IF MR.X DOES SHOW UP, YOU'RE CAPABLE OF DEALING WITH HIM! WE'LL LEAVE IT ALL TO YOU!

YOU BET... POLICE NOT INVITED... NOT POLITE TO GO WHERE NOT WANTED!

LET'S GO, WING! IT'S GETTING LATE!

THUS, AS THE HOUR OF MIDNIGHT DRAWS NEAR...

ALL QUIET, MIST' CLIMSON!

DON'T BE IMPATIENT, WING! OUR INVITATION IS FOR MIDNIGHT!

PAUL'S PAWNSHOP

THE MINUTES TICK SLOWLY BY, AND THEN...

OKAY, MIST'CLIMSON, HERE IS MIDNIGHT... AND STILL NOTHING DOING!

GIVE MR.X A CHANCE, WING... A MAN HAS A RIGHT TO BE A FEW MINUTES LATE!

BOOM BOOM

BUT TIME PASSES, AND...

JOKE ON US, MIST' CLIMSON! MIST'X NOT COMING!

I'M SURE WE WEREN'T LURED DOWN HERE AS A JOKE, WING! FOR SOME REASON, MR.X WANTED OUR PRESENCE HERE!

MAYBE SO HE BE SAFE TO PULL JOB SOMEWHERE ELSE!

NO, LOOK! THOSE PIGEONS!

3

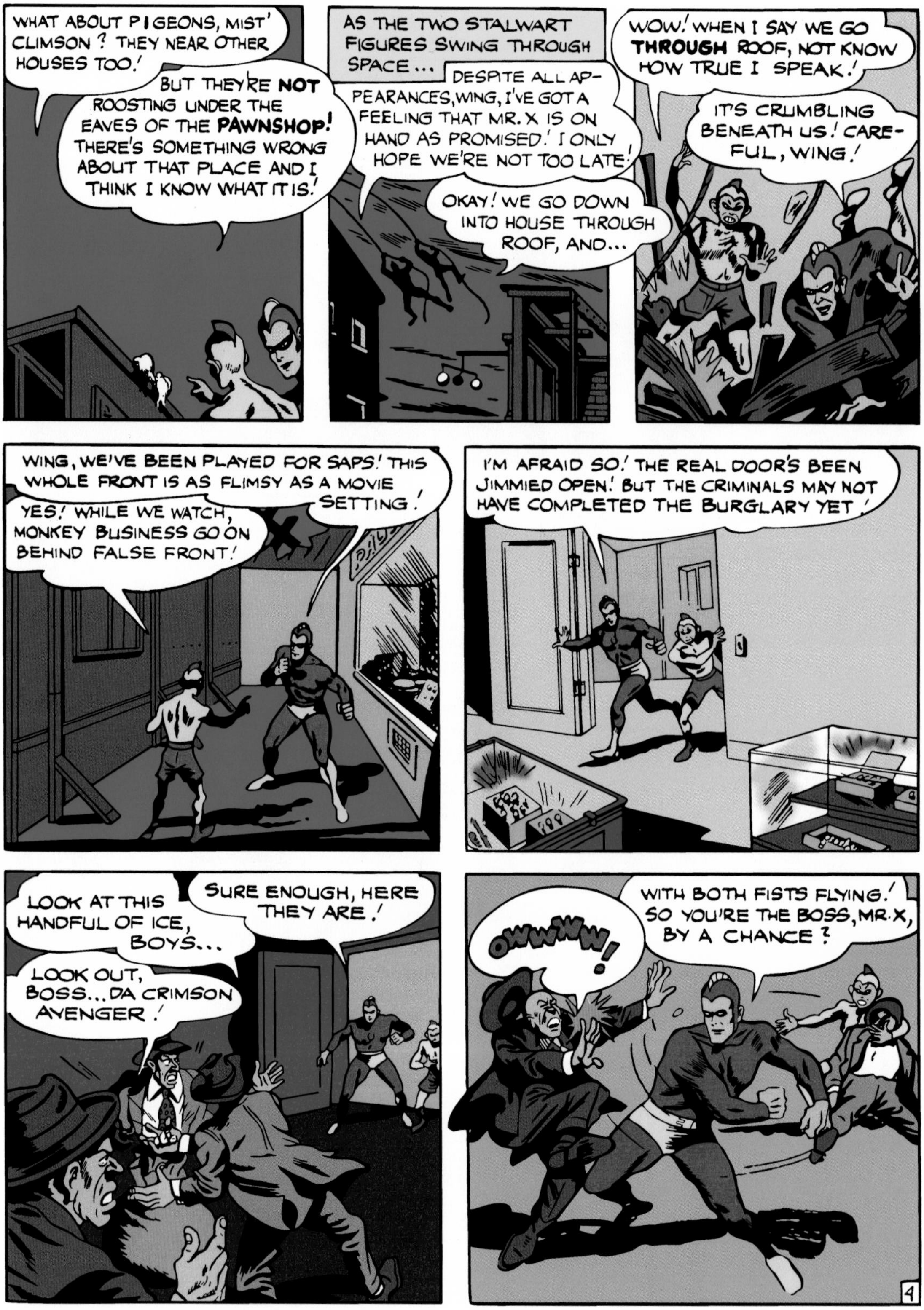
WHAT ABOUT PIGEONS, MIST' CLIMSON ? THEY NEAR OTHER HOUSES TOO!
BUT THEY'RE NOT ROOSTING UNDER THE EAVES OF THE PAWNSHOP! THERE'S SOMETHING WRONG ABOUT THAT PLACE AND I THINK I KNOW WHAT IT IS!
AS THE TWO STALWART FIGURES SWING THROUGH SPACE...
DESPITE ALL APPEARANCES, WING, I'VE GOT A FEELING THAT MR. X IS ON HAND AS PROMISED! I ONLY HOPE WE'RE NOT TOO LATE!
OKAY! WE GO DOWN INTO HOUSE THROUGH ROOF, AND...
WOW! WHEN I SAY WE GO THROUGH ROOF, NOT KNOW HOW TRUE I SPEAK!
IT'S CRUMBLING BENEATH US! CAREFUL, WING!
WING, WE'VE BEEN PLAYED FOR SAPS! THIS WHOLE FRONT IS AS FLIMSY AS A MOVIE SETTING!
YES! WHILE WE WATCH, MONKEY BUSINESS GO ON BEHIND FALSE FRONT!
I'M AFRAID SO! THE REAL DOOR'S BEEN JIMMIED OPEN! BUT THE CRIMINALS MAY NOT HAVE COMPLETED THE BURGLARY YET!
LOOK AT THIS HANDFUL OF ICE, BOYS...
SURE ENOUGH, HERE THEY ARE!
LOOK OUT, BOSS...DA CRIMSON AVENGER!
OWWWW!
WITH BOTH FISTS FLYING! SO YOU'RE THE BOSS, MR. X, BY A CHANCE?
4

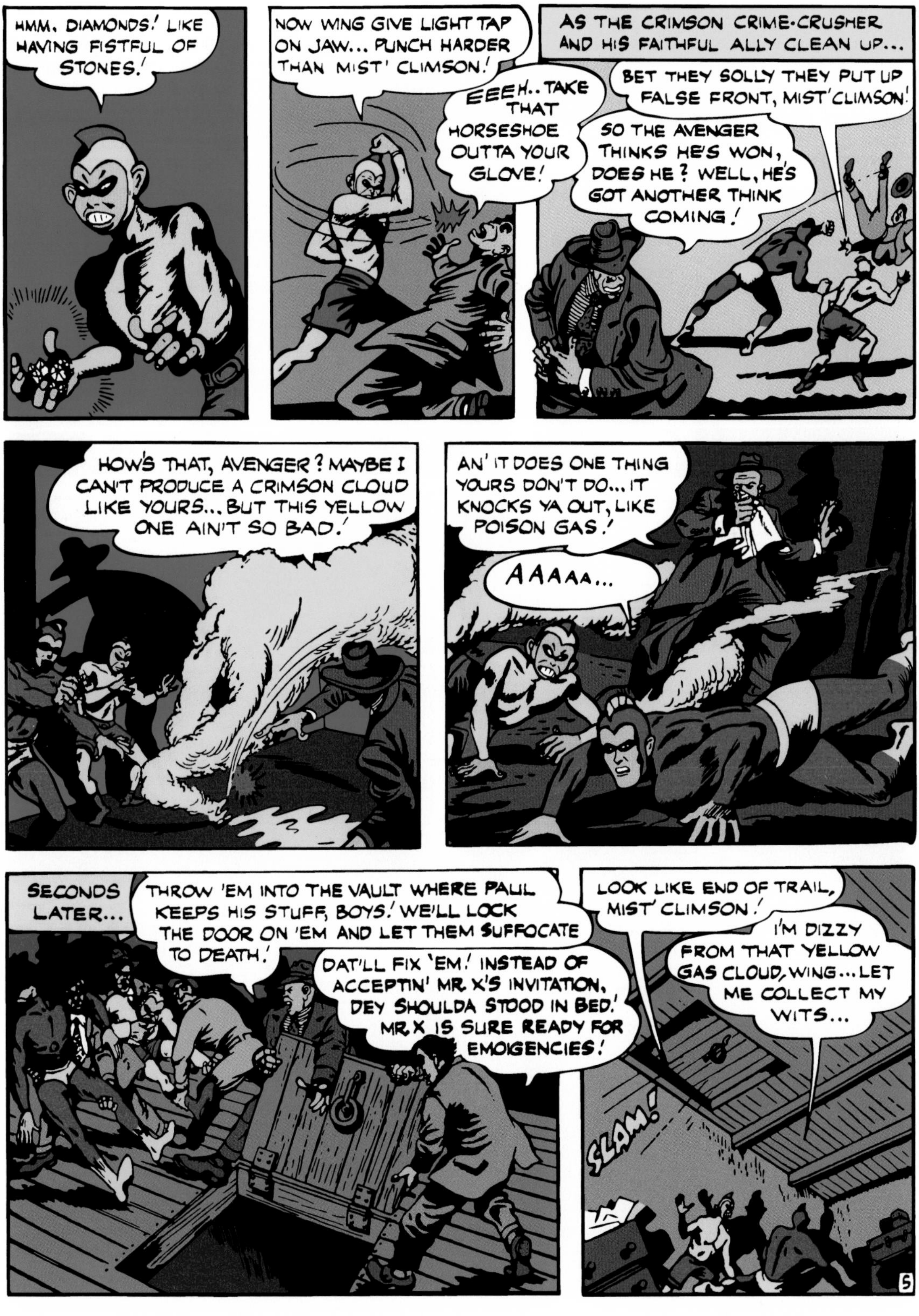
HMM, DIAMONDS! LIKE HAVING FISTFUL OF STONES!
NOW WING GIVE LIGHT TAP ON JAW... PUNCH HARDER THAN MIST' CLIMSON!
EEEH.. TAKE THAT HORSESHOE OUTTA YOUR GLOVE!
AS THE CRIMSON CRIME-CRUSHER AND HIS FAITHFUL ALLY CLEAN UP...
BET THEY SOLLY THEY PUT UP FALSE FRONT, MIST' CLIMSON!
SO THE AVENGER THINKS HE'S WON, DOES HE? WELL, HE'S GOT ANOTHER THINK COMING!
HOW'S THAT, AVENGER? MAYBE I CAN'T PRODUCE A CRIMSON CLOUD LIKE YOURS... BUT THIS YELLOW ONE AIN'T SO BAD!
AN' IT DOES ONE THING YOURS DON'T DO... IT KNOCKS YA OUT, LIKE POISON GAS!
AAAAA...
SECONDS LATER...
THROW 'EM INTO THE VAULT WHERE PAUL KEEPS HIS STUFF, BOYS! WE'LL LOCK THE DOOR ON 'EM AND LET THEM SUFFOCATE TO DEATH!
DAT'LL FIX 'EM! INSTEAD OF ACCEPTIN' MR. X'S INVITATION, DEY SHOULDA STOOD IN BED! MR. X IS SURE READY FOR EMOIGENCIES!
LOOK LIKE END OF TRAIL, MIST' CLIMSON!
I'M DIZZY FROM THAT YELLOW GAS CLOUD, WING... LET ME COLLECT MY WITS...
SLAM!
5

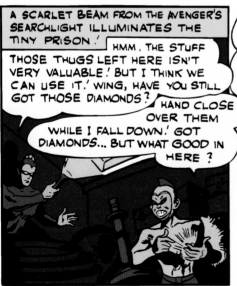

A SCARLET BEAM FROM THE AVENGER'S SEARCHLIGHT ILLUMINATES THE TINY PRISON.'

HMM. THE STUFF THOSE THUGS LEFT HERE ISN'T VERY VALUABLE.' BUT I THINK WE CAN USE IT.' WING, HAVE YOU STILL GOT THOSE DIAMONDS?

HAND CLOSE OVER THEM WHILE I FALL DOWN.' GOT DIAMONDS... BUT WHAT GOOD IN HERE?

PLENTY.' DIAMONDS ARE A LOT HARDER THAN STEEL... AND BY FITTING THEM FIRMLY INTO THIS CANDLESTICK, I'LL HAVE SOMETHING THAT CAN SERVE AS A DRILL!

THIS IS EASIER THAN DRILLING FROM THE OUTSIDE...WE DON'T HAVE TO CUT THROUGH SO MUCH STEEL TO REACH THE TUMBLERS.'

YOU MAKE GOOD SAFE-CLACKER, MIST' CLIMSON!

PRESENTLY...

AH, AT LAST.' BUT I WONDER IF THOSE THUGS ARE STILL AROUND.'

MAYBE THEY STOP TO PICK UP MORE LOOT.' MAYBE THEY THINK THEY GOT PLENTY TIME ...

YOU'RE RIGHT, WING.' HERE THEY ARE!

HEY, BOSS, LOOK.' THEY GOT OUT.' WHAT DID MR. X SAY TO DO?

HUH...? I DUNNO... HE DIDN'T FIGURE...

TOO BAD, CHUM.' IT'S TOO LATE FOR YOU TO DO ANY FIGURING NOW!

YOW!!

BY THIS TIME I'VE GOT YOUR NUMBER.'

I BETTER GET OUTTA HERE.' LOOKS LIKE IT DON'T PAY TO TANGLE WITH THE AVENGER TOO MUCH!

6

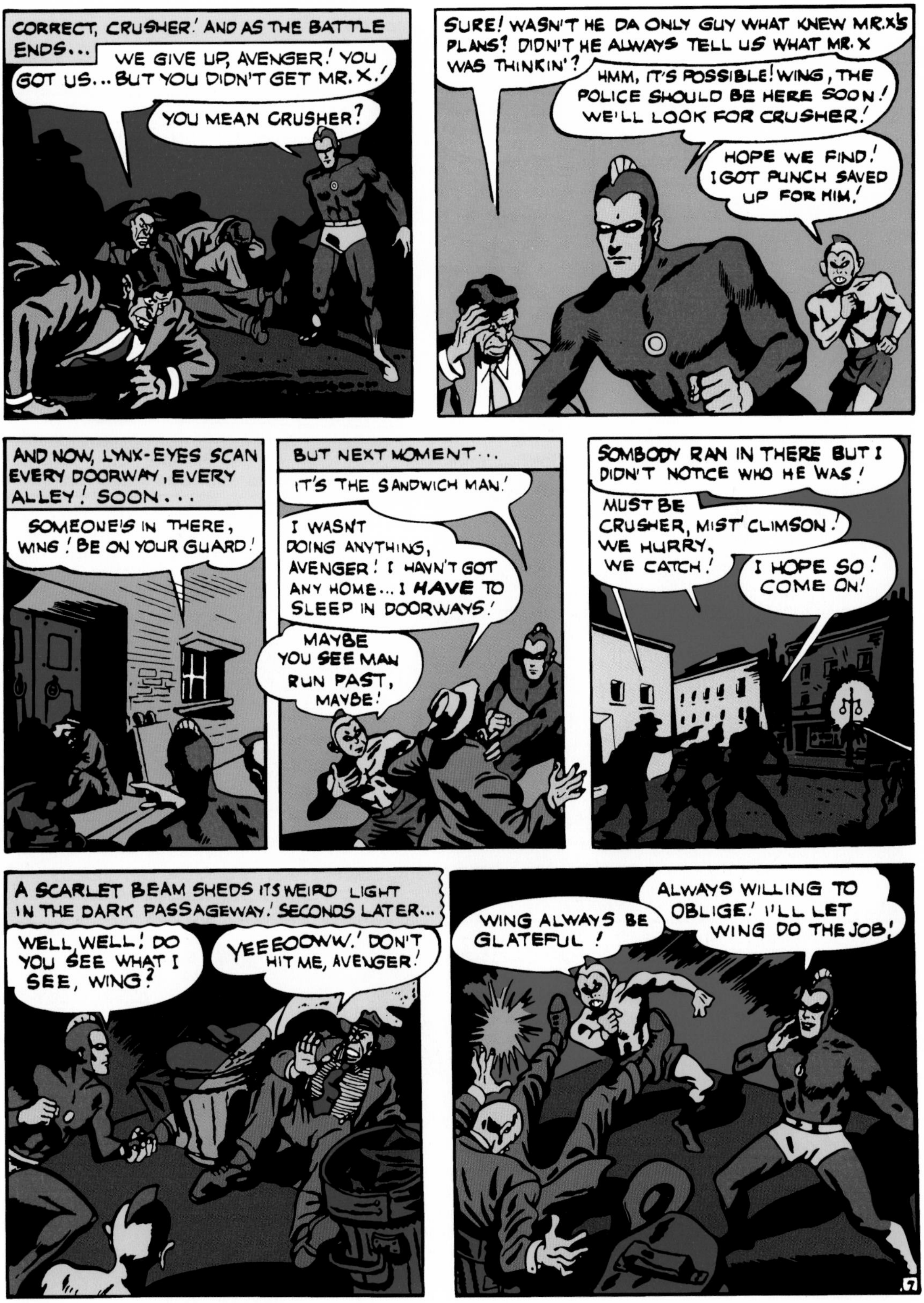
CORRECT, CRUSHER! AND AS THE BATTLE ENDS...
WE GIVE UP, AVENGER! YOU GOT US...BUT YOU DIDN'T GET MR. X.!
YOU MEAN CRUSHER?
SURE! WASN'T HE DA ONLY GUY WHAT KNEW MR.X'S PLANS? DIDN'T HE ALWAYS TELL US WHAT MR. X WAS THINKIN'?
HMM, IT'S POSSIBLE! WING, THE POLICE SHOULD BE HERE SOON! WE'LL LOOK FOR CRUSHER!
HOPE WE FIND! I GOT PUNCH SAVED UP FOR HIM!
AND NOW, LYNX-EYES SCAN EVERY DOORWAY, EVERY ALLEY! SOON...
SOMEONE'S IN THERE, WING! BE ON YOUR GUARD!
BUT NEXT MOMENT...
IT'S THE SANDWICH MAN!
I WASN'T DOING ANYTHING, AVENGER! I HAVN'T GOT ANY HOME...I HAVE TO SLEEP IN DOORWAYS!
MAYBE YOU SEE MAN RUN PAST, MAYBE!
SOMBODY RAN IN THERE BUT I DIDN'T NOTICE WHO HE WAS!
MUST BE CRUSHER, MIST' CLIMSON! WE HURRY, WE CATCH!
I HOPE SO! COME ON!
A SCARLET BEAM SHEDS ITS WEIRD LIGHT IN THE DARK PASSAGEWAY! SECONDS LATER...
WELL, WELL! DO YOU SEE WHAT I SEE, WING?
YEEEOOWW! DON'T HIT ME, AVENGER!
WING ALWAYS BE GLATEFUL!
ALWAYS WILLING TO OBLIGE! I'LL LET WING DO THE JOB!
7

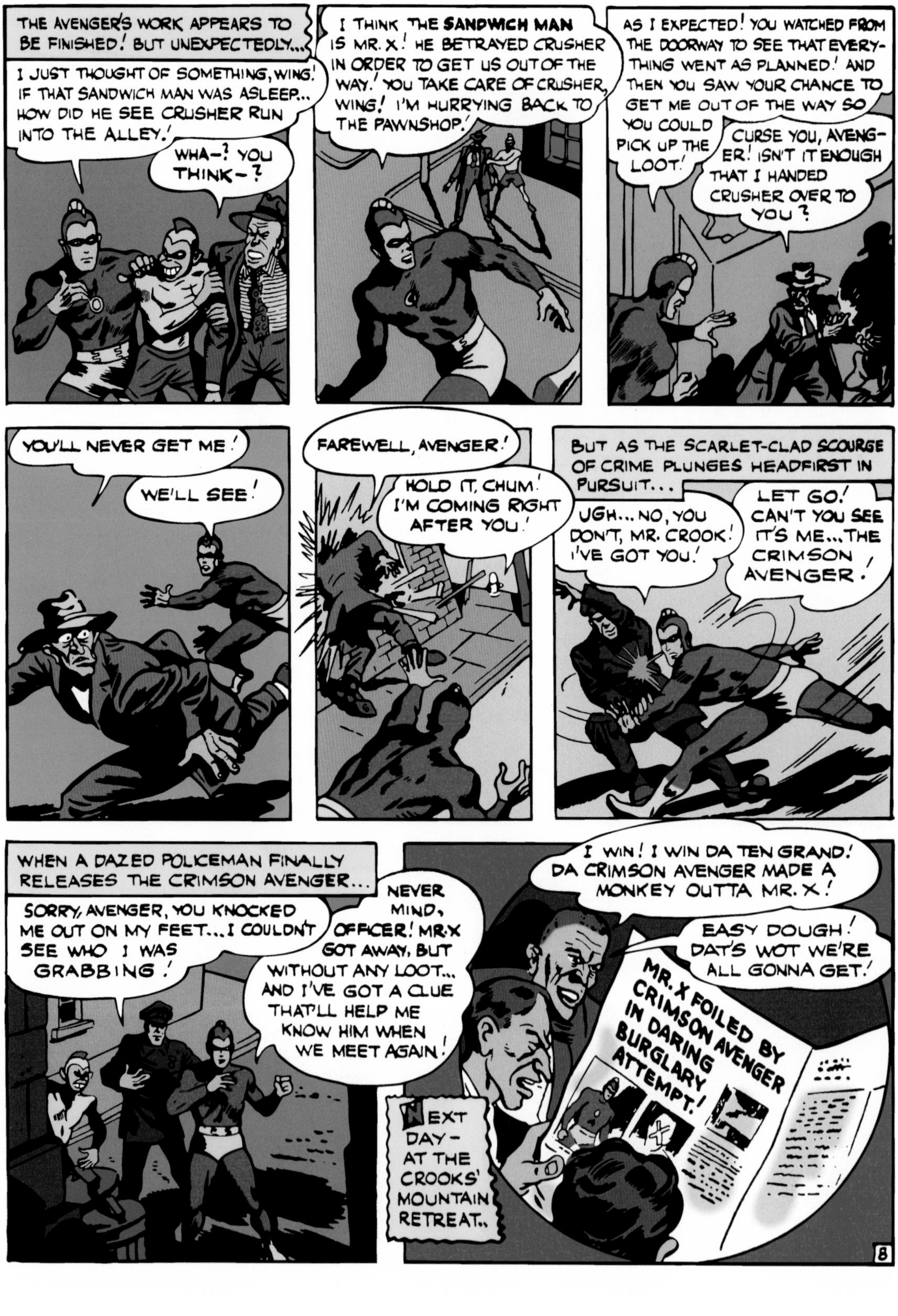
THE AVENGER'S WORK APPEARS TO BE FINISHED! BUT UNEXPECTEDLY...
I JUST THOUGHT OF SOMETHING, WING! IF THAT SANDWICH MAN WAS ASLEEP... HOW DID HE SEE CRUSHER RUN INTO THE ALLEY!
WHA-? YOU THINK-?
I THINK THE SANDWICH MAN IS MR. X! HE BETRAYED CRUSHER IN ORDER TO GET US OUT OF THE WAY! YOU TAKE CARE OF CRUSHER, WING! I'M HURRYING BACK TO THE PAWNSHOP!
AS I EXPECTED! YOU WATCHED FROM THE DOORWAY TO SEE THAT EVERYTHING WENT AS PLANNED! AND THEN YOU SAW YOUR CHANCE TO GET ME OUT OF THE WAY SO YOU COULD PICK UP THE LOOT!
CURSE YOU, AVENGER! ISN'T IT ENOUGH THAT I HANDED CRUSHER OVER TO YOU?
YOU'LL NEVER GET ME!
WE'LL SEE!
FAREWELL, AVENGER!
HOLD IT, CHUM! I'M COMING RIGHT AFTER YOU!
BUT AS THE SCARLET-CLAD SCOURGE OF CRIME PLUNGES HEADFIRST IN PURSUIT...
UGH... NO, YOU DON'T, MR. CROOK! I'VE GOT YOU!
LET GO! CAN'T YOU SEE IT'S ME... THE CRIMSON AVENGER!
WHEN A DAZED POLICEMAN FINALLY RELEASES THE CRIMSON AVENGER...
SORRY, AVENGER, YOU KNOCKED ME OUT ON MY FEET... I COULDN'T SEE WHO I WAS GRABBING!
NEVER MIND, OFFICER! MR. X GOT AWAY, BUT WITHOUT ANY LOOT... AND I'VE GOT A CLUE THAT'LL HELP ME KNOW HIM WHEN WE MEET AGAIN!
I WIN! I WIN DA TEN GRAND! DA CRIMSON AVENGER MADE A MONKEY OUTTA MR. X!
EASY DOUGH! DAT'S WOT WE'RE ALL GONNA GET!
MR. X FOILED BY CRIMSON AVENGER IN DARING BURGLARY ATTEMPT!
NEXT DAY- AT THE CROOKS' MOUNTAIN RETREAT..
8

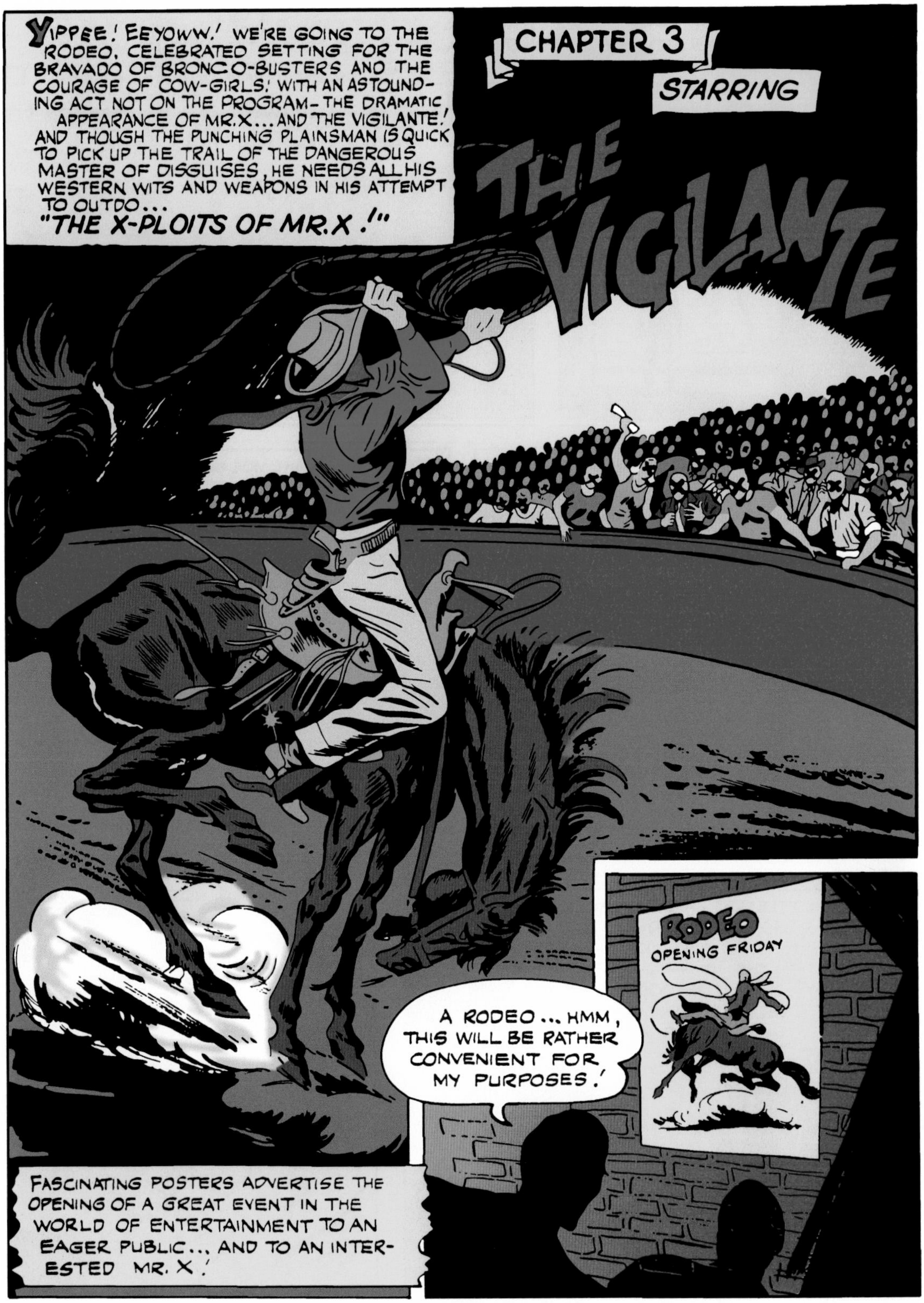
YIPPEE! EEYOWW! WE'RE GOING TO THE RODEO, CELEBRATED SETTING FOR THE BRAVADO OF BRONCO-BUSTERS AND THE COURAGE OF COW-GIRLS! WITH AN ASTOUNDING ACT NOT ON THE PROGRAM-THE DRAMATIC APPEARANCE OF MR.X... AND THE VIGILANTE! AND THOUGH THE PUNCHING PLAINSMAN IS QUICK TO PICK UP THE TRAIL OF THE DANGEROUS MASTER OF DISGUISES, HE NEEDS ALL HIS WESTERN WITS AND WEAPONS IN HIS ATTEMPT TO OUTDO...
"THE X-PLOITS OF MR.X !"
CHAPTER 3
STARRING
THE VIGILANTE
RODEO
OPENING FRIDAY
A RODEO... HMM, THIS WILL BE RATHER CONVENIENT FOR MY PURPOSES!
FASCINATING POSTERS ADVERTISE THE OPENING OF A GREAT EVENT IN THE WORLD OF ENTERTAINMENT TO AN EAGER PUBLIC... AND TO AN INTERESTED MR. X!

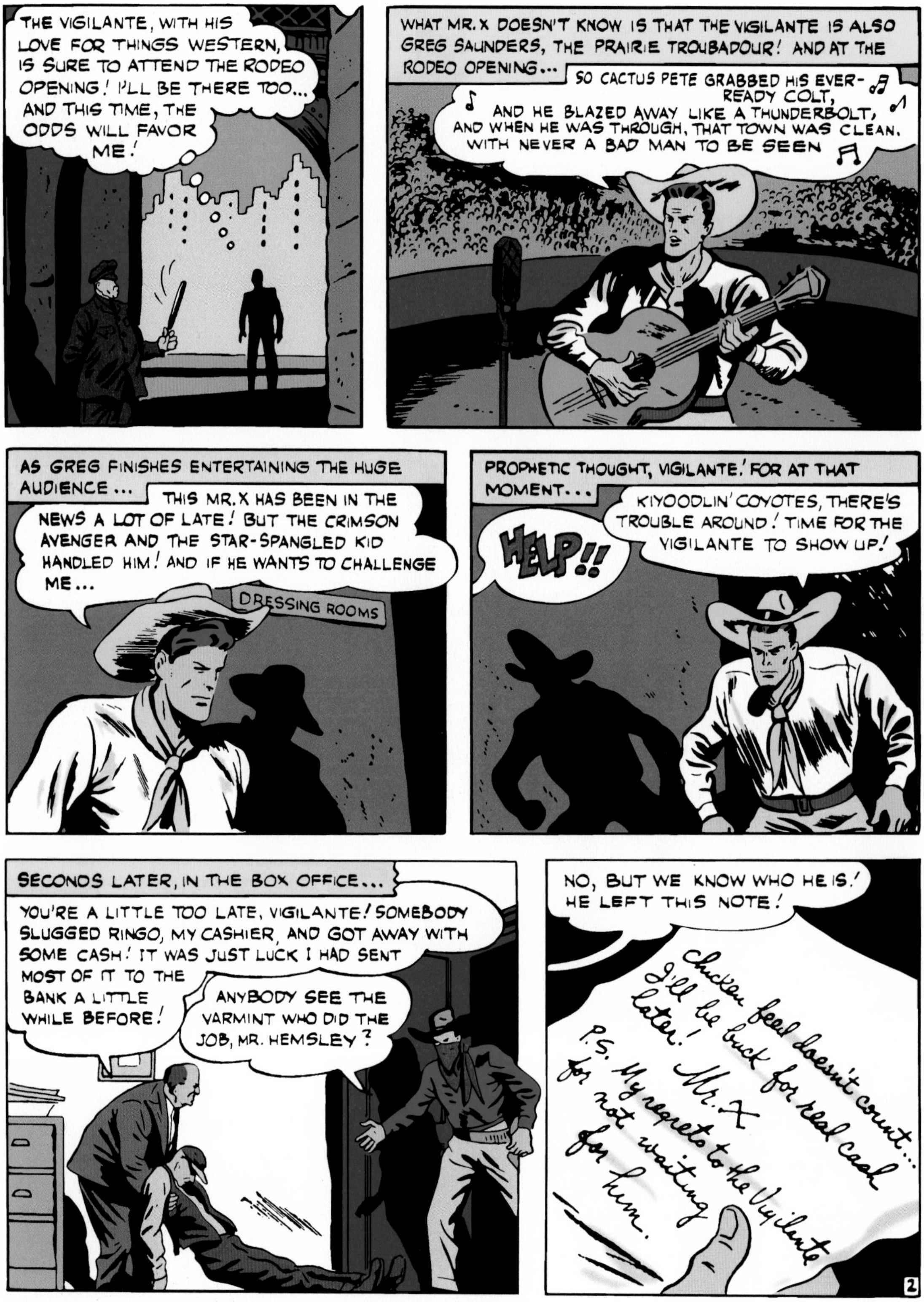
THE VIGILANTE, WITH HIS LOVE FOR THINGS WESTERN, IS SURE TO ATTEND THE RODEO OPENING! I'LL BE THERE TOO... AND THIS TIME, THE ODDS WILL FAVOR ME!
WHAT MR. X DOESN'T KNOW IS THAT THE VIGILANTE IS ALSO GREG SAUNDERS, THE PRAIRIE TROUBADOUR! AND AT THE RODEO OPENING...
SO CACTUS PETE GRABBED HIS EVER-READY COLT, AND HE BLAZED AWAY LIKE A THUNDERBOLT, AND WHEN HE WAS THROUGH, THAT TOWN WAS CLEAN. WITH NEVER A BAD MAN TO BE SEEN
AS GREG FINISHES ENTERTAINING THE HUGE AUDIENCE...
THIS MR. X HAS BEEN IN THE NEWS A LOT OF LATE! BUT THE CRIMSON AVENGER AND THE STAR-SPANGLED KID HANDLED HIM! AND IF HE WANTS TO CHALLENGE ME...
DRESSING ROOMS
PROPHETIC THOUGHT, VIGILANTE! FOR AT THAT MOMENT...
HELP!!
KIYOODLIN' COYOTES, THERE'S TROUBLE AROUND! TIME FOR THE VIGILANTE TO SHOW UP!
SECONDS LATER, IN THE BOX OFFICE...
YOU'RE A LITTLE TOO LATE, VIGILANTE! SOMEBODY SLUGGED RINGO, MY CASHIER, AND GOT AWAY WITH SOME CASH! IT WAS JUST LUCK I HAD SENT MOST OF IT TO THE BANK A LITTLE WHILE BEFORE!
ANYBODY SEE THE VARMINT WHO DID THE JOB, MR. HEMSLEY?
NO, BUT WE KNOW WHO HE IS! HE LEFT THIS NOTE!
Chicken feed doesn't count... I'll be back for real cash later! Mr. X
P.S. My regrets to the Vigilante for not waiting for him.
2

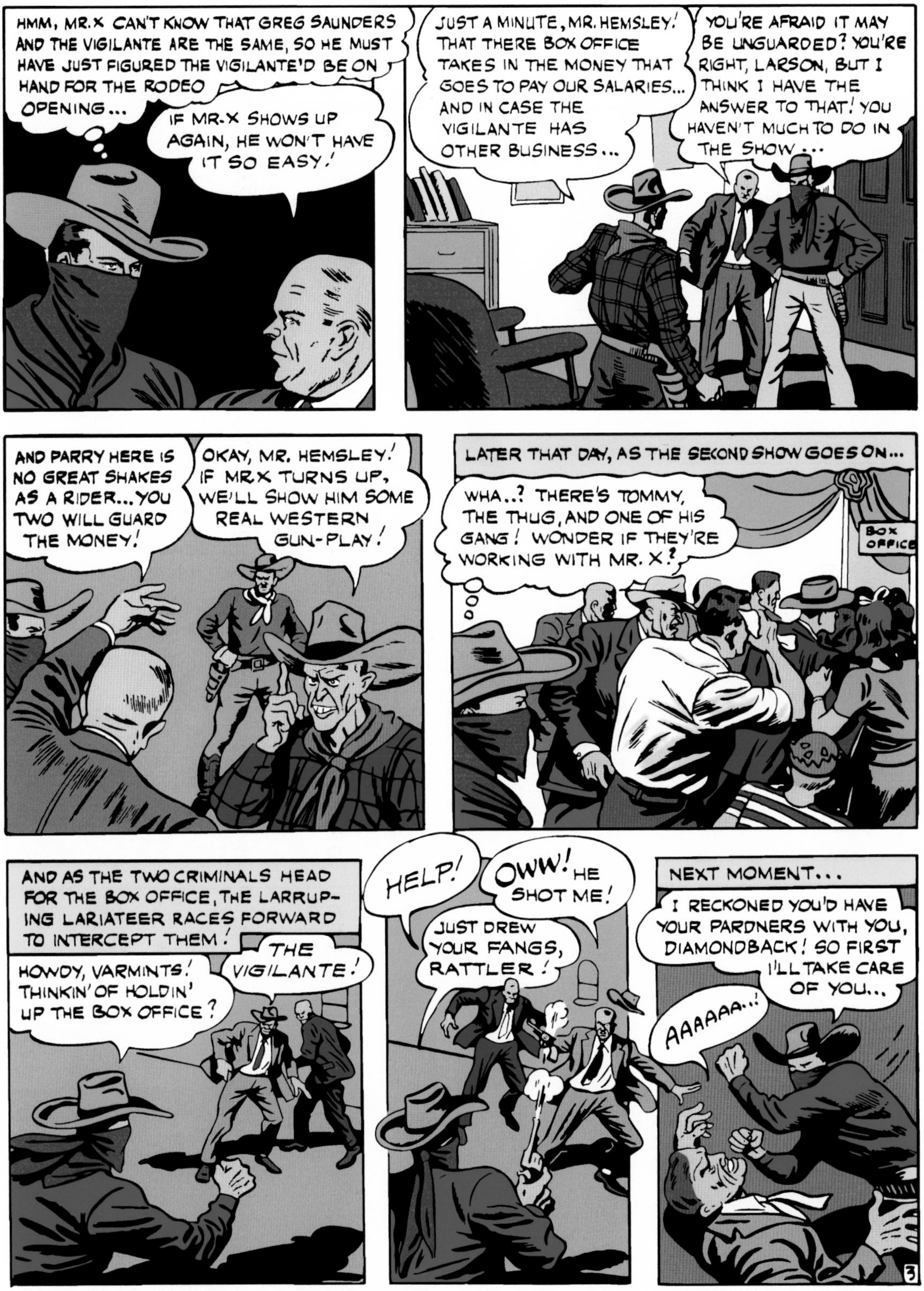
HMM, MR. X CAN'T KNOW THAT GREG SAUNDERS AND THE VIGILANTE ARE THE SAME, SO HE MUST HAVE JUST FIGURED THE VIGILANTE'D BE ON HAND FOR THE RODEO OPENING...
IF MR. X SHOWS UP AGAIN, HE WON'T HAVE IT SO EASY!
JUST A MINUTE, MR. HEMSLEY! THAT THERE BOX OFFICE TAKES IN THE MONEY THAT GOES TO PAY OUR SALARIES... AND IN CASE THE VIGILANTE HAS OTHER BUSINESS...
YOU'RE AFRAID IT MAY BE UNGUARDED? YOU'RE RIGHT, LARSON, BUT I THINK I HAVE THE ANSWER TO THAT! YOU HAVEN'T MUCH TO DO IN THE SHOW...
AND PARRY HERE IS NO GREAT SHAKES AS A RIDER... YOU TWO WILL GUARD THE MONEY!
OKAY, MR. HEMSLEY! IF MR. X TURNS UP, WE'LL SHOW HIM SOME REAL WESTERN GUN-PLAY!
LATER THAT DAY, AS THE SECOND SHOW GOES ON...
WHA..? THERE'S TOMMY, THE THUG, AND ONE OF HIS GANG! WONDER IF THEY'RE WORKING WITH MR. X?
BOX OFFICE
AND AS THE TWO CRIMINALS HEAD FOR THE BOX OFFICE, THE LARRUPING LARIATEER RACES FORWARD TO INTERCEPT THEM!
HOWDY, VARMINTS! THINKIN' OF HOLDIN' UP THE BOX OFFICE?
THE VIGILANTE!
HELP!
OWW! HE SHOT ME!
JUST DREW YOUR FANGS, RATTLER!
NEXT MOMENT...
I RECKONED YOU'D HAVE YOUR PARDNERS WITH YOU, DIAMONDBACK! SO FIRST I'LL TAKE CARE OF YOU...
AAAAAA..!
3

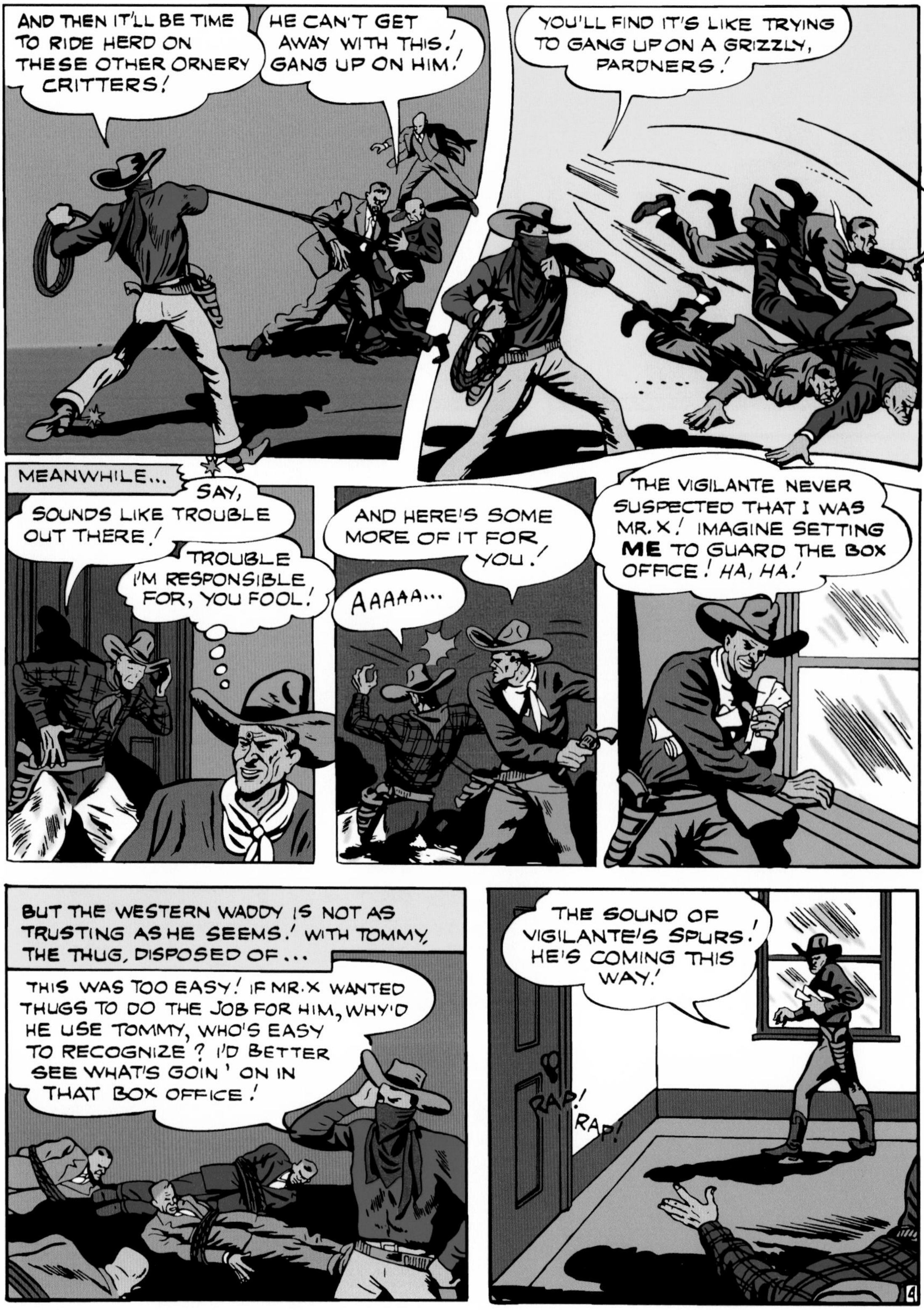
AND THEN IT'LL BE TIME TO RIDE HERD ON THESE OTHER ORNERY CRITTERS!
HE CAN'T GET AWAY WITH THIS! GANG UP ON HIM!
YOU'LL FIND IT'S LIKE TRYING TO GANG UP ON A GRIZZLY, PARDNERS!
MEANWHILE...
SAY, SOUNDS LIKE TROUBLE OUT THERE!
TROUBLE I'M RESPONSIBLE FOR, YOU FOOL!
AND HERE'S SOME MORE OF IT FOR YOU!
AAAAA...
THE VIGILANTE NEVER SUSPECTED THAT I WAS MR. X! IMAGINE SETTING ME TO GUARD THE BOX OFFICE! HA, HA!
BUT THE WESTERN WADDY IS NOT AS TRUSTING AS HE SEEMS! WITH TOMMY, THE THUG, DISPOSED OF...
THIS WAS TOO EASY! IF MR. X WANTED THUGS TO DO THE JOB FOR HIM, WHY'D HE USE TOMMY, WHO'S EASY TO RECOGNIZE? I'D BETTER SEE WHAT'S GOIN' ON IN THAT BOX OFFICE!
THE SOUND OF VIGILANTE'S SPURS! HE'S COMING THIS WAY!
RAP! RAP!
4

I'D BETTER PUT THIS ASIDE UNTIL I CAN GET RID OF HIM!

RAP! RAP!

NEXT MOMENT...

PARRY! WHAT HAPPENED?

WHO... WHAT... WHERE AM I?

YOU'RE RIGHT HERE IN THE OFFICE YOU WERE SUPPOSED TO WATCH! AN' NOT DOIN' A GOOD JOB OF IT!

IT WASN'T MY FAULT, VIG! SOMEBODY HIT ME FROM BEHIND! I DIDN'T HAVE TIME TO PULL MY GUN!

HE MUST HAVE RUN OUT THAT DOOR!

I DIDN'T NOTICE ANYBODY RUN OUT! SURE YOU DIDN'T SEE HIM?

WHY, NO...

PARRY, I'M SORRY I HIRED YOU THE OTHER DAY! YOU CAN'T RIDE, YOU CAN'T THROW A LARIAT...

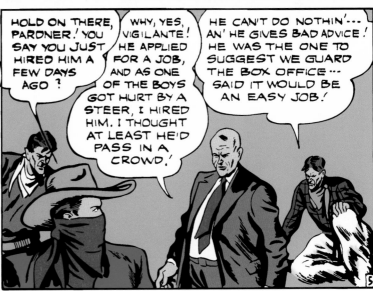

HOLD ON THERE, PARDNER! YOU SAY YOU JUST HIRED HIM A FEW DAYS AGO?

WHY, YES, VIGILANTE! HE APPLIED FOR A JOB, AND AS ONE OF THE BOYS GOT HURT BY A STEER, I HIRED HIM. I THOUGHT AT LEAST HE'D PASS IN A CROWD!

HE CAN'T DO NOTHIN'--- AN' HE GIVES BAD ADVICE! HE WAS THE ONE TO SUGGEST WE GUARD THE BOX OFFICE --- SAID IT WOULD BE AN EASY JOB!

5

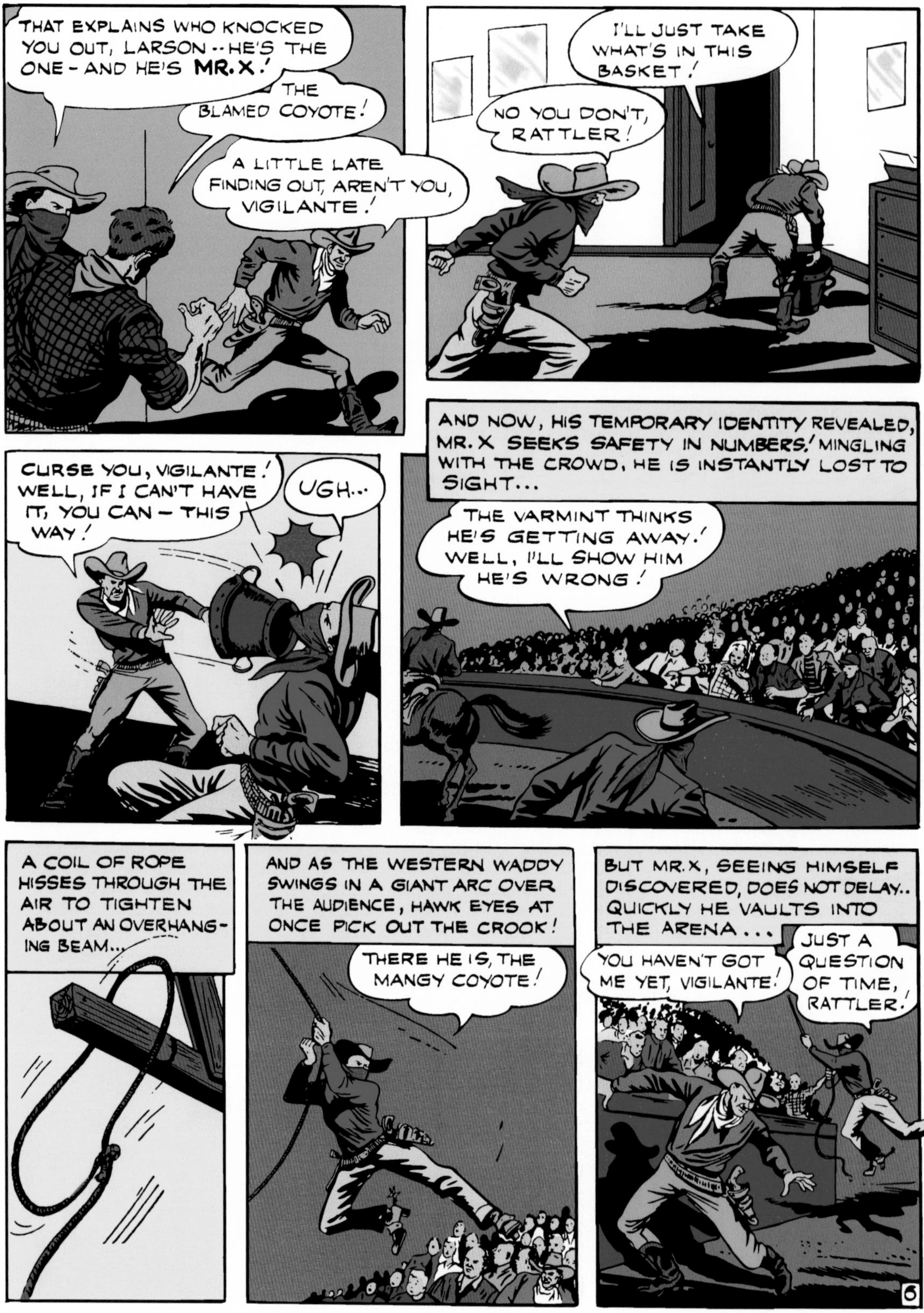
THAT EXPLAINS WHO KNOCKED YOU OUT, LARSON -- HE'S THE ONE - AND HE'S MR. X!
THE BLAMED COYOTE!
A LITTLE LATE FINDING OUT, AREN'T YOU, VIGILANTE!
I'LL JUST TAKE WHAT'S IN THIS BASKET!
NO YOU DON'T, RATTLER!
CURSE YOU, VIGILANTE! WELL, IF I CAN'T HAVE IT, YOU CAN - THIS WAY!
UGH...
AND NOW, HIS TEMPORARY IDENTITY REVEALED, MR. X SEEKS SAFETY IN NUMBERS! MINGLING WITH THE CROWD, HE IS INSTANTLY LOST TO SIGHT...
THE VARMINT THINKS HE'S GETTING AWAY! WELL, I'LL SHOW HIM HE'S WRONG!
A COIL OF ROPE HISSES THROUGH THE AIR TO TIGHTEN ABOUT AN OVERHANGING BEAM...
AND AS THE WESTERN WADDY SWINGS IN A GIANT ARC OVER THE AUDIENCE, HAWK EYES AT ONCE PICK OUT THE CROOK!
THERE HE IS, THE MANGY COYOTE!
BUT MR. X, SEEING HIMSELF DISCOVERED, DOES NOT DELAY.. QUICKLY HE VAULTS INTO THE ARENA...
YOU HAVEN'T GOT ME YET, VIGILANTE!
JUST A QUESTION OF TIME, RATTLER!
6

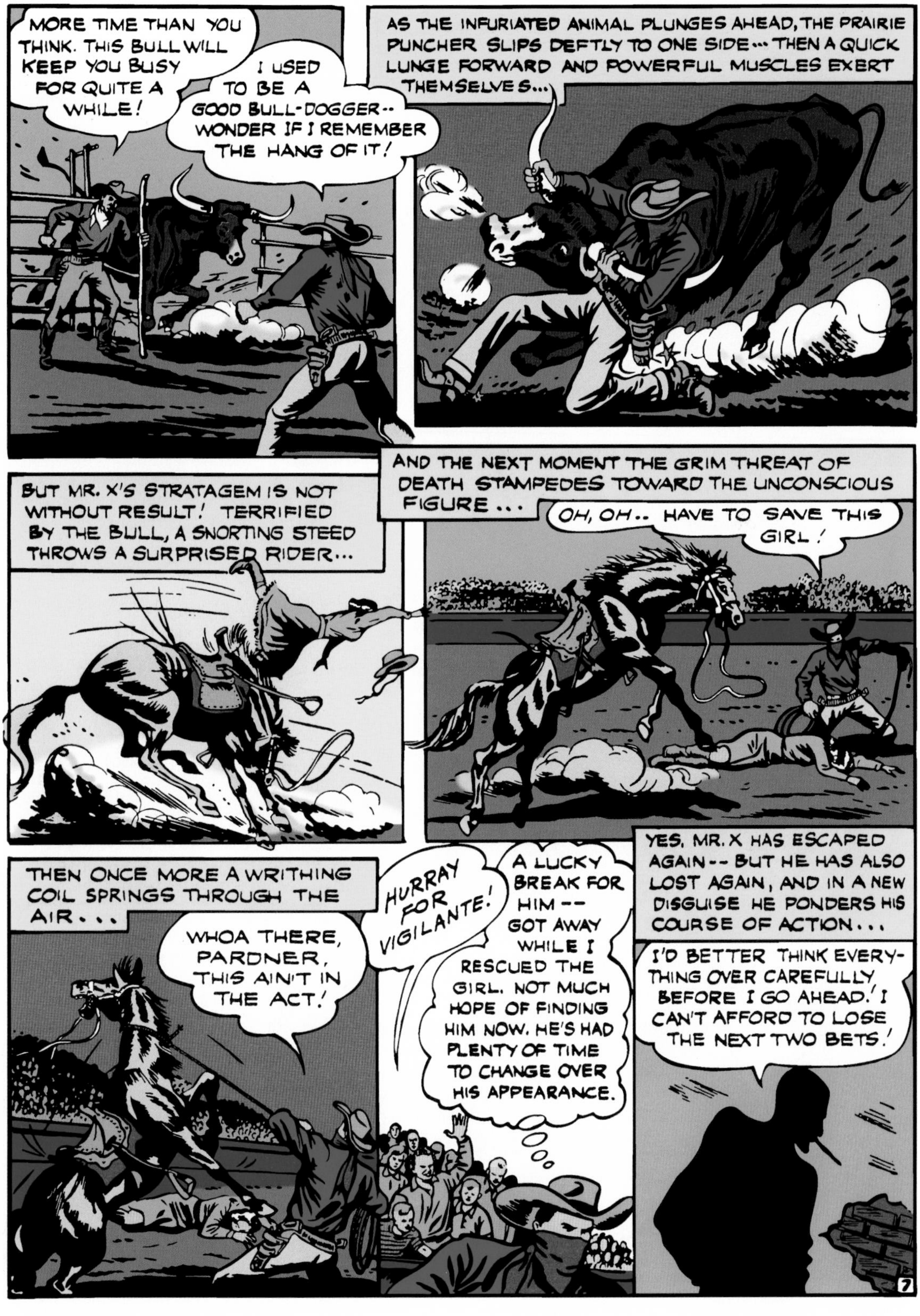
MORE TIME THAN YOU THINK. THIS BULL WILL KEEP YOU BUSY FOR QUITE A WHILE!
I USED TO BE A GOOD BULL-DOGGER-- WONDER IF I REMEMBER THE HANG OF IT!
AS THE INFURIATED ANIMAL PLUNGES AHEAD, THE PRAIRIE PUNCHER SLIPS DEFTLY TO ONE SIDE... THEN A QUICK LUNGE FORWARD AND POWERFUL MUSCLES EXERT THEMSELVES...
BUT MR. X'S STRATAGEM IS NOT WITHOUT RESULT! TERRIFIED BY THE BULL, A SNORTING STEED THROWS A SURPRISED RIDER...
AND THE NEXT MOMENT THE GRIM THREAT OF DEATH STAMPEDES TOWARD THE UNCONSCIOUS FIGURE...
OH, OH.. HAVE TO SAVE THIS GIRL!
THEN ONCE MORE A WRITHING COIL SPRINGS THROUGH THE AIR...
WHOA THERE, PARDNER, THIS AIN'T IN THE ACT!
HURRAY FOR VIGILANTE!
A LUCKY BREAK FOR HIM -- GOT AWAY WHILE I RESCUED THE GIRL. NOT MUCH HOPE OF FINDING HIM NOW. HE'S HAD PLENTY OF TIME TO CHANGE OVER HIS APPEARANCE.
YES, MR. X HAS ESCAPED AGAIN -- BUT HE HAS ALSO LOST AGAIN, AND IN A NEW DISGUISE HE PONDERS HIS COURSE OF ACTION...
I'D BETTER THINK EVERYTHING OVER CAREFULLY, BEFORE I GO AHEAD! I CAN'T AFFORD TO LOSE THE NEXT TWO BETS!
7

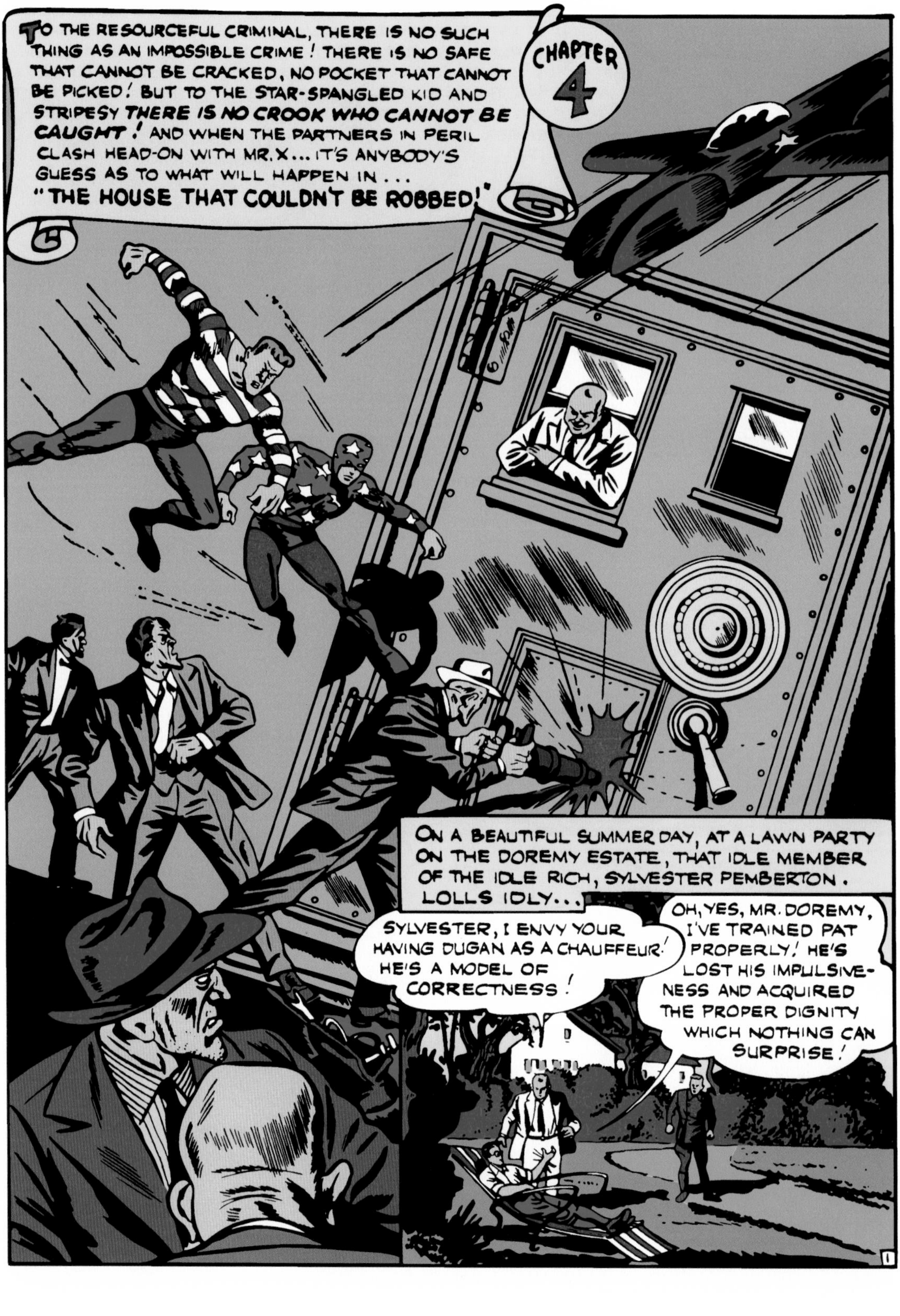
TO THE RESOURCEFUL CRIMINAL, THERE IS NO SUCH THING AS AN IMPOSSIBLE CRIME! THERE IS NO SAFE THAT CANNOT BE CRACKED, NO POCKET THAT CANNOT BE PICKED! BUT TO THE STAR-SPANGLED KID AND STRIPESY THERE IS NO CROOK WHO CANNOT BE CAUGHT! AND WHEN THE PARTNERS IN PERIL CLASH HEAD-ON WITH MR. X... IT'S ANYBODY'S GUESS AS TO WHAT WILL HAPPEN IN...
"THE HOUSE THAT COULDN'T BE ROBBED!"
CHAPTER 4
ON A BEAUTIFUL SUMMER DAY, AT A LAWN PARTY ON THE DOREMY ESTATE, THAT IDLE MEMBER OF THE IDLE RICH, SYLVESTER PEMBERTON, LOLLS IDLY...
SYLVESTER, I ENVY YOUR HAVING DUGAN AS A CHAUFFEUR! HE'S A MODEL OF CORRECTNESS!
OH, YES, MR. DOREMY, I'VE TRAINED PAT PROPERLY! HE'S LOST HIS IMPULSIVE-NESS AND ACQUIRED THE PROPER DIGNITY WHICH NOTHING CAN SURPRISE!
1

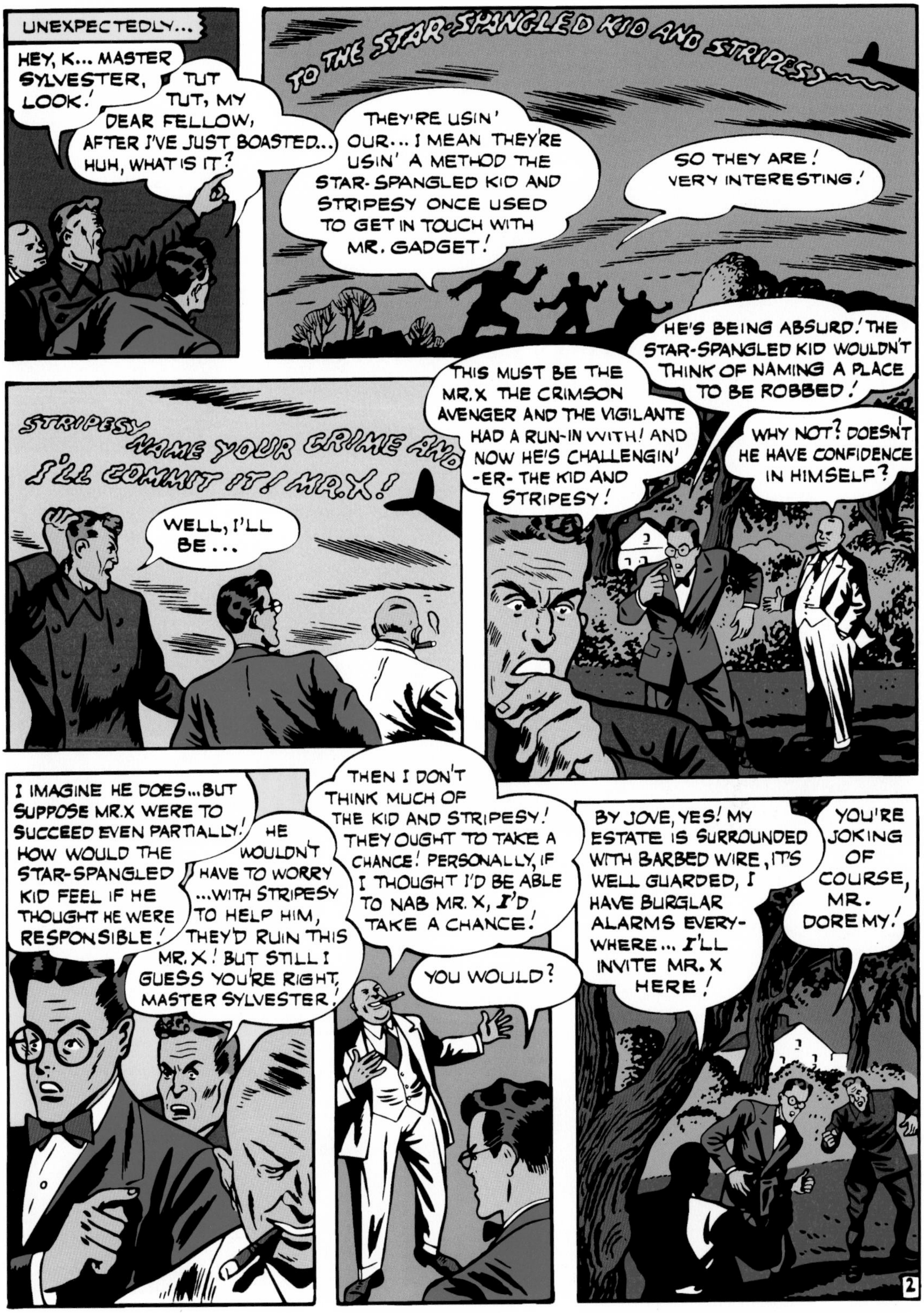
UNEXPECTEDLY...
HEY, K... MASTER SYLVESTER, LOOK!
TUT TUT, MY DEAR FELLOW, AFTER I'VE JUST BOASTED... HUH, WHAT IS IT?
TO THE STAR-SPANGLED KID AND STRIPESY
THEY'RE USIN' OUR... I MEAN THEY'RE USIN' A METHOD THE STAR-SPANGLED KID AND STRIPESY ONCE USED TO GET IN TOUCH WITH MR. GADGET!
SO THEY ARE! VERY INTERESTING!
STRIPESY NAME YOUR CRIME AND I'LL COMMIT IT! MR. X!
WELL, I'LL BE...
THIS MUST BE THE MR. X THE CRIMSON AVENGER AND THE VIGILANTE HAD A RUN-IN WITH! AND NOW HE'S CHALLENGIN' -ER- THE KID AND STRIPESY!
HE'S BEING ABSURD! THE STAR-SPANGLED KID WOULDN'T THINK OF NAMING A PLACE TO BE ROBBED!
WHY NOT? DOESN'T HE HAVE CONFIDENCE IN HIMSELF?
I IMAGINE HE DOES...BUT SUPPOSE MR. X WERE TO SUCCEED EVEN PARTIALLY! HOW WOULD THE STAR-SPANGLED KID FEEL IF HE THOUGHT HE WERE RESPONSIBLE!
HE WOULDN'T HAVE TO WORRY ...WITH STRIPESY TO HELP HIM, THEY'D RUIN THIS MR. X! BUT STILL I GUESS YOU'RE RIGHT, MASTER SYLVESTER!
THEN I DON'T THINK MUCH OF THE KID AND STRIPESY! THEY OUGHT TO TAKE A CHANCE! PERSONALLY, IF I THOUGHT I'D BE ABLE TO NAB MR. X, I'D TAKE A CHANCE!
YOU WOULD?
BY JOVE, YES! MY ESTATE IS SURROUNDED WITH BARBED WIRE, IT'S WELL GUARDED, I HAVE BURGLAR ALARMS EVERYWHERE... I'LL INVITE MR. X HERE!
YOU'RE JOKING OF COURSE, MR. DOREMY!
2

I AM **NOT!** THIS HOUSE CAN'T POSSIBLY BE ROBBED. MR. X NO DOUBT EXPECTS THE KID TO GET IN TOUCH WITH HIM VIA THE NEWSPAPER PERSONAL COLUMN. WELL, I'LL PUT IN AN AD AND SIGN THE KID'S NAME!

MR. DOREMY, DO YOU THINK THAT WOULD BE RIGHT!

IT'S **MY** HOUSE THAT WOULD BE ROBBED IF MR. X SUCCEEDED, SO WHY SHOULD THE STAR-SPANGLED KID OBJECT? I'M GOING TO DO IT!

AND MR. X IS THE GUY TO GIVE IT TO YOU!

THUS, LATER..

WH..WHAT DOES IT SAY, POICY? I AIN'T GOT ME GLASSES!

THE BEST GLASSES IN THE WORLD WOULDN'T HELP YOU READ, LAMEBRAIN! NOT UNLESS YOU WENT TO SCHOOL!

HAW, HAW! LOOK AT LAMEBRAIN, TRYIN' TO ACT EDUCATED!

PERSONAL

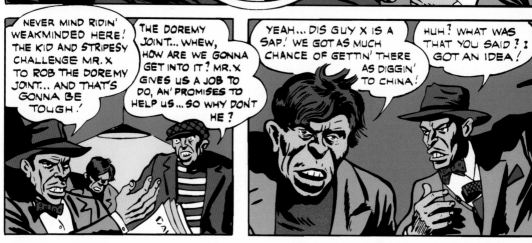

NEVER MIND RIDIN' WEAKMINDED HERE! THE KID AND STRIPESY CHALLENGE MR. X TO ROB THE DOREMY JOINT... AND THAT'S GONNA BE TOUGH!

THE DOREMY JOINT... WHEW, HOW ARE WE GONNA GET INTO IT? MR. X GIVES US A JOB TO DO, AN' PROMISES TO HELP US... SO WHY DON'T HE?

YEAH... DIS GUY X IS A SAP! WE GOT AS MUCH CHANCE OF GETTIN' THERE AS DIGGIN' TO CHINA!

HUH? WHAT WAS THAT YOU SAID?! I GOT AN IDEA!

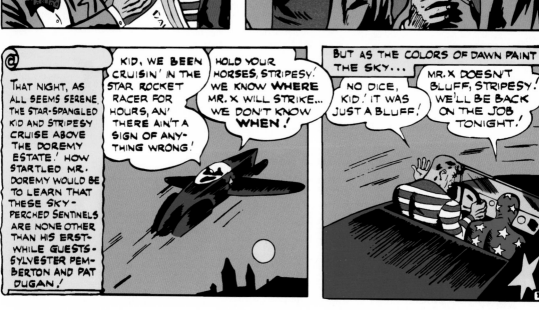

THAT NIGHT, AS ALL SEEMS SERENE, THE STAR-SPANGLED KID AND STRIPESY CRUISE ABOVE THE DOREMY ESTATE! HOW STARTLED MR. DOREMY WOULD BE TO LEARN THAT THESE SKY-PERCHED SENTINELS ARE NONE OTHER THAN HIS ERSTWHILE GUESTS— SYLVESTER PEMBERTON AND PAT DUGAN!

KID, WE BEEN CRUISIN' IN THE STAR ROCKET RACER FOR HOURS, AN' THERE AIN'T A SIGN OF ANYTHING WRONG!

HOLD YOUR HORSES, STRIPESY! WE KNOW **WHERE** MR. X WILL STRIKE... WE DON'T KNOW **WHEN!**

BUT AS THE COLORS OF DAWN PAINT THE SKY...

NO DICE, KID! IT WAS JUST A BLUFF!

MR. X DOESN'T BLUFF, STRIPESY! WE'LL BE BACK ON THE JOB TONIGHT!

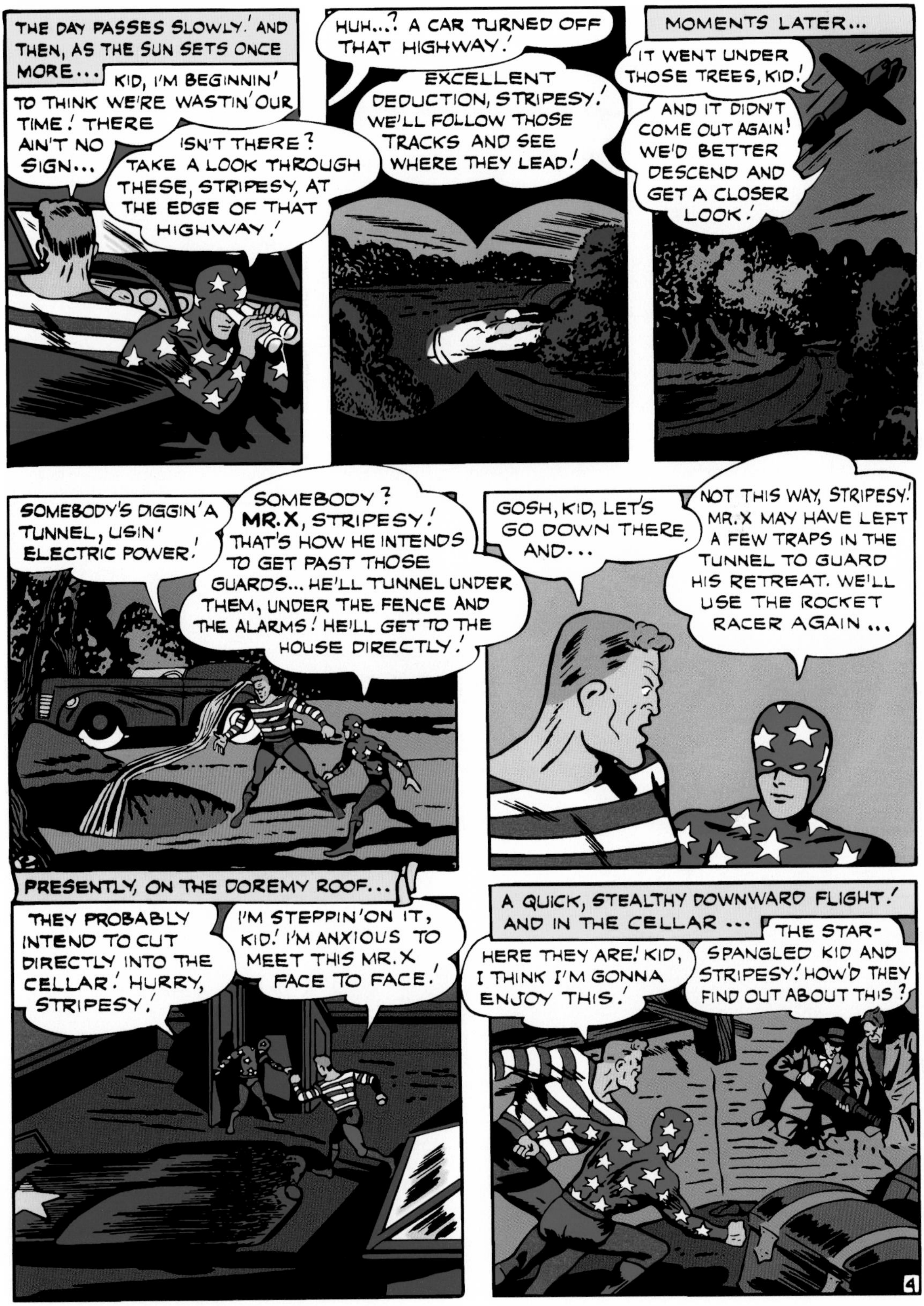
THE DAY PASSES SLOWLY! AND THEN, AS THE SUN SETS ONCE MORE...
KID, I'M BEGINNIN' TO THINK WE'RE WASTIN' OUR TIME! THERE AIN'T NO SIGN...
ISN'T THERE? TAKE A LOOK THROUGH THESE, STRIPESY, AT THE EDGE OF THAT HIGHWAY!
HUH...? A CAR TURNED OFF THAT HIGHWAY!
EXCELLENT DEDUCTION, STRIPESY! WE'LL FOLLOW THOSE TRACKS AND SEE WHERE THEY LEAD!
MOMENTS LATER...
IT WENT UNDER THOSE TREES, KID!
AND IT DIDN'T COME OUT AGAIN! WE'D BETTER DESCEND AND GET A CLOSER LOOK!
SOMEBODY'S DIGGIN' A TUNNEL, USIN' ELECTRIC POWER!
SOMEBODY? MR. X, STRIPESY! THAT'S HOW HE INTENDS TO GET PAST THOSE GUARDS... HE'LL TUNNEL UNDER THEM, UNDER THE FENCE AND THE ALARMS! HE'LL GET TO THE HOUSE DIRECTLY!
GOSH, KID, LET'S GO DOWN THERE, AND...
NOT THIS WAY, STRIPESY! MR. X MAY HAVE LEFT A FEW TRAPS IN THE TUNNEL TO GUARD HIS RETREAT. WE'LL USE THE ROCKET RACER AGAIN...
PRESENTLY, ON THE DOREMY ROOF...
THEY PROBABLY INTEND TO CUT DIRECTLY INTO THE CELLAR! HURRY, STRIPESY!
I'M STEPPIN' ON IT, KID! I'M ANXIOUS TO MEET THIS MR. X FACE TO FACE!
A QUICK, STEALTHY DOWNWARD FLIGHT! AND IN THE CELLAR...
HERE THEY ARE! KID, I THINK I'M GONNA ENJOY THIS!
THE STAR-SPANGLED KID AND STRIPESY! HOW'D THEY FIND OUT ABOUT THIS?
4

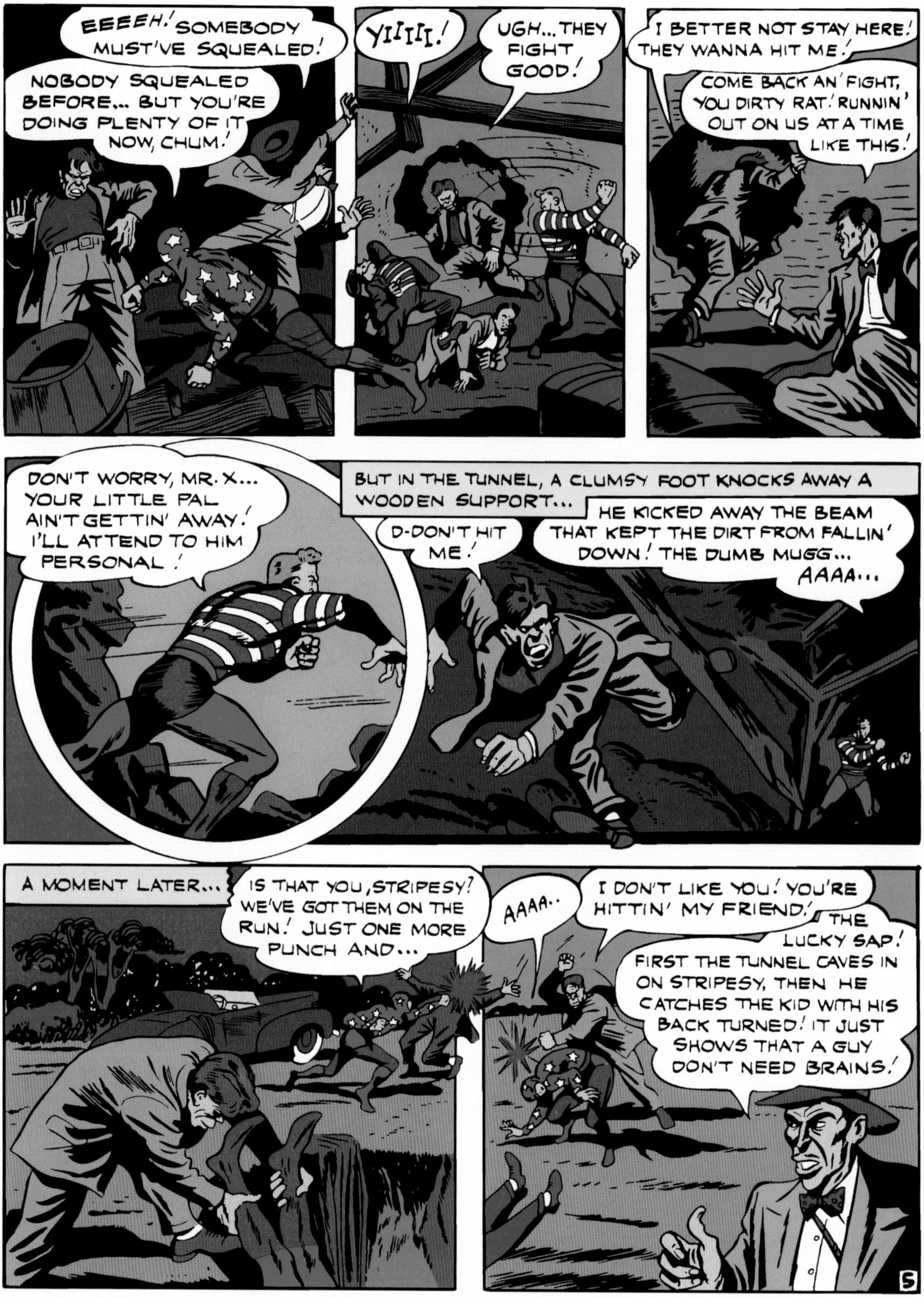
EEEEH! SOMEBODY MUST'VE SQUEALED!
NOBODY SQUEALED BEFORE... BUT YOU'RE DOING PLENTY OF IT NOW, CHUM!
YIIII!
UGH... THEY FIGHT GOOD!
I BETTER NOT STAY HERE! THEY WANNA HIT ME!
COME BACK AN' FIGHT, YOU DIRTY RAT! RUNNIN' OUT ON US AT A TIME LIKE THIS!
DON'T WORRY, MR. X... YOUR LITTLE PAL AIN'T GETTIN' AWAY! I'LL ATTEND TO HIM PERSONAL!
BUT IN THE TUNNEL, A CLUMSY FOOT KNOCKS AWAY A WOODEN SUPPORT...
D-DON'T HIT ME!
HE KICKED AWAY THE BEAM THAT KEPT THE DIRT FROM FALLIN' DOWN! THE DUMB MUGG... AAAA...
A MOMENT LATER...
IS THAT YOU, STRIPESY? WE'VE GOT THEM ON THE RUN! JUST ONE MORE PUNCH AND...
AAAA..
I DON'T LIKE YOU! YOU'RE HITTIN' MY FRIEND!
THE LUCKY SAP! FIRST THE TUNNEL CAVES IN ON STRIPESY, THEN HE CATCHES THE KID WITH HIS BACK TURNED! IT JUST SHOWS THAT A GUY DON'T NEED BRAINS!
5

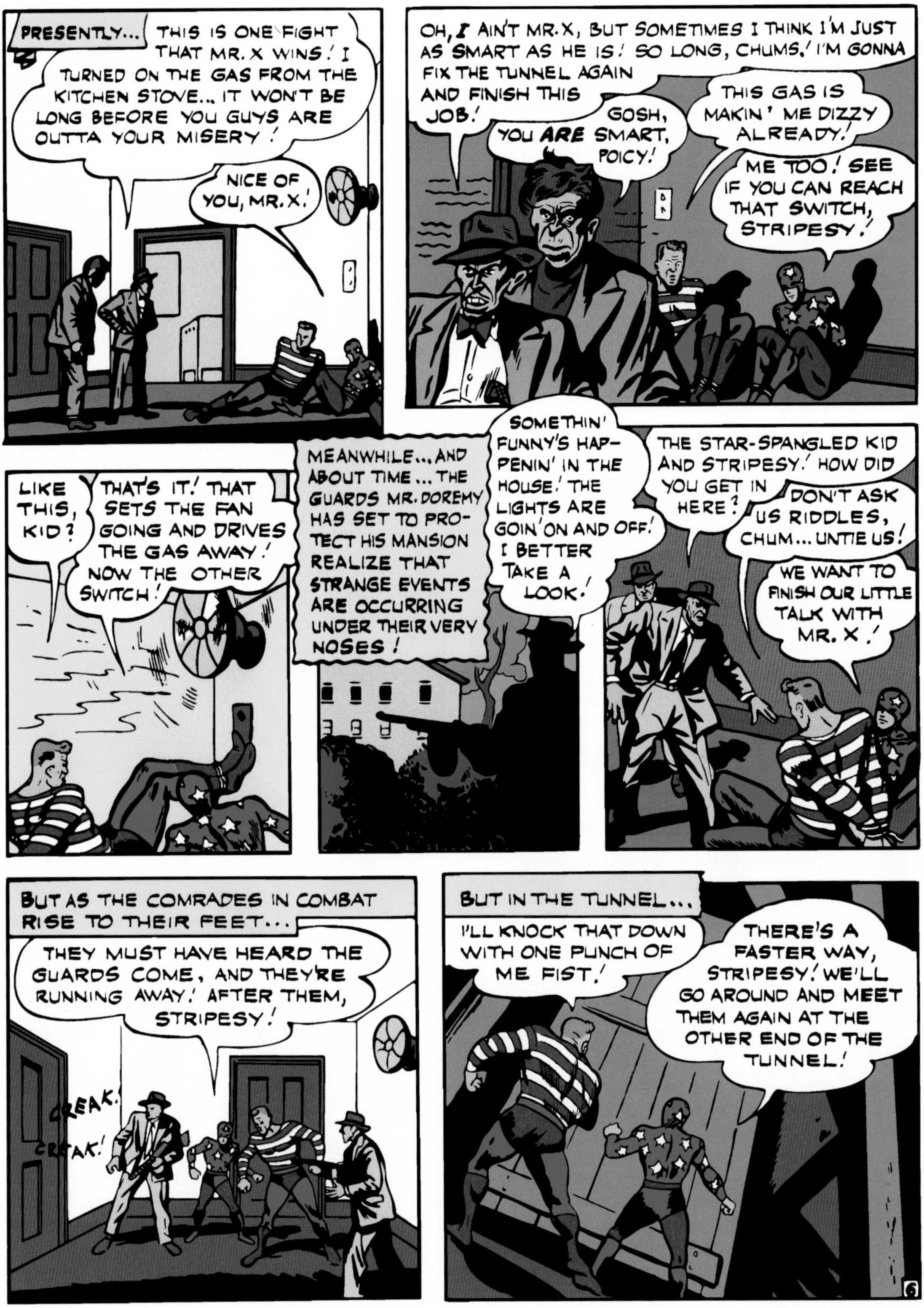
PRESENTLY...
THIS IS ONE FIGHT THAT MR. X WINS! I TURNED ON THE GAS FROM THE KITCHEN STOVE... IT WON'T BE LONG BEFORE YOU GUYS ARE OUTTA YOUR MISERY!
NICE OF YOU, MR. X!
OH, I AIN'T MR. X, BUT SOMETIMES I THINK I'M JUST AS SMART AS HE IS! SO LONG, CHUMS! I'M GONNA FIX THE TUNNEL AGAIN AND FINISH THIS JOB!
GOSH, YOU ARE SMART, POICY!
THIS GAS IS MAKIN' ME DIZZY ALREADY!
ME TOO! SEE IF YOU CAN REACH THAT SWITCH, STRIPESY!
LIKE THIS, KID?
THAT'S IT! THAT SETS THE FAN GOING AND DRIVES THE GAS AWAY! NOW THE OTHER SWITCH!
MEANWHILE... AND ABOUT TIME... THE GUARDS MR. DOREMY HAS SET TO PROTECT HIS MANSION REALIZE THAT STRANGE EVENTS ARE OCCURRING UNDER THEIR VERY NOSES!
SOMETHIN' FUNNY'S HAPPENIN' IN THE HOUSE! THE LIGHTS ARE GOIN' ON AND OFF! I BETTER TAKE A LOOK!
THE STAR-SPANGLED KID AND STRIPESY! HOW DID YOU GET IN HERE?
DON'T ASK US RIDDLES, CHUM... UNTIE US!
WE WANT TO FINISH OUR LITTLE TALK WITH MR. X!
BUT AS THE COMRADES IN COMBAT RISE TO THEIR FEET...
THEY MUST HAVE HEARD THE GUARDS COME, AND THEY'RE RUNNING AWAY! AFTER THEM, STRIPESY!
CREAK!
CREAK!
BUT IN THE TUNNEL...
I'LL KNOCK THAT DOWN WITH ONE PUNCH OF ME FIST!
THERE'S A FASTER WAY, STRIPESY! WE'LL GO AROUND AND MEET THEM AGAIN AT THE OTHER END OF THE TUNNEL!
6

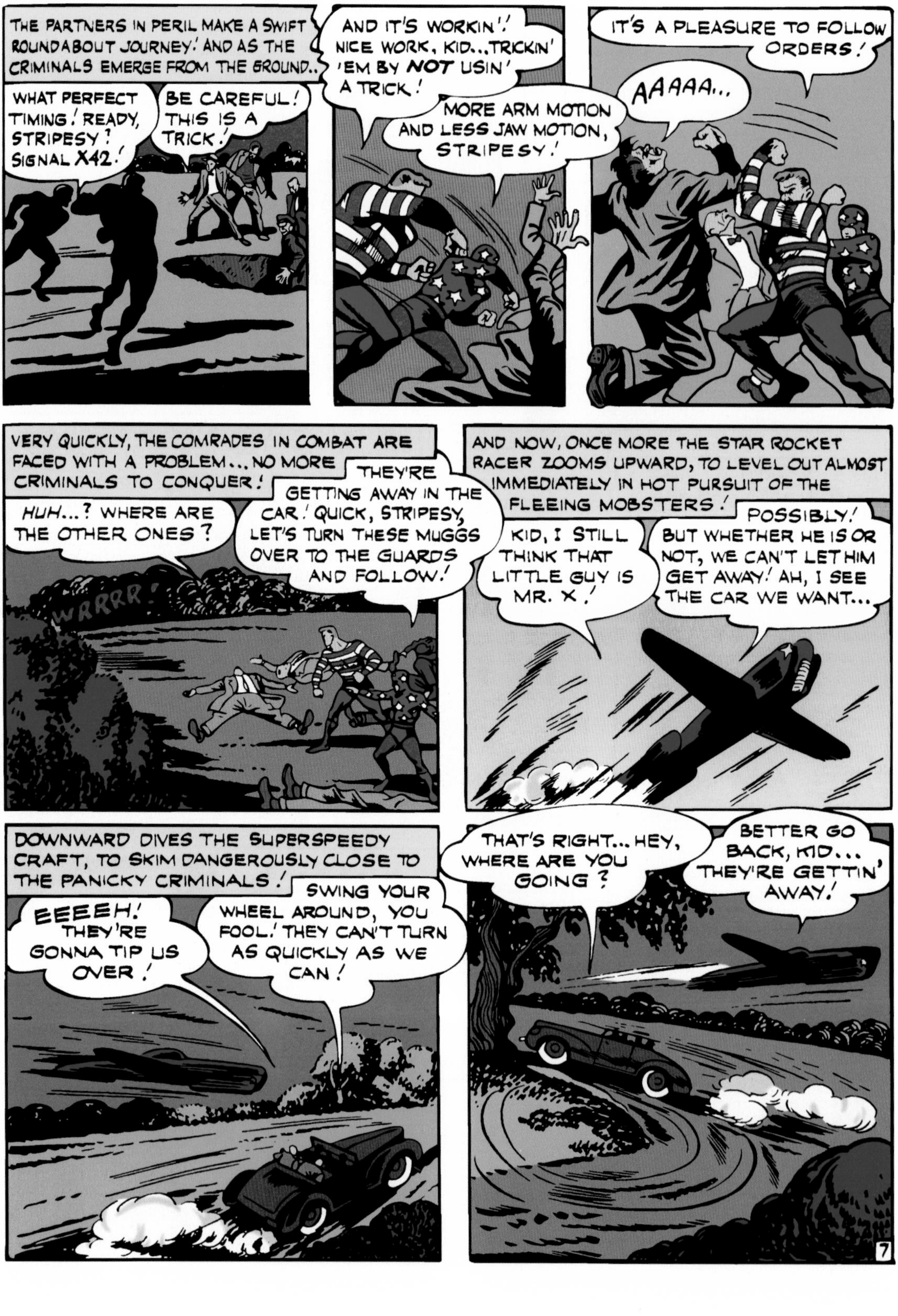
THE PARTNERS IN PERIL MAKE A SWIFT ROUNDABOUT JOURNEY! AND AS THE CRIMINALS EMERGE FROM THE GROUND..
WHAT PERFECT TIMING! READY, STRIPESY? SIGNAL X42!
BE CAREFUL! THIS IS A TRICK!
AND IT'S WORKIN'! NICE WORK, KID...TRICKIN' 'EM BY NOT USIN' A TRICK!
MORE ARM MOTION AND LESS JAW MOTION, STRIPESY!
IT'S A PLEASURE TO FOLLOW ORDERS!
AAAAA...
VERY QUICKLY, THE COMRADES IN COMBAT ARE FACED WITH A PROBLEM... NO MORE CRIMINALS TO CONQUER!
HUH...? WHERE ARE THE OTHER ONES?
THEY'RE GETTING AWAY IN THE CAR! QUICK, STRIPESY, LET'S TURN THESE MUGGS OVER TO THE GUARDS AND FOLLOW!
WRRRR!
AND NOW, ONCE MORE THE STAR ROCKET RACER ZOOMS UPWARD, TO LEVEL OUT ALMOST IMMEDIATELY IN HOT PURSUIT OF THE FLEEING MOBSTERS!
KID, I STILL THINK THAT LITTLE GUY IS MR. X!
POSSIBLY! BUT WHETHER HE IS OR NOT, WE CAN'T LET HIM GET AWAY! AH, I SEE THE CAR WE WANT...
DOWNWARD DIVES THE SUPERSPEEDY CRAFT, TO SKIM DANGEROUSLY CLOSE TO THE PANICKY CRIMINALS!
EEEEH! THEY'RE GONNA TIP US OVER!
SWING YOUR WHEEL AROUND, YOU FOOL! THEY CAN'T TURN AS QUICKLY AS WE CAN!
THAT'S RIGHT... HEY, WHERE ARE YOU GOING?
BETTER GO BACK, KID... THEY'RE GETTIN' AWAY!
7

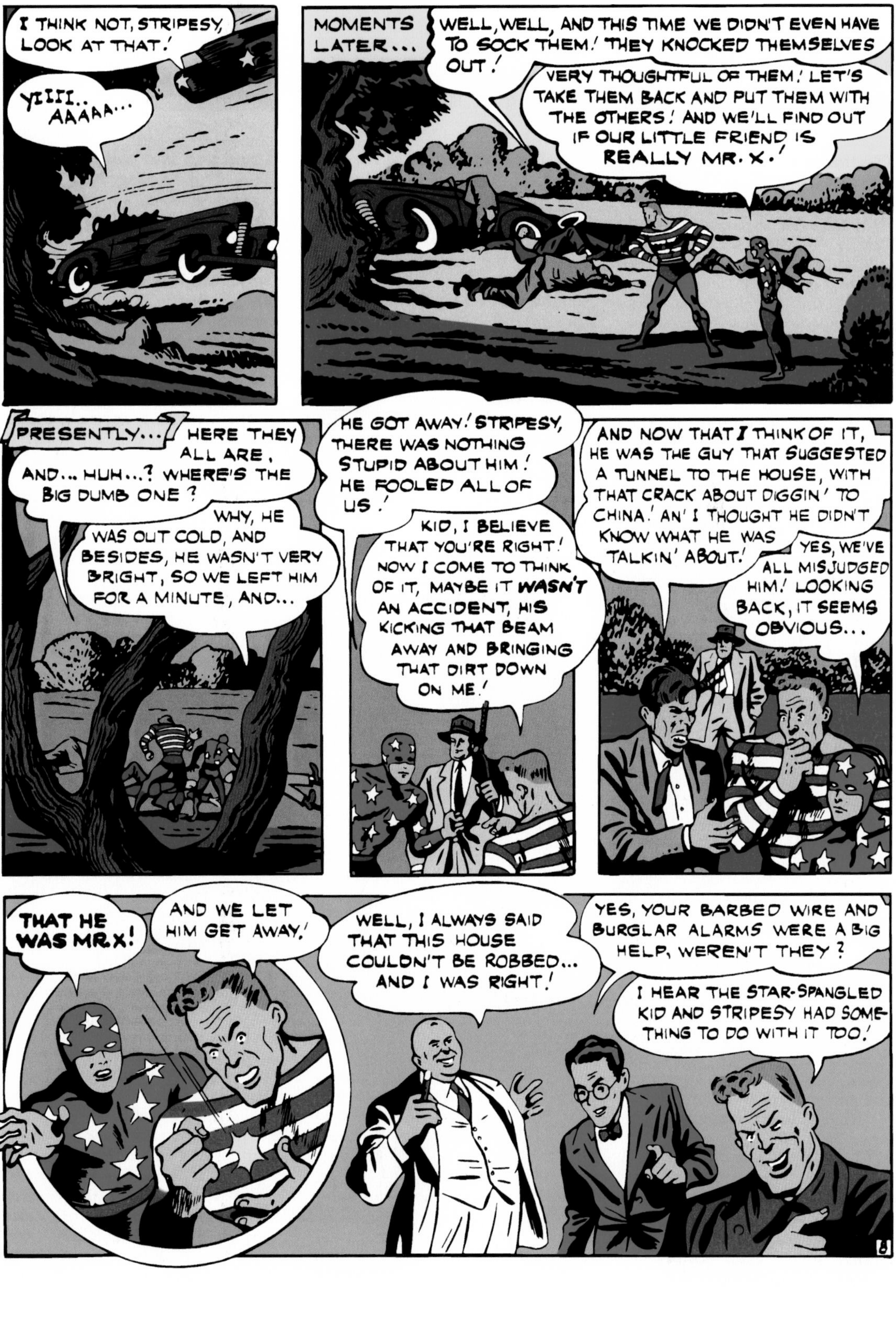
I THINK NOT, STRIPESY, LOOK AT THAT!
YIIII.. AAAAA...
MOMENTS LATER...
WELL, WELL, AND THIS TIME WE DIDN'T EVEN HAVE TO SOCK THEM! THEY KNOCKED THEMSELVES OUT!
VERY THOUGHTFUL OF THEM! LET'S TAKE THEM BACK AND PUT THEM WITH THE OTHERS! AND WE'LL FIND OUT IF OUR LITTLE FRIEND IS REALLY MR. X.!
PRESENTLY...
HERE THEY ALL ARE, AND... HUH...? WHERE'S THE BIG DUMB ONE?
WHY, HE WAS OUT COLD, AND BESIDES, HE WASN'T VERY BRIGHT, SO WE LEFT HIM FOR A MINUTE, AND...
HE GOT AWAY! STRIPESY, THERE WAS NOTHING STUPID ABOUT HIM! HE FOOLED ALL OF US!
KID, I BELIEVE THAT YOU'RE RIGHT! NOW I COME TO THINK OF IT, MAYBE IT WASN'T AN ACCIDENT, HIS KICKING THAT BEAM AWAY AND BRINGING THAT DIRT DOWN ON ME!
AND NOW THAT I THINK OF IT, HE WAS THE GUY THAT SUGGESTED A TUNNEL TO THE HOUSE, WITH THAT CRACK ABOUT DIGGIN' TO CHINA! AN' I THOUGHT HE DIDN'T KNOW WHAT HE WAS TALKIN' ABOUT!
YES, WE'VE ALL MISJUDGED HIM! LOOKING BACK, IT SEEMS OBVIOUS...
THAT HE WAS MR.X!
AND WE LET HIM GET AWAY!
WELL, I ALWAYS SAID THAT THIS HOUSE COULDN'T BE ROBBED... AND I WAS RIGHT!
YES, YOUR BARBED WIRE AND BURGLAR ALARMS WERE A BIG HELP, WEREN'T THEY?
I HEAR THE STAR-SPANGLED KID AND STRIPESY HAD SOMETHING TO DO WITH IT TOO!
8

Chapter V

INTERLUDE at HOODLUMS' HIDEOUT

IN the spacious lobby of the palatial hotel, the silence was broken by a slow chuckle. "If it ain't Mr. X," grinned Red Heister. "Come back to tell us how you put one over on the Crimson Avenger?"

"And the Star-Spangled Kid and Stripesy?" jeered Dodo the Dip. "I'm waitin' to hear how you-all hogtied the Vigilante," drawled Lazy Dyers, his slow voice full of malice.

The sardonic face of the master of disguises remained expressionless.

"I've failed," he admitted calmly. "I've failed three times Possibly I've been a bit overconfident. I've been too careful to warn my opponents when I intended to commit a crime, too careless once I secured a temporary advantage over them.

"But at least I haven't failed completely. I've come close to success, and in each case I've escaped from my opponent at the end."

"You're no slouch, Mr. X," conceded Blackie Kraul. "You had some good ideas, and against opposition that wasn't so high class, you'd have made out okay. But these babies are too much for you."

"Do you think so?" Mr. X turned a curious gaze on Blackie, and the uneasy thug squirmed under the glance. The two burning eyes that drilled into his made him think of the frightening face that might be hidden under the mask, and the thought sent shivers down his spine. His own eyes dropped and he muttered:

"Now, if you wanta call them other bets off . . ."

"The bets stand! But it's strange that you should have wanted to call them off. It's almost as if you'd heard my plans for the Shining Knight. "Mr. X smiled sadly. "Poor fellows."

Blackie swallowed anxiously.

Ten thousand dollars of his was riding on the Shining Knight. And from the way Mr. X spoke, that ten thousand dollars was as good as lost.

"Don't try to kid me, pal," he said nervously. "The Shinin' Knight can take care of hisself. He's stood up against some mighty tough hombres in his time. He ain't scared of no man alive."

"No man, perhaps." Again Mr. X smiled, showing white sharp teeth. "But there are certain animals . . ."

Blackie straightened up in alarm. "What do ya mean, animals?"

Mr. X leaned toward him, whispered. To the others, watching curiously, it was a shock to see Blackie turn pale. "You see," said Mr. X pleasantly, "he doesn't stand a chance."

Blackie gulped. "That depends. The Knight ain't no fool. Like I said, he knows how to look out for hisself."

"Ah, you wouldn't say that if you knew my entire plan." Again Mr. X leaned toward the burly thug, again his lips moved, his words inaudible to the others.

"Of course, Blackie," observed Mr. X in conclusion, "you won't say a thing about this to anybody. This is entirely between you and me."

"I'll keep me mouth shut."

"That's good of you." Mr. X faced the others. "You will excuse me, gentlemen. I must write a letter and be up early tomorrow morning to arrange my plans for the man of yesterday. I think that before I'm through with him, he'll wish he was back where he came from."

He sat down at a desk some distance away and the others began to talk normally once more, as if a weight had been lifted from their minds.

But Blackie could not join in the conversation. What Mr. X had told him weighed on his mind. The Shining Knight was a doomed man . . . and with him, Blackie's ten thousand dollars.

Slowly the others drifted away, until only Blackie and Mr. X were left. The latter seemed to be writing slowly. Then he too departed, and Blackie was alone, to pace up and down irritably, puffing on endless cigarettes. The lights in the different rooms winked out . . . and still Blackie prowled the lobby restlessly, unable to come to a decision.

He had never in his life squealed on a pal. There was nothing he despised more than a stoolpigeon. But never had the temptation to squeal been so strong. Beads of sweat stood out on his brow as the battle went on within him.

"It ain't like squealin' to the cops," he muttered to himself. "And it ain't like I was turnin' Mr. X in. It's just that I'll spoil his scheme, that's all."

But underneath, he was not deceiving himself. For, in order to give the Shining Knight information of any value, he would have to reveal enough about Mr. X's plans to make sure of their failure. And if those plans were ruined, Mr. X stood a good chance of being caught. His luck couldn't hold forever.

In the hotel, all was silent. Finally, Blackie growled savagely to himself. He had made up his mind.

Sitting down at a desk in the lobby, he carefully selected a sheet of paper. There was no letterhead on the white sheet, no printed matter by which to identify the hotel. Writing slowly and laboriously, he penned his message. Under the best of conditions, Blackie wrote with almost painful difficulty, and now, what with the necessity of disguising his handwriting, the ink almost dried under his pen before it had completed two words. Nevertheless, he persisted.

When he had finished, he sat back and regarded the product of his labors. No chance of the Knight falling into Mr. X's trap now, he thought grimly.

Now he produced two envelopes, one larger than the other. The outer one, in handwriting that he did not bother to disguise, he addressed to a friend of his. The inner one he addressed to Professor Moresby. All the world knew that the Professor had ways of reaching the Shining Knight.

The message he had so laboriously spelled out he placed within t h i s inner envelope, which he then sealed a n d stamped. The inner envelope, along with a short note, he placed in the large envelope.

The idea behind this procedure was simple. The large letter would first reach his friend, who would then remail the smaller letter to Professor Morseby. In this way, neither the Professor nor the Shining Knight would ever catch sight of the postmark of the nearby village which might give them a clue to the hideout. Nor would Mr. X, for that matter, ever be able to prove that it w a s Blackie who had betrayed him.

His letter finished, Blackie listened intently for a moment. The hotel was still quiet. Mr. X, no matter what strange powers he possessed, required sleep like any other man.

Silently, Blackie slipped out into the night. The moon overhead lighted the narrow path that led down the mountainside.

He moved cautiously, a black soundless shadow that was the only living thing in sight.

Unexpected r o c k s tripped him, brambles t o r e at his clothes. But he went swiftly for all that, and in little more than an hour he was at the nearby village, its tiny cluster of houses slumbering in the moonlight.

Not a soul was abroad. The shutter of the village letter box swung open, then shut again. Blackie's letter was in the mail.

With the same silence he had shown previously, he slipped back into the shadows, then began the slow climb up the mountainside, and back toward the hotel again.

In the hotel, sitting behind drawn shades, Mr. X chuckled. Through the narrow space at the side, he could see Blackie fearfully scrambling down the trail. He watched him to make sure Blackie did not turn back, then walked quickly out into the hotel corridor.

The thick luxurious r u g s deadened his footsteps as he descended into the lobby. At the writing desk, he found everything as he h a d expected. Where there had been seventeen envelopes, eight large and nine small, there were now fifteen. Two sheets of letter paper were missing.

From beneath the blotter, he removed a thin sheet of carbon paper, as well as a thicker sheet, both extending to the edge of the blotter. Because of Blackie's heavy-handed use of the pen, there was no difficulty in reading what he had written.

Mr. X's lips curled. "Exactly as I expected him to do. The

fool! Didn't he realize I wouldn't reveal my *real* plans to any one?"

A moment later, Mr. X climbed the stairs once more. From his room, some time afterward, he watched Blackie returning. He smiled with satisfaction as he noted that Blackie no longer had the letter.

✻   ✻   ✻

Next morning, as Mr. X took his seat in his plane, the others crowded around. Blackie's face was innocent and friendly.

"So long, pals," he said. "It'd cost me dough, but if you'd fix the Shinin' Knight's wagon, it'd be okay with me. I sure hate that guy."

"Thanks, Blackie," returned Mr. X. "I appreciate the way you feel."

The propeller became a droning blur, the plane taxied across the short landing field and into space. As it zoomed upward, Mr. X grinned.

"The idiot," he said, thinking of Blackie. "He's too stupid to understand why I told him my pretended plans. When I challenged the other Soldiers of Victory, I warned them where I intended to strike. This time Blackie, without realizing it, is doing the challenging for me. The Shining Knight learns nothing that I don't want him to know. Blackie gives him misleading information, s e t s him to watching for the wrong thing, distracts his attention from the right thing."

The plane settled down to level flight, the woods and valleys skimming past it far below.

"This," gloated Mr. X, "is one bet I can't lose!"

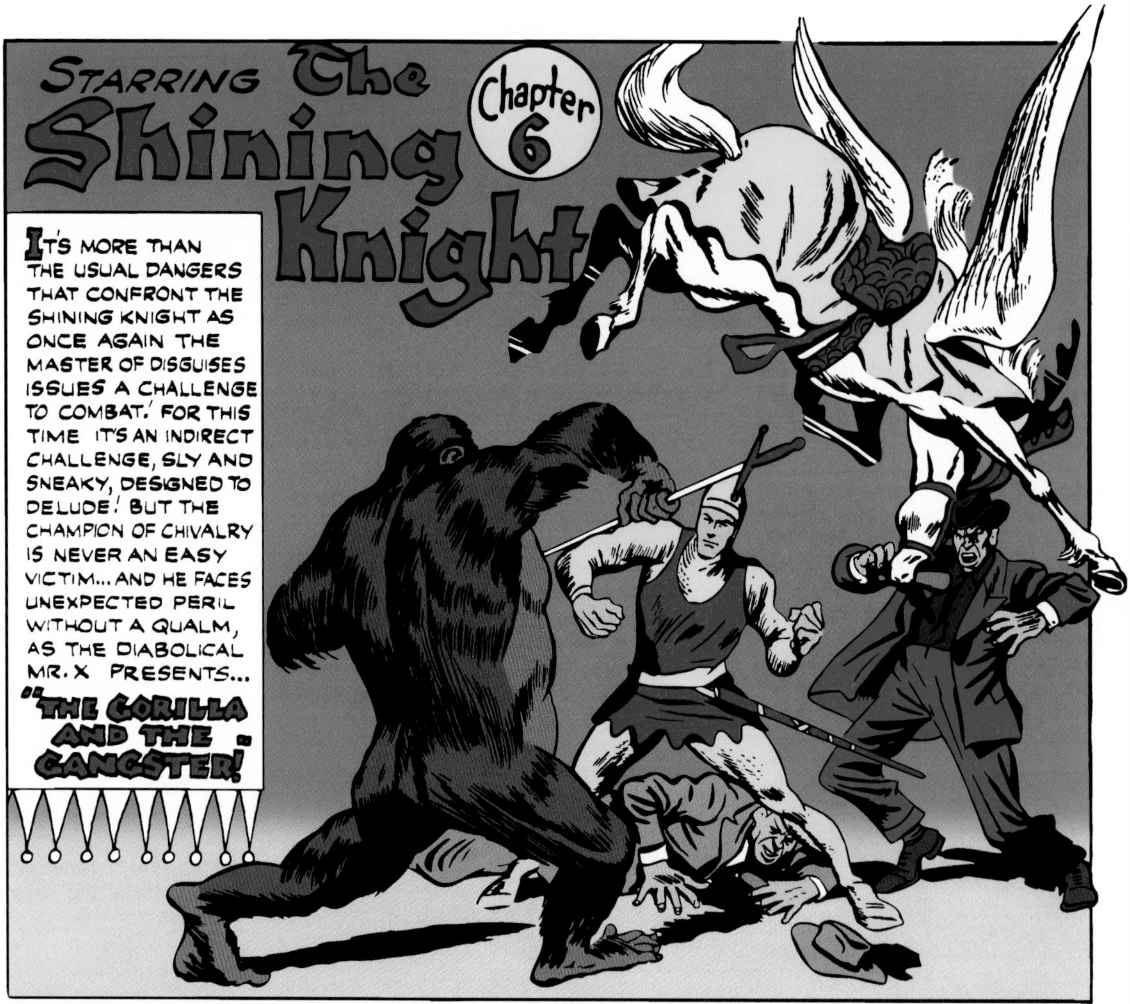
STARRING The Shining Knight
Chapter 6
IT'S MORE THAN THE USUAL DANGERS THAT CONFRONT THE SHINING KNIGHT AS ONCE AGAIN THE MASTER OF DISGUISES ISSUES A CHALLENGE TO COMBAT! FOR THIS TIME IT'S AN INDIRECT CHALLENGE, SLY AND SNEAKY, DESIGNED TO DELUDE! BUT THE CHAMPION OF CHIVALRY IS NEVER AN EASY VICTIM... AND HE FACES UNEXPECTED PERIL WITHOUT A QUALM, AS THE DIABOLICAL MR. X PRESENTS...
"THE GORILLA AND THE GANGSTER!"

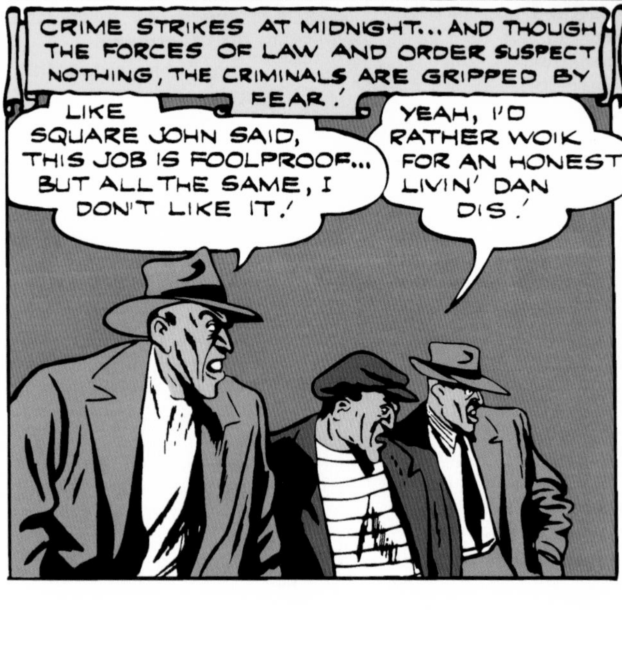
CRIME STRIKES AT MIDNIGHT... AND THOUGH THE FORCES OF LAW AND ORDER SUSPECT NOTHING, THE CRIMINALS ARE GRIPPED BY FEAR!
LIKE SQUARE JOHN SAID, THIS JOB IS FOOLPROOF... BUT ALL THE SAME, I DON'T LIKE IT!
YEAH, I'D RATHER WOIK FOR AN HONEST LIVIN' DAN DIS!

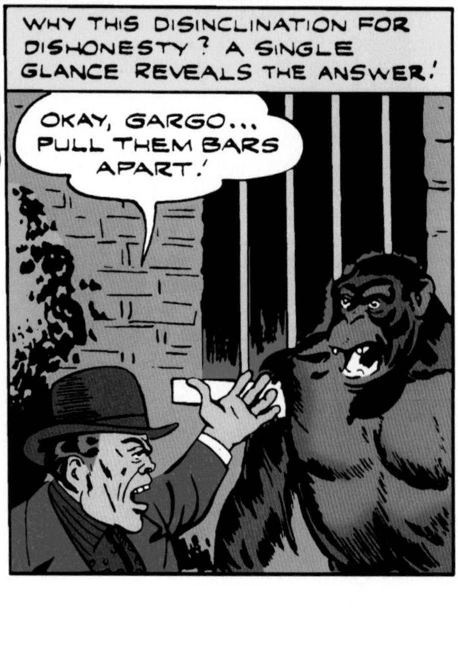
WHY THIS DISINCLINATION FOR DISHONESTY? A SINGLE GLANCE REVEALS THE ANSWER!
OKAY, GARGO... PULL THEM BARS APART!

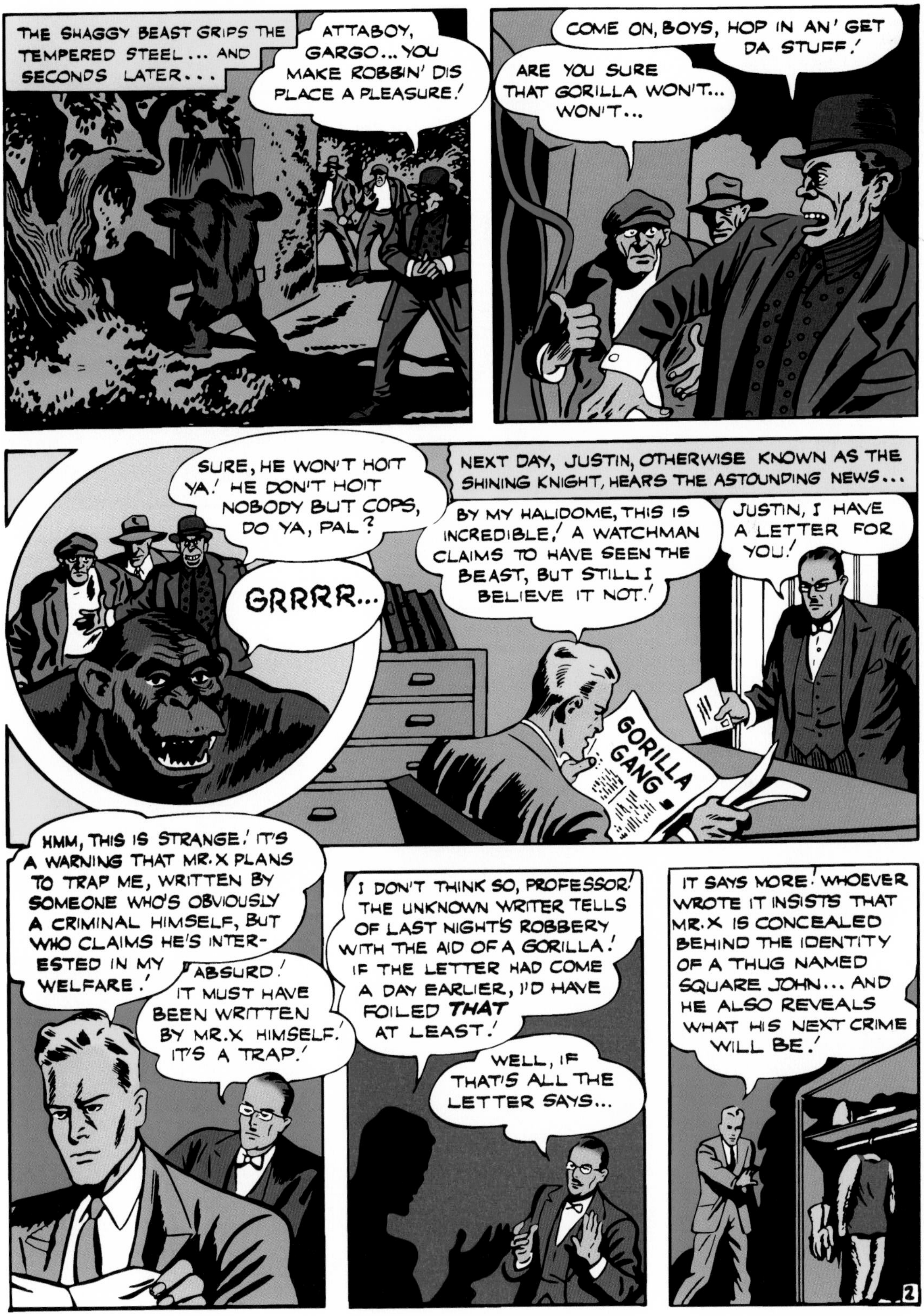
THE SHAGGY BEAST GRIPS THE TEMPERED STEEL... AND SECONDS LATER...
ATTABOY, GARGO... YOU MAKE ROBBIN' DIS PLACE A PLEASURE!
COME ON, BOYS, HOP IN AN' GET DA STUFF!
ARE YOU SURE THAT GORILLA WON'T... WON'T...
SURE, HE WON'T HOIT YA! HE DON'T HOIT NOBODY BUT COPS, DO YA, PAL?
GRRRR...
NEXT DAY, JUSTIN, OTHERWISE KNOWN AS THE SHINING KNIGHT, HEARS THE ASTOUNDING NEWS...
BY MY HALIDOME, THIS IS INCREDIBLE! A WATCHMAN CLAIMS TO HAVE SEEN THE BEAST, BUT STILL I BELIEVE IT NOT!
JUSTIN, I HAVE A LETTER FOR YOU!
GORILLA GANG
HMM, THIS IS STRANGE! IT'S A WARNING THAT MR. X PLANS TO TRAP ME, WRITTEN BY SOMEONE WHO'S OBVIOUSLY A CRIMINAL HIMSELF, BUT WHO CLAIMS HE'S INTERESTED IN MY WELFARE!
ABSURD! IT MUST HAVE BEEN WRITTEN BY MR. X HIMSELF! IT'S A TRAP!
I DON'T THINK SO, PROFESSOR! THE UNKNOWN WRITER TELLS OF LAST NIGHT'S ROBBERY WITH THE AID OF A GORILLA! IF THE LETTER HAD COME A DAY EARLIER, I'D HAVE FOILED THAT AT LEAST!
WELL, IF THAT'S ALL THE LETTER SAYS...
IT SAYS MORE! WHOEVER WROTE IT INSISTS THAT MR. X IS CONCEALED BEHIND THE IDENTITY OF A THUG NAMED SQUARE JOHN... AND HE ALSO REVEALS WHAT HIS NEXT CRIME WILL BE!
2

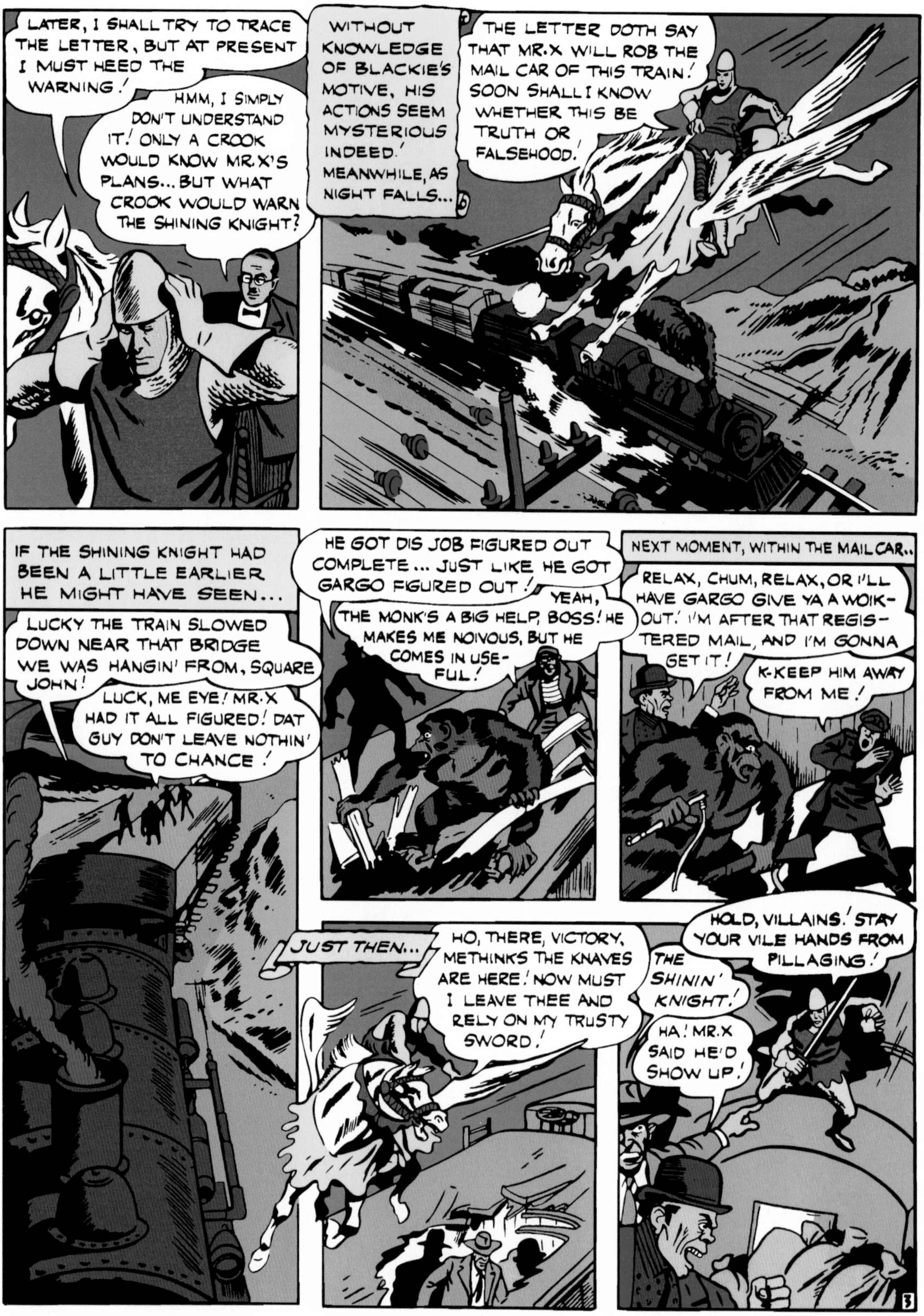
LATER, I SHALL TRY TO TRACE THE LETTER, BUT AT PRESENT I MUST HEED THE WARNING!
HMM, I SIMPLY DON'T UNDERSTAND IT! ONLY A CROOK WOULD KNOW MR. X'S PLANS... BUT WHAT CROOK WOULD WARN THE SHINING KNIGHT?
WITHOUT KNOWLEDGE OF BLACKIE'S MOTIVE, HIS ACTIONS SEEM MYSTERIOUS INDEED! MEANWHILE, AS NIGHT FALLS...
THE LETTER DOTH SAY THAT MR. X WILL ROB THE MAIL CAR OF THIS TRAIN! SOON SHALL I KNOW WHETHER THIS BE TRUTH OR FALSEHOOD!
IF THE SHINING KNIGHT HAD BEEN A LITTLE EARLIER HE MIGHT HAVE SEEN...
LUCKY THE TRAIN SLOWED DOWN NEAR THAT BRIDGE WE WAS HANGIN' FROM, SQUARE JOHN!
LUCK, ME EYE! MR. X HAD IT ALL FIGURED! DAT GUY DON'T LEAVE NOTHIN' TO CHANCE!
HE GOT DIS JOB FIGURED OUT COMPLETE... JUST LIKE HE GOT GARGO FIGURED OUT!
YEAH, THE MONK'S A BIG HELP, BOSS! HE MAKES ME NOIVOUS, BUT HE COMES IN USE-FUL!
NEXT MOMENT, WITHIN THE MAIL CAR..
RELAX, CHUM, RELAX, OR I'LL HAVE GARGO GIVE YA A WOIK-OUT! I'M AFTER THAT REGIS-TERED MAIL, AND I'M GONNA GET IT!
K-KEEP HIM AWAY FROM ME!
JUST THEN...
HO, THERE, VICTORY, METHINKS THE KNAVES ARE HERE! NOW MUST I LEAVE THEE AND RELY ON MY TRUSTY SWORD!
HOLD, VILLAINS! STAY YOUR VILE HANDS FROM PILLAGING!
THE SHININ' KNIGHT!
HA! MR. X SAID HE'D SHOW UP!
3

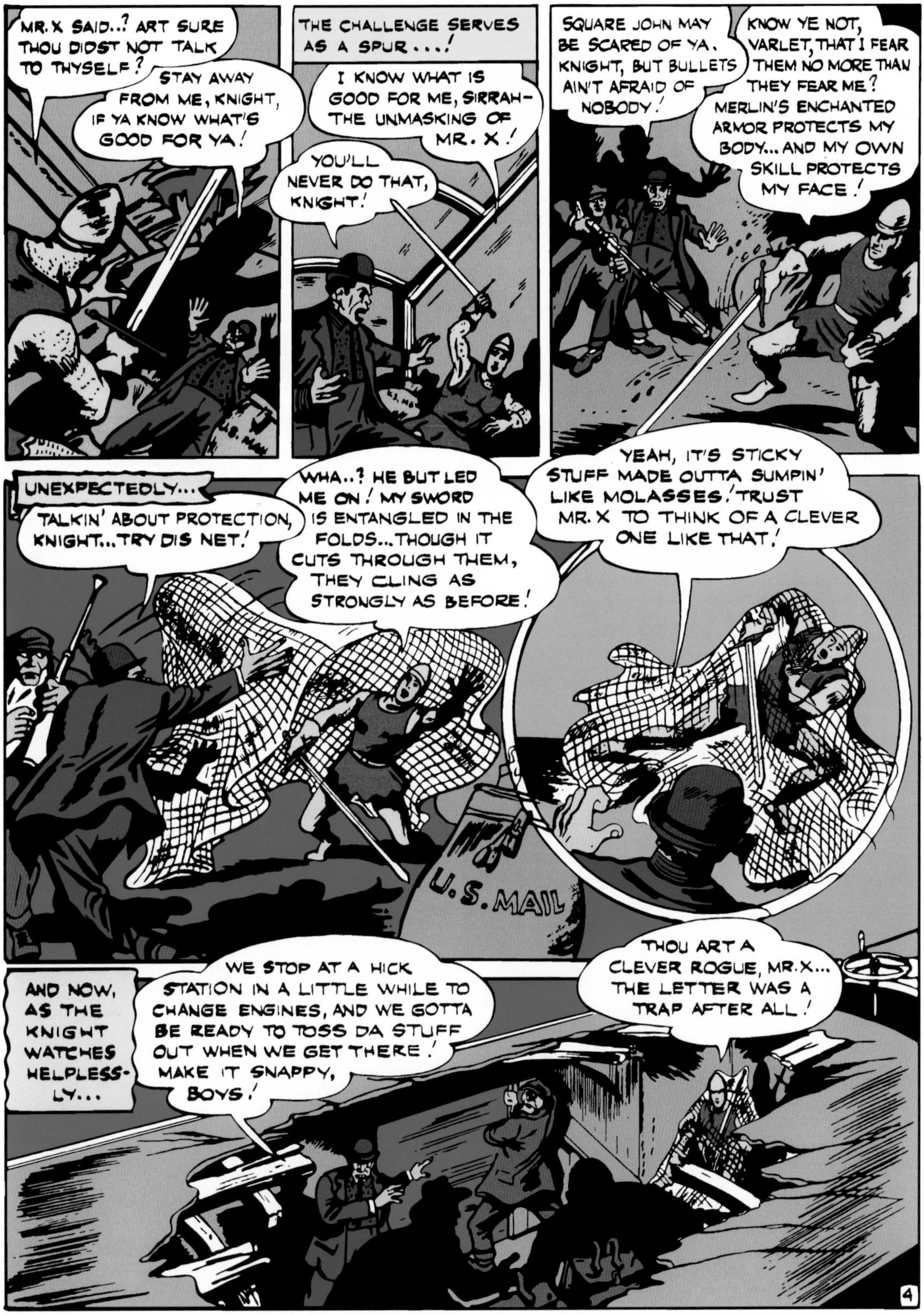
MR. X SAID..? ART SURE THOU DIDST NOT TALK TO THYSELF?
STAY AWAY FROM ME, KNIGHT, IF YA KNOW WHAT'S GOOD FOR YA!
THE CHALLENGE SERVES AS A SPUR...!
I KNOW WHAT IS GOOD FOR ME, SIRRAH-THE UNMASKING OF MR. X!
YOU'LL NEVER DO THAT, KNIGHT!
SQUARE JOHN MAY BE SCARED OF YA, KNIGHT, BUT BULLETS AIN'T AFRAID OF NOBODY!
KNOW YE NOT, VARLET, THAT I FEAR THEM NO MORE THAN THEY FEAR ME? MERLIN'S ENCHANTED ARMOR PROTECTS MY BODY... AND MY OWN SKILL PROTECTS MY FACE!
UNEXPECTEDLY...
TALKIN' ABOUT PROTECTION, KNIGHT... TRY DIS NET!
WHA..? HE BUT LED ME ON! MY SWORD IS ENTANGLED IN THE FOLDS... THOUGH IT CUTS THROUGH THEM, THEY CLING AS STRONGLY AS BEFORE!
YEAH, IT'S STICKY STUFF MADE OUTTA SUMPIN' LIKE MOLASSES! TRUST MR. X TO THINK OF A CLEVER ONE LIKE THAT!
U.S. MAIL
AND NOW, AS THE KNIGHT WATCHES HELPLESSLY...
WE STOP AT A HICK STATION IN A LITTLE WHILE TO CHANGE ENGINES, AND WE GOTTA BE READY TO TOSS DA STUFF OUT WHEN WE GET THERE! MAKE IT SNAPPY, BOYS!
THOU ART A CLEVER ROGUE, MR. X... THE LETTER WAS A TRAP AFTER ALL!
4

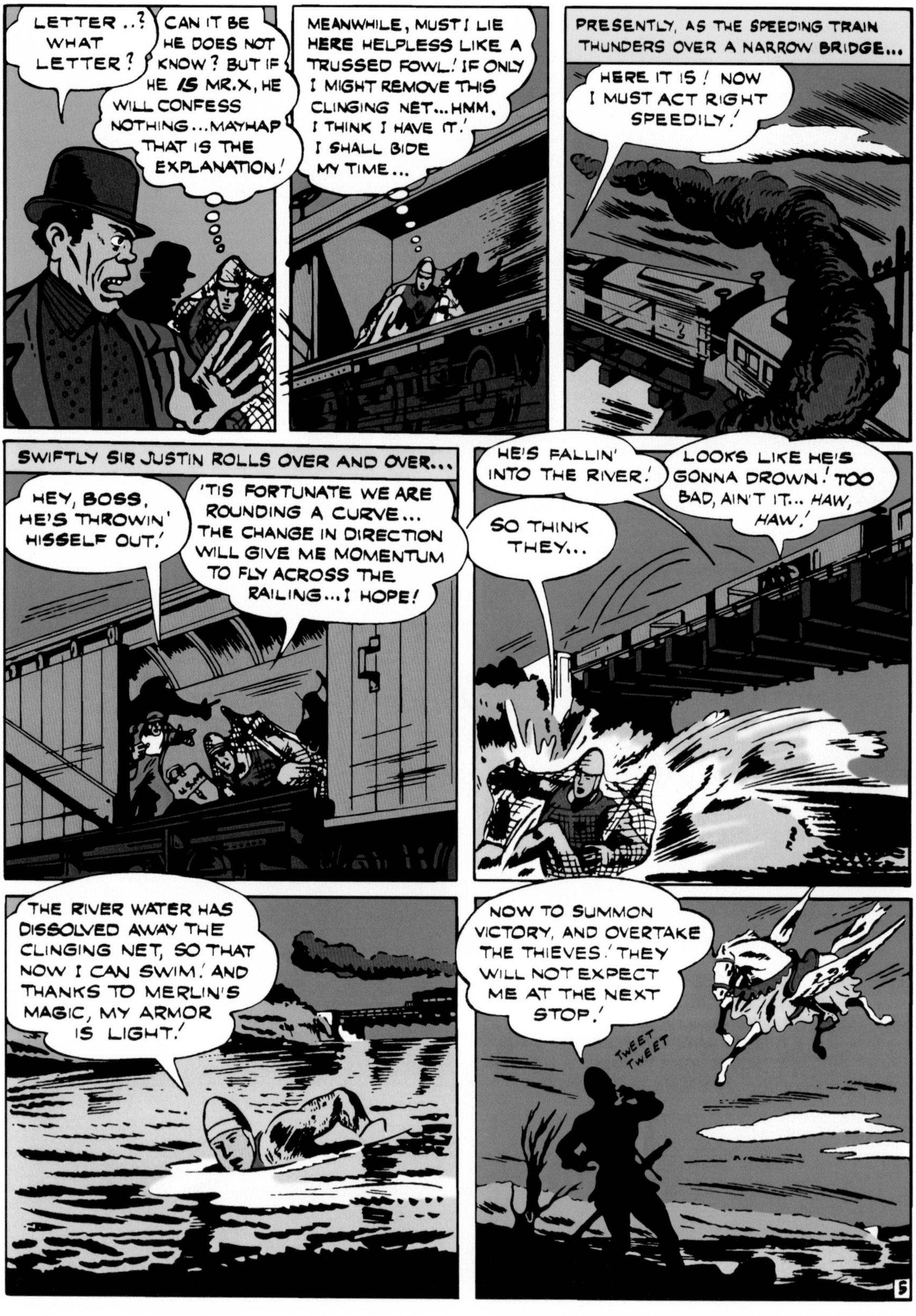
LETTER ..? WHAT LETTER?
CAN IT BE HE DOES NOT KNOW? BUT IF HE *IS* MR.X, HE WILL CONFESS NOTHING...MAYHAP THAT IS THE EXPLANATION!
MEANWHILE, MUST I LIE HERE HELPLESS LIKE A TRUSSED FOWL! IF ONLY I MIGHT REMOVE THIS CLINGING NET...HMM, I THINK I HAVE IT! I SHALL BIDE MY TIME...
PRESENTLY, AS THE SPEEDING TRAIN THUNDERS OVER A NARROW BRIDGE...
HERE IT IS! NOW I MUST ACT RIGHT SPEEDILY!
SWIFTLY SIR JUSTIN ROLLS OVER AND OVER...
HEY, BOSS, HE'S THROWIN' HISSELF OUT!
'TIS FORTUNATE WE ARE ROUNDING A CURVE... THE CHANGE IN DIRECTION WILL GIVE ME MOMENTUM TO FLY ACROSS THE RAILING...I HOPE!
HE'S FALLIN' INTO THE RIVER!
LOOKS LIKE HE'S GONNA DROWN! TOO BAD, AIN'T IT... *HAW, HAW!*
SO THINK THEY...
THE RIVER WATER HAS DISSOLVED AWAY THE CLINGING NET, SO THAT NOW I CAN SWIM! AND THANKS TO MERLIN'S MAGIC, MY ARMOR IS LIGHT!
NOW TO SUMMON VICTORY, AND OVERTAKE THE THIEVES! THEY WILL NOT EXPECT ME AT THE NEXT STOP!
TWEET TWEET
5

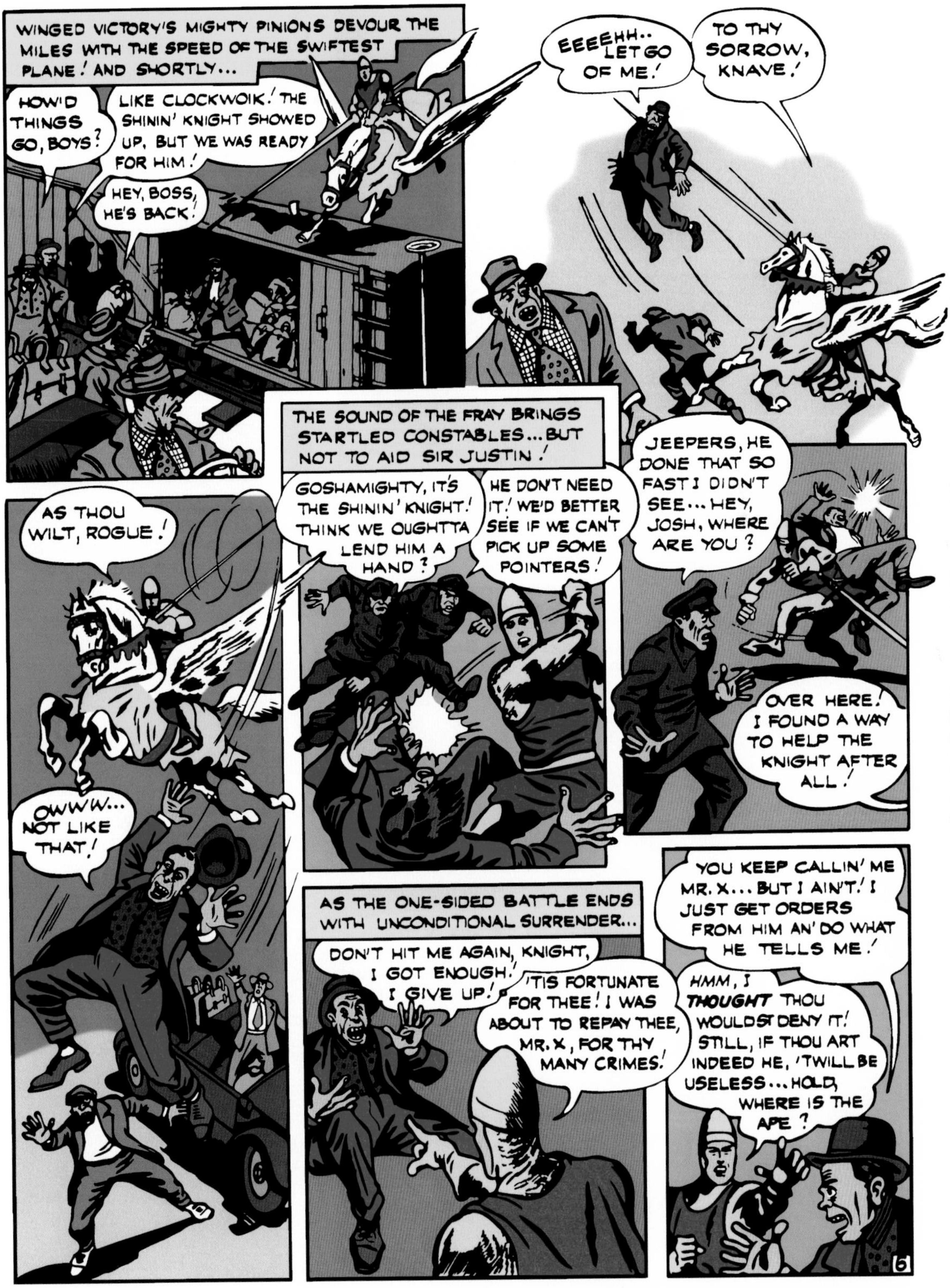
WINGED VICTORY'S MIGHTY PINIONS DEVOUR THE MILES WITH THE SPEED OF THE SWIFTEST PLANE! AND SHORTLY...
HOW'D THINGS GO, BOYS?
LIKE CLOCKWOIK! THE SHININ' KNIGHT SHOWED UP, BUT WE WAS READY FOR HIM!
HEY, BOSS, HE'S BACK!
EEEEHH.. LET GO OF ME!
TO THY SORROW, KNAVE!
AS THOU WILT, ROGUE!
OWWW... NOT LIKE THAT!
THE SOUND OF THE FRAY BRINGS STARTLED CONSTABLES... BUT NOT TO AID SIR JUSTIN!
GOSHAMIGHTY, IT'S THE SHININ' KNIGHT! THINK WE OUGHTTA LEND HIM A HAND?
HE DON'T NEED IT! WE'D BETTER SEE IF WE CAN'T PICK UP SOME POINTERS!
JEEPERS, HE DONE THAT SO FAST I DIDN'T SEE... HEY, JOSH, WHERE ARE YOU?
OVER HERE! I FOUND A WAY TO HELP THE KNIGHT AFTER ALL!
AS THE ONE-SIDED BATTLE ENDS WITH UNCONDITIONAL SURRENDER...
DON'T HIT ME AGAIN, KNIGHT, I GOT ENOUGH! I GIVE UP!
'TIS FORTUNATE FOR THEE! I WAS ABOUT TO REPAY THEE, MR. X, FOR THY MANY CRIMES!
YOU KEEP CALLIN' ME MR. X... BUT I AIN'T! I JUST GET ORDERS FROM HIM AN' DO WHAT HE TELLS ME!
HMM, I **THOUGHT** THOU WOULDST DENY IT! STILL, IF THOU ART INDEED HE, 'TWILL BE USELESS... HOLD, WHERE IS THE APE?
6

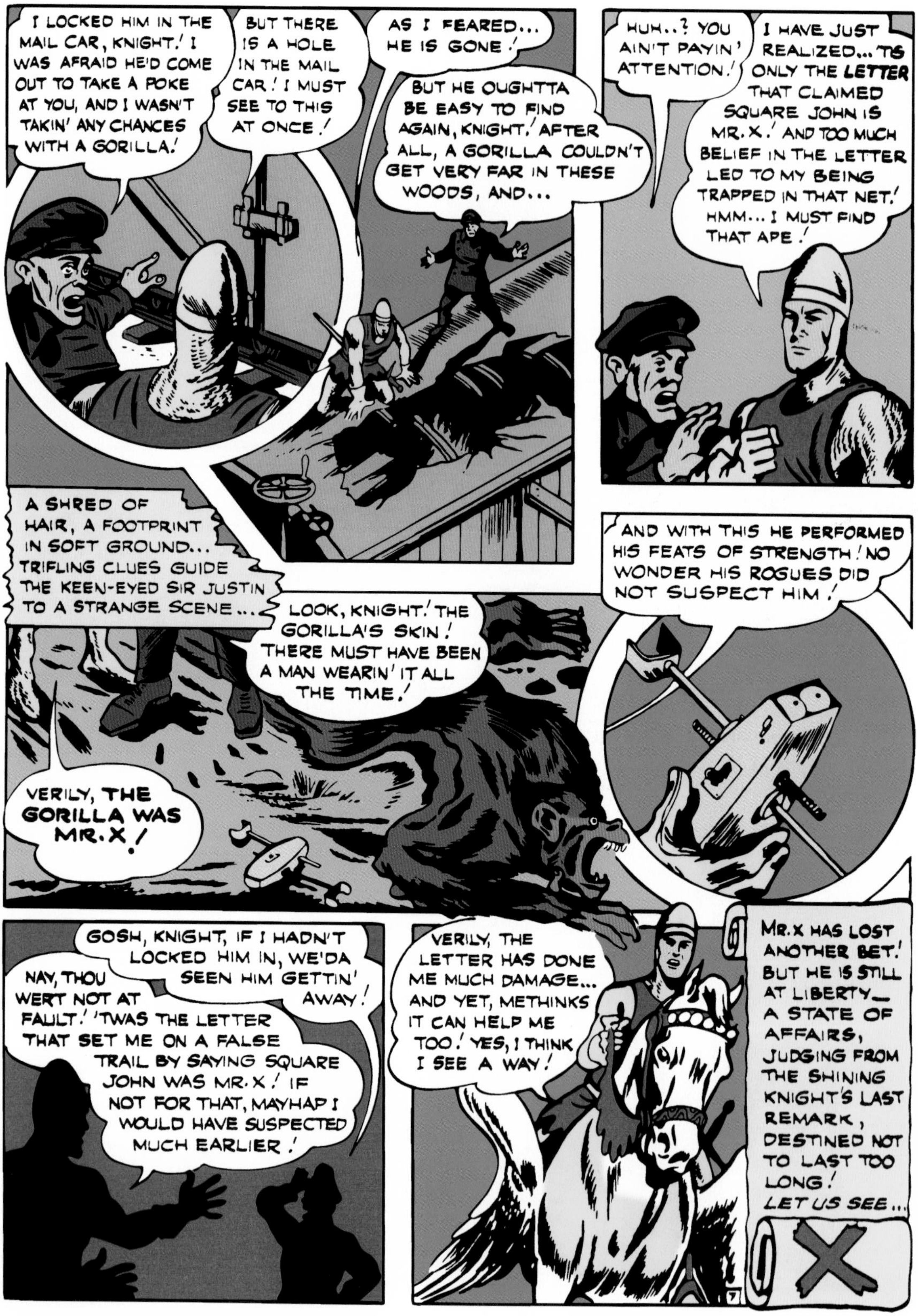
I LOCKED HIM IN THE MAIL CAR, KNIGHT! I WAS AFRAID HE'D COME OUT TO TAKE A POKE AT YOU, AND I WASN'T TAKIN' ANY CHANCES WITH A GORILLA!
BUT THERE IS A HOLE IN THE MAIL CAR! I MUST SEE TO THIS AT ONCE!
AS I FEARED... HE IS GONE!
BUT HE OUGHTTA BE EASY TO FIND AGAIN, KNIGHT! AFTER ALL, A GORILLA COULDN'T GET VERY FAR IN THESE WOODS, AND...
HUH..? YOU AIN'T PAYIN' ATTENTION!
I HAVE JUST REALIZED... 'TIS ONLY THE LETTER THAT CLAIMED SQUARE JOHN IS MR. X! AND TOO MUCH BELIEF IN THE LETTER LED TO MY BEING TRAPPED IN THAT NET! HMM... I MUST FIND THAT APE!
A SHRED OF HAIR, A FOOTPRINT IN SOFT GROUND... TRIFLING CLUES GUIDE THE KEEN-EYED SIR JUSTIN TO A STRANGE SCENE...
LOOK, KNIGHT! THE GORILLA'S SKIN! THERE MUST HAVE BEEN A MAN WEARIN' IT ALL THE TIME!
VERILY, THE GORILLA WAS MR. X!
AND WITH THIS HE PERFORMED HIS FEATS OF STRENGTH! NO WONDER HIS ROGUES DID NOT SUSPECT HIM!
GOSH, KNIGHT, IF I HADN'T LOCKED HIM IN, WE'DA SEEN HIM GETTIN' AWAY!
NAY, THOU WERT NOT AT FAULT! 'TWAS THE LETTER THAT SET ME ON A FALSE TRAIL BY SAYING SQUARE JOHN WAS MR. X! IF NOT FOR THAT, MAYHAP I WOULD HAVE SUSPECTED MUCH EARLIER!
VERILY, THE LETTER HAS DONE ME MUCH DAMAGE... AND YET, METHINKS IT CAN HELP ME TOO! YES, I THINK I SEE A WAY!
MR. X HAS LOST ANOTHER BET! BUT HE IS STILL AT LIBERTY_ A STATE OF AFFAIRS, JUDGING FROM THE SHINING KNIGHT'S LAST REMARK, DESTINED NOT TO LAST TOO LONG! LET US SEE...
X
7

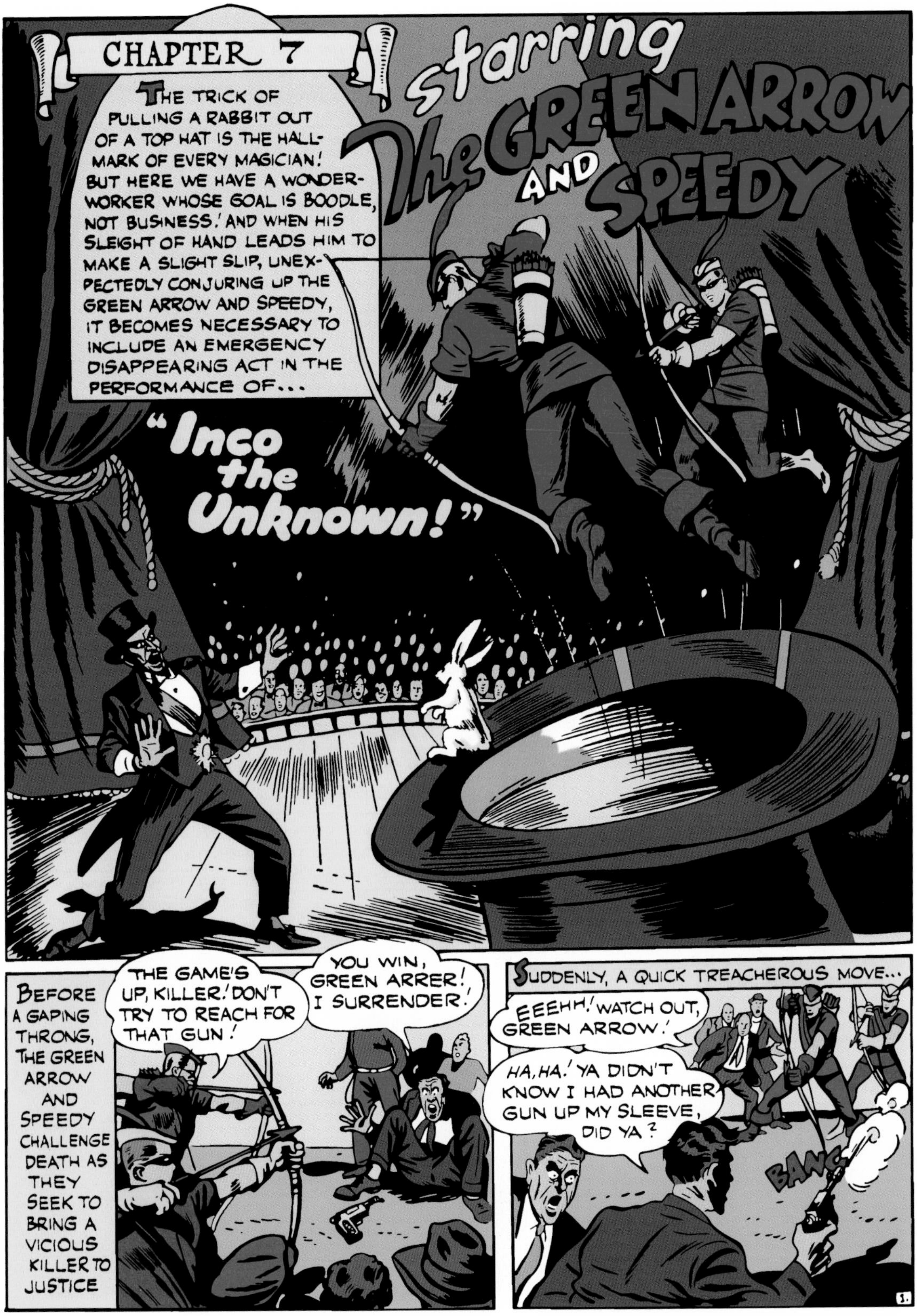
CHAPTER 7
THE TRICK OF PULLING A RABBIT OUT OF A TOP HAT IS THE HALL-MARK OF EVERY MAGICIAN! BUT HERE WE HAVE A WONDER-WORKER WHOSE GOAL IS BOODLE, NOT BUSINESS! AND WHEN HIS SLEIGHT OF HAND LEADS HIM TO MAKE A SLIGHT SLIP, UNEX-PECTEDLY CONJURING UP THE GREEN ARROW AND SPEEDY, IT BECOMES NECESSARY TO INCLUDE AN EMERGENCY DISAPPEARING ACT IN THE PERFORMANCE OF...
starring The GREEN ARROW AND SPEEDY
"Inco the Unknown!"
BEFORE A GAPING THRONG, THE GREEN ARROW AND SPEEDY CHALLENGE DEATH AS THEY SEEK TO BRING A VICIOUS KILLER TO JUSTICE
THE GAME'S UP, KILLER! DON'T TRY TO REACH FOR THAT GUN!
YOU WIN, GREEN ARRER! I SURRENDER!
SUDDENLY, A QUICK TREACHEROUS MOVE...
EEEHH! WATCH OUT, GREEN ARROW!
HA, HA! YA DIDN'T KNOW I HAD ANOTHER GUN UP MY SLEEVE, DID YA?
BANG
1.

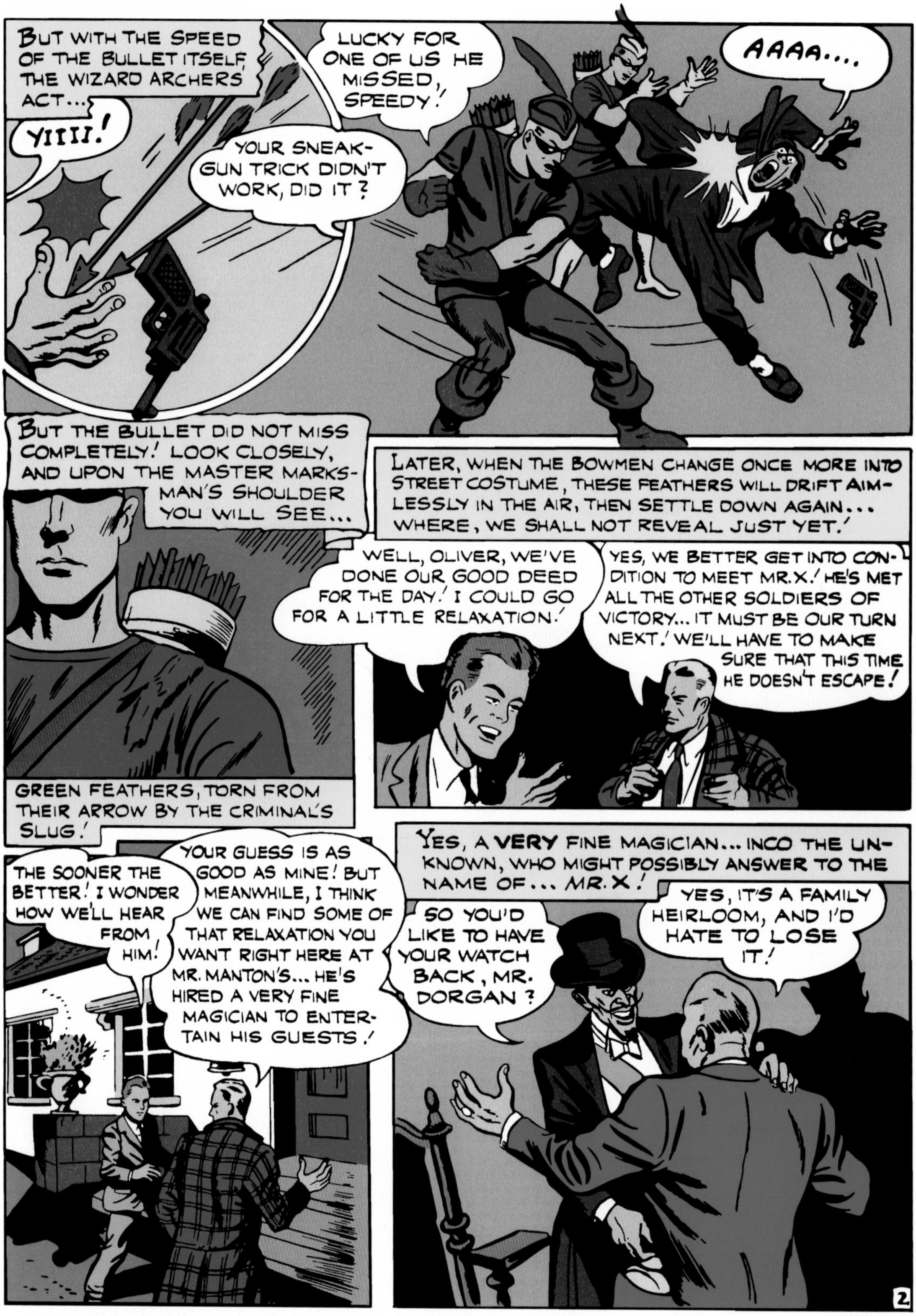
BUT WITH THE SPEED OF THE BULLET ITSELF, THE WIZARD ARCHERS ACT...
YIIII!
LUCKY FOR ONE OF US HE MISSED, SPEEDY!
YOUR SNEAK-GUN TRICK DIDN'T WORK, DID IT?
AAAA....
BUT THE BULLET DID NOT MISS COMPLETELY! LOOK CLOSELY, AND UPON THE MASTER MARKSMAN'S SHOULDER YOU WILL SEE...
GREEN FEATHERS, TORN FROM THEIR ARROW BY THE CRIMINAL'S SLUG!
LATER, WHEN THE BOWMEN CHANGE ONCE MORE INTO STREET COSTUME, THESE FEATHERS WILL DRIFT AIMLESSLY IN THE AIR, THEN SETTLE DOWN AGAIN... WHERE, WE SHALL NOT REVEAL JUST YET!
WELL, OLIVER, WE'VE DONE OUR GOOD DEED FOR THE DAY! I COULD GO FOR A LITTLE RELAXATION!
YES, WE BETTER GET INTO CONDITION TO MEET MR.X! HE'S MET ALL THE OTHER SOLDIERS OF VICTORY... IT MUST BE OUR TURN NEXT! WE'LL HAVE TO MAKE SURE THAT THIS TIME HE DOESN'T ESCAPE!
THE SOONER THE BETTER! I WONDER HOW WE'LL HEAR FROM HIM!
YOUR GUESS IS AS GOOD AS MINE! BUT MEANWHILE, I THINK WE CAN FIND SOME OF THAT RELAXATION YOU WANT RIGHT HERE AT MR. MANTON'S... HE'S HIRED A VERY FINE MAGICIAN TO ENTERTAIN HIS GUESTS!
YES, A VERY FINE MAGICIAN... INCO THE UNKNOWN, WHO MIGHT POSSIBLY ANSWER TO THE NAME OF... MR. X!
SO YOU'D LIKE TO HAVE YOUR WATCH BACK, MR. DORGAN?
YES, IT'S A FAMILY HEIRLOOM, AND I'D HATE TO LOSE IT!
2

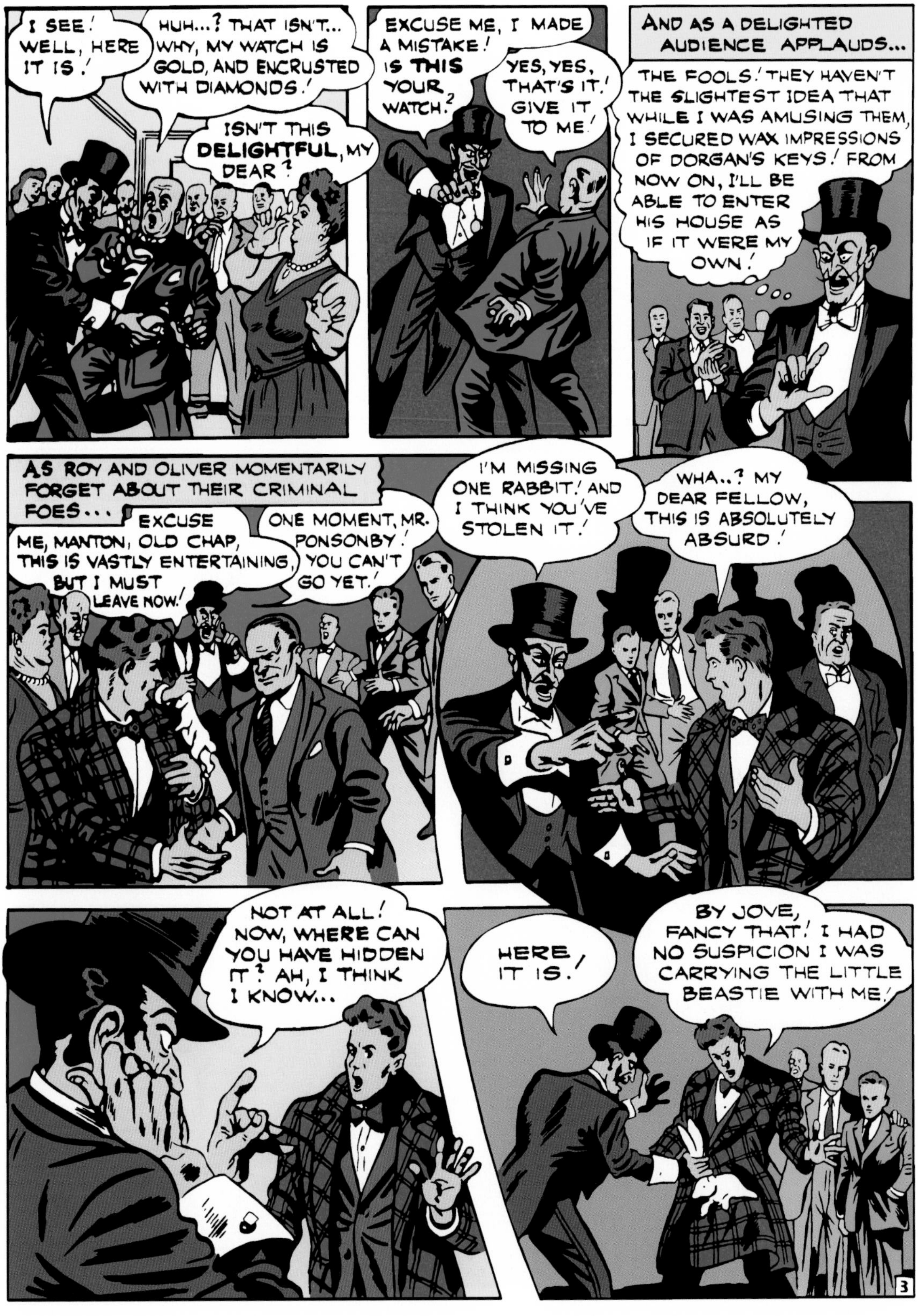
I SEE! WELL, HERE IT IS!
HUH...? THAT ISN'T... WHY, MY WATCH IS GOLD, AND ENCRUSTED WITH DIAMONDS!
ISN'T THIS DELIGHTFUL, MY DEAR?
EXCUSE ME, I MADE A MISTAKE! IS THIS YOUR WATCH?
YES, YES, THAT'S IT! GIVE IT TO ME!
AND AS A DELIGHTED AUDIENCE APPLAUDS...
THE FOOLS! THEY HAVEN'T THE SLIGHTEST IDEA THAT WHILE I WAS AMUSING THEM, I SECURED WAX IMPRESSIONS OF DORGAN'S KEYS! FROM NOW ON, I'LL BE ABLE TO ENTER HIS HOUSE AS IF IT WERE MY OWN!
AS ROY AND OLIVER MOMENTARILY FORGET ABOUT THEIR CRIMINAL FOES...
EXCUSE ME, MANTON, OLD CHAP, THIS IS VASTLY ENTERTAINING, BUT I MUST LEAVE NOW!
ONE MOMENT, MR. PONSONBY! YOU CAN'T GO YET!
I'M MISSING ONE RABBIT! AND I THINK YOU'VE STOLEN IT!
WHA..? MY DEAR FELLOW, THIS IS ABSOLUTELY ABSURD!
NOT AT ALL! NOW, WHERE CAN YOU HAVE HIDDEN IT? AH, I THINK I KNOW...
HERE, IT IS!
BY JOVE, FANCY THAT! I HAD NO SUSPICION I WAS CARRYING THE LITTLE BEASTIE WITH ME!
3

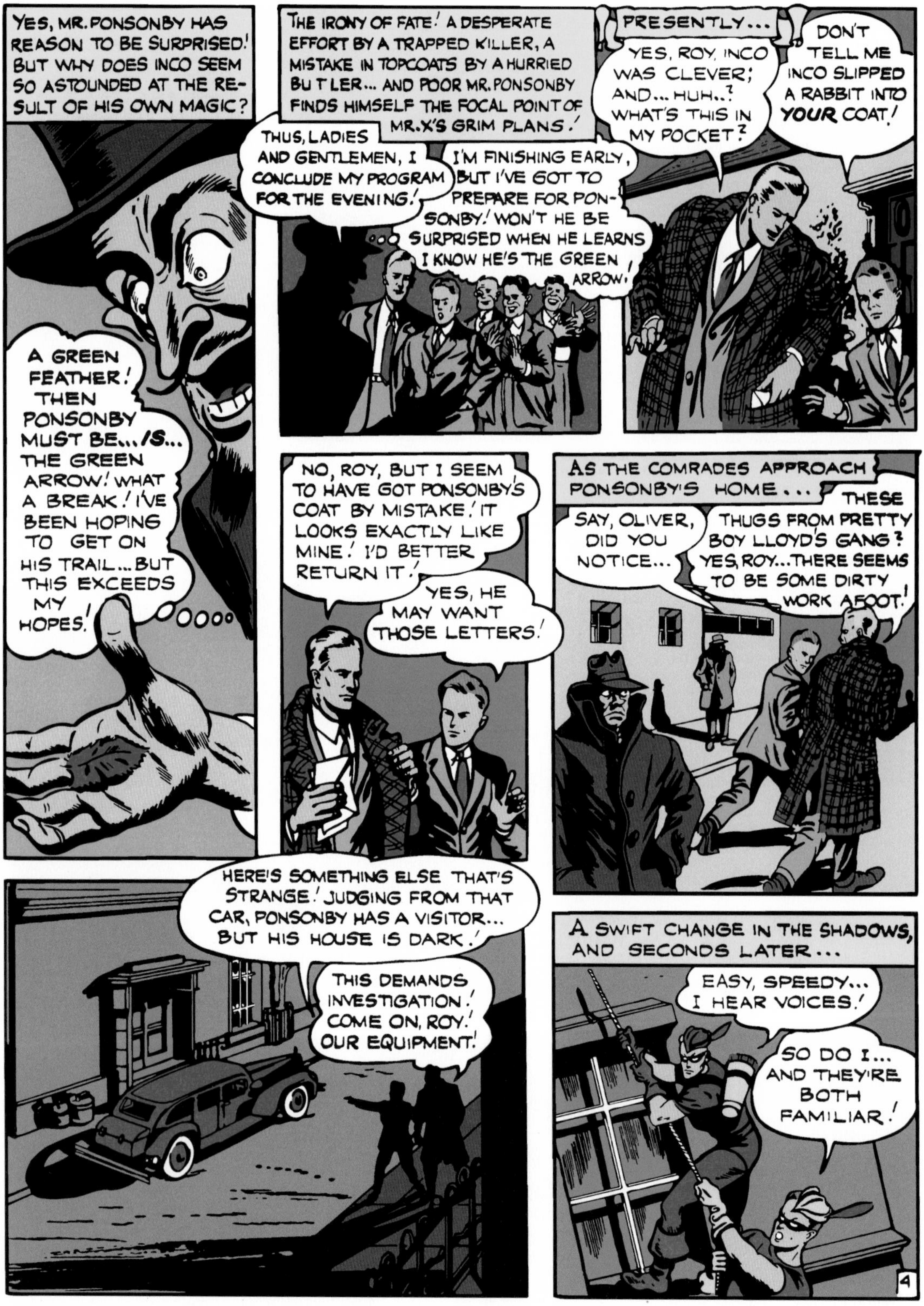
YES, MR. PONSONBY HAS REASON TO BE SURPRISED! BUT WHY DOES INCO SEEM SO ASTOUNDED AT THE RESULT OF HIS OWN MAGIC?
A GREEN FEATHER! THEN PONSONBY MUST BE.../S... THE GREEN ARROW! WHAT A BREAK! I'VE BEEN HOPING TO GET ON HIS TRAIL...BUT THIS EXCEEDS MY HOPES!
THE IRONY OF FATE! A DESPERATE EFFORT BY A TRAPPED KILLER, A MISTAKE IN TOPCOATS BY A HURRIED BUTLER... AND POOR MR. PONSONBY FINDS HIMSELF THE FOCAL POINT OF MR. X'S GRIM PLANS!
THUS, LADIES AND GENTLEMEN, I CONCLUDE MY PROGRAM FOR THE EVENING!
I'M FINISHING EARLY, BUT I'VE GOT TO PREPARE FOR PONSONBY! WON'T HE BE SURPRISED WHEN HE LEARNS I KNOW HE'S THE GREEN ARROW!
PRESENTLY...
YES, ROY, INCO WAS CLEVER; AND... HUH..? WHAT'S THIS IN MY POCKET?
DON'T TELL ME INCO SLIPPED A RABBIT INTO YOUR COAT!
NO, ROY, BUT I SEEM TO HAVE GOT PONSONBY'S COAT BY MISTAKE! IT LOOKS EXACTLY LIKE MINE! I'D BETTER RETURN IT!
YES, HE MAY WANT THOSE LETTERS!
AS THE COMRADES APPROACH PONSONBY'S HOME...
SAY, OLIVER, DID YOU NOTICE...
THESE THUGS FROM PRETTY BOY LLOYD'S GANG? YES, ROY...THERE SEEMS TO BE SOME DIRTY WORK AFOOT!
HERE'S SOMETHING ELSE THAT'S STRANGE! JUDGING FROM THAT CAR, PONSONBY HAS A VISITOR... BUT HIS HOUSE IS DARK!
THIS DEMANDS INVESTIGATION! COME ON, ROY! OUR EQUIPMENT!
A SWIFT CHANGE IN THE SHADOWS, AND SECONDS LATER...
EASY, SPEEDY... I HEAR VOICES!
SO DO I... AND THEY'RE BOTH FAMILIAR!
4

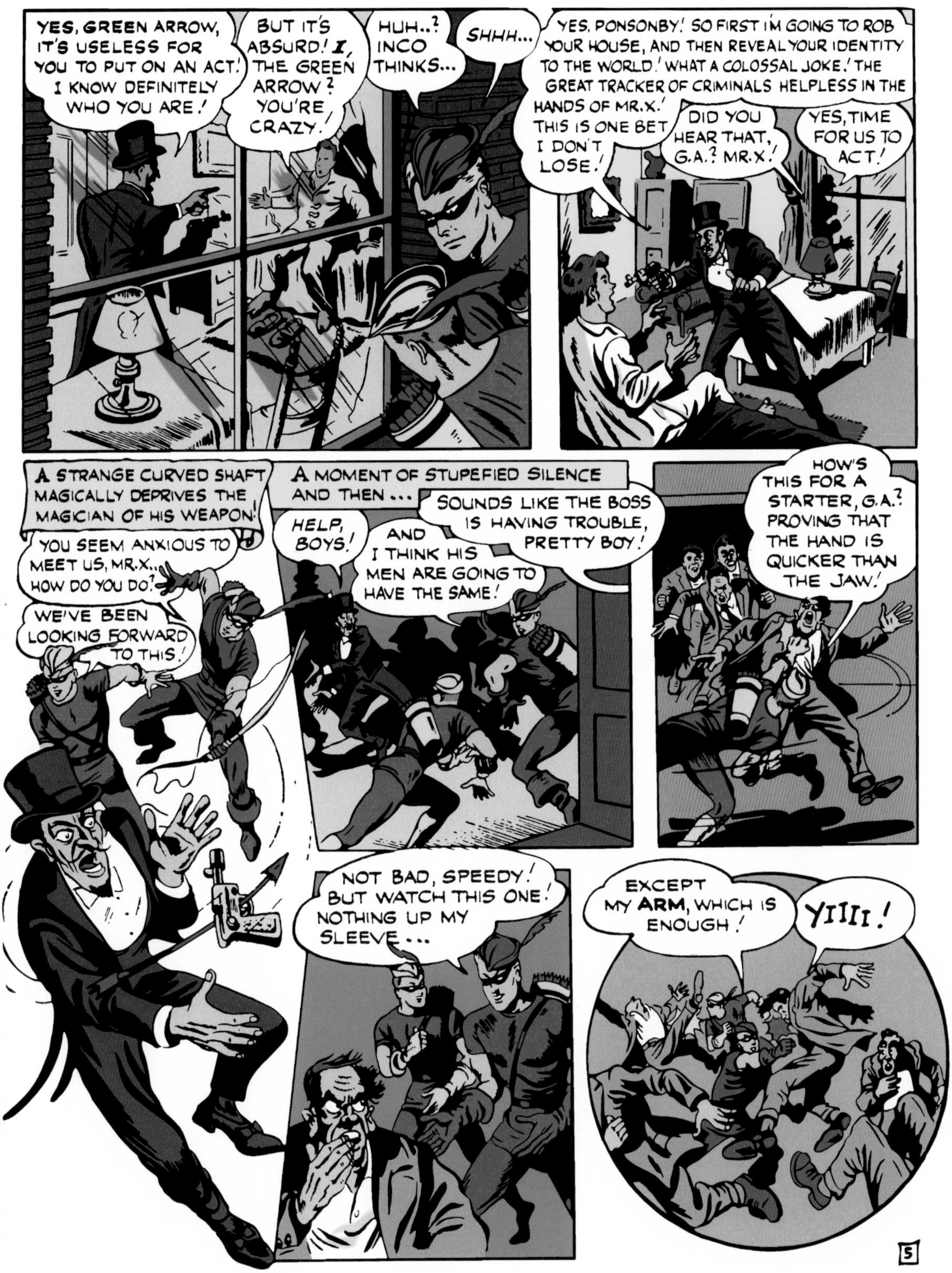
YES, GREEN ARROW, IT'S USELESS FOR YOU TO PUT ON AN ACT! I KNOW DEFINITELY WHO YOU ARE!
BUT IT'S ABSURD! I, THE GREEN ARROW? YOU'RE CRAZY!
HUH..? INCO THINKS...
SHHH...
YES, PONSONBY! SO FIRST I'M GOING TO ROB YOUR HOUSE, AND THEN REVEAL YOUR IDENTITY TO THE WORLD! WHAT A COLOSSAL JOKE! THE GREAT TRACKER OF CRIMINALS HELPLESS IN THE HANDS OF MR.X! THIS IS ONE BET I DON'T LOSE!
DID YOU HEAR THAT, G.A.? MR.X!
YES, TIME FOR US TO ACT!
A STRANGE CURVED SHAFT MAGICALLY DEPRIVES THE MAGICIAN OF HIS WEAPON!
YOU SEEM ANXIOUS TO MEET US, MR.X.. HOW DO YOU DO?
WE'VE BEEN LOOKING FORWARD TO THIS!
A MOMENT OF STUPEFIED SILENCE AND THEN...
HELP, BOYS!
SOUNDS LIKE THE BOSS IS HAVING TROUBLE, PRETTY BOY!
AND I THINK HIS MEN ARE GOING TO HAVE THE SAME!
HOW'S THIS FOR A STARTER, G.A.? PROVING THAT THE HAND IS QUICKER THAN THE JAW!
NOT BAD, SPEEDY! BUT WATCH THIS ONE! NOTHING UP MY SLEEVE...
EXCEPT MY ARM, WHICH IS ENOUGH!
YIIII!
5

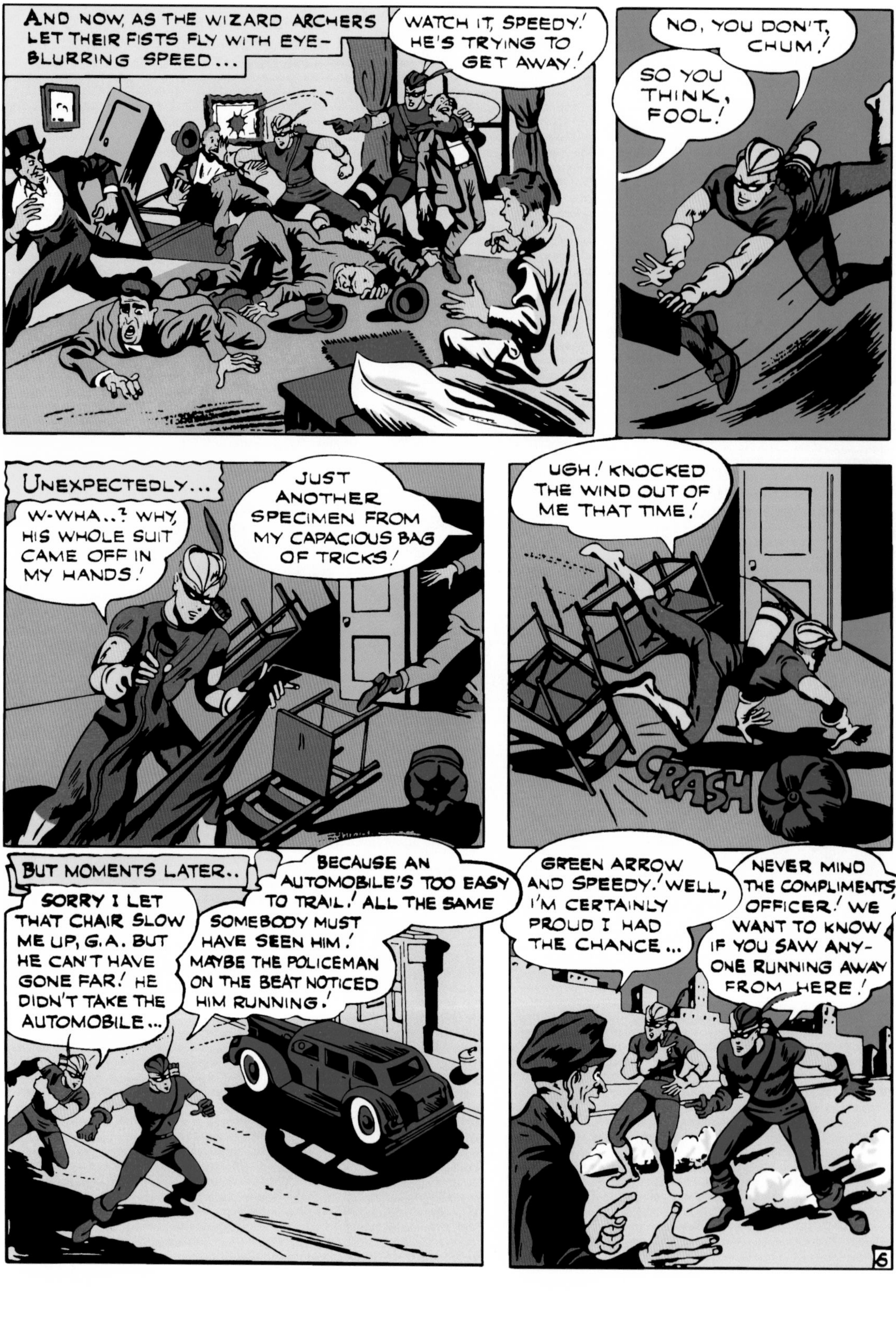
AND NOW, AS THE WIZARD ARCHERS LET THEIR FISTS FLY WITH EYE-BLURRING SPEED...
WATCH IT, SPEEDY! HE'S TRYING TO GET AWAY!
NO, YOU DON'T, CHUM!
SO YOU THINK, FOOL!
UNEXPECTEDLY...
W-WHA..? WHY, HIS WHOLE SUIT CAME OFF IN MY HANDS!
JUST ANOTHER SPECIMEN FROM MY CAPACIOUS BAG OF TRICKS!
UGH! KNOCKED THE WIND OUT OF ME THAT TIME!
CRASH
BUT MOMENTS LATER..
SORRY I LET THAT CHAIR SLOW ME UP, G.A. BUT HE CAN'T HAVE GONE FAR! HE DIDN'T TAKE THE AUTOMOBILE...
BECAUSE AN AUTOMOBILE'S TOO EASY TO TRAIL! ALL THE SAME SOMEBODY MUST HAVE SEEN HIM! MAYBE THE POLICEMAN ON THE BEAT NOTICED HIM RUNNING!
GREEN ARROW AND SPEEDY! WELL, I'M CERTAINLY PROUD I HAD THE CHANCE...
NEVER MIND THE COMPLIMENTS, OFFICER! WE WANT TO KNOW IF YOU SAW ANYONE RUNNING AWAY FROM HERE!
6

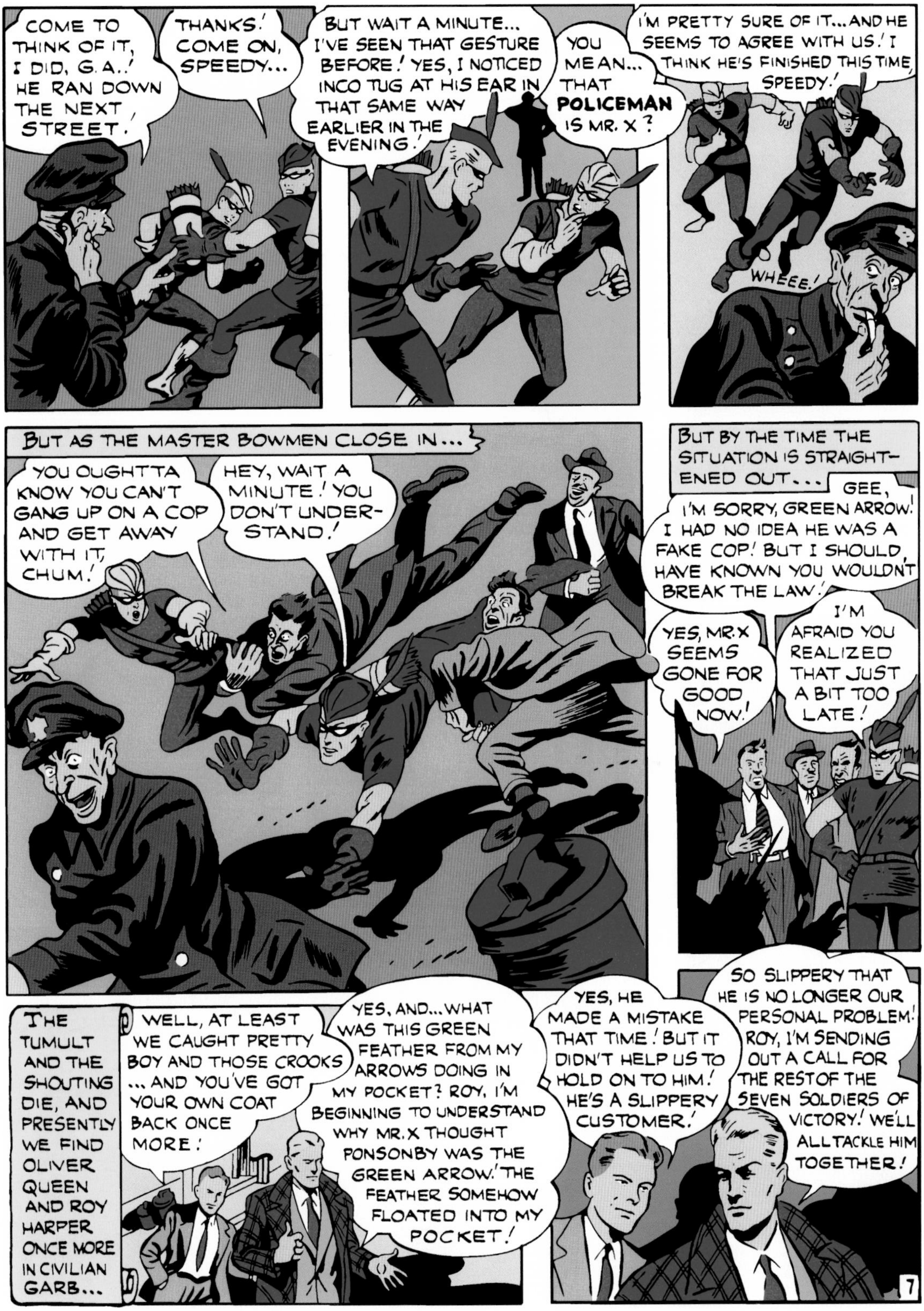
COME TO THINK OF IT, I DID, G.A..! HE RAN DOWN THE NEXT STREET!
THANKS! COME ON, SPEEDY...
BUT WAIT A MINUTE... I'VE SEEN THAT GESTURE BEFORE! YES, I NOTICED INCO TUG AT HIS EAR IN THAT SAME WAY EARLIER IN THE EVENING!
YOU MEAN... THAT POLICEMAN IS MR. X?
I'M PRETTY SURE OF IT...AND HE SEEMS TO AGREE WITH US! I THINK HE'S FINISHED THIS TIME, SPEEDY!
WHEEE!
BUT AS THE MASTER BOWMEN CLOSE IN...
YOU OUGHTTA KNOW YOU CAN'T GANG UP ON A COP AND GET AWAY WITH IT, CHUM!
HEY, WAIT A MINUTE! YOU DON'T UNDERSTAND!
BUT BY THE TIME THE SITUATION IS STRAIGHTENED OUT...
GEE, I'M SORRY, GREEN ARROW! I HAD NO IDEA HE WAS A FAKE COP! BUT I SHOULD HAVE KNOWN YOU WOULDN'T BREAK THE LAW!
YES, MR. X SEEMS GONE FOR GOOD NOW!
I'M AFRAID YOU REALIZED THAT JUST A BIT TOO LATE!
THE TUMULT AND THE SHOUTING DIE, AND PRESENTLY WE FIND OLIVER QUEEN AND ROY HARPER ONCE MORE IN CIVILIAN GARB...
WELL, AT LEAST WE CAUGHT PRETTY BOY AND THOSE CROOKS ... AND YOU'VE GOT YOUR OWN COAT BACK ONCE MORE!
YES, AND...WHAT WAS THIS GREEN FEATHER FROM MY ARROWS DOING IN MY POCKET? ROY, I'M BEGINNING TO UNDERSTAND WHY MR. X THOUGHT PONSONBY WAS THE GREEN ARROW! THE FEATHER SOMEHOW FLOATED INTO MY POCKET!
YES, HE MADE A MISTAKE THAT TIME! BUT IT DIDN'T HELP US TO HOLD ON TO HIM! HE'S A SLIPPERY CUSTOMER!
SO SLIPPERY THAT HE IS NO LONGER OUR PERSONAL PROBLEM! ROY, I'M SENDING OUT A CALL FOR THE REST OF THE SEVEN SOLDIERS OF VICTORY! WE'LL ALL TACKLE HIM TOGETHER!
7

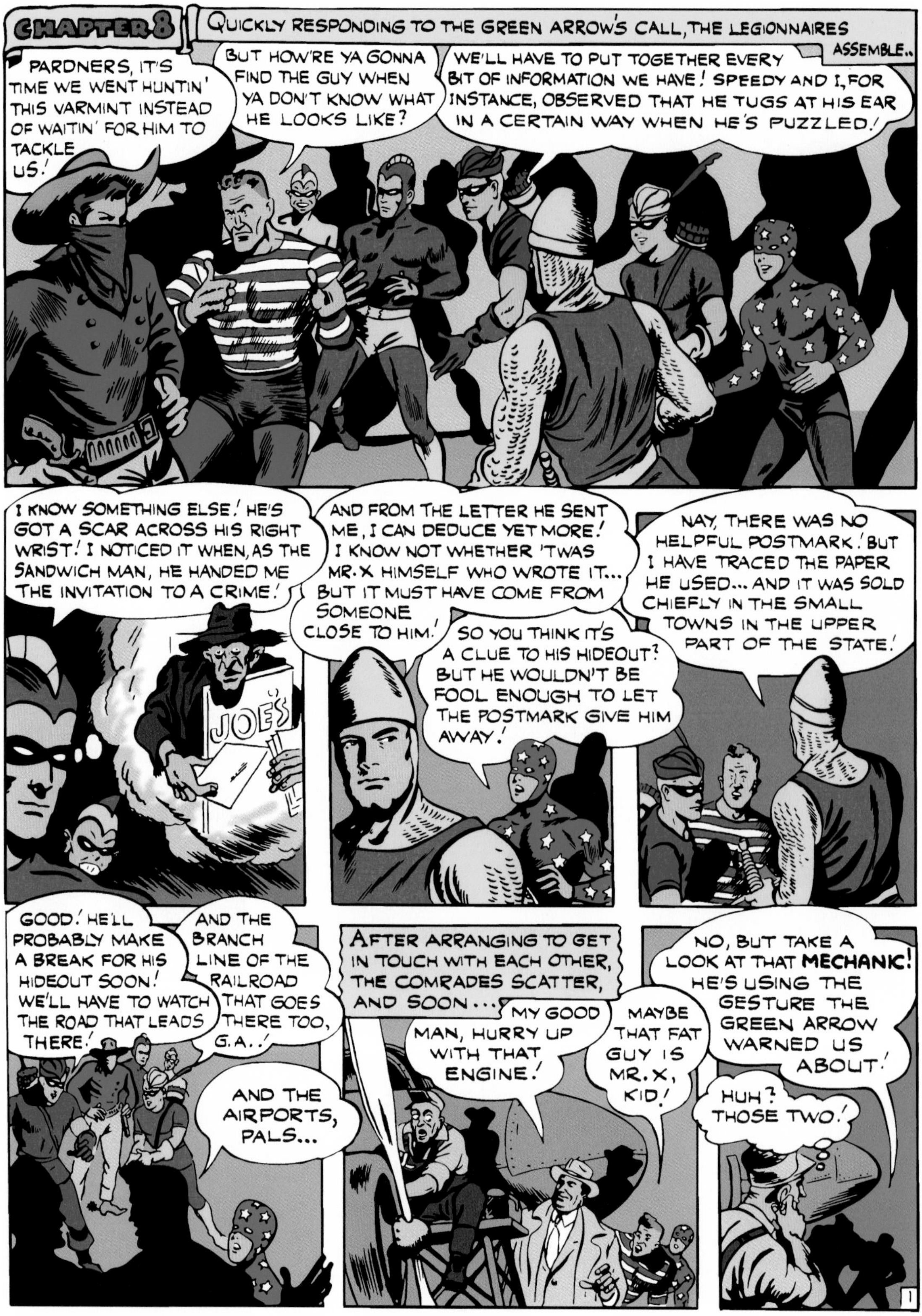
CHAPTER 8
QUICKLY RESPONDING TO THE GREEN ARROW'S CALL, THE LEGIONNAIRES ASSEMBLE..
PARDNERS, IT'S TIME WE WENT HUNTIN' THIS VARMINT INSTEAD OF WAITIN' FOR HIM TO TACKLE US!
BUT HOW'RE YA GONNA FIND THE GUY WHEN YA DON'T KNOW WHAT HE LOOKS LIKE?
WE'LL HAVE TO PUT TOGETHER EVERY BIT OF INFORMATION WE HAVE! SPEEDY AND I, FOR INSTANCE, OBSERVED THAT HE TUGS AT HIS EAR IN A CERTAIN WAY WHEN HE'S PUZZLED!
I KNOW SOMETHING ELSE! HE'S GOT A SCAR ACROSS HIS RIGHT WRIST! I NOTICED IT WHEN, AS THE SANDWICH MAN, HE HANDED ME THE INVITATION TO A CRIME!
JOE'S
AND FROM THE LETTER HE SENT ME, I CAN DEDUCE YET MORE! I KNOW NOT WHETHER 'TWAS MR. X HIMSELF WHO WROTE IT... BUT IT MUST HAVE COME FROM SOMEONE CLOSE TO HIM!
SO YOU THINK IT'S A CLUE TO HIS HIDEOUT? BUT HE WOULDN'T BE FOOL ENOUGH TO LET THE POSTMARK GIVE HIM AWAY!
NAY, THERE WAS NO HELPFUL POSTMARK! BUT I HAVE TRACED THE PAPER HE USED... AND IT WAS SOLD CHIEFLY IN THE SMALL TOWNS IN THE UPPER PART OF THE STATE!
GOOD! HE'LL PROBABLY MAKE A BREAK FOR HIS HIDEOUT SOON! WE'LL HAVE TO WATCH THE ROAD THAT LEADS THERE!
AND THE BRANCH LINE OF THE RAILROAD THAT GOES THERE TOO, G.A..!
AND THE AIRPORTS, PALS...
AFTER ARRANGING TO GET IN TOUCH WITH EACH OTHER, THE COMRADES SCATTER, AND SOON...
MY GOOD MAN, HURRY UP WITH THAT ENGINE!
MAYBE THAT FAT GUY IS MR. X, KID!
NO, BUT TAKE A LOOK AT THAT MECHANIC! HE'S USING THE GESTURE THE GREEN ARROW WARNED US ABOUT!
HUH? THOSE TWO!
1

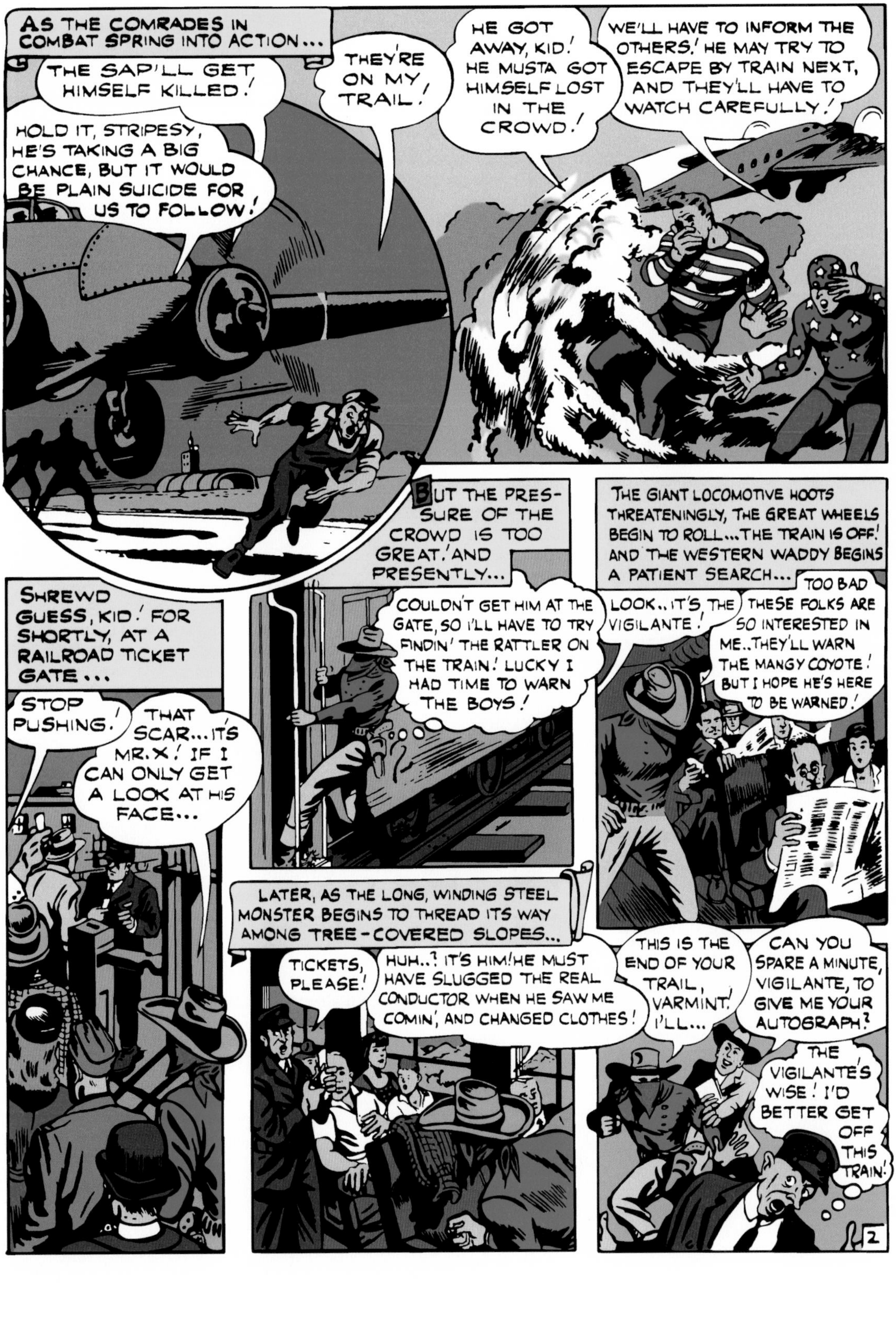
AS THE COMRADES IN COMBAT SPRING INTO ACTION...
THE SAP'LL GET HIMSELF KILLED!
HOLD IT, STRIPESY, HE'S TAKING A BIG CHANCE, BUT IT WOULD BE PLAIN SUICIDE FOR US TO FOLLOW!
THEY'RE ON MY TRAIL!
HE GOT AWAY, KID! HE MUSTA GOT HIMSELF LOST IN THE CROWD!
WE'LL HAVE TO INFORM THE OTHERS! HE MAY TRY TO ESCAPE BY TRAIN NEXT, AND THEY'LL HAVE TO WATCH CAREFULLY!
BUT THE PRESSURE OF THE CROWD IS TOO GREAT! AND PRESENTLY...
THE GIANT LOCOMOTIVE HOOTS THREATENINGLY, THE GREAT WHEELS BEGIN TO ROLL...THE TRAIN IS OFF! AND THE WESTERN WADDY BEGINS A PATIENT SEARCH...
SHREWD GUESS, KID! FOR SHORTLY, AT A RAILROAD TICKET GATE...
STOP PUSHING!
THAT SCAR...IT'S MR.X! IF I CAN ONLY GET A LOOK AT HIS FACE...
UH
COULDN'T GET HIM AT THE GATE, SO I'LL HAVE TO TRY FINDIN' THE RATTLER ON THE TRAIN! LUCKY I HAD TIME TO WARN THE BOYS!
LOOK.. IT'S THE VIGILANTE!
TOO BAD THESE FOLKS ARE SO INTERESTED IN ME..THEY'LL WARN THE MANGY COYOTE! BUT I HOPE HE'S HERE TO BE WARNED!
LATER, AS THE LONG, WINDING STEEL MONSTER BEGINS TO THREAD ITS WAY AMONG TREE-COVERED SLOPES...
TICKETS, PLEASE!
HUH..? IT'S HIM! HE MUST HAVE SLUGGED THE REAL CONDUCTOR WHEN HE SAW ME COMIN', AND CHANGED CLOTHES!
THIS IS THE END OF YOUR TRAIL, VARMINT. I'LL...
CAN YOU SPARE A MINUTE, VIGILANTE, TO GIVE ME YOUR AUTOGRAPH?
THE VIGILANTE'S WISE! I'D BETTER GET OFF THIS TRAIN!
2

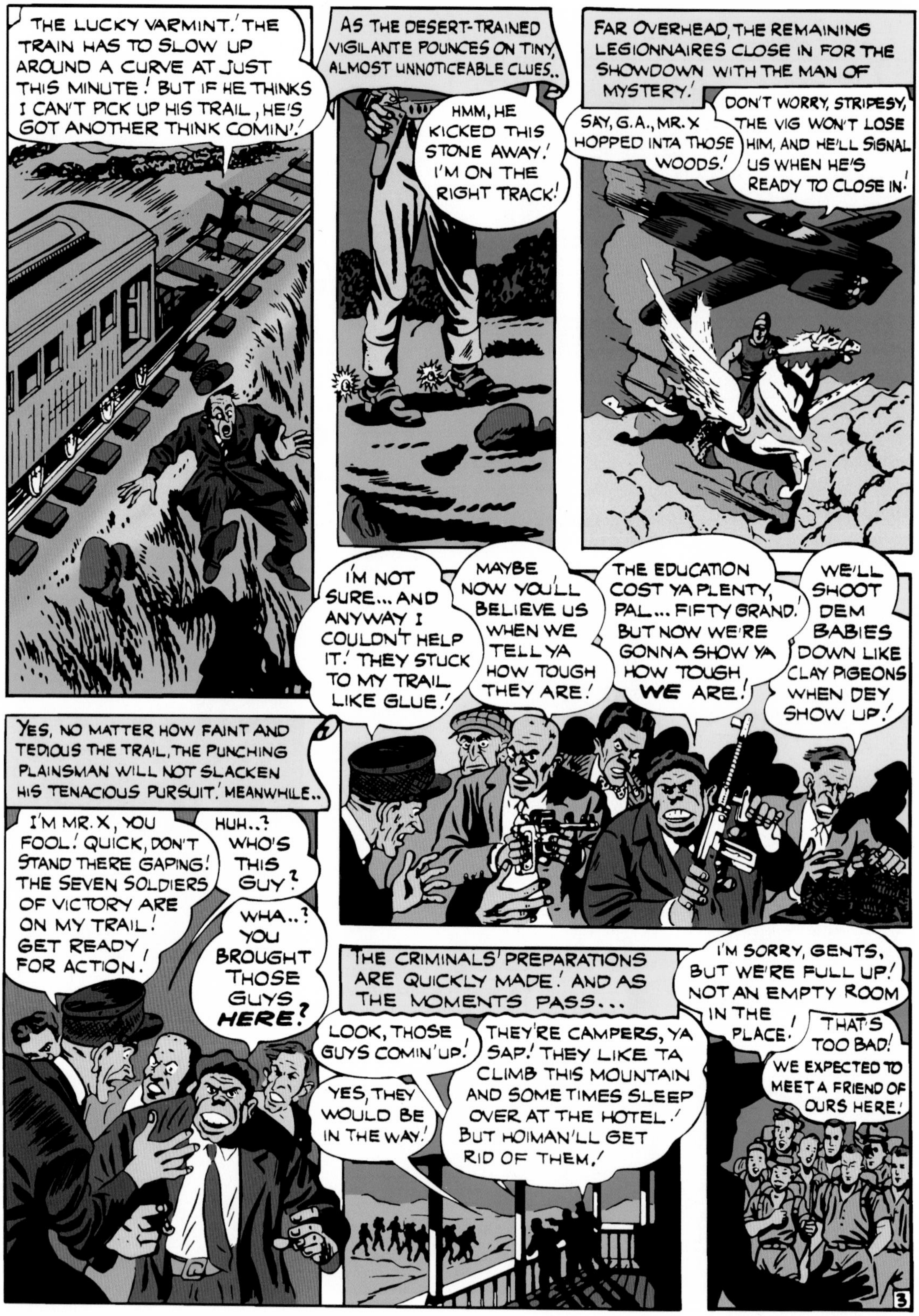
THE LUCKY VARMINT! THE TRAIN HAS TO SLOW UP AROUND A CURVE AT JUST THIS MINUTE! BUT IF HE THINKS I CAN'T PICK UP HIS TRAIL, HE'S GOT ANOTHER THINK COMIN'!
AS THE DESERT-TRAINED VIGILANTE POUNCES ON TINY, ALMOST UNNOTICEABLE CLUES..
HMM, HE KICKED THIS STONE AWAY! I'M ON THE RIGHT TRACK!
FAR OVERHEAD, THE REMAINING LEGIONNAIRES CLOSE IN FOR THE SHOWDOWN WITH THE MAN OF MYSTERY!
SAY, G.A., MR. X HOPPED INTA THOSE WOODS!
DON'T WORRY, STRIPESY, THE VIG WON'T LOSE HIM, AND HE'LL SIGNAL US WHEN HE'S READY TO CLOSE IN!
YES, NO MATTER HOW FAINT AND TEDIOUS THE TRAIL, THE PUNCHING PLAINSMAN WILL NOT SLACKEN HIS TENACIOUS PURSUIT! MEANWHILE..
I'M MR. X, YOU FOOL! QUICK, DON'T STAND THERE GAPING! THE SEVEN SOLDIERS OF VICTORY ARE ON MY TRAIL! GET READY FOR ACTION!
HUH..? WHO'S THIS GUY?
WHA..? YOU BROUGHT THOSE GUYS HERE?
I'M NOT SURE... AND ANYWAY I COULDN'T HELP IT! THEY STUCK TO MY TRAIL LIKE GLUE!
MAYBE NOW YOU'LL BELIEVE US WHEN WE TELL YA HOW TOUGH THEY ARE!
THE EDUCATION COST YA PLENTY, PAL... FIFTY GRAND! BUT NOW WE'RE GONNA SHOW YA HOW TOUGH WE ARE!
WE'LL SHOOT DEM BABIES DOWN LIKE CLAY PIGEONS WHEN DEY SHOW UP!
THE CRIMINALS' PREPARATIONS ARE QUICKLY MADE! AND AS THE MOMENTS PASS...
LOOK, THOSE GUYS COMIN' UP!
YES, THEY WOULD BE IN THE WAY!
THEY'RE CAMPERS, YA SAP! THEY LIKE TA CLIMB THIS MOUNTAIN AND SOME TIMES SLEEP OVER AT THE HOTEL! BUT HOIMAN'LL GET RID OF THEM!
I'M SORRY, GENTS, BUT WE'RE FULL UP! NOT AN EMPTY ROOM IN THE PLACE!
THAT'S TOO BAD! WE EXPECTED TO MEET A FRIEND OF OURS HERE!
3

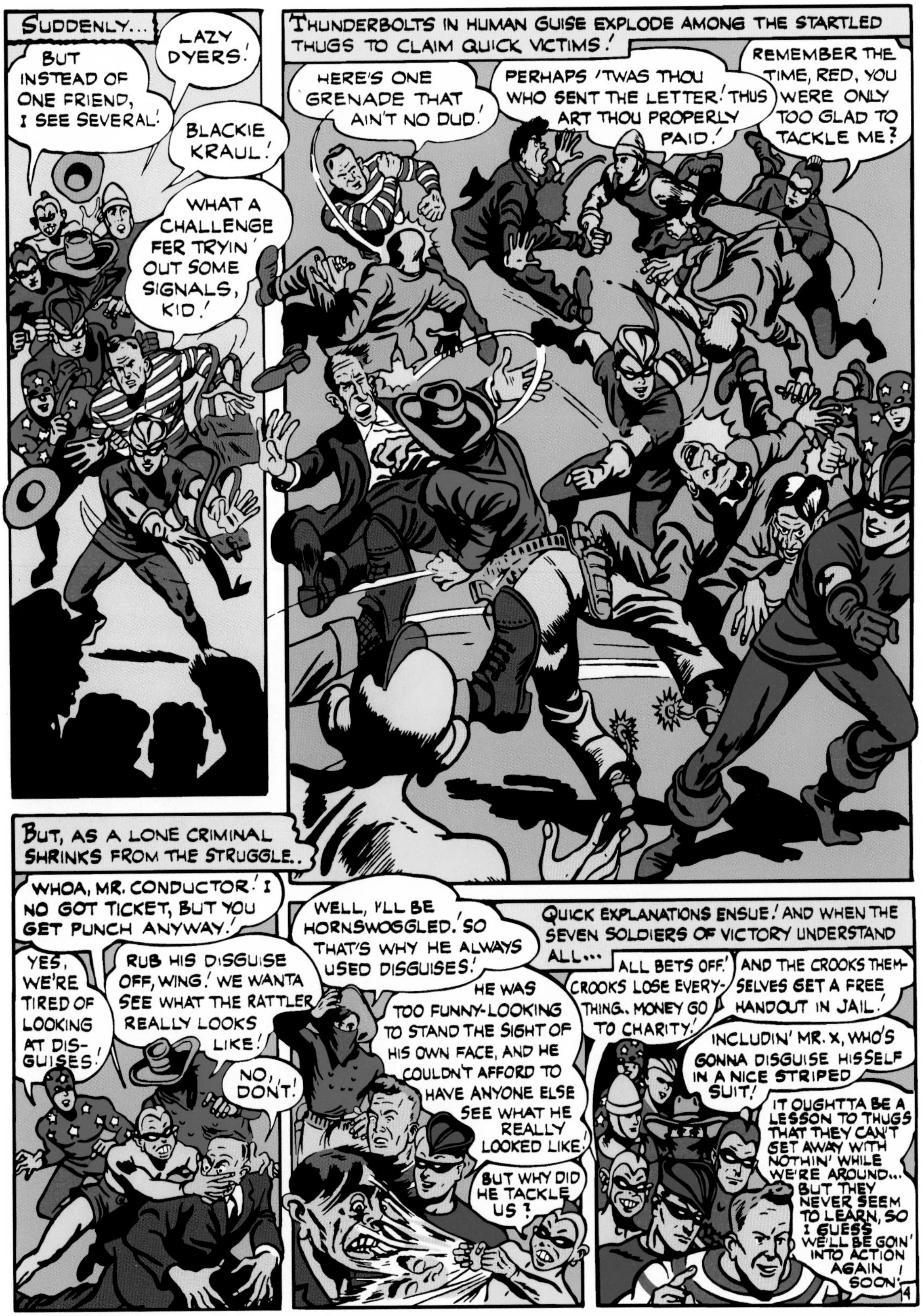
SUDDENLY...
LAZY DYERS!
BUT INSTEAD OF ONE FRIEND, I SEE SEVERAL!
BLACKIE KRAUL!
WHAT A CHALLENGE FER TRYIN' OUT SOME SIGNALS, KID!
THUNDERBOLTS IN HUMAN GUISE EXPLODE AMONG THE STARTLED THUGS TO CLAIM QUICK VICTIMS!
HERE'S ONE GRENADE THAT AIN'T NO DUD!
PERHAPS 'TWAS THOU WHO SENT THE LETTER! THUS ART THOU PROPERLY PAID!
REMEMBER THE TIME, RED, YOU WERE ONLY TOO GLAD TO TACKLE ME?
BUT, AS A LONE CRIMINAL SHRINKS FROM THE STRUGGLE..
WHOA, MR. CONDUCTOR! I NO GOT TICKET, BUT YOU GET PUNCH ANYWAY!
YES, WE'RE TIRED OF LOOKING AT DISGUISES!
RUB HIS DISGUISE OFF, WING! WE WANTA SEE WHAT THE RATTLER REALLY LOOKS LIKE!
NO, DON'T!
WELL, I'LL BE HORNSWOGGLED! SO THAT'S WHY HE ALWAYS USED DISGUISES!
HE WAS TOO FUNNY-LOOKING TO STAND THE SIGHT OF HIS OWN FACE, AND HE COULDN'T AFFORD TO HAVE ANYONE ELSE SEE WHAT HE REALLY LOOKED LIKE.
BUT WHY DID HE TACKLE US?
QUICK EXPLANATIONS ENSUE! AND WHEN THE SEVEN SOLDIERS OF VICTORY UNDERSTAND ALL...
ALL BETS OFF! CROOKS LOSE EVERY-THING.. MONEY GO TO CHARITY!
AND THE CROOKS THEM-SELVES GET A FREE HANDOUT IN JAIL!
INCLUDIN' MR. X, WHO'S GONNA DISGUISE HISSELF IN A NICE STRIPED SUIT!
IT OUGHTTA BE A LESSON TO THUGS THAT THEY CAN'T GET AWAY WITH NOTHIN' WHILE WE'RE AROUND... BUT THEY NEVER SEEM TO LEARN, SO I GUESS WE'LL BE GOIN' INTO ACTION AGAIN SOON!
14

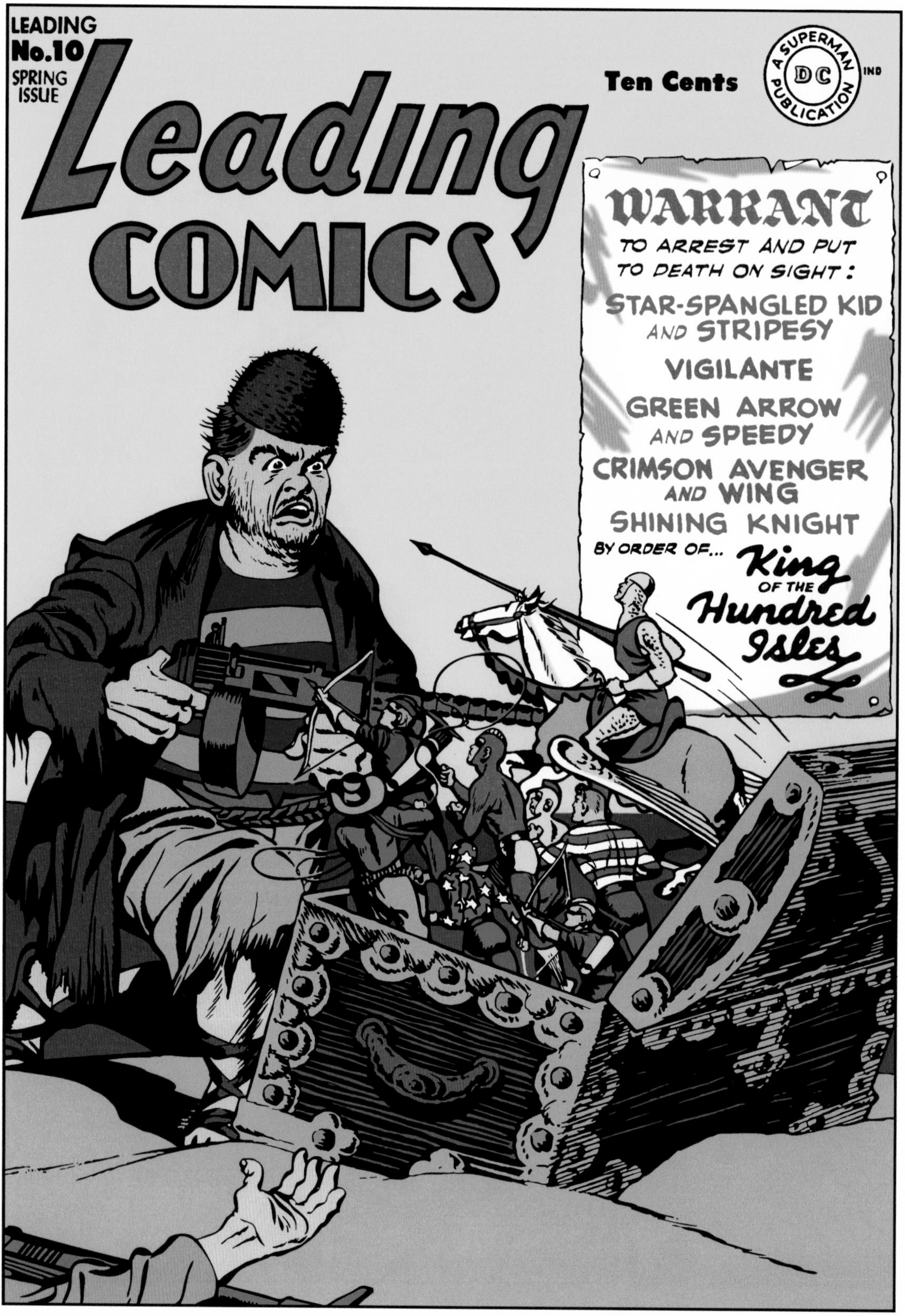
LEADING
No.10
SPRING ISSUE
Leading COMICS
Ten Cents
A SUPERMAN DC PUBLICATION
IND
WARRANT
TO ARREST AND PUT TO DEATH ON SIGHT:
STAR-SPANGLED KID AND STRIPESY
VIGILANTE
GREEN ARROW AND SPEEDY
CRIMSON AVENGER AND WING
SHINING KNIGHT
BY ORDER OF... King OF THE Hundred Isles

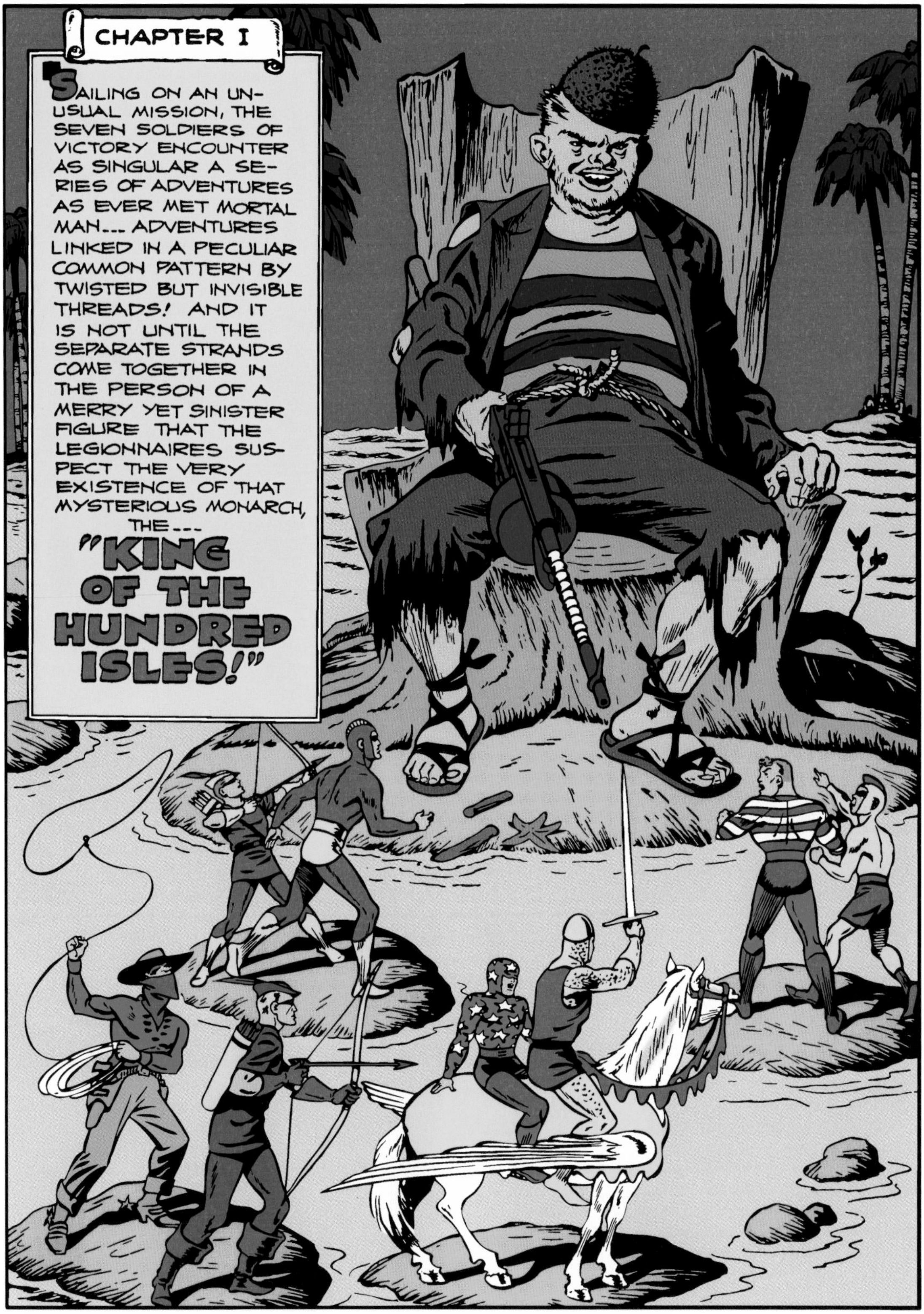
CHAPTER I
"SAILING ON AN UNUSUAL MISSION, THE SEVEN SOLDIERS OF VICTORY ENCOUNTER AS SINGULAR A SERIES OF ADVENTURES AS EVER MET MORTAL MAN... ADVENTURES LINKED IN A PECULIAR COMMON PATTERN BY TWISTED BUT INVISIBLE THREADS! AND IT IS NOT UNTIL THE SEPARATE STRANDS COME TOGETHER IN THE PERSON OF A MERRY YET SINISTER FIGURE THAT THE LEGIONNAIRES SUSPECT THE VERY EXISTENCE OF THAT MYSTERIOUS MONARCH, THE---
"KING OF THE HUNDRED ISLES!"

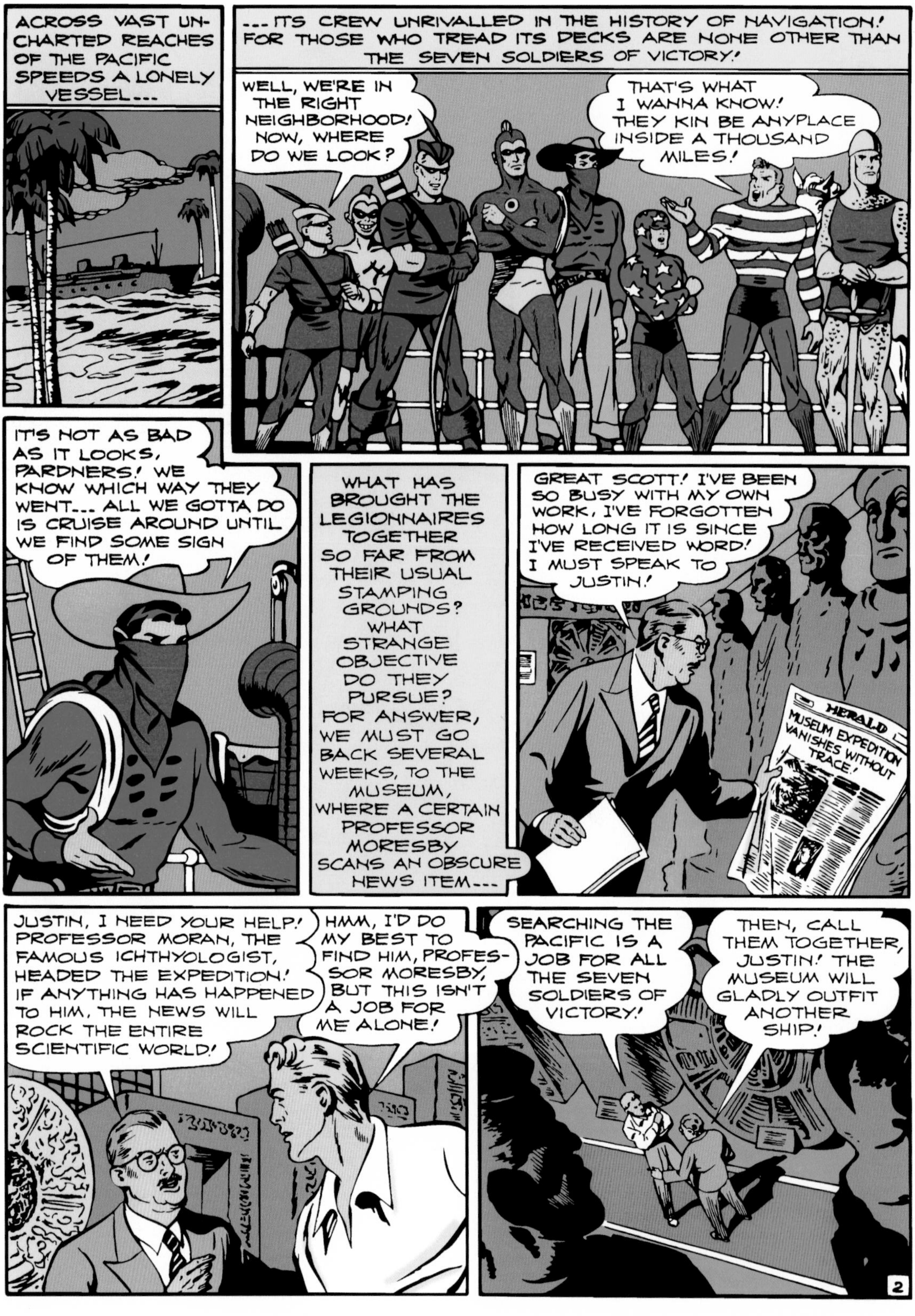
ACROSS VAST UN-CHARTED REACHES OF THE PACIFIC SPEEDS A LONELY VESSEL...
...ITS CREW UNRIVALLED IN THE HISTORY OF NAVIGATION! FOR THOSE WHO TREAD ITS DECKS ARE NONE OTHER THAN THE SEVEN SOLDIERS OF VICTORY!
WELL, WE'RE IN THE RIGHT NEIGHBORHOOD! NOW, WHERE DO WE LOOK?
THAT'S WHAT I WANNA KNOW! THEY KIN BE ANYPLACE INSIDE A THOUSAND MILES!
IT'S NOT AS BAD AS IT LOOKS, PARDNERS! WE KNOW WHICH WAY THEY WENT... ALL WE GOTTA DO IS CRUISE AROUND UNTIL WE FIND SOME SIGN OF THEM!
WHAT HAS BROUGHT THE LEGIONNAIRES TOGETHER SO FAR FROM THEIR USUAL STAMPING GROUNDS? WHAT STRANGE OBJECTIVE DO THEY PURSUE? FOR ANSWER, WE MUST GO BACK SEVERAL WEEKS, TO THE MUSEUM, WHERE A CERTAIN PROFESSOR MORESBY SCANS AN OBSCURE NEWS ITEM...
GREAT SCOTT! I'VE BEEN SO BUSY WITH MY OWN WORK, I'VE FORGOTTEN HOW LONG IT IS SINCE I'VE RECEIVED WORD! I MUST SPEAK TO JUSTIN!
HERALD
MUSEUM EXPEDITION VANISHES WITHOUT TRACE!
JUSTIN, I NEED YOUR HELP! PROFESSOR MORAN, THE FAMOUS ICHTHYOLOGIST, HEADED THE EXPEDITION! IF ANYTHING HAS HAPPENED TO HIM, THE NEWS WILL ROCK THE ENTIRE SCIENTIFIC WORLD!
HMM, I'D DO MY BEST TO FIND HIM, PROFES-SOR MORESBY, BUT THIS ISN'T A JOB FOR ME ALONE!
SEARCHING THE PACIFIC IS A JOB FOR ALL THE SEVEN SOLDIERS OF VICTORY!
THEN, CALL THEM TOGETHER, JUSTIN! THE MUSEUM WILL GLADLY OUTFIT ANOTHER SHIP!
2

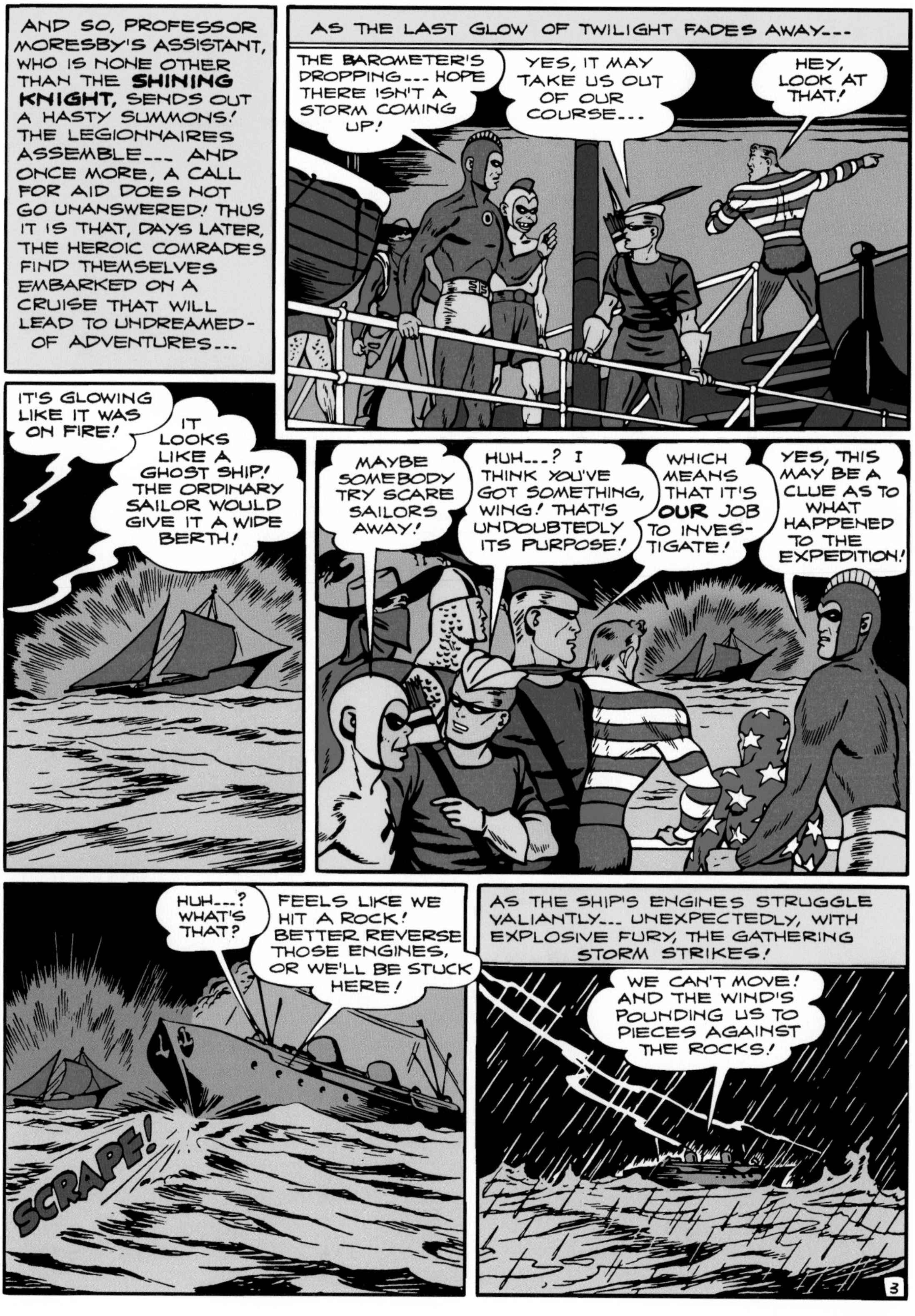
AND SO, PROFESSOR MORESBY'S ASSISTANT, WHO IS NONE OTHER THAN THE **SHINING KNIGHT,** SENDS OUT A HASTY SUMMONS! THE LEGIONNAIRES ASSEMBLE--- AND ONCE MORE, A CALL FOR AID DOES NOT GO UNANSWERED! THUS IT IS THAT, DAYS LATER, THE HEROIC COMRADES FIND THEMSELVES EMBARKED ON A CRUISE THAT WILL LEAD TO UNDREAMED-OF ADVENTURES---
AS THE LAST GLOW OF TWILIGHT FADES AWAY---
THE BAROMETER'S DROPPING--- HOPE THERE ISN'T A STORM COMING UP!
YES, IT MAY TAKE US OUT OF OUR COURSE---
HEY, LOOK AT THAT!
IT'S GLOWING LIKE IT WAS ON FIRE!
IT LOOKS LIKE A GHOST SHIP! THE ORDINARY SAILOR WOULD GIVE IT A WIDE BERTH!
MAYBE SOMEBODY TRY SCARE SAILORS AWAY!
HUH---? I THINK YOU'VE GOT SOMETHING, WING! THAT'S UNDOUBTEDLY ITS PURPOSE!
WHICH MEANS THAT IT'S **OUR** JOB TO INVESTIGATE!
YES, THIS MAY BE A CLUE AS TO WHAT HAPPENED TO THE EXPEDITION!
HUH---? WHAT'S THAT?
FEELS LIKE WE HIT A ROCK! BETTER REVERSE THOSE ENGINES, OR WE'LL BE STUCK HERE!
SCRAPE!
AS THE SHIP'S ENGINES STRUGGLE VALIANTLY--- UNEXPECTEDLY, WITH EXPLOSIVE FURY, THE GATHERING STORM STRIKES!
WE CAN'T MOVE! AND THE WIND'S POUNDING US TO PIECES AGAINST THE ROCKS!
3

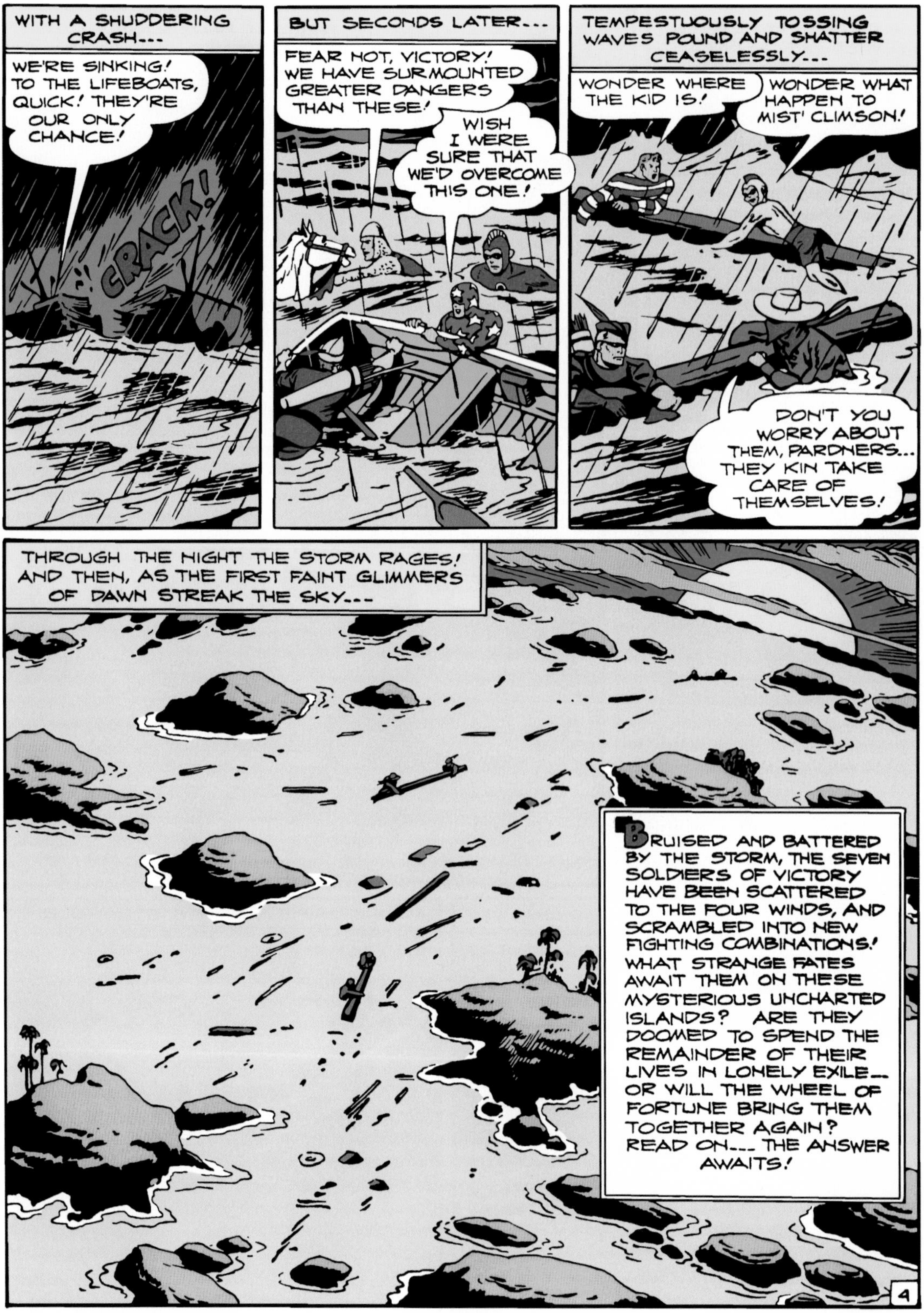
WITH A SHUDDERING CRASH...
WE'RE SINKING! TO THE LIFEBOATS, QUICK! THEY'RE OUR ONLY CHANCE!
CRACK!
BUT SECONDS LATER...
FEAR NOT, VICTORY! WE HAVE SURMOUNTED GREATER DANGERS THAN THESE!
WISH I WERE SURE THAT WE'D OVERCOME THIS ONE!
TEMPESTUOUSLY TOSSING WAVES POUND AND SHATTER CEASELESSLY...
WONDER WHERE THE KID IS!
WONDER WHAT HAPPEN TO MIST' CLIMSON!
DON'T YOU WORRY ABOUT THEM, PARDNERS... THEY KIN TAKE CARE OF THEMSELVES!
THROUGH THE NIGHT THE STORM RAGES! AND THEN, AS THE FIRST FAINT GLIMMERS OF DAWN STREAK THE SKY...
BRUISED AND BATTERED BY THE STORM, THE SEVEN SOLDIERS OF VICTORY HAVE BEEN SCATTERED TO THE FOUR WINDS, AND SCRAMBLED INTO NEW FIGHTING COMBINATIONS! WHAT STRANGE FATES AWAIT THEM ON THESE MYSTERIOUS UNCHARTED ISLANDS? ARE THEY DOOMED TO SPEND THE REMAINDER OF THEIR LIVES IN LONELY EXILE... OR WILL THE WHEEL OF FORTUNE BRING THEM TOGETHER AGAIN? READ ON... THE ANSWER AWAITS!
4

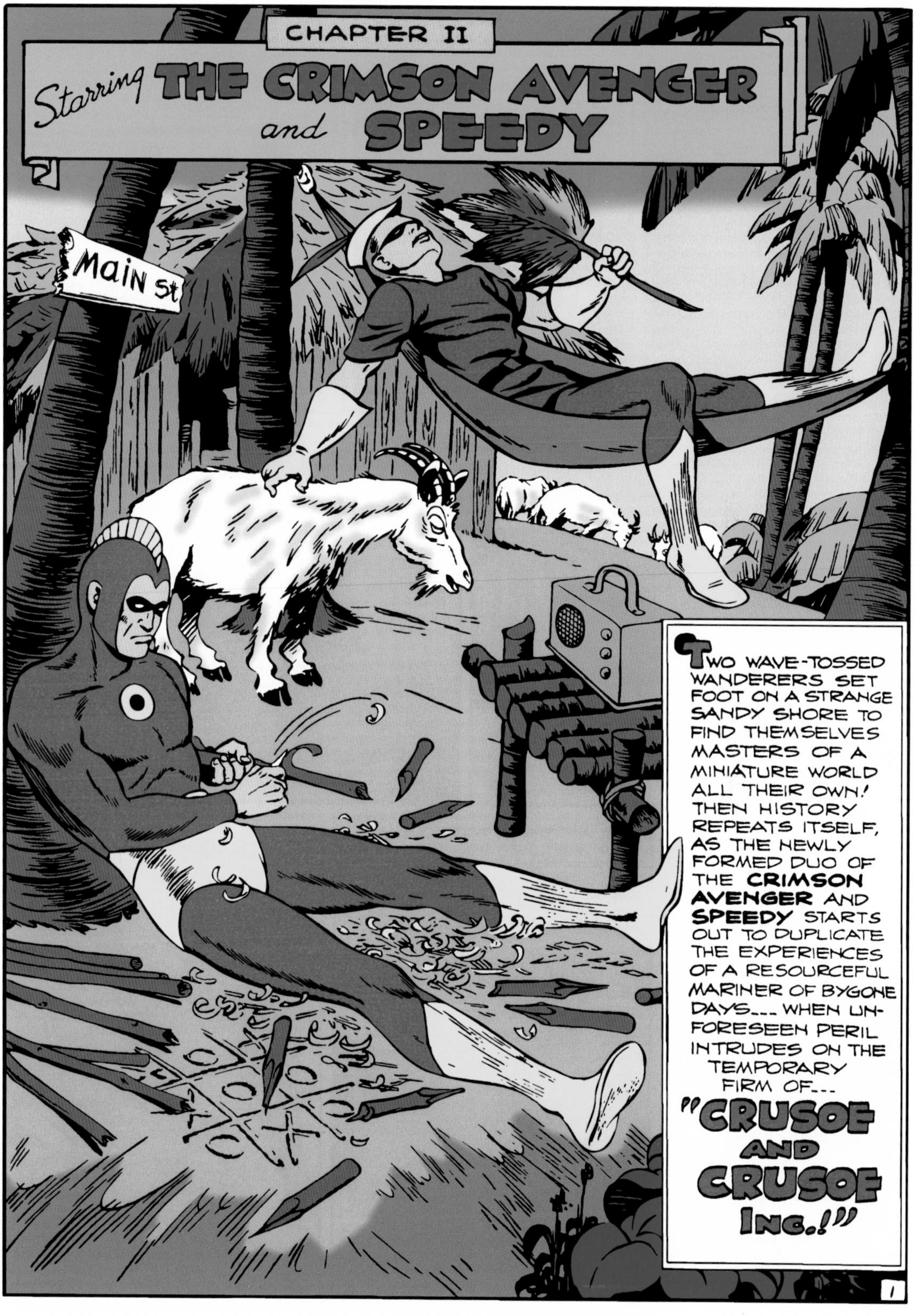
CHAPTER II
Starring THE CRIMSON AVENGER and SPEEDY
Main St
TWO WAVE-TOSSED WANDERERS SET FOOT ON A STRANGE SANDY SHORE TO FIND THEMSELVES MASTERS OF A MINIATURE WORLD ALL THEIR OWN! THEN HISTORY REPEATS ITSELF, AS THE NEWLY FORMED DUO OF THE CRIMSON AVENGER AND SPEEDY STARTS OUT TO DUPLICATE THE EXPERIENCES OF A RESOURCEFUL MARINER OF BYGONE DAYS... WHEN UNFORESEEN PERIL INTRUDES ON THE TEMPORARY FIRM OF...
"CRUSOE AND CRUSOE INC.!"
1

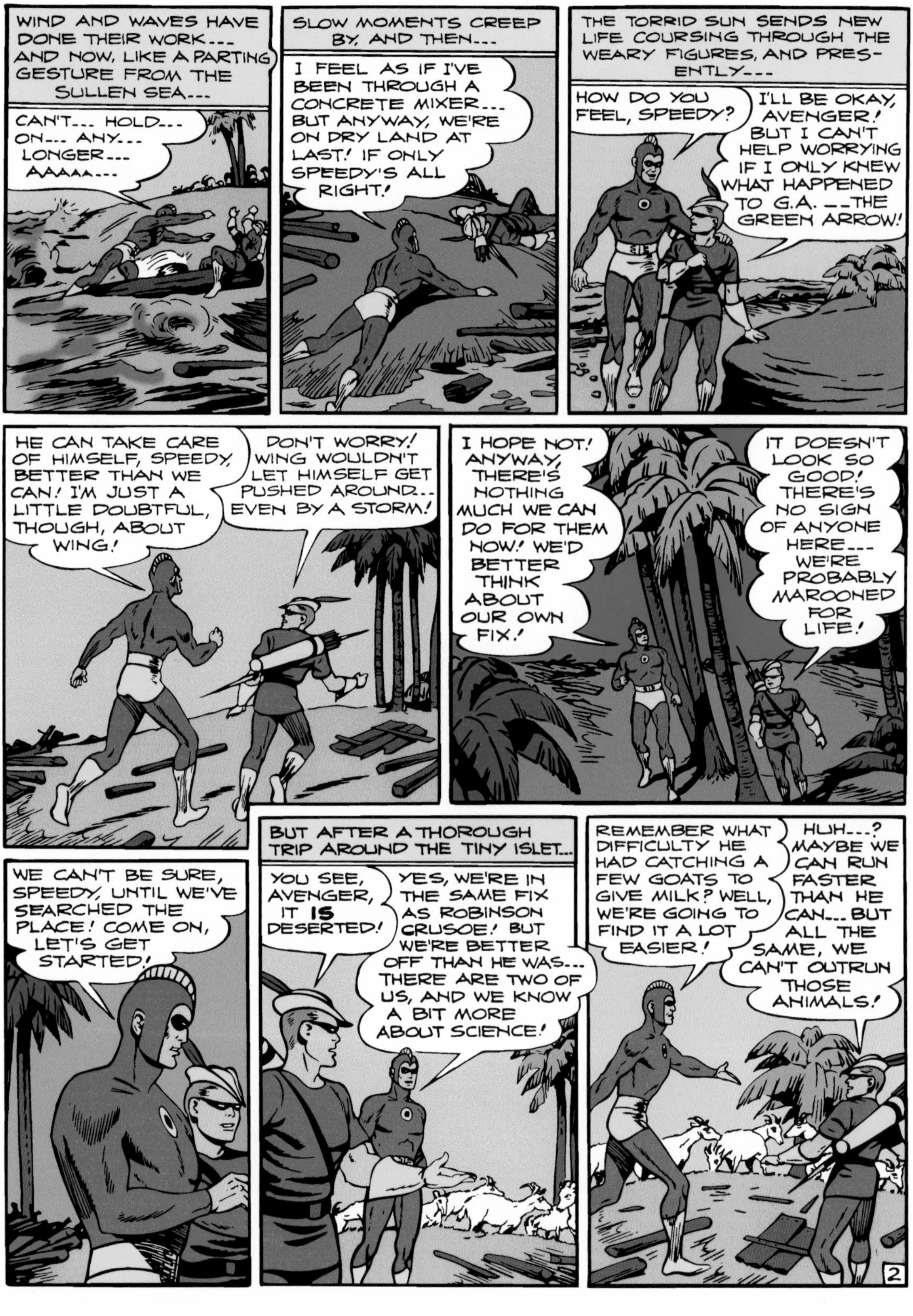
WIND AND WAVES HAVE DONE THEIR WORK--- AND NOW, LIKE A PARTING GESTURE FROM THE SULLEN SEA---
CAN'T--- HOLD--- ON--- ANY--- LONGER--- AAAAA---
SLOW MOMENTS CREEP BY, AND THEN---
I FEEL AS IF I'VE BEEN THROUGH A CONCRETE MIXER--- BUT ANYWAY, WE'RE ON DRY LAND AT LAST! IF ONLY SPEEDY'S ALL RIGHT!
THE TORRID SUN SENDS NEW LIFE COURSING THROUGH THE WEARY FIGURES, AND PRESENTLY---
HOW DO YOU FEEL, SPEEDY?
I'LL BE OKAY, AVENGER! BUT I CAN'T HELP WORRYING IF I ONLY KNEW WHAT HAPPENED TO G.A. --THE GREEN ARROW!
HE CAN TAKE CARE OF HIMSELF, SPEEDY, BETTER THAN WE CAN! I'M JUST A LITTLE DOUBTFUL, THOUGH, ABOUT WING!
DON'T WORRY! WING WOULDN'T LET HIMSELF GET PUSHED AROUND-- EVEN BY A STORM!
I HOPE NOT! ANYWAY, THERE'S NOTHING MUCH WE CAN DO FOR THEM NOW! WE'D BETTER THINK ABOUT OUR OWN FIX!
IT DOESN'T LOOK SO GOOD! THERE'S NO SIGN OF ANYONE HERE--- WE'RE PROBABLY MAROONED FOR LIFE!
WE CAN'T BE SURE, SPEEDY, UNTIL WE'VE SEARCHED THE PLACE! COME ON, LET'S GET STARTED!
BUT AFTER A THOROUGH TRIP AROUND THE TINY ISLET...
YOU SEE, AVENGER, IT IS DESERTED!
YES, WE'RE IN THE SAME FIX AS ROBINSON CRUSOE! BUT WE'RE BETTER OFF THAN HE WAS--- THERE ARE TWO OF US, AND WE KNOW A BIT MORE ABOUT SCIENCE!
REMEMBER WHAT DIFFICULTY HE HAD CATCHING A FEW GOATS TO GIVE MILK? WELL, WE'RE GOING TO FIND IT A LOT EASIER!
HUH---? MAYBE WE CAN RUN FASTER THAN HE CAN--- BUT ALL THE SAME, WE CAN'T OUTRUN THOSE ANIMALS!
2

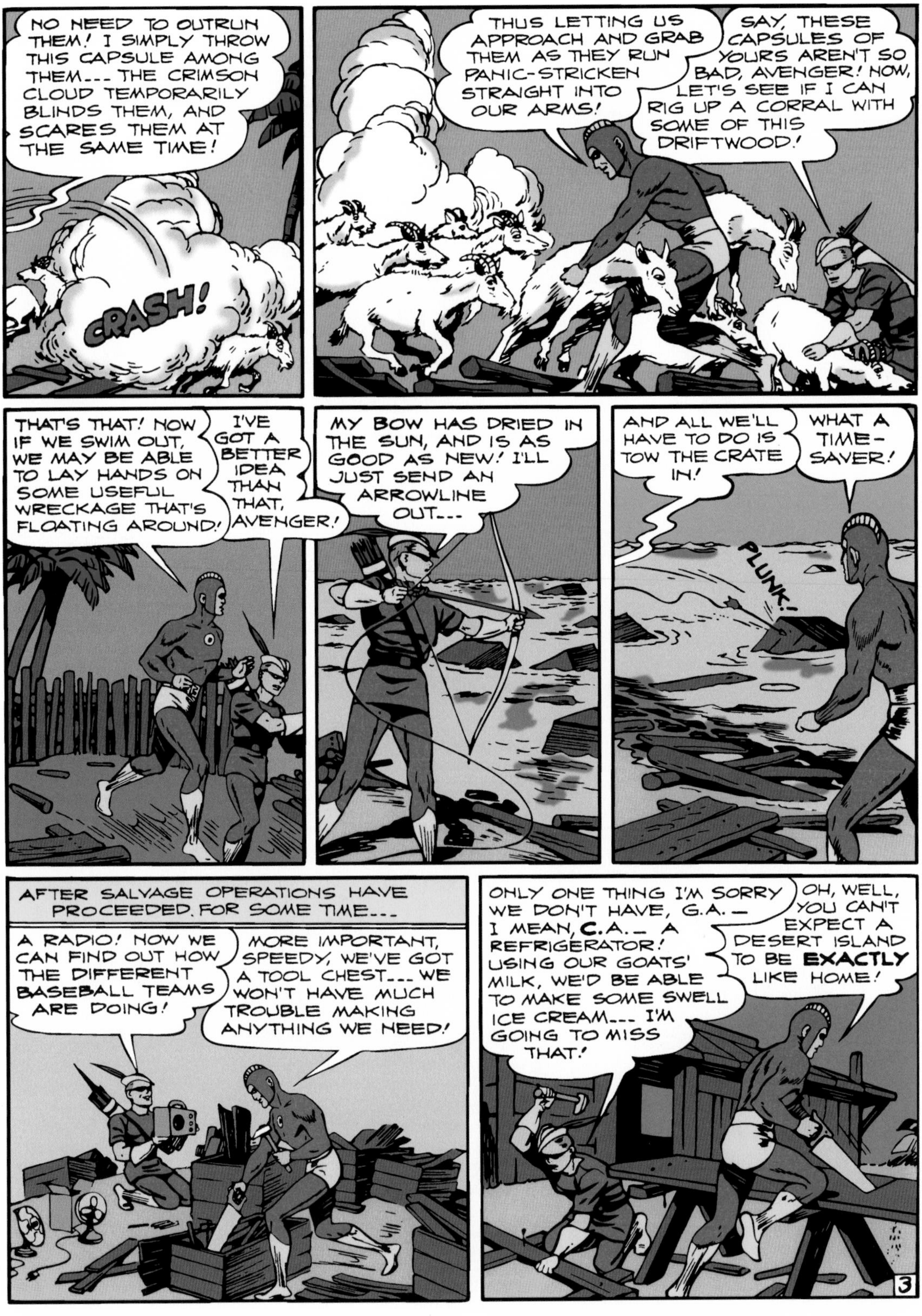
NO NEED TO OUTRUN THEM! I SIMPLY THROW THIS CAPSULE AMONG THEM--- THE CRIMSON CLOUD TEMPORARILY BLINDS THEM, AND SCARES THEM AT THE SAME TIME!
CRASH!
THUS LETTING US APPROACH AND GRAB THEM AS THEY RUN PANIC-STRICKEN STRAIGHT INTO OUR ARMS!
SAY, THESE CAPSULES OF YOURS AREN'T SO BAD, AVENGER! NOW, LET'S SEE IF I CAN RIG UP A CORRAL WITH SOME OF THIS DRIFTWOOD!
THAT'S THAT! NOW IF WE SWIM OUT, WE MAY BE ABLE TO LAY HANDS ON SOME USEFUL WRECKAGE THAT'S FLOATING AROUND!
I'VE GOT A BETTER IDEA THAN THAT, AVENGER!
MY BOW HAS DRIED IN THE SUN, AND IS AS GOOD AS NEW! I'LL JUST SEND AN ARROWLINE OUT---
AND ALL WE'LL HAVE TO DO IS TOW THE CRATE IN!
PLUNK!
WHAT A TIME-SAVER!
AFTER SALVAGE OPERATIONS HAVE PROCEEDED FOR SOME TIME---
A RADIO! NOW WE CAN FIND OUT HOW THE DIFFERENT BASEBALL TEAMS ARE DOING!
MORE IMPORTANT, SPEEDY, WE'VE GOT A TOOL CHEST--- WE WON'T HAVE MUCH TROUBLE MAKING ANYTHING WE NEED!
ONLY ONE THING I'M SORRY WE DON'T HAVE, G.A. — I MEAN, C.A. — A REFRIGERATOR! USING OUR GOATS' MILK, WE'D BE ABLE TO MAKE SOME SWELL ICE CREAM--- I'M GOING TO MISS THAT!
OH, WELL, YOU CAN'T EXPECT A DESERT ISLAND TO BE EXACTLY LIKE HOME!
3

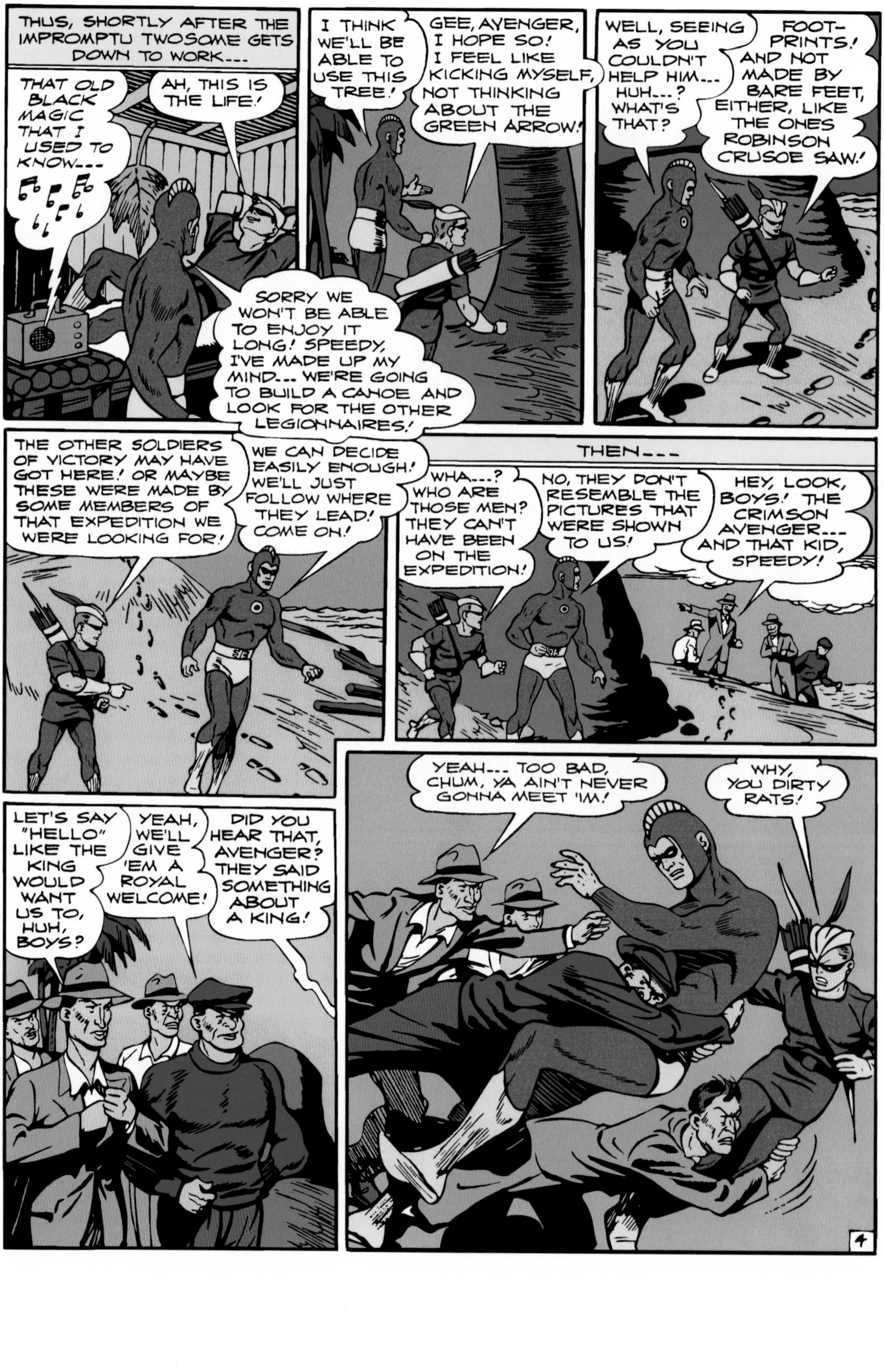
THUS, SHORTLY AFTER THE IMPROMPTU TWOSOME GETS DOWN TO WORK...
THAT OLD BLACK MAGIC THAT I USED TO KNOW...
AH, THIS IS THE LIFE!
SORRY WE WON'T BE ABLE TO ENJOY IT LONG! SPEEDY, I'VE MADE UP MY MIND... WE'RE GOING TO BUILD A CANOE AND LOOK FOR THE OTHER LEGIONNAIRES!
I THINK WE'LL BE ABLE TO USE THIS TREE!
GEE, AVENGER, I HOPE SO! I FEEL LIKE KICKING MYSELF, NOT THINKING ABOUT THE GREEN ARROW!
WELL, SEEING AS YOU COULDN'T HELP HIM... HUH...? WHAT'S THAT?
FOOT-PRINTS! AND NOT MADE BY BARE FEET, EITHER, LIKE THE ONES ROBINSON CRUSOE SAW!
THE OTHER SOLDIERS OF VICTORY MAY HAVE GOT HERE! OR MAYBE THESE WERE MADE BY SOME MEMBERS OF THAT EXPEDITION WE WERE LOOKING FOR!
WE CAN DECIDE EASILY ENOUGH! WE'LL JUST FOLLOW WHERE THEY LEAD! COME ON!
THEN...
WHA...? WHO ARE THOSE MEN? THEY CAN'T HAVE BEEN ON THE EXPEDITION!
NO, THEY DON'T RESEMBLE THE PICTURES THAT WERE SHOWN TO US!
HEY, LOOK, BOYS! THE CRIMSON AVENGER... AND THAT KID, SPEEDY!
LET'S SAY "HELLO" LIKE THE KING WOULD WANT US TO, HUH, BOYS?
YEAH, WE'LL GIVE 'EM A ROYAL WELCOME!
DID YOU HEAR THAT, AVENGER? THEY SAID SOMETHING ABOUT A KING!
YEAH... TOO BAD, CHUM, YA AIN'T NEVER GONNA MEET 'IM!
WHY, YOU DIRTY RATS!
4

SURPRISED BY THE TREACHEROUS ONSLAUGHT, THE HEROIC DUO IS QUICKLY OVERWHELMED...

TAKE IT EASY, AVENGER... DESE TROPICAL ISLES IS DA PLACE TO RELAX!

AAAAA...

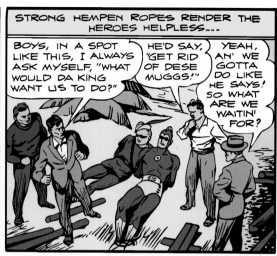

STRONG HEMPEN ROPES RENDER THE HEROES HELPLESS...

BOYS, IN A SPOT LIKE THIS, I ALWAYS ASK MYSELF, "WHAT WOULD DA KING WANT US TO DO?"

HE'D SAY, "GET RID OF DESE MUGGS!"

YEAH, AN' WE GOTTA DO LIKE HE SAYS! SO WHAT ARE WE WAITIN' FOR?

PRESENTLY...

SO LONG, CHUMS! WHEN DA TIDE COMES UP, YOU'RE GOIN' FER A NICE LONG SWIM... DOWN TO THE BOTTOM OF DA OCEAN!

DON'T BE SO SURE OF THAT, RATS... WE'VE GOT OUT OF TIGHTER SPOTS THAN THIS BEFORE!

GEE, AVENGER, I TRIED TO SOUND CONFIDENT--- BUT WE DON'T STAND A CHANCE! IF ONLY THE GREEN ARROW... I DON'T MEAN ANY REFLECTION ON YOU, AVENGER, BUT---

HMM. I KNOW HOW YOU FEEL, SPEEDY, BUT DON'T GIVE UP YET!

I THINK THESE LITTLE TROPICAL FISH CAN HELP US!

HUH...?

QUITE SURE! BY PRESSING MY SEARCHLIGHT AGAINST THE ROCK, I CAN TURN ON THE LIGHT!

I THINK I'M BEGINNING TO GET IT!

THE RED BEAM ATTRACTS THE FISH, BRINGS THEM NOSING AROUND!

THAT'S RIGHT! AND WHEN YOU BRING YOUR ROPES CLOSE TO THE LENS... THEY NOSE AROUND THEM TOO!

5

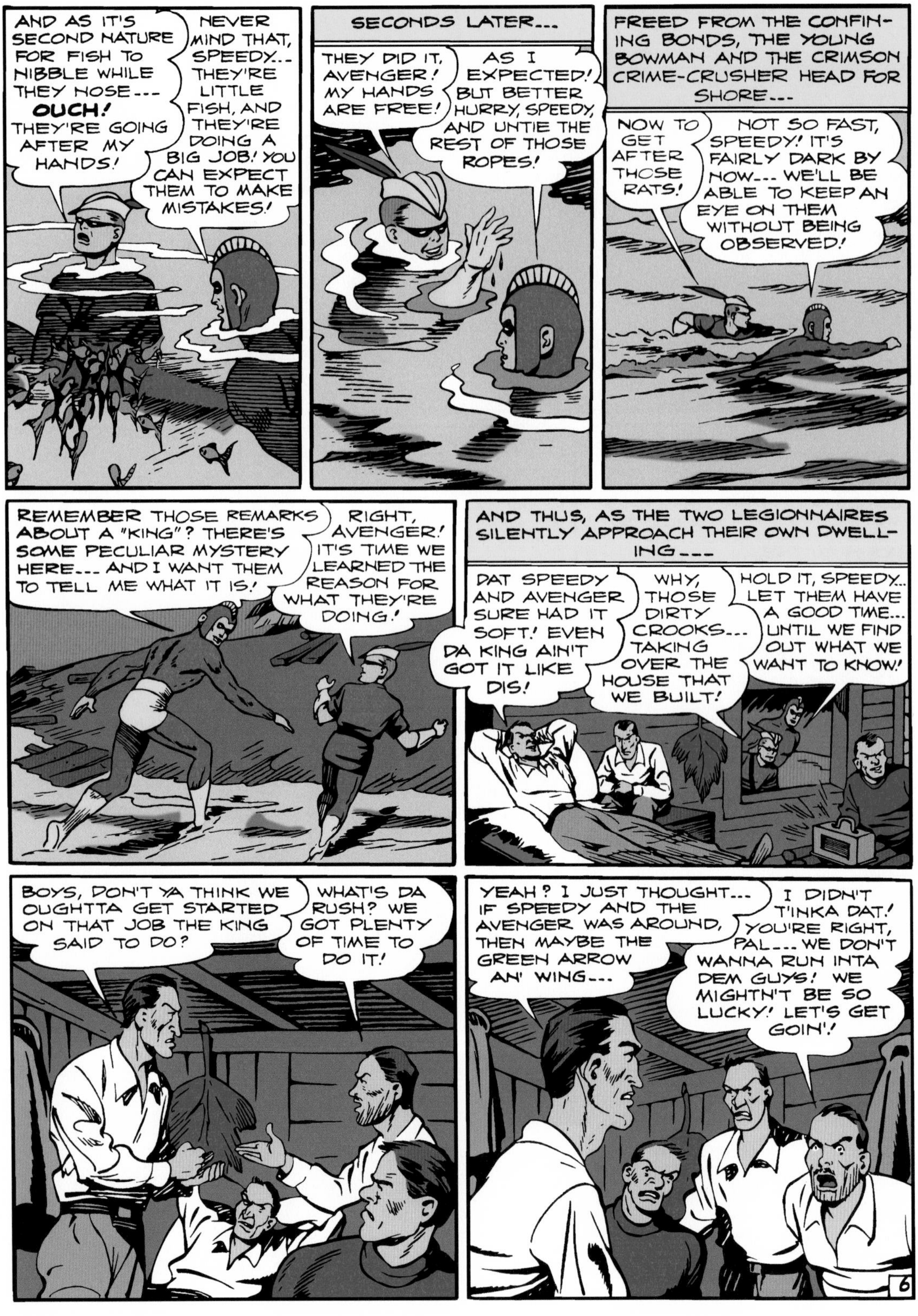
AND AS IT'S SECOND NATURE FOR FISH TO NIBBLE WHILE THEY NOSE--- OUCH! THEY'RE GOING AFTER MY HANDS!
NEVER MIND THAT, SPEEDY-- THEY'RE LITTLE FISH, AND THEY'RE DOING A BIG JOB! YOU CAN EXPECT THEM TO MAKE MISTAKES!
SECONDS LATER...
THEY DID IT, AVENGER! MY HANDS ARE FREE!
AS I EXPECTED! BUT BETTER HURRY, SPEEDY, AND UNTIE THE REST OF THOSE ROPES!
FREED FROM THE CONFINING BONDS, THE YOUNG BOWMAN AND THE CRIMSON CRIME-CRUSHER HEAD FOR SHORE---
NOW TO GET AFTER THOSE RATS!
NOT SO FAST, SPEEDY! IT'S FAIRLY DARK BY NOW--- WE'LL BE ABLE TO KEEP AN EYE ON THEM WITHOUT BEING OBSERVED!
REMEMBER THOSE REMARKS ABOUT A "KING"? THERE'S SOME PECULIAR MYSTERY HERE--- AND I WANT THEM TO TELL ME WHAT IT IS!
RIGHT, AVENGER! IT'S TIME WE LEARNED THE REASON FOR WHAT THEY'RE DOING!
AND THUS, AS THE TWO LEGIONNAIRES SILENTLY APPROACH THEIR OWN DWELLING---
DAT SPEEDY AND AVENGER SURE HAD IT SOFT! EVEN DA KING AIN'T GOT IT LIKE DIS!
WHY, THOSE DIRTY CROOKS--- TAKING OVER THE HOUSE THAT WE BUILT!
HOLD IT, SPEEDY.. LET THEM HAVE A GOOD TIME... UNTIL WE FIND OUT WHAT WE WANT TO KNOW!
BOYS, DON'T YA THINK WE OUGHTTA GET STARTED ON THAT JOB THE KING SAID TO DO?
WHAT'S DA RUSH? WE GOT PLENTY OF TIME TO DO IT!
YEAH? I JUST THOUGHT--- IF SPEEDY AND THE AVENGER WAS AROUND, THEN MAYBE THE GREEN ARROW AN' WING---
I DIDN'T T'INKA DAT! YOU'RE RIGHT, PAL--- WE DON'T WANNA RUN INTA DEM GUYS! WE MIGHTN'T BE SO LUCKY! LET'S GET GOIN'!
6

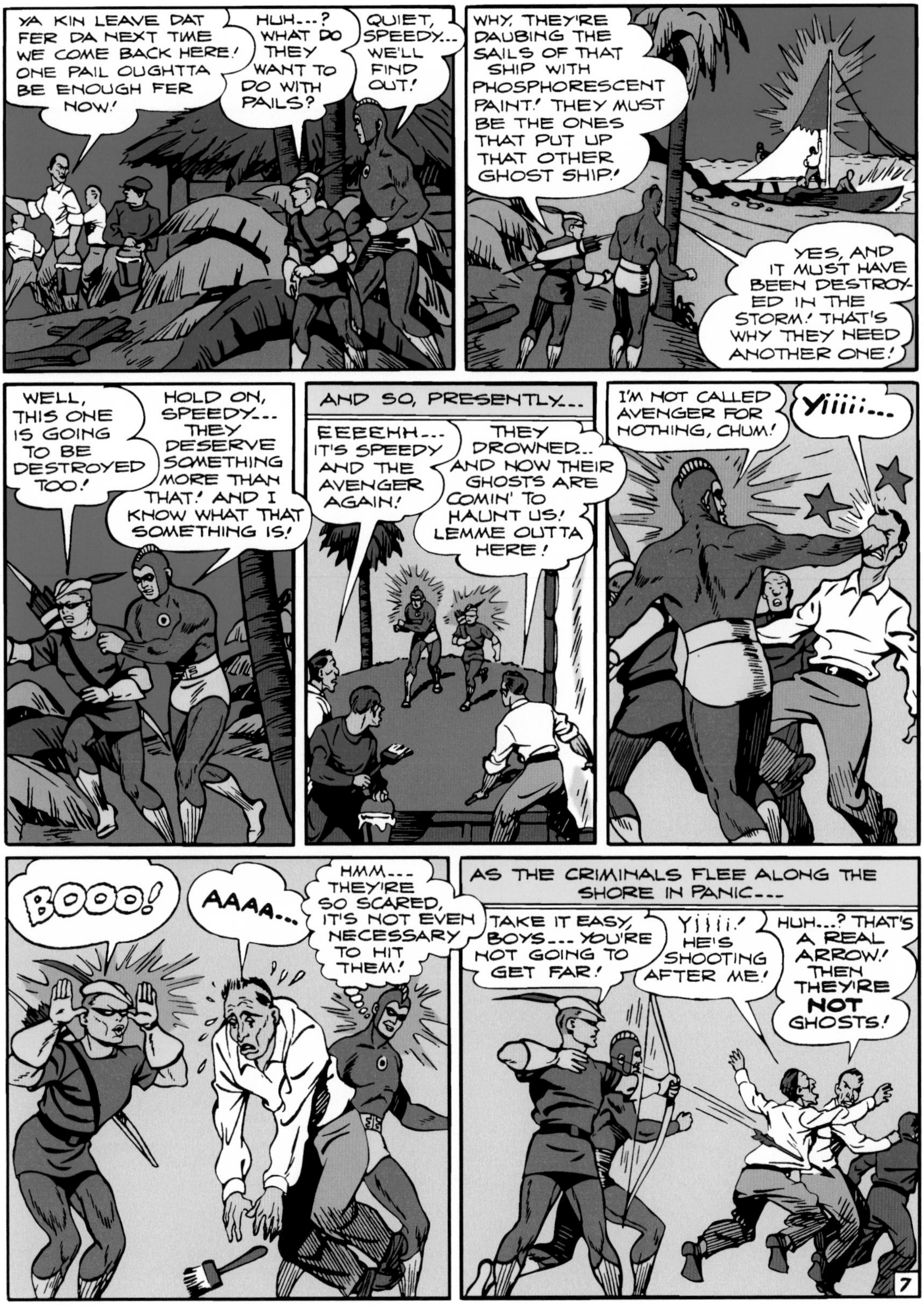
YA KIN LEAVE DAT FER DA NEXT TIME WE COME BACK HERE! ONE PAIL OUGHTTA BE ENOUGH FER NOW!
HUH...? WHAT DO THEY WANT TO DO WITH PAILS?
QUIET, SPEEDY... WE'LL FIND OUT!
WHY, THEY'RE DAUBING THE SAILS OF THAT SHIP WITH PHOSPHORESCENT PAINT! THEY MUST BE THE ONES THAT PUT UP THAT OTHER GHOST SHIP!
YES, AND IT MUST HAVE BEEN DESTROYED IN THE STORM! THAT'S WHY THEY NEED ANOTHER ONE!
WELL, THIS ONE IS GOING TO BE DESTROYED TOO!
HOLD ON, SPEEDY... THEY DESERVE SOMETHING MORE THAN THAT! AND I KNOW WHAT THAT SOMETHING IS!
AND SO, PRESENTLY...
EEEEHH... IT'S SPEEDY AND THE AVENGER AGAIN!
THEY DROWNED... AND NOW THEIR GHOSTS ARE COMIN' TO HAUNT US! LEMME OUTTA HERE!
I'M NOT CALLED AVENGER FOR NOTHING, CHUM!
Yiiiii...
BOOO!
AAAA...
HMM... THEY'RE SO SCARED, IT'S NOT EVEN NECESSARY TO HIT THEM!
AS THE CRIMINALS FLEE ALONG THE SHORE IN PANIC...
TAKE IT EASY, BOYS... YOU'RE NOT GOING TO GET FAR!
Yiiii! HE'S SHOOTING AFTER ME!
HUH...? THAT'S A REAL ARROW! THEN THEY'RE NOT GHOSTS!
7

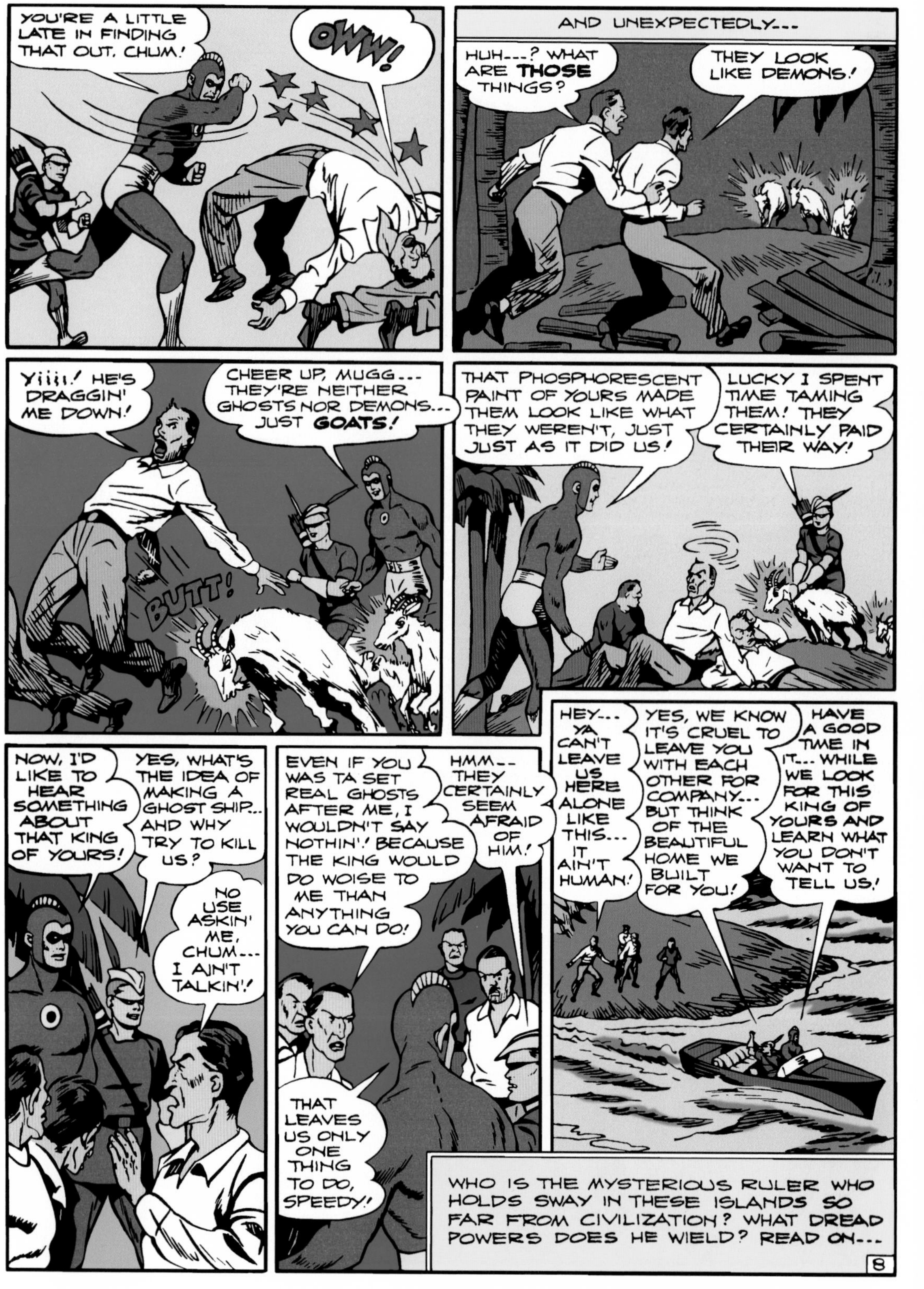
YOU'RE A LITTLE LATE IN FINDING THAT OUT, CHUM!
OWW!
AND UNEXPECTEDLY---
HUH---? WHAT ARE THOSE THINGS?
THEY LOOK LIKE DEMONS!
Yiiii! HE'S DRAGGIN' ME DOWN!
CHEER UP, MUGG--- THEY'RE NEITHER GHOSTS NOR DEMONS--- JUST GOATS!
BUTT!
THAT PHOSPHORESCENT PAINT OF YOURS MADE THEM LOOK LIKE WHAT THEY WEREN'T, JUST JUST AS IT DID US!
LUCKY I SPENT TIME TAMING THEM! THEY CERTAINLY PAID THEIR WAY!
NOW, I'D LIKE TO HEAR SOMETHING ABOUT THAT KING OF YOURS!
YES, WHAT'S THE IDEA OF MAKING A GHOST SHIP-- AND WHY TRY TO KILL US?
NO USE ASKIN' ME, CHUM--- I AIN'T TALKIN'!
EVEN IF YOU WAS TA SET REAL GHOSTS AFTER ME, I WOULDN'T SAY NOTHIN'! BECAUSE THE KING WOULD DO WOISE TO ME THAN ANYTHING YOU CAN DO!
HMM-- THEY CERTAINLY SEEM AFRAID OF HIM!
THAT LEAVES US ONLY ONE THING TO DO, SPEEDY!
HEY--- YA CAN'T LEAVE US HERE ALONE LIKE THIS--- IT AIN'T HUMAN!
YES, WE KNOW IT'S CRUEL TO LEAVE YOU WITH EACH OTHER FOR COMPANY--- BUT THINK OF THE BEAUTIFUL HOME WE BUILT FOR YOU!
HAVE A GOOD TIME IN IT--- WHILE WE LOOK FOR THIS KING OF YOURS AND LEARN WHAT YOU DON'T WANT TO TELL US!
WHO IS THE MYSTERIOUS RULER WHO HOLDS SWAY IN THESE ISLANDS SO FAR FROM CIVILIZATION? WHAT DREAD POWERS DOES HE WIELD? READ ON---
8

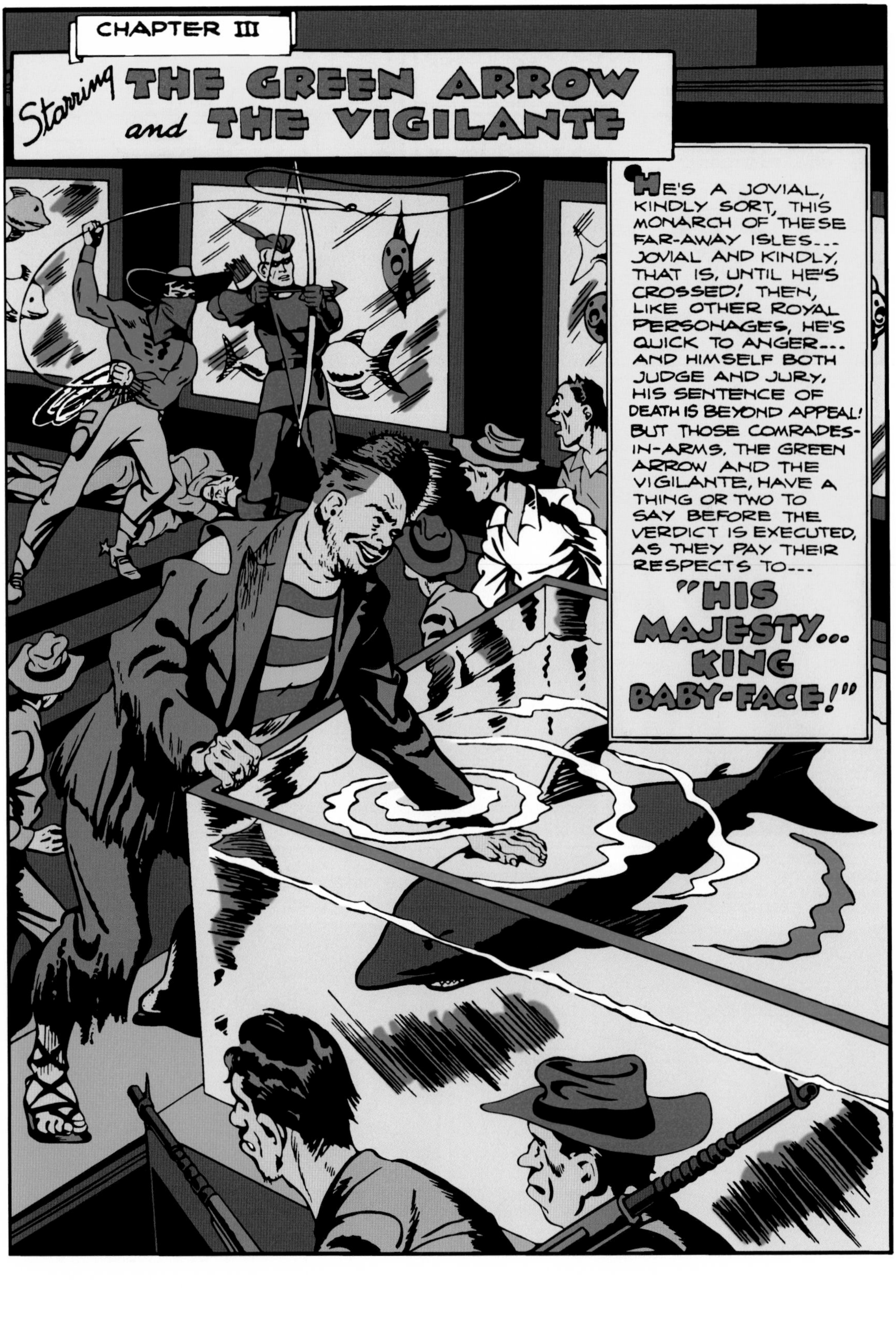
CHAPTER III
Starring THE GREEN ARROW and THE VIGILANTE
HE'S A JOVIAL, KINDLY SORT, THIS MONARCH OF THESE FAR-AWAY ISLES... JOVIAL AND KINDLY, THAT IS, UNTIL HE'S CROSSED! THEN, LIKE OTHER ROYAL PERSONAGES, HE'S QUICK TO ANGER... AND HIMSELF BOTH JUDGE AND JURY, HIS SENTENCE OF DEATH IS BEYOND APPEAL! BUT THOSE COMRADES-IN-ARMS, THE GREEN ARROW AND THE VIGILANTE, HAVE A THING OR TWO TO SAY BEFORE THE VERDICT IS EXECUTED, AS THEY PAY THEIR RESPECTS TO...
"HIS MAJESTY... KING BABY-FACE!"

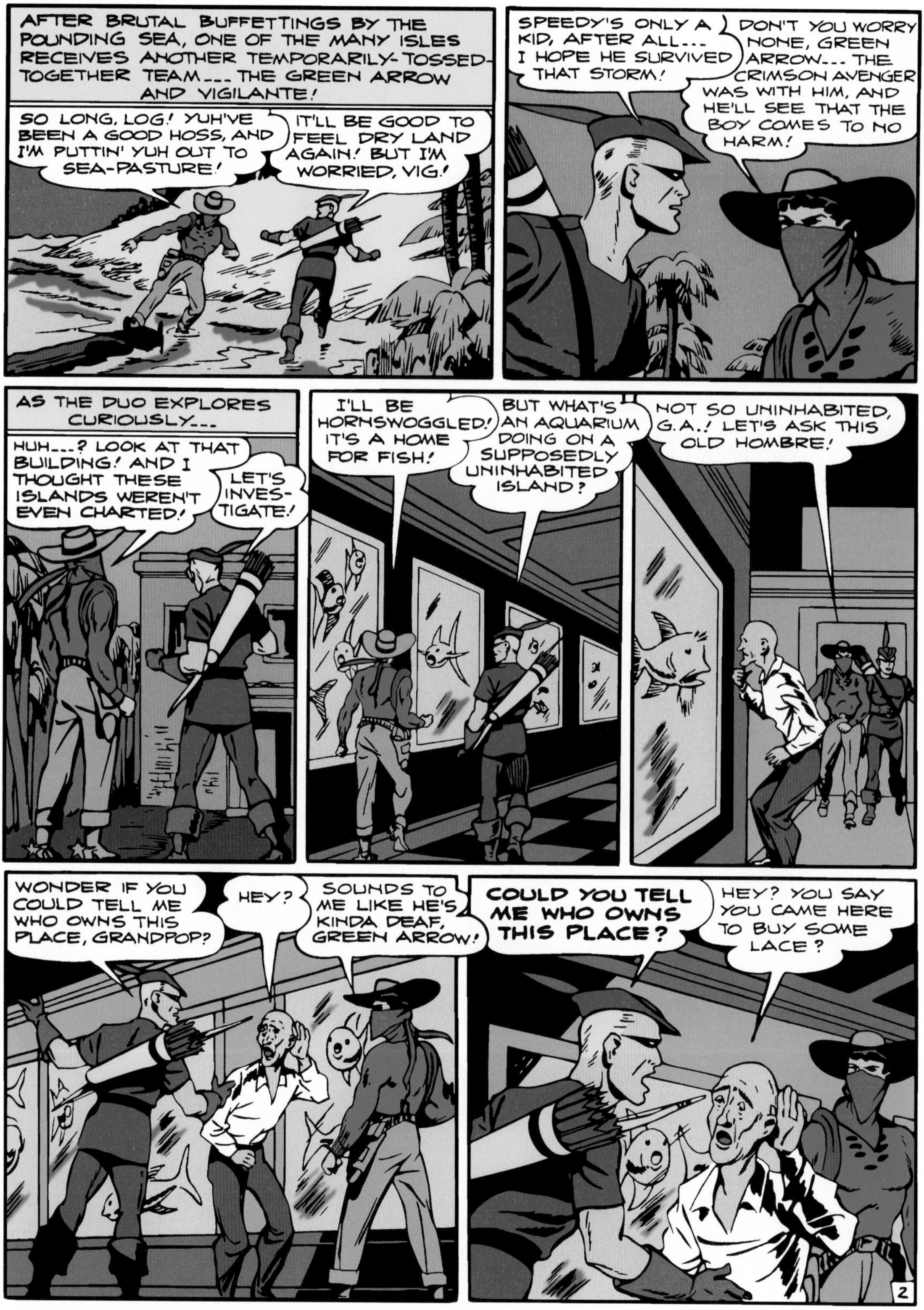
AFTER BRUTAL BUFFETTINGS BY THE POUNDING SEA, ONE OF THE MANY ISLES RECEIVES ANOTHER TEMPORARILY-TOSSED-TOGETHER TEAM... THE GREEN ARROW AND VIGILANTE!
SO LONG, LOG! YUH'VE BEEN A GOOD HOSS, AND I'M PUTTIN' YUH OUT TO SEA-PASTURE!
IT'LL BE GOOD TO FEEL DRY LAND AGAIN! BUT I'M WORRIED, VIG!
SPEEDY'S ONLY A KID, AFTER ALL... I HOPE HE SURVIVED THAT STORM!
DON'T YOU WORRY NONE, GREEN ARROW... THE CRIMSON AVENGER WAS WITH HIM, AND HE'LL SEE THAT THE BOY COMES TO NO HARM!
AS THE DUO EXPLORES CURIOUSLY...
HUH...? LOOK AT THAT BUILDING! AND I THOUGHT THESE ISLANDS WEREN'T EVEN CHARTED!
LET'S INVES-TIGATE!
I'LL BE HORNSWOGGLED! IT'S A HOME FOR FISH!
BUT WHAT'S AN AQUARIUM DOING ON A SUPPOSEDLY UNINHABITED ISLAND?
NOT SO UNINHABITED, G.A.! LET'S ASK THIS OLD HOMBRE!
WONDER IF YOU COULD TELL ME WHO OWNS THIS PLACE, GRANDPOP?
HEY?
SOUNDS TO ME LIKE HE'S KINDA DEAF, GREEN ARROW!
COULD YOU TELL ME WHO OWNS THIS PLACE?
HEY? YOU SAY YOU CAME HERE TO BUY SOME LACE?
2

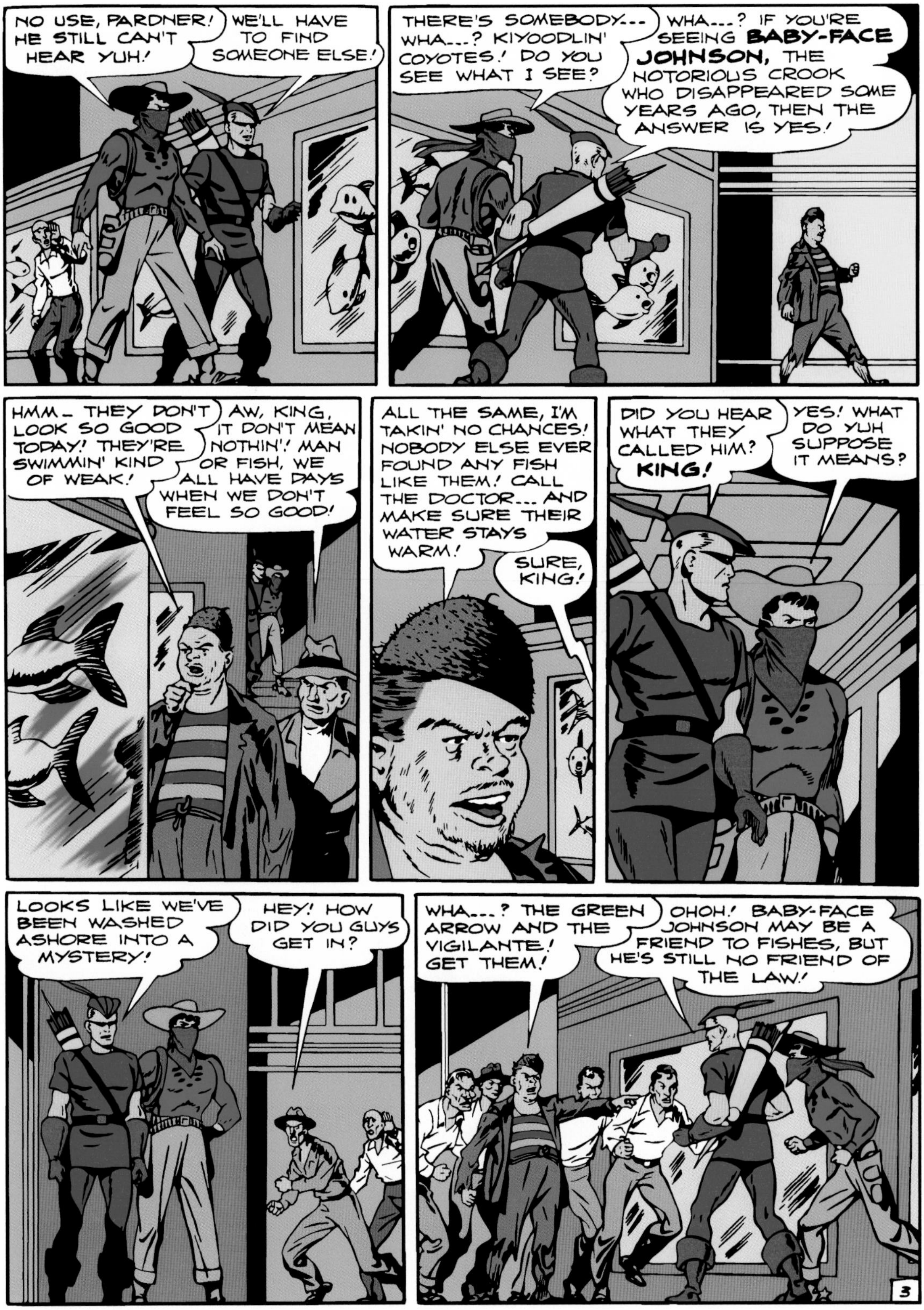
NO USE, PARDNER! HE STILL CAN'T HEAR YUH!
WE'LL HAVE TO FIND SOMEONE ELSE!
THERE'S SOMEBODY--- WHA---? KIYOODLIN' COYOTES! DO YOU SEE WHAT I SEE?
WHA---? IF YOU'RE SEEING BABY-FACE JOHNSON, THE NOTORIOUS CROOK WHO DISAPPEARED SOME YEARS AGO, THEN THE ANSWER IS YES!
HMM - THEY DON'T LOOK SO GOOD TODAY! THEY'RE SWIMMIN' KIND OF WEAK!
AW, KING, IT DON'T MEAN NOTHIN'! MAN OR FISH, WE ALL HAVE DAYS WHEN WE DON'T FEEL SO GOOD!
ALL THE SAME, I'M TAKIN' NO CHANCES! NOBODY ELSE EVER FOUND ANY FISH LIKE THEM! CALL THE DOCTOR--- AND MAKE SURE THEIR WATER STAYS WARM!
SURE, KING!
DID YOU HEAR WHAT THEY CALLED HIM? KING!
YES! WHAT DO YUH SUPPOSE IT MEANS?
LOOKS LIKE WE'VE BEEN WASHED ASHORE INTO A MYSTERY!
HEY! HOW DID YOU GUYS GET IN?
WHA---? THE GREEN ARROW AND THE VIGILANTE! GET THEM!
OHOH! BABY-FACE JOHNSON MAY BE A FRIEND TO FISHES, BUT HE'S STILL NO FRIEND OF THE LAW!
3

IF YO'RE ANGLIN' FOR TROUBLE, YOU'VE GOT IT!

Yiii!

WATCH OUT, VIG--- THEY'RE TRYING TO USE THEIR GUNS!

I RECKONED THEY WOULD, GREEN ARROW... BUT THEY'RE KINDA SLOW ON THE DRAW!

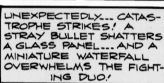

UNEXPECTEDLY... CATASTROPHE STRIKES! A STRAY BULLET SHATTERS A GLASS PANEL... AND A MINIATURE WATERFALL OVERWHELMS THE FIGHTING DUO!

HUH?

WE GOT 'EM ON THE RUN! COME ON, BOYS!

SECONDS LATER...

THE DIRTY BUMS! THEY COME HERE WITHOUT NO INVITATION AN' WHAT DO THEY DO? THEY DRIVE A BUNCH OF POOR LITTLE FISHES OUTTA THEIR HOME!

YOUR FISHES WOULD STILL HAVE THEIR TANK IF YOUR THUGS DIDN'T TRY---

QUIET! DON'T TRY TO ARGUE WITH ME--- I'M KING HERE!

AN' ON ACCOUNT OF YOU GUYS ACTIN' LIKE CRIMINALS, YOU GOT TO BE PUNISHED! I'M HANDIN' OUT SOME ROYAL JUSTICE!

4

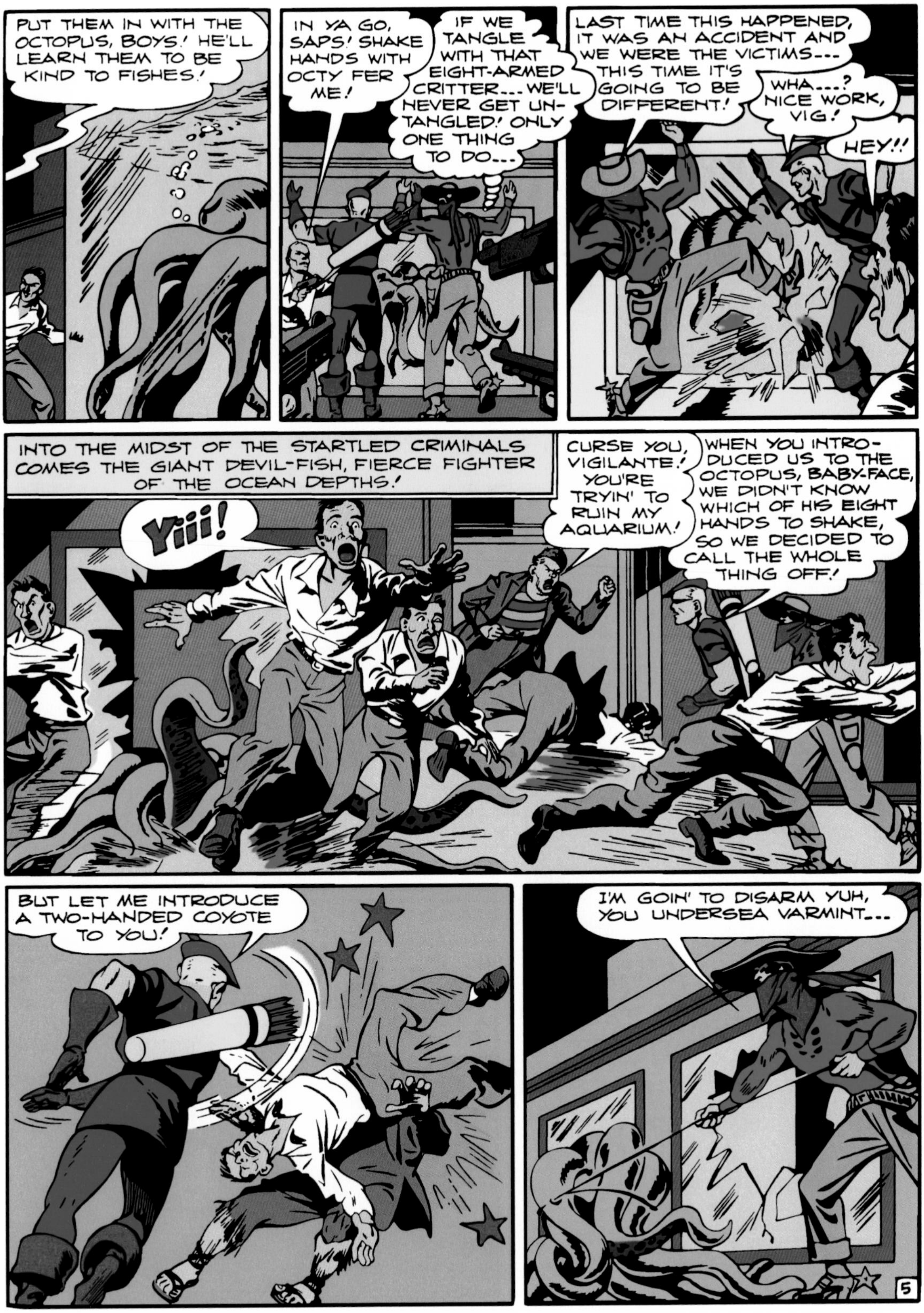
PUT THEM IN WITH THE OCTOPUS, BOYS! HE'LL LEARN THEM TO BE KIND TO FISHES!
IN YA GO, SAPS! SHAKE HANDS WITH OCTY FER ME!
IF WE TANGLE WITH THAT EIGHT-ARMED CRITTER... WE'LL NEVER GET UN-TANGLED! ONLY ONE THING TO DO...
LAST TIME THIS HAPPENED, IT WAS AN ACCIDENT AND WE WERE THE VICTIMS--- THIS TIME IT'S GOING TO BE DIFFERENT!
WHA...? NICE WORK, VIG!
HEY!!
INTO THE MIDST OF THE STARTLED CRIMINALS COMES THE GIANT DEVIL-FISH, FIERCE FIGHTER OF THE OCEAN DEPTHS!
YIII!
CURSE YOU, VIGILANTE! YOU'RE TRYIN' TO RUIN MY AQUARIUM!
WHEN YOU INTRO-DUCED US TO THE OCTOPUS, BABY-FACE, WE DIDN'T KNOW WHICH OF HIS EIGHT HANDS TO SHAKE, SO WE DECIDED TO CALL THE WHOLE THING OFF!
BUT LET ME INTRODUCE A TWO-HANDED COYOTE TO YOU!
I'M GOIN' TO DISARM YUH, YOU UNDERSEA VARMINT...
5

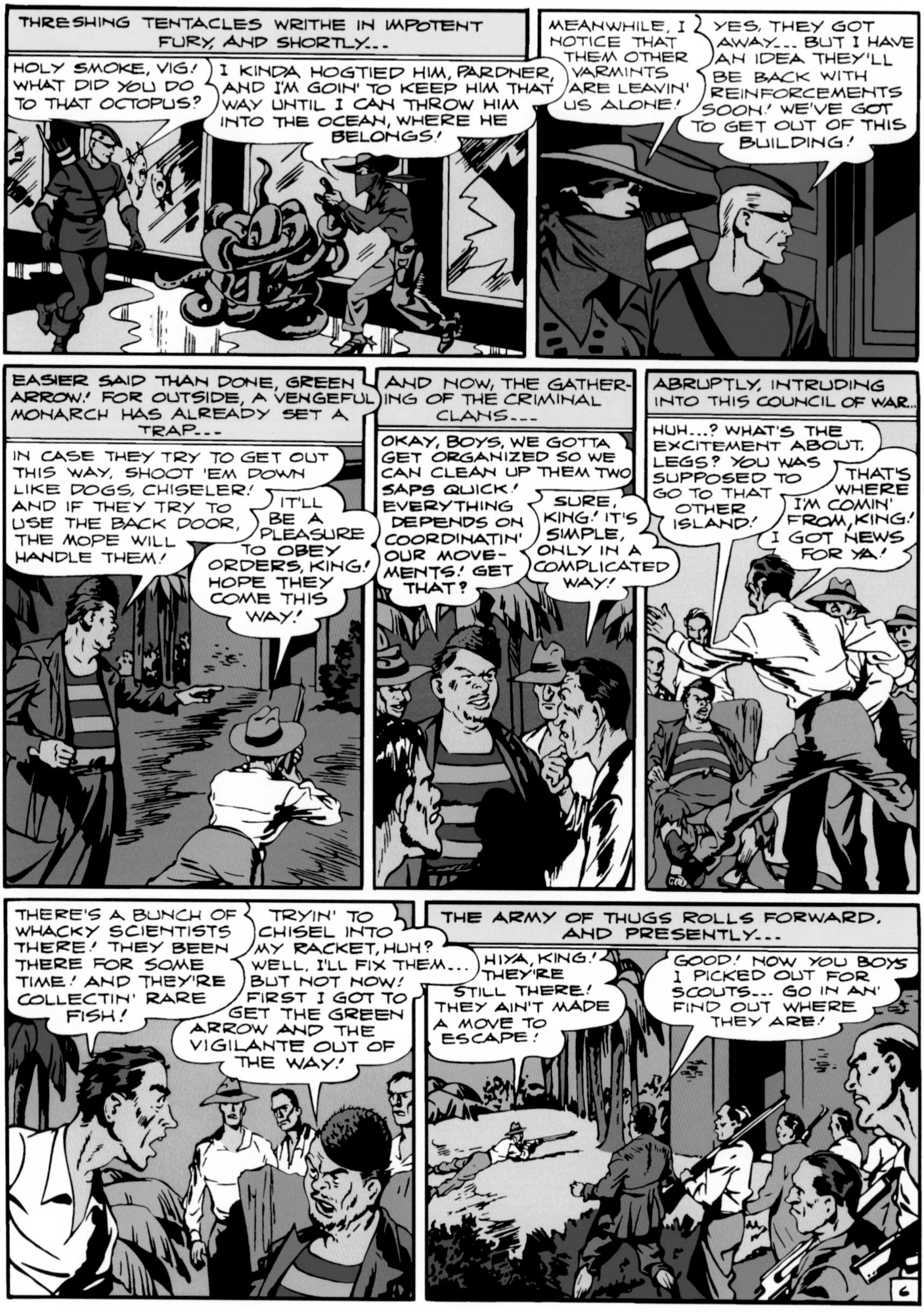
THRESHING TENTACLES WRITHE IN IMPOTENT FURY, AND SHORTLY...
HOLY SMOKE, VIG! WHAT DID YOU DO TO THAT OCTOPUS?
I KINDA HOGTIED HIM, PARDNER, AND I'M GOIN' TO KEEP HIM THAT WAY UNTIL I CAN THROW HIM INTO THE OCEAN, WHERE HE BELONGS!
MEANWHILE, I NOTICE THAT THEM OTHER VARMINTS ARE LEAVIN' US ALONE!
YES, THEY GOT AWAY... BUT I HAVE AN IDEA THEY'LL BE BACK WITH REINFORCEMENTS SOON! WE'VE GOT TO GET OUT OF THIS BUILDING!
EASIER SAID THAN DONE, GREEN ARROW! FOR OUTSIDE, A VENGEFUL MONARCH HAS ALREADY SET A TRAP...
IN CASE THEY TRY TO GET OUT THIS WAY, SHOOT 'EM DOWN LIKE DOGS, CHISELER! AND IF THEY TRY TO USE THE BACK DOOR, THE MOPE WILL HANDLE THEM!
IT'LL BE A PLEASURE TO OBEY ORDERS, KING! HOPE THEY COME THIS WAY!
AND NOW, THE GATHERING OF THE CRIMINAL CLANS...
OKAY, BOYS, WE GOTTA GET ORGANIZED SO WE CAN CLEAN UP THEM TWO SAPS QUICK! EVERYTHING DEPENDS ON COORDINATIN' OUR MOVEMENTS! GET THAT?
SURE, KING! IT'S SIMPLE, ONLY IN A COMPLICATED WAY!
ABRUPTLY, INTRUDING INTO THIS COUNCIL OF WAR...
HUH...? WHAT'S THE EXCITEMENT ABOUT, LEGS? YOU WAS SUPPOSED TO GO TO THAT OTHER ISLAND!
THAT'S WHERE I'M COMIN' FROM, KING! I GOT NEWS FOR YA!
THERE'S A BUNCH OF WHACKY SCIENTISTS THERE! THEY BEEN THERE FOR SOME TIME! AND THEY'RE COLLECTIN' RARE FISH!
TRYIN' TO CHISEL INTO MY RACKET, HUH? WELL, I'LL FIX THEM... BUT NOT NOW! FIRST I GOT TO GET THE GREEN ARROW AND THE VIGILANTE OUT OF THE WAY!
THE ARMY OF THUGS ROLLS FORWARD, AND PRESENTLY...
HIYA, KING! THEY'RE STILL THERE! THEY AIN'T MADE A MOVE TO ESCAPE!
GOOD! NOW YOU BOYS I PICKED OUT FOR SCOUTS... GO IN AN' FIND OUT WHERE THEY ARE!
6

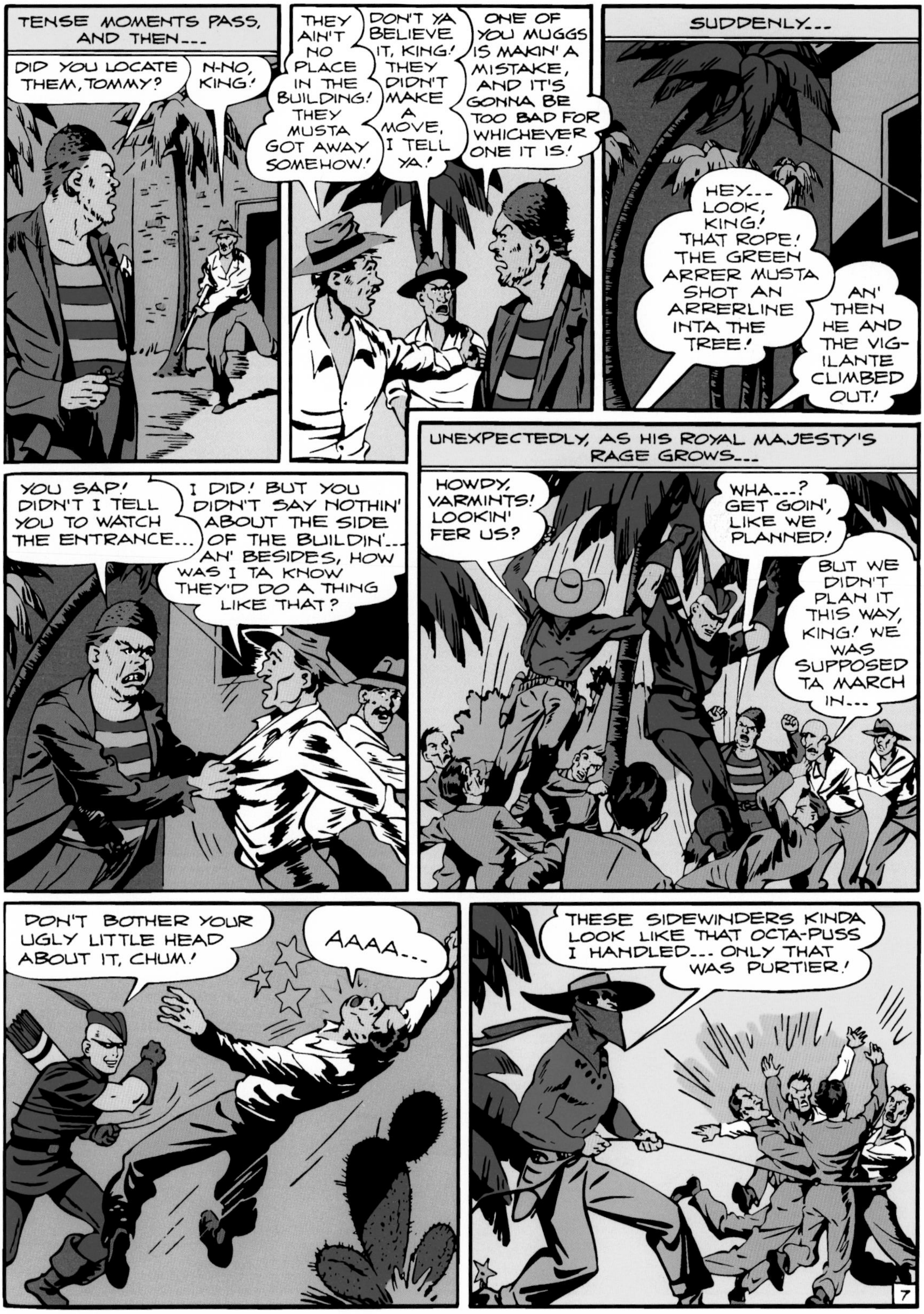
TENSE MOMENTS PASS, AND THEN---
DID YOU LOCATE THEM, TOMMY?
N-NO, KING!
THEY AIN'T NO PLACE IN THE BUILDING! THEY MUSTA GOT AWAY SOMEHOW!
DON'T YA BELIEVE IT, KING! THEY DIDN'T MAKE A MOVE, I TELL YA!
ONE OF YOU MUGGS IS MAKIN' A MISTAKE, AND IT'S GONNA BE TOO BAD FOR WHICHEVER ONE IT IS!
SUDDENLY---
HEY--- LOOK, KING! THAT ROPE! THE GREEN ARRER MUSTA SHOT AN ARRERLINE INTA THE TREE!
AN' THEN HE AND THE VIG-ILANTE CLIMBED OUT!
YOU SAP! DIDN'T I TELL YOU TO WATCH THE ENTRANCE...
I DID! BUT YOU DIDN'T SAY NOTHIN' ABOUT THE SIDE OF THE BUILDIN'--- AN' BESIDES, HOW WAS I TA KNOW THEY'D DO A THING LIKE THAT?
UNEXPECTEDLY, AS HIS ROYAL MAJESTY'S RAGE GROWS---
HOWDY, VARMINTS! LOOKIN' FER US?
WHA---? GET GOIN', LIKE WE PLANNED!
BUT WE DIDN'T PLAN IT THIS WAY, KING! WE WAS SUPPOSED TA MARCH IN---
DON'T BOTHER YOUR UGLY LITTLE HEAD ABOUT IT, CHUM!
AAAA---
THESE SIDEWINDERS KINDA LOOK LIKE THAT OCTA-PUSS I HANDLED--- ONLY THAT WAS PURTIER!
7

AS A FEAR-STRICKEN RULER ATTEMPTS FLIGHT...

NOT SO FAST, BABY-FACE! WE'VE GOT A FEW QUESTIONS TO ASK YOU... AND THIS TIME YOU'RE ANSWERING THEM!

BUT LIKE A BOLT FROM THE BLUE, WITH TERRIFYING SUDDENNESS...

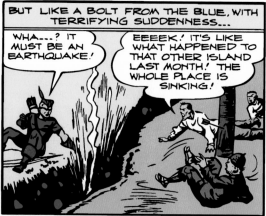

WHA---? IT MUST BE AN EARTHQUAKE!

EEEEK! IT'S LIKE WHAT HAPPENED TO THAT OTHER ISLAND LAST MONTH! THE WHOLE PLACE IS SINKING!

TALL TREES TREMBLE AND CRASH! MOLTEN LAVA ERUPTS THROUGH CRACKS IN THE SHATTERED GROUND! AND AS THE DOOMED ISLAND SINKS LOWER AND LOWER, A GREAT WALL OF WATER RACES IN FROM THE HEAVING OCEAN...

AND AFTER THE FINAL RIPPLES OF CATASTROPHE HAVE DIED AWAY...

HEY, PULL ME IN, KING, WILL YA?

ALL THE FISH I BEEN COLLECTIN'.. THEY'RE BACK IN THE OCEAN ONCE MORE! SO MUCH HARD WORK WASTED... THAT'S LIFE!

NEVER MIND, KING--- DERE'S DAT EXPEDITION OF WHACKY SCIENTISTS ON DAT ISLAND I CAME FROM! DEY'LL HELP YA START A NEW COLLECTION!

WHILE A SHORT DISTANCE AWAY...

HERE WE ARE AGAIN, PARDNER! WE MIGHT JUST AS WELL NEVER HAVE LANDED!

CHEER UP, VIG, WE'RE SURE TO RUN ACROSS ANOTHER ISLAND! AND WHEN WE DO, WE'LL MAKE IT OUR BUSINESS TO SOLVE THE MYSTERY OF "KING" BABY-FACE! SOMETHING BESIDES FISH IS KEEPING HIM IN THESE ISLANDS! FROM NOW ON OUR MOTTO IS GOING TO BE— "DOWN WITH THE KING!"

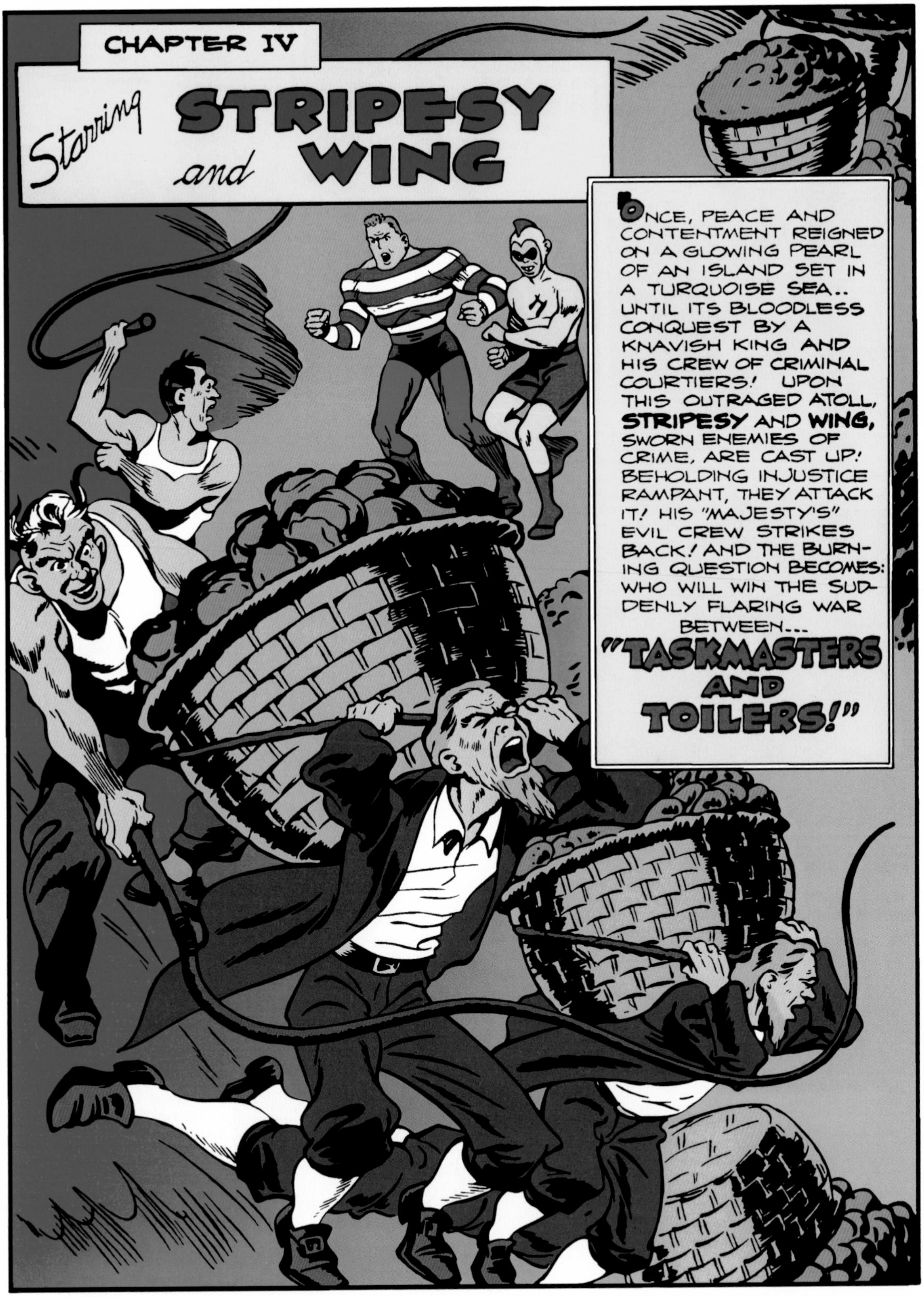
CHAPTER IV
Starring STRIPESY and WING
ONCE, PEACE AND CONTENTMENT REIGNED ON A GLOWING PEARL OF AN ISLAND SET IN A TURQUOISE SEA.. UNTIL ITS BLOODLESS CONQUEST BY A KNAVISH KING AND HIS CREW OF CRIMINAL COURTIERS! UPON THIS OUTRAGED ATOLL, STRIPESY AND WING, SWORN ENEMIES OF CRIME, ARE CAST UP! BEHOLDING INJUSTICE RAMPANT, THEY ATTACK IT! HIS "MAJESTY'S" EVIL CREW STRIKES BACK! AND THE BURNING QUESTION BECOMES: WHO WILL WIN THE SUDDENLY FLARING WAR BETWEEN...
"TASKMASTERS AND TOILERS!"

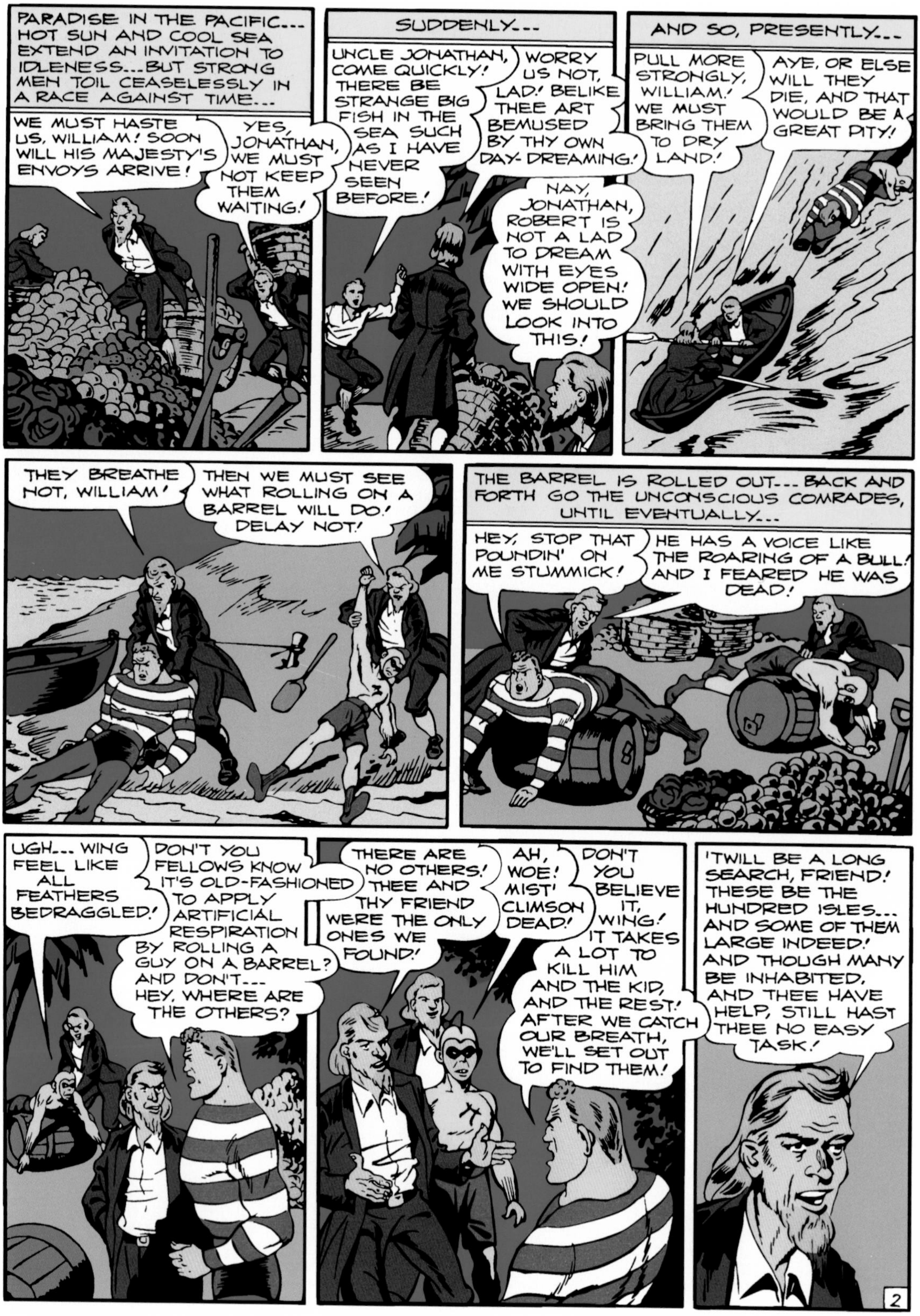
PARADISE IN THE PACIFIC... HOT SUN AND COOL SEA EXTEND AN INVITATION TO IDLENESS...BUT STRONG MEN TOIL CEASELESSLY IN A RACE AGAINST TIME...
WE MUST HASTE US, WILLIAM! SOON WILL HIS MAJESTY'S ENVOYS ARRIVE!
YES, JONATHAN, WE MUST NOT KEEP THEM WAITING!
SUDDENLY...
UNCLE JONATHAN, COME QUICKLY! THERE BE STRANGE BIG FISH IN THE SEA SUCH AS I HAVE NEVER SEEN BEFORE!
WORRY US NOT, LAD! BELIKE THEE ART BEMUSED BY THY OWN DAY-DREAMING!
NAY, JONATHAN, ROBERT IS NOT A LAD TO DREAM WITH EYES WIDE OPEN! WE SHOULD LOOK INTO THIS!
AND SO, PRESENTLY...
PULL MORE STRONGLY, WILLIAM! WE MUST BRING THEM TO DRY LAND!
AYE, OR ELSE WILL THEY DIE, AND THAT WOULD BE A GREAT PITY!
THEY BREATHE NOT, WILLIAM!
THEN WE MUST SEE WHAT ROLLING ON A BARREL WILL DO! DELAY NOT!
THE BARREL IS ROLLED OUT... BACK AND FORTH GO THE UNCONSCIOUS COMRADES, UNTIL EVENTUALLY...
HEY, STOP THAT POUNDIN' ON ME STUMMICK!
HE HAS A VOICE LIKE THE ROARING OF A BULL! AND I FEARED HE WAS DEAD!
UGH... WING FEEL LIKE ALL FEATHERS BEDRAGGLED!
DON'T YOU FELLOWS KNOW IT'S OLD-FASHIONED TO APPLY ARTIFICIAL RESPIRATION BY ROLLING A GUY ON A BARREL? AND DON'T... HEY, WHERE ARE THE OTHERS?
THERE ARE NO OTHERS! THEE AND THY FRIEND WERE THE ONLY ONES WE FOUND!
AH, WOE! MIST' CLIMSON DEAD!
DON'T YOU BELIEVE IT, WING! IT TAKES A LOT TO KILL HIM AND THE KID, AND THE REST! AFTER WE CATCH OUR BREATH, WE'LL SET OUT TO FIND THEM!
'TWILL BE A LONG SEARCH, FRIEND! THESE BE THE HUNDRED ISLES... AND SOME OF THEM LARGE INDEED! AND THOUGH MANY BE INHABITED, AND THEE HAVE HELP, STILL HAST THEE NO EASY TASK!
2

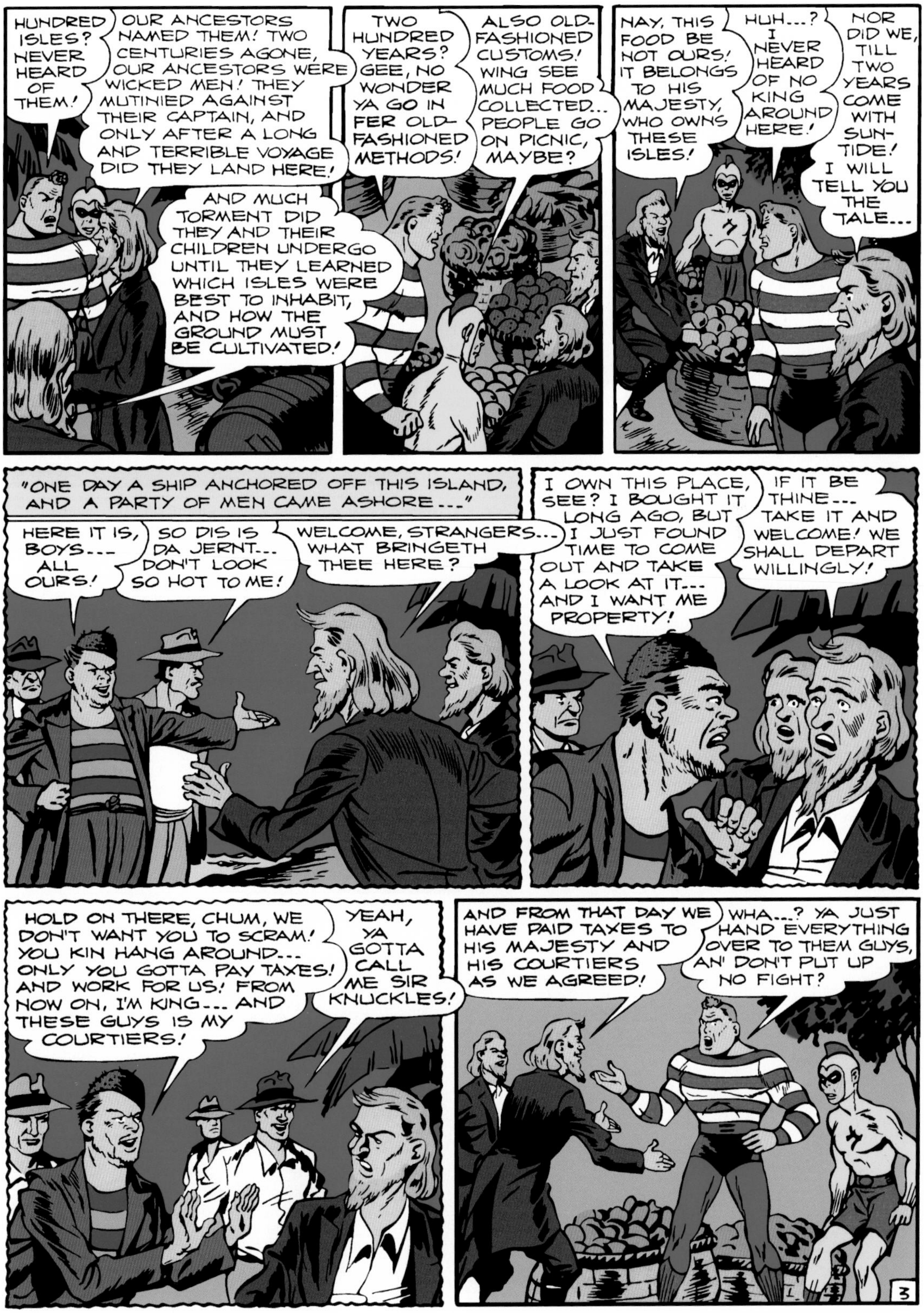
HUNDRED ISLES? NEVER HEARD OF THEM!
OUR ANCESTORS NAMED THEM! TWO CENTURIES AGONE, OUR ANCESTORS WERE WICKED MEN! THEY MUTINIED AGAINST THEIR CAPTAIN, AND ONLY AFTER A LONG AND TERRIBLE VOYAGE DID THEY LAND HERE!
AND MUCH TORMENT DID THEY AND THEIR CHILDREN UNDERGO UNTIL THEY LEARNED WHICH ISLES WERE BEST TO INHABIT, AND HOW THE GROUND MUST BE CULTIVATED!
TWO HUNDRED YEARS? GEE, NO WONDER YA GO IN FER OLD-FASHIONED METHODS!
ALSO OLD-FASHIONED CUSTOMS! WING SEE MUCH FOOD COLLECTED... PEOPLE GO ON PICNIC, MAYBE?
NAY, THIS FOOD BE NOT OURS! IT BELONGS TO HIS MAJESTY, WHO OWNS THESE ISLES!
HUH...? I NEVER HEARD OF NO KING AROUND HERE!
NOR DID WE, TILL TWO YEARS COME WITH SUN-TIDE! I WILL TELL YOU THE TALE...
"ONE DAY A SHIP ANCHORED OFF THIS ISLAND, AND A PARTY OF MEN CAME ASHORE..."
HERE IT IS, BOYS... ALL OURS!
SO DIS IS DA JERNT... DON'T LOOK SO HOT TO ME!
WELCOME, STRANGERS... WHAT BRINGETH THEE HERE?
I OWN THIS PLACE, SEE? I BOUGHT IT LONG AGO, BUT I JUST FOUND TIME TO COME OUT AND TAKE A LOOK AT IT... AND I WANT ME PROPERTY!
IF IT BE THINE... TAKE IT AND WELCOME! WE SHALL DEPART WILLINGLY!
HOLD ON THERE, CHUM, WE DON'T WANT YOU TO SCRAM! YOU KIN HANG AROUND... ONLY YOU GOTTA PAY TAXES! AND WORK FOR US! FROM NOW ON, I'M KING... AND THESE GUYS IS MY COURTIERS!
YEAH, YA GOTTA CALL ME SIR KNUCKLES!
AND FROM THAT DAY WE HAVE PAID TAXES TO HIS MAJESTY AND HIS COURTIERS AS WE AGREED!
WHA...? YA JUST HAND EVERYTHING OVER TO THEM GUYS, AN' DON'T PUT UP NO FIGHT?
3

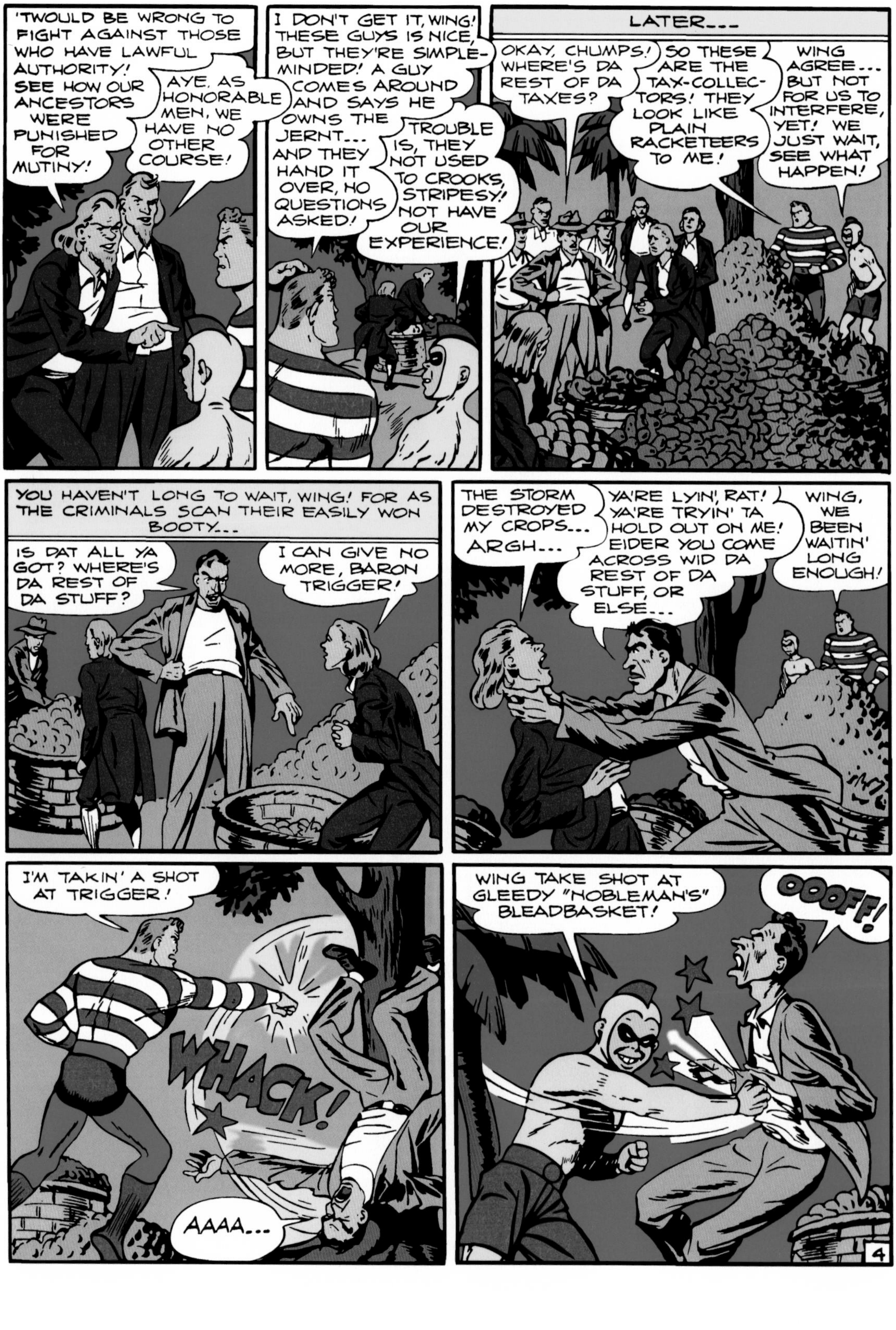
'TWOULD BE WRONG TO FIGHT AGAINST THOSE WHO HAVE LAWFUL AUTHORITY! SEE HOW OUR ANCESTORS WERE PUNISHED FOR MUTINY!
AYE, AS HONORABLE MEN, WE HAVE NO OTHER COURSE!
I DON'T GET IT, WING! THESE GUYS IS NICE, BUT THEY'RE SIMPLE-MINDED! A GUY COMES AROUND AND SAYS HE OWNS THE JERNT... AND THEY HAND IT OVER, NO QUESTIONS ASKED!
TROUBLE IS, THEY NOT USED TO CROOKS, STRIPESY! NOT HAVE OUR EXPERIENCE!
LATER...
OKAY, CHUMPS! WHERE'S DA REST OF DA TAXES?
SO THESE ARE THE TAX-COLLECTORS! THEY LOOK LIKE PLAIN RACKETEERS TO ME!
WING AGREE... BUT NOT FOR US TO INTERFERE, YET! WE JUST WAIT, SEE WHAT HAPPEN!
YOU HAVEN'T LONG TO WAIT, WING! FOR AS THE CRIMINALS SCAN THEIR EASILY WON BOOTY...
IS DAT ALL YA GOT? WHERE'S DA REST OF DA STUFF?
I CAN GIVE NO MORE, BARON TRIGGER!
THE STORM DESTROYED MY CROPS... ARGH...
YA'RE LYIN', RAT! YA'RE TRYIN' TA HOLD OUT ON ME! EIDER YOU COME ACROSS WID DA REST OF DA STUFF, OR ELSE...
WING, WE BEEN WAITIN' LONG ENOUGH!
I'M TAKIN' A SHOT AT TRIGGER!
WHACK!
AAAA...
WING TAKE SHOT AT GLEEDY "NOBLEMAN'S" BLEADBASKET!
OOOFF!
4

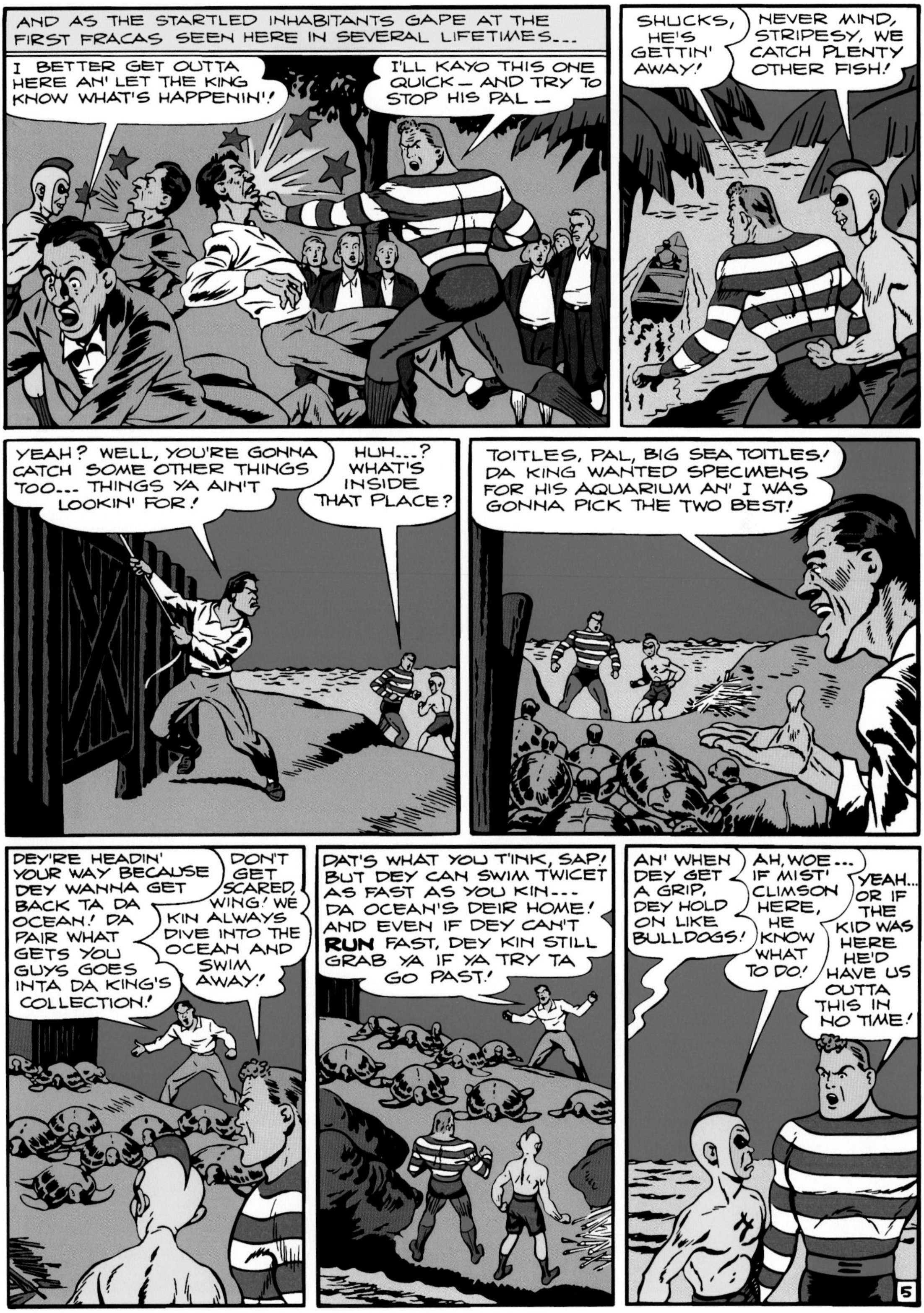
AND AS THE STARTLED INHABITANTS GAPE AT THE FIRST FRACAS SEEN HERE IN SEVERAL LIFETIMES...
I BETTER GET OUTTA HERE AN' LET THE KING KNOW WHAT'S HAPPENIN'!
I'LL KAYO THIS ONE QUICK — AND TRY TO STOP HIS PAL —
SHUCKS, HE'S GETTIN' AWAY!
NEVER MIND, STRIPESY, WE CATCH PLENTY OTHER FISH!
YEAH? WELL, YOU'RE GONNA CATCH SOME OTHER THINGS TOO... THINGS YA AIN'T LOOKIN' FOR!
HUH...? WHAT'S INSIDE THAT PLACE?
TOITLES, PAL, BIG SEA TOITLES! DA KING WANTED SPECIMENS FOR HIS AQUARIUM AN' I WAS GONNA PICK THE TWO BEST!
DEY'RE HEADIN' YOUR WAY BECAUSE DEY WANNA GET BACK TA DA OCEAN! DA PAIR WHAT GETS YOU GUYS GOES INTA DA KING'S COLLECTION!
DON'T GET SCARED, WING! WE KIN ALWAYS DIVE INTO THE OCEAN AND SWIM AWAY!
DAT'S WHAT YOU T'INK, SAP! BUT DEY CAN SWIM TWICET AS FAST AS YOU KIN... DA OCEAN'S DEIR HOME! AND EVEN IF DEY CAN'T RUN FAST, DEY KIN STILL GRAB YA IF YA TRY TA GO PAST!
AN' WHEN DEY GET A GRIP, DEY HOLD ON LIKE BULLDOGS!
AH, WOE... IF MIST' CLIMSON HERE, HE KNOW WHAT TO DO!
YEAH... OR IF THE KID WAS HERE HE'D HAVE US OUTTA THIS IN NO TIME!
5

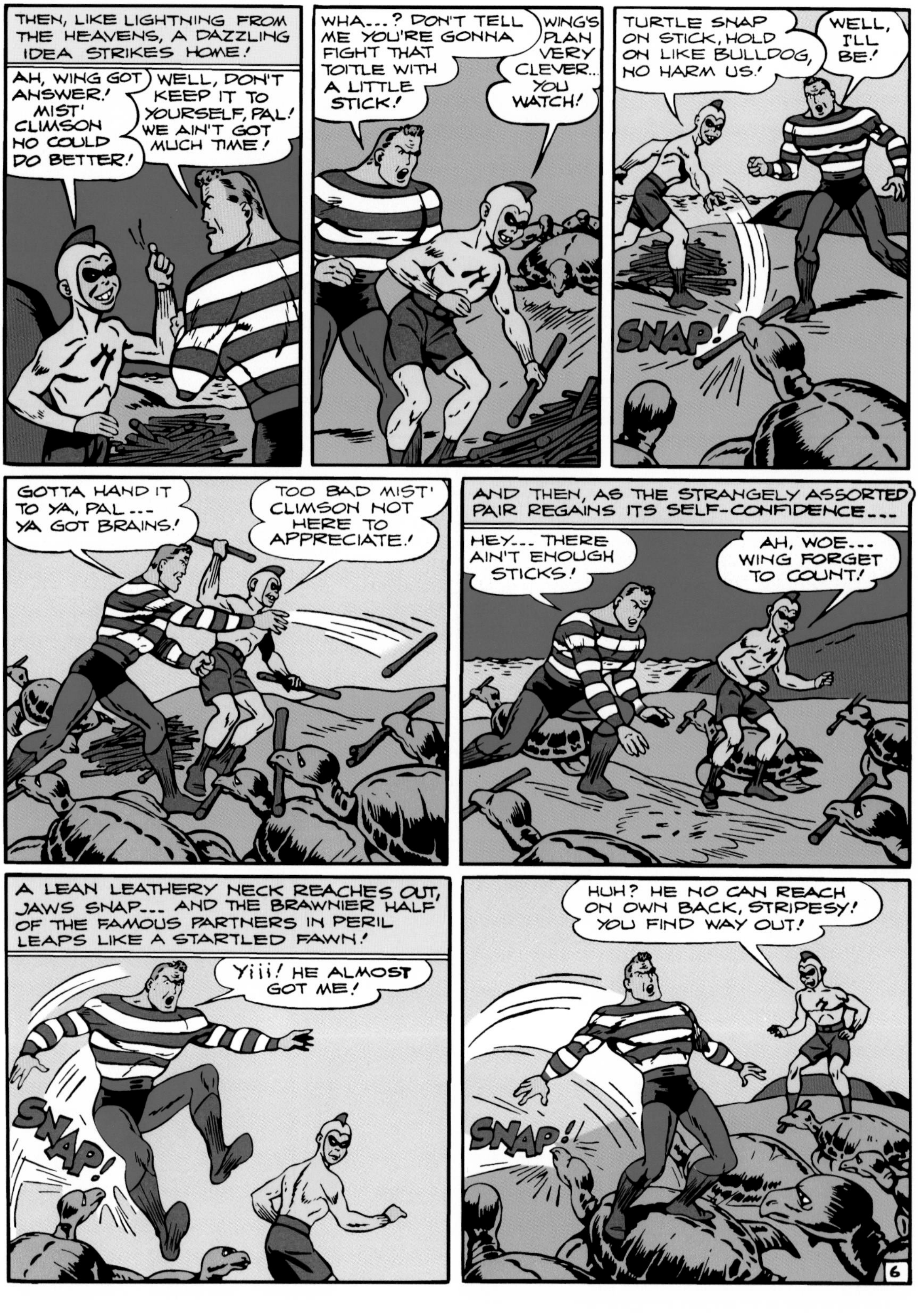
THEN, LIKE LIGHTNING FROM THE HEAVENS, A DAZZLING IDEA STRIKES HOME!
AH, WING GOT ANSWER! MIST' CLIMSON HO COULD DO BETTER!
WELL, DON'T KEEP IT TO YOURSELF, PAL! WE AIN'T GOT MUCH TIME!
WHA...? DON'T TELL ME YOU'RE GONNA FIGHT THAT TOITLE WITH A LITTLE STICK!
WING'S PLAN VERY CLEVER... YOU WATCH!
TURTLE SNAP ON STICK, HOLD ON LIKE BULLDOG, NO HARM US!
WELL, I'LL BE!
SNAP!
GOTTA HAND IT TO YA, PAL... YA GOT BRAINS!
TOO BAD MIST' CLIMSON NOT HERE TO APPRECIATE!
AND THEN, AS THE STRANGELY ASSORTED PAIR REGAINS ITS SELF-CONFIDENCE...
HEY... THERE AIN'T ENOUGH STICKS!
AH, WOE... WING FORGET TO COUNT!
A LEAN LEATHERY NECK REACHES OUT, JAWS SNAP... AND THE BRAWNIER HALF OF THE FAMOUS PARTNERS IN PERIL LEAPS LIKE A STARTLED FAWN!
Yiii! HE ALMOST GOT ME!
SNAP!
HUH? HE NO CAN REACH ON OWN BACK, STRIPESY! YOU FIND WAY OUT!
SNAP!
6

LEAPING HITHER, LEAPING THITHER, LIKE ELIZA CROSSING THE ICE, THE TWO NEW COMRADES IN COMBAT TRACE A PERILOUS PATH TO SAFETY!
GOT TO KEEP ON TOES FOR THIS!
IT'S LIKE REHOISIN' FER UNCLE TOM'S CABIN!
AND NOW IT'S YOUR TURN TO ENTER THE SCENE, SIMON LEGREE!
HIT HARD, STRIPESY... HIM BAD ACTOR!
YOU'RE TAKIN' DA KID'S PLACE POIFECT, WING! WE MIGHTA BEEN PRACTICIN' THIS FER YEARS!
NICE TO HAVE CLOOK TO PRACTICE ON!
YOU DONE ENOUGH PRACTICIN' ON ME, CHUM! I'M GETTIN' UP HERE OUTTA THE WAY!
BUT ALAS, THERE IS NO SECURITY IN THIS WORLD! SUDDENLY...
EEEHH... HELP!
AAAA...
UGH...
DON'T HIT ME, DON'T...
CLUNK!
HUH...? THEY'RE OUT COLD!
NICE WOIK, PAL! DAT WAS USIN' YOUR COCONUT, ALL RIGHT!
THIS TIME THEY AIN'T GETTIN' AWAY! WE'LL FINISH 'EM RIGHT... AND WE'LL MAKE SURE THEY DIE PAINFUL!
WHAT NAMELESS FATE IS IN STORE FOR THE UNFORTUNATE DUO, TRAPPED BEYOND HOPE OF ESCAPE? ARE THE PEACEFUL INHABITANTS OF THIS ISLE DOOMED TO ENDLESS OPPRESSIONS UNDER THE HEELS OF AN UNDERWORLD KING AND HIS IGNOBLE "NOBLES?" FOR THE ANSWER TO THESE AND OTHER QUESTIONS, READ ON...
7

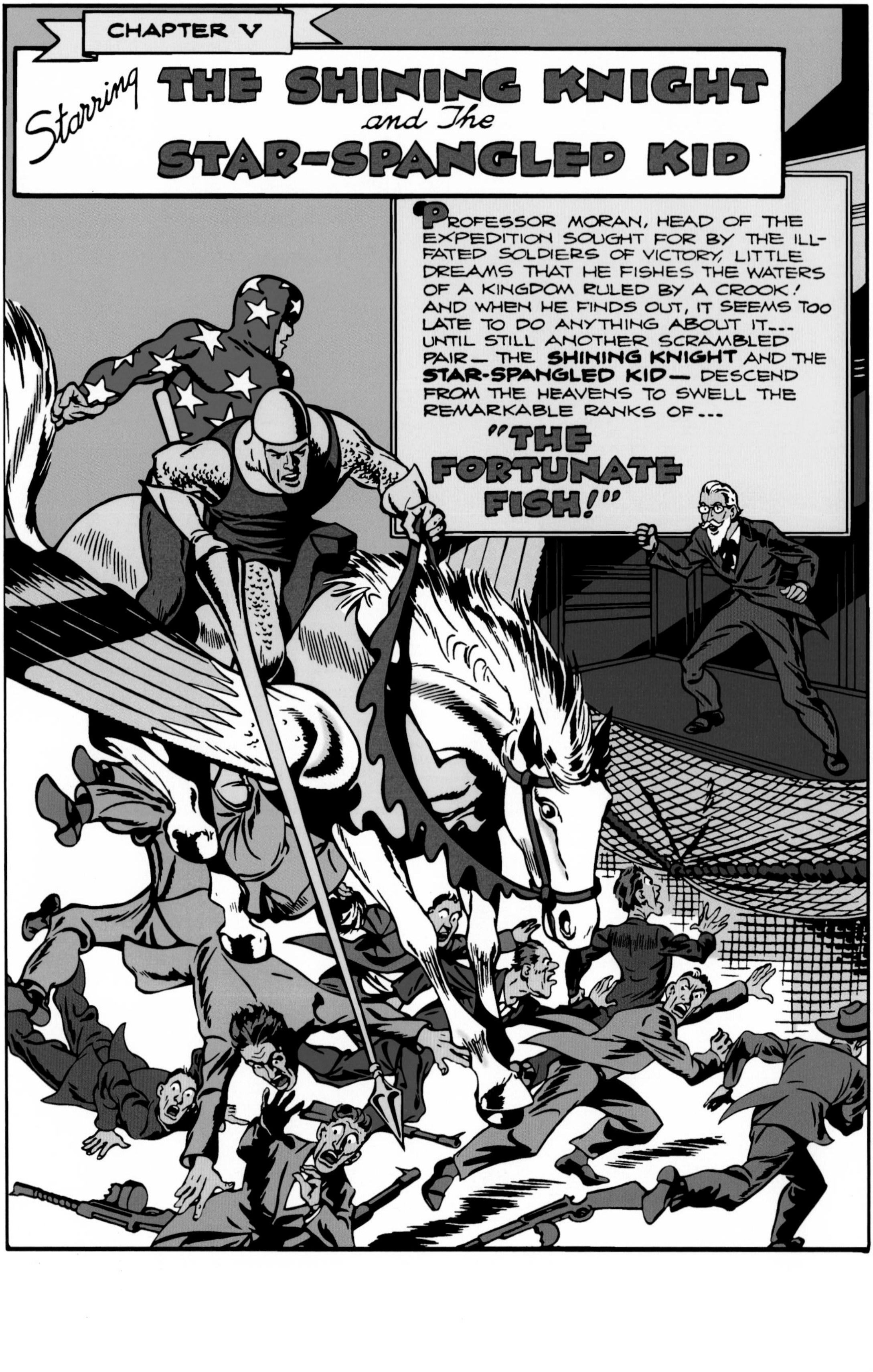
CHAPTER V
Starring THE SHINING KNIGHT and The STAR-SPANGLED KID
PROFESSOR MORAN, HEAD OF THE EXPEDITION SOUGHT FOR BY THE ILL-FATED SOLDIERS OF VICTORY, LITTLE DREAMS THAT HE FISHES THE WATERS OF A KINGDOM RULED BY A CROOK! AND WHEN HE FINDS OUT, IT SEEMS TOO LATE TO DO ANYTHING ABOUT IT... UNTIL STILL ANOTHER SCRAMBLED PAIR-- THE SHINING KNIGHT AND THE STAR-SPANGLED KID-- DESCEND FROM THE HEAVENS TO SWELL THE REMARKABLE RANKS OF...
"THE FORTUNATE FISH!"

DID YOU EVER SEE A FISH LOST IN THOUGHT? TAKE A LOOK AT THIS FINE FINNY SPECIMEN...

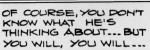

OF COURSE, YOU DON'T KNOW WHAT HE'S THINKING ABOUT... BUT YOU WILL, YOU WILL...

THE SIGHT OF A MAN USUALLY SPELLS DANGER... YET THIS UNDAUNTED DWELLER OF THE DEPTHS DARTS FEARLESSLY FORWARD...

A SPECIMEN SUCH AS I HAVE NEVER SEEN BEFORE! I SHALL NAME IT AFTER ME!

NEXT SECOND, THE TRAP CLOSES!

HOW TO GET BACK TO THE SURFACE, AND LET THEM SEE MY PRIZE!

SNAP!

WHA---? PROFESSOR MORAN BACK SO SOON?

GENTLEMEN, I HAVE HAD ASTONISHING SUCCESS! I HAVE DISCOVERED A NEW GENUS OF PISCES! IT SHALL BE NAMED ARTHROPODOPHAGUS MORANENSIS, AFTER MYSELF!

STAY THERE, MY FRIEND, UNTIL I CAN BRING YOU BACK TO CIVILIZATION AND ASTOUND THE SCIENTIFIC WORLD!

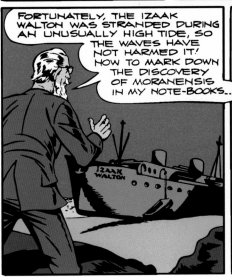

FORTUNATELY, THE IZAAK WALTON WAS STRANDED DURING AN UNUSUALLY HIGH TIDE, SO THE WAVES HAVE NOT HARMED IT! HOW TO MARK DOWN THE DISCOVERY OF MORANENSIS IN MY NOTE-BOOKS...

IZAAK WALTON

WHA---? A MOTOR-LAUNCH! THEN THERE'S CIVILIZED LIFE IN THESE ISLANDS!

2

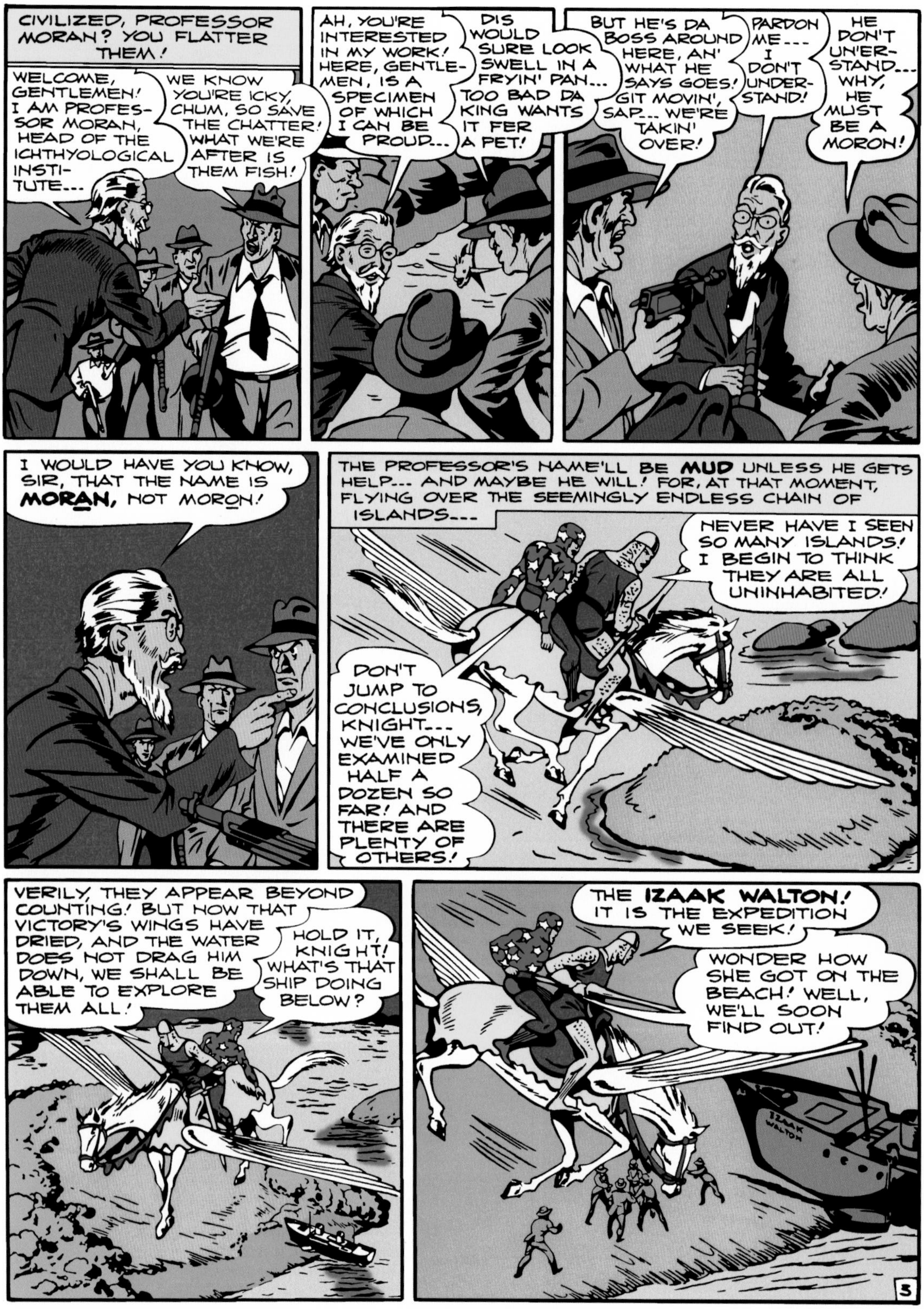
CIVILIZED, PROFESSOR MORAN? YOU FLATTER THEM!
WELCOME, GENTLEMEN! I AM PROFESSOR MORAN, HEAD OF THE ICHTHYOLOGICAL INSTITUTE...
WE KNOW YOU'RE ICKY, CHUM, SO SAVE THE CHATTER! WHAT WE'RE AFTER IS THEM FISH!
AH, YOU'RE INTERESTED IN MY WORK! HERE, GENTLEMEN, IS A SPECIMEN OF WHICH I CAN BE PROUD...
DIS WOULD SURE LOOK SWELL IN A FRYIN' PAN... TOO BAD DA KING WANTS IT FER A PET!
BUT HE'S DA BOSS AROUND HERE, AN' WHAT HE SAYS GOES! GIT MOVIN', SAP... WE'RE TAKIN' OVER!
PARDON ME... I DON'T UNDERSTAND!
HE DON'T UN'ERSTAND... WHY, HE MUST BE A MORON!
I WOULD HAVE YOU KNOW, SIR, THAT THE NAME IS MORAN, NOT MORON!
THE PROFESSOR'S NAME'LL BE MUD UNLESS HE GETS HELP... AND MAYBE HE WILL! FOR, AT THAT MOMENT, FLYING OVER THE SEEMINGLY ENDLESS CHAIN OF ISLANDS...
NEVER HAVE I SEEN SO MANY ISLANDS! I BEGIN TO THINK THEY ARE ALL UNINHABITED!
DON'T JUMP TO CONCLUSIONS, KNIGHT... WE'VE ONLY EXAMINED HALF A DOZEN SO FAR! AND THERE ARE PLENTY OF OTHERS!
VERILY, THEY APPEAR BEYOND COUNTING! BUT NOW THAT VICTORY'S WINGS HAVE DRIED, AND THE WATER DOES NOT DRAG HIM DOWN, WE SHALL BE ABLE TO EXPLORE THEM ALL!
HOLD IT, KNIGHT! WHAT'S THAT SHIP DOING BELOW?
THE IZAAK WALTON! IT IS THE EXPEDITION WE SEEK!
WONDER HOW SHE GOT ON THE BEACH! WELL, WE'LL SOON FIND OUT!
IZAAK WALTON
3

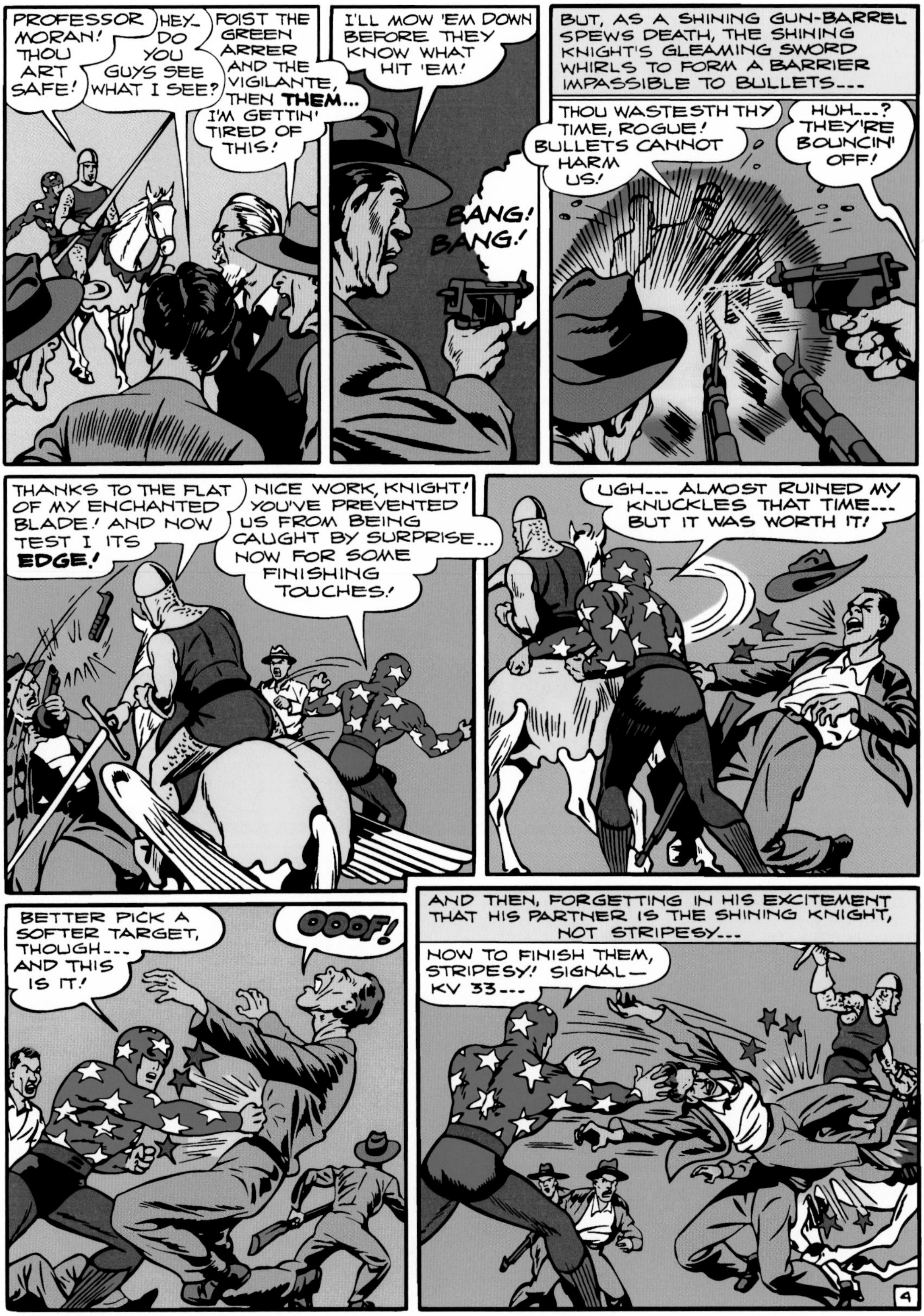
PROFESSOR MORAN! THOU ART SAFE!
HEY-- DO YOU GUYS SEE WHAT I SEE?
FOIST THE GREEN ARRER AND THE VIGILANTE, THEN THEM... I'M GETTIN' TIRED OF THIS!
I'LL MOW 'EM DOWN BEFORE THEY KNOW WHAT HIT 'EM!
BANG! BANG!
BUT, AS A SHINING GUN-BARREL SPEWS DEATH, THE SHINING KNIGHT'S GLEAMING SWORD WHIRLS TO FORM A BARRIER IMPASSIBLE TO BULLETS---
THOU WASTESTH THY TIME, ROGUE! BULLETS CANNOT HARM US!
HUH---? THEY'RE BOUNCIN' OFF!
THANKS TO THE FLAT OF MY ENCHANTED BLADE! AND NOW TEST I ITS EDGE!
NICE WORK, KNIGHT! YOU'VE PREVENTED US FROM BEING CAUGHT BY SURPRISE... NOW FOR SOME FINISHING TOUCHES!
UGH--- ALMOST RUINED MY KNUCKLES THAT TIME--- BUT IT WAS WORTH IT!
BETTER PICK A SOFTER TARGET, THOUGH--- AND THIS IS IT!
OOOF!
AND THEN, FORGETTING IN HIS EXCITEMENT THAT HIS PARTNER IS THE SHINING KNIGHT, NOT STRIPESY---
NOW TO FINISH THEM, STRIPESY! SIGNAL-- KV 33---
4

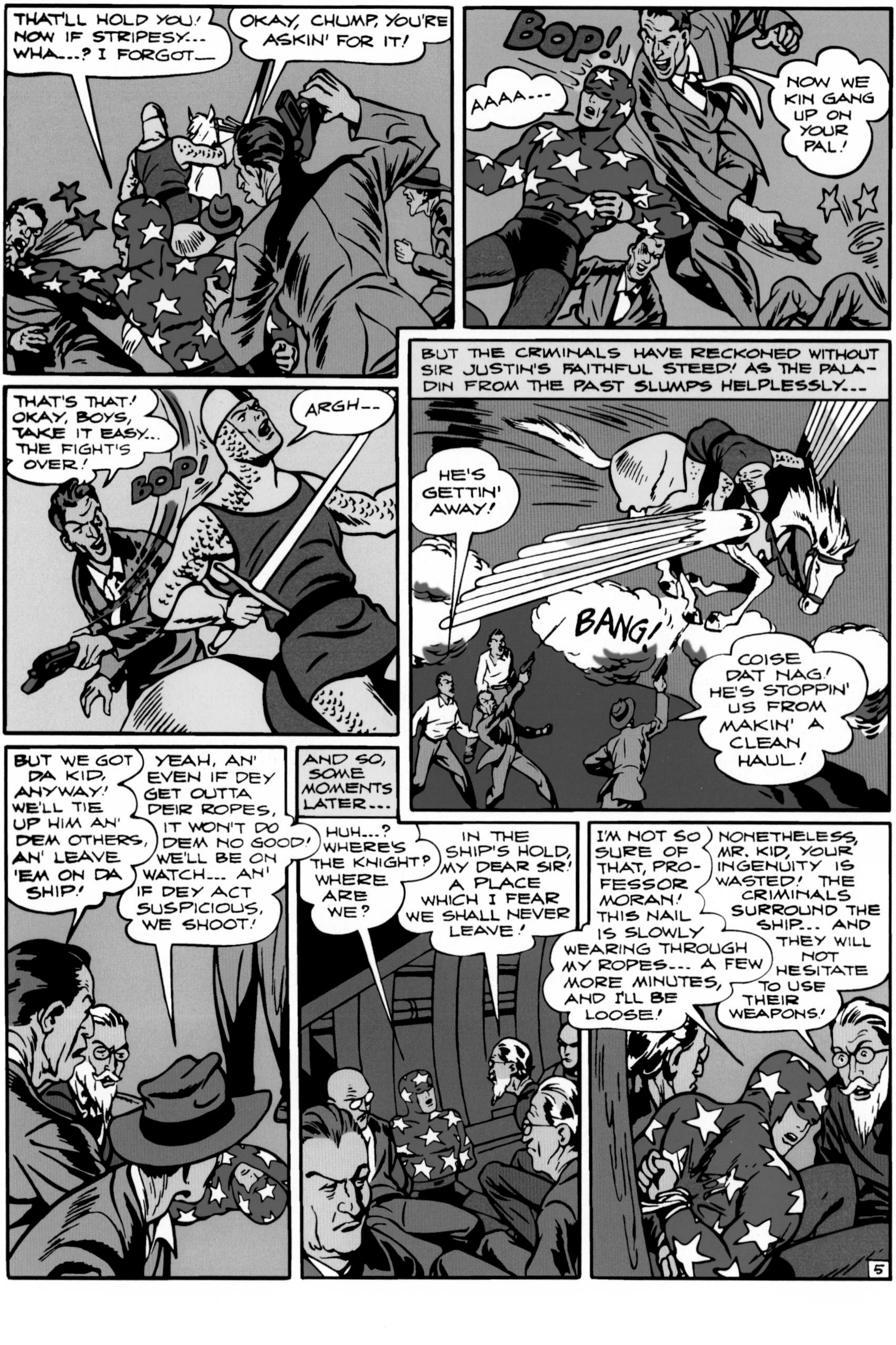
THAT'LL HOLD YOU! NOW IF STRIPESY... WHA...? I FORGOT—
OKAY, CHUMP, YOU'RE ASKIN' FOR IT!
BOP!
AAAA...
NOW WE KIN GANG UP ON YOUR PAL!
THAT'S THAT! OKAY, BOYS, TAKE IT EASY... THE FIGHT'S OVER!
ARGH--
BOP!
BUT THE CRIMINALS HAVE RECKONED WITHOUT SIR JUSTIN'S FAITHFUL STEED! AS THE PALADIN FROM THE PAST SLUMPS HELPLESSLY...
HE'S GETTIN' AWAY!
BANG!
COISE DAT NAG! HE'S STOPPIN' US FROM MAKIN' A CLEAN HAUL!
BUT WE GOT DA KID, ANYWAY! WE'LL TIE UP HIM AN' DEM OTHERS, AN' LEAVE 'EM ON DA SHIP!
YEAH, AN' EVEN IF DEY GET OUTTA DEIR ROPES, IT WON'T DO DEM NO GOOD! WE'LL BE ON WATCH... AN' IF DEY ACT SUSPICIOUS, WE SHOOT!
AND SO, SOME MOMENTS LATER...
HUH...? WHERE'S THE KNIGHT? WHERE ARE WE?
IN THE SHIP'S HOLD, MY DEAR SIR! A PLACE WHICH I FEAR WE SHALL NEVER LEAVE!
I'M NOT SO SURE OF THAT, PROFESSOR MORAN! THIS NAIL IS SLOWLY WEARING THROUGH MY ROPES... A FEW MORE MINUTES, AND I'LL BE LOOSE!
NONETHELESS, MR. KID, YOUR INGENUITY IS WASTED! THE CRIMINALS SURROUND THE SHIP... AND THEY WILL NOT HESITATE TO USE THEIR WEAPONS!
5

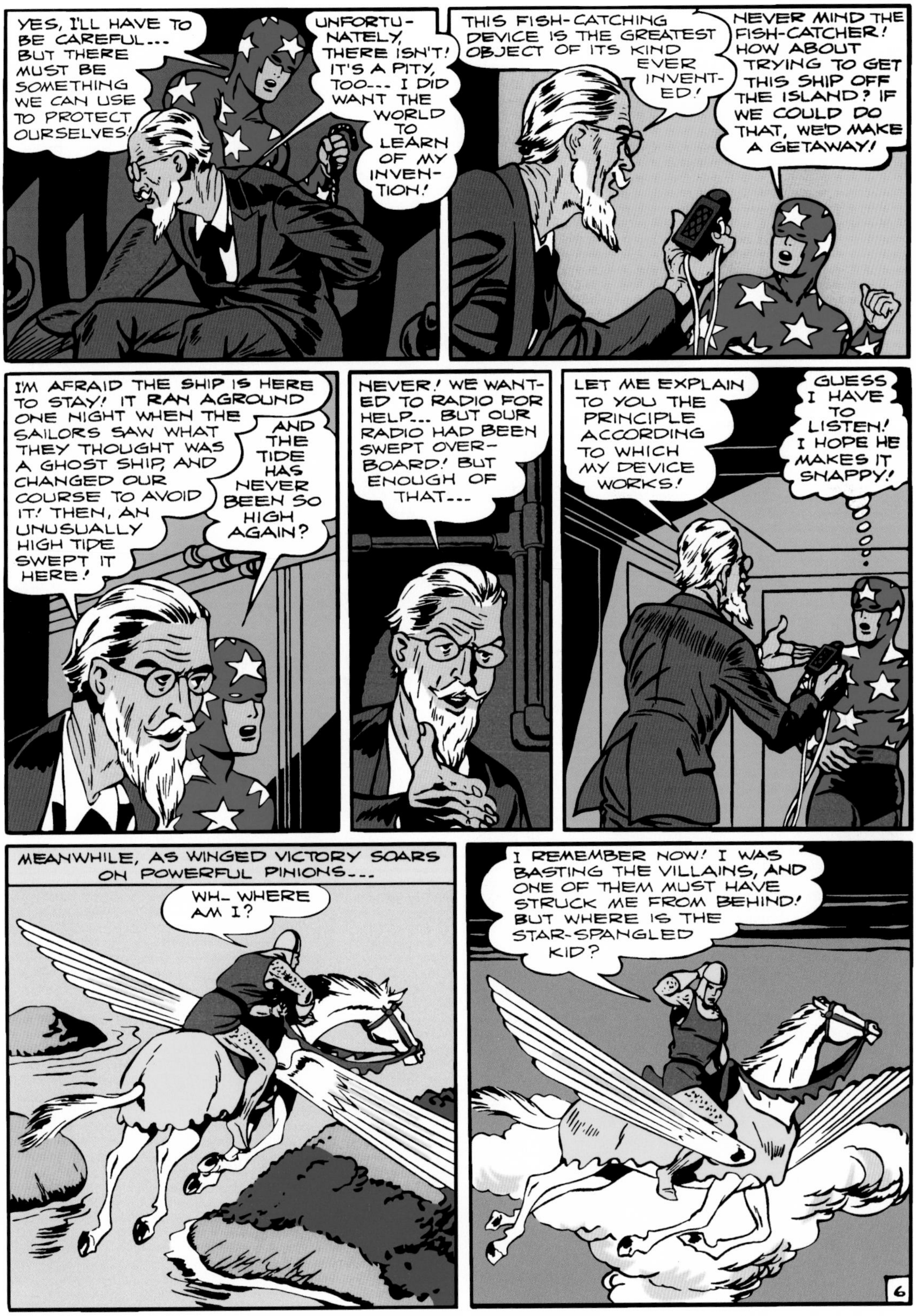
YES, I'LL HAVE TO BE CAREFUL... BUT THERE MUST BE SOMETHING WE CAN USE TO PROTECT OURSELVES!
UNFORTUNATELY, THERE ISN'T! IT'S A PITY, TOO... I DID WANT THE WORLD TO LEARN OF MY INVENTION!
THIS FISH-CATCHING DEVICE IS THE GREATEST OBJECT OF ITS KIND EVER INVENTED!
NEVER MIND THE FISH-CATCHER! HOW ABOUT TRYING TO GET THIS SHIP OFF THE ISLAND? IF WE COULD DO THAT, WE'D MAKE A GETAWAY!
I'M AFRAID THE SHIP IS HERE TO STAY! IT RAN AGROUND ONE NIGHT WHEN THE SAILORS SAW WHAT THEY THOUGHT WAS A GHOST SHIP, AND CHANGED OUR COURSE TO AVOID IT! THEN, AN UNUSUALLY HIGH TIDE SWEPT IT HERE!
AND THE TIDE HAS NEVER BEEN SO HIGH AGAIN?
NEVER! WE WANTED TO RADIO FOR HELP... BUT OUR RADIO HAD BEEN SWEPT OVERBOARD! BUT ENOUGH OF THAT...
LET ME EXPLAIN TO YOU THE PRINCIPLE ACCORDING TO WHICH MY DEVICE WORKS!
GUESS I HAVE TO LISTEN! I HOPE HE MAKES IT SNAPPY!
MEANWHILE, AS WINGED VICTORY SOARS ON POWERFUL PINIONS...
WH- WHERE AM I?
I REMEMBER NOW! I WAS BASTING THE VILLAINS, AND ONE OF THEM MUST HAVE STRUCK ME FROM BEHIND! BUT WHERE IS THE STAR-SPANGLED KID?
6

HE MUST DEEM ME A VILE COWARD TO HAVE LEFT HIM SO IN THE LURCH WHEN HE MOST NEEDED ME! BACK, BRAVE STEED! WE MUST SEE WHAT HAS HAPPENED TO OUR COMRADE!

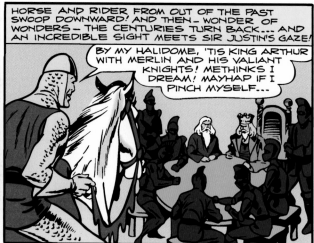

HORSE AND RIDER FROM OUT OF THE PAST SWOOP DOWNWARD! AND THEN—WONDER OF WONDERS—THE CENTURIES TURN BACK.... AND AN INCREDIBLE SIGHT MEETS SIR JUSTIN'S GAZE!

BY MY HALIDOME, 'TIS KING ARTHUR WITH MERLIN AND HIS VALIANT KNIGHTS! METHINKS I DREAM! MAYHAP IF I PINCH MYSELF...

WELCOME, SIR JUSTIN! WHERE HAST THOU BEEN THESE MANY YEARS?

MY GOOD LIEGE WELCOMES ME! I KNOW NOT WHAT TO THINK!

UNEXPECTEDLY, A STARTLED STEED BRAKES IN MID-AIR... AND A RIDER CAUGHT UNAWARES GOES PLUMMETING DOWNWARD...

HHHNNNNMMM!

'TIS NO DREAM! VICTORY HAS SEEN IT TOO, AND CANNOT BELIEVE HIS EYES!

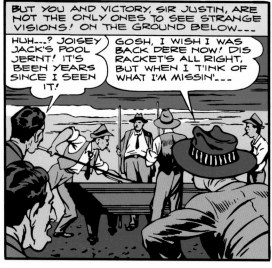

BUT YOU AND VICTORY, SIR JUSTIN, ARE NOT THE ONLY ONES TO SEE STRANGE VISIONS! ON THE GROUND BELOW___

HUH...? JOISEY JACK'S POOL JERNT! IT'S BEEN YEARS SINCE I SEEN IT!

GOSH, I WISH I WAS BACK DERE NOW! DIS RACKET'S ALL RIGHT, BUT WHEN I T'INK OF WHAT I'M MISSIN'___

GEE, I NEVER T' OUGHT I COULD BE SO HOMESICK FER A PLACE!

SO I SAYS TA HIM, "LISTEN, COPPER, HOW'D YA LIKE TA RUN INTA SOME BRASS KNUCKLES?"

HAW, HAW! COPPER... BRASS KNUCKLES... YA SURE GOT A SENSE OF HUMOR, PAL!

7

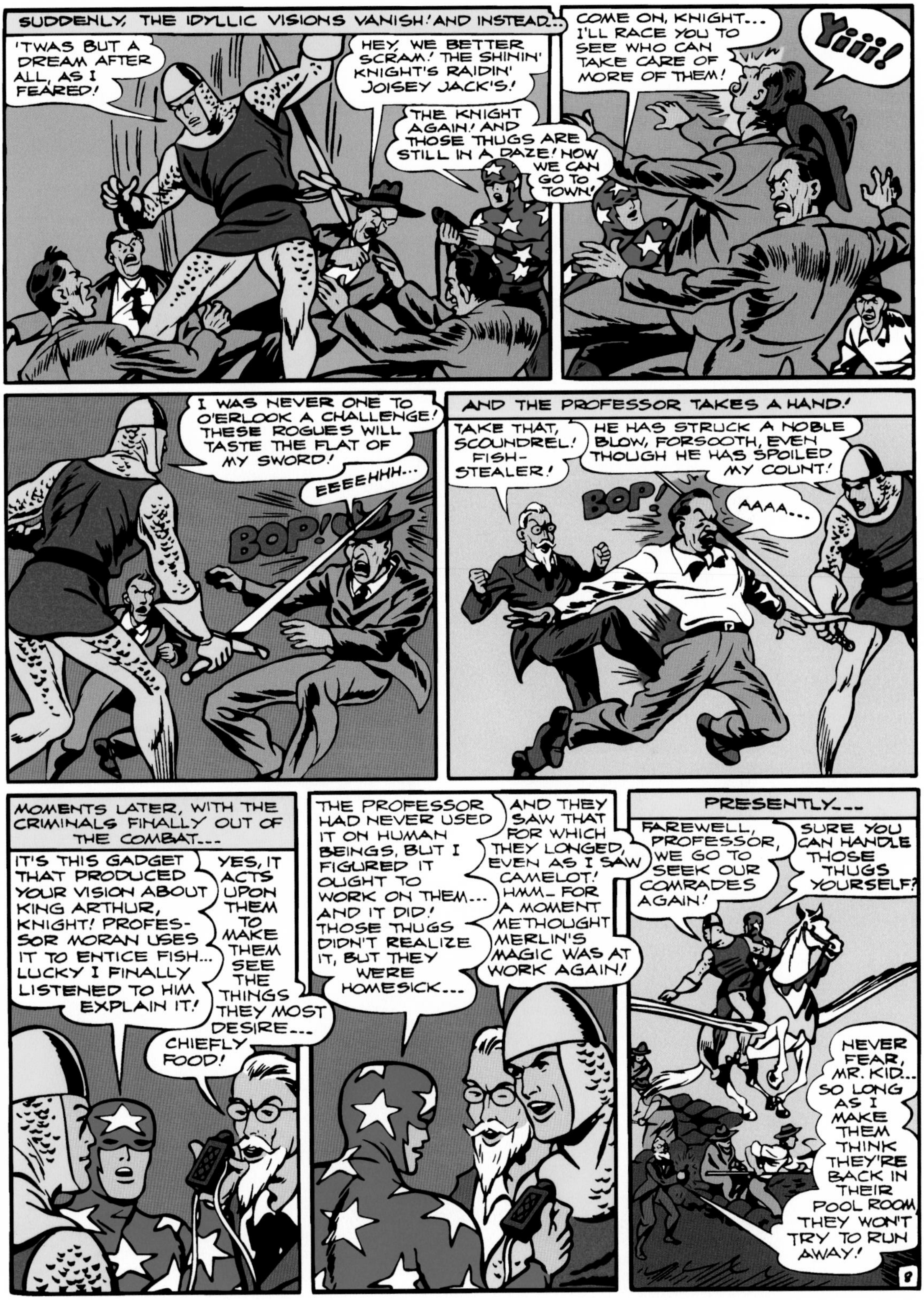
SUDDENLY, THE IDYLLIC VISIONS VANISH! AND INSTEAD...
'TWAS BUT A DREAM AFTER ALL, AS I FEARED!
HEY, WE BETTER SCRAM! THE SHININ' KNIGHT'S RAIDIN' JOISEY JACK'S!
THE KNIGHT AGAIN! AND THOSE THUGS ARE STILL IN A DAZE! NOW WE CAN GO TO TOWN!
COME ON, KNIGHT... I'LL RACE YOU TO SEE WHO CAN TAKE CARE OF MORE OF THEM!
Yiiii!
I WAS NEVER ONE TO O'ERLOOK A CHALLENGE! THESE ROGUES WILL TASTE THE FLAT OF MY SWORD!
EEEEHHH...
BOP!
AND THE PROFESSOR TAKES A HAND!
TAKE THAT, SCOUNDREL! FISH-STEALER!
HE HAS STRUCK A NOBLE BLOW, FORSOOTH, EVEN THOUGH HE HAS SPOILED MY COUNT!
BOP!
AAAA...
MOMENTS LATER, WITH THE CRIMINALS FINALLY OUT OF THE COMBAT...
IT'S THIS GADGET THAT PRODUCED YOUR VISION ABOUT KING ARTHUR, KNIGHT! PROFESSOR MORAN USES IT TO ENTICE FISH... LUCKY I FINALLY LISTENED TO HIM EXPLAIN IT!
YES, IT ACTS UPON THEM TO MAKE THEM SEE THE THINGS THEY MOST DESIRE...
CHIEFLY FOOD!
THE PROFESSOR HAD NEVER USED IT ON HUMAN BEINGS, BUT I FIGURED IT OUGHT TO WORK ON THEM... AND IT DID! THOSE THUGS DIDN'T REALIZE IT, BUT THEY WERE HOMESICK...
AND THEY SAW THAT FOR WHICH THEY LONGED, EVEN AS I SAW CAMELOT! HMM-- FOR A MOMENT METHOUGHT MERLIN'S MAGIC WAS AT WORK AGAIN!
PRESENTLY...
FAREWELL, PROFESSOR, WE GO TO SEEK OUR COMRADES AGAIN!
SURE YOU CAN HANDLE THOSE THUGS YOURSELF?
NEVER FEAR, MR. KID... SO LONG AS I MAKE THEM THINK THEY'RE BACK IN THEIR POOL ROOM THEY WON'T TRY TO RUN AWAY!
8

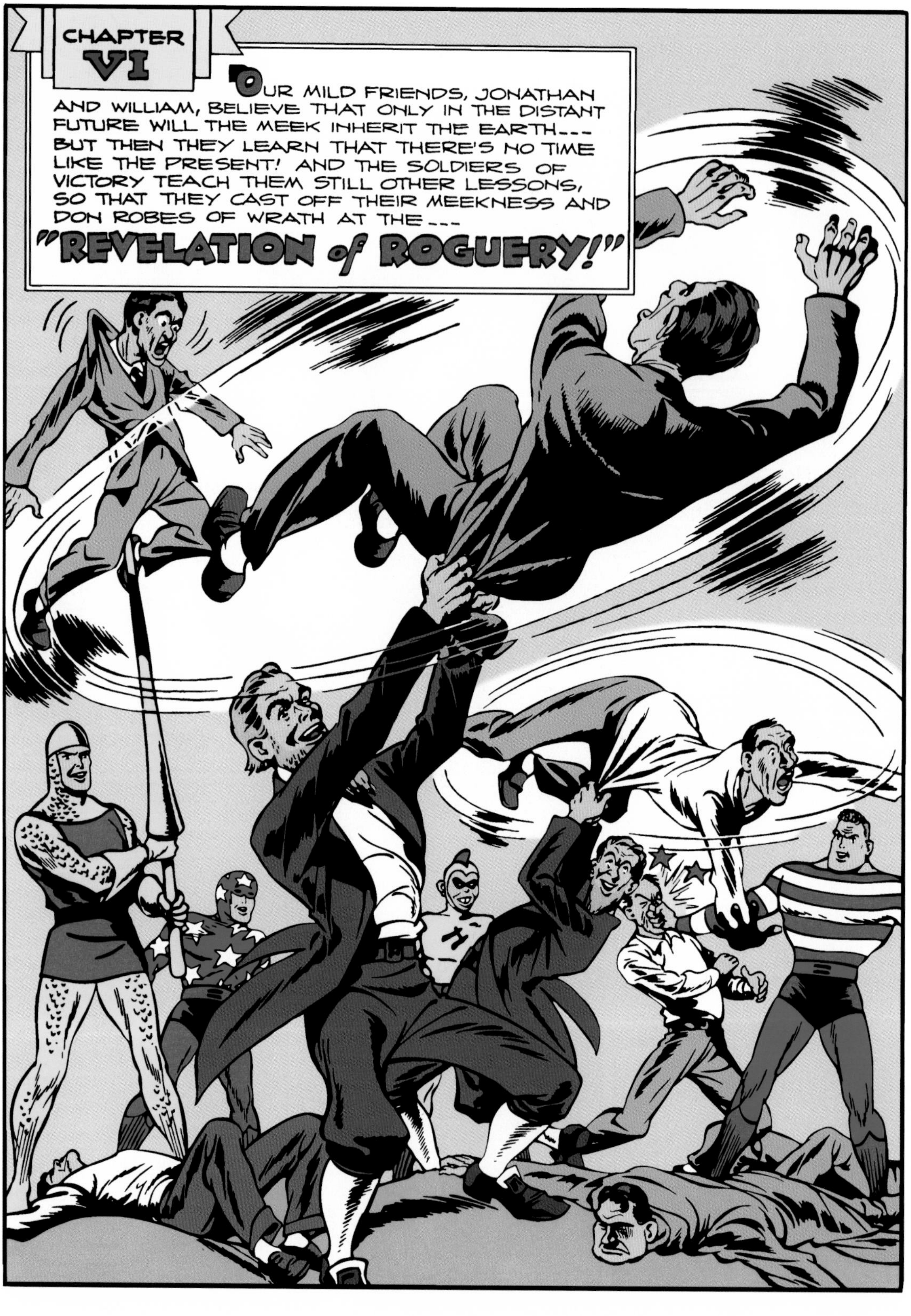
CHAPTER VI
OUR MILD FRIENDS, JONATHAN AND WILLIAM, BELIEVE THAT ONLY IN THE DISTANT FUTURE WILL THE MEEK INHERIT THE EARTH--- BUT THEN THEY LEARN THAT THERE'S NO TIME LIKE THE PRESENT! AND THE SOLDIERS OF VICTORY TEACH THEM STILL OTHER LESSONS, SO THAT THEY CAST OFF THEIR MEEKNESS AND DON ROBES OF WRATH AT THE---
"REVELATION of ROGUERY!"

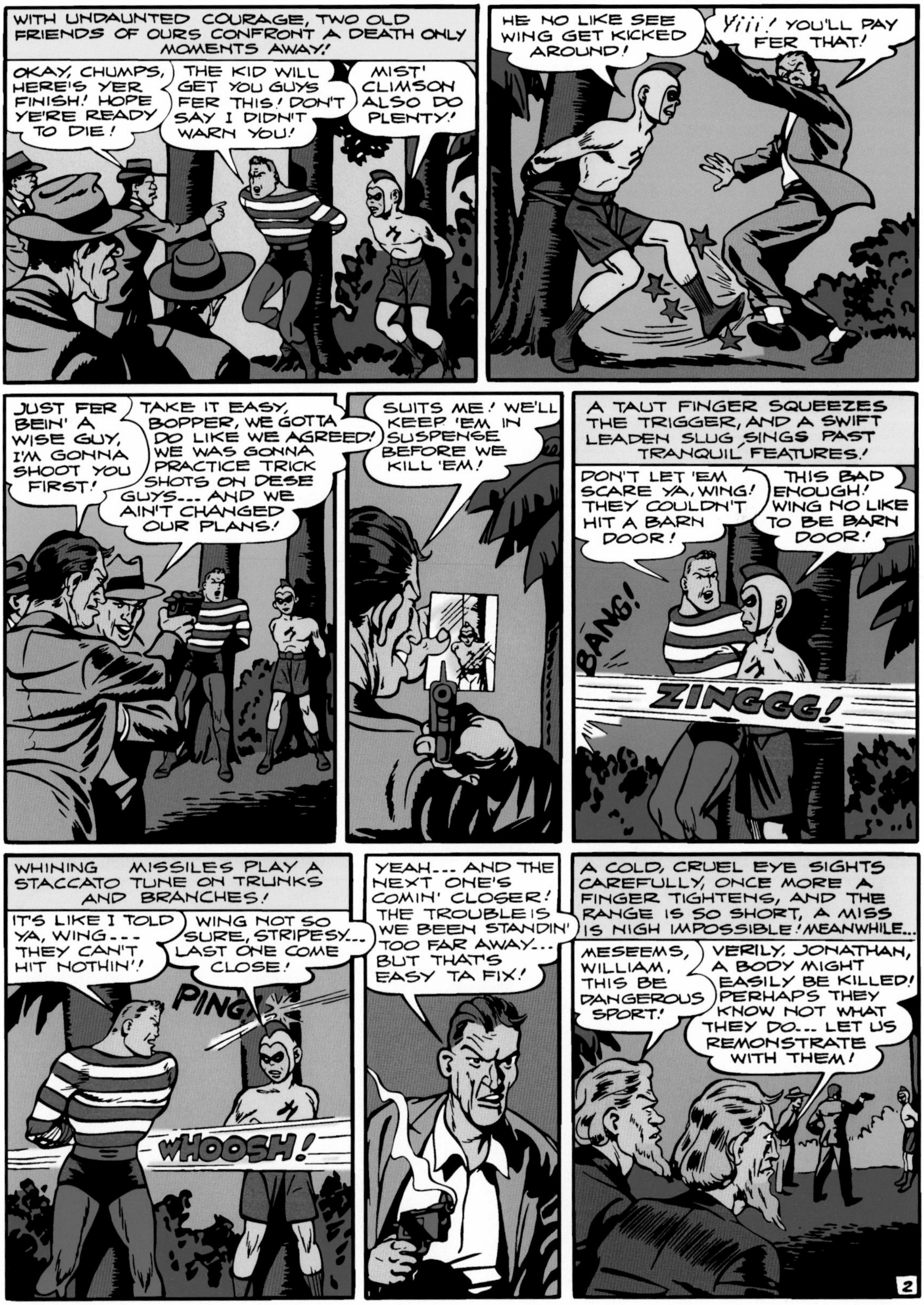
WITH UNDAUNTED COURAGE, TWO OLD FRIENDS OF OURS CONFRONT A DEATH ONLY MOMENTS AWAY!
OKAY, CHUMPS, HERE'S YER FINISH! HOPE YE'RE READY TO DIE!
THE KID WILL GET YOU GUYS FER THIS! DON'T SAY I DIDN'T WARN YOU!
MIST' CLIMSON ALSO DO PLENTY!
HE NO LIKE SEE WING GET KICKED AROUND!
YIII! YOU'LL PAY FER THAT!
JUST FER BEIN' A WISE GUY, I'M GONNA SHOOT YOU FIRST!
TAKE IT EASY, BOPPER, WE GOTTA DO LIKE WE AGREED! WE WAS GONNA PRACTICE TRICK SHOTS ON DESE GUYS... AND WE AIN'T CHANGED OUR PLANS!
SUITS ME! WE'LL KEEP 'EM IN SUSPENSE BEFORE WE KILL 'EM!
A TAUT FINGER SQUEEZES THE TRIGGER, AND A SWIFT LEADEN SLUG SINGS PAST TRANQUIL FEATURES!
DON'T LET 'EM SCARE YA, WING! THEY COULDN'T HIT A BARN DOOR!
THIS BAD ENOUGH! WING NO LIKE TO BE BARN DOOR!
BANG!
ZINGGG!
WHINING MISSILES PLAY A STACCATO TUNE ON TRUNKS AND BRANCHES!
IT'S LIKE I TOLD YA, WING--- THEY CAN'T HIT NOTHIN'!
WING NOT SO SURE, STRIPESY... LAST ONE COME CLOSE!
PING!
WHOOSH!
YEAH--- AND THE NEXT ONE'S COMIN' CLOSER! THE TROUBLE IS WE BEEN STANDIN' TOO FAR AWAY... BUT THAT'S EASY TA FIX!
A COLD, CRUEL EYE SIGHTS CAREFULLY, ONCE MORE A FINGER TIGHTENS, AND THE RANGE IS SO SHORT, A MISS IS NIGH IMPOSSIBLE! MEANWHILE...
MESEEMS, WILLIAM, THIS BE DANGEROUS SPORT!
VERILY, JONATHAN, A BODY MIGHT EASILY BE KILLED! PERHAPS THEY KNOW NOT WHAT THEY DO... LET US REMONSTRATE WITH THEM!
2

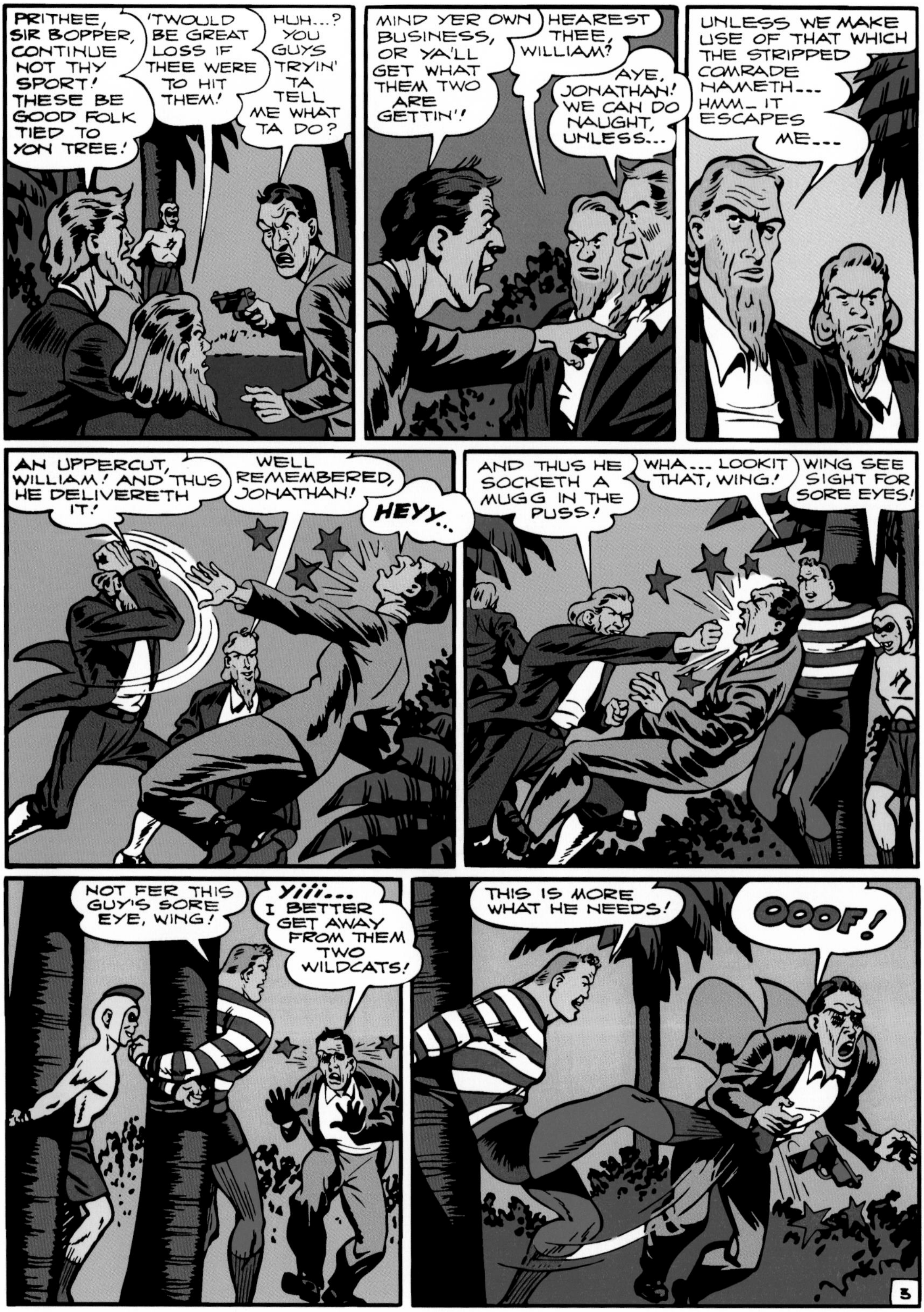
PRITHEE, SIR BOPPER, CONTINUE NOT THY SPORT! THESE BE GOOD FOLK TIED TO YON TREE!
'TWOULD BE GREAT LOSS IF THEE WERE TO HIT THEM!
HUH...? YOU GUYS TRYIN' TA TELL ME WHAT TA DO?
MIND YER OWN BUSINESS, OR YA'LL GET WHAT THEM TWO ARE GETTIN'!
HEAREST THEE, WILLIAM?
AYE, JONATHAN! WE CAN DO NAUGHT, UNLESS...
UNLESS WE MAKE USE OF THAT WHICH THE STRIPPED COMRADE NAMETH... HMM.. IT ESCAPES ME...
AN UPPERCUT, WILLIAM! AND THUS HE DELIVERETH IT!
WELL REMEMBERED, JONATHAN!
HEYY...
AND THUS HE SOCKETH A MUGG IN THE PUSS!
WHA... LOOKIT THAT, WING!
WING SEE SIGHT FOR SORE EYES!
NOT FER THIS GUY'S SORE EYE, WING!
YIII... I BETTER GET AWAY FROM THEM TWO WILDCATS!
THIS IS MORE WHAT HE NEEDS!
OOOF!
3

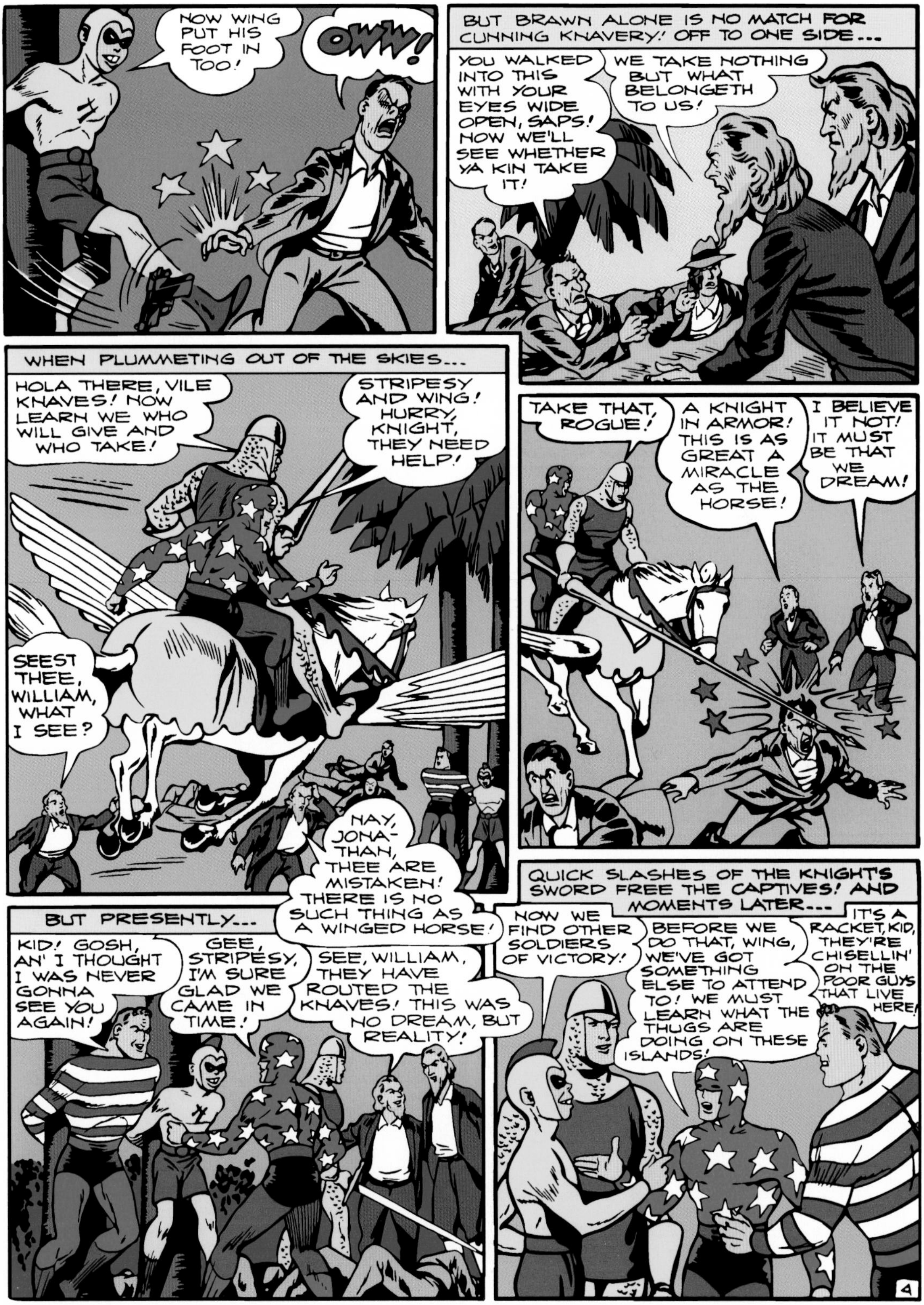
NOW WING PUT HIS FOOT IN TOO!
OWW!
BUT BRAWN ALONE IS NO MATCH FOR CUNNING KNAVERY! OFF TO ONE SIDE...
YOU WALKED INTO THIS WITH YOUR EYES WIDE OPEN, SAPS! NOW WE'LL SEE WHETHER YA KIN TAKE IT!
WE TAKE NOTHING BUT WHAT BELONGETH TO US!
WHEN PLUMMETING OUT OF THE SKIES...
HOLA THERE, VILE KNAVES! NOW LEARN WE WHO WILL GIVE AND WHO TAKE!
STRIPESY AND WING! HURRY, KNIGHT, THEY NEED HELP!
SEEST THEE, WILLIAM, WHAT I SEE?
NAY, JONATHAN, THEE ARE MISTAKEN! THERE IS NO SUCH THING AS A WINGED HORSE!
TAKE THAT, ROGUE!
A KNIGHT IN ARMOR! THIS IS AS GREAT A MIRACLE AS THE HORSE!
I BELIEVE IT NOT! IT MUST BE THAT WE DREAM!
BUT PRESENTLY...
KID! GOSH, AN' I THOUGHT I WAS NEVER GONNA SEE YOU AGAIN!
GEE, STRIPESY, I'M SURE GLAD WE CAME IN TIME!
SEE, WILLIAM, THEY HAVE ROUTED THE KNAVES! THIS WAS NO DREAM, BUT REALITY!
QUICK SLASHES OF THE KNIGHT'S SWORD FREE THE CAPTIVES! AND MOMENTS LATER...
NOW WE FIND OTHER SOLDIERS OF VICTORY!
BEFORE WE DO THAT, WING, WE'VE GOT SOMETHING ELSE TO ATTEND TO! WE MUST LEARN WHAT THE THUGS ARE DOING ON THESE ISLANDS!
IT'S A RACKET, KID, THEY'RE CHISELLIN' ON THE POOR GUYS THAT LIVE HERE!
4

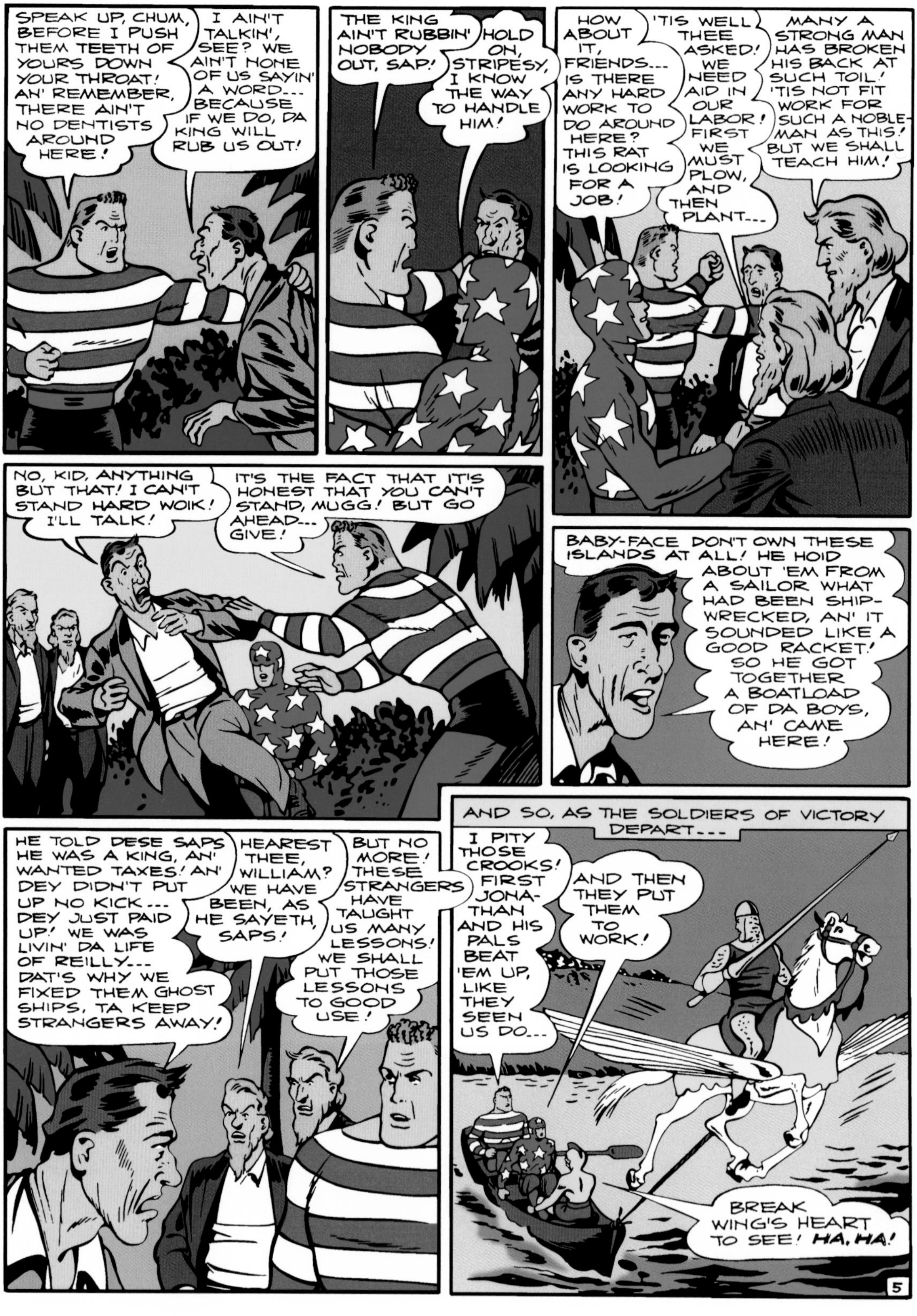
SPEAK UP, CHUM, BEFORE I PUSH THEM TEETH OF YOURS DOWN YOUR THROAT! AN' REMEMBER, THERE AIN'T NO DENTISTS AROUND HERE!
I AIN'T TALKIN', SEE? WE AIN'T NONE OF US SAYIN' A WORD... BECAUSE IF WE DO, DA KING WILL RUB US OUT!
THE KING AIN'T RUBBIN' NOBODY OUT, SAP!
HOLD ON, STRIPESY, I KNOW THE WAY TO HANDLE HIM!
HOW ABOUT IT, FRIENDS... IS THERE ANY HARD WORK TO DO AROUND HERE? THIS RAT IS LOOKING FOR A JOB!
'TIS WELL THEE ASKED! WE NEED AID IN OUR LABOR! FIRST WE MUST PLOW, AND THEN PLANT...
MANY A STRONG MAN HAS BROKEN HIS BACK AT SUCH TOIL! 'TIS NOT FIT WORK FOR SUCH A NOBLEMAN AS THIS! BUT WE SHALL TEACH HIM!
NO, KID, ANYTHING BUT THAT! I CAN'T STAND HARD WOIK! I'LL TALK!
IT'S THE FACT THAT IT'S HONEST THAT YOU CAN'T STAND, MUGG! BUT GO AHEAD... GIVE!
BABY-FACE DON'T OWN THESE ISLANDS AT ALL! HE HOID ABOUT 'EM FROM A SAILOR WHAT HAD BEEN SHIPWRECKED, AN' IT SOUNDED LIKE A GOOD RACKET! SO HE GOT TOGETHER A BOATLOAD OF DA BOYS, AN' CAME HERE!
HE TOLD DESE SAPS HE WAS A KING, AN' WANTED TAXES! AN' DEY DIDN'T PUT UP NO KICK... DEY JUST PAID UP! WE WAS LIVIN' DA LIFE OF REILLY... DAT'S WHY WE FIXED THEM GHOST SHIPS, TA KEEP STRANGERS AWAY!
HEAREST THEE, WILLIAM? WE HAVE BEEN, AS HE SAYETH, SAPS!
BUT NO MORE! THESE STRANGERS HAVE TAUGHT US MANY LESSONS! WE SHALL PUT THOSE LESSONS TO GOOD USE!
AND SO, AS THE SOLDIERS OF VICTORY DEPART...
I PITY THOSE CROOKS! FIRST JONATHAN AND HIS PALS BEAT 'EM UP, LIKE THEY SEEN US DO...
AND THEN THEY PUT THEM TO WORK!
BREAK WING'S HEART TO SEE! HA, HA!
5

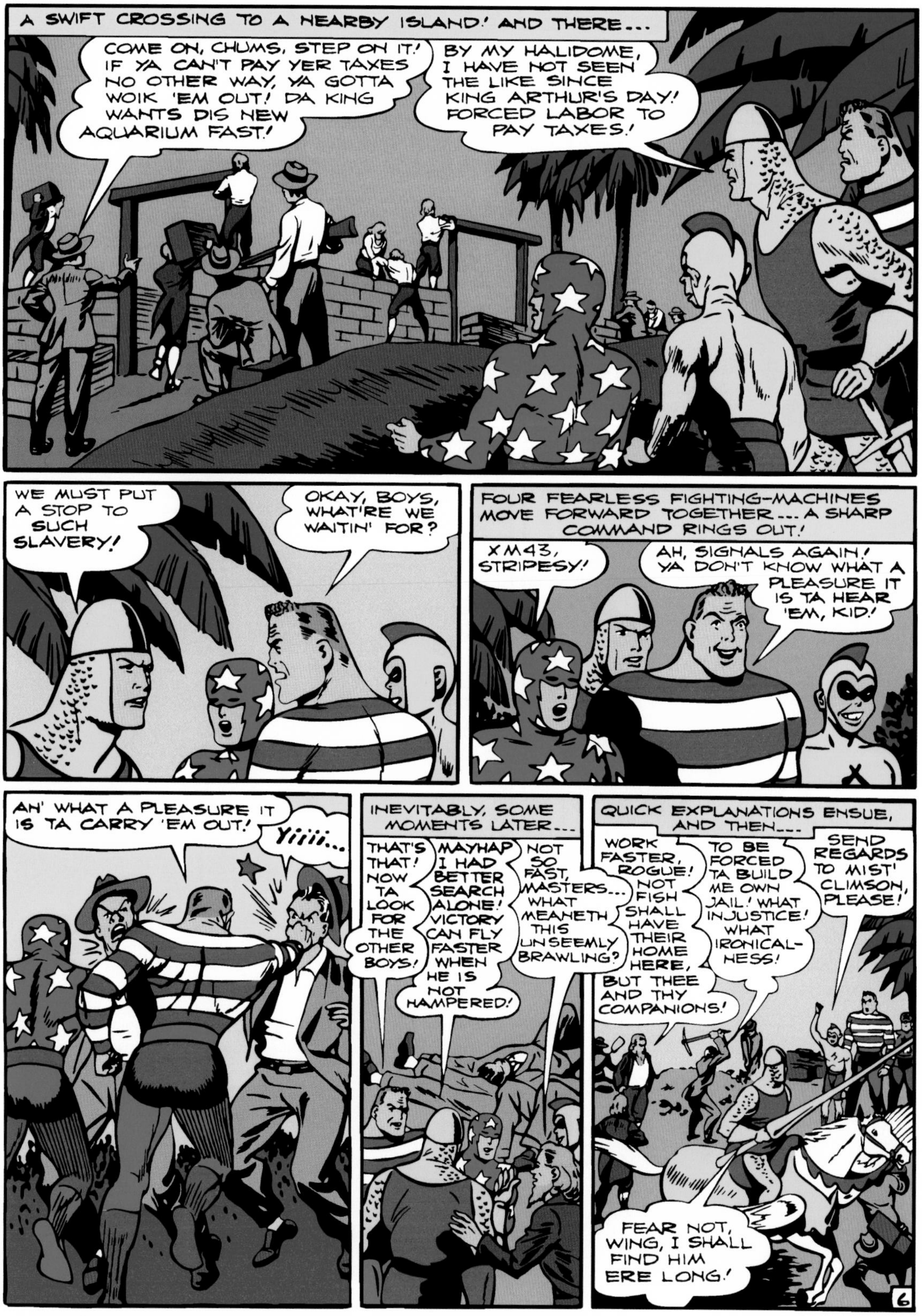
A SWIFT CROSSING TO A NEARBY ISLAND! AND THERE...
COME ON, CHUMS, STEP ON IT! IF YA CAN'T PAY YER TAXES NO OTHER WAY, YA GOTTA WOIK 'EM OUT! DA KING WANTS DIS NEW AQUARIUM FAST!
BY MY HALIDOME, I HAVE NOT SEEN THE LIKE SINCE KING ARTHUR'S DAY! FORCED LABOR TO PAY TAXES!
WE MUST PUT A STOP TO SUCH SLAVERY!
OKAY, BOYS, WHAT'RE WE WAITIN' FOR?
FOUR FEARLESS FIGHTING-MACHINES MOVE FORWARD TOGETHER... A SHARP COMMAND RINGS OUT!
XM43, STRIPESY!
AH, SIGNALS AGAIN! YA DON'T KNOW WHAT A PLEASURE IT IS TA HEAR 'EM, KID!
AN' WHAT A PLEASURE IT IS TA CARRY 'EM OUT!
Yiiii...
INEVITABLY, SOME MOMENTS LATER...
THAT'S THAT! NOW TA LOOK FOR THE OTHER BOYS!
MAYHAP I HAD BETTER SEARCH ALONE! VICTORY CAN FLY FASTER WHEN HE IS NOT HAMPERED!
NOT SO FAST, MASTERS... WHAT MEANETH THIS UNSEEMLY BRAWLING?
QUICK EXPLANATIONS ENSUE, AND THEN...
WORK FASTER, ROGUE! NOT FISH SHALL HAVE THEIR HOME HERE, BUT THEE AND THY COMPANIONS!
TO BE FORCED TA BUILD ME OWN JAIL! WHAT INJUSTICE! WHAT IRONICAL-NESS!
SEND REGARDS TO MIST' CLIMSON, PLEASE!
FEAR NOT, WING, I SHALL FIND HIM ERE LONG!
6

MEANWHILE, ON THE ISLAND WHERE PROFESSOR MORAN HAS BEEN LEFT IN CHARGE OF THE MOBSTERS...

STEP ON IT, YOU MUGGS, OR I SHALL REGRETFULLY BE FORCED TO LET YOU HAVE IT!

OKAY, CHUM, OKAY! ANYTHING YOU SAY... BUT DON'T POINT THEM RODS AT US!

WID A GUY WHAT KNEW HOW TO HANDLE 'EM, WE WOULDN'T BE SCARED... BUT DIS PERFESSER'S LIABLE TO LET GO ACCIDENTAL! A GUY'S LIFE AIN'T SAFE AROUN' HERE!

IT REQUIRED THE STAR-SPANGLED KID'S REMARKS TO MAKE ME REALIZE THE POSSIBILITY OF SALVAGING THE SHIP! THIS CHANNEL WILL PERMIT THE NEXT HIGH TIDE TO REFLOAT IT!

ALSO, RATHER CLEVER THE WAY I'M HANDLING THESE CRIMINALS! IF THEY REBEL, I THREATEN TO SHOOT THEM! IF THEY OBEY ORDERS, I REWARD THEM WITH AN HOUR IN THEIR IMAGINARY POOL ROOM!

DA SAP TINKS HE'S SMART! HE DON'T REALIZE WE GOT PLANS OF OUR OWN!

YES, PROFESSOR MORAN, THERE ARE OTHER CLEVER PEOPLE IN THE WORLD BESIDES YOURSELF! WHEN HIGH TIDE FINALLY ARRIVES...

THE SHIP'S FLOATING! WONDERFUL WORK, PROFESSOR MORAN!

YES, I FLATTER MYSELF THAT I AM A BIT MORE INTELLIGENT THAN THE AVERAGE PERSON!

IZAAK WALTON

UNEXPECTEDLY...

YEAH, YOU'RE DA SMARTEST SAP I EVER SEEN! HAW, HAW! DAT'LL LEARN YA NOT TO TAKE YOUR EYES OFF US! NOW WE'LL GO TA MEET DA KING!

AAAA...

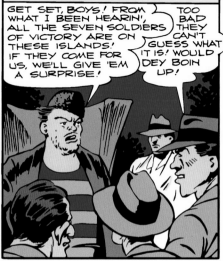

AND NOT FAR AWAY...

GET SET, BOYS! FROM WHAT I BEEN HEARIN', ALL THE SEVEN SOLDIERS OF VICTORY ARE ON THESE ISLANDS! IF THEY COME FOR US, WE'LL GIVE 'EM A SURPRISE!

TOO BAD THEY CAN'T GUESS WHAT IT IS! WOULD DEY BOIN UP!

ANOTHER STORM IS GATHERING, THIS TIME A STORM BREWED OF HUMAN FEAR, AND HATE, AND THE DESIRE FOR VENGEANCE! BUT THE LEGIONNAIRES, TOO, ARE PREPARING!
=
ON A NEIGHBORING ISLAND...

7

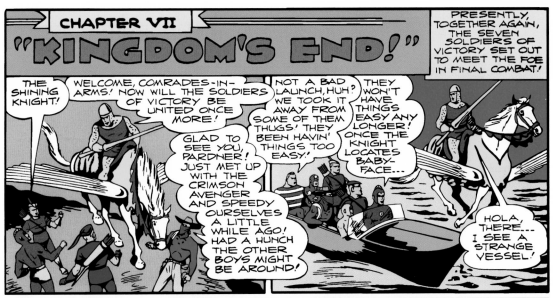

CHAPTER VII

"KINGDOM'S END!"

PRESENTLY, TOGETHER AGAIN, THE SEVEN SOLDIERS OF VICTORY SET OUT TO MEET THE FOE IN FINAL COMBAT!

THE SHINING KNIGHT!

WELCOME, COMRADES-IN-ARMS! NOW WILL THE SOLDIERS OF VICTORY BE UNITED ONCE MORE!

GLAD TO SEE YOU, PARDNER! JUST MET UP WITH THE CRIMSON AVENGER AND SPEEDY OURSELVES A LITTLE WHILE AGO! HAD A HUNCH THE OTHER BOY'S MIGHT BE AROUND!

NOT A BAD LAUNCH, HUH? WE TOOK IT AWAY FROM SOME OF THEM THUGS! THEY BEEN HAVIN' THINGS TOO EASY!

THEY WON'T HAVE THINGS EASY ANY LONGER! ONCE THE KNIGHT LOCATES BABY-FACE...

HOLA, THERE... I SEE A STRANGE VESSEL!

PROFESSOR MORAN'S BOAT! HE'S MANAGED TO FLOAT IT!

GOSH, KID, NOW WE'LL BE ABLE TO GET HOME!

BUT AS THE EVER ALERT CHAMPION OF CHIVALRY FLIES FORWARD TO GREET THE APPROACHING CRAFT...

WHA...? THESE ARE NO FRIENDS! ON GUARD, COMRADES!

LUCKY THE KNIGHT WARNED US! WE JUMPED JUST IN TIME!

WONDER WHAT HAPPENED TO PROFESSOR MORAN! HE HAD THE THUGS UNDER CONTROL LAST WE SAW OF HIM!

RAM!

AS THE GLOATING CRIMINALS PREPARE TO PICK OFF THEIR HELPLESS PREY...

DIS IS GONNA BE A PLEASURE! LIKE SHOOTIN' FISH IN A BARREL!

THE VILE ROGUES WOULD SHOOT HELP-LESS MEN! I MUST ACT RAPIDLY!

I MEANT TO SAVE THESE FOR THE CHIEF VILLAIN... BUT NOW I HAVE NO CHOICE!

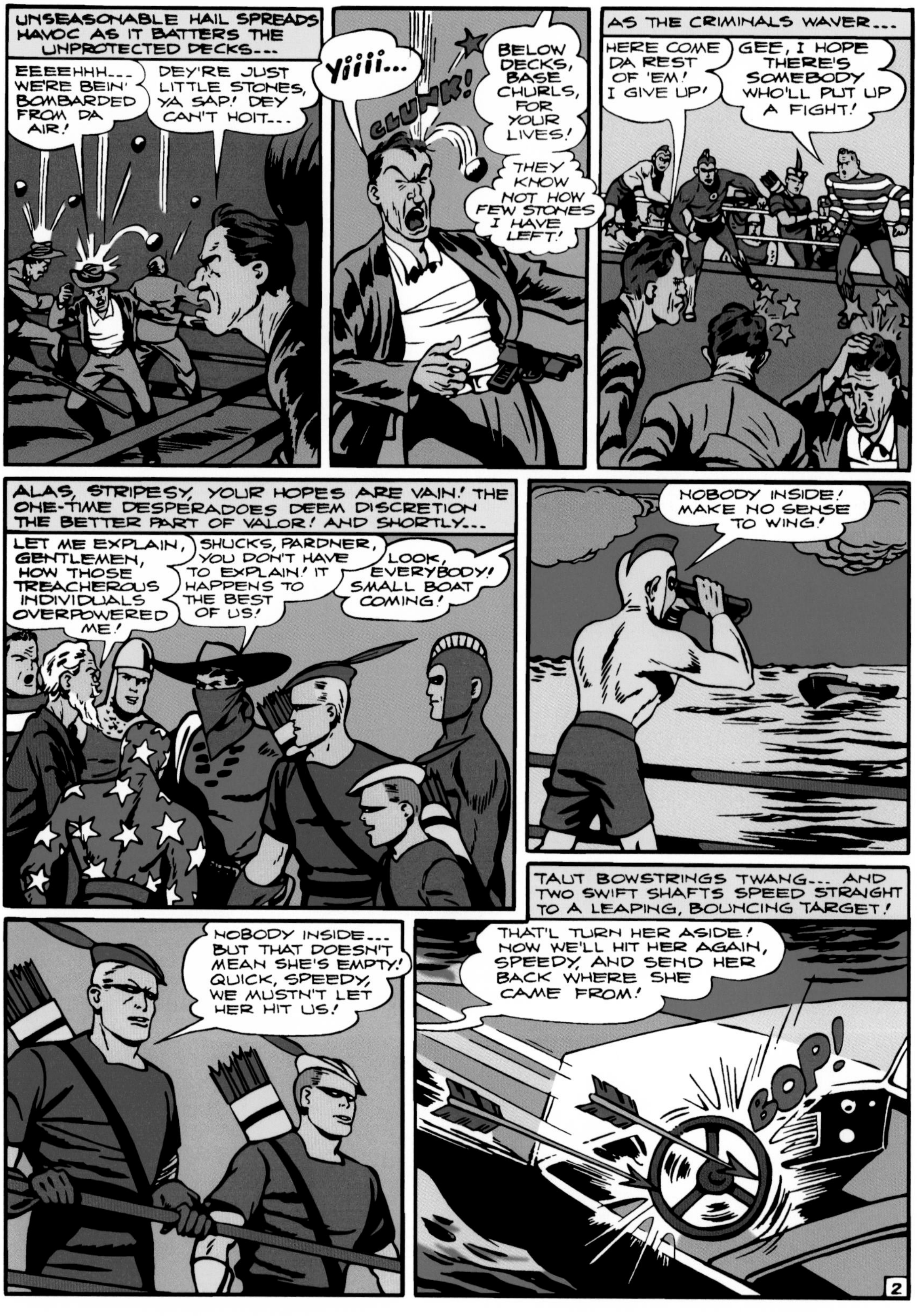
UNSEASONABLE HAIL SPREADS HAVOC AS IT BATTERS THE UNPROTECTED DECKS...
EEEEHHH... WE'RE BEIN' BOMBARDED FROM DA AIR!
DEY'RE JUST LITTLE STONES, YA SAP! DEY CAN'T HOIT...
Yiiii...
CLUNK!
BELOW DECKS, BASE CHURLS, FOR YOUR LIVES!
THEY KNOW NOT HOW FEW STONES I HAVE LEFT!
AS THE CRIMINALS WAVER...
HERE COME DA REST OF 'EM! I GIVE UP!
GEE, I HOPE THERE'S SOMEBODY WHO'LL PUT UP A FIGHT!
ALAS, STRIPESY, YOUR HOPES ARE VAIN! THE ONE-TIME DESPERADOES DEEM DISCRETION THE BETTER PART OF VALOR! AND SHORTLY...
LET ME EXPLAIN, GENTLEMEN, HOW THOSE TREACHEROUS INDIVIDUALS OVERPOWERED ME!
SHUCKS, PARDNER, YOU DON'T HAVE TO EXPLAIN! IT HAPPENS TO THE BEST OF US!
LOOK, EVERYBODY! SMALL BOAT COMING!
NOBODY INSIDE! MAKE NO SENSE TO WING!
TAUT BOWSTRINGS TWANG... AND TWO SWIFT SHAFTS SPEED STRAIGHT TO A LEAPING, BOUNCING TARGET!
NOBODY INSIDE... BUT THAT DOESN'T MEAN SHE'S EMPTY! QUICK, SPEEDY, WE MUSTN'T LET HER HIT US!
THAT'L TURN HER ASIDE! NOW WE'LL HIT HER AGAIN, SPEEDY, AND SEND HER BACK WHERE SHE CAME FROM!
BOP!
2

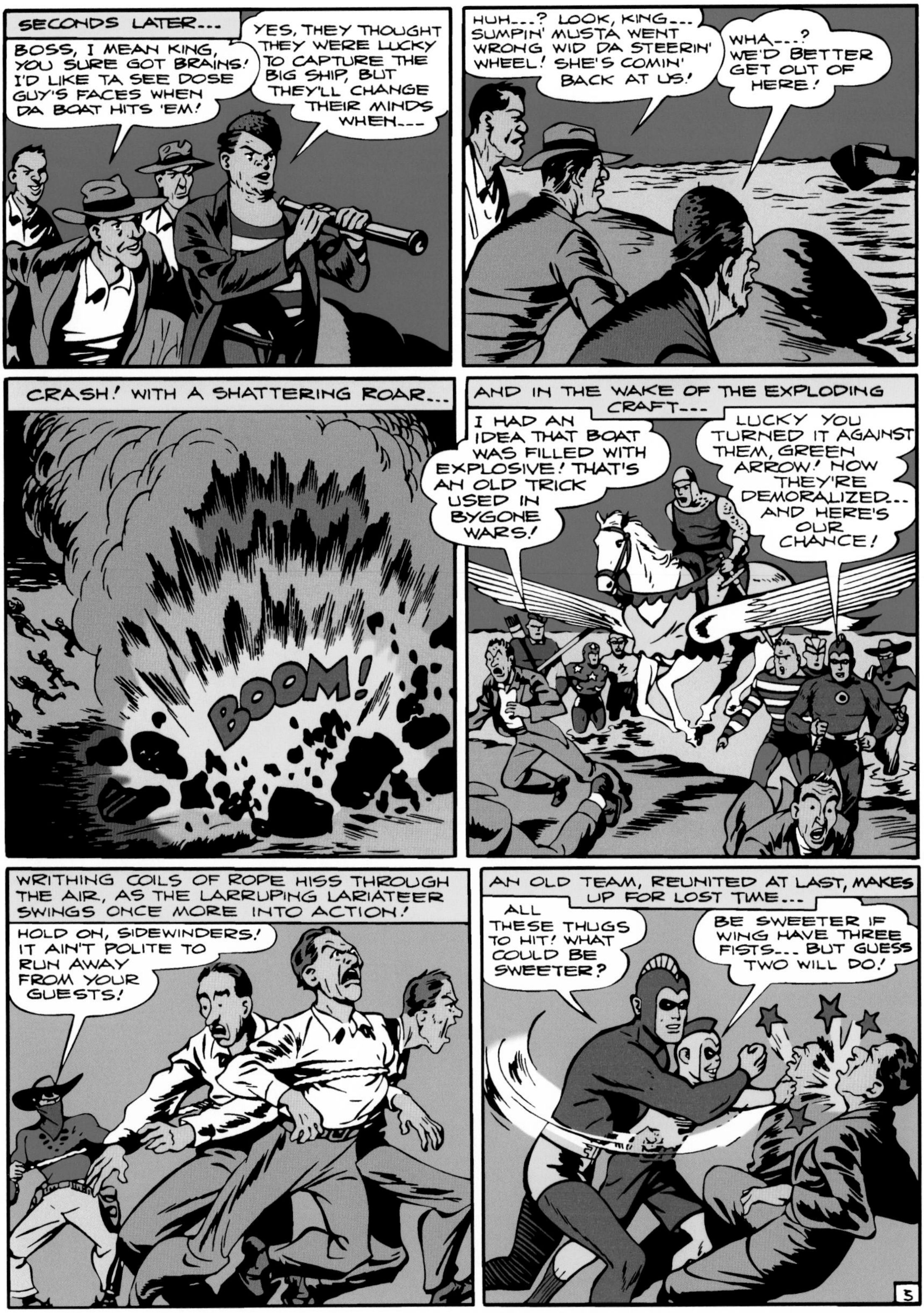
SECONDS LATER...
BOSS, I MEAN KING, YOU SURE GOT BRAINS! I'D LIKE TA SEE DOSE GUY'S FACES WHEN DA BOAT HITS 'EM!
YES, THEY THOUGHT THEY WERE LUCKY TO CAPTURE THE BIG SHIP, BUT THEY'LL CHANGE THEIR MINDS WHEN---
HUH---? LOOK, KING--- SUMPIN' MUSTA WENT WRONG WID DA STEERIN' WHEEL! SHE'S COMIN' BACK AT US!
WHA---? WE'D BETTER GET OUT OF HERE!
CRASH! WITH A SHATTERING ROAR...
BOOM!
AND IN THE WAKE OF THE EXPLODING CRAFT---
I HAD AN IDEA THAT BOAT WAS FILLED WITH EXPLOSIVE! THAT'S AN OLD TRICK USED IN BYGONE WARS!
LUCKY YOU TURNED IT AGAINST THEM, GREEN ARROW! NOW THEY'RE DEMORALIZED... AND HERE'S OUR CHANCE!
WRITHING COILS OF ROPE HISS THROUGH THE AIR, AS THE LARRUPING LARIATEER SWINGS ONCE MORE INTO ACTION!
HOLD ON, SIDEWINDERS! IT AIN'T POLITE TO RUN AWAY FROM YOUR GUESTS!
AN OLD TEAM, REUNITED AT LAST, MAKES UP FOR LOST TIME...
ALL THESE THUGS TO HIT! WHAT COULD BE SWEETER?
BE SWEETER IF WING HAVE THREE FISTS... BUT GUESS TWO WILL DO!
5

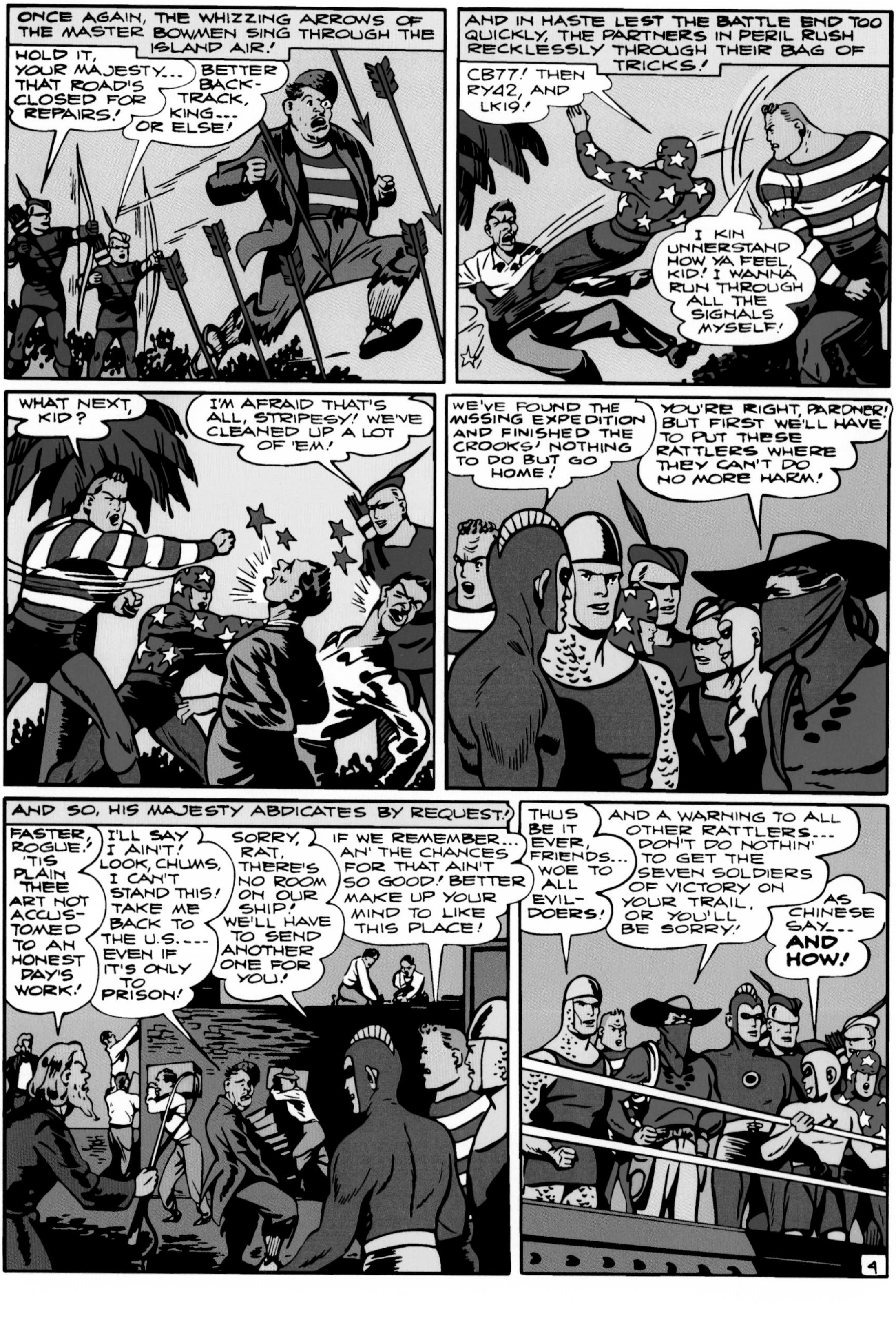
ONCE AGAIN, THE WHIZZING ARROWS OF THE MASTER BOWMEN SING THROUGH THE ISLAND AIR!
HOLD IT, YOUR MAJESTY... THAT ROAD'S CLOSED FOR REPAIRS!
BETTER BACK-TRACK, KING... OR ELSE!
AND IN HASTE LEST THE BATTLE END TOO QUICKLY, THE PARTNERS IN PERIL RUSH RECKLESSLY THROUGH THEIR BAG OF TRICKS!
CB77! THEN RY42, AND LK19!
I KIN UNNERSTAND HOW YA FEEL, KID! I WANNA RUN THROUGH ALL THE SIGNALS MYSELF!
WHAT NEXT, KID?
I'M AFRAID THAT'S ALL, STRIPESY! WE'VE CLEANED UP A LOT OF 'EM!
WE'VE FOUND THE MISSING EXPEDITION AND FINISHED THE CROOKS! NOTHING TO DO BUT GO HOME!
YOU'RE RIGHT, PARDNER! BUT FIRST WE'LL HAVE TO PUT THESE RATTLERS WHERE THEY CAN'T DO NO MORE HARM!
AND SO, HIS MAJESTY ABDICATES BY REQUEST!
FASTER, ROGUE! 'TIS PLAIN THEE ART NOT ACCUS-TOMED TO AN HONEST DAY'S WORK!
I'LL SAY I AIN'T! LOOK, CHUMS, I CAN'T STAND THIS! TAKE ME BACK TO THE U.S.--- EVEN IF IT'S ONLY TO PRISON!
SORRY, RAT, THERE'S NO ROOM ON OUR SHIP! WE'LL HAVE TO SEND ANOTHER ONE FOR YOU!
IF WE REMEMBER... AN' THE CHANCES FOR THAT AIN'T SO GOOD! BETTER MAKE UP YOUR MIND TO LIKE THIS PLACE!
THUS BE IT EVER, FRIENDS... WOE TO ALL EVIL-DOERS!
AND A WARNING TO ALL OTHER RATTLERS... DON'T DO NOTHIN' TO GET THE SEVEN SOLDIERS OF VICTORY ON YOUR TRAIL, OR YOU'LL BE SORRY!
AS CHINESE SAY... AND HOW!
4

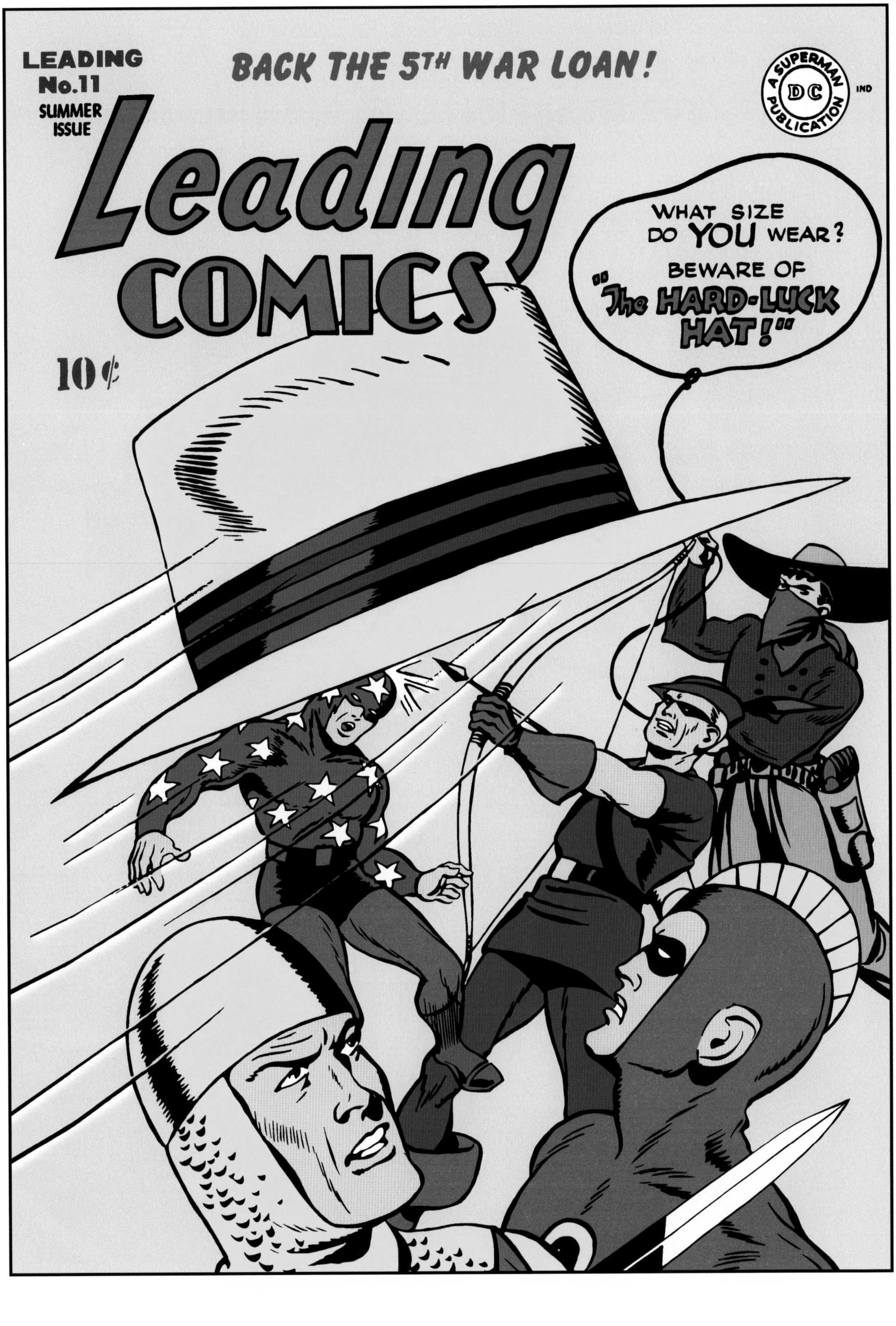
LEADING
No.11
SUMMER ISSUE
BACK THE 5TH WAR LOAN!
A SUPERMAN DC PUBLICATION
IND
Leading
COMICS
10¢
WHAT SIZE DO YOU WEAR?
BEWARE OF
"The HARD-LUCK HAT!"

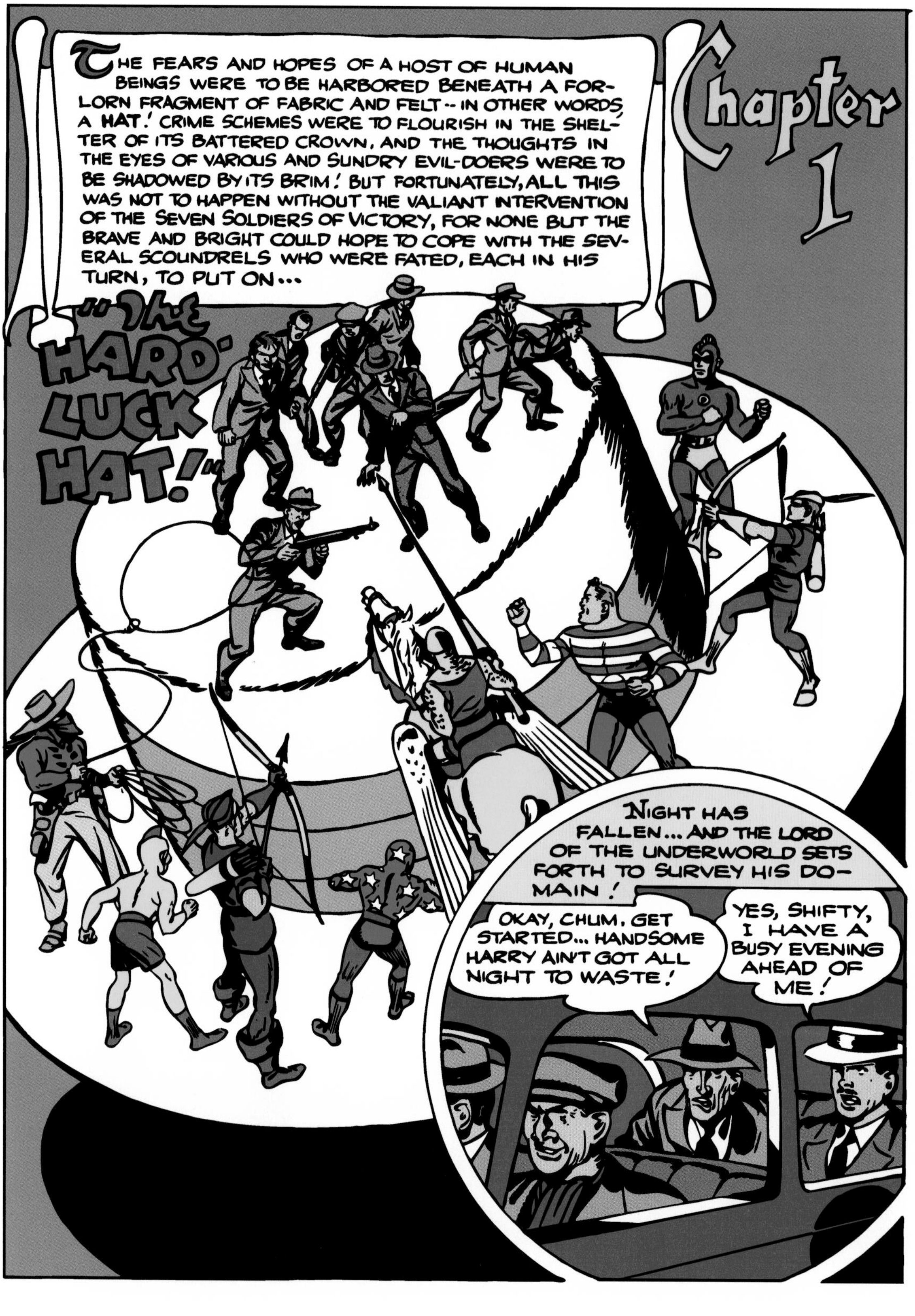
THE FEARS AND HOPES OF A HOST OF HUMAN BEINGS WERE TO BE HARBORED BENEATH A FORLORN FRAGMENT OF FABRIC AND FELT -- IN OTHER WORDS, A HAT! CRIME SCHEMES WERE TO FLOURISH IN THE SHELTER OF ITS BATTERED CROWN, AND THE THOUGHTS IN THE EYES OF VARIOUS AND SUNDRY EVIL-DOERS WERE TO BE SHADOWED BY ITS BRIM! BUT FORTUNATELY, ALL THIS WAS NOT TO HAPPEN WITHOUT THE VALIANT INTERVENTION OF THE SEVEN SOLDIERS OF VICTORY, FOR NONE BUT THE BRAVE AND BRIGHT COULD HOPE TO COPE WITH THE SEVERAL SCOUNDRELS WHO WERE FATED, EACH IN HIS TURN, TO PUT ON...
Chapter 1
"The HARD-LUCK HAT!"
NIGHT HAS FALLEN... AND THE LORD OF THE UNDERWORLD SETS FORTH TO SURVEY HIS DOMAIN!
OKAY, CHUM, GET STARTED... HANDSOME HARRY AIN'T GOT ALL NIGHT TO WASTE!
YES, SHIFTY, I HAVE A BUSY EVENING AHEAD OF ME!

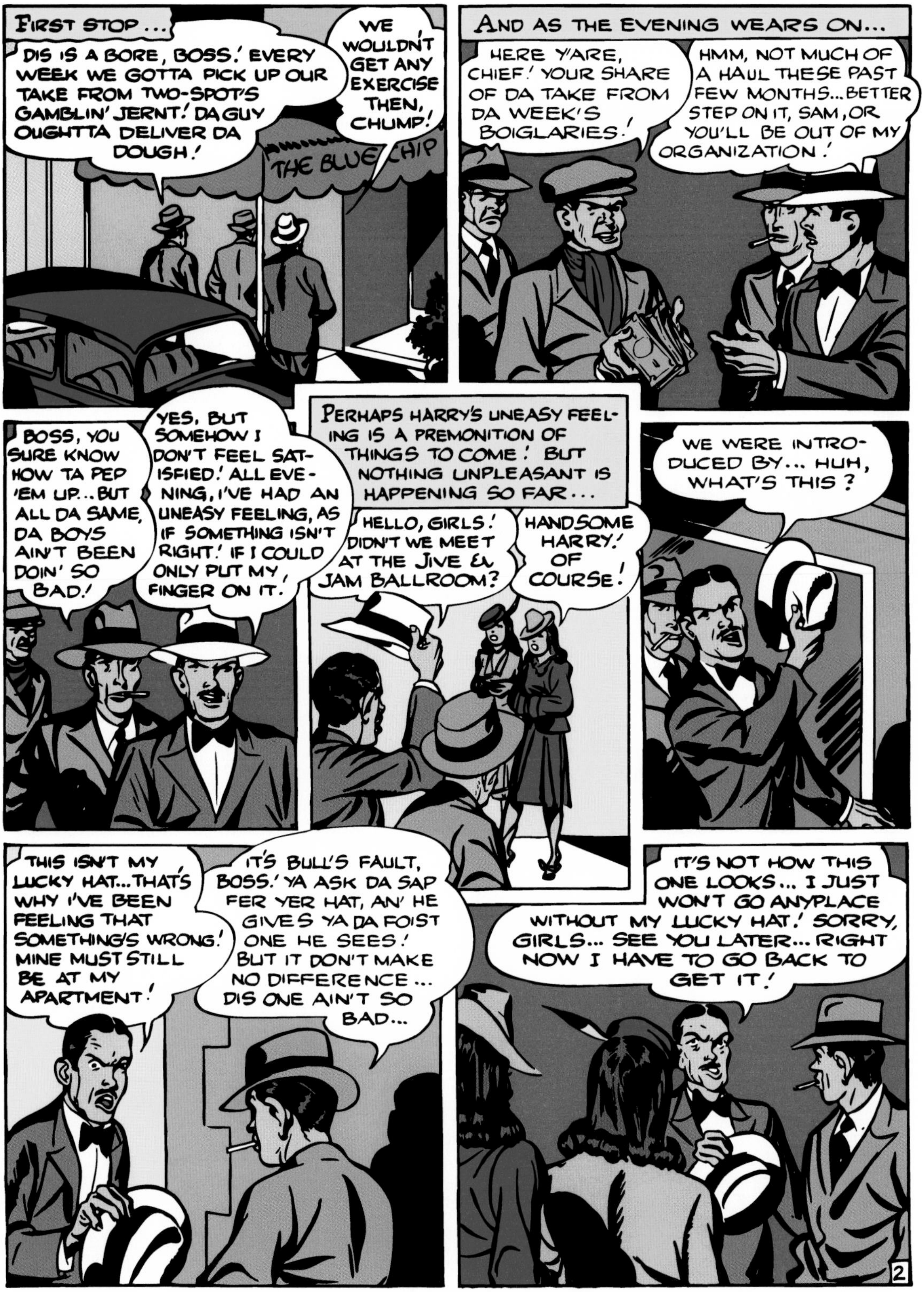
FIRST STOP...
DIS IS A BORE, BOSS! EVERY WEEK WE GOTTA PICK UP OUR TAKE FROM TWO-SPOT'S GAMBLIN' JERNT! DA GUY OUGHTTA DELIVER DA DOUGH!
WE WOULDN'T GET ANY EXERCISE THEN, CHUMP!
THE BLUE CHIP
AND AS THE EVENING WEARS ON...
HERE Y'ARE, CHIEF! YOUR SHARE OF DA TAKE FROM DA WEEK'S BOIGLARIES!
HMM, NOT MUCH OF A HAUL THESE PAST FEW MONTHS...BETTER STEP ON IT, SAM, OR YOU'LL BE OUT OF MY ORGANIZATION!
BOSS, YOU SURE KNOW HOW TA PEP 'EM UP...BUT ALL DA SAME, DA BOYS AIN'T BEEN DOIN' SO BAD!
YES, BUT SOMEHOW I DON'T FEEL SATISFIED! ALL EVENING, I'VE HAD AN UNEASY FEELING, AS IF SOMETHING ISN'T RIGHT! IF I COULD ONLY PUT MY FINGER ON IT!
PERHAPS HARRY'S UNEASY FEELING IS A PREMONITION OF THINGS TO COME! BUT NOTHING UNPLEASANT IS HAPPENING SO FAR...
HELLO, GIRLS! DIDN'T WE MEET AT THE JIVE & JAM BALLROOM?
HANDSOME HARRY! OF COURSE!
WE WERE INTRODUCED BY... HUH, WHAT'S THIS?
THIS ISN'T MY LUCKY HAT...THAT'S WHY I'VE BEEN FEELING THAT SOMETHING'S WRONG! MINE MUST STILL BE AT MY APARTMENT!
IT'S BULL'S FAULT, BOSS! YA ASK DA SAP FER YER HAT, AN' HE GIVES YA DA FOIST ONE HE SEES! BUT IT DON'T MAKE NO DIFFERENCE... DIS ONE AIN'T SO BAD...
IT'S NOT HOW THIS ONE LOOKS... I JUST WON'T GO ANYPLACE WITHOUT MY LUCKY HAT! SORRY, GIRLS... SEE YOU LATER... RIGHT NOW I HAVE TO GO BACK TO GET IT!
2

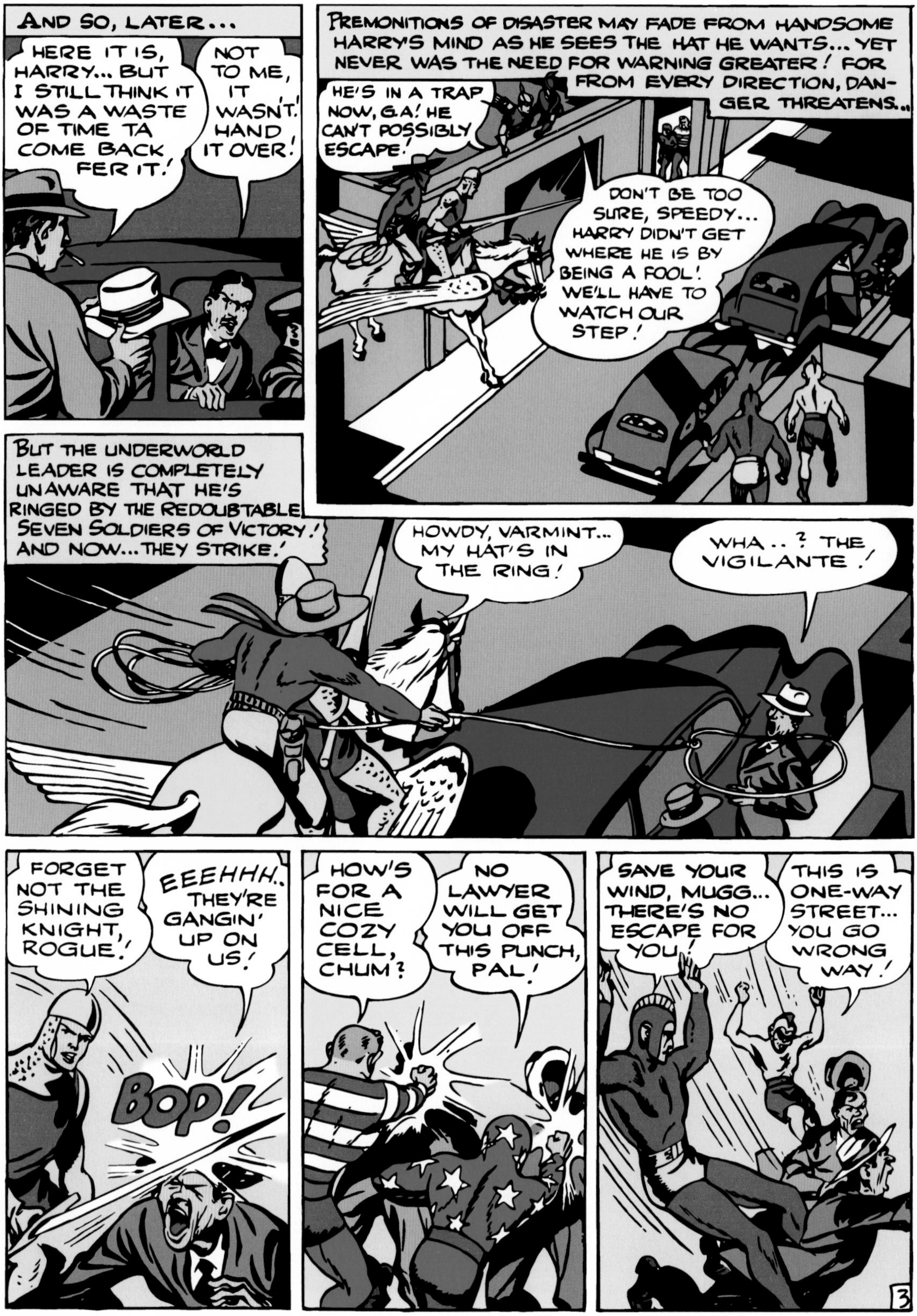
AND SO, LATER...
HERE IT IS, HARRY... BUT I STILL THINK IT WAS A WASTE OF TIME TA COME BACK FER IT!
NOT TO ME, IT WASN'T! HAND IT OVER!
PREMONITIONS OF DISASTER MAY FADE FROM HANDSOME HARRY'S MIND AS HE SEES THE HAT HE WANTS... YET NEVER WAS THE NEED FOR WARNING GREATER! FOR FROM EVERY DIRECTION, DANGER THREATENS...
HE'S IN A TRAP NOW, G.A! HE CAN'T POSSIBLY ESCAPE!
DON'T BE TOO SURE, SPEEDY... HARRY DIDN'T GET WHERE HE IS BY BEING A FOOL! WE'LL HAVE TO WATCH OUR STEP!
BUT THE UNDERWORLD LEADER IS COMPLETELY UNAWARE THAT HE'S RINGED BY THE REDOUBTABLE SEVEN SOLDIERS OF VICTORY! AND NOW...THEY STRIKE!
HOWDY, VARMINT... MY HAT'S IN THE RING!
WHA..? THE VIGILANTE!
FORGET NOT THE SHINING KNIGHT, ROGUE!
EEEHHH.. THEY'RE GANGIN' UP ON US!
BOP!
HOW'S FOR A NICE COZY CELL, CHUM?
NO LAWYER WILL GET YOU OFF THIS PUNCH, PAL!
SAVE YOUR WIND, MUGG... THERE'S NO ESCAPE FOR YOU!
THIS IS ONE-WAY STREET... YOU GO WRONG WAY!
3

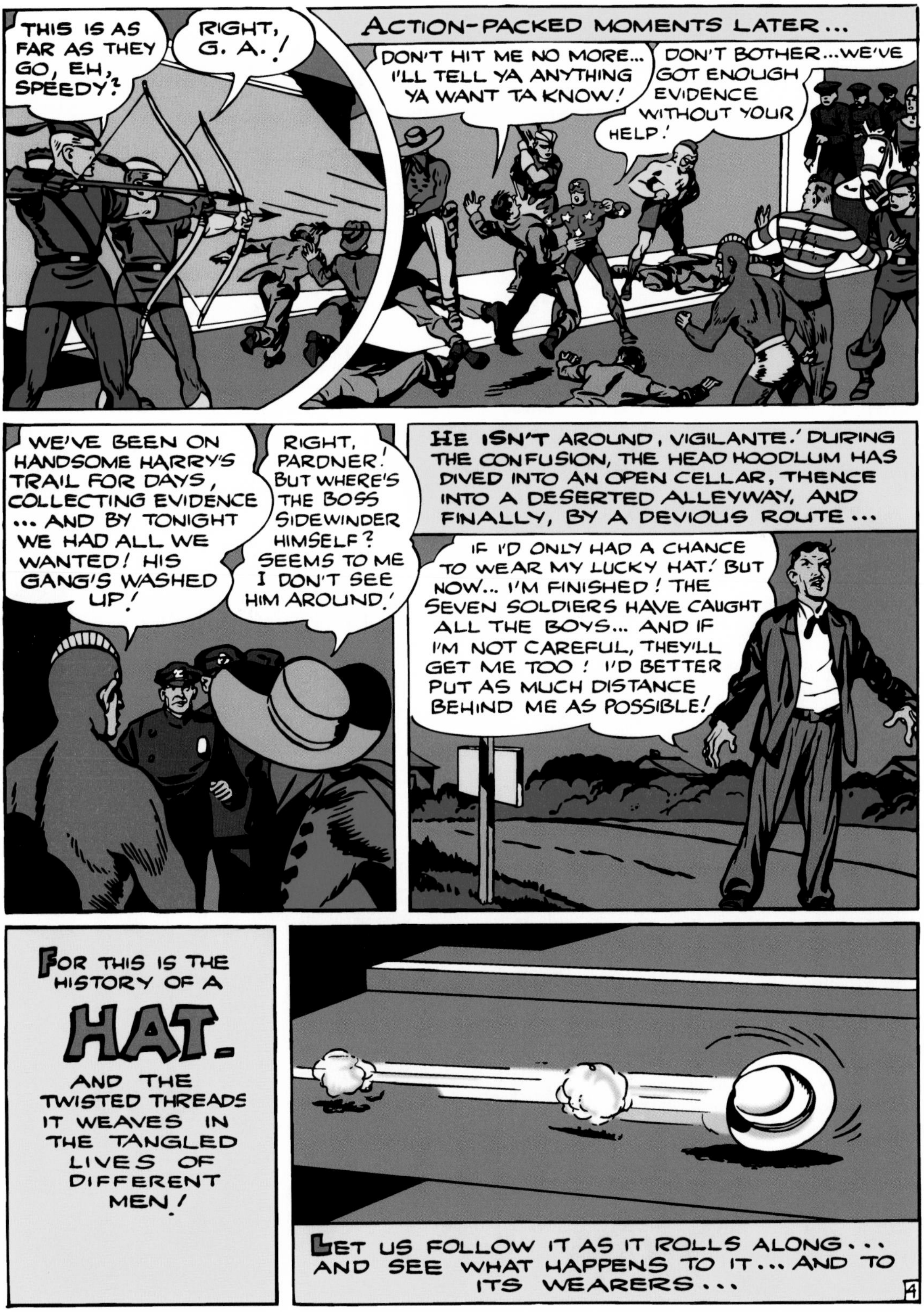
THIS IS AS FAR AS THEY GO, EH, SPEEDY?
RIGHT, G. A.!
ACTION-PACKED MOMENTS LATER...
DON'T HIT ME NO MORE... I'LL TELL YA ANYTHING YA WANT TA KNOW!
DON'T BOTHER...WE'VE GOT ENOUGH EVIDENCE WITHOUT YOUR HELP!
WE'VE BEEN ON HANDSOME HARRY'S TRAIL FOR DAYS, COLLECTING EVIDENCE ... AND BY TONIGHT WE HAD ALL WE WANTED! HIS GANG'S WASHED UP!
RIGHT, PARDNER! BUT WHERE'S THE BOSS SIDEWINDER HIMSELF? SEEMS TO ME I DON'T SEE HIM AROUND!
HE ISN'T AROUND, VIGILANTE! DURING THE CONFUSION, THE HEAD HOODLUM HAS DIVED INTO AN OPEN CELLAR, THENCE INTO A DESERTED ALLEYWAY, AND FINALLY, BY A DEVIOUS ROUTE...
IF I'D ONLY HAD A CHANCE TO WEAR MY LUCKY HAT! BUT NOW... I'M FINISHED! THE SEVEN SOLDIERS HAVE CAUGHT ALL THE BOYS... AND IF I'M NOT CAREFUL, THEY'LL GET ME TOO! I'D BETTER PUT AS MUCH DISTANCE BEHIND ME AS POSSIBLE!
FOR THIS IS THE HISTORY OF A
HAT.
AND THE TWISTED THREADS IT WEAVES IN THE TANGLED LIVES OF DIFFERENT MEN!
LET US FOLLOW IT AS IT ROLLS ALONG... AND SEE WHAT HAPPENS TO IT... AND TO ITS WEARERS...
4

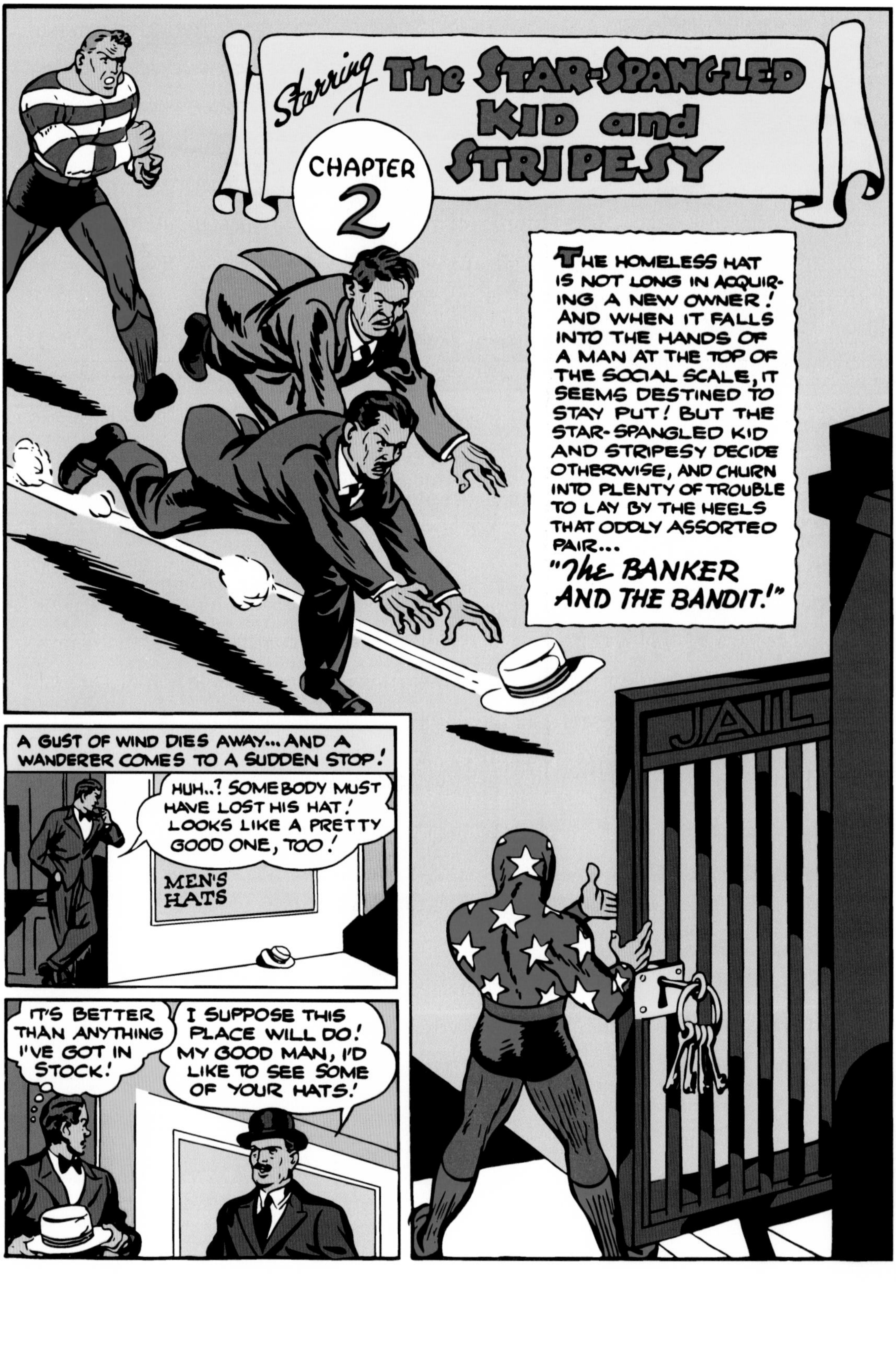
Starring The STAR-SPANGLED KID and STRIPESY
CHAPTER 2
THE HOMELESS HAT IS NOT LONG IN ACQUIRING A NEW OWNER! AND WHEN IT FALLS INTO THE HANDS OF A MAN AT THE TOP OF THE SOCIAL SCALE, IT SEEMS DESTINED TO STAY PUT! BUT THE STAR-SPANGLED KID AND STRIPESY DECIDE OTHERWISE, AND CHURN INTO PLENTY OF TROUBLE TO LAY BY THE HEELS THAT ODDLY ASSORTED PAIR...
"The BANKER AND THE BANDIT!"
JAIL
A GUST OF WIND DIES AWAY... AND A WANDERER COMES TO A SUDDEN STOP!
HUH..? SOMEBODY MUST HAVE LOST HIS HAT! LOOKS LIKE A PRETTY GOOD ONE, TOO!
MEN'S HATS
IT'S BETTER THAN ANYTHING I'VE GOT IN STOCK!
I SUPPOSE THIS PLACE WILL DO! MY GOOD MAN, I'D LIKE TO SEE SOME OF YOUR HATS!

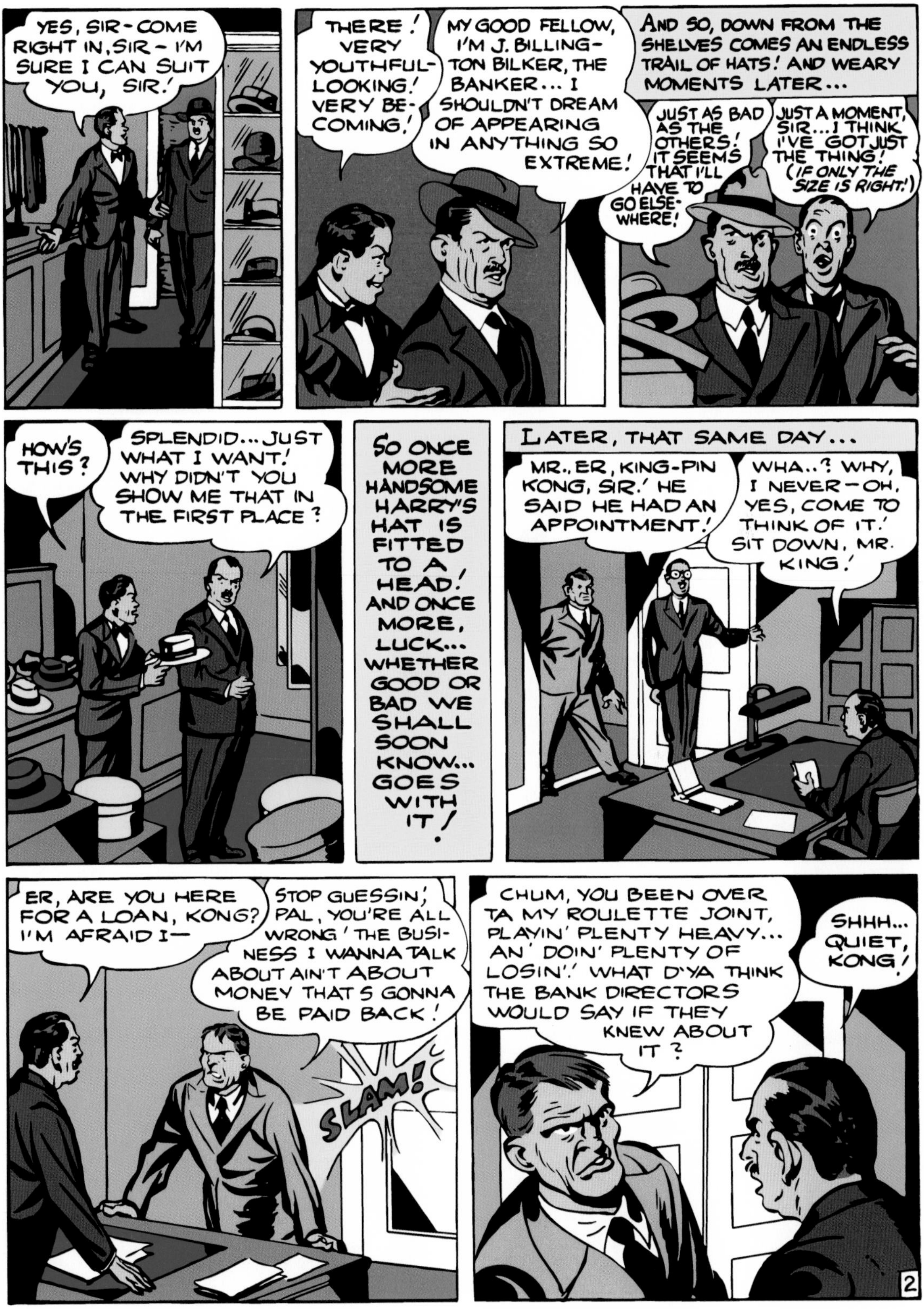
YES, SIR-COME RIGHT IN, SIR - I'M SURE I CAN SUIT YOU, SIR!
THERE! VERY YOUTHFUL-LOOKING! VERY BE-COMING!
MY GOOD FELLOW, I'M J. BILLINGTON BILKER, THE BANKER... I SHOULDN'T DREAM OF APPEARING IN ANYTHING SO EXTREME!
AND SO, DOWN FROM THE SHELVES COMES AN ENDLESS TRAIL OF HATS! AND WEARY MOMENTS LATER...
JUST AS BAD AS THE OTHERS! IT SEEMS THAT I'LL HAVE TO GO ELSEWHERE!
JUST A MOMENT, SIR... I THINK I'VE GOT JUST THE THING! (IF ONLY THE SIZE IS RIGHT!)
HOW'S THIS?
SPLENDID... JUST WHAT I WANT! WHY DIDN'T YOU SHOW ME THAT IN THE FIRST PLACE?
SO ONCE MORE HANDSOME HARRY'S HAT IS FITTED TO A HEAD! AND ONCE MORE, LUCK... WHETHER GOOD OR BAD WE SHALL SOON KNOW... GOES WITH IT!
LATER, THAT SAME DAY...
MR., ER, KING-PIN KONG, SIR! HE SAID HE HAD AN APPOINTMENT!
WHA..? WHY, I NEVER-OH, YES, COME TO THINK OF IT! SIT DOWN, MR. KING!
ER, ARE YOU HERE FOR A LOAN, KONG? I'M AFRAID I—
STOP GUESSIN', PAL, YOU'RE ALL WRONG! THE BUSINESS I WANNA TALK ABOUT AIN'T ABOUT MONEY THAT'S GONNA BE PAID BACK!
SLAM!
CHUM, YOU BEEN OVER TA MY ROULETTE JOINT, PLAYIN' PLENTY HEAVY... AN' DOIN' PLENTY OF LOSIN'! WHAT D'YA THINK THE BANK DIRECTORS WOULD SAY IF THEY KNEW ABOUT IT?
SHHH... QUIET, KONG!
2

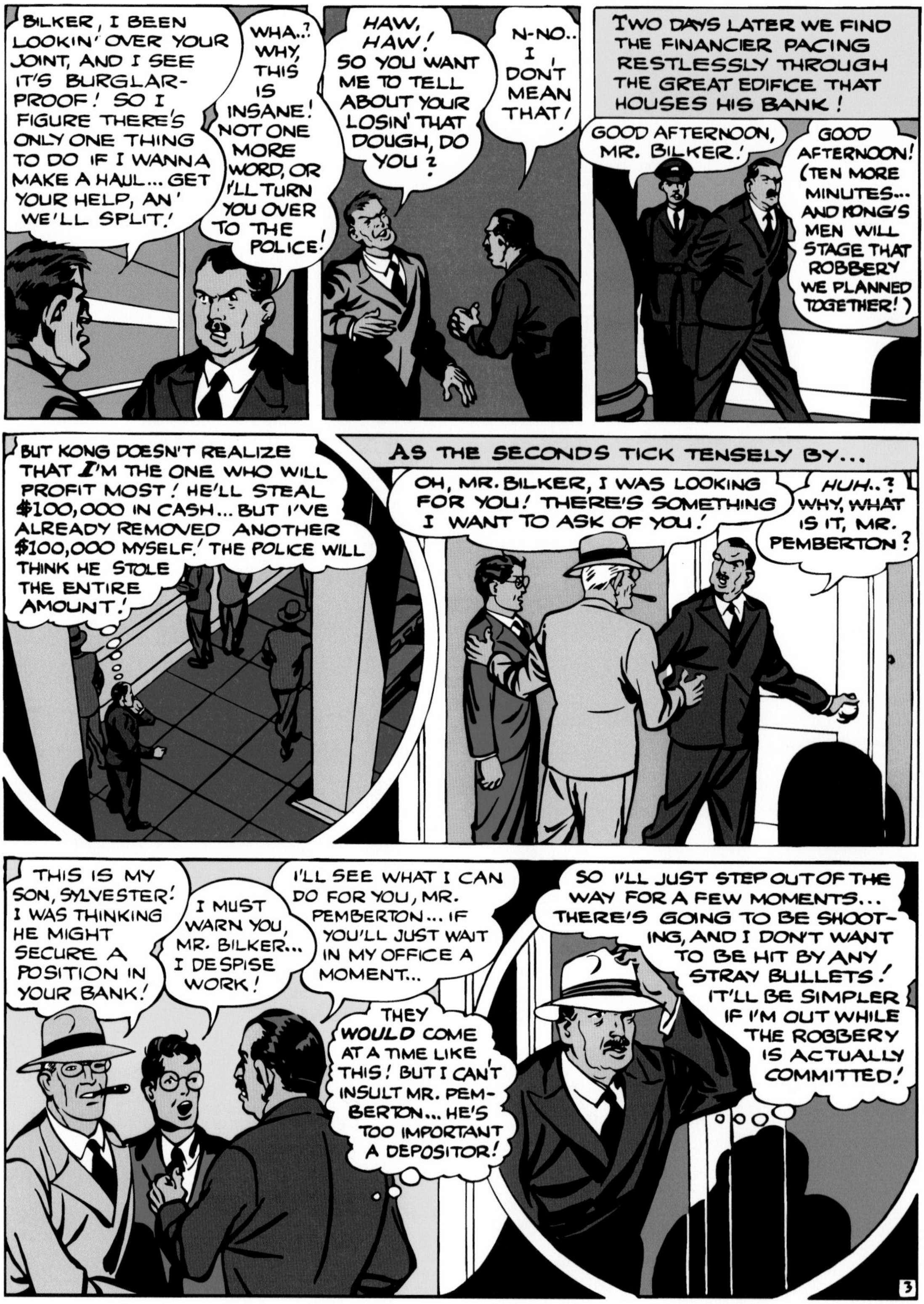
BILKER, I BEEN LOOKIN' OVER YOUR JOINT, AND I SEE IT'S BURGLAR-PROOF! SO I FIGURE THERE'S ONLY ONE THING TO DO IF I WANNA MAKE A HAUL... GET YOUR HELP, AN' WE'LL SPLIT!
WHA..? WHY, THIS IS INSANE! NOT ONE MORE WORD, OR I'LL TURN YOU OVER TO THE POLICE!
HAW, HAW! SO YOU WANT ME TO TELL ABOUT YOUR LOSIN' THAT DOUGH, DO YOU?
N-NO.. I DON'T MEAN THAT!
TWO DAYS LATER WE FIND THE FINANCIER PACING RESTLESSLY THROUGH THE GREAT EDIFICE THAT HOUSES HIS BANK!
GOOD AFTERNOON, MR. BILKER!
GOOD AFTERNOON! (TEN MORE MINUTES... AND KONG'S MEN WILL STAGE THAT ROBBERY WE PLANNED TOGETHER!)
BUT KONG DOESN'T REALIZE THAT I'M THE ONE WHO WILL PROFIT MOST! HE'LL STEAL $100,000 IN CASH... BUT I'VE ALREADY REMOVED ANOTHER $100,000 MYSELF! THE POLICE WILL THINK HE STOLE THE ENTIRE AMOUNT!
AS THE SECONDS TICK TENSELY BY...
OH, MR. BILKER, I WAS LOOKING FOR YOU! THERE'S SOMETHING I WANT TO ASK OF YOU!
HUH..? WHY, WHAT IS IT, MR. PEMBERTON?
THIS IS MY SON, SYLVESTER! I WAS THINKING HE MIGHT SECURE A POSITION IN YOUR BANK!
I MUST WARN YOU, MR. BILKER... I DESPISE WORK!
I'LL SEE WHAT I CAN DO FOR YOU, MR. PEMBERTON... IF YOU'LL JUST WAIT IN MY OFFICE A MOMENT...
THEY WOULD COME AT A TIME LIKE THIS! BUT I CAN'T INSULT MR. PEMBERTON... HE'S TOO IMPORTANT A DEPOSITOR!
SO I'LL JUST STEP OUT OF THE WAY FOR A FEW MOMENTS... THERE'S GOING TO BE SHOOTING, AND I DON'T WANT TO BE HIT BY ANY STRAY BULLETS! IT'LL BE SIMPLER IF I'M OUT WHILE THE ROBBERY IS ACTUALLY COMMITTED!
3

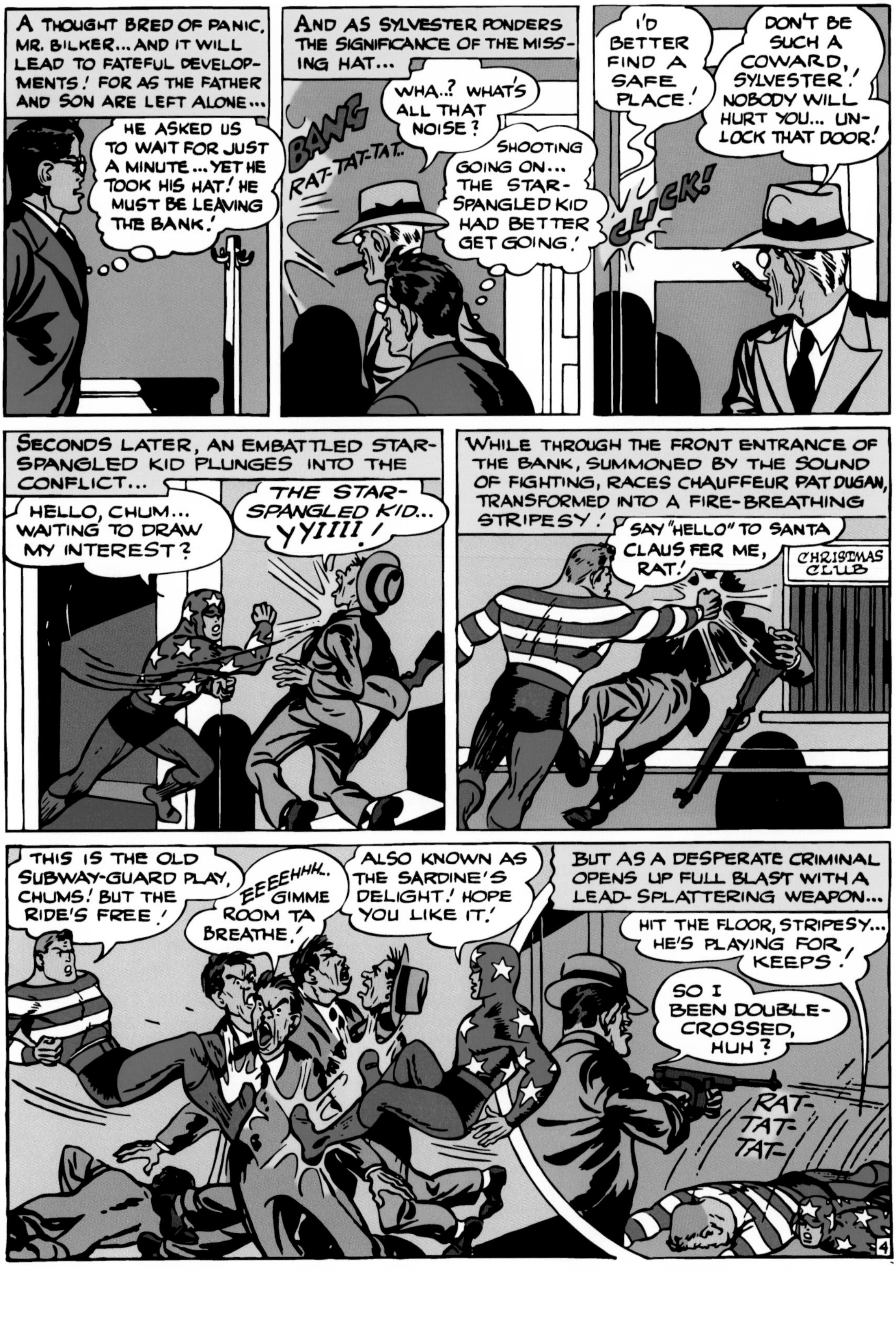
A THOUGHT BRED OF PANIC, MR. BILKER... AND IT WILL LEAD TO FATEFUL DEVELOPMENTS! FOR AS THE FATHER AND SON ARE LEFT ALONE...
HE ASKED US TO WAIT FOR JUST A MINUTE... YET HE TOOK HIS HAT! HE MUST BE LEAVING THE BANK!
AND AS SYLVESTER PONDERS THE SIGNIFICANCE OF THE MISSING HAT...
BANG
RAT-TAT-TAT..
WHA..? WHAT'S ALL THAT NOISE?
SHOOTING GOING ON... THE STAR-SPANGLED KID HAD BETTER GET GOING!
I'D BETTER FIND A SAFE PLACE!
DON'T BE SUCH A COWARD, SYLVESTER! NOBODY WILL HURT YOU... UNLOCK THAT DOOR!
CLICK!
SECONDS LATER, AN EMBATTLED STAR-SPANGLED KID PLUNGES INTO THE CONFLICT...
HELLO, CHUM... WAITING TO DRAW MY INTEREST?
THE STAR-SPANGLED KID... YYIIII!
WHILE THROUGH THE FRONT ENTRANCE OF THE BANK, SUMMONED BY THE SOUND OF FIGHTING, RACES CHAUFFEUR PAT DUGAN, TRANSFORMED INTO A FIRE-BREATHING STRIPESY!
SAY "HELLO" TO SANTA CLAUS FER ME, RAT!
CHRISTMAS CLUB
THIS IS THE OLD SUBWAY-GUARD PLAY, CHUMS! BUT THE RIDE'S FREE!
EEEEHHH.. GIMME ROOM TA BREATHE!
ALSO KNOWN AS THE SARDINE'S DELIGHT! HOPE YOU LIKE IT!
BUT AS A DESPERATE CRIMINAL OPENS UP FULL BLAST WITH A LEAD-SPLATTERING WEAPON...
HIT THE FLOOR, STRIPESY... HE'S PLAYING FOR KEEPS!
SO I BEEN DOUBLE-CROSSED, HUH?
RAT-TAT-TAT-
4

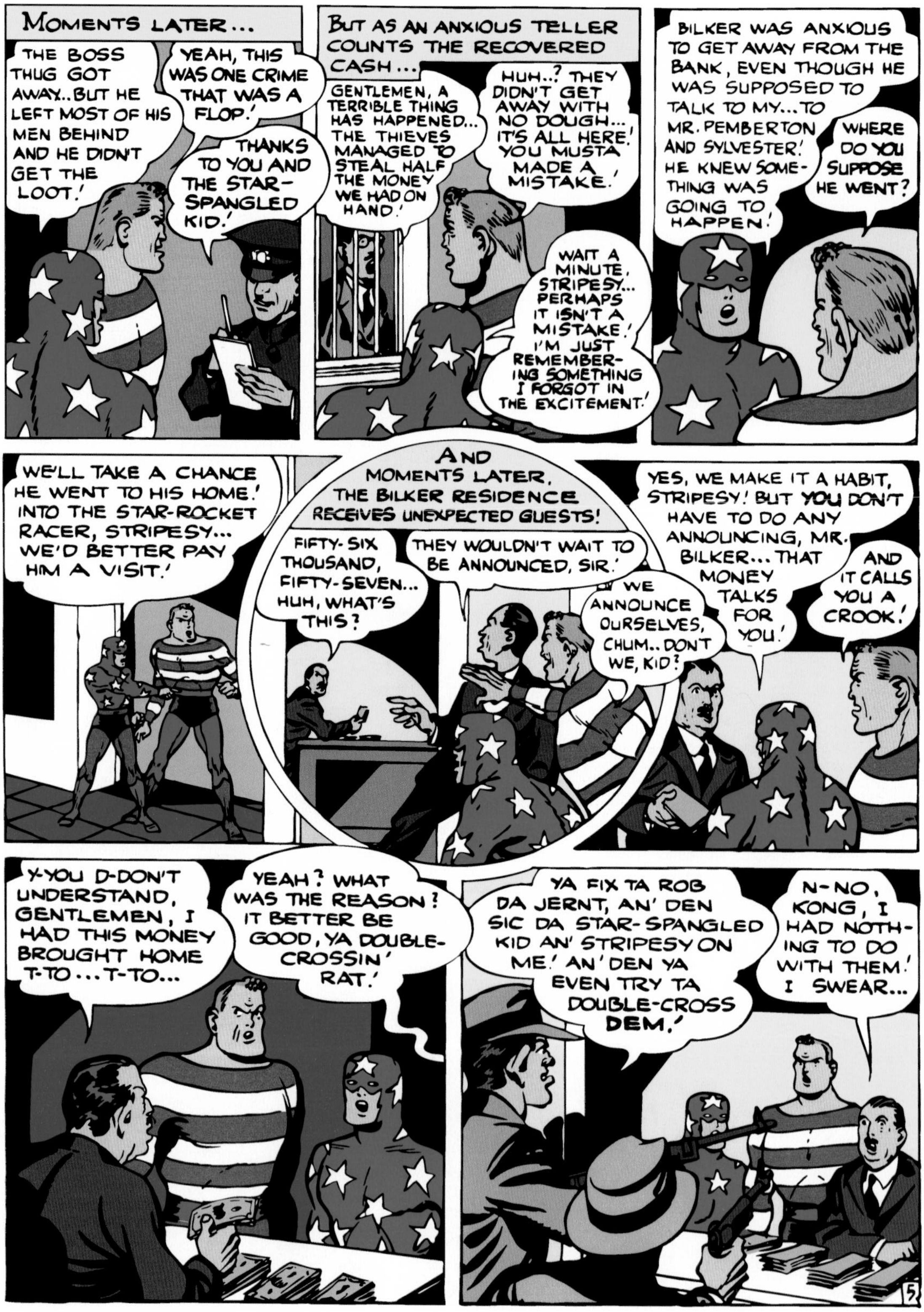
MOMENTS LATER...
THE BOSS THUG GOT AWAY..BUT HE LEFT MOST OF HIS MEN BEHIND AND HE DIDN'T GET THE LOOT!
YEAH, THIS WAS ONE CRIME THAT WAS A FLOP!
THANKS TO YOU AND THE STAR-SPANGLED KID!
BUT AS AN ANXIOUS TELLER COUNTS THE RECOVERED CASH...
GENTLEMEN, A TERRIBLE THING HAS HAPPENED... THE THIEVES MANAGED TO STEAL HALF THE MONEY WE HAD ON HAND!
HUH..? THEY DIDN'T GET AWAY WITH NO DOUGH... IT'S ALL HERE! YOU MUSTA MADE A MISTAKE!
WAIT A MINUTE, STRIPESY... PERHAPS IT ISN'T A MISTAKE! I'M JUST REMEMBERING SOMETHING I FORGOT IN THE EXCITEMENT!
BILKER WAS ANXIOUS TO GET AWAY FROM THE BANK, EVEN THOUGH HE WAS SUPPOSED TO TALK TO MY...TO MR. PEMBERTON AND SYLVESTER! HE KNEW SOMETHING WAS GOING TO HAPPEN!
WHERE DO YOU SUPPOSE HE WENT?
WE'LL TAKE A CHANCE HE WENT TO HIS HOME! INTO THE STAR-ROCKET RACER, STRIPESY... WE'D BETTER PAY HIM A VISIT!
AND MOMENTS LATER, THE BILKER RESIDENCE RECEIVES UNEXPECTED GUESTS!
FIFTY-SIX THOUSAND, FIFTY-SEVEN... HUH, WHAT'S THIS?
THEY WOULDN'T WAIT TO BE ANNOUNCED, SIR!
WE ANNOUNCE OURSELVES, CHUM.. DON'T WE, KID?
YES, WE MAKE IT A HABIT, STRIPESY! BUT YOU DON'T HAVE TO DO ANY ANNOUNCING, MR. BILKER... THAT MONEY TALKS FOR YOU!
AND IT CALLS YOU A CROOK!
Y-YOU D-DON'T UNDERSTAND, GENTLEMEN, I HAD THIS MONEY BROUGHT HOME T-TO... T-TO...
YEAH? WHAT WAS THE REASON? IT BETTER BE GOOD, YA DOUBLE-CROSSIN' RAT!
YA FIX TA ROB DA JERNT, AN' DEN SIC DA STAR-SPANGLED KID AN' STRIPESY ON ME! AN' DEN YA EVEN TRY TA DOUBLE-CROSS DEM!
N-NO, KONG, I HAD NOTHING TO DO WITH THEM! I SWEAR...
5

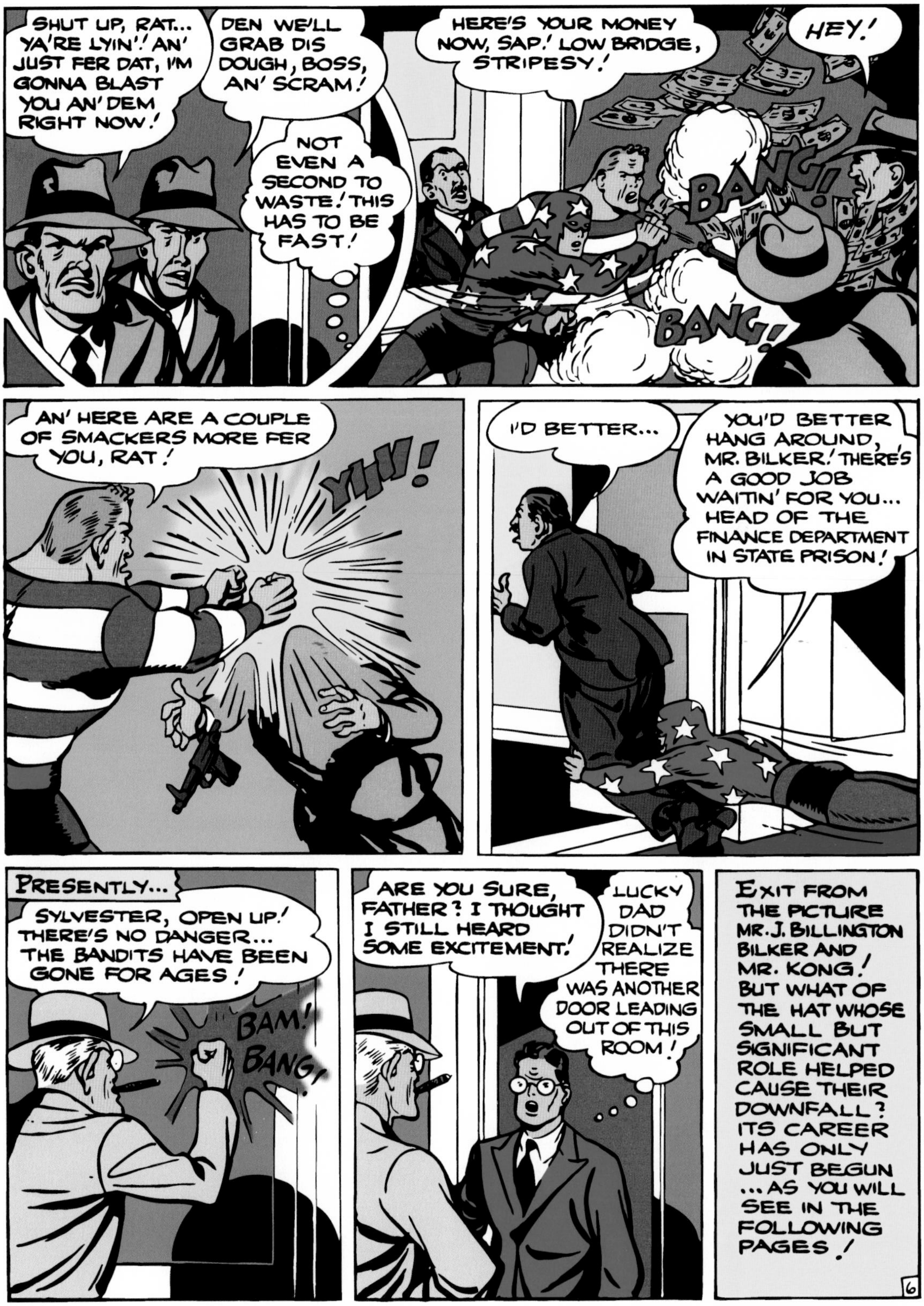
SHUT UP, RAT... YA'RE LYIN'! AN' JUST FER DAT, I'M GONNA BLAST YOU AN' DEM RIGHT NOW!
DEN WE'LL GRAB DIS DOUGH, BOSS, AN' SCRAM!
NOT EVEN A SECOND TO WASTE! THIS HAS TO BE FAST!
HERE'S YOUR MONEY NOW, SAP! LOW BRIDGE, STRIPESY!
HEY!
BANG!
BANG!
AN' HERE ARE A COUPLE OF SMACKERS MORE FER YOU, RAT!
YIII!
I'D BETTER...
YOU'D BETTER HANG AROUND, MR. BILKER! THERE'S A GOOD JOB WAITIN' FOR YOU... HEAD OF THE FINANCE DEPARTMENT IN STATE PRISON!
PRESENTLY...
SYLVESTER, OPEN UP! THERE'S NO DANGER... THE BANDITS HAVE BEEN GONE FOR AGES!
BAM! BANG!
ARE YOU SURE, FATHER? I THOUGHT I STILL HEARD SOME EXCITEMENT!
LUCKY DAD DIDN'T REALIZE THERE WAS ANOTHER DOOR LEADING OUT OF THIS ROOM!
EXIT FROM THE PICTURE MR. J. BILLINGTON BILKER AND MR. KONG! BUT WHAT OF THE HAT WHOSE SMALL BUT SIGNIFICANT ROLE HELPED CAUSE THEIR DOWNFALL? ITS CAREER HAS ONLY JUST BEGUN ...AS YOU WILL SEE IN THE FOLLOWING PAGES!
6

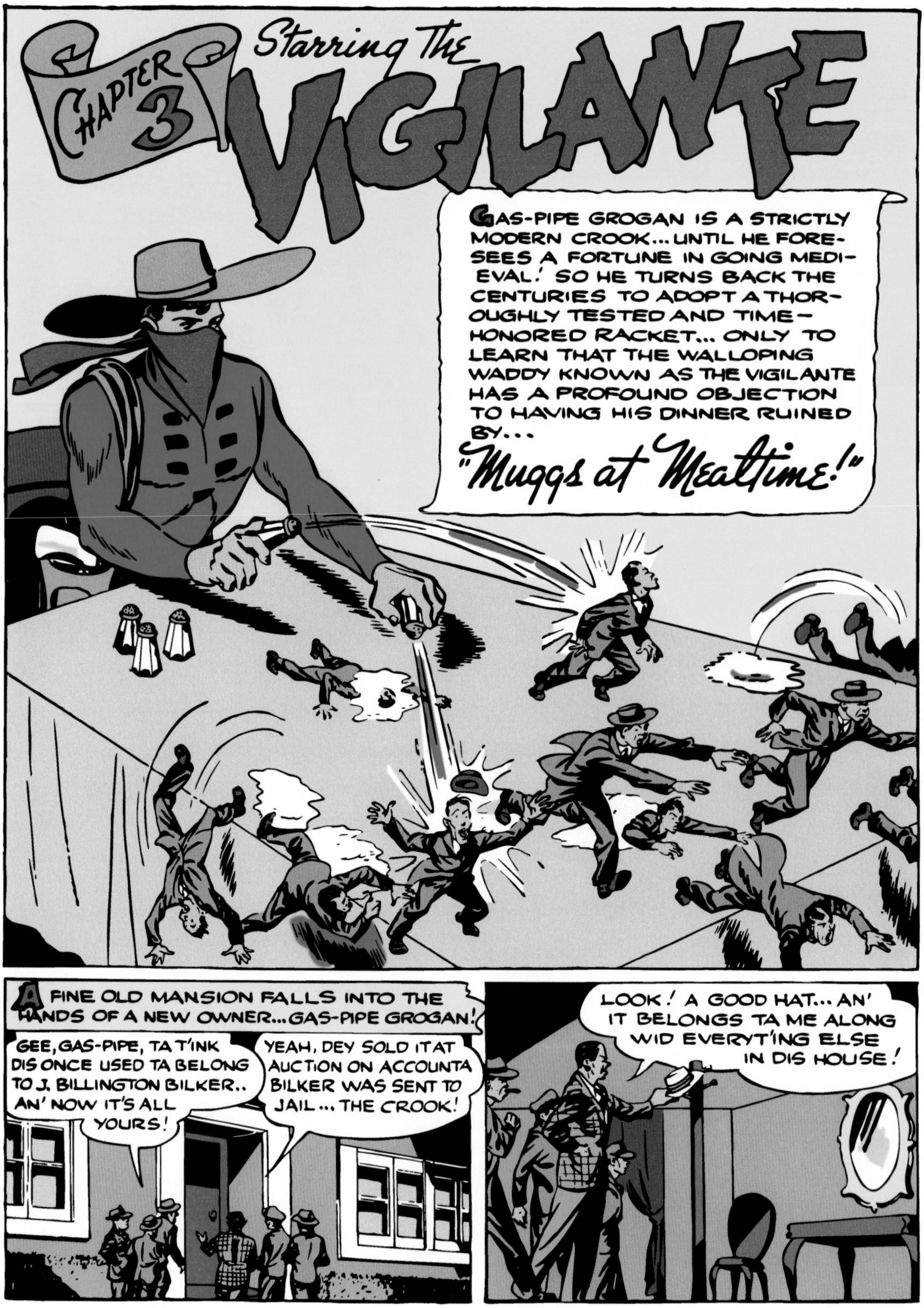
CHAPTER 3
Starring The
VIGILANTE
GAS-PIPE GROGAN IS A STRICTLY MODERN CROOK... UNTIL HE FORESEES A FORTUNE IN GOING MEDIEVAL! SO HE TURNS BACK THE CENTURIES TO ADOPT A THOROUGHLY TESTED AND TIME-HONORED RACKET... ONLY TO LEARN THAT THE WALLOPING WADDY KNOWN AS THE VIGILANTE HAS A PROFOUND OBJECTION TO HAVING HIS DINNER RUINED BY...
"Muggs at Mealtime!"
A FINE OLD MANSION FALLS INTO THE HANDS OF A NEW OWNER...GAS-PIPE GROGAN!
GEE, GAS-PIPE, TA T'INK DIS ONCE USED TA BELONG TO J. BILLINGTON BILKER.. AN' NOW IT'S ALL YOURS!
YEAH, DEY SOLD IT AT AUCTION ON ACCOUNTA BILKER WAS SENT TO JAIL... THE CROOK!
LOOK! A GOOD HAT... AN' IT BELONGS TA ME ALONG WID EVERYT'ING ELSE IN DIS HOUSE!

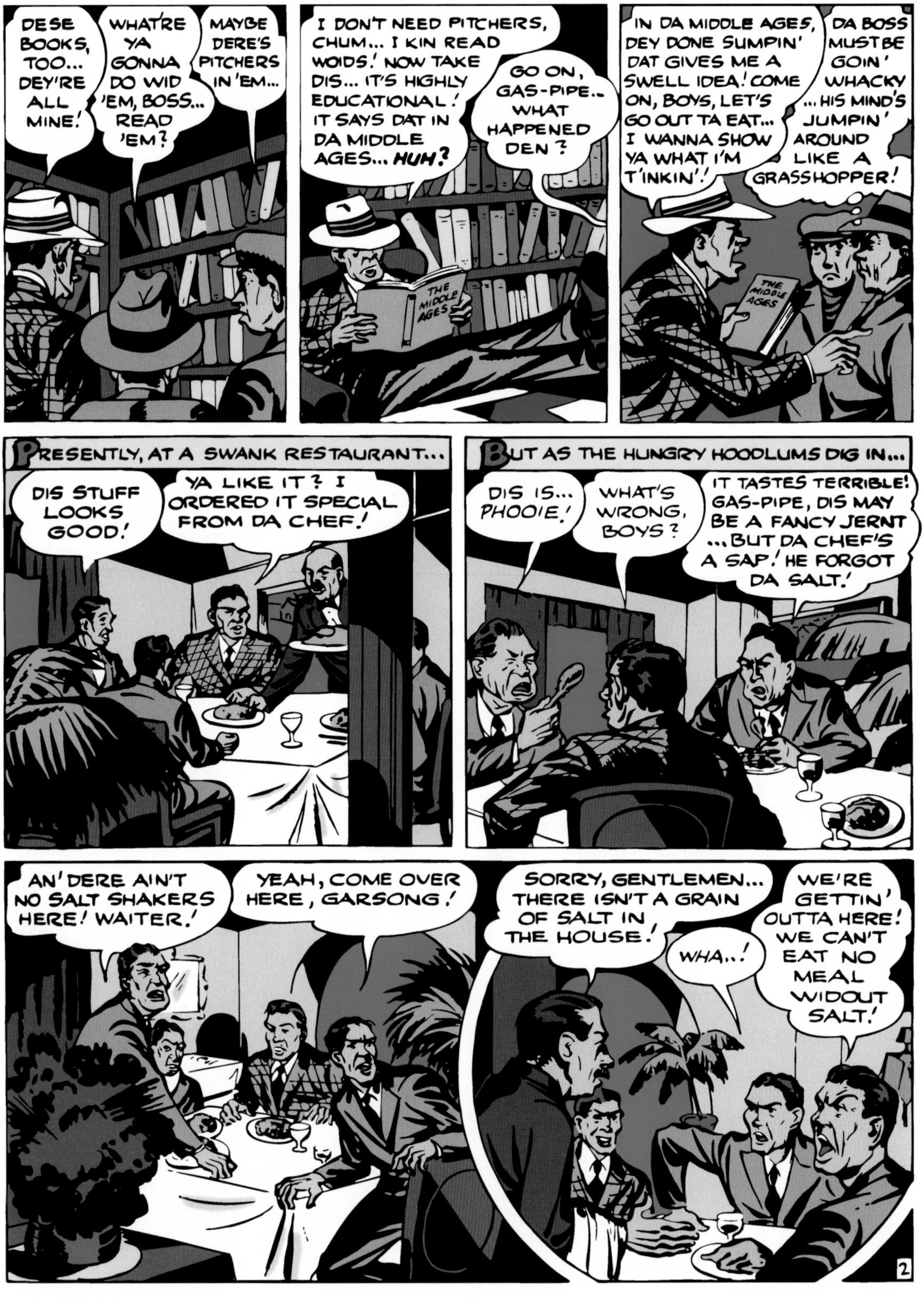
DESE BOOKS, TOO... DEY'RE ALL MINE!
WHAT'RE YA GONNA DO WID 'EM, BOSS... READ 'EM?
MAYBE DERE'S PITCHERS IN 'EM...
I DON'T NEED PITCHERS, CHUM... I KIN READ WOIDS! NOW TAKE DIS... IT'S HIGHLY EDUCATIONAL! IT SAYS DAT IN DA MIDDLE AGES... HUH?
GO ON, GAS-PIPE.. WHAT HAPPENED DEN?
THE MIDDLE AGES
IN DA MIDDLE AGES, DEY DONE SUMPIN' DAT GIVES ME A SWELL IDEA! COME ON, BOYS, LET'S GO OUT TA EAT... I WANNA SHOW YA WHAT I'M T'INKIN'!
DA BOSS MUST BE GOIN' WHACKY ...HIS MIND'S JUMPIN' AROUND LIKE A GRASSHOPPER!
THE MIDDLE AGES
PRESENTLY, AT A SWANK RESTAURANT...
DIS STUFF LOOKS GOOD!
YA LIKE IT? I ORDERED IT SPECIAL FROM DA CHEF!
BUT AS THE HUNGRY HOODLUMS DIG IN...
DIS IS... PHOOIE!
WHAT'S WRONG, BOYS?
IT TASTES TERRIBLE! GAS-PIPE, DIS MAY BE A FANCY JERNT ...BUT DA CHEF'S A SAP! HE FORGOT DA SALT!
AN' DERE AIN'T NO SALT SHAKERS HERE! WAITER!
YEAH, COME OVER HERE, GARSONG!
SORRY, GENTLEMEN... THERE ISN'T A GRAIN OF SALT IN THE HOUSE!
WHA..!
WE'RE GETTIN' OUTTA HERE! WE CAN'T EAT NO MEAL WIDOUT SALT!
2

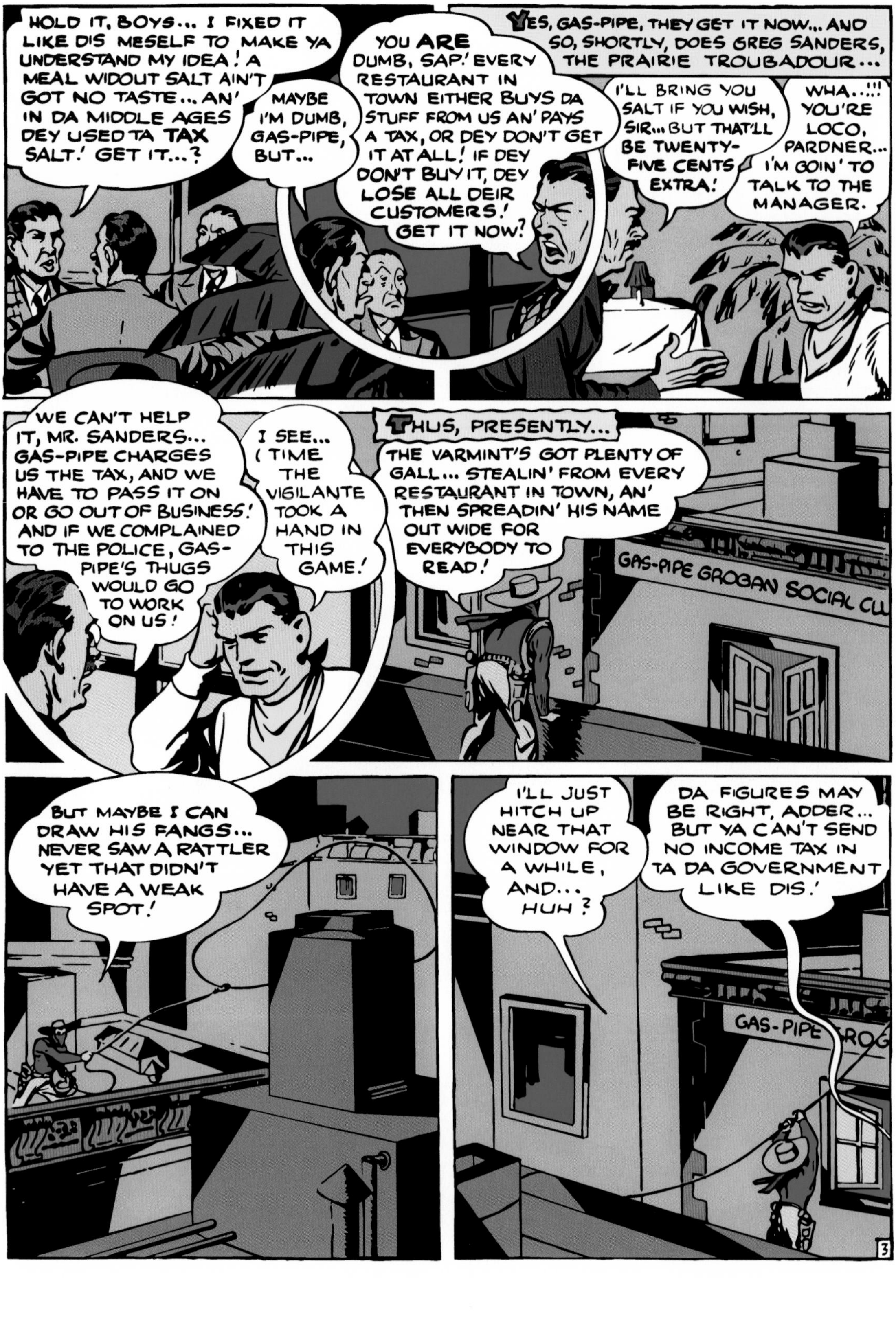
HOLD IT, BOYS... I FIXED IT LIKE DIS MESELF TO MAKE YA UNDERSTAND MY IDEA! A MEAL WIDOUT SALT AIN'T GOT NO TASTE... AN' IN DA MIDDLE AGES DEY USED TA TAX SALT! GET IT...?
MAYBE I'M DUMB, GAS-PIPE, BUT...
YOU ARE DUMB, SAP! EVERY RESTAURANT IN TOWN EITHER BUYS DA STUFF FROM US AN' PAYS A TAX, OR DEY DON'T GET IT AT ALL! IF DEY DON'T BUY IT, DEY LOSE ALL DEIR CUSTOMERS! GET IT NOW?
YES, GAS-PIPE, THEY GET IT NOW... AND SO, SHORTLY, DOES GREG SANDERS, THE PRAIRIE TROUBADOUR...
I'LL BRING YOU SALT IF YOU WISH, SIR... BUT THAT'LL BE TWENTY-FIVE CENTS EXTRA!
WHA..!!! YOU'RE LOCO, PARDNER... I'M GOIN' TO TALK TO THE MANAGER.
WE CAN'T HELP IT, MR. SANDERS... GAS-PIPE CHARGES US THE TAX, AND WE HAVE TO PASS IT ON OR GO OUT OF BUSINESS! AND IF WE COMPLAINED TO THE POLICE, GAS-PIPE'S THUGS WOULD GO TO WORK ON US!
I SEE... (TIME THE VIGILANTE TOOK A HAND IN THIS GAME!
THUS, PRESENTLY...
THE VARMINT'S GOT PLENTY OF GALL... STEALIN' FROM EVERY RESTAURANT IN TOWN, AN' THEN SPREADIN' HIS NAME OUT WIDE FOR EVERYBODY TO READ!
GAS-PIPE GROGAN SOCIAL CL
BUT MAYBE I CAN DRAW HIS FANGS... NEVER SAW A RATTLER YET THAT DIDN'T HAVE A WEAK SPOT!
I'LL JUST HITCH UP NEAR THAT WINDOW FOR A WHILE, AND... HUH?
DA FIGURES MAY BE RIGHT, ADDER... BUT YA CAN'T SEND NO INCOME TAX IN TA DA GOVERNMENT LIKE DIS!
GAS-PIPE GROG
3

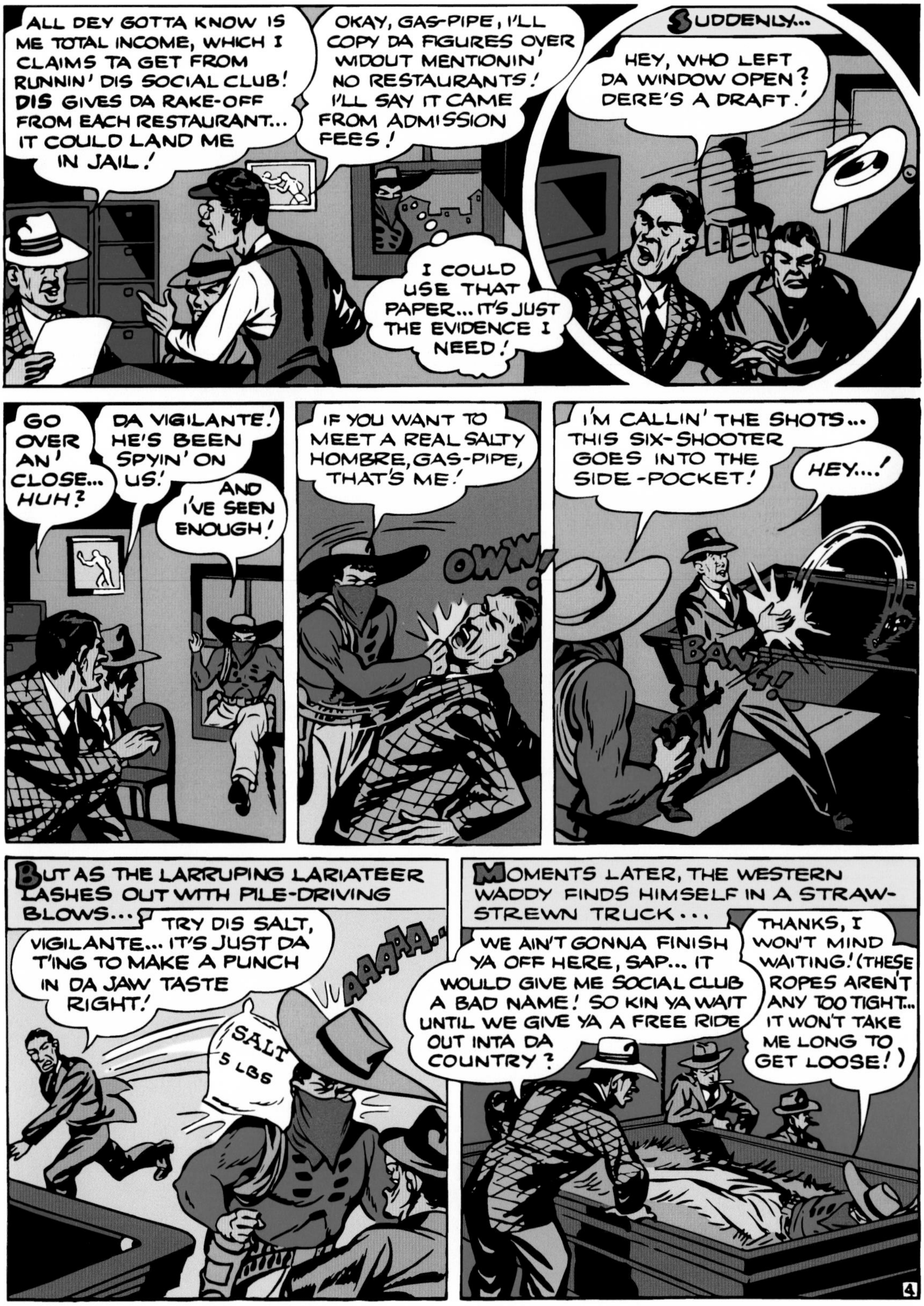
ALL DEY GOTTA KNOW IS ME TOTAL INCOME, WHICH I CLAIMS TA GET FROM RUNNIN' DIS SOCIAL CLUB! DIS GIVES DA RAKE-OFF FROM EACH RESTAURANT... IT COULD LAND ME IN JAIL!
OKAY, GAS-PIPE, I'LL COPY DA FIGURES OVER WIDOUT MENTIONIN' NO RESTAURANTS! I'LL SAY IT CAME FROM ADMISSION FEES!
I COULD USE THAT PAPER... IT'S JUST THE EVIDENCE I NEED!
SUDDENLY...
HEY, WHO LEFT DA WINDOW OPEN? DERE'S A DRAFT!
GO OVER AN' CLOSE... HUH?
DA VIGILANTE! HE'S BEEN SPYIN' ON US!
AND I'VE SEEN ENOUGH!
IF YOU WANT TO MEET A REAL SALTY HOMBRE, GAS-PIPE, THAT'S ME!
OWW!
I'M CALLIN' THE SHOTS... THIS SIX-SHOOTER GOES INTO THE SIDE-POCKET!
HEY...!
BANG!
BUT AS THE LARRUPING LARIATEER LASHES OUT WITH PILE-DRIVING BLOWS...
TRY DIS SALT, VIGILANTE... IT'S JUST DA T'ING TO MAKE A PUNCH IN DA JAW TASTE RIGHT!
AAAAA...
SALT 5 LBS
MOMENTS LATER, THE WESTERN WADDY FINDS HIMSELF IN A STRAW-STREWN TRUCK...
WE AIN'T GONNA FINISH YA OFF HERE, SAP... IT WOULD GIVE ME SOCIAL CLUB A BAD NAME! SO KIN YA WAIT UNTIL WE GIVE YA A FREE RIDE OUT INTA DA COUNTRY?
THANKS, I WON'T MIND WAITING! (THESE ROPES AREN'T ANY TOO TIGHT... IT WON'T TAKE ME LONG TO GET LOOSE!)
4

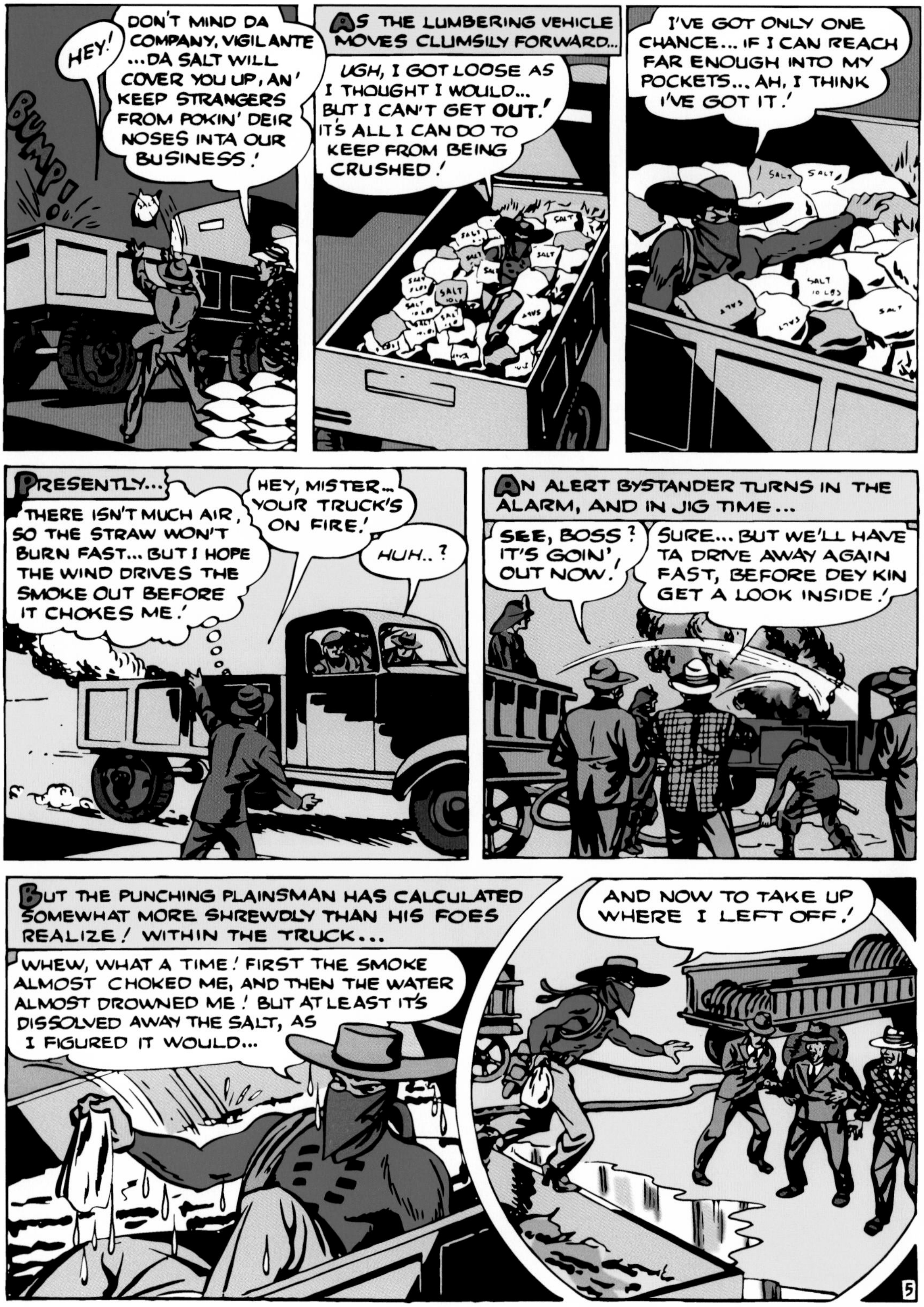
HEY!
DON'T MIND DA COMPANY, VIGILANTE ...DA SALT WILL COVER YOU UP, AN' KEEP STRANGERS FROM POKIN' DEIR NOSES INTA OUR BUSINESS!
BUMP!
AS THE LUMBERING VEHICLE MOVES CLUMSILY FORWARD...
UGH, I GOT LOOSE AS I THOUGHT I WOULD... BUT I CAN'T GET OUT! IT'S ALL I CAN DO TO KEEP FROM BEING CRUSHED!
I'VE GOT ONLY ONE CHANCE... IF I CAN REACH FAR ENOUGH INTO MY POCKETS... AH, I THINK I'VE GOT IT!
PRESENTLY...
THERE ISN'T MUCH AIR, SO THE STRAW WON'T BURN FAST... BUT I HOPE THE WIND DRIVES THE SMOKE OUT BEFORE IT CHOKES ME!
HEY, MISTER... YOUR TRUCK'S ON FIRE!
HUH..?
AN ALERT BYSTANDER TURNS IN THE ALARM, AND IN JIG TIME...
SEE, BOSS? IT'S GOIN' OUT NOW!
SURE... BUT WE'LL HAVE TA DRIVE AWAY AGAIN FAST, BEFORE DEY KIN GET A LOOK INSIDE!
BUT THE PUNCHING PLAINSMAN HAS CALCULATED SOMEWHAT MORE SHREWDLY THAN HIS FOES REALIZE! WITHIN THE TRUCK...
WHEW, WHAT A TIME! FIRST THE SMOKE ALMOST CHOKED ME, AND THEN THE WATER ALMOST DROWNED ME! BUT AT LEAST IT'S DISSOLVED AWAY THE SALT, AS I FIGURED IT WOULD...
AND NOW TO TAKE UP WHERE I LEFT OFF!
5

HOW DO YOU LIKE THIS SACK IN THE JAW, DIAMOND-BACK?

AS THE REMAINING CRIMINALS ATTEMPT FLIGHT...

LOOKS LIKE YOU'RE ALL WET, PARDNER!

HEY...!!!

SECONDS LATER... YA CAN'T HOLD US, VIGILANTE, BECAUSE YA CAN'T PROVE WE DONE NOTHIN'! ME LAWYER WILL GET US OUTTA JAIL IN NO TIME!

I KINDA DOUBT THAT, VARMINT ... BECAUSE BEFORE I'M FINISHED WITH YOU, I'M GOIN' TO HAVE PROOF OF WHAT YOU'VE DONE!

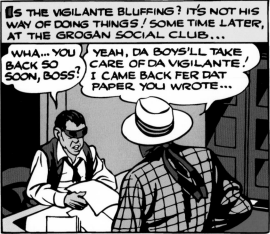

IS THE VIGILANTE BLUFFING? IT'S NOT HIS WAY OF DOING THINGS! SOME TIME LATER, AT THE GROGAN SOCIAL CLUB...

WHA... YOU BACK SO SOON, BOSS?

YEAH, DA BOYS'LL TAKE CARE OF DA VIGILANTE! I CAME BACK FER DAT PAPER YOU WROTE...

I FINISHED COPYIN' DA FIGURES, AN' I WAS JUST GONNA TEAR IT UP, BUT HERE IT IS...WHA..? YOU AIN'T...

THANKS, PARDNER... I AIN'T! I WAS JUST WEARING HIS HAT!

OKAY, WISE GUY, YOU ASKED FER IT!

BAD EYE, VARMINT... YUH HIT YOUR BOSS'S HAT, NOT ME!

BANG!

BUT *I* DON'T MISS!

AAAA...

FINIS TO THE CAREER OF GAS-PIPE GROGAN! THE HARD-LUCK HAT HAS BROUGHT HIM HIS QUOTA OF MISFORTUNE... AND THOUGH IT HAS ACQUIRED A PAIR OF BULLETHOLES IN THE PROCESS, THESE ARE MORE EASILY MENDED THAN THE WRECK IT HAS MADE, AND IS STILL DESTINED TO MAKE, IN THE LIVES OF MEN!

6

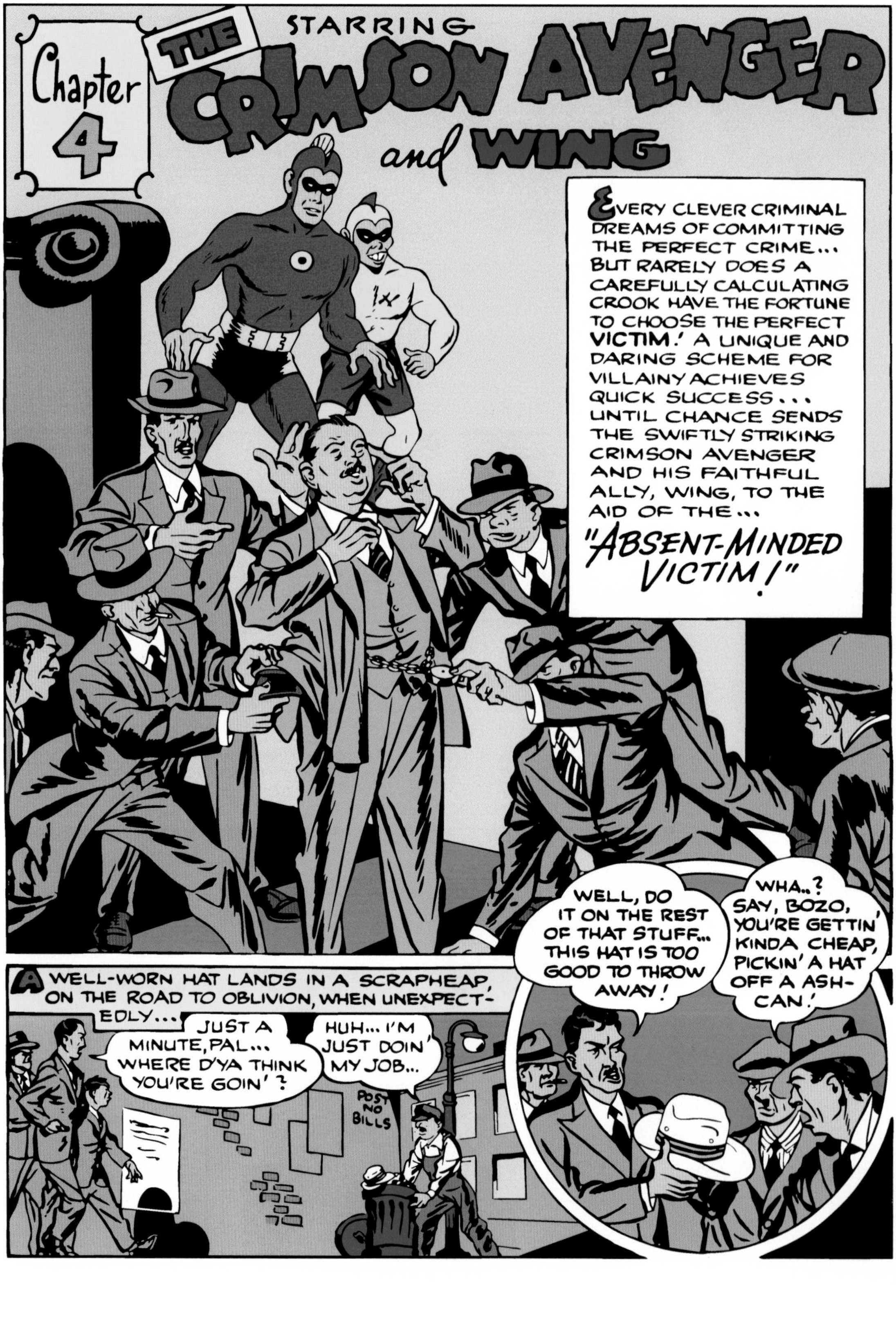
Chapter 4
STARRING
THE CRIMSON AVENGER and WING
EVERY CLEVER CRIMINAL DREAMS OF COMMITTING THE PERFECT CRIME... BUT RARELY DOES A CAREFULLY CALCULATING CROOK HAVE THE FORTUNE TO CHOOSE THE PERFECT VICTIM! A UNIQUE AND DARING SCHEME FOR VILLAINY ACHIEVES QUICK SUCCESS... UNTIL CHANCE SENDS THE SWIFTLY STRIKING CRIMSON AVENGER AND HIS FAITHFUL ALLY, WING, TO THE AID OF THE...
"ABSENT-MINDED VICTIM!"
A WELL-WORN HAT LANDS IN A SCRAPHEAP, ON THE ROAD TO OBLIVION, WHEN UNEXPECTEDLY...
JUST A MINUTE, PAL... WHERE D'YA THINK YOU'RE GOIN'?
HUH... I'M JUST DOIN' MY JOB...
POST NO BILLS
WELL, DO IT ON THE REST OF THAT STUFF... THIS HAT IS TOO GOOD TO THROW AWAY!
WHA..? SAY, BOZO, YOU'RE GETTIN' KINDA CHEAP, PICKIN' A HAT OFF A ASH-CAN!

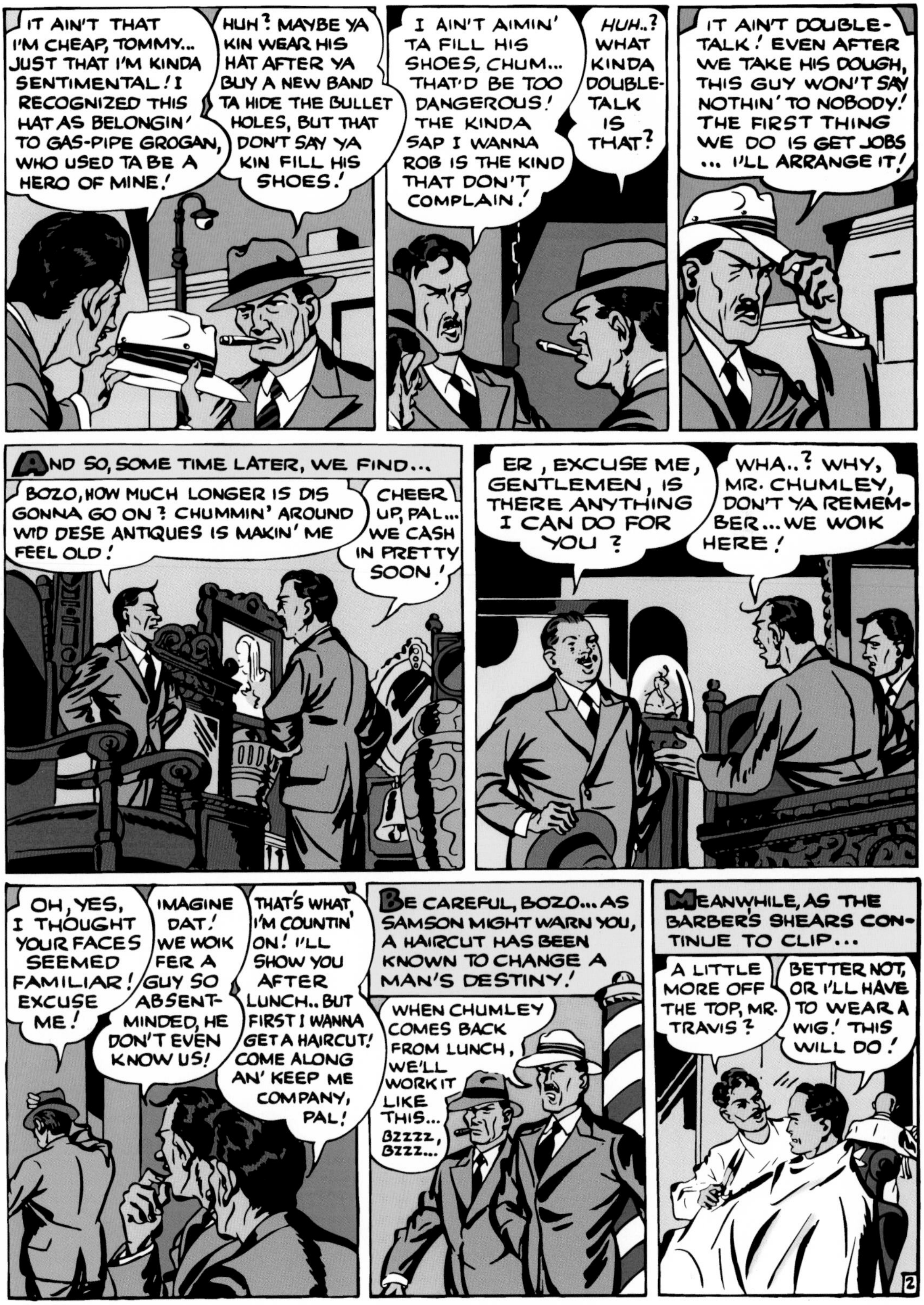
IT AIN'T THAT I'M CHEAP, TOMMY... JUST THAT I'M KINDA SENTIMENTAL! I RECOGNIZED THIS HAT AS BELONGIN' TO GAS-PIPE GROGAN, WHO USED TA BE A HERO OF MINE!
HUH? MAYBE YA KIN WEAR HIS HAT AFTER YA BUY A NEW BAND TA HIDE THE BULLET HOLES, BUT THAT DON'T SAY YA KIN FILL HIS SHOES!
I AIN'T AIMIN' TA FILL HIS SHOES, CHUM... THAT'D BE TOO DANGEROUS! THE KINDA SAP I WANNA ROB IS THE KIND THAT DON'T COMPLAIN!
HUH..? WHAT KINDA DOUBLE-TALK IS THAT?
IT AIN'T DOUBLE-TALK! EVEN AFTER WE TAKE HIS DOUGH, THIS GUY WON'T SAY NOTHIN' TO NOBODY! THE FIRST THING WE DO IS GET JOBS ... I'LL ARRANGE IT!
AND SO, SOME TIME LATER, WE FIND...
BOZO, HOW MUCH LONGER IS DIS GONNA GO ON? CHUMMIN' AROUND WID DESE ANTIQUES IS MAKIN' ME FEEL OLD!
CHEER UP, PAL... WE CASH IN PRETTY SOON!
ER, EXCUSE ME, GENTLEMEN, IS THERE ANYTHING I CAN DO FOR YOU?
WHA..? WHY, MR. CHUMLEY, DON'T YA REMEMBER... WE WOIK HERE!
OH, YES, I THOUGHT YOUR FACES SEEMED FAMILIAR! EXCUSE ME!
IMAGINE DAT! WE WOIK FER A GUY SO ABSENT-MINDED, HE DON'T EVEN KNOW US!
THAT'S WHAT I'M COUNTIN' ON! I'LL SHOW YOU AFTER LUNCH.. BUT FIRST I WANNA GET A HAIRCUT! COME ALONG AN' KEEP ME COMPANY, PAL!
BE CAREFUL, BOZO... AS SAMSON MIGHT WARN YOU, A HAIRCUT HAS BEEN KNOWN TO CHANGE A MAN'S DESTINY!
WHEN CHUMLEY COMES BACK FROM LUNCH, WE'LL WORK IT LIKE THIS... BZZZZ, BZZZ...
MEANWHILE, AS THE BARBER'S SHEARS CONTINUE TO CLIP...
A LITTLE MORE OFF THE TOP, MR. TRAVIS?
BETTER NOT, OR I'LL HAVE TO WEAR A WIG! THIS WILL DO!
2

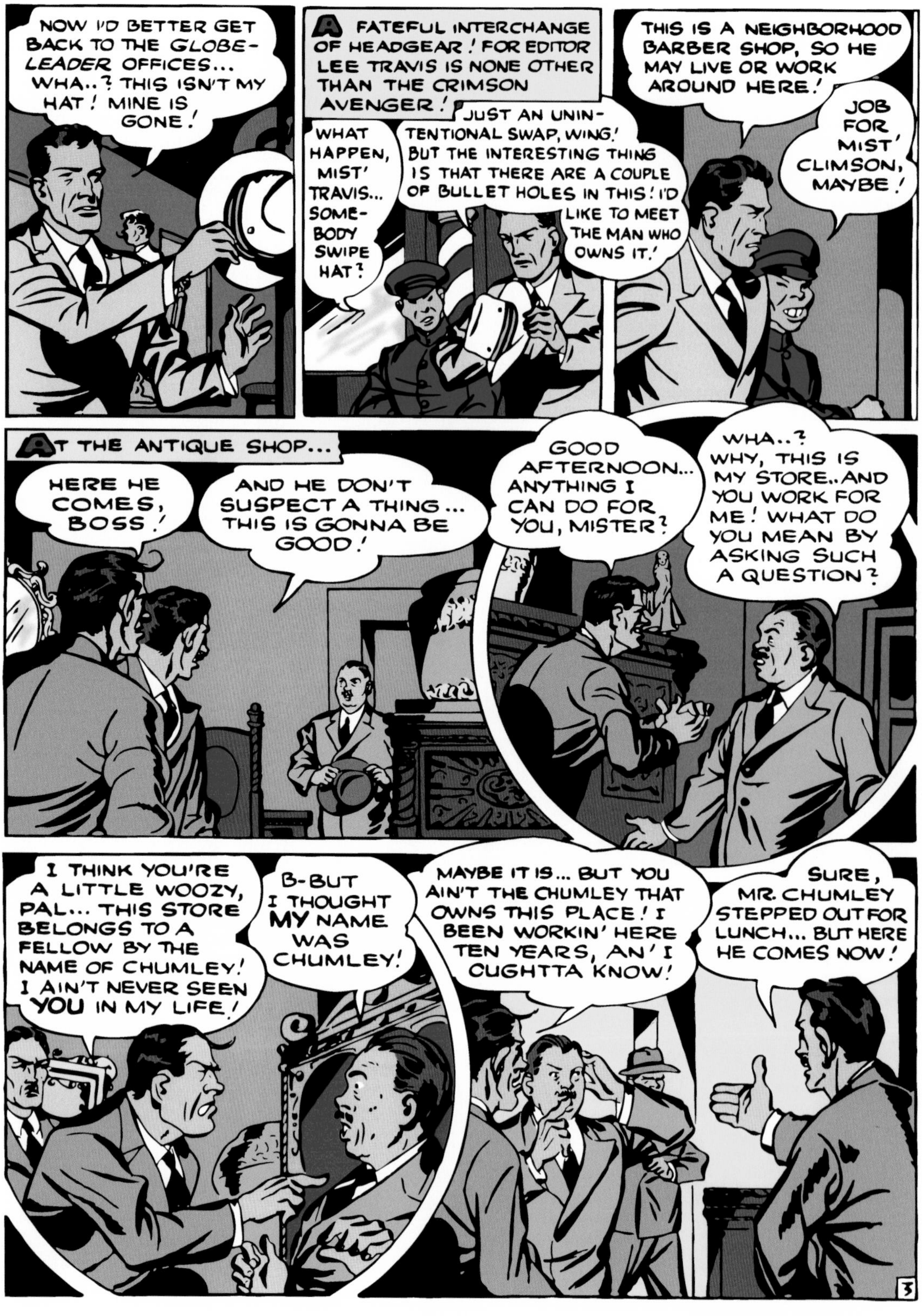
NOW I'D BETTER GET BACK TO THE GLOBE-LEADER OFFICES... WHA..? THIS ISN'T MY HAT! MINE IS GONE!
A FATEFUL INTERCHANGE OF HEADGEAR! FOR EDITOR LEE TRAVIS IS NONE OTHER THAN THE CRIMSON AVENGER!
WHAT HAPPEN, MIST' TRAVIS... SOMEBODY SWIPE HAT?
JUST AN UNINTENTIONAL SWAP, WING! BUT THE INTERESTING THING IS THAT THERE ARE A COUPLE OF BULLET HOLES IN THIS! I'D LIKE TO MEET THE MAN WHO OWNS IT!
THIS IS A NEIGHBORHOOD BARBER SHOP, SO HE MAY LIVE OR WORK AROUND HERE!
JOB FOR, MIST' CLIMSON, MAYBE!
AT THE ANTIQUE SHOP...
HERE HE COMES, BOSS!
AND HE DON'T SUSPECT A THING... THIS IS GONNA BE GOOD!
GOOD AFTERNOON... ANYTHING I CAN DO FOR YOU, MISTER?
WHA..? WHY, THIS IS MY STORE.. AND YOU WORK FOR ME! WHAT DO YOU MEAN BY ASKING SUCH A QUESTION?
I THINK YOU'RE A LITTLE WOOZY, PAL... THIS STORE BELONGS TO A FELLOW BY THE NAME OF CHUMLEY! I AIN'T NEVER SEEN YOU IN MY LIFE!
B-BUT I THOUGHT MY NAME WAS CHUMLEY!
MAYBE IT IS... BUT YOU AIN'T THE CHUMLEY THAT OWNS THIS PLACE! I BEEN WORKIN' HERE TEN YEARS, AN' I OUGHTTA KNOW!
SURE, MR. CHUMLEY STEPPED OUT FOR LUNCH... BUT HERE HE COMES NOW!
3

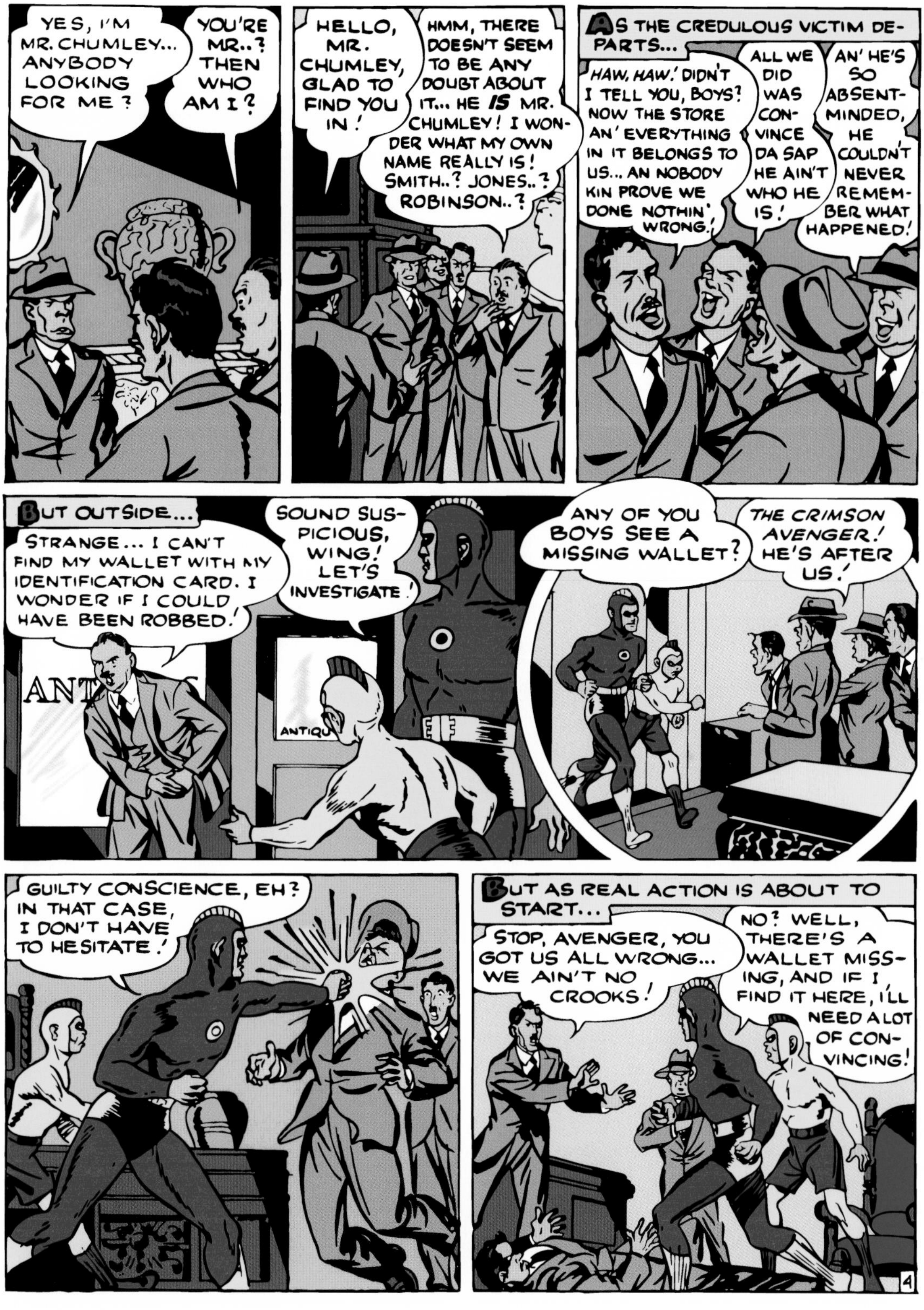
YES, I'M MR. CHUMLEY... ANYBODY LOOKING FOR ME?
YOU'RE MR..? THEN WHO AM I?
HELLO, MR. CHUMLEY, GLAD TO FIND YOU IN!
HMM, THERE DOESN'T SEEM TO BE ANY DOUBT ABOUT IT... HE *IS* MR. CHUMLEY! I WONDER WHAT MY OWN NAME REALLY IS! SMITH..? JONES..? ROBINSON..?
AS THE CREDULOUS VICTIM DEPARTS...
HAW, HAW! DIDN'T I TELL YOU, BOYS? NOW THE STORE AN' EVERYTHING IN IT BELONGS TO US... AN NOBODY KIN PROVE WE DONE NOTHIN' WRONG!
ALL WE DID WAS CONVINCE DA SAP HE AIN'T WHO HE IS!
AN' HE'S SO ABSENT-MINDED, HE COULDN'T NEVER REMEMBER WHAT HAPPENED!
BUT OUTSIDE...
STRANGE... I CAN'T FIND MY WALLET WITH MY IDENTIFICATION CARD. I WONDER IF I COULD HAVE BEEN ROBBED!
ANT
SOUND SUSPICIOUS, WING! LET'S INVESTIGATE!
ANTIQU
ANY OF YOU BOYS SEE A MISSING WALLET?
THE CRIMSON AVENGER! HE'S AFTER US!
GUILTY CONSCIENCE, EH? IN THAT CASE, I DON'T HAVE TO HESITATE!
BUT AS REAL ACTION IS ABOUT TO START...
STOP, AVENGER, YOU GOT US ALL WRONG... WE AIN'T NO CROOKS!
NO? WELL, THERE'S A WALLET MISSING, AND IF I FIND IT HERE, I'LL NEED A LOT OF CONVINCING!
4

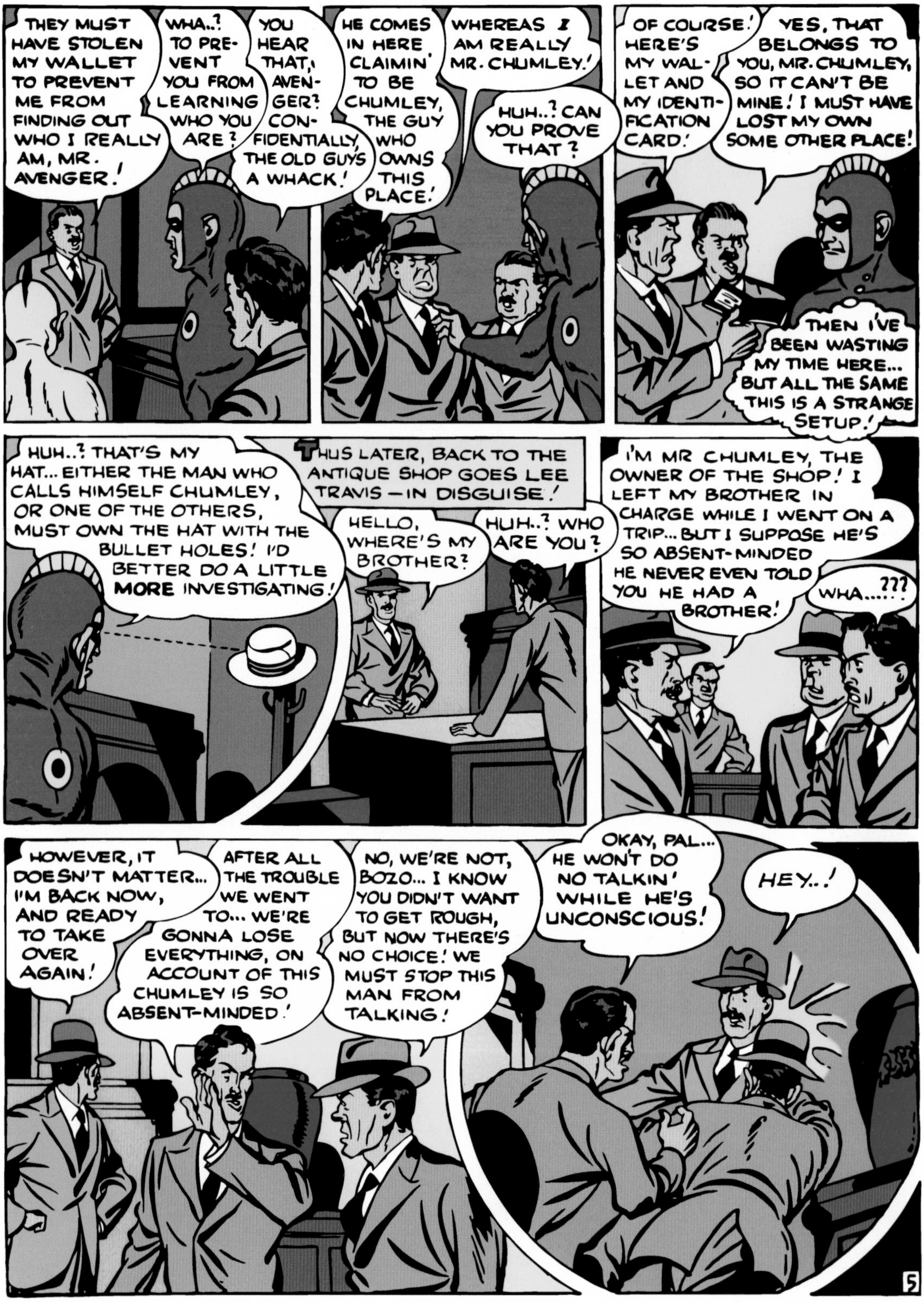
THEY MUST HAVE STOLEN MY WALLET TO PREVENT ME FROM FINDING OUT WHO I REALLY AM, MR. AVENGER!
WHA..? TO PREVENT YOU FROM LEARNING WHO YOU ARE?
YOU HEAR THAT, AVENGER? CONFIDENTIALLY, THE OLD GUY'S A WHACK!
HE COMES IN HERE CLAIMIN' TO BE CHUMLEY, THE GUY WHO OWNS THIS PLACE!
WHEREAS I AM REALLY MR. CHUMLEY!
HUH..? CAN YOU PROVE THAT?
OF COURSE! HERE'S MY WALLET AND MY IDENTIFICATION CARD!
YES, THAT BELONGS TO YOU, MR. CHUMLEY, SO IT CAN'T BE MINE! I MUST HAVE LOST MY OWN SOME OTHER PLACE!
THEN I'VE BEEN WASTING MY TIME HERE... BUT ALL THE SAME THIS IS A STRANGE SETUP!
HUH..? THAT'S MY HAT... EITHER THE MAN WHO CALLS HIMSELF CHUMLEY, OR ONE OF THE OTHERS, MUST OWN THE HAT WITH THE BULLET HOLES! I'D BETTER DO A LITTLE MORE INVESTIGATING!
THUS LATER, BACK TO THE ANTIQUE SHOP GOES LEE TRAVIS — IN DISGUISE!
HELLO, WHERE'S MY BROTHER?
HUH..? WHO ARE YOU?
I'M MR CHUMLEY, THE OWNER OF THE SHOP! I LEFT MY BROTHER IN CHARGE WHILE I WENT ON A TRIP... BUT I SUPPOSE HE'S SO ABSENT-MINDED HE NEVER EVEN TOLD YOU HE HAD A BROTHER!
WHA...???
HOWEVER, IT DOESN'T MATTER... I'M BACK NOW, AND READY TO TAKE OVER AGAIN!
AFTER ALL THE TROUBLE WE WENT TO... WE'RE GONNA LOSE EVERYTHING, ON ACCOUNT OF THIS CHUMLEY IS SO ABSENT-MINDED!
NO, WE'RE NOT, BOZO... I KNOW YOU DIDN'T WANT TO GET ROUGH, BUT NOW THERE'S NO CHOICE! WE MUST STOP THIS MAN FROM TALKING!
OKAY, PAL... HE WON'T DO NO TALKIN' WHILE HE'S UNCONSCIOUS!
HEY..!
5

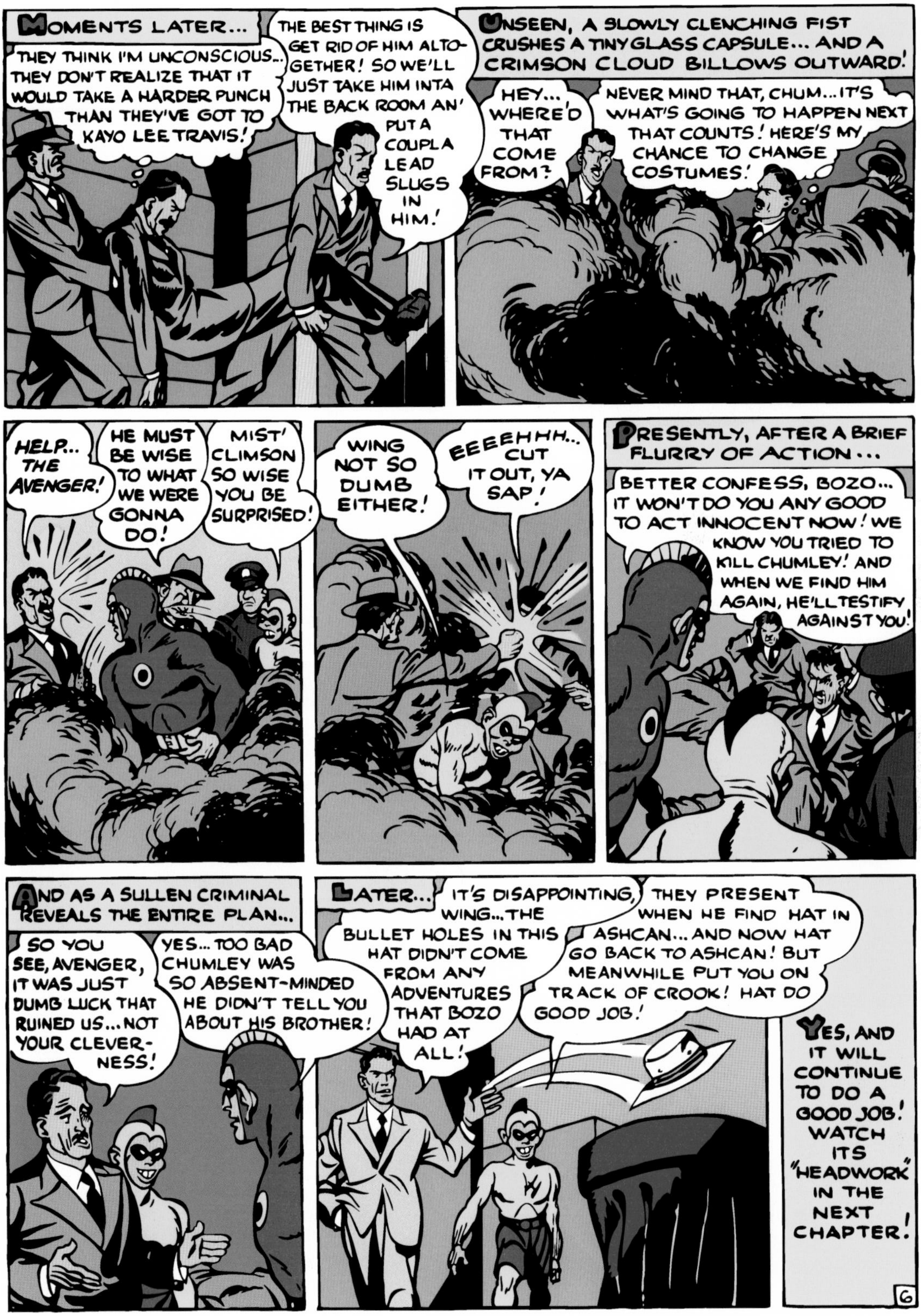
MOMENTS LATER...
THEY THINK I'M UNCONSCIOUS... THEY DON'T REALIZE THAT IT WOULD TAKE A HARDER PUNCH THAN THEY'VE GOT TO KAYO LEE TRAVIS!
THE BEST THING IS GET RID OF HIM ALTOGETHER! SO WE'LL JUST TAKE HIM INTA THE BACK ROOM AN' PUT A COUPLA LEAD SLUGS IN HIM!
UNSEEN, A SLOWLY CLENCHING FIST CRUSHES A TINY GLASS CAPSULE... AND A CRIMSON CLOUD BILLOWS OUTWARD!
HEY... WHERE'D THAT COME FROM?
NEVER MIND THAT, CHUM... IT'S WHAT'S GOING TO HAPPEN NEXT THAT COUNTS! HERE'S MY CHANCE TO CHANGE COSTUMES!
HELP.. THE AVENGER!
HE MUST BE WISE TO WHAT WE WERE GONNA DO!
MIST' CLIMSON SO WISE YOU BE SURPRISED!
WING NOT SO DUMB EITHER!
EEEEHHH... CUT IT OUT, YA SAP!
PRESENTLY, AFTER A BRIEF FLURRY OF ACTION...
BETTER CONFESS, BOZO... IT WON'T DO YOU ANY GOOD TO ACT INNOCENT NOW! WE KNOW YOU TRIED TO KILL CHUMLEY! AND WHEN WE FIND HIM AGAIN, HE'LL TESTIFY AGAINST YOU!
AND AS A SULLEN CRIMINAL REVEALS THE ENTIRE PLAN...
SO YOU SEE, AVENGER, IT WAS JUST DUMB LUCK THAT RUINED US... NOT YOUR CLEVERNESS!
YES... TOO BAD CHUMLEY WAS SO ABSENT-MINDED HE DIDN'T TELL YOU ABOUT HIS BROTHER!
LATER...
IT'S DISAPPOINTING, WING... THE BULLET HOLES IN THIS HAT DIDN'T COME FROM ANY ADVENTURES THAT BOZO HAD AT ALL!
THEY PRESENT WHEN HE FIND HAT IN ASHCAN... AND NOW HAT GO BACK TO ASHCAN! BUT MEANWHILE PUT YOU ON TRACK OF CROOK! HAT DO GOOD JOB!
YES, AND IT WILL CONTINUE TO DO A GOOD JOB! WATCH ITS "HEADWORK" IN THE NEXT CHAPTER!
6

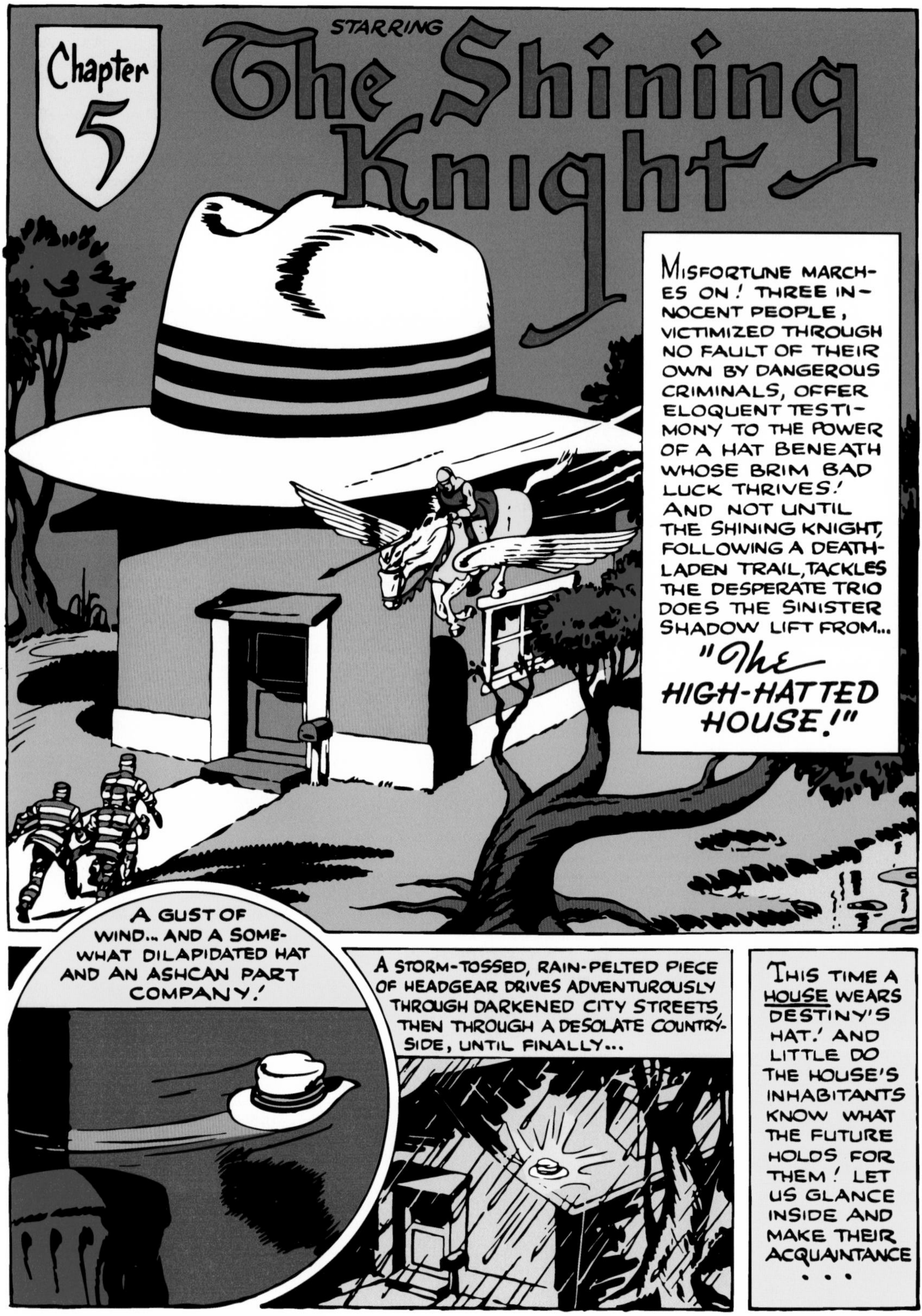
Chapter 5
STARRING
The Shining Knight
MISFORTUNE MARCHES ON! THREE INNOCENT PEOPLE, VICTIMIZED THROUGH NO FAULT OF THEIR OWN BY DANGEROUS CRIMINALS, OFFER ELOQUENT TESTIMONY TO THE POWER OF A HAT BENEATH WHOSE BRIM BAD LUCK THRIVES! AND NOT UNTIL THE SHINING KNIGHT, FOLLOWING A DEATH-LADEN TRAIL, TACKLES THE DESPERATE TRIO DOES THE SINISTER SHADOW LIFT FROM...
"THE HIGH-HATTED HOUSE!"
A GUST OF WIND... AND A SOMEWHAT DILAPIDATED HAT AND AN ASHCAN PART COMPANY!
A STORM-TOSSED, RAIN-PELTED PIECE OF HEADGEAR DRIVES ADVENTUROUSLY THROUGH DARKENED CITY STREETS, THEN THROUGH A DESOLATE COUNTRYSIDE, UNTIL FINALLY...
THIS TIME A HOUSE WEARS DESTINY'S HAT! AND LITTLE DO THE HOUSE'S INHABITANTS KNOW WHAT THE FUTURE HOLDS FOR THEM! LET US GLANCE INSIDE AND MAKE THEIR ACQUAINTANCE . . .

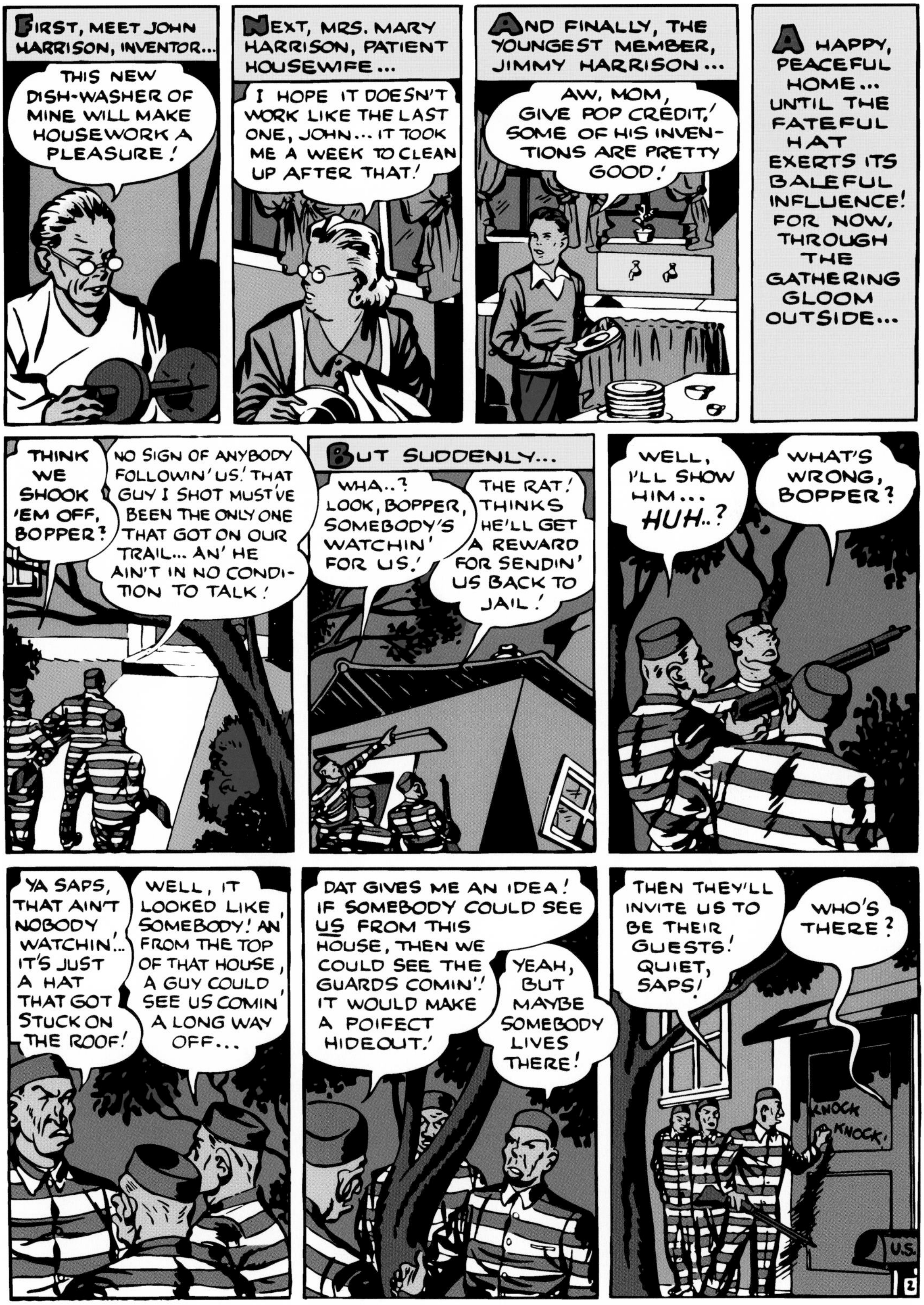
FIRST, MEET JOHN HARRISON, INVENTOR...
THIS NEW DISH-WASHER OF MINE WILL MAKE HOUSEWORK A PLEASURE!
NEXT, MRS. MARY HARRISON, PATIENT HOUSEWIFE...
I HOPE IT DOESN'T WORK LIKE THE LAST ONE, JOHN... IT TOOK ME A WEEK TO CLEAN UP AFTER THAT!
AND FINALLY, THE YOUNGEST MEMBER, JIMMY HARRISON...
AW, MOM, GIVE POP CREDIT! SOME OF HIS INVENTIONS ARE PRETTY GOOD!
A HAPPY, PEACEFUL HOME... UNTIL THE FATEFUL HAT EXERTS ITS BALEFUL INFLUENCE! FOR NOW, THROUGH THE GATHERING GLOOM OUTSIDE...
THINK WE SHOOK 'EM OFF, BOPPER?
NO SIGN OF ANYBODY FOLLOWIN' US! THAT GUY I SHOT MUST'VE BEEN THE ONLY ONE THAT GOT ON OUR TRAIL... AN' HE AIN'T IN NO CONDITION TO TALK!
BUT SUDDENLY...
WHA..? LOOK, BOPPER, SOMEBODY'S WATCHIN' FOR US!
THE RAT! THINKS HE'LL GET A REWARD FOR SENDIN' US BACK TO JAIL!
WELL, I'LL SHOW HIM... HUH..?
WHAT'S WRONG, BOPPER?
YA SAPS, THAT AIN'T NOBODY WATCHIN'... IT'S JUST A HAT THAT GOT STUCK ON THE ROOF!
WELL, IT LOOKED LIKE SOMEBODY! AN' FROM THE TOP OF THAT HOUSE, A GUY COULD SEE US COMIN' A LONG WAY OFF...
DAT GIVES ME AN IDEA! IF SOMEBODY COULD SEE US FROM THIS HOUSE, THEN WE COULD SEE THE GUARDS COMIN'! IT WOULD MAKE A POIFECT HIDEOUT!
YEAH, BUT MAYBE SOMEBODY LIVES THERE!
THEN THEY'LL INVITE US TO BE THEIR GUESTS! QUIET, SAPS!
WHO'S THERE?
KNOCK KNOCK!
U.S.
2

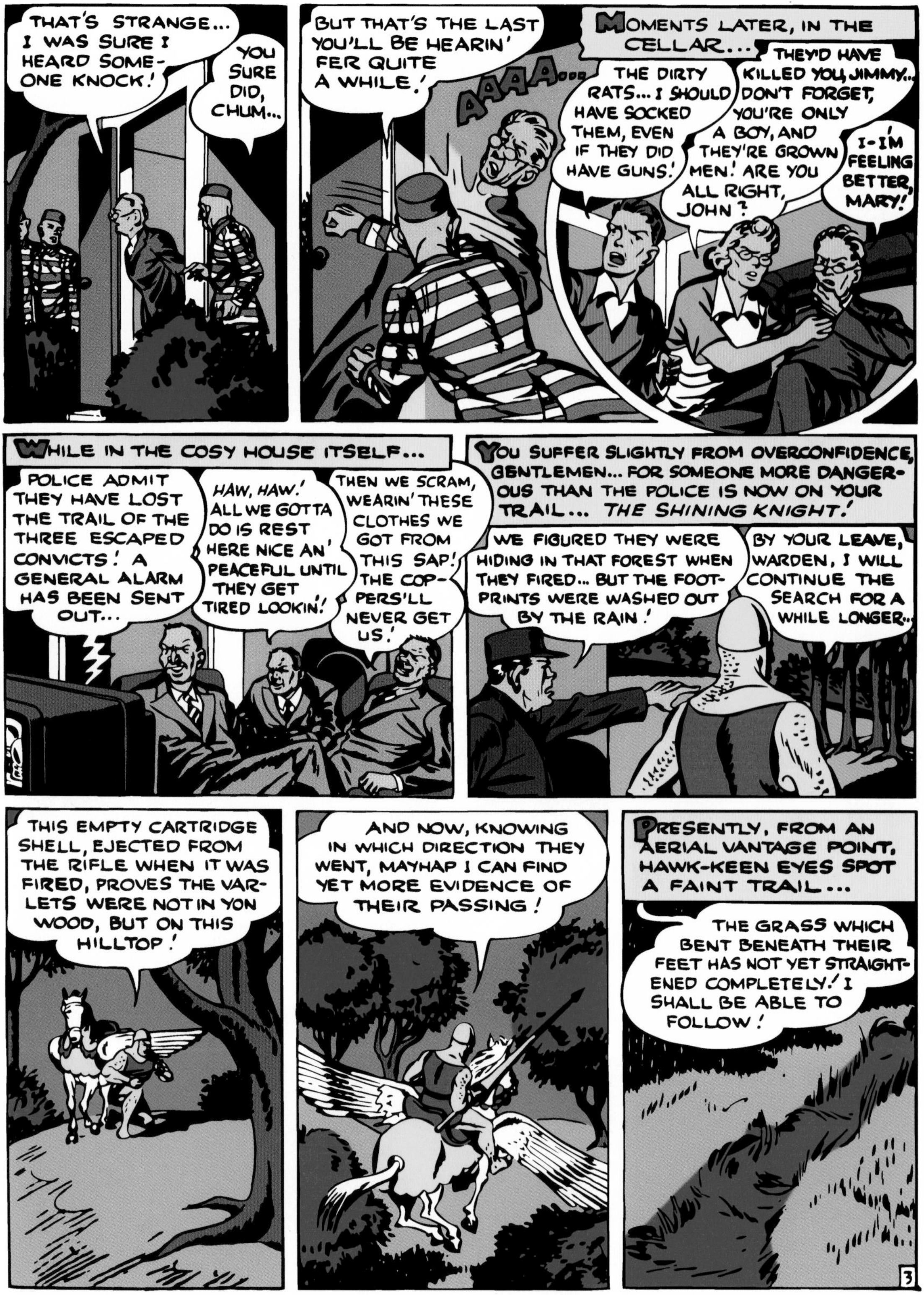
THAT'S STRANGE... I WAS SURE I HEARD SOME-ONE KNOCK!
YOU SURE DID, CHUM...
BUT THAT'S THE LAST YOU'LL BE HEARIN' FER QUITE A WHILE!
AAAA...
MOMENTS LATER, IN THE CELLAR...
THE DIRTY RATS... I SHOULD HAVE SOCKED THEM, EVEN IF THEY DID HAVE GUNS!
THEY'D HAVE KILLED YOU, JIMMY... DON'T FORGET, YOU'RE ONLY A BOY, AND THEY'RE GROWN MEN! ARE YOU ALL RIGHT, JOHN?
I-I'M FEELING BETTER, MARY!
WHILE IN THE COSY HOUSE ITSELF...
POLICE ADMIT THEY HAVE LOST THE TRAIL OF THE THREE ESCAPED CONVICTS! A GENERAL ALARM HAS BEEN SENT OUT...
HAW, HAW! ALL WE GOTTA DO IS REST HERE NICE AN' PEACEFUL UNTIL THEY GET TIRED LOOKIN'!
THEN WE SCRAM, WEARIN' THESE CLOTHES WE GOT FROM THIS SAP! THE COP-PERS'LL NEVER GET US!
YOU SUFFER SLIGHTLY FROM OVERCONFIDENCE, GENTLEMEN... FOR SOMEONE MORE DANGER-OUS THAN THE POLICE IS NOW ON YOUR TRAIL... THE SHINING KNIGHT!
WE FIGURED THEY WERE HIDING IN THAT FOREST WHEN THEY FIRED... BUT THE FOOT-PRINTS WERE WASHED OUT BY THE RAIN!
BY YOUR LEAVE, WARDEN, I WILL CONTINUE THE SEARCH FOR A WHILE LONGER...
THIS EMPTY CARTRIDGE SHELL, EJECTED FROM THE RIFLE WHEN IT WAS FIRED, PROVES THE VAR-LETS WERE NOT IN YON WOOD, BUT ON THIS HILLTOP!
AND NOW, KNOWING IN WHICH DIRECTION THEY WENT, MAYHAP I CAN FIND YET MORE EVIDENCE OF THEIR PASSING!
PRESENTLY, FROM AN AERIAL VANTAGE POINT, HAWK-KEEN EYES SPOT A FAINT TRAIL...
THE GRASS WHICH BENT BENEATH THEIR FEET HAS NOT YET STRAIGHT-ENED COMPLETELY! I SHALL BE ABLE TO FOLLOW!
3

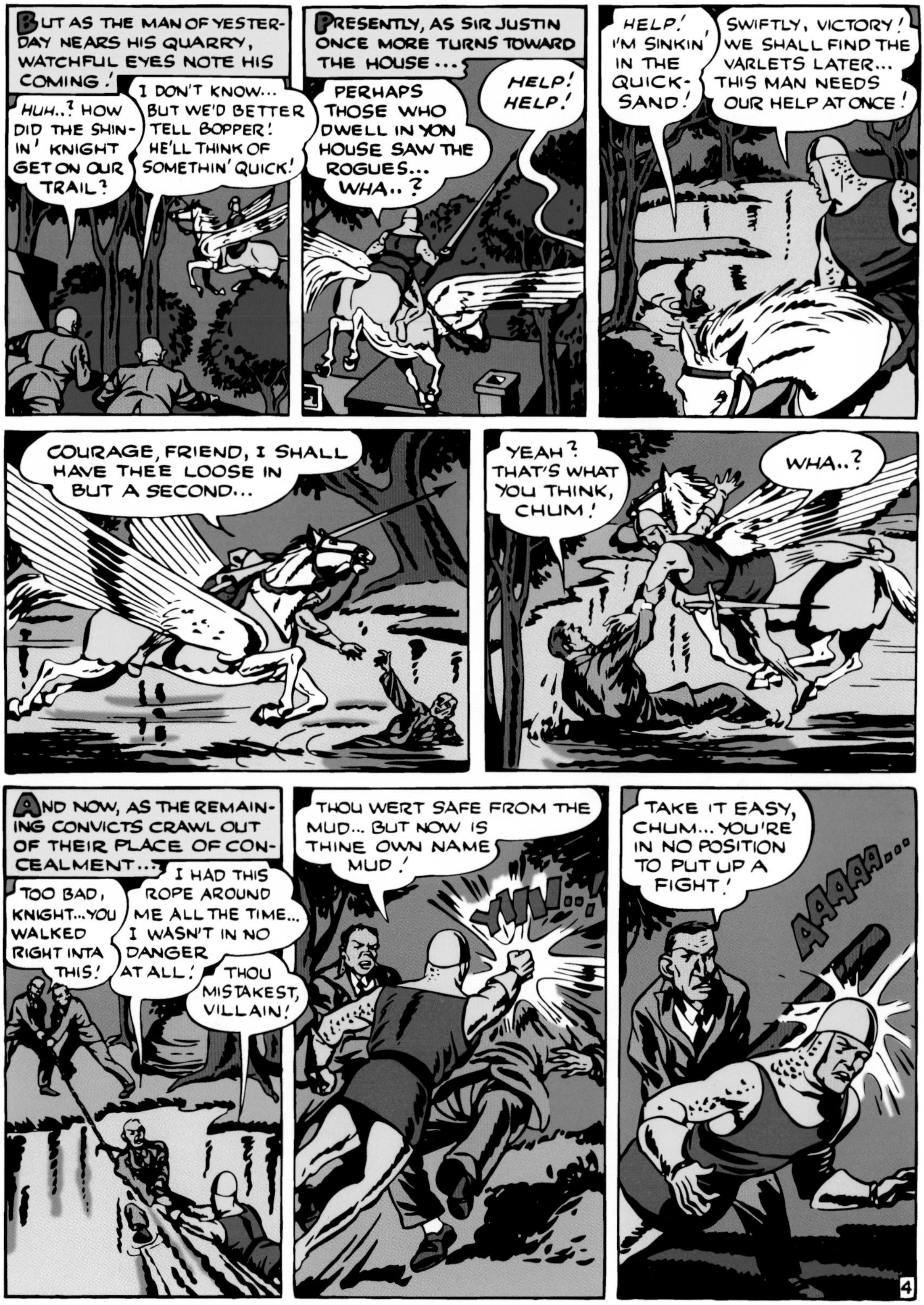
BUT AS THE MAN OF YESTERDAY NEARS HIS QUARRY, WATCHFUL EYES NOTE HIS COMING!
HUH..? HOW DID THE SHININ' KNIGHT GET ON OUR TRAIL?
I DON'T KNOW... BUT WE'D BETTER TELL BOPPER! HE'LL THINK OF SOMETHIN' QUICK!
PRESENTLY, AS SIR JUSTIN ONCE MORE TURNS TOWARD THE HOUSE...
PERHAPS THOSE WHO DWELL IN YON HOUSE SAW THE ROGUES... WHA..?
HELP! HELP!
HELP! I'M SINKIN' IN THE QUICK-SAND!
SWIFTLY, VICTORY! WE SHALL FIND THE VARLETS LATER... THIS MAN NEEDS OUR HELP AT ONCE!
COURAGE, FRIEND, I SHALL HAVE THEE LOOSE IN BUT A SECOND...
YEAH? THAT'S WHAT YOU THINK, CHUM!
WHA..?
AND NOW, AS THE REMAINING CONVICTS CRAWL OUT OF THEIR PLACE OF CONCEALMENT...
TOO BAD, KNIGHT...YOU WALKED RIGHT INTA THIS!
I HAD THIS ROPE AROUND ME ALL THE TIME... I WASN'T IN NO DANGER AT ALL!
THOU MISTAKEST, VILLAIN!
THOU WERT SAFE FROM THE MUD... BUT NOW IS THINE OWN NAME MUD!
YIIII..!
TAKE IT EASY, CHUM... YOU'RE IN NO POSITION TO PUT UP A FIGHT!
AAAAA...
4

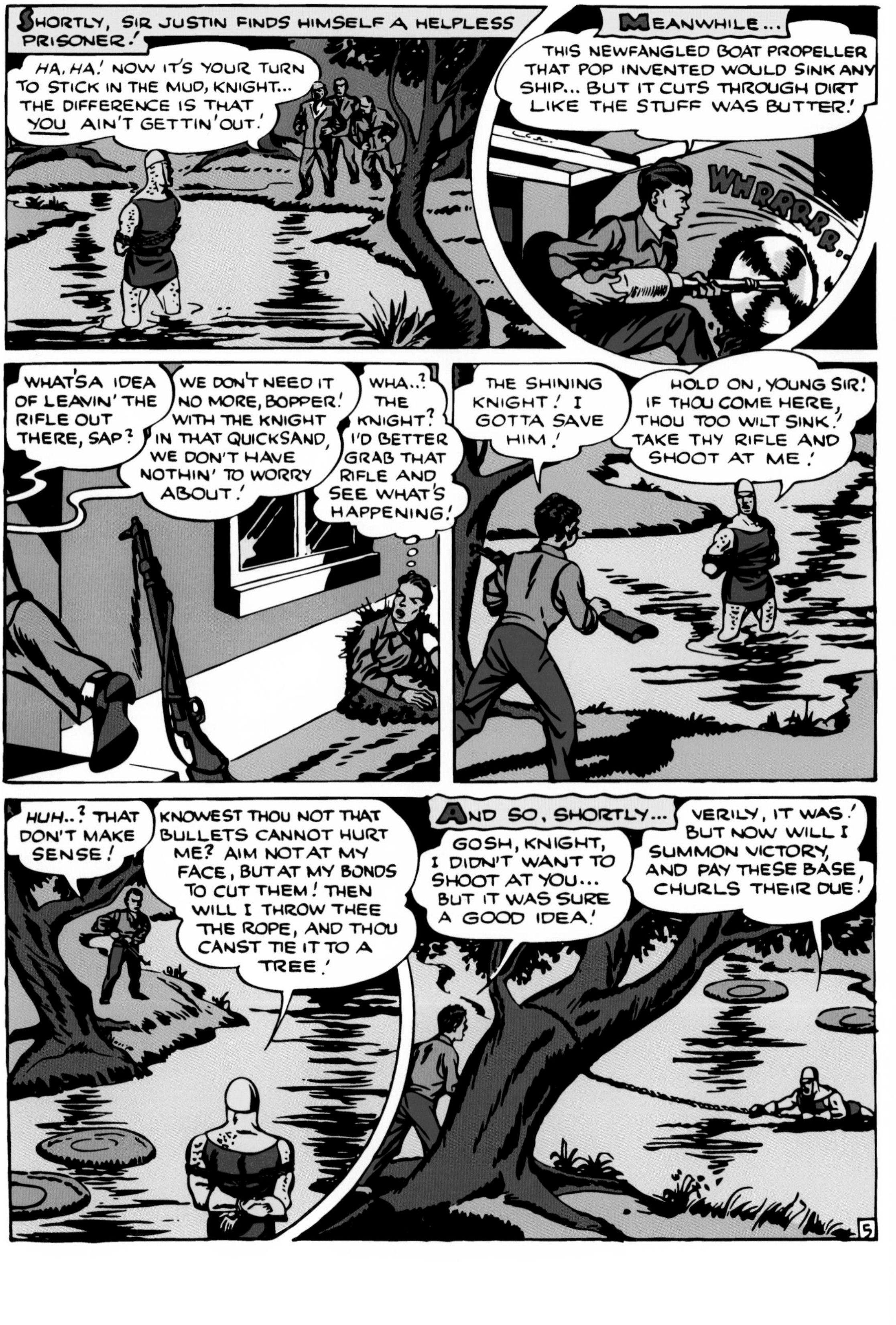
SHORTLY, SIR JUSTIN FINDS HIMSELF A HELPLESS PRISONER!
HA, HA! NOW IT'S YOUR TURN TO STICK IN THE MUD, KNIGHT... THE DIFFERENCE IS THAT YOU AIN'T GETTIN' OUT!
MEANWHILE...
THIS NEWFANGLED BOAT PROPELLER THAT POP INVENTED WOULD SINK ANY SHIP... BUT IT CUTS THROUGH DIRT LIKE THE STUFF WAS BUTTER!
WHRRRRR..
WHAT'SA IDEA OF LEAVIN' THE RIFLE OUT THERE, SAP?
WE DON'T NEED IT NO MORE, BOPPER! WITH THE KNIGHT IN THAT QUICKSAND, WE DON'T HAVE NOTHIN' TO WORRY ABOUT!
WHA..? THE KNIGHT? I'D BETTER GRAB THAT RIFLE AND SEE WHAT'S HAPPENING!
THE SHINING KNIGHT! I GOTTA SAVE HIM!
HOLD ON, YOUNG SIR! IF THOU COME HERE, THOU TOO WILT SINK! TAKE THY RIFLE AND SHOOT AT ME!
HUH..? THAT DON'T MAKE SENSE!
KNOWEST THOU NOT THAT BULLETS CANNOT HURT ME? AIM NOT AT MY FACE, BUT AT MY BONDS TO CUT THEM! THEN WILL I THROW THEE THE ROPE, AND THOU CANST TIE IT TO A TREE!
AND SO, SHORTLY...
GOSH, KNIGHT, I DIDN'T WANT TO SHOOT AT YOU... BUT IT WAS SURE A GOOD IDEA!
VERILY, IT WAS! BUT NOW WILL I SUMMON VICTORY, AND PAY THESE BASE CHURLS THEIR DUE!
5

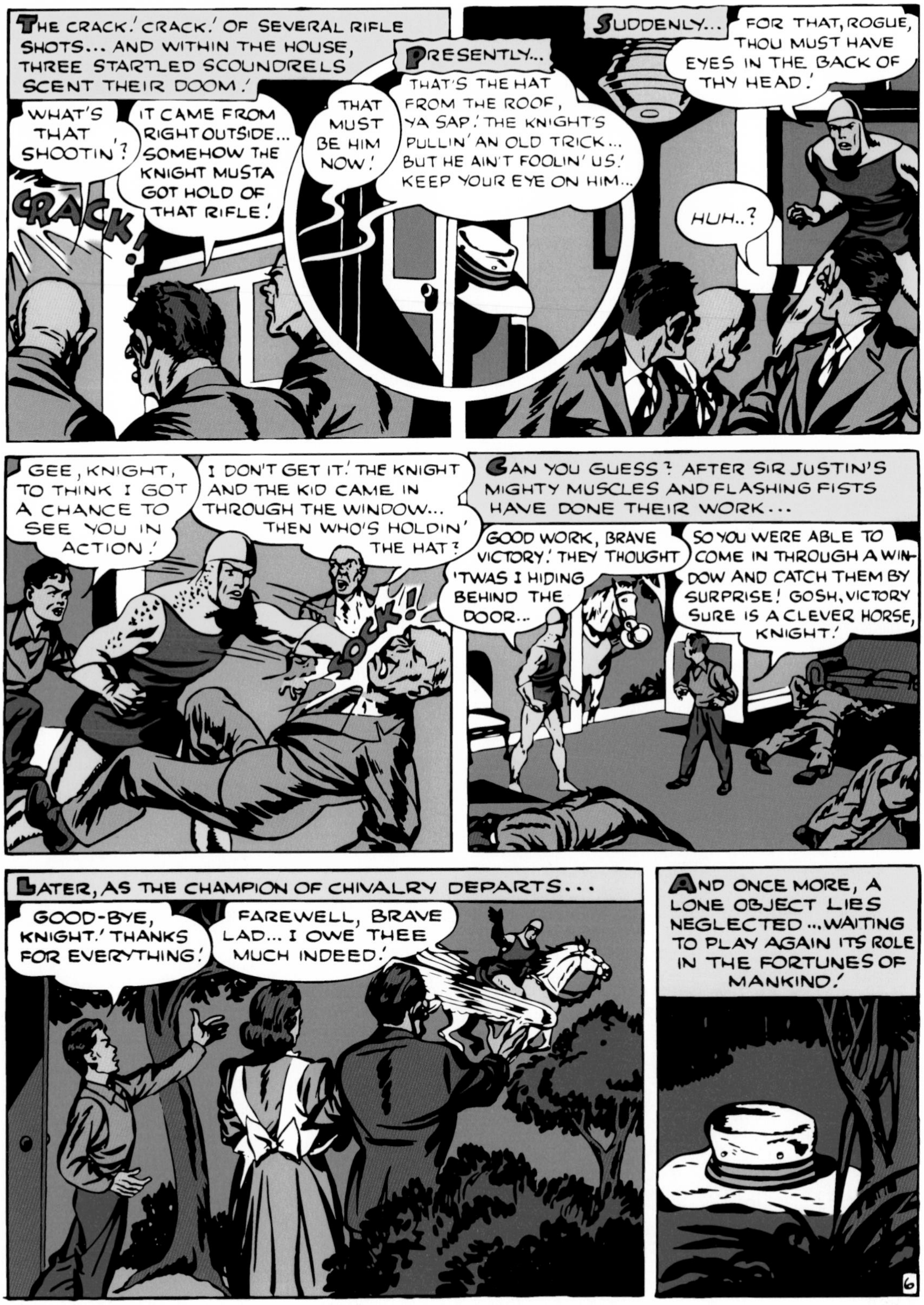
THE CRACK! CRACK! OF SEVERAL RIFLE SHOTS... AND WITHIN THE HOUSE, THREE STARTLED SCOUNDRELS SCENT THEIR DOOM!
WHAT'S THAT SHOOTIN'?
IT CAME FROM RIGHT OUTSIDE... SOMEHOW THE KNIGHT MUSTA GOT HOLD OF THAT RIFLE!
CRACK!
PRESENTLY...
THAT MUST BE HIM NOW!
THAT'S THE HAT FROM THE ROOF, YA SAP! THE KNIGHT'S PULLIN' AN OLD TRICK... BUT HE AIN'T FOOLIN' US! KEEP YOUR EYE ON HIM...
SUDDENLY...
FOR THAT, ROGUE, THOU MUST HAVE EYES IN THE BACK OF THY HEAD!
HUH..?
GEE, KNIGHT, TO THINK I GOT A CHANCE TO SEE YOU IN ACTION!
I DON'T GET IT! THE KNIGHT AND THE KID CAME IN THROUGH THE WINDOW... THEN WHO'S HOLDIN' THE HAT?
SOCK!!
CAN YOU GUESS? AFTER SIR JUSTIN'S MIGHTY MUSCLES AND FLASHING FISTS HAVE DONE THEIR WORK...
GOOD WORK, BRAVE VICTORY! THEY THOUGHT 'TWAS I HIDING BEHIND THE DOOR...
SO YOU WERE ABLE TO COME IN THROUGH A WINDOW AND CATCH THEM BY SURPRISE! GOSH, VICTORY SURE IS A CLEVER HORSE, KNIGHT!
LATER, AS THE CHAMPION OF CHIVALRY DEPARTS...
GOOD-BYE, KNIGHT! THANKS FOR EVERYTHING!
FAREWELL, BRAVE LAD... I OWE THEE MUCH INDEED!
AND ONCE MORE, A LONE OBJECT LIES NEGLECTED ...WAITING TO PLAY AGAIN ITS ROLE IN THE FORTUNES OF MANKIND!
6

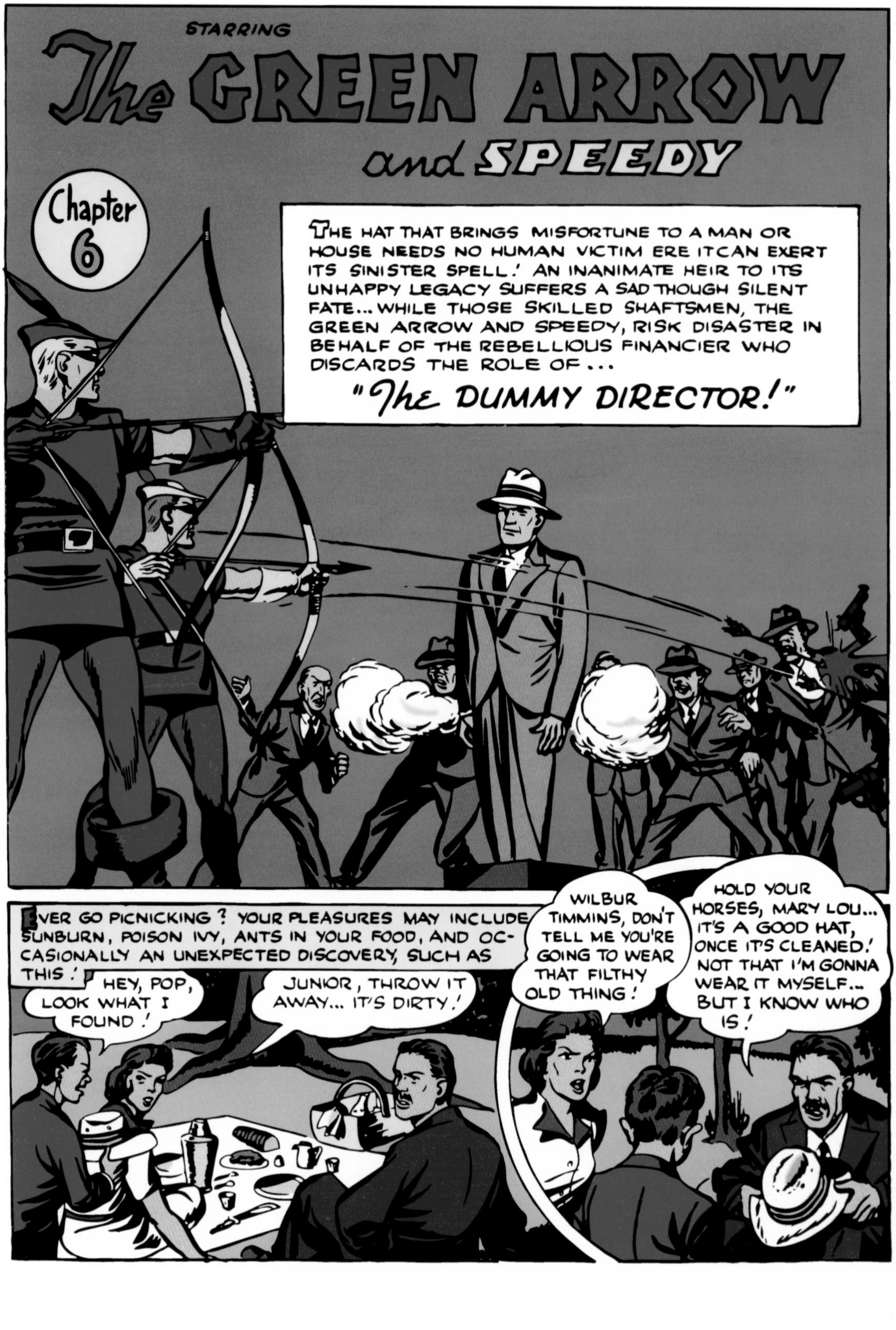
STARRING
The GREEN ARROW
and SPEEDY
Chapter 6
THE HAT THAT BRINGS MISFORTUNE TO A MAN OR HOUSE NEEDS NO HUMAN VICTIM ERE IT CAN EXERT ITS SINISTER SPELL! AN INANIMATE HEIR TO ITS UNHAPPY LEGACY SUFFERS A SAD THOUGH SILENT FATE... WHILE THOSE SKILLED SHAFTSMEN, THE GREEN ARROW AND SPEEDY, RISK DISASTER IN BEHALF OF THE REBELLIOUS FINANCIER WHO DISCARDS THE ROLE OF...
"The DUMMY DIRECTOR!"
EVER GO PICNICKING? YOUR PLEASURES MAY INCLUDE SUNBURN, POISON IVY, ANTS IN YOUR FOOD, AND OCCASIONALLY AN UNEXPECTED DISCOVERY, SUCH AS THIS!
HEY, POP, LOOK WHAT I FOUND!
JUNIOR, THROW IT AWAY... IT'S DIRTY!
WILBUR TIMMINS, DON'T TELL ME YOU'RE GOING TO WEAR THAT FILTHY OLD THING!
HOLD YOUR HORSES, MARY LOU... IT'S A GOOD HAT, ONCE IT'S CLEANED! NOT THAT I'M GONNA WEAR IT MYSELF... BUT I KNOW WHO IS!

AND ON THE FOLLOWING MONDAY...

THAT HAT SURE DRESSES YOU UP, DUMMY, OLD BOY... IT'S JUST WHAT YOU NEEDED!

WILBUR TIMMINS

FIRST CLASS SECOND-HAND CLOTHES

A SAD COME-DOWN FOR THE ONCE PROUD PROPERTY OF HANDSOME HARRY! AND YET... THE FUTURE STILL HOLDS STRANGE THINGS IN STORE!

ARE YOU THE PROPRIETOR OF THIS STORE?

SURE... YOU WANT TO BUY SOME SECOND-HAND CLOTHES?

I WANT TO BUY THIS DUMMY, AND EVERYTHING HE'S WEARING!

WHA..? MISTER, ARE YOU TRYIN' TO KID ME?

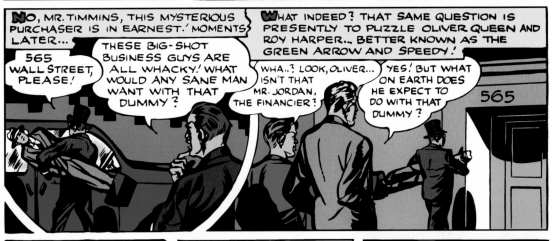

NO, MR. TIMMINS, THIS MYSTERIOUS PURCHASER IS IN EARNEST! MOMENTS LATER...

565 WALL STREET, PLEASE!

THESE BIG-SHOT BUSINESS GUYS ARE ALL WHACKY! WHAT WOULD ANY SANE MAN WANT WITH THAT DUMMY?

WHAT INDEED? THAT SAME QUESTION IS PRESENTLY TO PUZZLE OLIVER QUEEN AND ROY HARPER... BETTER KNOWN AS THE GREEN ARROW AND SPEEDY!

WHA..? LOOK, OLIVER... ISN'T THAT MR. JORDAN, THE FINANCIER?

YES! BUT WHAT ON EARTH DOES HE EXPECT TO DO WITH THAT DUMMY?

565

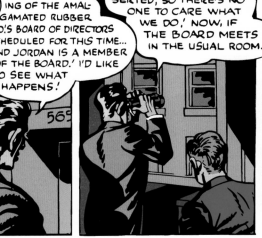

MAYBE HE WANTS IT FOR SOME SORT OF PRACTICAL JOKE! THEY SAY HE USED TO BE A PLAYBOY BEFORE HE WENT INTO WALL STREET!

I WONDER..! ROY, I READ ABOUT A MEETING OF THE AMALGAMATED RUBBER CO.'S BOARD OF DIRECTORS SCHEDULED FOR THIS TIME... AND JORDAN IS A MEMBER OF THE BOARD! I'D LIKE TO SEE WHAT HAPPENS!

PRESENTLY...

THIS OFFICE IS DESERTED, SO THERE'S NO ONE TO CARE WHAT WE DO! NOW, IF THE BOARD MEETS IN THE USUAL ROOM...

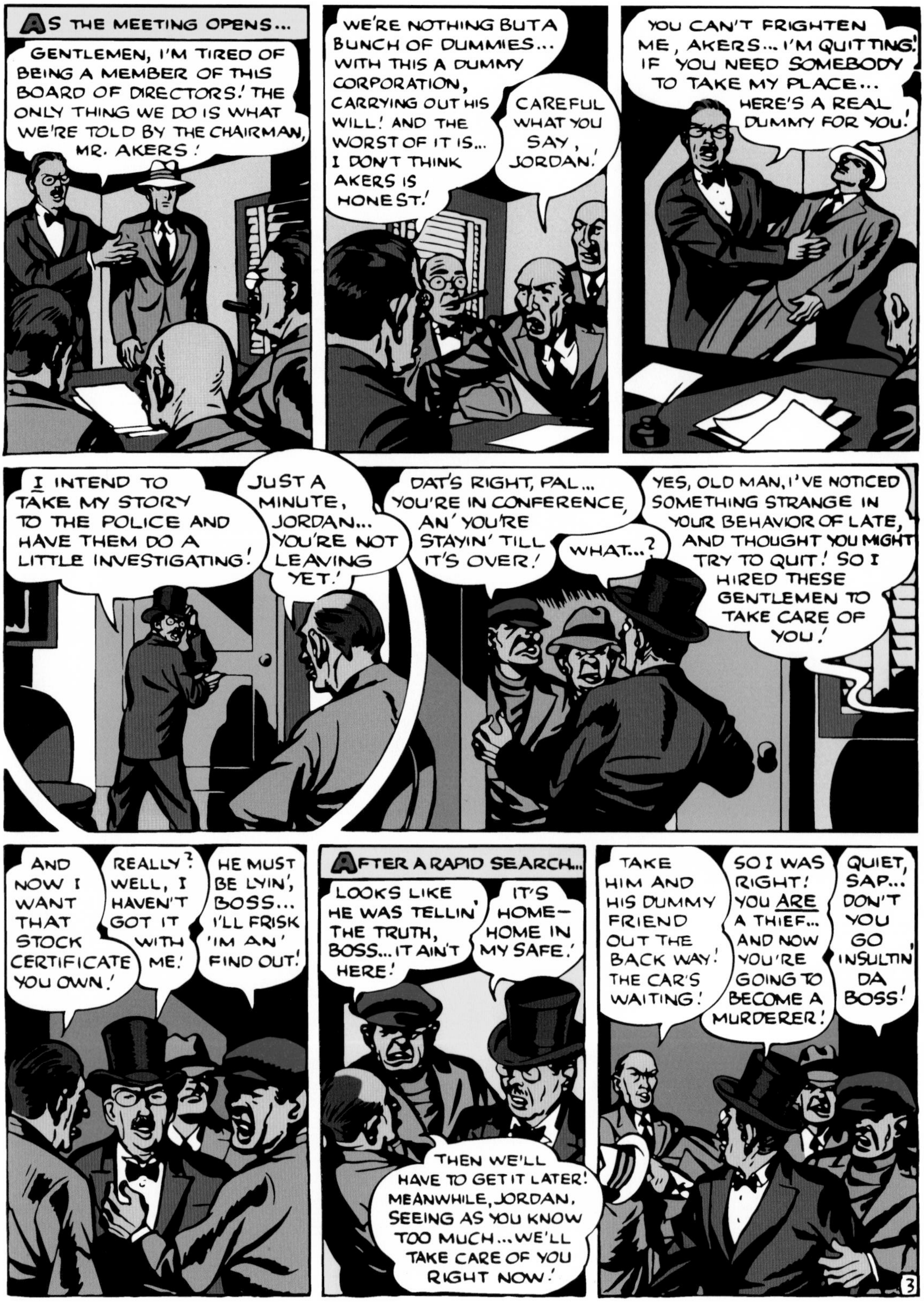
AS THE MEETING OPENS...
GENTLEMEN, I'M TIRED OF BEING A MEMBER OF THIS BOARD OF DIRECTORS! THE ONLY THING WE DO IS WHAT WE'RE TOLD BY THE CHAIRMAN, MR. AKERS!
WE'RE NOTHING BUT A BUNCH OF DUMMIES... WITH THIS A DUMMY CORPORATION, CARRYING OUT HIS WILL! AND THE WORST OF IT IS... I DON'T THINK AKERS IS HONEST!
CAREFUL WHAT YOU SAY, JORDAN!
YOU CAN'T FRIGHTEN ME, AKERS... I'M QUITTING! IF YOU NEED SOMEBODY TO TAKE MY PLACE... HERE'S A REAL DUMMY FOR YOU!
I INTEND TO TAKE MY STORY TO THE POLICE AND HAVE THEM DO A LITTLE INVESTIGATING!
JUST A MINUTE, JORDAN... YOU'RE NOT LEAVING YET!
DAT'S RIGHT, PAL... YOU'RE IN CONFERENCE, AN' YOU'RE STAYIN' TILL IT'S OVER!
WHAT...?
YES, OLD MAN, I'VE NOTICED SOMETHING STRANGE IN YOUR BEHAVIOR OF LATE, AND THOUGHT YOU MIGHT TRY TO QUIT! SO I HIRED THESE GENTLEMEN TO TAKE CARE OF YOU!
AND NOW I WANT THAT STOCK CERTIFICATE YOU OWN!
REALLY? WELL, I HAVEN'T GOT IT WITH ME!
HE MUST BE LYIN', BOSS... I'LL FRISK 'IM AN' FIND OUT!
AFTER A RAPID SEARCH...
LOOKS LIKE HE WAS TELLIN' THE TRUTH, BOSS... IT AIN'T HERE!
IT'S HOME-HOME IN MY SAFE!
THEN WE'LL HAVE TO GET IT LATER! MEANWHILE, JORDAN, SEEING AS YOU KNOW TOO MUCH... WE'LL TAKE CARE OF YOU RIGHT NOW!
TAKE HIM AND HIS DUMMY FRIEND OUT THE BACK WAY! THE CAR'S WAITING!
SO I WAS RIGHT! YOU ARE A THIEF... AND NOW YOU'RE GOING TO BECOME A MURDERER!
QUIET, SAP... DON'T YOU GO INSULTIN' DA BOSS!
3

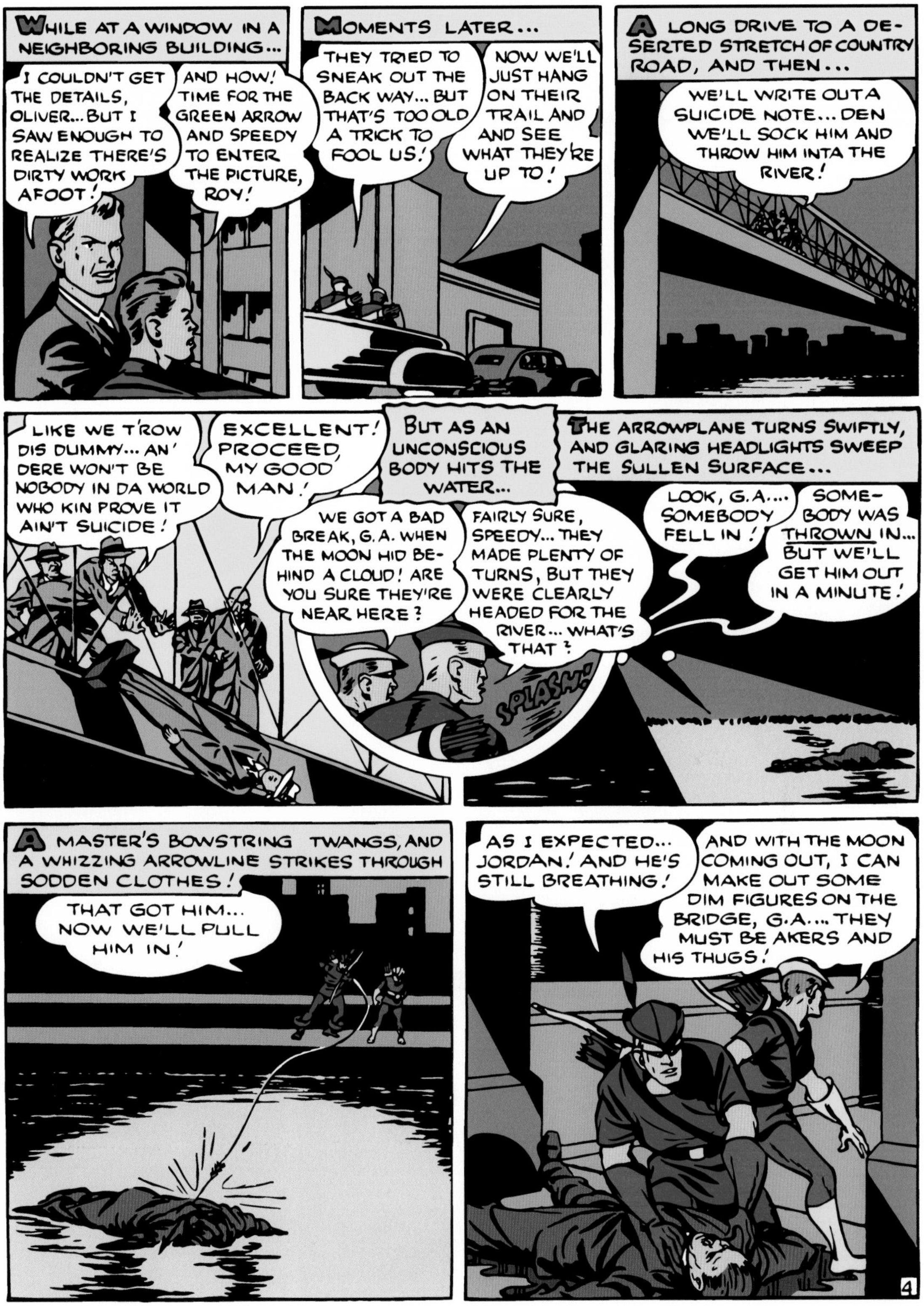
WHILE AT A WINDOW IN A NEIGHBORING BUILDING...
I COULDN'T GET THE DETAILS, OLIVER...BUT I SAW ENOUGH TO REALIZE THERE'S DIRTY WORK AFOOT!
AND HOW! TIME FOR THE GREEN ARROW AND SPEEDY TO ENTER THE PICTURE, ROY!
MOMENTS LATER...
THEY TRIED TO SNEAK OUT THE BACK WAY... BUT THAT'S TOO OLD A TRICK TO FOOL US!
NOW WE'LL JUST HANG ON THEIR TRAIL AND SEE WHAT THEY'RE UP TO!
A LONG DRIVE TO A DESERTED STRETCH OF COUNTRY ROAD, AND THEN...
WE'LL WRITE OUT A SUICIDE NOTE... DEN WE'LL SOCK HIM AND THROW HIM INTA THE RIVER!
LIKE WE T'ROW DIS DUMMY... AN' DERE WON'T BE NOBODY IN DA WORLD WHO KIN PROVE IT AIN'T SUICIDE!
EXCELLENT! PROCEED, MY GOOD MAN!
BUT AS AN UNCONSCIOUS BODY HITS THE WATER...
WE GOT A BAD BREAK, G.A. WHEN THE MOON HID BEHIND A CLOUD! ARE YOU SURE THEY'RE NEAR HERE?
FAIRLY SURE, SPEEDY... THEY MADE PLENTY OF TURNS, BUT THEY WERE CLEARLY HEADED FOR THE RIVER... WHAT'S THAT?
SPLASH!
THE ARROWPLANE TURNS SWIFTLY, AND GLARING HEADLIGHTS SWEEP THE SULLEN SURFACE...
LOOK, G.A.... SOMEBODY FELL IN!
SOMEBODY WAS THROWN IN... BUT WE'LL GET HIM OUT IN A MINUTE!
A MASTER'S BOWSTRING TWANGS, AND A WHIZZING ARROWLINE STRIKES THROUGH SODDEN CLOTHES!
THAT GOT HIM... NOW WE'LL PULL HIM IN!
AS I EXPECTED... JORDAN! AND HE'S STILL BREATHING!
AND WITH THE MOON COMING OUT, I CAN MAKE OUT SOME DIM FIGURES ON THE BRIDGE, G.A.... THEY MUST BE AKERS AND HIS THUGS!
4

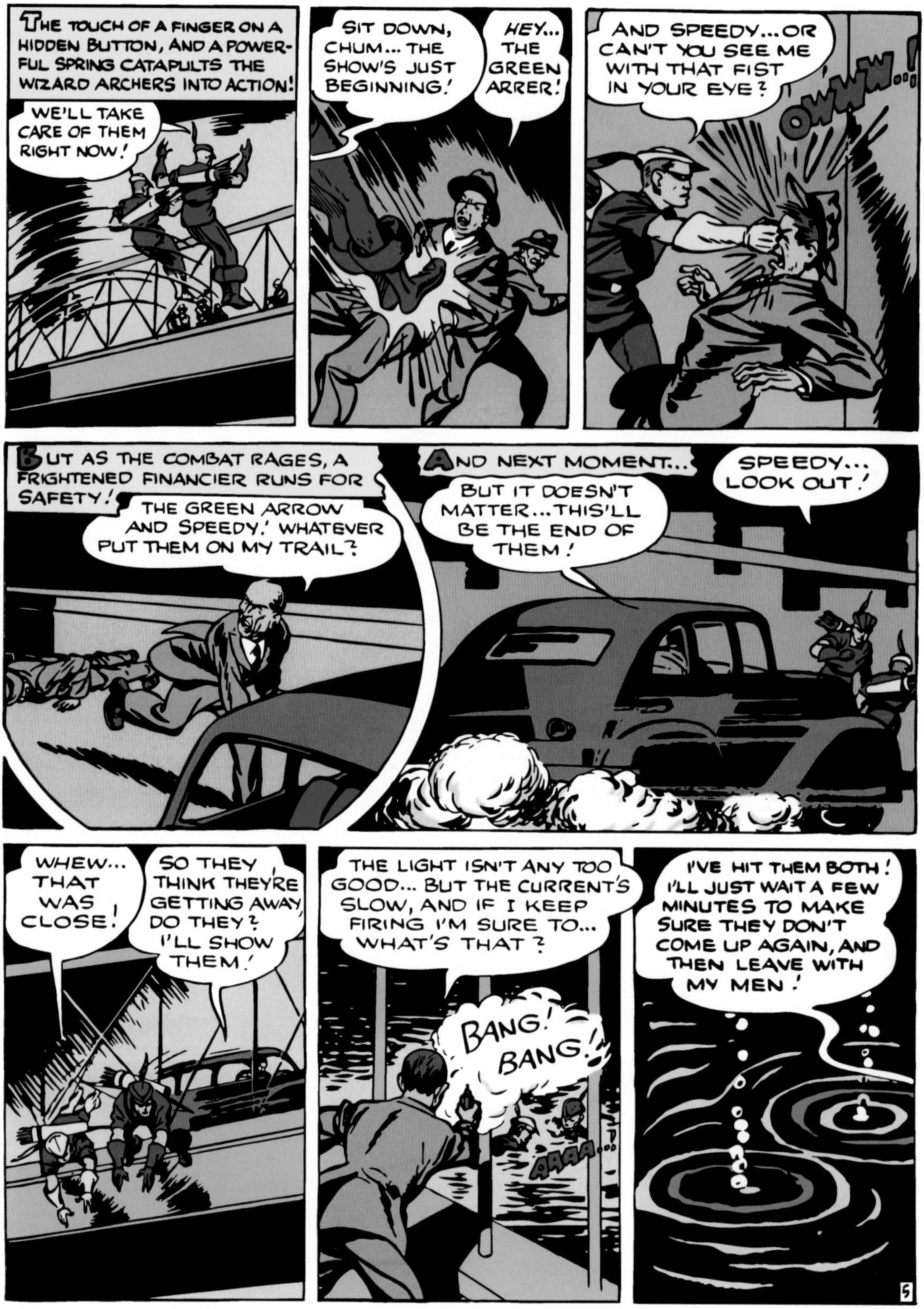
THE TOUCH OF A FINGER ON A HIDDEN BUTTON, AND A POWERFUL SPRING CATAPULTS THE WIZARD ARCHERS INTO ACTION!
WE'LL TAKE CARE OF THEM RIGHT NOW!
SIT DOWN, CHUM... THE SHOW'S JUST BEGINNING!
HEY... THE GREEN ARRER!
AND SPEEDY... OR CAN'T YOU SEE ME WITH THAT FIST IN YOUR EYE?
OWWW..!
BUT AS THE COMBAT RAGES, A FRIGHTENED FINANCIER RUNS FOR SAFETY!
THE GREEN ARROW AND SPEEDY! WHATEVER PUT THEM ON MY TRAIL?
AND NEXT MOMENT...
BUT IT DOESN'T MATTER... THIS'LL BE THE END OF THEM!
SPEEDY... LOOK OUT!
WHEW... THAT WAS CLOSE!
SO THEY THINK THEY'RE GETTING AWAY, DO THEY? I'LL SHOW THEM!
THE LIGHT ISN'T ANY TOO GOOD... BUT THE CURRENT'S SLOW, AND IF I KEEP FIRING I'M SURE TO... WHAT'S THAT?
BANG! BANG!
AAAA...!
I'VE HIT THEM BOTH! I'LL JUST WAIT A FEW MINUTES TO MAKE SURE THEY DON'T COME UP AGAIN, AND THEN LEAVE WITH MY MEN!
5

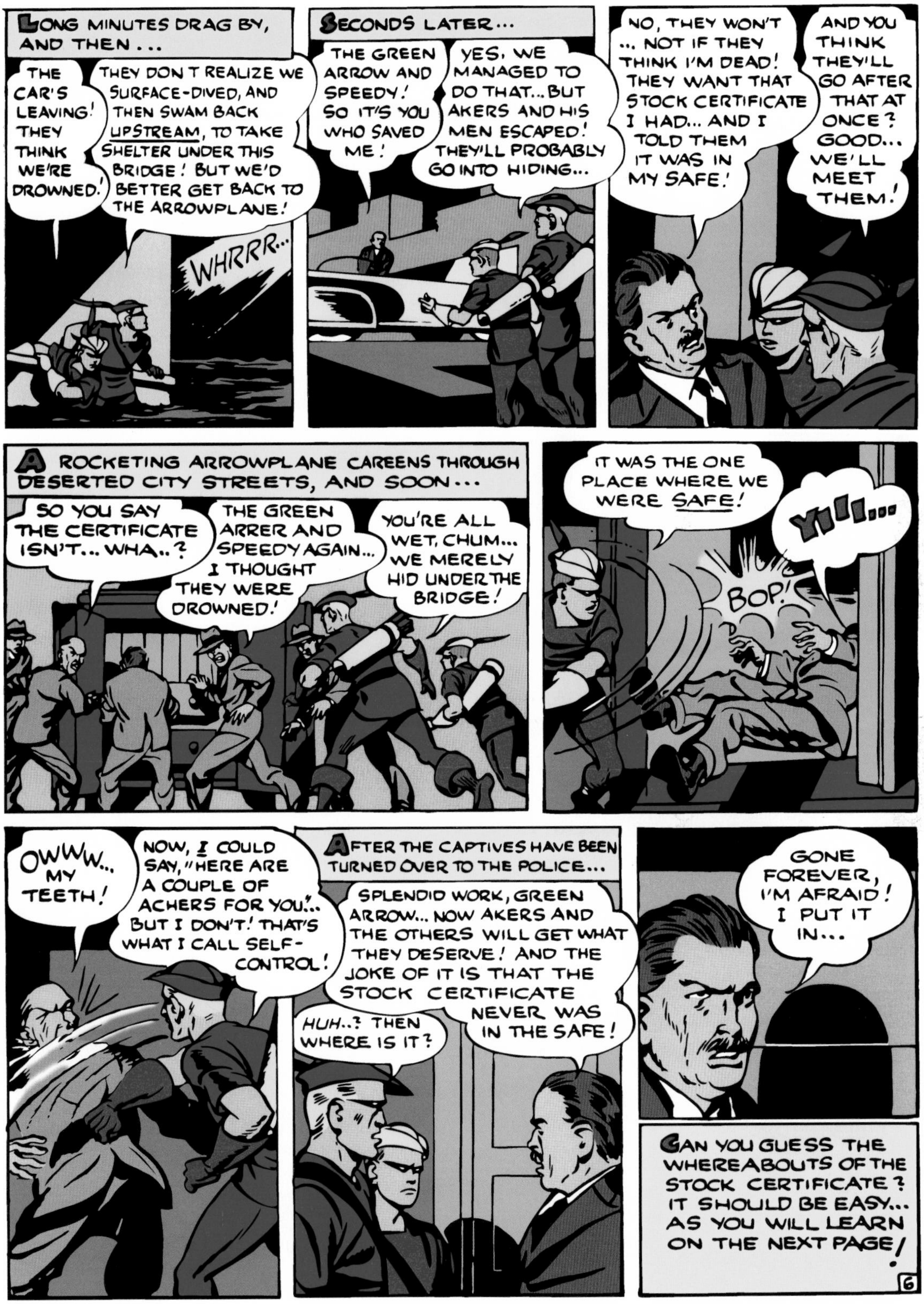
LONG MINUTES DRAG BY, AND THEN ...
THE CAR'S LEAVING! THEY THINK WE'RE DROWNED!
THEY DON'T REALIZE WE SURFACE-DIVED, AND THEN SWAM BACK UPSTREAM, TO TAKE SHELTER UNDER THIS BRIDGE! BUT WE'D BETTER GET BACK TO THE ARROWPLANE!
WHRRR...
SECONDS LATER...
THE GREEN ARROW AND SPEEDY! SO IT'S YOU WHO SAVED ME!
YES, WE MANAGED TO DO THAT... BUT AKERS AND HIS MEN ESCAPED! THEY'LL PROBABLY GO INTO HIDING...
NO, THEY WON'T ... NOT IF THEY THINK I'M DEAD! THEY WANT THAT STOCK CERTIFICATE I HAD... AND I TOLD THEM IT WAS IN MY SAFE!
AND YOU THINK THEY'LL GO AFTER THAT AT ONCE? GOOD... WE'LL MEET THEM!
A ROCKETING ARROWPLANE CAREENS THROUGH DESERTED CITY STREETS, AND SOON...
SO YOU SAY THE CERTIFICATE ISN'T... WHA..?
THE GREEN ARRER AND SPEEDY AGAIN... I THOUGHT THEY WERE DROWNED!
YOU'RE ALL WET, CHUM... WE MERELY HID UNDER THE BRIDGE!
IT WAS THE ONE PLACE WHERE WE WERE SAFE!
YI!!...
BOP!
OWWW... MY TEETH!
NOW, I COULD SAY, "HERE ARE A COUPLE OF ACHERS FOR YOU!"... BUT I DON'T! THAT'S WHAT I CALL SELF-CONTROL!
AFTER THE CAPTIVES HAVE BEEN TURNED OVER TO THE POLICE...
SPLENDID WORK, GREEN ARROW... NOW AKERS AND THE OTHERS WILL GET WHAT THEY DESERVE! AND THE JOKE OF IT IS THAT THE STOCK CERTIFICATE NEVER WAS IN THE SAFE!
HUH..? THEN WHERE IS IT?
GONE FOREVER, I'M AFRAID! I PUT IT IN...
CAN YOU GUESS THE WHEREABOUTS OF THE STOCK CERTIFICATE? IT SHOULD BE EASY... AS YOU WILL LEARN ON THE NEXT PAGE!
6

CHAPTER 7
HAT'S HAVEN

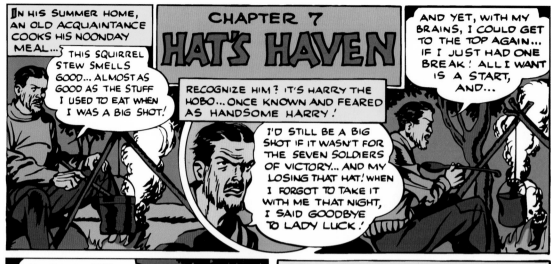

In his summer home, an old acquaintance cooks his noonday meal...

THIS SQUIRREL STEW SMELLS GOOD... ALMOST AS GOOD AS THE STUFF I USED TO EAT WHEN I WAS A BIG SHOT!

RECOGNIZE HIM? IT'S HARRY THE HOBO... ONCE KNOWN AND FEARED AS HANDSOME HARRY!

I'D STILL BE A BIG SHOT IF IT WASN'T FOR THE SEVEN SOLDIERS OF VICTORY... AND MY LOSING THAT HAT! WHEN I FORGOT TO TAKE IT WITH ME THAT NIGHT, I SAID GOODBYE TO LADY LUCK!

AND YET, WITH MY BRAINS, I COULD GET TO THE TOP AGAIN... IF I JUST HAD ONE BREAK! ALL I WANT IS A START, AND...

HUH... WHAT'S THAT ON THE RIVER? I MUST BE DREAMING!

NO HARRY, IT'S NO DREAM... YOUR HAT HAS RETURNED TO YOU! BUT HAS IT BROUGHT THE GOOD LUCK YOU EXPECT? ONLY TIME WILL TELL!

IT'S THE BREAK I WAS LOOKING FOR! MY GOOD LUCK IS WITH ME AGAIN! NOW NOTHING CAN HOLD ME BACK... NOTHING!

I'LL START IN A SMALL WAY... I NEED A LITTLE DOUGH, BUT SOMEHOW OR OTHER, I'M SURE TO GET THAT... WHA..? THE HAT DON'T FEEL RIGHT!

THERE WAS A STOCK CERTIFICATE HIDDEN IN THE LINING! I CAN SELL IT THROUGH A FENCE AND GET ALL THE DOUGH I NEED! MY LUCK'S WORKING ALREADY!

AMALGAMATED RUBBER

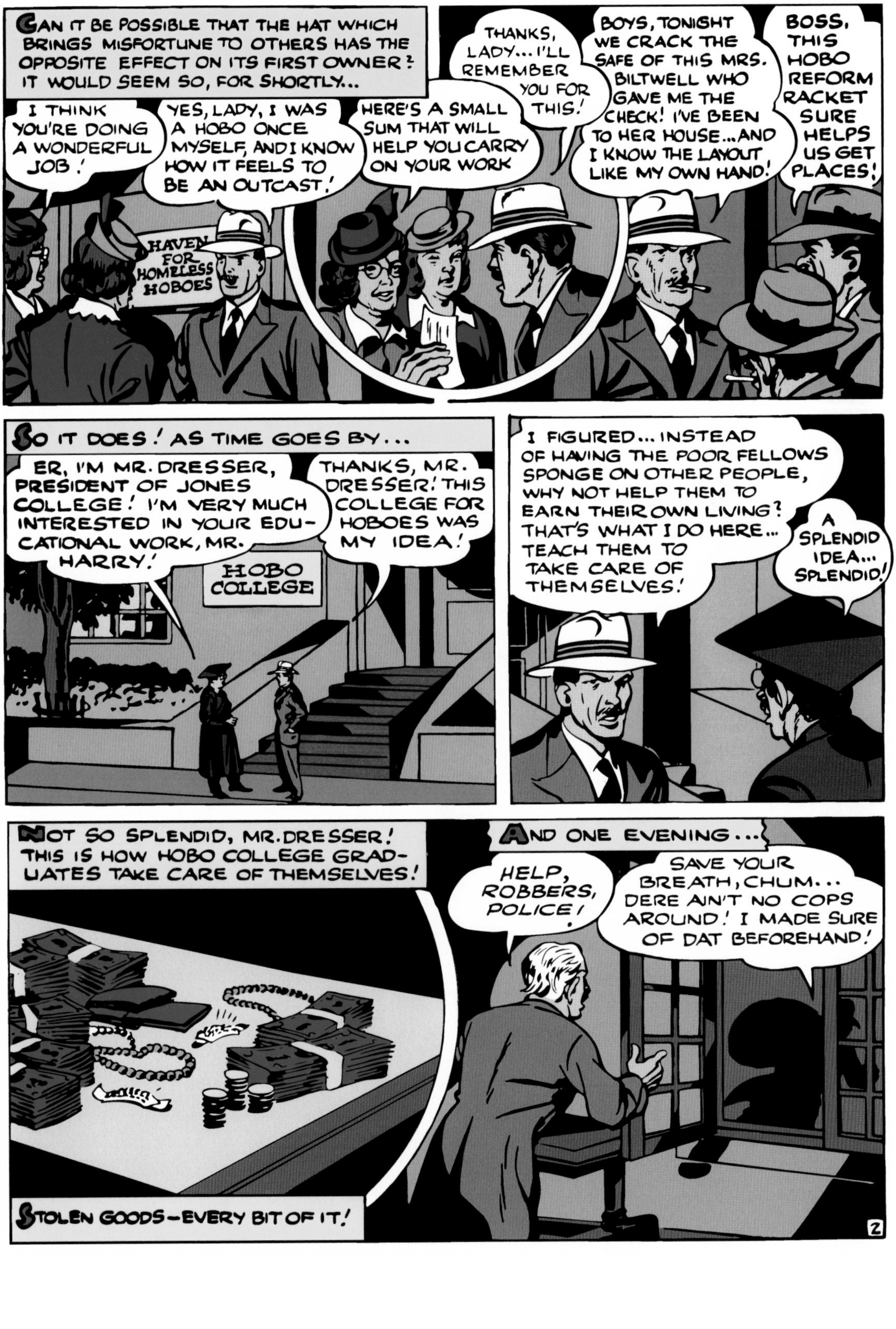
CAN IT BE POSSIBLE THAT THE HAT WHICH BRINGS MISFORTUNE TO OTHERS HAS THE OPPOSITE EFFECT ON ITS FIRST OWNER? IT WOULD SEEM SO, FOR SHORTLY...
I THINK YOU'RE DOING A WONDERFUL JOB!
YES, LADY, I WAS A HOBO ONCE MYSELF, AND I KNOW HOW IT FEELS TO BE AN OUTCAST!
HAVEN FOR HOMELESS HOBOES
HERE'S A SMALL SUM THAT WILL HELP YOU CARRY ON YOUR WORK
THANKS, LADY... I'LL REMEMBER YOU FOR THIS!
BOYS, TONIGHT WE CRACK THE SAFE OF THIS MRS. BILTWELL WHO GAVE ME THE CHECK! I'VE BEEN TO HER HOUSE... AND I KNOW THE LAYOUT LIKE MY OWN HAND!
BOSS, THIS HOBO REFORM RACKET SURE HELPS US GET PLACES!
SO IT DOES! AS TIME GOES BY...
ER, I'M MR. DRESSER, PRESIDENT OF JONES COLLEGE! I'M VERY MUCH INTERESTED IN YOUR EDUCATIONAL WORK, MR. HARRY!
THANKS, MR. DRESSER! THIS COLLEGE FOR HOBOES WAS MY IDEA!
HOBO COLLEGE
I FIGURED... INSTEAD OF HAVING THE POOR FELLOWS SPONGE ON OTHER PEOPLE, WHY NOT HELP THEM TO EARN THEIR OWN LIVING? THAT'S WHAT I DO HERE... TEACH THEM TO TAKE CARE OF THEMSELVES!
A SPLENDID IDEA... SPLENDID!
NOT SO SPLENDID, MR. DRESSER! THIS IS HOW HOBO COLLEGE GRADUATES TAKE CARE OF THEMSELVES!
STOLEN GOODS—EVERY BIT OF IT!
AND ONE EVENING...
HELP, ROBBERS, POLICE!
SAVE YOUR BREATH, CHUM... DERE AIN'T NO COPS AROUND! I MADE SURE OF DAT BEFOREHAND!
2

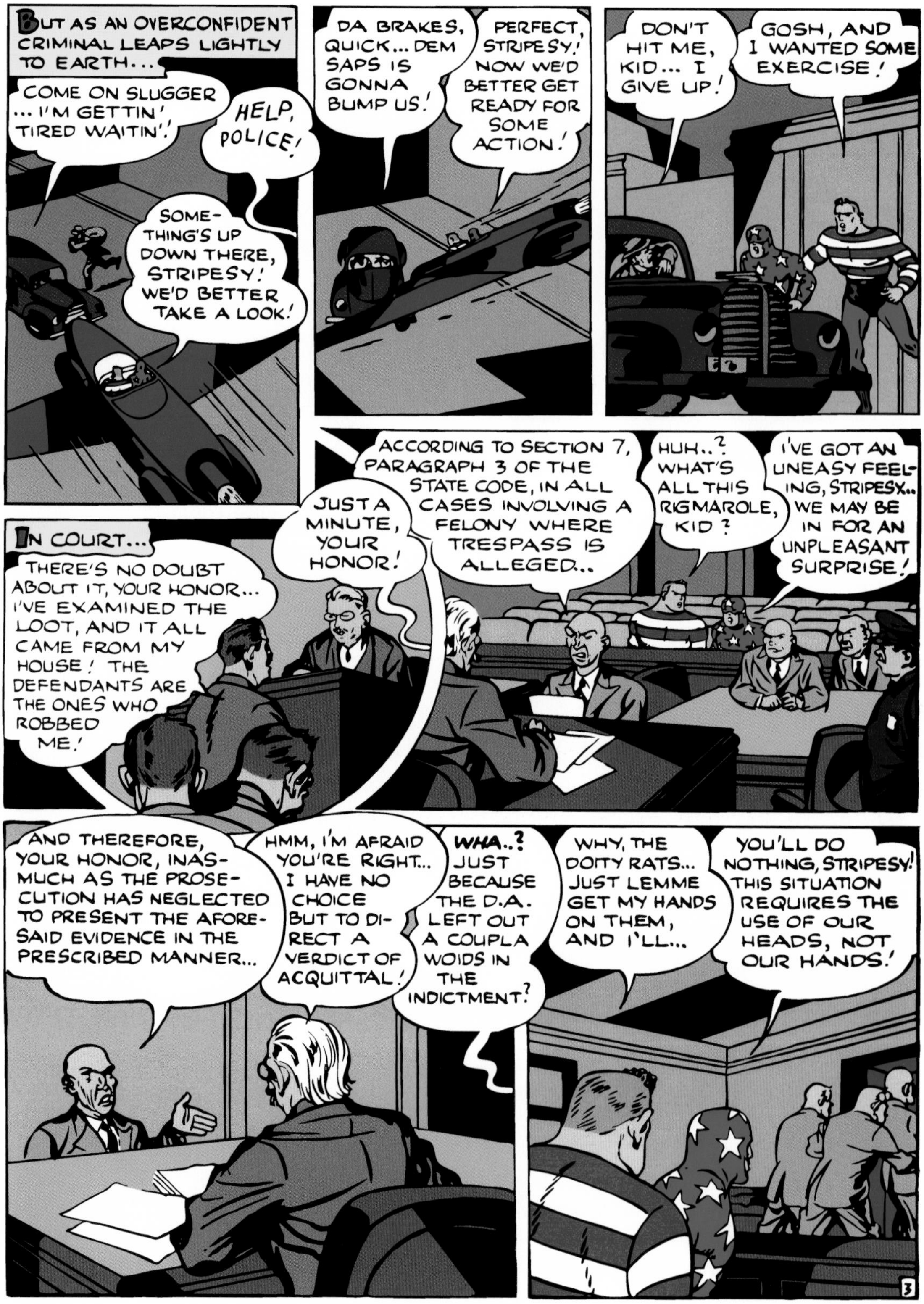
BUT AS AN OVERCONFIDENT CRIMINAL LEAPS LIGHTLY TO EARTH...
COME ON SLUGGER ... I'M GETTIN' TIRED WAITIN'!
HELP, POLICE!
SOME-THING'S UP DOWN THERE, STRIPESY! WE'D BETTER TAKE A LOOK!
DA BRAKES, QUICK... DEM SAPS IS GONNA BUMP US!
PERFECT, STRIPESY! NOW WE'D BETTER GET READY FOR SOME ACTION!
DON'T HIT ME, KID... I GIVE UP!
GOSH, AND I WANTED SOME EXERCISE!
IN COURT...
THERE'S NO DOUBT ABOUT IT, YOUR HONOR... I'VE EXAMINED THE LOOT, AND IT ALL CAME FROM MY HOUSE! THE DEFENDANTS ARE THE ONES WHO ROBBED ME!
JUST A MINUTE, YOUR HONOR!
ACCORDING TO SECTION 7, PARAGRAPH 3 OF THE STATE CODE, IN ALL CASES INVOLVING A FELONY WHERE TRESPASS IS ALLEGED..
HUH..? WHAT'S ALL THIS RIGMAROLE, KID?
I'VE GOT AN UNEASY FEELING, STRIPESY.. WE MAY BE IN FOR AN UNPLEASANT SURPRISE!
AND THEREFORE, YOUR HONOR, INASMUCH AS THE PROSECUTION HAS NEGLECTED TO PRESENT THE AFORESAID EVIDENCE IN THE PRESCRIBED MANNER...
HMM, I'M AFRAID YOU'RE RIGHT... I HAVE NO CHOICE BUT TO DIRECT A VERDICT OF ACQUITTAL!
WHA..? JUST BECAUSE THE D.A. LEFT OUT A COUPLA WOIDS IN THE INDICTMENT?
WHY, THE DOITY RATS... JUST LEMME GET MY HANDS ON THEM, AND I'LL...
YOU'LL DO NOTHING, STRIPESY! THIS SITUATION REQUIRES THE USE OF OUR HEADS, NOT OUR HANDS!
3

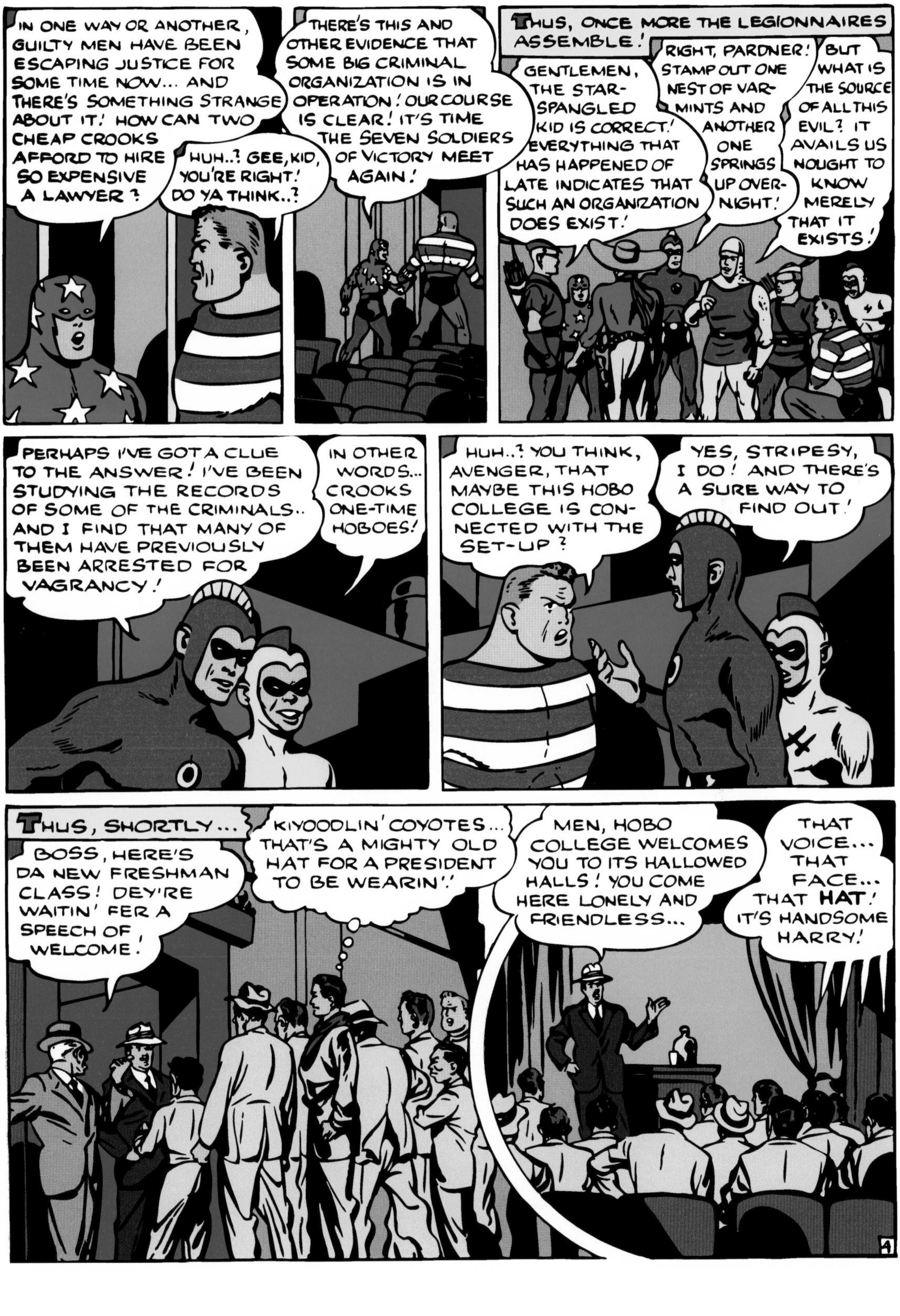
IN ONE WAY OR ANOTHER, GUILTY MEN HAVE BEEN ESCAPING JUSTICE FOR SOME TIME NOW... AND THERE'S SOMETHING STRANGE ABOUT IT! HOW CAN TWO CHEAP CROOKS AFFORD TO HIRE SO EXPENSIVE A LAWYER?
HUH..? GEE, KID, YOU'RE RIGHT! DO YA THINK..?
THERE'S THIS AND OTHER EVIDENCE THAT SOME BIG CRIMINAL ORGANIZATION IS IN OPERATION! OUR COURSE IS CLEAR! IT'S TIME THE SEVEN SOLDIERS OF VICTORY MEET AGAIN!
THUS, ONCE MORE THE LEGIONNAIRES ASSEMBLE!
GENTLEMEN, THE STAR-SPANGLED KID IS CORRECT! EVERYTHING THAT HAS HAPPENED OF LATE INDICATES THAT SUCH AN ORGANIZATION DOES EXIST!
RIGHT, PARDNER! STAMP OUT ONE NEST OF VARMINTS AND ANOTHER ONE SPRINGS UP OVERNIGHT!
BUT WHAT IS THE SOURCE OF ALL THIS EVIL? IT AVAILS US NOUGHT TO KNOW MERELY THAT IT EXISTS!
PERHAPS I'VE GOT A CLUE TO THE ANSWER! I'VE BEEN STUDYING THE RECORDS OF SOME OF THE CRIMINALS.. AND I FIND THAT MANY OF THEM HAVE PREVIOUSLY BEEN ARRESTED FOR VAGRANCY!
IN OTHER WORDS... CROOKS ONE-TIME HOBOES!
HUH..? YOU THINK, AVENGER, THAT MAYBE THIS HOBO COLLEGE IS CONNECTED WITH THE SET-UP?
YES, STRIPESY, I DO! AND THERE'S A SURE WAY TO FIND OUT!
THUS, SHORTLY...
BOSS, HERE'S DA NEW FRESHMAN CLASS! DEY'RE WAITIN' FER A SPEECH OF WELCOME!
KIYOODLIN' COYOTES... THAT'S A MIGHTY OLD HAT FOR A PRESIDENT TO BE WEARIN'!
MEN, HOBO COLLEGE WELCOMES YOU TO ITS HALLOWED HALLS! YOU COME HERE LONELY AND FRIENDLESS...
THAT VOICE... THAT FACE... THAT HAT! IT'S HANDSOME HARRY!
4

MOMENTS LATER, IN THE HOBO DORMITORY...

BOYS, NOW THAT WE'VE RECOGNIZED HANDSOME HARRY, THERE'S NO NEED TO WAIT AND GATHER EVIDENCE! WE'VE GOT ENOUGH ON HIM TO SEND HIM TO JAIL RIGHT NOW!

AND WITH HIM OUT OF THE WAY, HIS ENTIRE ORGANIZATION WILL FALL TO PIECES, EXACTLY AS BEFORE!

WHILE IN THE OFFICE OF THE PRESIDENT...

SOME OF THOSE FRESHMEN LOOKED ALMOST **TOO** TOUGH! I'LL JUST LISTEN IN ON THEM WITH THIS DICTAPHONE, AND... **WHA—?**

NOW THAT WE'VE RECOGNIZED HANDSOME HARRY...

THEY KNOW ME...AND THEY'RE AFTER ME!

A TREMBLING FINGER FUMBLES FRANTICALLY FOR A BUTTON, AND A SHRILL CLAMOR AROUSES THE CAMPUS!

WE WON'T BOTHER WITH THE SMALL FRY, PARDNERS... WHAT'S THAT?

RRRIIIINNNGG!

AN ALARM! MAYBE HARRY CAUGHT WISE TO US!

WE'D BETTER ACT BEFORE HE CAN GET HIS MEN TOGETHER!

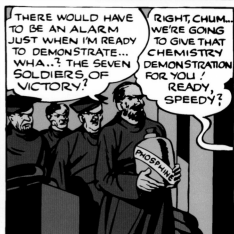

THERE WOULD HAVE TO BE AN ALARM JUST WHEN I'M READY TO DEMONSTRATE... WHA..? THE SEVEN SOLDIERS OF VICTORY?

RIGHT, CHUM... WE'RE GOING TO GIVE THAT CHEMISTRY DEMONSTRATION FOR YOU! READY, SPEEDY?

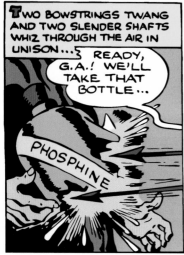

TWO BOWSTRINGS TWANG AND TWO SLENDER SHAFTS WHIZ THROUGH THE AIR IN UNISON...

READY, G.A.! WE'LL TAKE THAT BOTTLE...

PHOSPHINE

AND SHOW EVERYBODY THAT PHOSPHINE BURSTS INTO FLAME WHEN IT HITS THE AIR!

WELL DONE, COMRADES! NOW TEACH I THESE ROGUES DIVERS LESSONS FROM ANCIENT HISTORY!

5

WHILE **WE** HAND OUT A LITTLE INSTRUCTION IN PHYSICS!

WE DEMONSTRATE LAW OF PENDULUM!

MATHEMATICS IS MY SPECIALTY, PARDNERS! I AIM TO PROVE THAT RATTLERS IN THIS CIRCLE AIN'T ON THE SQUARE!

GOSH, KID, NOTHIN' ELSE FOR US TA DO BUT TEACH GYM!

IT'S QUITE A TRICK AT THAT, STRIPESY, SHOWING DUMBBELLS HOW TO TURN SOMERSAULTS!

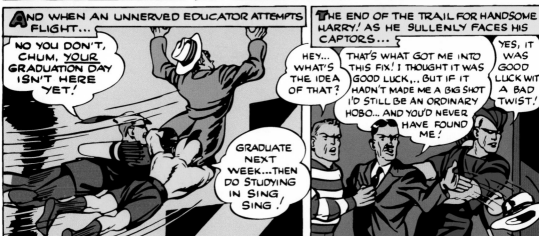

AND WHEN AN UNNERVED EDUCATOR ATTEMPTS FLIGHT...

NO YOU DON'T, CHUM, YOUR GRADUATION DAY ISN'T HERE YET!

GRADUATE NEXT WEEK...THEN DO STUDYING IN SING SING!

THE END OF THE TRAIL FOR HANDSOME HARRY! AS HE SULLENLY FACES HIS CAPTORS...

HEY... WHAT'S THE IDEA OF THAT?

THAT'S WHAT GOT ME INTO THIS FIX! I THOUGHT IT WAS GOOD LUCK,.. BUT IF IT HADN'T MADE ME A BIG SHOT I'D STILL BE AN ORDINARY HOBO... AND YOU'D NEVER HAVE FOUND ME!

YES, IT WAS GOOD LUCK WITH A BAD TWIST!

WHICH IS ABOUT AS MUCH LUCK AS ANY CROOK CAN EXPECT WHEN THE SEVEN SOLDIERS OF VICTORY GET AFTER HIM!

AS WE HAVE OFT PROVED BEFORE... AND AS WE SHALL PROVE AGAIN!

THUS, ON THE DESERTED HOBO CAMPUS, THE HARD-LUCK HAT FINDS ITS FINAL HAVEN!

AND THERE LET US LEAVE IT, ITS POWER FOR EVIL GONE AT LAST! 6

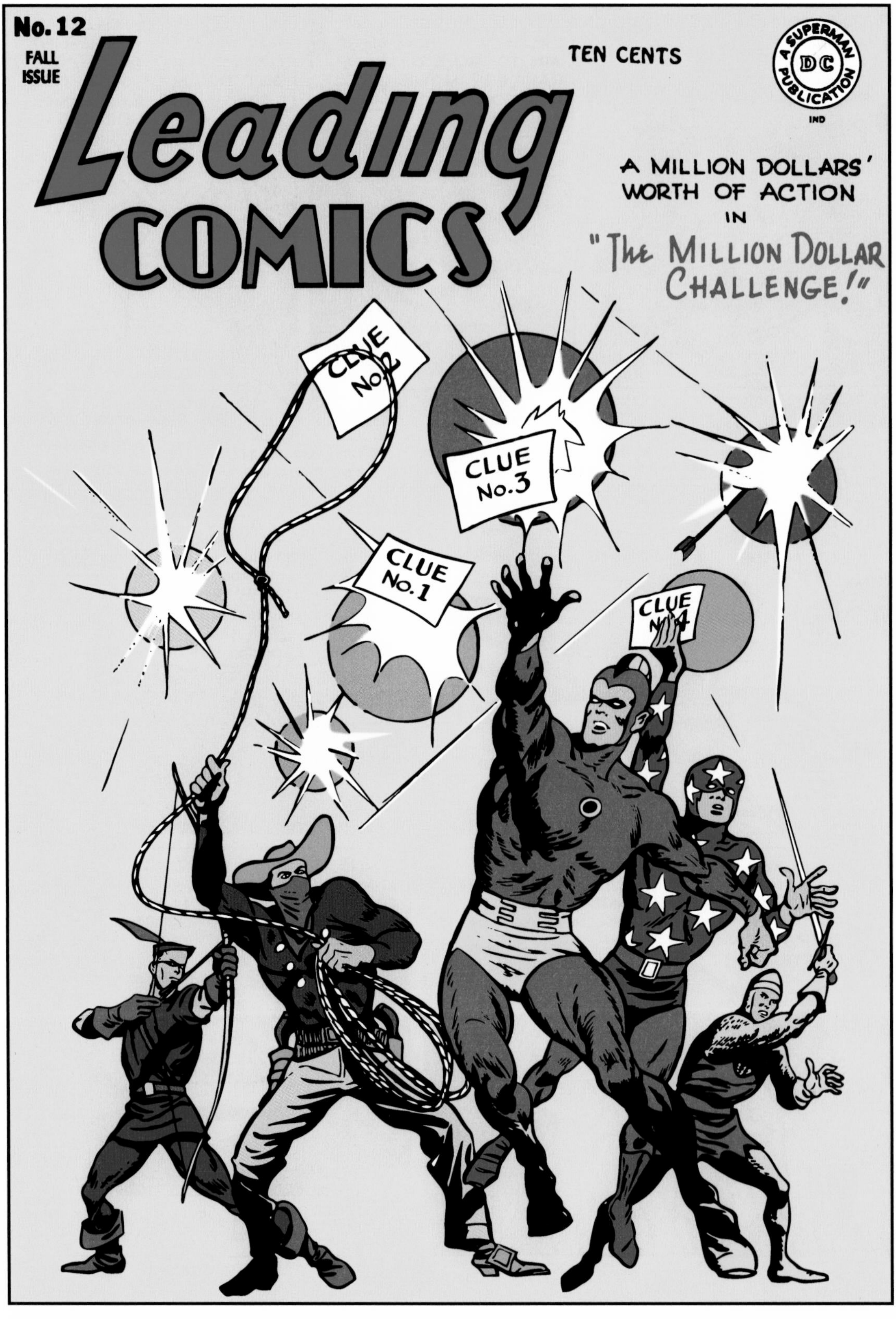
No. 12
FALL ISSUE
TEN CENTS
A SUPERMAN DC PUBLICATION
IND
Leading COMICS
A MILLION DOLLARS' WORTH OF ACTION IN
"The MILLION DOLLAR CHALLENGE!"
CLUE No. 2
CLUE No. 3
CLUE No. 1
CLUE No. 4

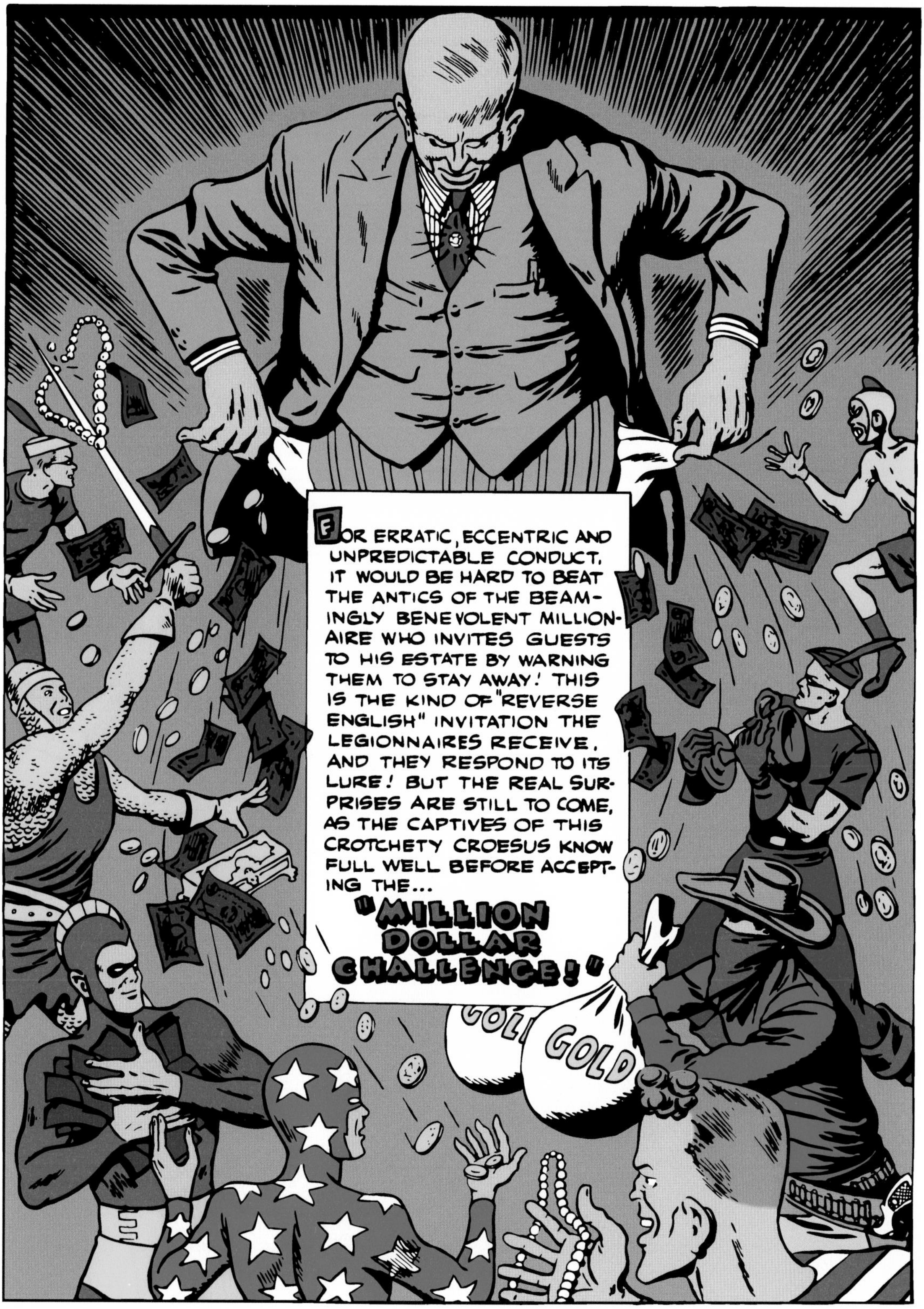
FOR ERRATIC, ECCENTRIC AND UNPREDICTABLE CONDUCT, IT WOULD BE HARD TO BEAT THE ANTICS OF THE BEAMINGLY BENEVOLENT MILLIONAIRE WHO INVITES GUESTS TO HIS ESTATE BY WARNING THEM TO STAY AWAY! THIS IS THE KIND OF "REVERSE ENGLISH" INVITATION THE LEGIONNAIRES RECEIVE, AND THEY RESPOND TO ITS LURE! BUT THE REAL SURPRISES ARE STILL TO COME, AS THE CAPTIVES OF THIS CROTCHETY CROESUS KNOW FULL WELL BEFORE ACCEPTING THE...
"MILLION DOLLAR CHALLENGE!"
GOLD
GOLD

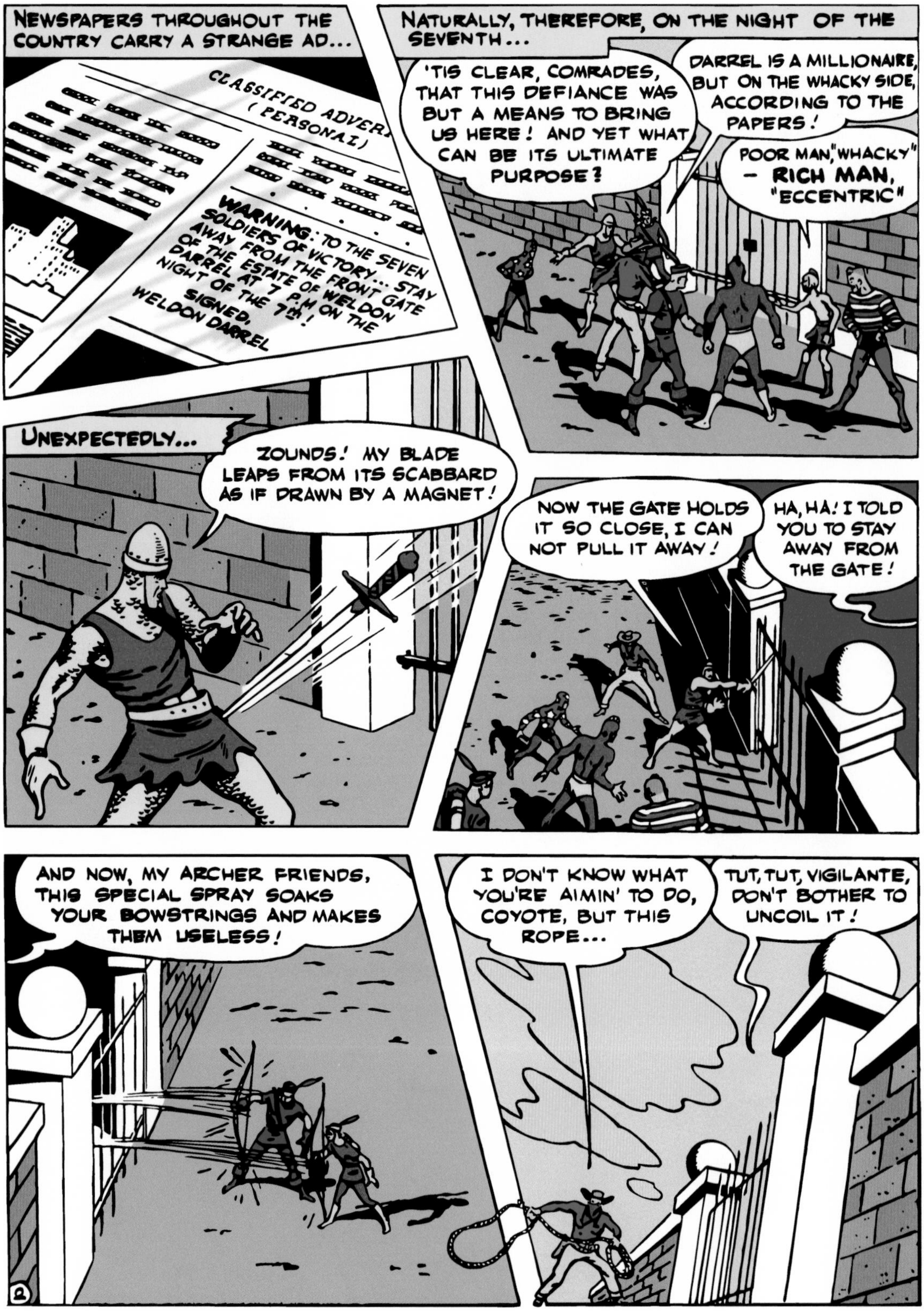
NEWSPAPERS THROUGHOUT THE COUNTRY CARRY A STRANGE AD...
CLASSIFIED ADVER
(PERSONAL)
WARNING: TO THE SEVEN SOLDIERS OF VICTORY... STAY AWAY FROM THE FRONT GATE OF THE ESTATE OF WELDON DARREL AT 7 P.M ON THE NIGHT OF THE 7TH!
SIGNED, WELDON DARREL
NATURALLY, THEREFORE, ON THE NIGHT OF THE SEVENTH...
'TIS CLEAR, COMRADES, THAT THIS DEFIANCE WAS BUT A MEANS TO BRING US HERE! AND YET WHAT CAN BE ITS ULTIMATE PURPOSE?
DARREL IS A MILLIONAIRE, BUT ON THE WHACKY SIDE, ACCORDING TO THE PAPERS!
POOR MAN, "WHACKY" – RICH MAN, "ECCENTRIC"
UNEXPECTEDLY...
ZOUNDS! MY BLADE LEAPS FROM ITS SCABBARD AS IF DRAWN BY A MAGNET!
NOW THE GATE HOLDS IT SO CLOSE, I CAN NOT PULL IT AWAY!
HA, HA! I TOLD YOU TO STAY AWAY FROM THE GATE!
AND NOW, MY ARCHER FRIENDS, THIS SPECIAL SPRAY SOAKS YOUR BOWSTRINGS AND MAKES THEM USELESS!
2
I DON'T KNOW WHAT YOU'RE AIMIN' TO DO, COYOTE, BUT THIS ROPE...
TUT, TUT, VIGILANTE, DON'T BOTHER TO UNCOIL IT!

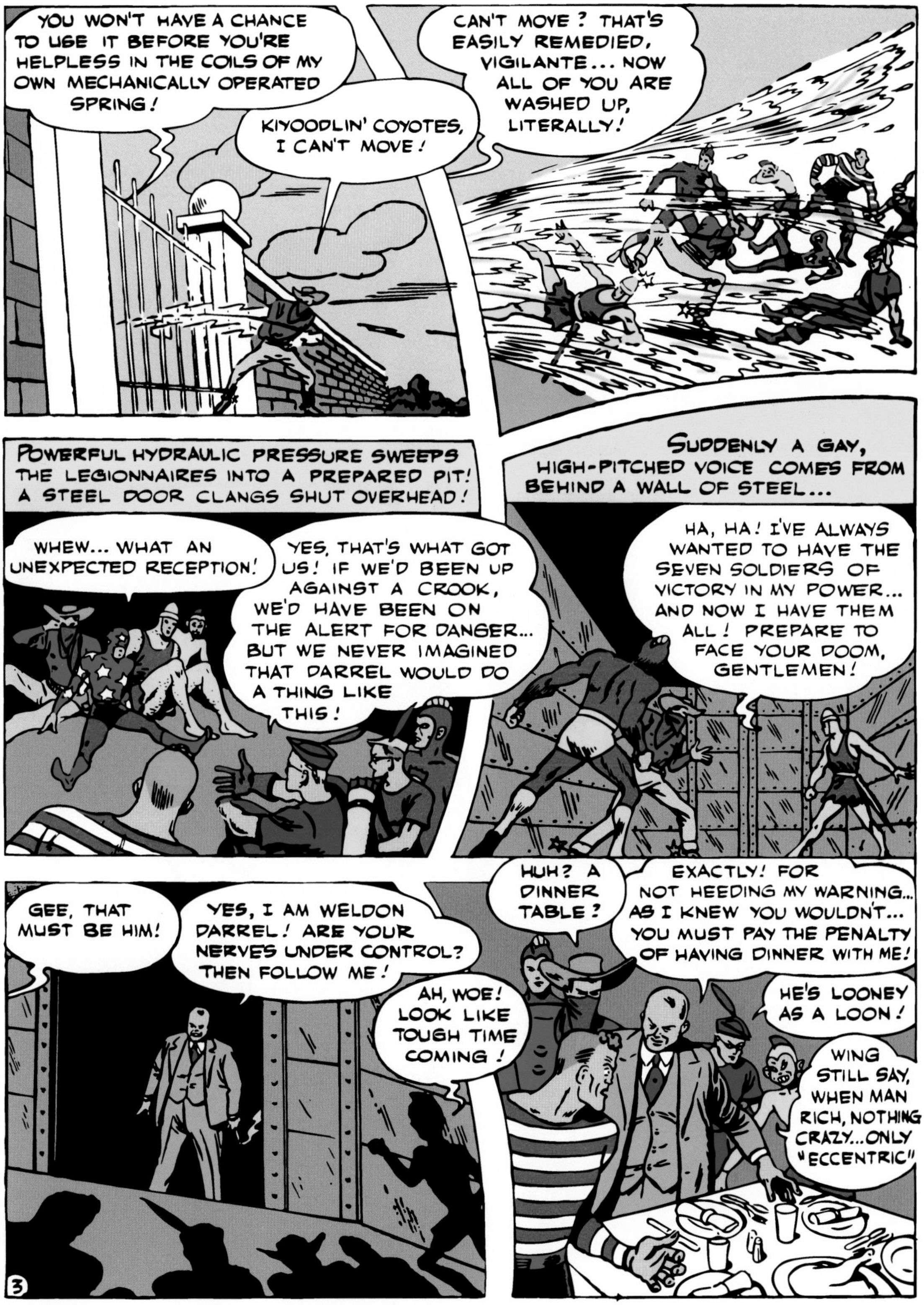
YOU WON'T HAVE A CHANCE TO USE IT BEFORE YOU'RE HELPLESS IN THE COILS OF MY OWN MECHANICALLY OPERATED SPRING!
KIYOODLIN' COYOTES, I CAN'T MOVE!
CAN'T MOVE? THAT'S EASILY REMEDIED, VIGILANTE... NOW ALL OF YOU ARE WASHED UP, LITERALLY!
POWERFUL HYDRAULIC PRESSURE SWEEPS THE LEGIONNAIRES INTO A PREPARED PIT! A STEEL DOOR CLANGS SHUT OVERHEAD!
WHEW... WHAT AN UNEXPECTED RECEPTION!
YES, THAT'S WHAT GOT US! IF WE'D BEEN UP AGAINST A CROOK, WE'D HAVE BEEN ON THE ALERT FOR DANGER... BUT WE NEVER IMAGINED THAT DARREL WOULD DO A THING LIKE THIS!
SUDDENLY A GAY, HIGH-PITCHED VOICE COMES FROM BEHIND A WALL OF STEEL...
HA, HA! I'VE ALWAYS WANTED TO HAVE THE SEVEN SOLDIERS OF VICTORY IN MY POWER... AND NOW I HAVE THEM ALL! PREPARE TO FACE YOUR DOOM, GENTLEMEN!
GEE, THAT MUST BE HIM!
YES, I AM WELDON DARREL! ARE YOUR NERVES UNDER CONTROL? THEN FOLLOW ME!
AH, WOE! LOOK LIKE TOUGH TIME COMING!
3
HUH? A DINNER TABLE?
EXACTLY! FOR NOT HEEDING MY WARNING... AS I KNEW YOU WOULDN'T... YOU MUST PAY THE PENALTY OF HAVING DINNER WITH ME!
HE'S LOONEY AS A LOON!
WING STILL SAY, WHEN MAN RICH, NOTHING CRAZY...ONLY "ECCENTRIC"

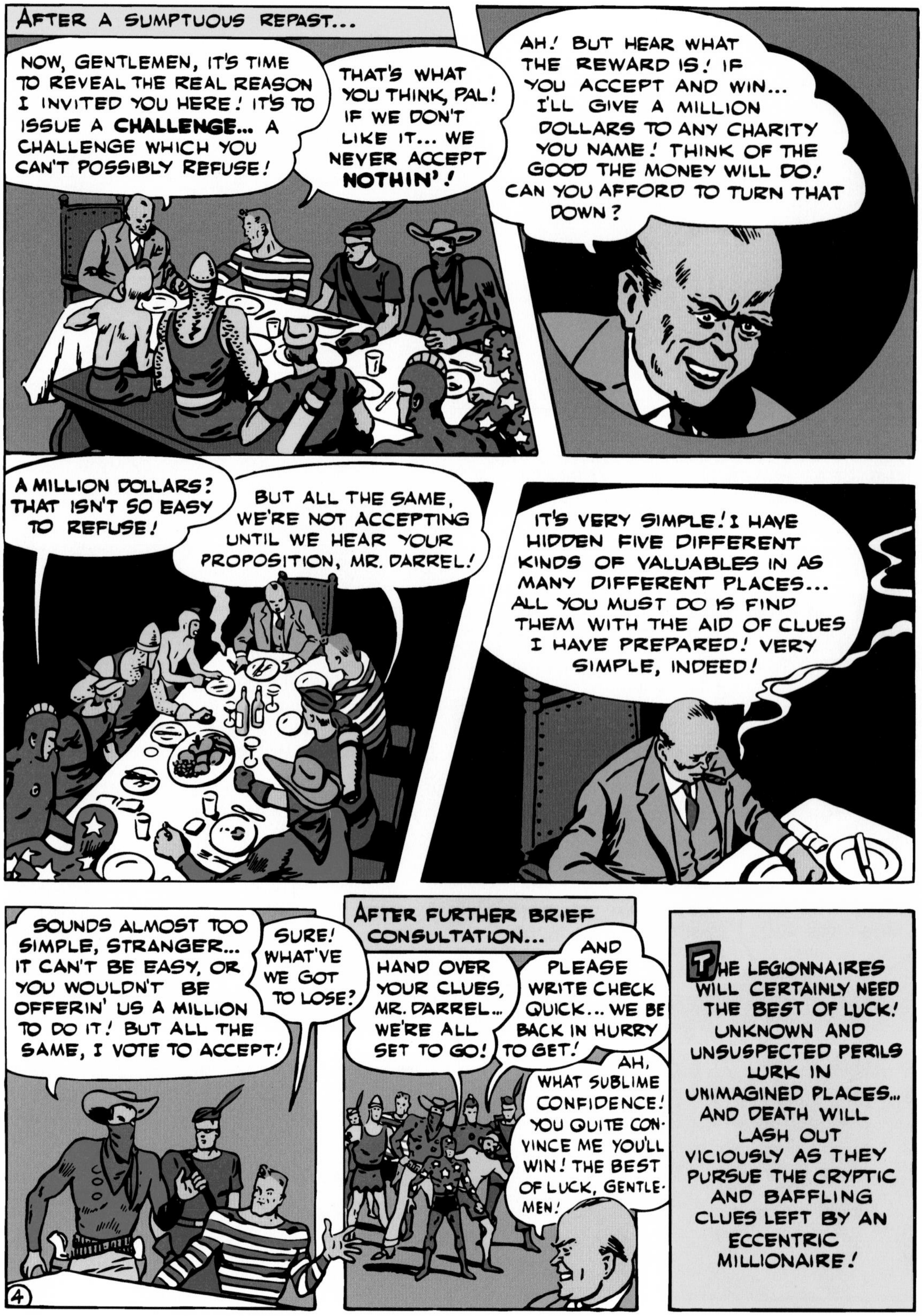
AFTER A SUMPTUOUS REPAST...
NOW, GENTLEMEN, IT'S TIME TO REVEAL THE REAL REASON I INVITED YOU HERE! IT'S TO ISSUE A **CHALLENGE...** A CHALLENGE WHICH YOU CAN'T POSSIBLY REFUSE!
THAT'S WHAT YOU THINK, PAL! IF WE DON'T LIKE IT... WE NEVER ACCEPT **NOTHIN'**!
AH! BUT HEAR WHAT THE REWARD IS! IF YOU ACCEPT AND WIN... I'LL GIVE A MILLION DOLLARS TO ANY CHARITY YOU NAME! THINK OF THE GOOD THE MONEY WILL DO! CAN YOU AFFORD TO TURN THAT DOWN?
A MILLION DOLLARS? THAT ISN'T SO EASY TO REFUSE!
BUT ALL THE SAME, WE'RE NOT ACCEPTING UNTIL WE HEAR YOUR PROPOSITION, MR. DARREL!
IT'S VERY SIMPLE! I HAVE HIDDEN FIVE DIFFERENT KINDS OF VALUABLES IN AS MANY DIFFERENT PLACES... ALL YOU MUST DO IS FIND THEM WITH THE AID OF CLUES I HAVE PREPARED! VERY SIMPLE, INDEED!
SOUNDS ALMOST TOO SIMPLE, STRANGER... IT CAN'T BE EASY, OR YOU WOULDN'T BE OFFERIN' US A MILLION TO DO IT! BUT ALL THE SAME, I VOTE TO ACCEPT!
SURE! WHAT'VE WE GOT TO LOSE?
4
AFTER FURTHER BRIEF CONSULTATION...
HAND OVER YOUR CLUES, MR. DARREL... WE'RE ALL SET TO GO!
AND PLEASE WRITE CHECK QUICK... WE BE BACK IN HURRY TO GET!
AH, WHAT SUBLIME CONFIDENCE! YOU QUITE CONVINCE ME YOU'LL WIN! THE BEST OF LUCK, GENTLEMEN!
THE LEGIONNAIRES WILL CERTAINLY NEED THE BEST OF LUCK! UNKNOWN AND UNSUSPECTED PERILS LURK IN UNIMAGINED PLACES... AND DEATH WILL LASH OUT VICIOUSLY AS THEY PURSUE THE CRYPTIC AND BAFFLING CLUES LEFT BY AN ECCENTRIC MILLIONAIRE!

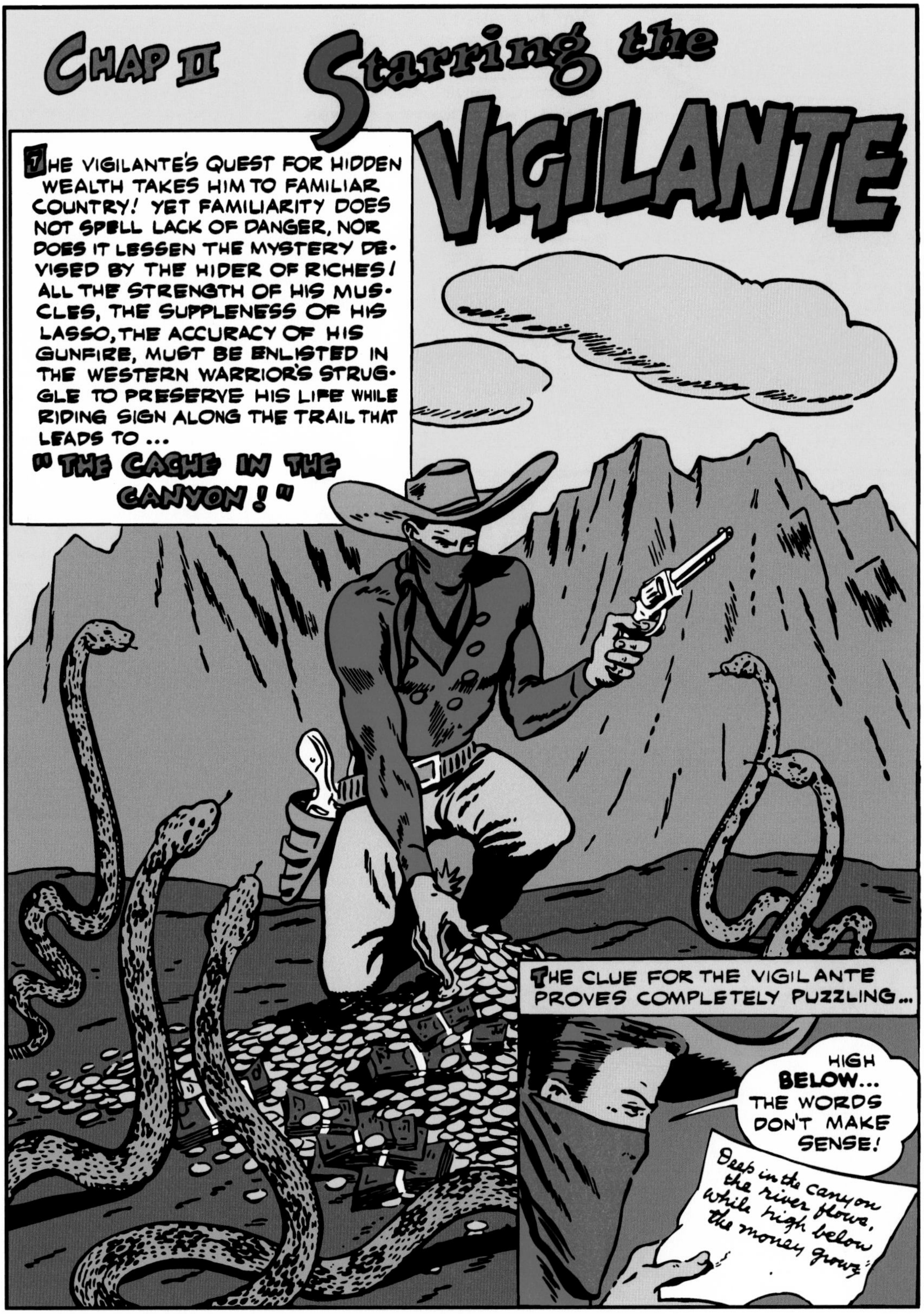

CHAP II
Starring the VIGILANTE
THE VIGILANTE'S QUEST FOR HIDDEN WEALTH TAKES HIM TO FAMILIAR COUNTRY! YET FAMILIARITY DOES NOT SPELL LACK OF DANGER, NOR DOES IT LESSEN THE MYSTERY DE-VISED BY THE HIDER OF RICHES! ALL THE STRENGTH OF HIS MUS-CLES, THE SUPPLENESS OF HIS LASSO, THE ACCURACY OF HIS GUNFIRE, MUST BE ENLISTED IN THE WESTERN WARRIOR'S STRUG-GLE TO PRESERVE HIS LIFE WHILE RIDING SIGN ALONG THE TRAIL THAT LEADS TO ...
"THE CACHE IN THE CANYON!"
THE CLUE FOR THE VIGILANTE PROVES COMPLETELY PUZZLING...
HIGH BELOW... THE WORDS DON'T MAKE SENSE!
Deep in the canyon the river flows, while high below the money grows!

IN FACT THIS DON'T HELP AT ALL! THE WEST'S FULL OF CANYONS...

BUT THE WESTERN WADDY PUTS HIS BRAIN TO WORK ON THE PROBLEM...

DARREL OWNS LAND ALL OVER THE COUNTRY... MAYBE HE OWNS SOME IN THE WEST TOO! I'LL TELEGRAPH THE DIFFERENT STATE LAND-OFFICES AND WAIT FOR THE ANSWERS!

A LITTLE LATER...

AH... THE OLD COOT OWNS A MINING CLAIM IN WYOMING THAT STRETCHES RIGHT UP TO A CANYON! AND IT WAS NEVER WORKED! MAYBE THAT'S THE ONE!

UNION TELEG
DARREL OWNER OF

AND SO THE VIGILANTE TRAVELS WEST! PRESENTLY...

I STILL CAN'T FIGGER WHAT "HIGH BELOW" CAN MEAN... BUT MAYBE I WILL WHEN I SEE THAT CANYON! FASTER, OLD HOSS!

BUT FROM BEHIND A NEARBY RIDGE, THE PUNCHING PLAINSMAN'S PROGRESS IS OBSERVED BY TWO PAIRS OF KEEN, COLD EYES...

THE VIGILANTE! WHAT'S HE DOIN' HERE, BOSS?

I DON'T KNOW, PETE... BUT I GOT AN IDEAR HE MAY BE AFTER US! MAYBE SOMEBODY SUSPECTS WHERE THAT GOLD DUST IS COMIN' FROM!

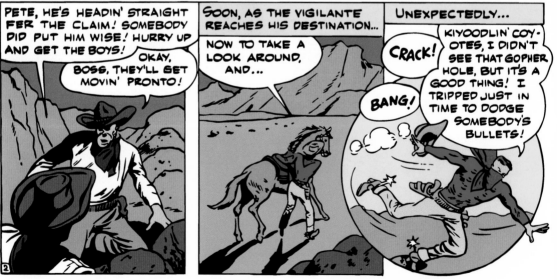

PETE, HE'S HEADIN' STRAIGHT FER THE CLAIM! SOMEBODY DID PUT HIM WISE! HURRY UP AND GET THE BOYS!

OKAY, BOSS, THEY'LL GET MOVIN' PRONTO!

SOON, AS THE VIGILANTE REACHES HIS DESTINATION...

NOW TO TAKE A LOOK AROUND, AND...

UNEXPECTEDLY...

CRACK!

BANG!

KIYOODLIN' COYOTES, I DIDN'T SEE THAT GOPHER HOLE, BUT IT'S A GOOD THING! I TRIPPED JUST IN TIME TO DODGE SOMEBODY'S BULLETS!

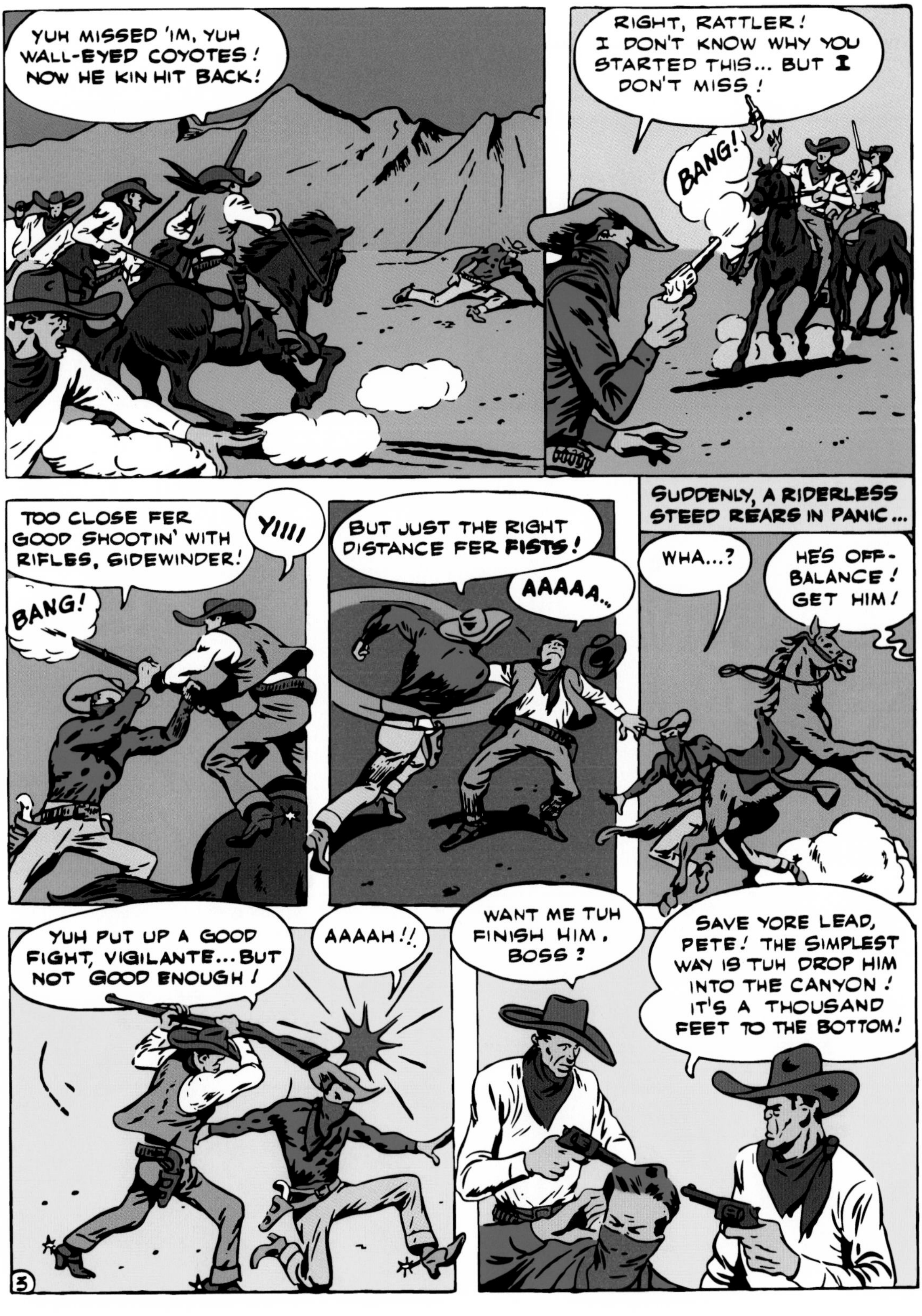
YUH MISSED 'IM, YUH WALL-EYED COYOTES! NOW HE KIN HIT BACK!
RIGHT, RATTLER! I DON'T KNOW WHY YOU STARTED THIS... BUT I DON'T MISS!
BANG!
TOO CLOSE FER GOOD SHOOTIN' WITH RIFLES, SIDEWINDER!
YIIII
BANG!
BUT JUST THE RIGHT DISTANCE FER FISTS!
AAAAA...
SUDDENLY, A RIDERLESS STEED REARS IN PANIC...
WHA...?
HE'S OFF-BALANCE! GET HIM!
YUH PUT UP A GOOD FIGHT, VIGILANTE... BUT NOT GOOD ENOUGH!
AAAAH!!
3
WANT ME TUH FINISH HIM, BOSS?
SAVE YORE LEAD, PETE! THE SIMPLEST WAY IS TUH DROP HIM INTO THE CANYON! IT'S A THOUSAND FEET TO THE BOTTOM!

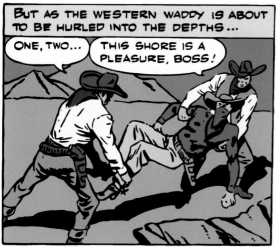

BUT AS THE WESTERN WADDY IS ABOUT TO BE HURLED INTO THE DEPTHS...

ONE, TWO...

THIS SHORE IS A PLEASURE, BOSS!

THREE...YIII! HE'S PULLIN' ME AFTER HIM!

MIGHT BE LONELY DOWN IN THE CANYON, VARMINT... I'M AIMIN' TO HAVE COMPANY!

I GOT YUH, BOSS! SHOOT THE VIGILANTE, SOMEBODY... MAKE 'IM LET GO!

HUH..? RECKON HE COULDN'T HOLD ON NO LONGER! PUT AWAY YORE COLTS, BOYS... THE VIGILANTE'S FINISHED!

HE'S SO FAR DOWN, YUH CAN'T EVEN SEE HIM CLEAR! HE LOOKS LIKE JUST A BLACK SPECK! BUT HE SHORE MAKES A PURTY SOUND!

YEAH! AND NOW WE CAN GO BACK TO WORK! COME ON, BOYS!

CRASH!

IS THE VIGILANTE FINISHED? ONLY SOMEONE IGNORANT OF THE LARRUPING LARIATEER'S WILES COULD BELIEVE THAT!

LUCKY THIS LEDGE WAS HERE! ALL I HAD TO DO WAS SHOVE A ROCK OVER... AND THEY THOUGHT THE CRASH CAME FROM ME! WONDER WHY THEY WANTED TO KILL ME, ANYWAY?

④

THIS IS A KIND OF FUNNY PLACE TO FIND HERE, AT THAT! HIGH UP ABOVE THE CANYON, AND JUST BELOW THE TOP... GALLOPIN' GOPHERS, WHAT DID I JUST SAY?

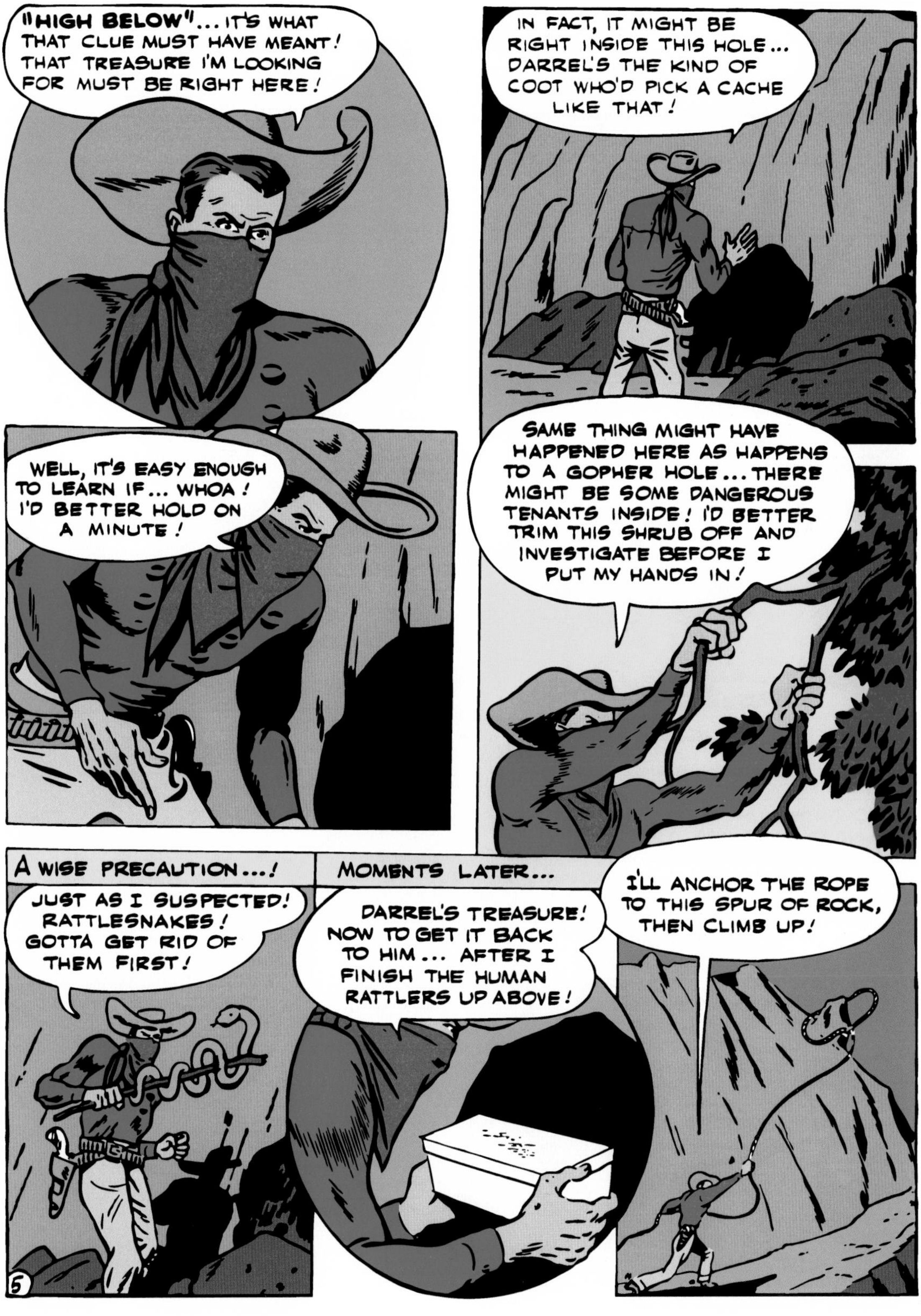
"HIGH BELOW"... IT'S WHAT THAT CLUE MUST HAVE MEANT! THAT TREASURE I'M LOOKING FOR MUST BE RIGHT HERE!
IN FACT, IT MIGHT BE RIGHT INSIDE THIS HOLE... DARREL'S THE KIND OF COOT WHO'D PICK A CACHE LIKE THAT!
WELL, IT'S EASY ENOUGH TO LEARN IF... WHOA! I'D BETTER HOLD ON A MINUTE!
SAME THING MIGHT HAVE HAPPENED HERE AS HAPPENS TO A GOPHER HOLE... THERE MIGHT BE SOME DANGEROUS TENANTS INSIDE! I'D BETTER TRIM THIS SHRUB OFF AND INVESTIGATE BEFORE I PUT MY HANDS IN!
A WISE PRECAUTION...!
JUST AS I SUSPECTED! RATTLESNAKES! GOTTA GET RID OF THEM FIRST!
5
MOMENTS LATER...
DARREL'S TREASURE! NOW TO GET IT BACK TO HIM... AFTER I FINISH THE HUMAN RATTLERS UP ABOVE!
I'LL ANCHOR THE ROPE TO THIS SPUR OF ROCK, THEN CLIMB UP!

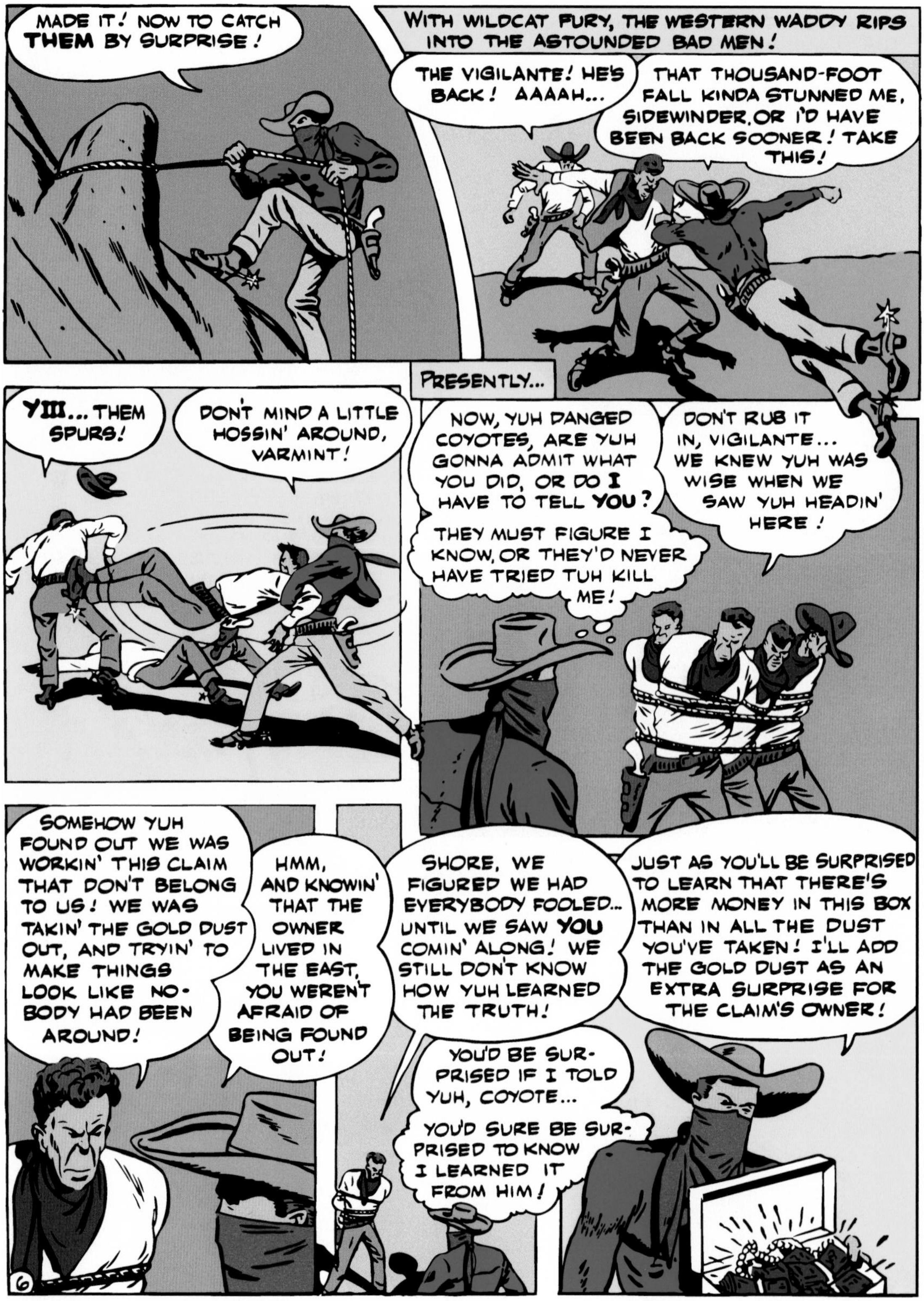
MADE IT! NOW TO CATCH THEM BY SURPRISE!
WITH WILDCAT FURY, THE WESTERN WADDY RIPS INTO THE ASTOUNDED BAD MEN!
THE VIGILANTE! HE'S BACK! AAAAH...
THAT THOUSAND-FOOT FALL KINDA STUNNED ME, SIDEWINDER, OR I'D HAVE BEEN BACK SOONER! TAKE THIS!
YIII... THEM SPURS!
DON'T MIND A LITTLE HOSSIN' AROUND, VARMINT!
PRESENTLY...
NOW, YUH DANGED COYOTES, ARE YUH GONNA ADMIT WHAT YOU DID, OR DO I HAVE TO TELL YOU?
THEY MUST FIGURE I KNOW, OR THEY'D NEVER HAVE TRIED TUH KILL ME!
DON'T RUB IT IN, VIGILANTE... WE KNEW YUH WAS WISE WHEN WE SAW YUH HEADIN' HERE!
SOMEHOW YUH FOUND OUT WE WAS WORKIN' THIS CLAIM THAT DON'T BELONG TO US! WE WAS TAKIN' THE GOLD DUST OUT, AND TRYIN' TO MAKE THINGS LOOK LIKE NO-BODY HAD BEEN AROUND!
HMM, AND KNOWIN' THAT THE OWNER LIVED IN THE EAST, YOU WEREN'T AFRAID OF BEING FOUND OUT!
SHORE, WE FIGURED WE HAD EVERYBODY FOOLED... UNTIL WE SAW YOU COMIN' ALONG! WE STILL DON'T KNOW HOW YUH LEARNED THE TRUTH!
YOU'D BE SUR-PRISED IF I TOLD YUH, COYOTE...
YOU'D SURE BE SUR-PRISED TO KNOW I LEARNED IT FROM HIM!
JUST AS YOU'LL BE SURPRISED TO LEARN THAT THERE'S MORE MONEY IN THIS BOX THAN IN ALL THE DUST YOU'VE TAKEN! I'LL ADD THE GOLD DUST AS AN EXTRA SURPRISE FOR THE CLAIM'S OWNER!
6

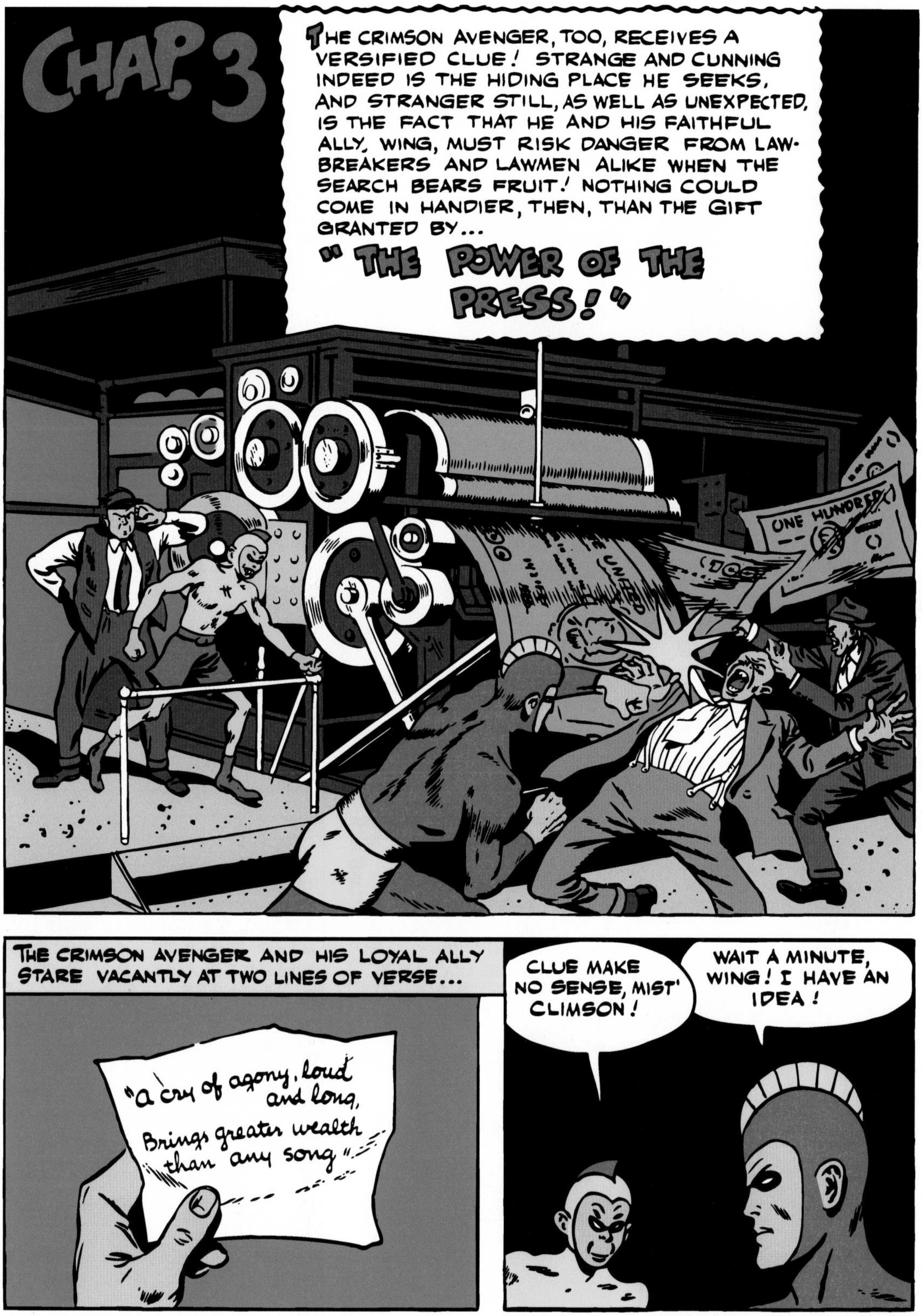
CHAP. 3
THE CRIMSON AVENGER, TOO, RECEIVES A VERSIFIED CLUE! STRANGE AND CUNNING INDEED IS THE HIDING PLACE HE SEEKS, AND STRANGER STILL, AS WELL AS UNEXPECTED, IS THE FACT THAT HE AND HIS FAITHFUL ALLY, WING, MUST RISK DANGER FROM LAW-BREAKERS AND LAWMEN ALIKE WHEN THE SEARCH BEARS FRUIT! NOTHING COULD COME IN HANDIER, THEN, THAN THE GIFT GRANTED BY...
"THE POWER OF THE PRESS!"
ONE HUNDRED
THE CRIMSON AVENGER AND HIS LOYAL ALLY STARE VACANTLY AT TWO LINES OF VERSE...
"a cry of agony, loud and long, Brings greater wealth than any song"
CLUE MAKE NO SENSE, MIST' CLIMSON!
WAIT A MINUTE, WING! I HAVE AN IDEA!

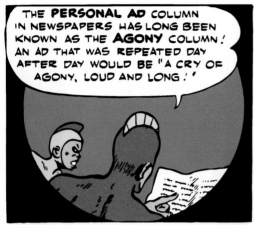

THE **PERSONAL AD** COLUMN IN NEWSPAPERS HAS LONG BEEN KNOWN AS THE **AGONY** COLUMN! AN AD THAT WAS REPEATED DAY AFTER DAY WOULD BE "A CRY OF AGONY, LOUD AND LONG."

BUT AFTER A SEARCH THROUGH SEVERAL DAYS' EDITIONS...

TOO BAD, MIST' CLIMSON! IDEA SOUND GOOD BUT NO WORK!

I WAS SURE I HAD HIT IT, BUT THERE'S NO SUCH AD IN ANY OF THESE PAPERS!

MAYBE IN SOME OTHER NEWSPAPER, BUT WE NOT GOT TIME TO LOOK AT ALL PAPERS IN COUNTRY!

SOME OTHER NEWS-PAPER? WING, I THINK YOU'VE GOT IT!

DARREL ONCE GOT ANGRY AT THE OWNER OF A SMALL COUNTRY PAPER NEAR HIS SUMMER HOME, AND BOUGHT IT! I REMEMBER BECAUSE HE PAID SUCH A HIGH PRICE FOR IT!

AND YOU THINK HE PLINT AGONY AD IN OWN PAPER? OKAY, MIST'CLIMSON,.. WE GO SEE!

SO PRESENTLY, IN THE OFFICE OF A SMALL COUNTRY WEEKLY...

THE CRIMSON AVENGER AND WING! GOSHAMIGHTY! THIS VISIT WILL SURE MAKE A FINE NEWS STORY!

WE CAME HERE TO ASK A FAVOR, MR. BLAKE. WE WANT TO LOOK THROUGH YOUR FILES FOR THE PAST FEW MONTHS!

GO RIGHT AHEAD, AVENGER, I'M NOT ASHAMED OF THE SHEET! OF COURSE, MR. DARREL DIDN'T GIVE ME MUCH MONEY TO RUN IT WITH...

EDITOR

2

"RUN IT AS BEST YOU CAN," HE SAID! "IF YOU'VE GOT BRAINS, YOU WON'T HAVE ANY TROUBLE FINDING MONEY!" BUT IT WASN'T SO EASY, AVENGER!

LOOK, WING... I THINK THIS IS IT!

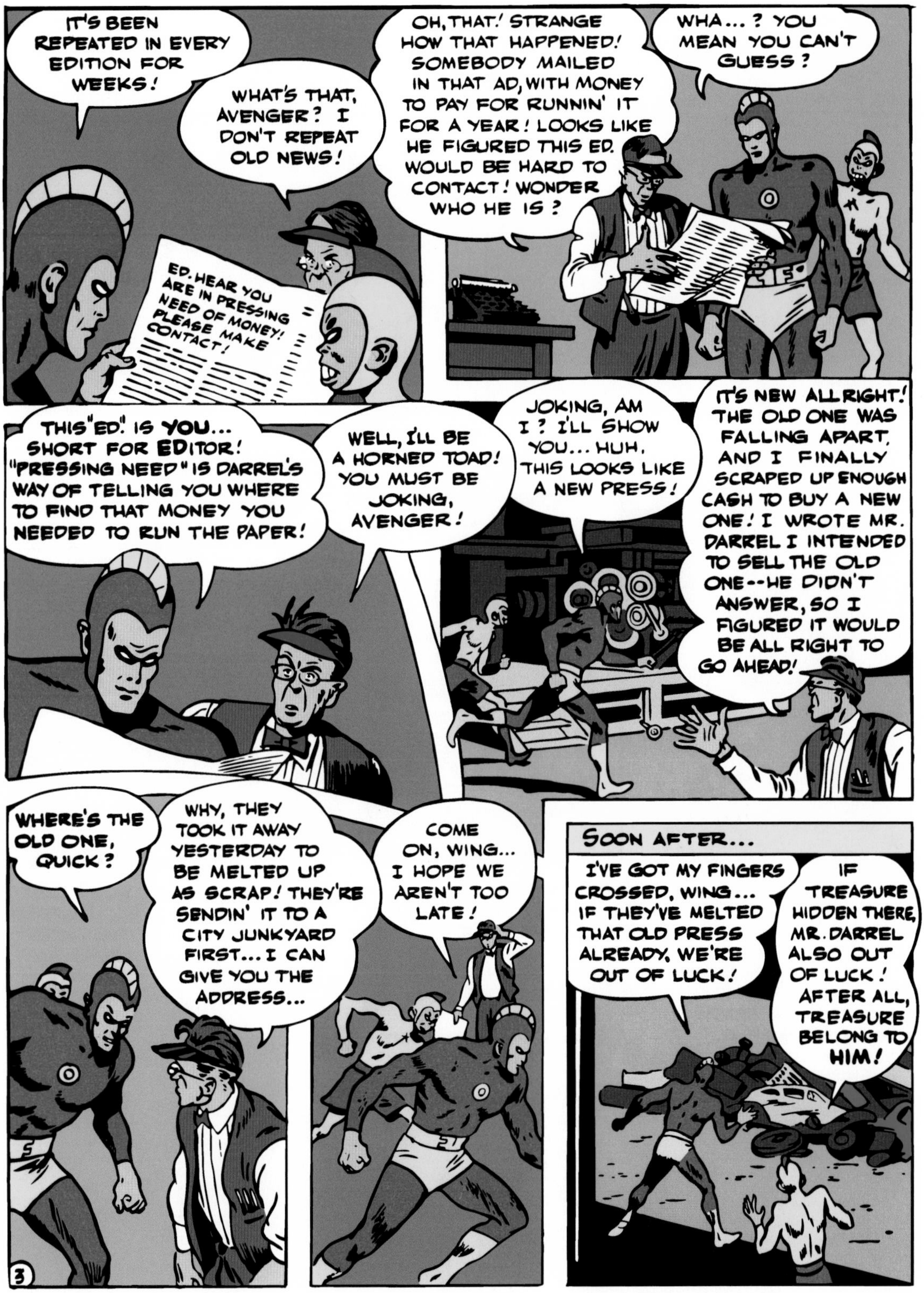
IT'S BEEN REPEATED IN EVERY EDITION FOR WEEKS!
WHAT'S THAT, AVENGER? I DON'T REPEAT OLD NEWS!
ED. HEAR YOU ARE IN PRESSING NEED OF MONEY! PLEASE MAKE CONTACT!
OH, THAT! STRANGE HOW THAT HAPPENED! SOMEBODY MAILED IN THAT AD, WITH MONEY TO PAY FOR RUNNIN' IT FOR A YEAR! LOOKS LIKE HE FIGURED THIS ED. WOULD BE HARD TO CONTACT! WONDER WHO HE IS?
WHA...? YOU MEAN YOU CAN'T GUESS?
THIS "ED." IS YOU... SHORT FOR EDITOR! "PRESSING NEED" IS DARREL'S WAY OF TELLING YOU WHERE TO FIND THAT MONEY YOU NEEDED TO RUN THE PAPER!
WELL, I'LL BE A HORNED TOAD! YOU MUST BE JOKING, AVENGER!
JOKING, AM I? I'LL SHOW YOU... HUH, THIS LOOKS LIKE A NEW PRESS!
IT'S NEW ALL RIGHT! THE OLD ONE WAS FALLING APART, AND I FINALLY SCRAPED UP ENOUGH CASH TO BUY A NEW ONE! I WROTE MR. DARREL I INTENDED TO SELL THE OLD ONE--HE DIDN'T ANSWER, SO I FIGURED IT WOULD BE ALL RIGHT TO GO AHEAD!
WHERE'S THE OLD ONE, QUICK?
WHY, THEY TOOK IT AWAY YESTERDAY TO BE MELTED UP AS SCRAP! THEY'RE SENDIN' IT TO A CITY JUNKYARD FIRST... I CAN GIVE YOU THE ADDRESS...
COME ON, WING... I HOPE WE AREN'T TOO LATE!
SOON AFTER...
I'VE GOT MY FINGERS CROSSED, WING... IF THEY'VE MELTED THAT OLD PRESS ALREADY, WE'RE OUT OF LUCK!
IF TREASURE HIDDEN THERE, MR. DARREL ALSO OUT OF LUCK! AFTER ALL, TREASURE BELONG TO HIM!
3

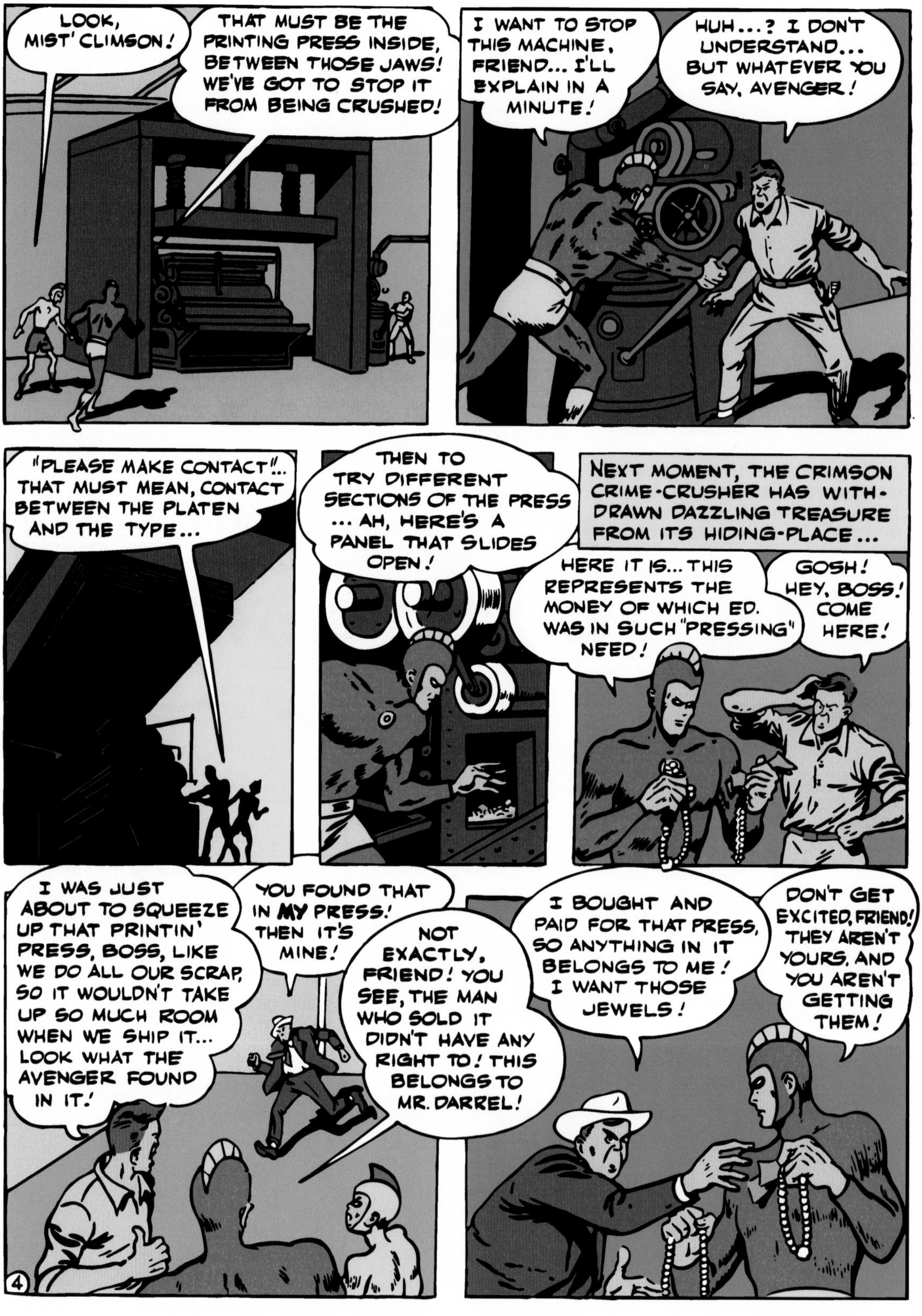
LOOK, MIST' CLIMSON!
THAT MUST BE THE PRINTING PRESS INSIDE, BETWEEN THOSE JAWS! WE'VE GOT TO STOP IT FROM BEING CRUSHED!
I WANT TO STOP THIS MACHINE, FRIEND... I'LL EXPLAIN IN A MINUTE!
HUH...? I DON'T UNDERSTAND... BUT WHATEVER YOU SAY, AVENGER!
"PLEASE MAKE CONTACT"!... THAT MUST MEAN, CONTACT BETWEEN THE PLATEN AND THE TYPE...
THEN TO TRY DIFFERENT SECTIONS OF THE PRESS ... AH, HERE'S A PANEL THAT SLIDES OPEN!
NEXT MOMENT, THE CRIMSON CRIME-CRUSHER HAS WITHDRAWN DAZZLING TREASURE FROM ITS HIDING-PLACE...
HERE IT IS... THIS REPRESENTS THE MONEY OF WHICH ED. WAS IN SUCH "PRESSING" NEED!
GOSH! HEY, BOSS! COME HERE!
I WAS JUST ABOUT TO SQUEEZE UP THAT PRINTIN' PRESS, BOSS, LIKE WE DO ALL OUR SCRAP, SO IT WOULDN'T TAKE UP SO MUCH ROOM WHEN WE SHIP IT... LOOK WHAT THE AVENGER FOUND IN IT!
YOU FOUND THAT IN MY PRESS! THEN IT'S MINE!
NOT EXACTLY, FRIEND! YOU SEE, THE MAN WHO SOLD IT DIDN'T HAVE ANY RIGHT TO! THIS BELONGS TO MR. DARREL!
4
I BOUGHT AND PAID FOR THAT PRESS, SO ANYTHING IN IT BELONGS TO ME! I WANT THOSE JEWELS!
DON'T GET EXCITED, FRIEND! THEY AREN'T YOURS, AND YOU AREN'T GETTING THEM!

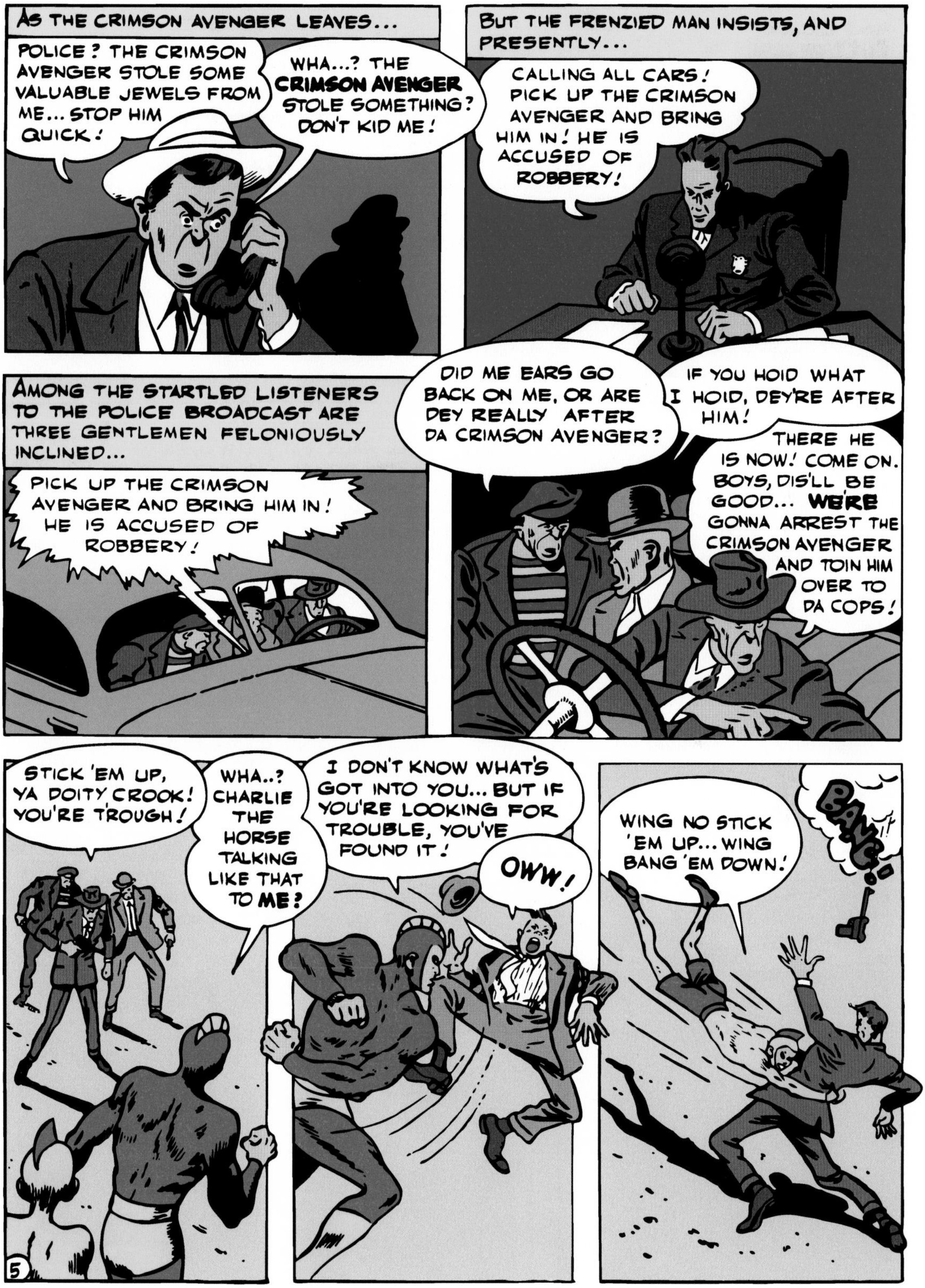
AS THE CRIMSON AVENGER LEAVES...
POLICE? THE CRIMSON AVENGER STOLE SOME VALUABLE JEWELS FROM ME... STOP HIM QUICK!
WHA...? THE CRIMSON AVENGER STOLE SOMETHING? DON'T KID ME!
BUT THE FRENZIED MAN INSISTS, AND PRESENTLY...
CALLING ALL CARS! PICK UP THE CRIMSON AVENGER AND BRING HIM IN! HE IS ACCUSED OF ROBBERY!
AMONG THE STARTLED LISTENERS TO THE POLICE BROADCAST ARE THREE GENTLEMEN FELONIOUSLY INCLINED...
PICK UP THE CRIMSON AVENGER AND BRING HIM IN! HE IS ACCUSED OF ROBBERY!
DID ME EARS GO BACK ON ME, OR ARE DEY REALLY AFTER DA CRIMSON AVENGER?
IF YOU HOID WHAT I HOID, DEY'RE AFTER HIM!
THERE HE IS NOW! COME ON, BOYS, DIS'LL BE GOOD... WE'RE GONNA ARREST THE CRIMSON AVENGER AND TOIN HIM OVER TO DA COPS!
STICK 'EM UP, YA DOITY CROOK! YOU'RE TROUGH!
WHA..? CHARLIE THE HORSE TALKING LIKE THAT TO ME?
I DON'T KNOW WHAT'S GOT INTO YOU... BUT IF YOU'RE LOOKING FOR TROUBLE, YOU'VE FOUND IT!
OWW!
WING NO STICK 'EM UP... WING BANG 'EM DOWN!
BANG!
5

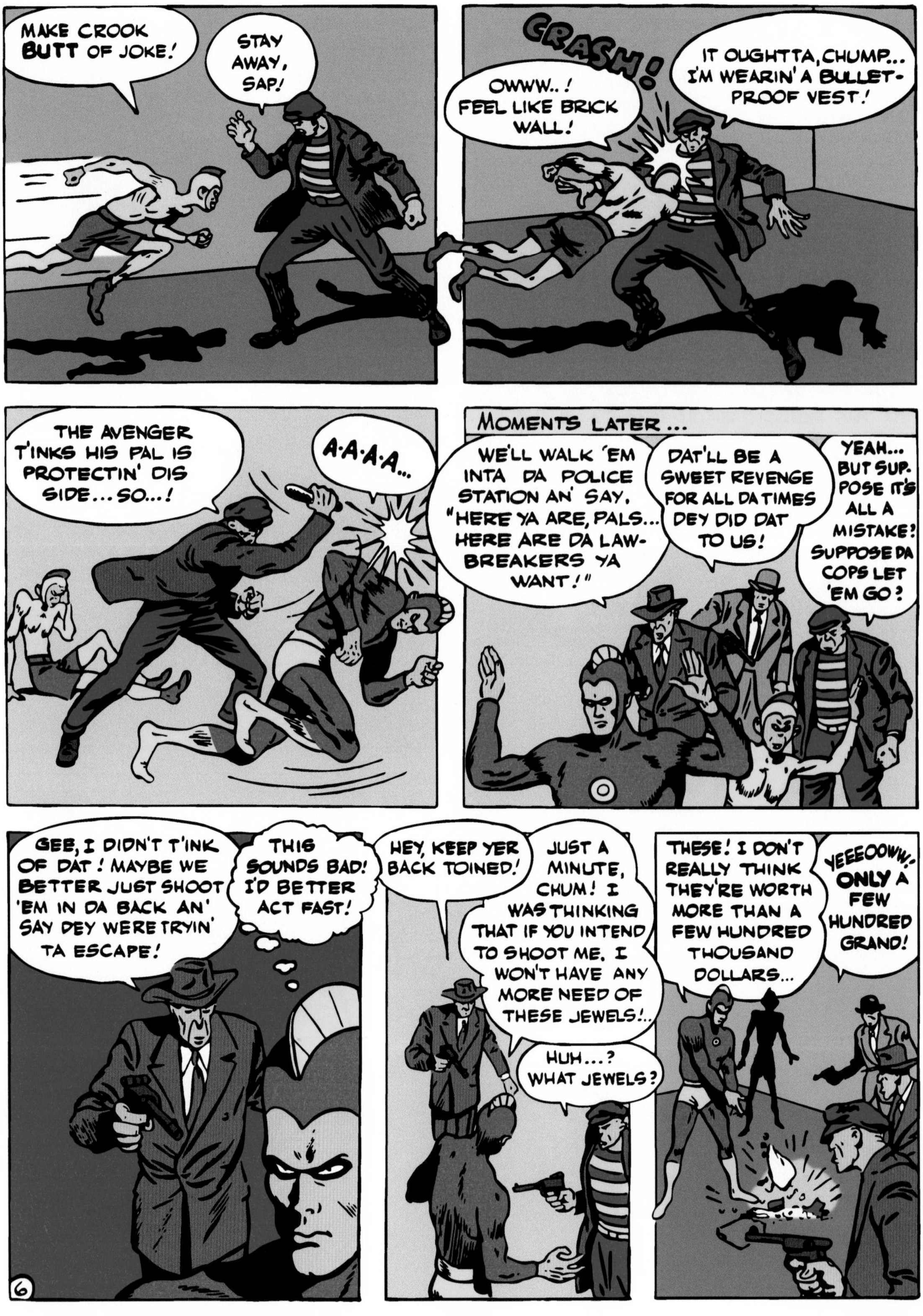
MAKE CROOK BUTT OF JOKE!
STAY AWAY, SAP!
CRASH!
OWWW..! FEEL LIKE BRICK WALL!
IT OUGHTTA, CHUMP... I'M WEARIN' A BULLET-PROOF VEST!
THE AVENGER T'INKS HIS PAL IS PROTECTIN' DIS SIDE... SO...!
A·A·A·A...
MOMENTS LATER...
WE'LL WALK 'EM INTA DA POLICE STATION AN' SAY, "HERE YA ARE, PALS... HERE ARE DA LAW-BREAKERS YA WANT!"
DAT'LL BE A SWEET REVENGE FOR ALL DA TIMES DEY DID DAT TO US!
YEAH... BUT SUP-POSE IT'S ALL A MISTAKE? SUPPOSE DA COPS LET 'EM GO?
GEE, I DIDN'T T'INK OF DAT! MAYBE WE BETTER JUST SHOOT 'EM IN DA BACK AN' SAY DEY WERE TRYIN' TA ESCAPE!
THIS SOUNDS BAD! I'D BETTER ACT FAST!
6
HEY, KEEP YER BACK TOINED!
JUST A MINUTE, CHUM! I WAS THINKING THAT IF YOU INTEND TO SHOOT ME, I WON'T HAVE ANY MORE NEED OF THESE JEWELS!..
HUH...? WHAT JEWELS?
THESE! I DON'T REALLY THINK THEY'RE WORTH MORE THAN A FEW HUNDRED THOUSAND DOLLARS...
YEEEOOWW! ONLY A FEW HUNDRED GRAND!

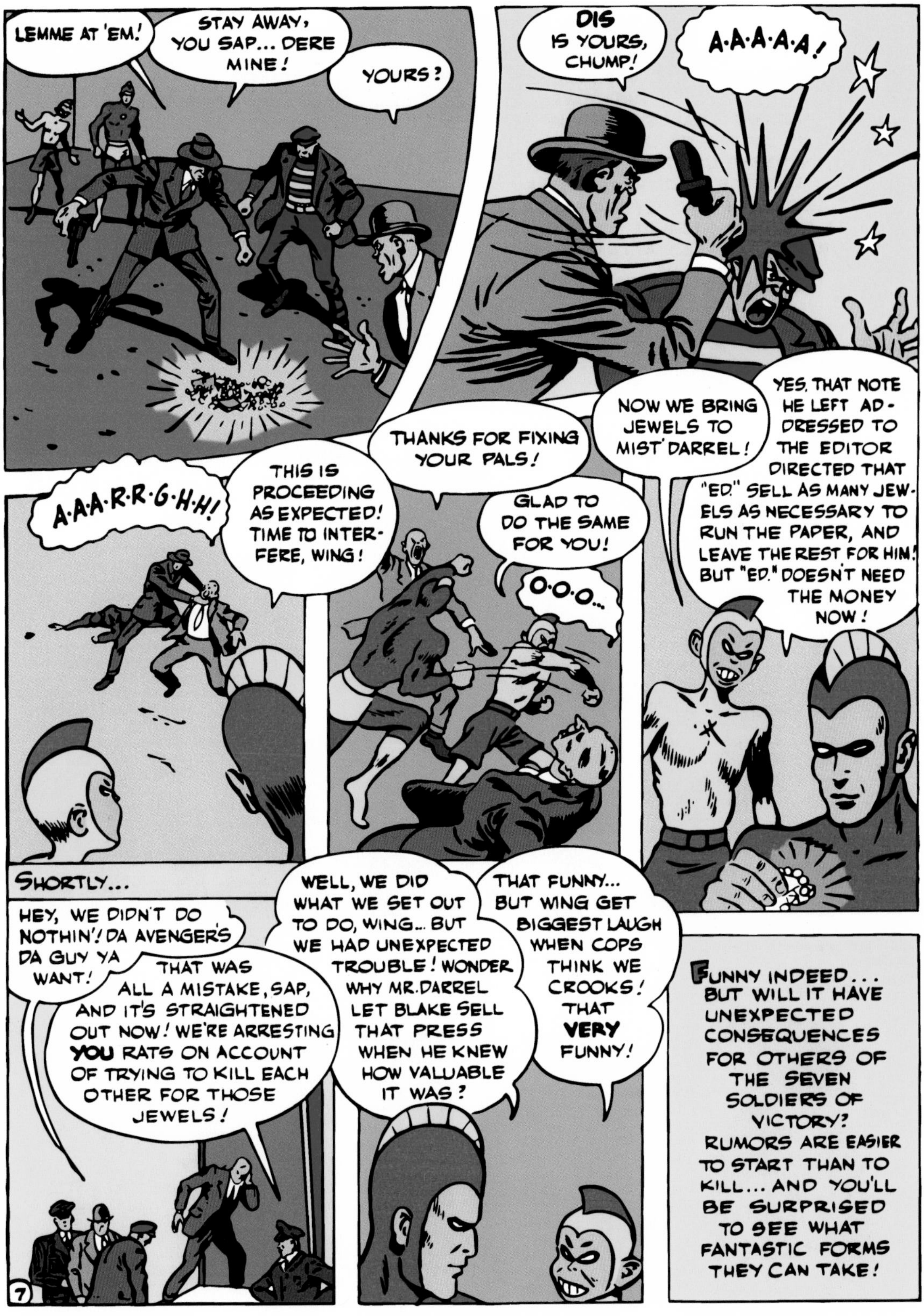
LEMME AT 'EM!
STAY AWAY, YOU SAP... DERE MINE!
YOURS?
DIS IS YOURS, CHUMP!
A-A-A-A-A!
A-A-A-R-R-G-H-H!
THIS IS PROCEEDING AS EXPECTED! TIME TO INTERFERE, WING!
THANKS FOR FIXING YOUR PALS!
GLAD TO DO THE SAME FOR YOU!
O-O-O...
NOW WE BRING JEWELS TO MIST' DARREL!
YES, THAT NOTE HE LEFT ADDRESSED TO THE EDITOR DIRECTED THAT "ED." SELL AS MANY JEWELS AS NECESSARY TO RUN THE PAPER, AND LEAVE THE REST FOR HIM! BUT "ED." DOESN'T NEED THE MONEY NOW!
SHORTLY...
HEY, WE DIDN'T DO NOTHIN'! DA AVENGER'S DA GUY YA WANT!
THAT WAS ALL A MISTAKE, SAP, AND IT'S STRAIGHTENED OUT NOW! WE'RE ARRESTING YOU RATS ON ACCOUNT OF TRYING TO KILL EACH OTHER FOR THOSE JEWELS!
7
WELL, WE DID WHAT WE SET OUT TO DO, WING... BUT WE HAD UNEXPECTED TROUBLE! WONDER WHY MR. DARREL LET BLAKE SELL THAT PRESS WHEN HE KNEW HOW VALUABLE IT WAS?
THAT FUNNY... BUT WING GET BIGGEST LAUGH WHEN COPS THINK WE CROOKS! THAT VERY FUNNY!
FUNNY INDEED... BUT WILL IT HAVE UNEXPECTED CONSEQUENCES FOR OTHERS OF THE SEVEN SOLDIERS OF VICTORY? RUMORS ARE EASIER TO START THAN TO KILL... AND YOU'LL BE SURPRISED TO SEE WHAT FANTASTIC FORMS THEY CAN TAKE!

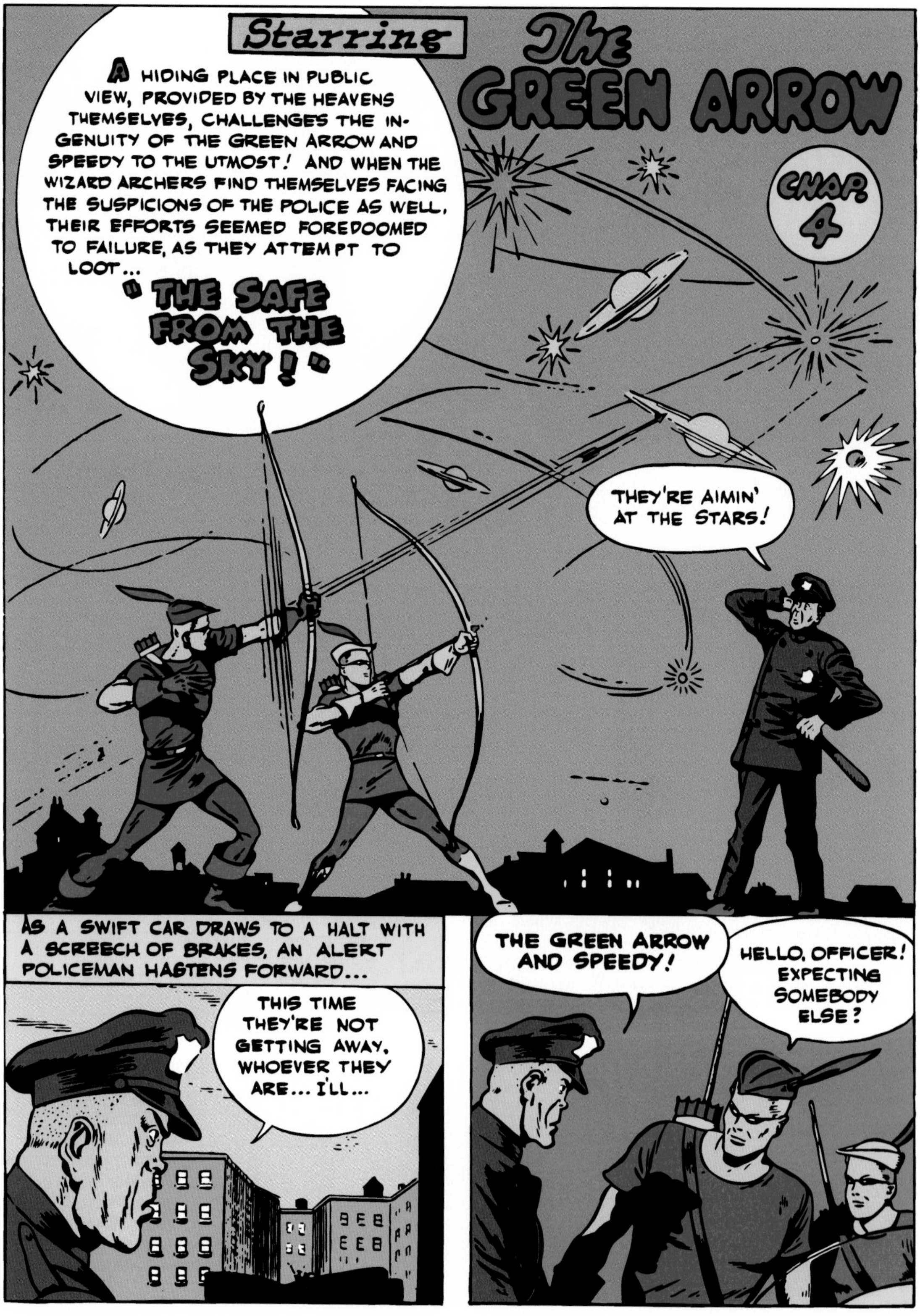
Starring
The GREEN ARROW
A HIDING PLACE IN PUBLIC VIEW, PROVIDED BY THE HEAVENS THEMSELVES, CHALLENGES THE INGENUITY OF THE GREEN ARROW AND SPEEDY TO THE UTMOST! AND WHEN THE WIZARD ARCHERS FIND THEMSELVES FACING THE SUSPICIONS OF THE POLICE AS WELL, THEIR EFFORTS SEEMED FOREDOOMED TO FAILURE, AS THEY ATTEMPT TO LOOT...
"THE SAFE FROM THE SKY!"
CHAP. 4
THEY'RE AIMIN' AT THE STARS!
AS A SWIFT CAR DRAWS TO A HALT WITH A SCREECH OF BRAKES, AN ALERT POLICEMAN HASTENS FORWARD...
THIS TIME THEY'RE NOT GETTING AWAY, WHOEVER THEY ARE... I'LL...
THE GREEN ARROW AND SPEEDY!
HELLO, OFFICER! EXPECTING SOMEBODY ELSE?

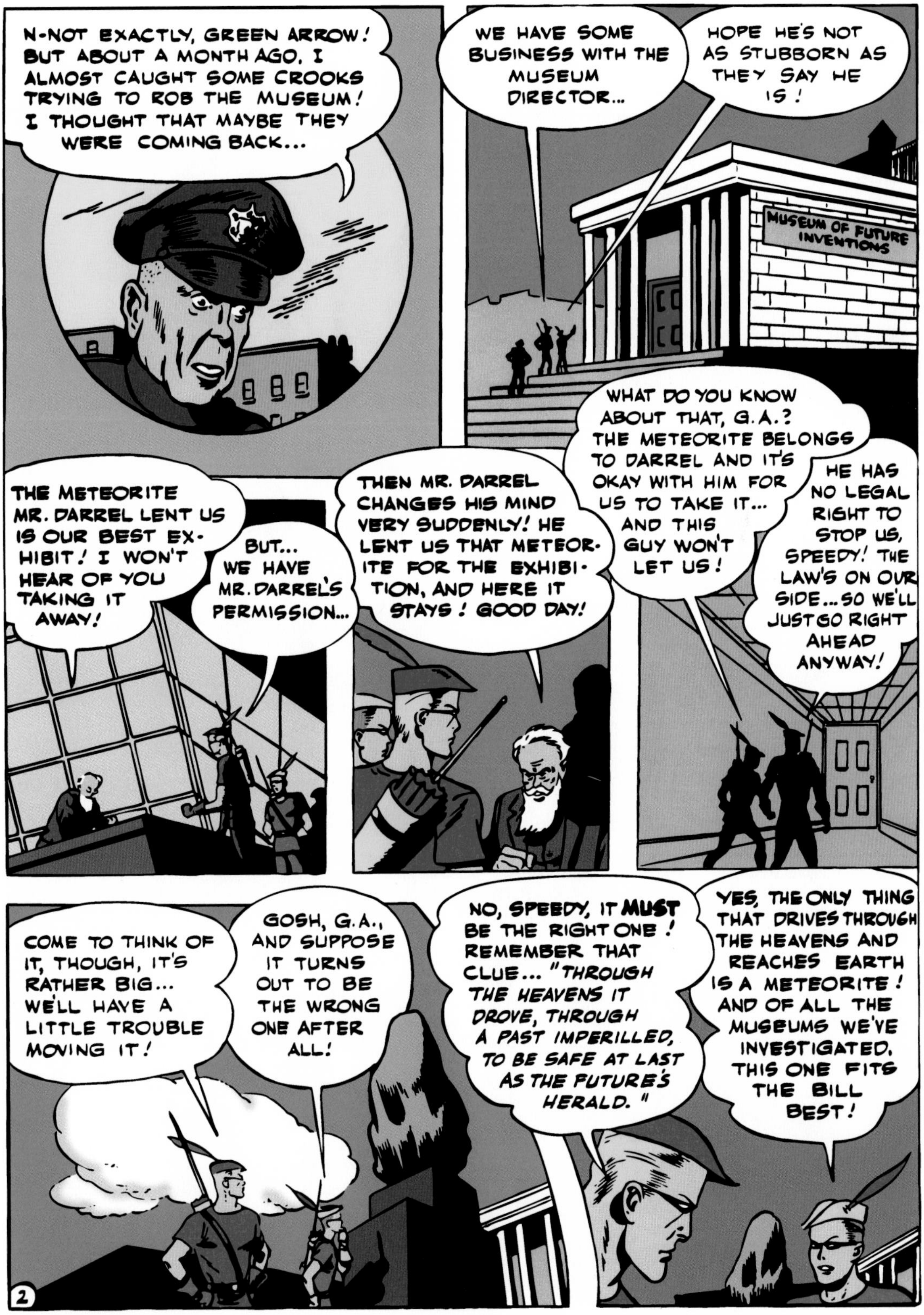
N-NOT EXACTLY, GREEN ARROW! BUT ABOUT A MONTH AGO, I ALMOST CAUGHT SOME CROOKS TRYING TO ROB THE MUSEUM! I THOUGHT THAT MAYBE THEY WERE COMING BACK...
WE HAVE SOME BUSINESS WITH THE MUSEUM DIRECTOR...
HOPE HE'S NOT AS STUBBORN AS THEY SAY HE IS!
MUSEUM OF FUTURE INVENTIONS
THE METEORITE MR. DARREL LENT US IS OUR BEST EXHIBIT! I WON'T HEAR OF YOU TAKING IT AWAY!
BUT... WE HAVE MR. DARREL'S PERMISSION...
THEN MR. DARREL CHANGES HIS MIND VERY SUDDENLY! HE LENT US THAT METEORITE FOR THE EXHIBITION, AND HERE IT STAYS! GOOD DAY!
WHAT DO YOU KNOW ABOUT THAT, G.A.? THE METEORITE BELONGS TO DARREL AND IT'S OKAY WITH HIM FOR US TO TAKE IT... AND THIS GUY WON'T LET US!
HE HAS NO LEGAL RIGHT TO STOP US, SPEEDY! THE LAW'S ON OUR SIDE...SO WE'LL JUST GO RIGHT AHEAD ANYWAY!
COME TO THINK OF IT, THOUGH, IT'S RATHER BIG... WE'LL HAVE A LITTLE TROUBLE MOVING IT!
GOSH, G.A., AND SUPPOSE IT TURNS OUT TO BE THE WRONG ONE AFTER ALL!
NO, SPEEDY, IT MUST BE THE RIGHT ONE! REMEMBER THAT CLUE... "THROUGH THE HEAVENS IT DROVE, THROUGH A PAST IMPERILLED, TO BE SAFE AT LAST AS THE FUTURE'S HERALD."
YES, THE ONLY THING THAT DRIVES THROUGH THE HEAVENS AND REACHES EARTH IS A METEORITE! AND OF ALL THE MUSEUMS WE'VE INVESTIGATED, THIS ONE FITS THE BILL BEST!
2

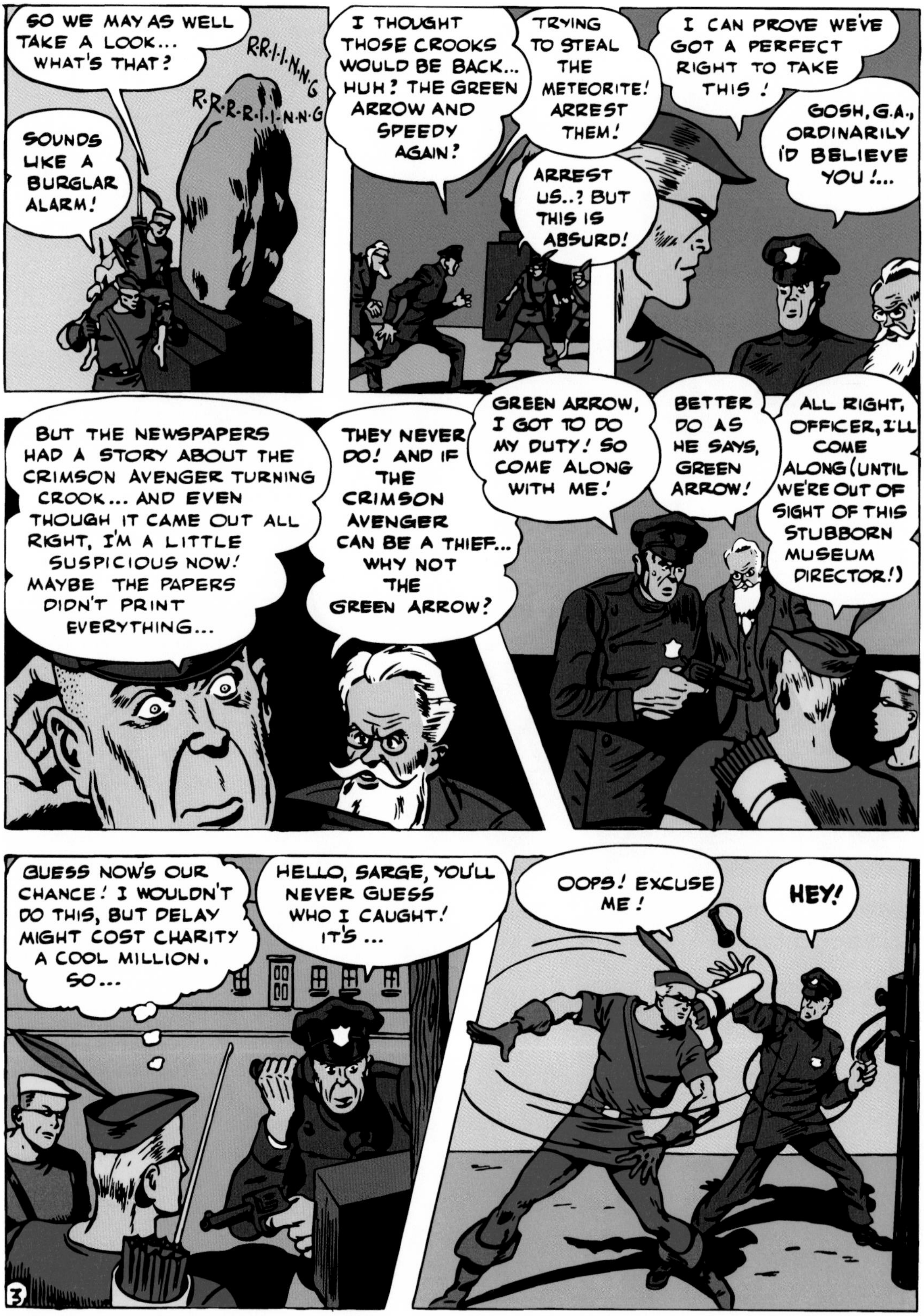
SO WE MAY AS WELL TAKE A LOOK... WHAT'S THAT?
R-R-I-I-N-N-G
R-R-R-R-I-I-N-N-G
SOUNDS LIKE A BURGLAR ALARM!
I THOUGHT THOSE CROOKS WOULD BE BACK... HUH? THE GREEN ARROW AND SPEEDY AGAIN?
TRYING TO STEAL THE METEORITE! ARREST THEM!
ARREST US..? BUT THIS IS ABSURD!
I CAN PROVE WE'VE GOT A PERFECT RIGHT TO TAKE THIS!
GOSH, G.A., ORDINARILY I'D BELIEVE YOU!...
BUT THE NEWSPAPERS HAD A STORY ABOUT THE CRIMSON AVENGER TURNING CROOK... AND EVEN THOUGH IT CAME OUT ALL RIGHT, I'M A LITTLE SUSPICIOUS NOW! MAYBE THE PAPERS DIDN'T PRINT EVERYTHING...
THEY NEVER DO! AND IF THE CRIMSON AVENGER CAN BE A THIEF... WHY NOT THE GREEN ARROW?
GREEN ARROW, I GOT TO DO MY DUTY! SO COME ALONG WITH ME!
BETTER DO AS HE SAYS, GREEN ARROW!
ALL RIGHT, OFFICER, I'LL COME ALONG (UNTIL WE'RE OUT OF SIGHT OF THIS STUBBORN MUSEUM DIRECTOR!)
GUESS NOW'S OUR CHANCE! I WOULDN'T DO THIS, BUT DELAY MIGHT COST CHARITY A COOL MILLION. SO...
HELLO, SARGE, YOU'LL NEVER GUESS WHO I CAUGHT! IT'S ...
3
OOPS! EXCUSE ME!
HEY!

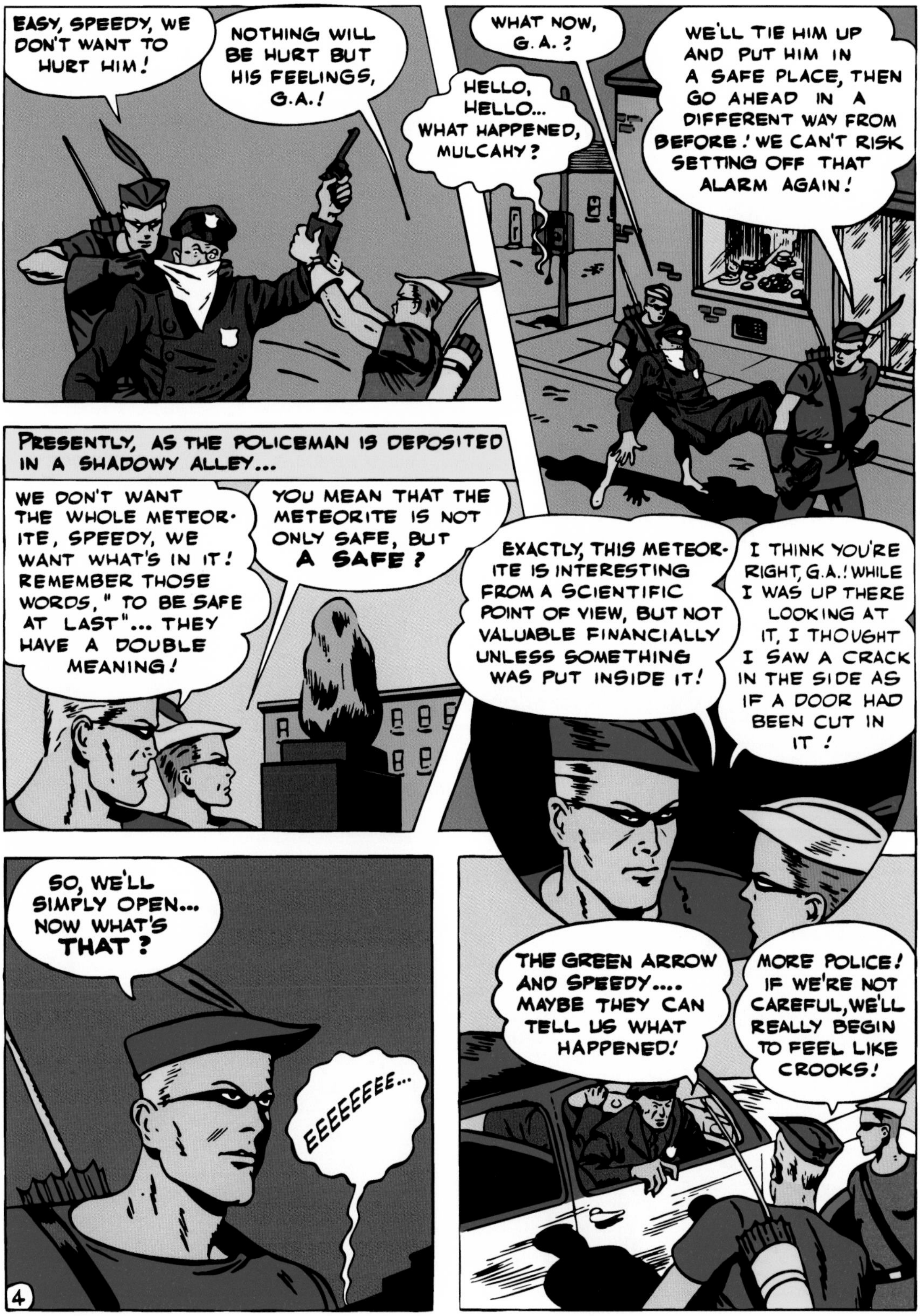
EASY, SPEEDY, WE DON'T WANT TO HURT HIM!
NOTHING WILL BE HURT BUT HIS FEELINGS, G.A.!
WHAT NOW, G.A.?
HELLO, HELLO... WHAT HAPPENED, MULCAHY?
WE'LL TIE HIM UP AND PUT HIM IN A SAFE PLACE, THEN GO AHEAD IN A DIFFERENT WAY FROM BEFORE! WE CAN'T RISK SETTING OFF THAT ALARM AGAIN!
PRESENTLY, AS THE POLICEMAN IS DEPOSITED IN A SHADOWY ALLEY...
WE DON'T WANT THE WHOLE METEORITE, SPEEDY, WE WANT WHAT'S IN IT! REMEMBER THOSE WORDS, "TO BE SAFE AT LAST"... THEY HAVE A DOUBLE MEANING!
YOU MEAN THAT THE METEORITE IS NOT ONLY SAFE, BUT A SAFE?
EXACTLY, THIS METEORITE IS INTERESTING FROM A SCIENTIFIC POINT OF VIEW, BUT NOT VALUABLE FINANCIALLY UNLESS SOMETHING WAS PUT INSIDE IT!
I THINK YOU'RE RIGHT, G.A.! WHILE I WAS UP THERE LOOKING AT IT, I THOUGHT I SAW A CRACK IN THE SIDE AS IF A DOOR HAD BEEN CUT IN IT!
SO, WE'LL SIMPLY OPEN... NOW WHAT'S THAT?
EEEEEEEE...
4
THE GREEN ARROW AND SPEEDY.... MAYBE THEY CAN TELL US WHAT HAPPENED!
MORE POLICE! IF WE'RE NOT CAREFUL, WE'LL REALLY BEGIN TO FEEL LIKE CROOKS!

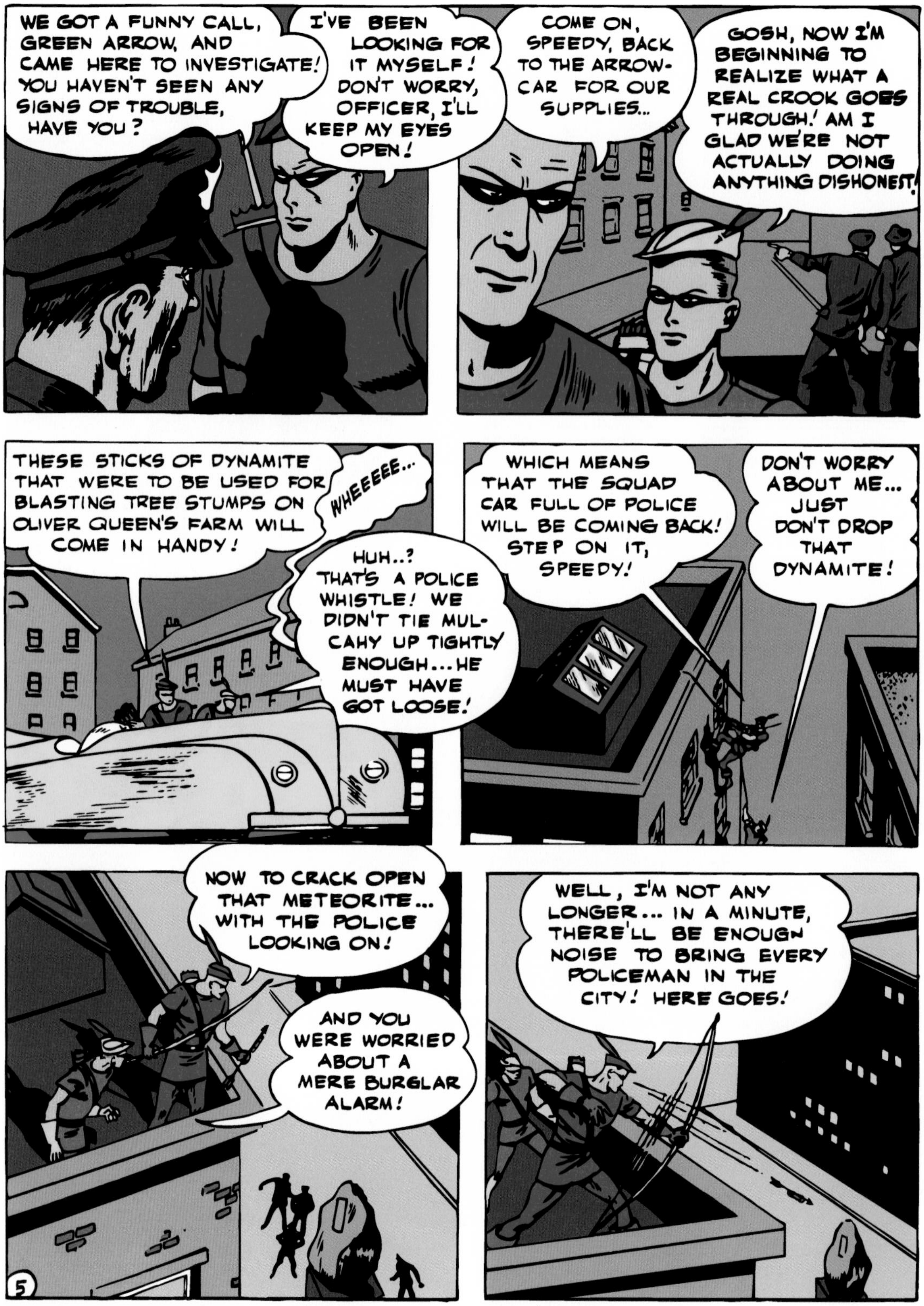
WE GOT A FUNNY CALL, GREEN ARROW, AND CAME HERE TO INVESTIGATE! YOU HAVEN'T SEEN ANY SIGNS OF TROUBLE, HAVE YOU?
I'VE BEEN LOOKING FOR IT MYSELF! DON'T WORRY, OFFICER, I'LL KEEP MY EYES OPEN!
COME ON, SPEEDY, BACK TO THE ARROW-CAR FOR OUR SUPPLIES...
GOSH, NOW I'M BEGINNING TO REALIZE WHAT A REAL CROOK GOES THROUGH! AM I GLAD WE'RE NOT ACTUALLY DOING ANYTHING DISHONEST!
THESE STICKS OF DYNAMITE THAT WERE TO BE USED FOR BLASTING TREE STUMPS ON OLIVER QUEEN'S FARM WILL COME IN HANDY!
WHEEEEE...
HUH..? THAT'S A POLICE WHISTLE! WE DIDN'T TIE MULCAHY UP TIGHTLY ENOUGH... HE MUST HAVE GOT LOOSE!
WHICH MEANS THAT THE SQUAD CAR FULL OF POLICE WILL BE COMING BACK! STEP ON IT, SPEEDY!
DON'T WORRY ABOUT ME... JUST DON'T DROP THAT DYNAMITE!
NOW TO CRACK OPEN THAT METEORITE... WITH THE POLICE LOOKING ON!
AND YOU WERE WORRIED ABOUT A MERE BURGLAR ALARM!
5
WELL, I'M NOT ANY LONGER... IN A MINUTE, THERE'LL BE ENOUGH NOISE TO BRING EVERY POLICEMAN IN THE CITY! HERE GOES!

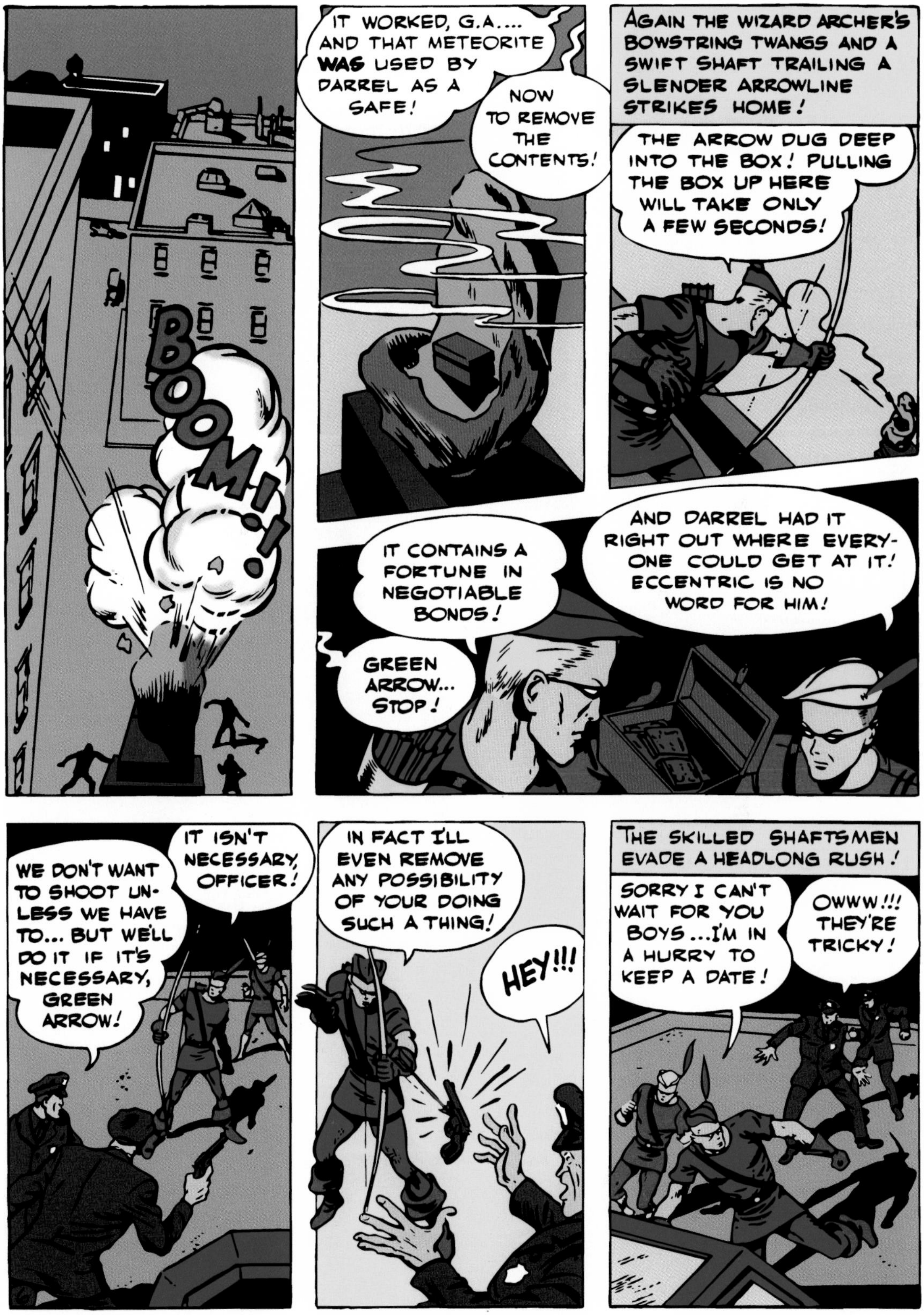
BOOM!
IT WORKED, G.A.... AND THAT METEORITE WAS USED BY DARREL AS A SAFE!
NOW TO REMOVE THE CONTENTS!
AGAIN THE WIZARD ARCHER'S BOWSTRING TWANGS AND A SWIFT SHAFT TRAILING A SLENDER ARROWLINE STRIKES HOME!
THE ARROW DUG DEEP INTO THE BOX! PULLING THE BOX UP HERE WILL TAKE ONLY A FEW SECONDS!
IT CONTAINS A FORTUNE IN NEGOTIABLE BONDS!
AND DARREL HAD IT RIGHT OUT WHERE EVERY-ONE COULD GET AT IT! ECCENTRIC IS NO WORD FOR HIM!
GREEN ARROW... STOP!
WE DON'T WANT TO SHOOT UN-LESS WE HAVE TO... BUT WE'LL DO IT IF IT'S NECESSARY, GREEN ARROW!
IT ISN'T NECESSARY, OFFICER!
IN FACT I'LL EVEN REMOVE ANY POSSIBILITY OF YOUR DOING SUCH A THING!
HEY!!!
THE SKILLED SHAFTSMEN EVADE A HEADLONG RUSH!
SORRY I CAN'T WAIT FOR YOU BOYS...I'M IN A HURRY TO KEEP A DATE!
OWWW!!! THEY'RE TRICKY!

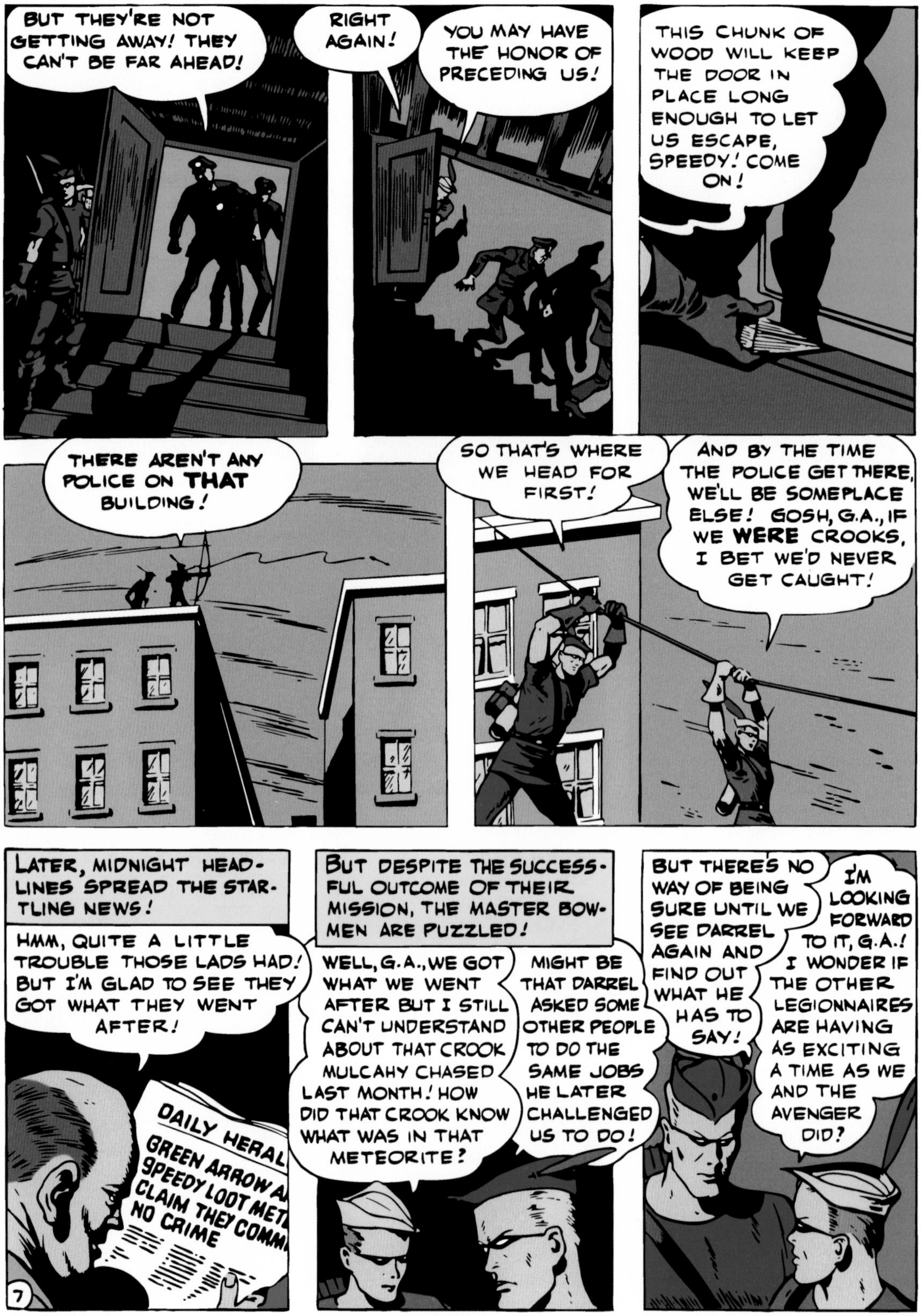
BUT THEY'RE NOT GETTING AWAY! THEY CAN'T BE FAR AHEAD!
RIGHT AGAIN!
YOU MAY HAVE THE HONOR OF PRECEDING US!
THIS CHUNK OF WOOD WILL KEEP THE DOOR IN PLACE LONG ENOUGH TO LET US ESCAPE, SPEEDY! COME ON!
THERE AREN'T ANY POLICE ON THAT BUILDING!
SO THAT'S WHERE WE HEAD FOR FIRST!
AND BY THE TIME THE POLICE GET THERE, WE'LL BE SOMEPLACE ELSE! GOSH, G.A., IF WE WERE CROOKS, I BET WE'D NEVER GET CAUGHT!
LATER, MIDNIGHT HEADLINES SPREAD THE STARTLING NEWS!
HMM, QUITE A LITTLE TROUBLE THOSE LADS HAD! BUT I'M GLAD TO SEE THEY GOT WHAT THEY WENT AFTER!
DAILY HERAL
GREEN ARROW A
SPEEDY LOOT MET
CLAIM THEY COMM
NO CRIME
7
BUT DESPITE THE SUCCESSFUL OUTCOME OF THEIR MISSION, THE MASTER BOWMEN ARE PUZZLED!
WELL, G.A., WE GOT WHAT WE WENT AFTER BUT I STILL CAN'T UNDERSTAND ABOUT THAT CROOK MULCAHY CHASED LAST MONTH! HOW DID THAT CROOK KNOW WHAT WAS IN THAT METEORITE?
MIGHT BE THAT DARREL ASKED SOME OTHER PEOPLE TO DO THE SAME JOBS HE LATER CHALLENGED US TO DO!
BUT THERE'S NO WAY OF BEING SURE UNTIL WE SEE DARREL AGAIN AND FIND OUT WHAT HE HAS TO SAY!
I'M LOOKING FORWARD TO IT, G.A.! I WONDER IF THE OTHER LEGIONNAIRES ARE HAVING AS EXCITING A TIME AS WE AND THE AVENGER DID?

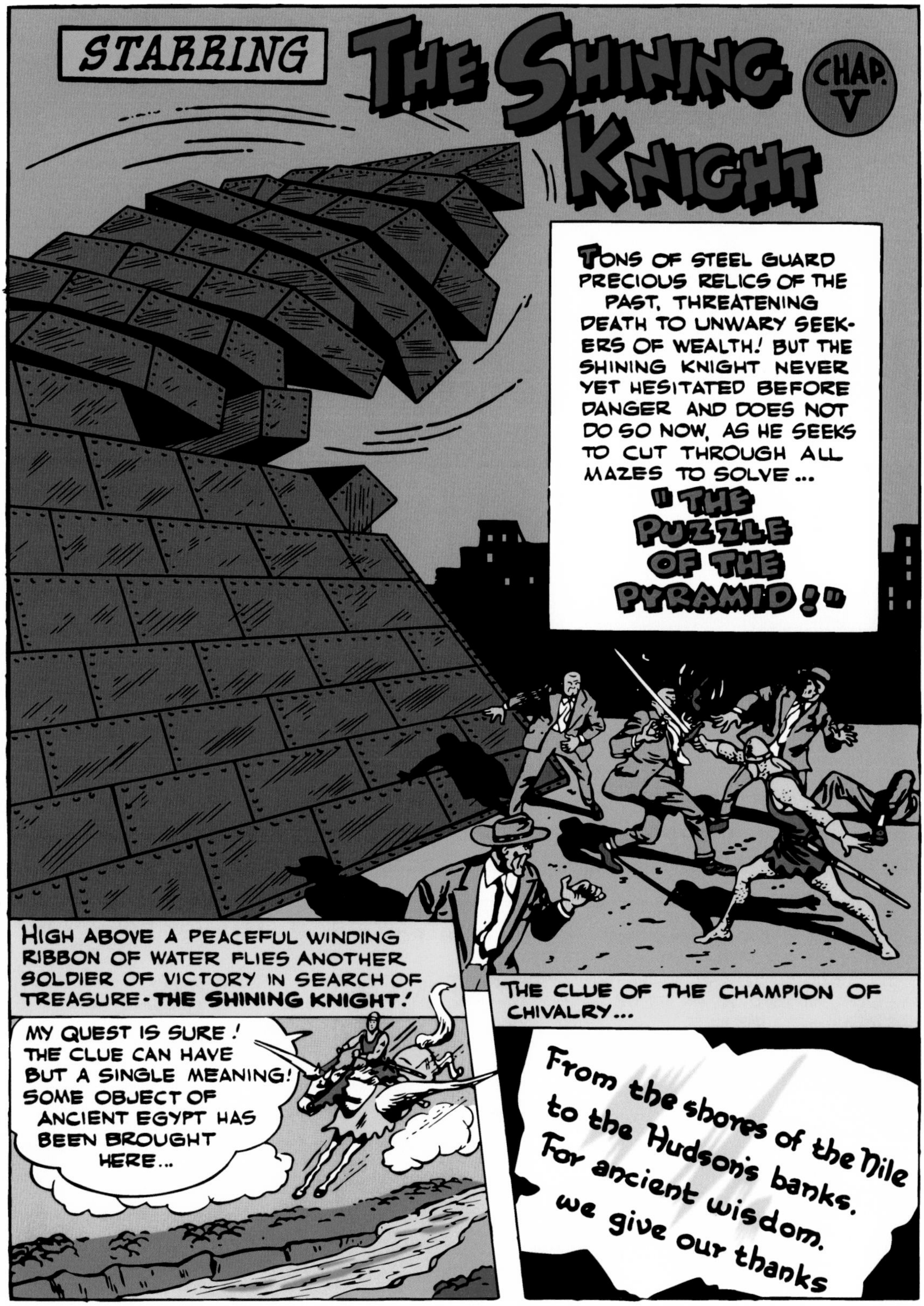
STARRING
THE SHINING KNIGHT
CHAP. V
TONS OF STEEL GUARD PRECIOUS RELICS OF THE PAST, THREATENING DEATH TO UNWARY SEEKERS OF WEALTH! BUT THE SHINING KNIGHT NEVER YET HESITATED BEFORE DANGER AND DOES NOT DO SO NOW, AS HE SEEKS TO CUT THROUGH ALL MAZES TO SOLVE ...
"THE PUZZLE OF THE PYRAMID!"
HIGH ABOVE A PEACEFUL WINDING RIBBON OF WATER FLIES ANOTHER SOLDIER OF VICTORY IN SEARCH OF TREASURE - THE SHINING KNIGHT!
MY QUEST IS SURE! THE CLUE CAN HAVE BUT A SINGLE MEANING! SOME OBJECT OF ANCIENT EGYPT HAS BEEN BROUGHT HERE...
THE CLUE OF THE CHAMPION OF CHIVALRY...
From the shores of the Nile to the Hudson's banks. For ancient wisdom. we give our thanks

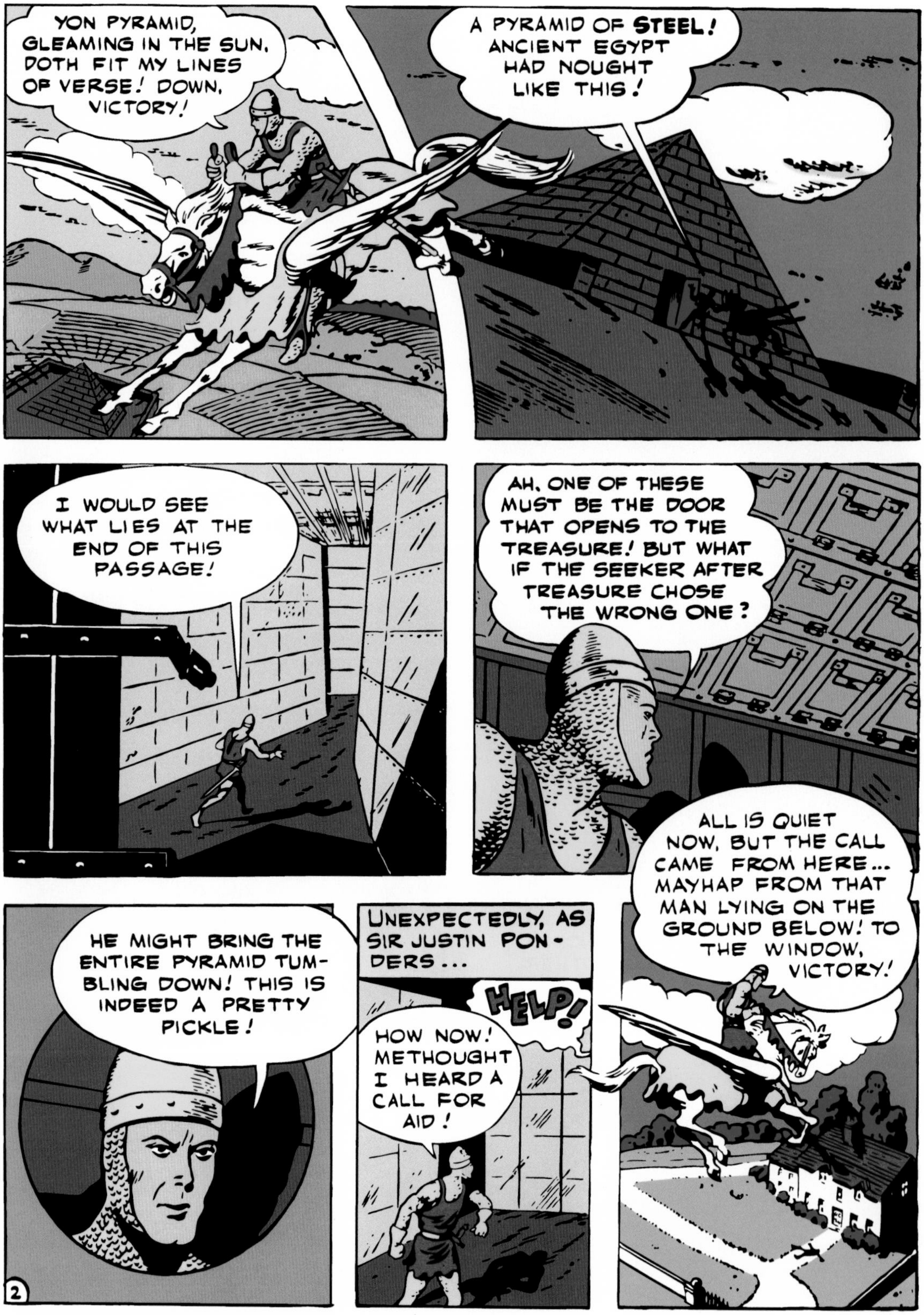
YON PYRAMID, GLEAMING IN THE SUN, DOTH FIT MY LINES OF VERSE! DOWN, VICTORY!
A PYRAMID OF STEEL! ANCIENT EGYPT HAD NOUGHT LIKE THIS!
I WOULD SEE WHAT LIES AT THE END OF THIS PASSAGE!
AH, ONE OF THESE MUST BE THE DOOR THAT OPENS TO THE TREASURE! BUT WHAT IF THE SEEKER AFTER TREASURE CHOSE THE WRONG ONE?
HE MIGHT BRING THE ENTIRE PYRAMID TUMBLING DOWN! THIS IS INDEED A PRETTY PICKLE!
2
UNEXPECTEDLY, AS SIR JUSTIN PONDERS...
HELP!
HOW NOW! METHOUGHT I HEARD A CALL FOR AID!
ALL IS QUIET NOW, BUT THE CALL CAME FROM HERE... MAYHAP FROM THAT MAN LYING ON THE GROUND BELOW! TO THE WINDOW, VICTORY!

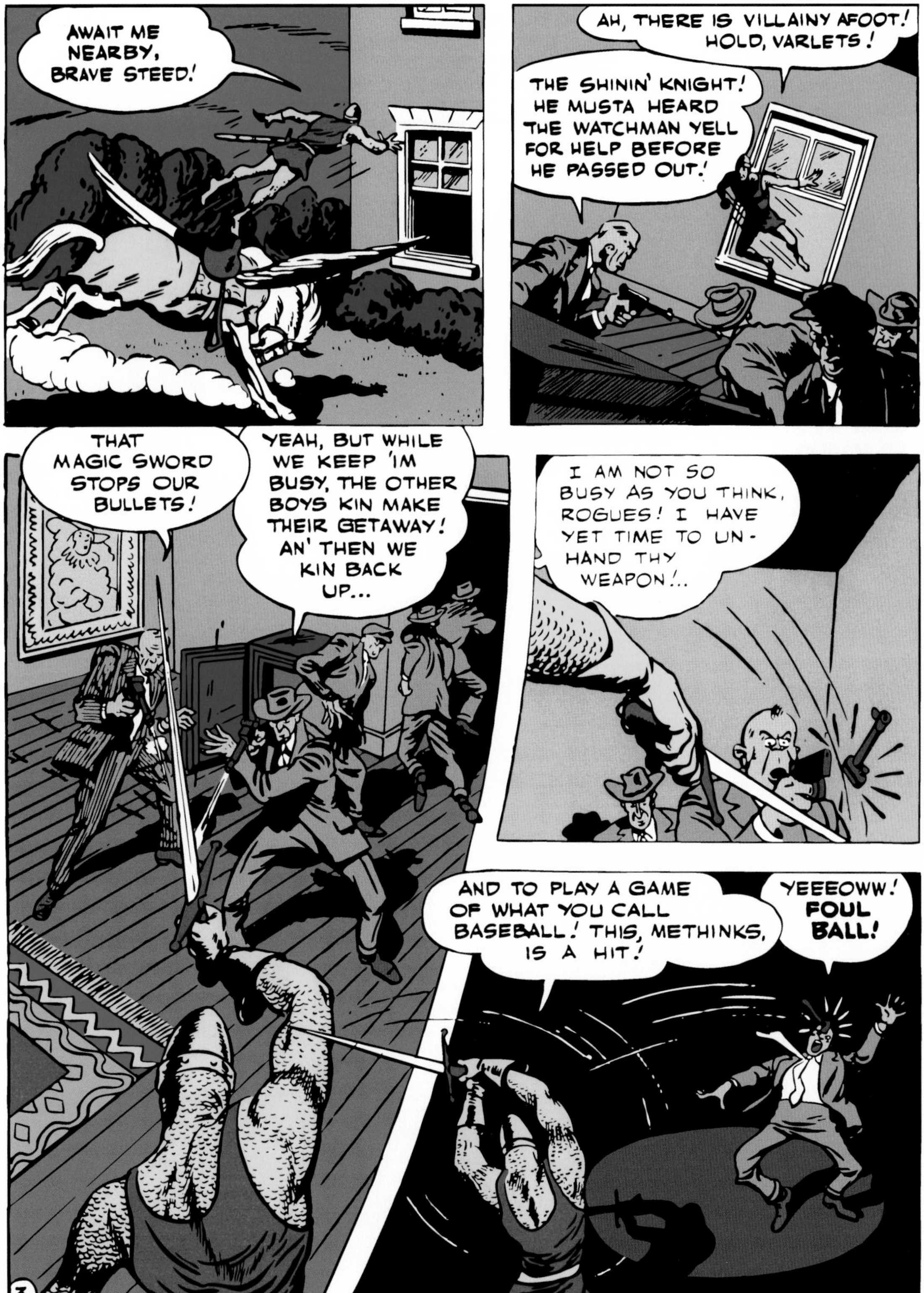
AWAIT ME NEARBY, BRAVE STEED!
AH, THERE IS VILLAINY AFOOT! HOLD, VARLETS!
THE SHININ' KNIGHT! HE MUSTA HEARD THE WATCHMAN YELL FOR HELP BEFORE HE PASSED OUT!
THAT MAGIC SWORD STOPS OUR BULLETS!
YEAH, BUT WHILE WE KEEP 'IM BUSY, THE OTHER BOYS KIN MAKE THEIR GETAWAY! AN' THEN WE KIN BACK UP...
I AM NOT SO BUSY AS YOU THINK, ROGUES! I HAVE YET TIME TO UN-HAND THY WEAPON!..
AND TO PLAY A GAME OF WHAT YOU CALL BASEBALL! THIS, METHINKS, IS A HIT!
YEEEOWW! FOUL BALL!
3

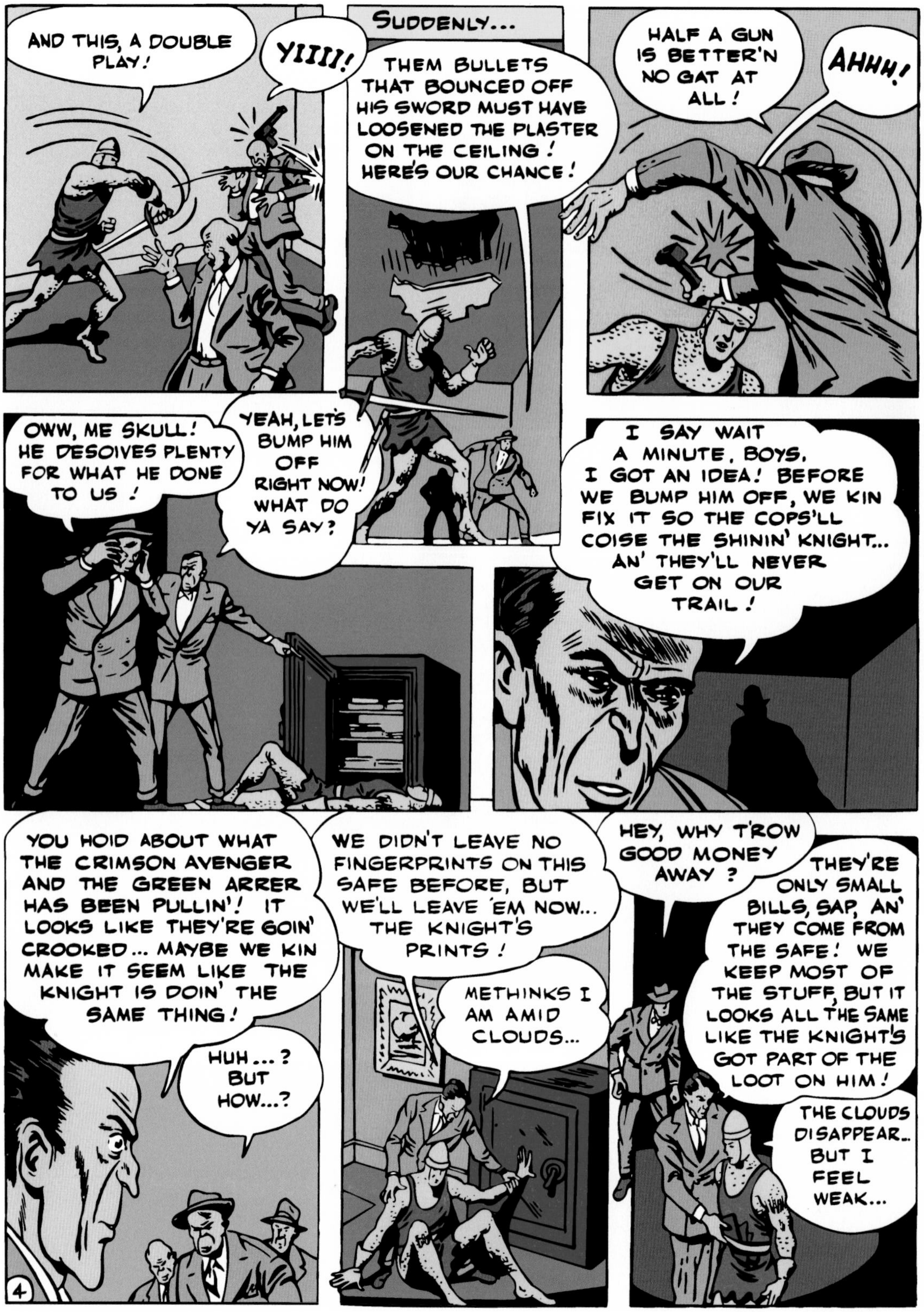
AND THIS, A DOUBLE PLAY!
YIIII!
SUDDENLY...
THEM BULLETS THAT BOUNCED OFF HIS SWORD MUST HAVE LOOSENED THE PLASTER ON THE CEILING! HERE'S OUR CHANCE!
HALF A GUN IS BETTER'N NO GAT AT ALL!
AHHH!
OWW, ME SKULL! HE DESOIVES PLENTY FOR WHAT HE DONE TO US!
YEAH, LET'S BUMP HIM OFF RIGHT NOW! WHAT DO YA SAY?
I SAY WAIT A MINUTE, BOYS. I GOT AN IDEA! BEFORE WE BUMP HIM OFF, WE KIN FIX IT SO THE COPS'LL COISE THE SHININ' KNIGHT... AN' THEY'LL NEVER GET ON OUR TRAIL!
YOU HOID ABOUT WHAT THE CRIMSON AVENGER AND THE GREEN ARRER HAS BEEN PULLIN'! IT LOOKS LIKE THEY'RE GOIN' CROOKED... MAYBE WE KIN MAKE IT SEEM LIKE THE KNIGHT IS DOIN' THE SAME THING!
HUH...? BUT HOW...?
4
WE DIDN'T LEAVE NO FINGERPRINTS ON THIS SAFE BEFORE, BUT WE'LL LEAVE 'EM NOW... THE KNIGHT'S PRINTS!
METHINKS I AM AMID CLOUDS...
HEY, WHY T'ROW GOOD MONEY AWAY?
THEY'RE ONLY SMALL BILLS, SAP, AN' THEY COME FROM THE SAFE! WE KEEP MOST OF THE STUFF, BUT IT LOOKS ALL THE SAME LIKE THE KNIGHT'S GOT PART OF THE LOOT ON HIM!
THE CLOUDS DISAPPEAR... BUT I FEEL WEAK...

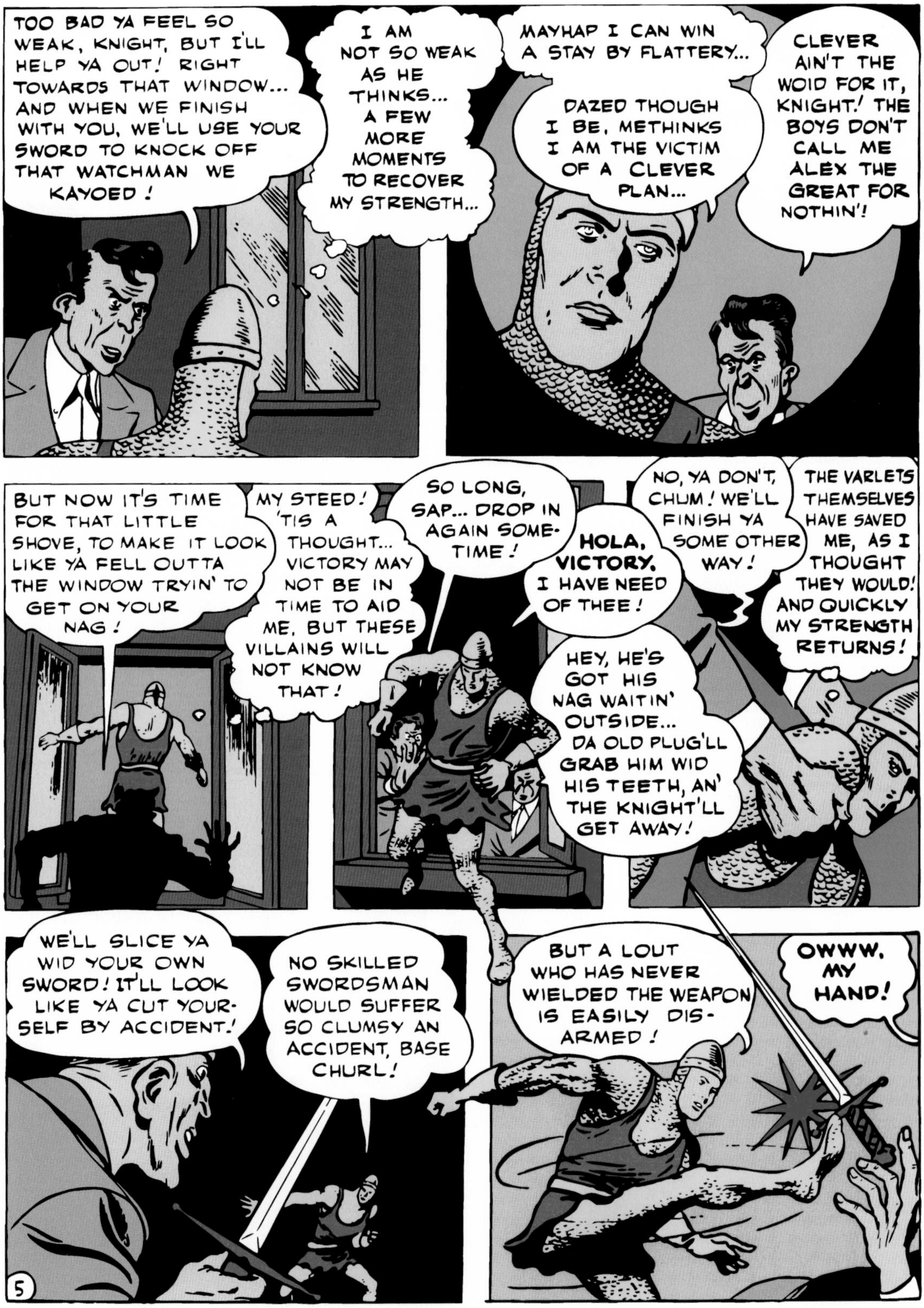
TOO BAD YA FEEL SO WEAK, KNIGHT, BUT I'LL HELP YA OUT! RIGHT TOWARDS THAT WINDOW... AND WHEN WE FINISH WITH YOU, WE'LL USE YOUR SWORD TO KNOCK OFF THAT WATCHMAN WE KAYOED!
I AM NOT SO WEAK AS HE THINKS... A FEW MORE MOMENTS TO RECOVER MY STRENGTH...
MAYHAP I CAN WIN A STAY BY FLATTERY...
DAZED THOUGH I BE, METHINKS I AM THE VICTIM OF A CLEVER PLAN...
CLEVER AIN'T THE WOID FOR IT, KNIGHT! THE BOYS DON'T CALL ME ALEX THE GREAT FOR NOTHIN'!
BUT NOW IT'S TIME FOR THAT LITTLE SHOVE, TO MAKE IT LOOK LIKE YA FELL OUTTA THE WINDOW TRYIN' TO GET ON YOUR NAG!
MY STEED! 'TIS A THOUGHT... VICTORY MAY NOT BE IN TIME TO AID ME, BUT THESE VILLAINS WILL NOT KNOW THAT!
SO LONG, SAP... DROP IN AGAIN SOME-TIME!
HOLA, VICTORY, I HAVE NEED OF THEE!
HEY, HE'S GOT HIS NAG WAITIN' OUTSIDE... DA OLD PLUG'LL GRAB HIM WID HIS TEETH, AN' THE KNIGHT'LL GET AWAY!
NO, YA DON'T, CHUM! WE'LL FINISH YA SOME OTHER WAY!
THE VARLETS THEMSELVES HAVE SAVED ME, AS I THOUGHT THEY WOULD! AND QUICKLY MY STRENGTH RETURNS!
WE'LL SLICE YA WID YOUR OWN SWORD! IT'LL LOOK LIKE YA CUT YOUR-SELF BY ACCIDENT!
NO SKILLED SWORDSMAN WOULD SUFFER SO CLUMSY AN ACCIDENT, BASE CHURL!
5
BUT A LOUT WHO HAS NEVER WIELDED THE WEAPON IS EASILY DIS-ARMED!
OWWW, MY HAND!

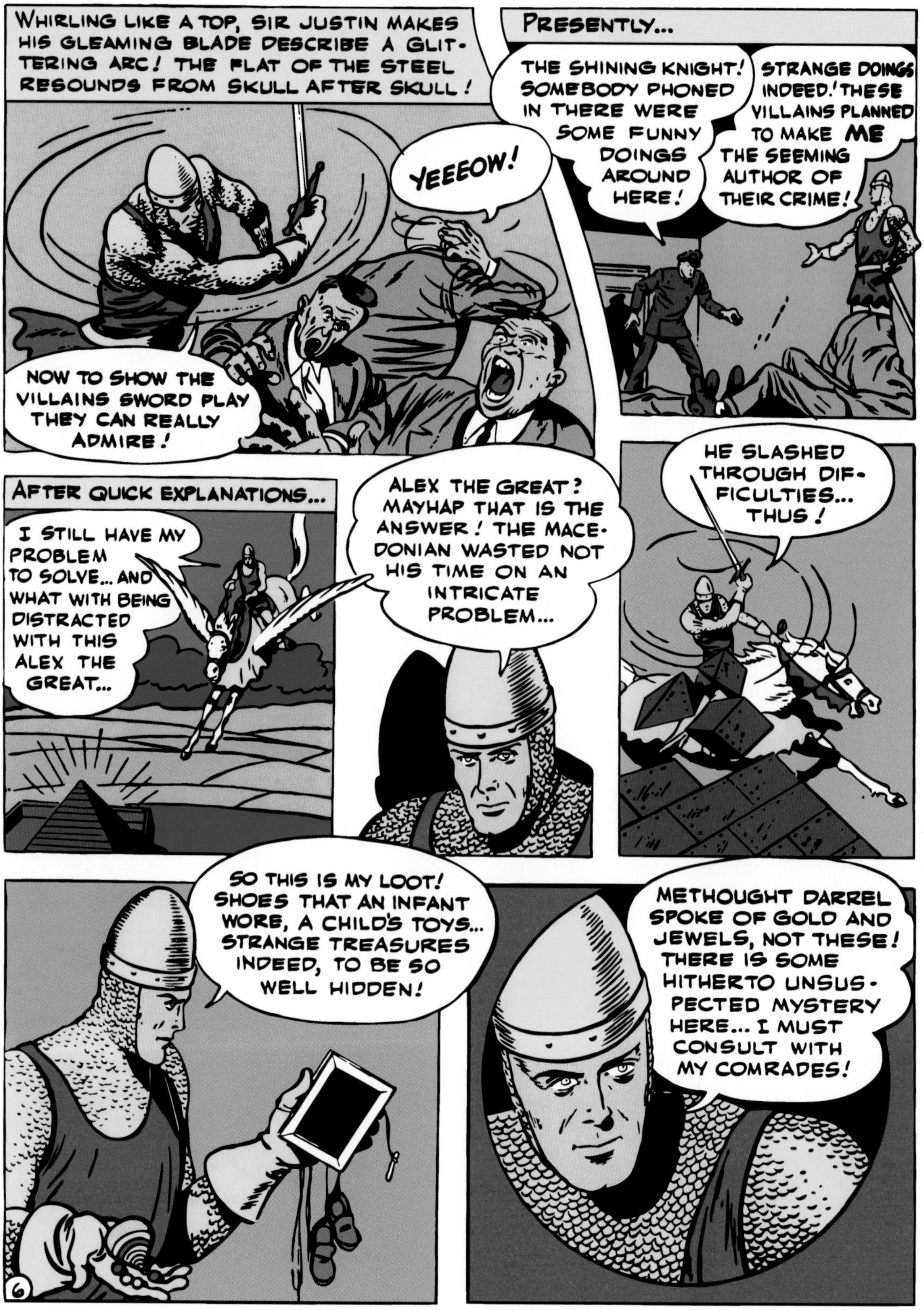
WHIRLING LIKE A TOP, SIR JUSTIN MAKES HIS GLEAMING BLADE DESCRIBE A GLITTERING ARC! THE FLAT OF THE STEEL RESOUNDS FROM SKULL AFTER SKULL!
YEEEOW!
NOW TO SHOW THE VILLAINS SWORD PLAY THEY CAN REALLY ADMIRE!
PRESENTLY...
THE SHINING KNIGHT! SOMEBODY PHONED IN THERE WERE SOME FUNNY DOINGS AROUND HERE!
STRANGE DOINGS INDEED! THESE VILLAINS PLANNED TO MAKE ME THE SEEMING AUTHOR OF THEIR CRIME!
AFTER QUICK EXPLANATIONS...
I STILL HAVE MY PROBLEM TO SOLVE... AND WHAT WITH BEING DISTRACTED WITH THIS ALEX THE GREAT...
ALEX THE GREAT? MAYHAP THAT IS THE ANSWER! THE MACEDONIAN WASTED NOT HIS TIME ON AN INTRICATE PROBLEM...
HE SLASHED THROUGH DIFFICULTIES... THUS!
SO THIS IS MY LOOT! SHOES THAT AN INFANT WORE, A CHILD'S TOYS... STRANGE TREASURES INDEED, TO BE SO WELL HIDDEN!
METHOUGHT DARREL SPOKE OF GOLD AND JEWELS, NOT THESE! THERE IS SOME HITHERTO UNSUSPECTED MYSTERY HERE... I MUST CONSULT WITH MY COMRADES!
6

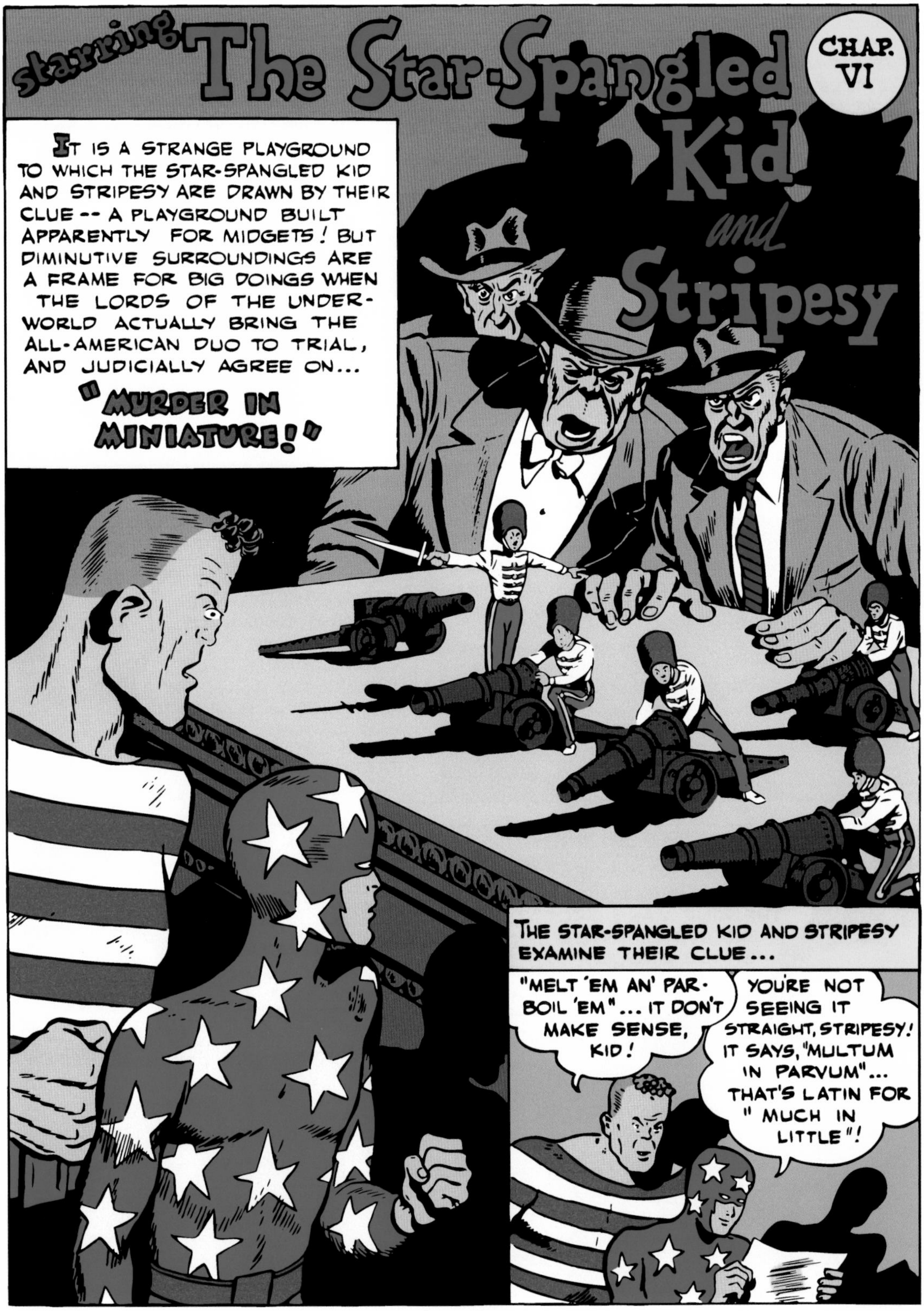
starring The Star-Spangled Kid and Stripesy
CHAP. VI
IT IS A STRANGE PLAYGROUND TO WHICH THE STAR-SPANGLED KID AND STRIPESY ARE DRAWN BY THEIR CLUE -- A PLAYGROUND BUILT APPARENTLY FOR MIDGETS! BUT DIMINUTIVE SURROUNDINGS ARE A FRAME FOR BIG DOINGS WHEN THE LORDS OF THE UNDER-WORLD ACTUALLY BRING THE ALL-AMERICAN DUO TO TRIAL, AND JUDICIALLY AGREE ON...
"MURDER IN MINIATURE!"
THE STAR-SPANGLED KID AND STRIPESY EXAMINE THEIR CLUE...
"MELT 'EM AN' PAR-BOIL 'EM"... IT DON'T MAKE SENSE, KID!
YOU'RE NOT SEEING IT STRAIGHT, STRIPESY! IT SAYS, "MULTUM IN PARVUM"... THAT'S LATIN FOR "MUCH IN LITTLE"!

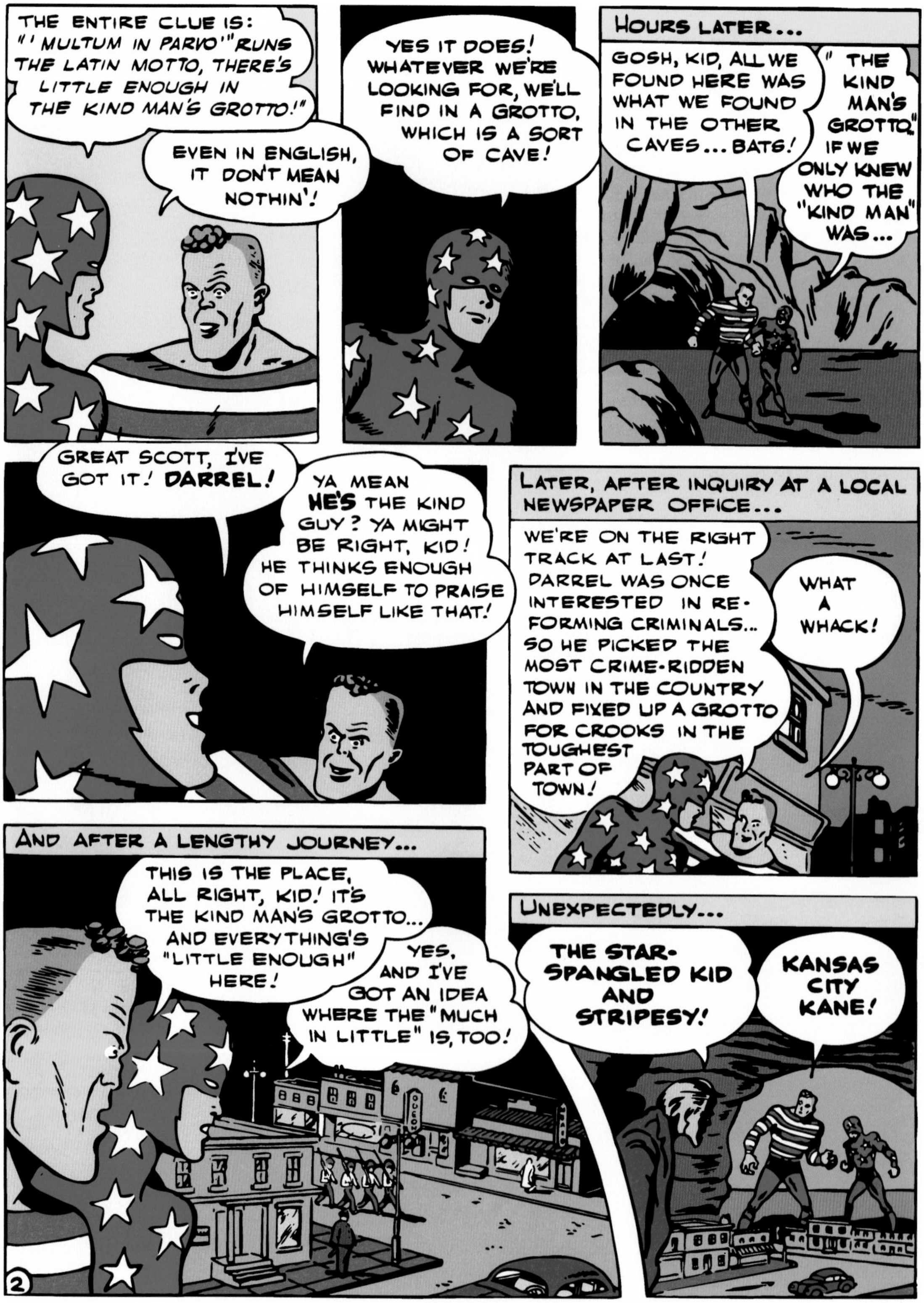
THE ENTIRE CLUE IS: "'MULTUM IN PARVO'" RUNS THE LATIN MOTTO, THERE'S LITTLE ENOUGH IN THE KIND MAN'S GROTTO!"
EVEN IN ENGLISH, IT DON'T MEAN NOTHIN'!
YES IT DOES! WHATEVER WE'RE LOOKING FOR, WE'LL FIND IN A GROTTO, WHICH IS A SORT OF CAVE!
HOURS LATER...
GOSH, KID, ALL WE FOUND HERE WAS WHAT WE FOUND IN THE OTHER CAVES... BATS!
"THE KIND MAN'S GROTTO," IF WE ONLY KNEW WHO THE "KIND MAN" WAS...
GREAT SCOTT, I'VE GOT IT! DARREL!
YA MEAN HE'S THE KIND GUY? YA MIGHT BE RIGHT, KID! HE THINKS ENOUGH OF HIMSELF TO PRAISE HIMSELF LIKE THAT!
LATER, AFTER INQUIRY AT A LOCAL NEWSPAPER OFFICE...
WE'RE ON THE RIGHT TRACK AT LAST! DARREL WAS ONCE INTERESTED IN RE-FORMING CRIMINALS... SO HE PICKED THE MOST CRIME-RIDDEN TOWN IN THE COUNTRY AND FIXED UP A GROTTO FOR CROOKS IN THE TOUGHEST PART OF TOWN!
WHAT A WHACK!
AND AFTER A LENGTHY JOURNEY...
THIS IS THE PLACE, ALL RIGHT, KID! IT'S THE KIND MAN'S GROTTO... AND EVERYTHING'S "LITTLE ENOUGH" HERE!
YES, AND I'VE GOT AN IDEA WHERE THE "MUCH IN LITTLE" IS, TOO!
2
UNEXPECTEDLY...
THE STAR-SPANGLED KID AND STRIPESY!
KANSAS CITY KANE!

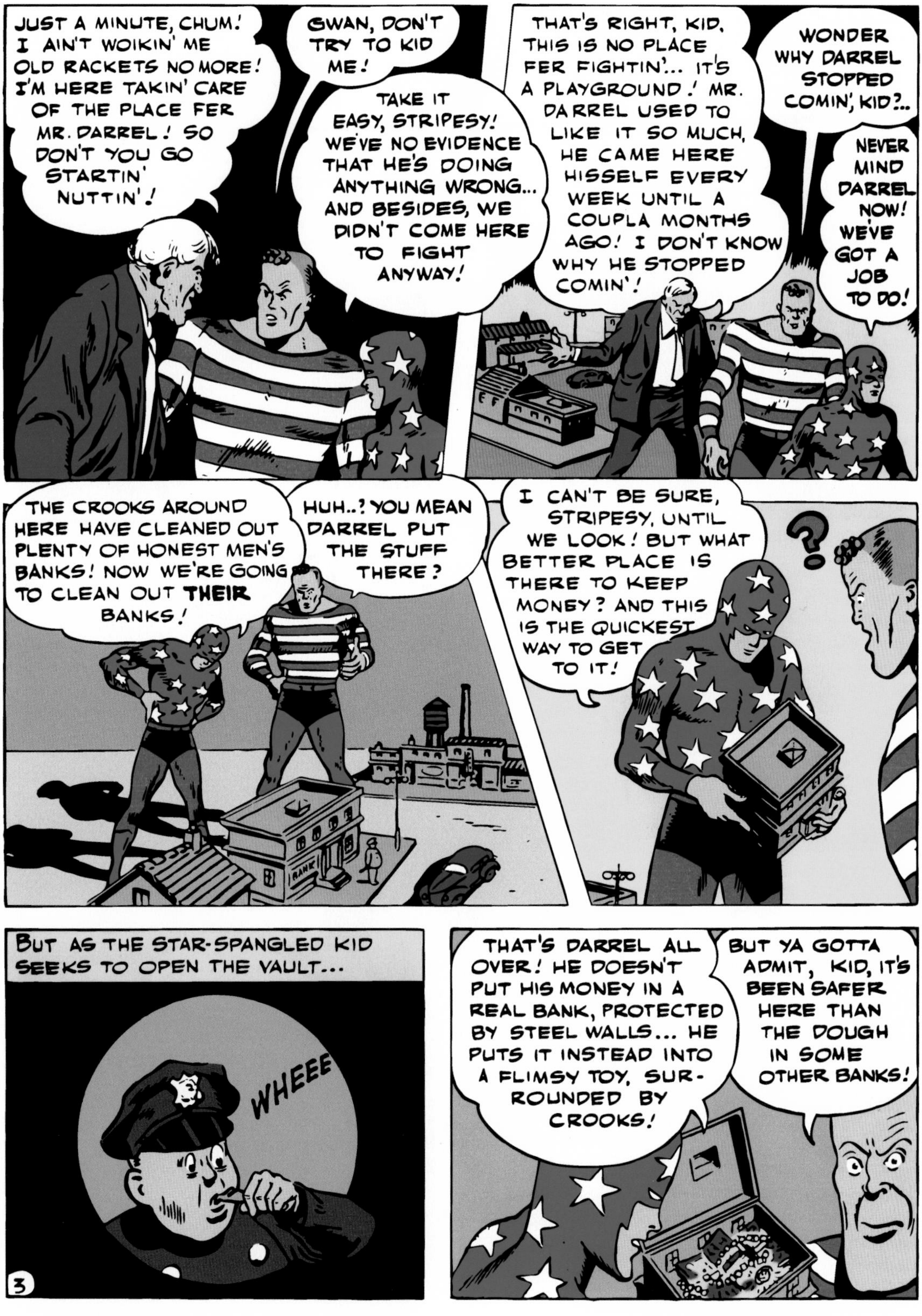
JUST A MINUTE, CHUM! I AIN'T WOIKIN' ME OLD RACKETS NO MORE! I'M HERE TAKIN' CARE OF THE PLACE FER MR. DARREL! SO DON'T YOU GO STARTIN' NUTTIN'!
GWAN, DON'T TRY TO KID ME!
TAKE IT EASY, STRIPESY! WE'VE NO EVIDENCE THAT HE'S DOING ANYTHING WRONG... AND BESIDES, WE DIDN'T COME HERE TO FIGHT ANYWAY!
THAT'S RIGHT, KID, THIS IS NO PLACE FER FIGHTIN'... IT'S A PLAYGROUND! MR. DARREL USED TO LIKE IT SO MUCH, HE CAME HERE HISSELF EVERY WEEK UNTIL A COUPLA MONTHS AGO! I DON'T KNOW WHY HE STOPPED COMIN'!
WONDER WHY DARREL STOPPED COMIN', KID?..
NEVER MIND DARREL NOW! WE'VE GOT A JOB TO DO!
THE CROOKS AROUND HERE HAVE CLEANED OUT PLENTY OF HONEST MEN'S BANKS! NOW WE'RE GOING TO CLEAN OUT THEIR BANKS!
HUH..? YOU MEAN DARREL PUT THE STUFF THERE?
I CAN'T BE SURE, STRIPESY, UNTIL WE LOOK! BUT WHAT BETTER PLACE IS THERE TO KEEP MONEY? AND THIS IS THE QUICKEST WAY TO GET TO IT!
BANK
BUT AS THE STAR-SPANGLED KID SEEKS TO OPEN THE VAULT...
WHEEE
3
THAT'S DARREL ALL OVER! HE DOESN'T PUT HIS MONEY IN A REAL BANK, PROTECTED BY STEEL WALLS... HE PUTS IT INSTEAD INTO A FLIMSY TOY, SURROUNDED BY CROOKS!
BUT YA GOTTA ADMIT, KID, IT'S BEEN SAFER HERE THAN THE DOUGH IN SOME OTHER BANKS!

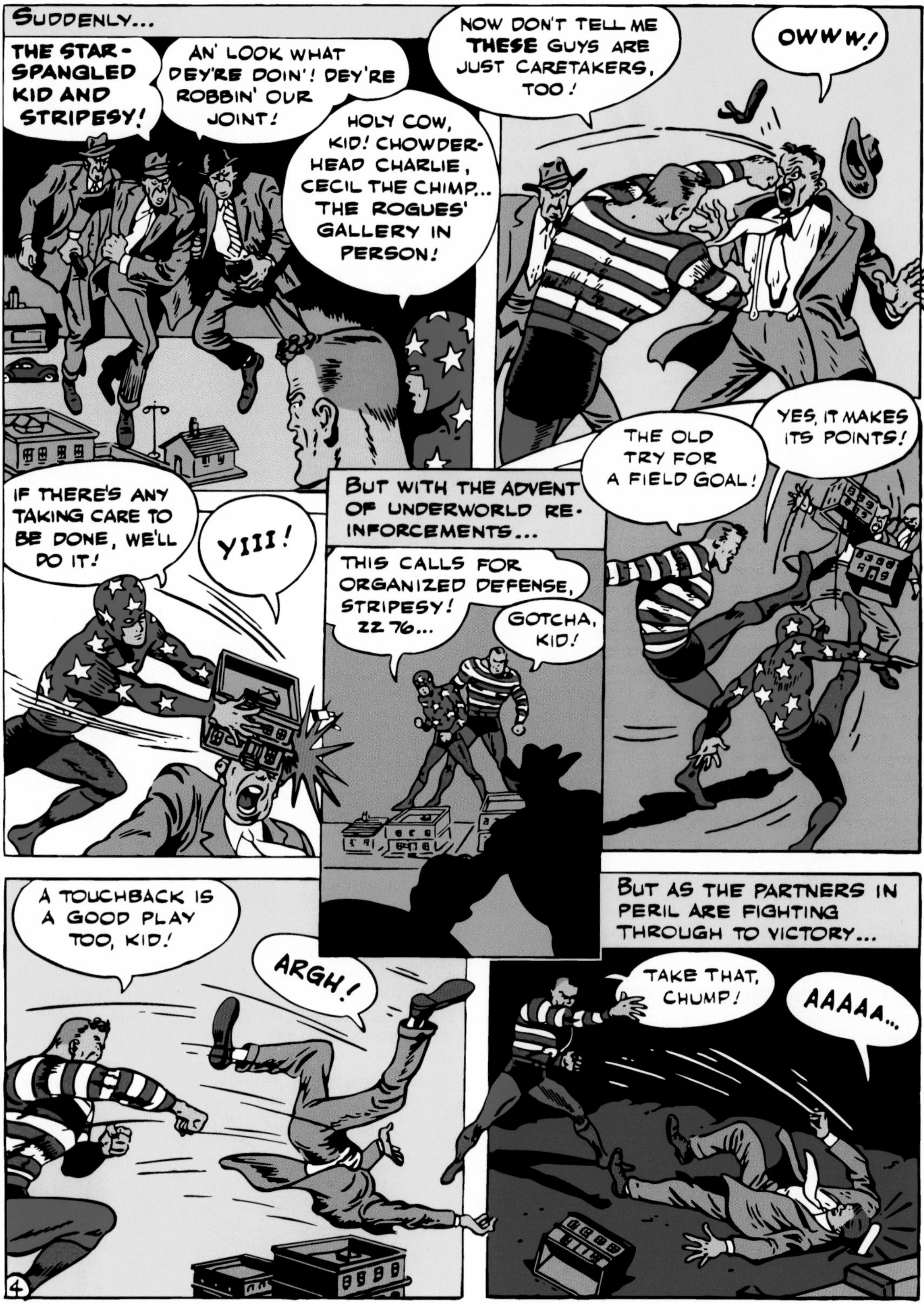
SUDDENLY...
THE STAR-SPANGLED KID AND STRIPESY!
AN' LOOK WHAT DEY'RE DOIN'! DEY'RE ROBBIN' OUR JOINT!
HOLY COW, KID! CHOWDER-HEAD CHARLIE, CECIL THE CHIMP... THE ROGUES' GALLERY IN PERSON!
NOW DON'T TELL ME THESE GUYS ARE JUST CARETAKERS, TOO!
OWWW!
IF THERE'S ANY TAKING CARE TO BE DONE, WE'LL DO IT!
YIII!
BUT WITH THE ADVENT OF UNDERWORLD RE-INFORCEMENTS...
THIS CALLS FOR ORGANIZED DEFENSE, STRIPESY! 22 76...
GOTCHA, KID!
THE OLD TRY FOR A FIELD GOAL!
YES, IT MAKES ITS POINTS!
A TOUCHBACK IS A GOOD PLAY TOO, KID!
ARGH!
BUT AS THE PARTNERS IN PERIL ARE FIGHTING THROUGH TO VICTORY...
TAKE THAT, CHUMP!
AAAAA...
4

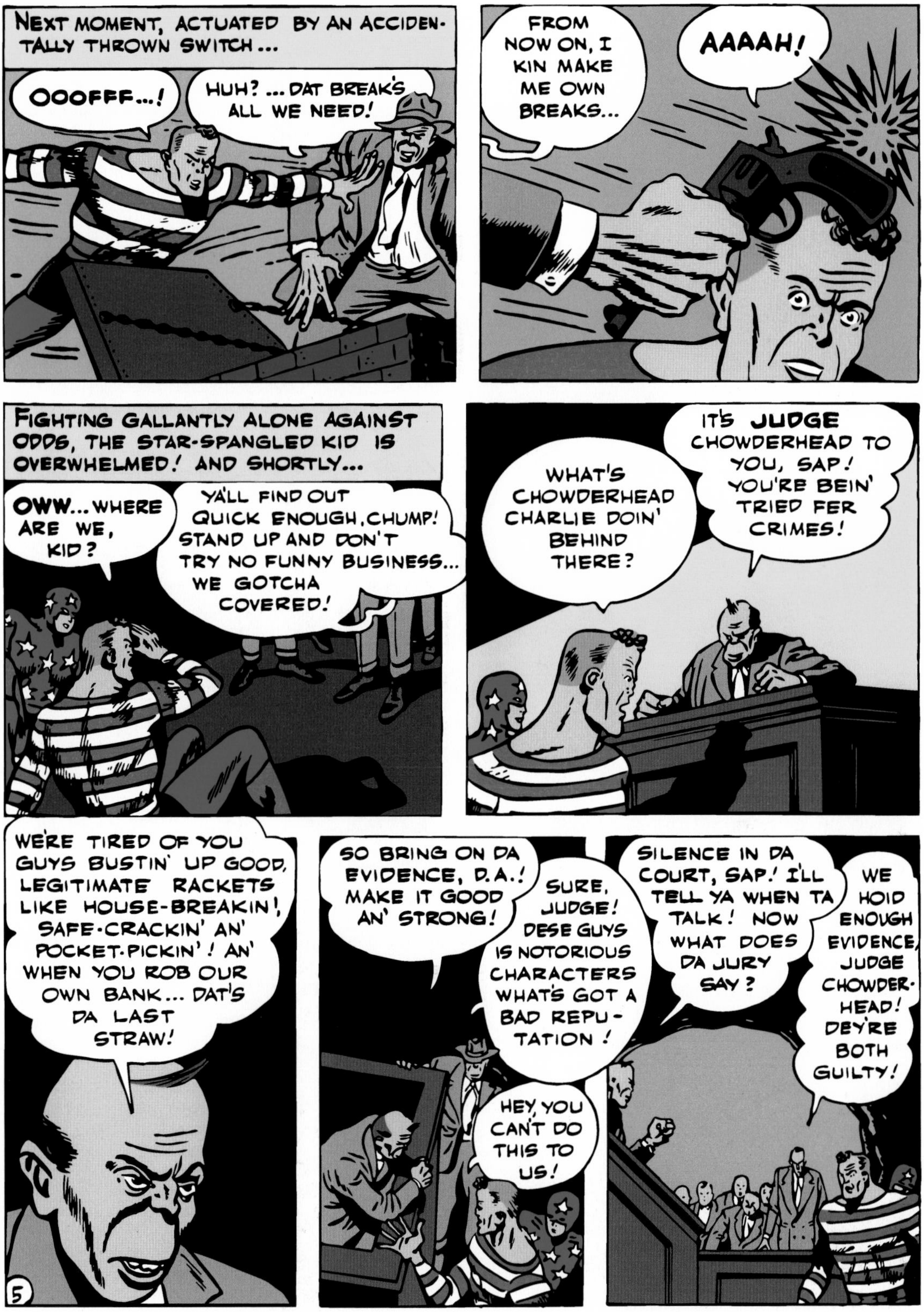
NEXT MOMENT, ACTUATED BY AN ACCIDENTALLY THROWN SWITCH...
OOOFFF...!
HUH? ... DAT BREAK'S ALL WE NEED!
FROM NOW ON, I KIN MAKE ME OWN BREAKS...
AAAAH!
FIGHTING GALLANTLY ALONE AGAINST ODDS, THE STAR-SPANGLED KID IS OVERWHELMED! AND SHORTLY...
OWW... WHERE ARE WE, KID?
YA'LL FIND OUT QUICK ENOUGH, CHUMP! STAND UP AND DON'T TRY NO FUNNY BUSINESS... WE GOTCHA COVERED!
WHAT'S CHOWDERHEAD CHARLIE DOIN' BEHIND THERE?
IT'S JUDGE CHOWDERHEAD TO YOU, SAP! YOU'RE BEIN' TRIED FER CRIMES!
WE'RE TIRED OF YOU GUYS BUSTIN' UP GOOD, LEGITIMATE RACKETS LIKE HOUSE-BREAKIN', SAFE-CRACKIN' AN' POCKET-PICKIN'! AN' WHEN YOU ROB OUR OWN BANK... DAT'S DA LAST STRAW!
5
SO BRING ON DA EVIDENCE, D.A.! MAKE IT GOOD AN' STRONG!
SURE, JUDGE! DESE GUYS IS NOTORIOUS CHARACTERS WHAT'S GOT A BAD REPUTATION!
HEY, YOU CAN'T DO THIS TO US!
SILENCE IN DA COURT, SAP! I'LL TELL YA WHEN TA TALK! NOW WHAT DOES DA JURY SAY?
WE HOID ENOUGH EVIDENCE, JUDGE CHOWDERHEAD! DEY'RE BOTH GUILTY!

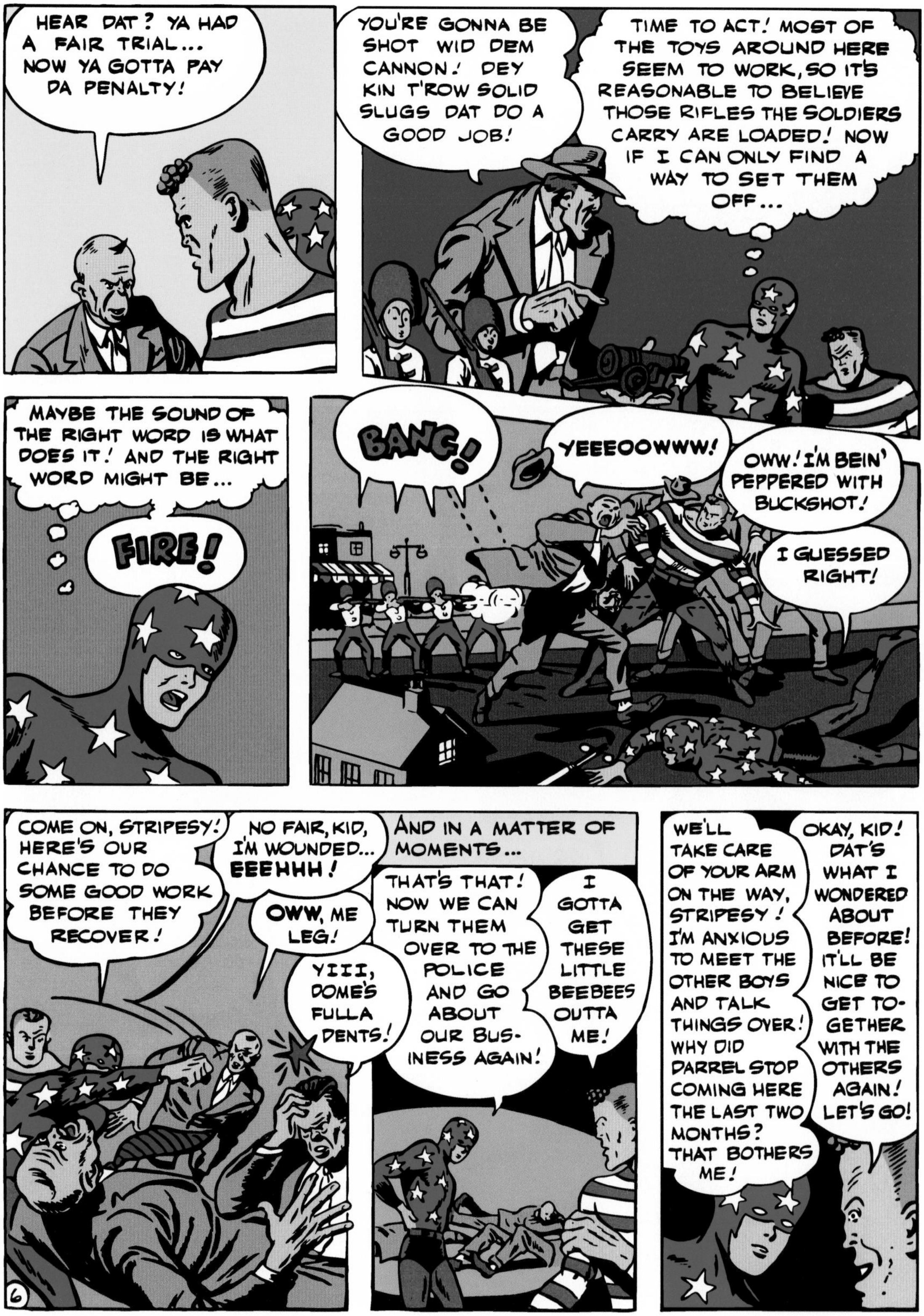
HEAR DAT? YA HAD A FAIR TRIAL... NOW YA GOTTA PAY DA PENALTY!
YOU'RE GONNA BE SHOT WID DEM CANNON! DEY KIN T'ROW SOLID SLUGS DAT DO A GOOD JOB!
TIME TO ACT! MOST OF THE TOYS AROUND HERE SEEM TO WORK, SO IT'S REASONABLE TO BELIEVE THOSE RIFLES THE SOLDIERS CARRY ARE LOADED! NOW IF I CAN ONLY FIND A WAY TO SET THEM OFF...
MAYBE THE SOUND OF THE RIGHT WORD IS WHAT DOES IT! AND THE RIGHT WORD MIGHT BE...
FIRE!
BANG!
YEEEOOWWW!
OWW! I'M BEIN' PEPPERED WITH BUCKSHOT!
I GUESSED RIGHT!
COME ON, STRIPESY! HERE'S OUR CHANCE TO DO SOME GOOD WORK BEFORE THEY RECOVER!
NO FAIR, KID, I'M WOUNDED... EEEHHH!
OWW, ME LEG!
YIII, DOME'S FULLA DENTS!
6
AND IN A MATTER OF MOMENTS...
THAT'S THAT! NOW WE CAN TURN THEM OVER TO THE POLICE AND GO ABOUT OUR BUSINESS AGAIN!
I GOTTA GET THESE LITTLE BEEBEES OUTTA ME!
WE'LL TAKE CARE OF YOUR ARM ON THE WAY, STRIPESY! I'M ANXIOUS TO MEET THE OTHER BOYS AND TALK THINGS OVER! WHY DID DARREL STOP COMING HERE THE LAST TWO MONTHS? THAT BOTHERS ME!
OKAY, KID! DAT'S WHAT I WONDERED ABOUT BEFORE! IT'LL BE NICE TO GET TOGETHER WITH THE OTHERS AGAIN! LET'S GO!

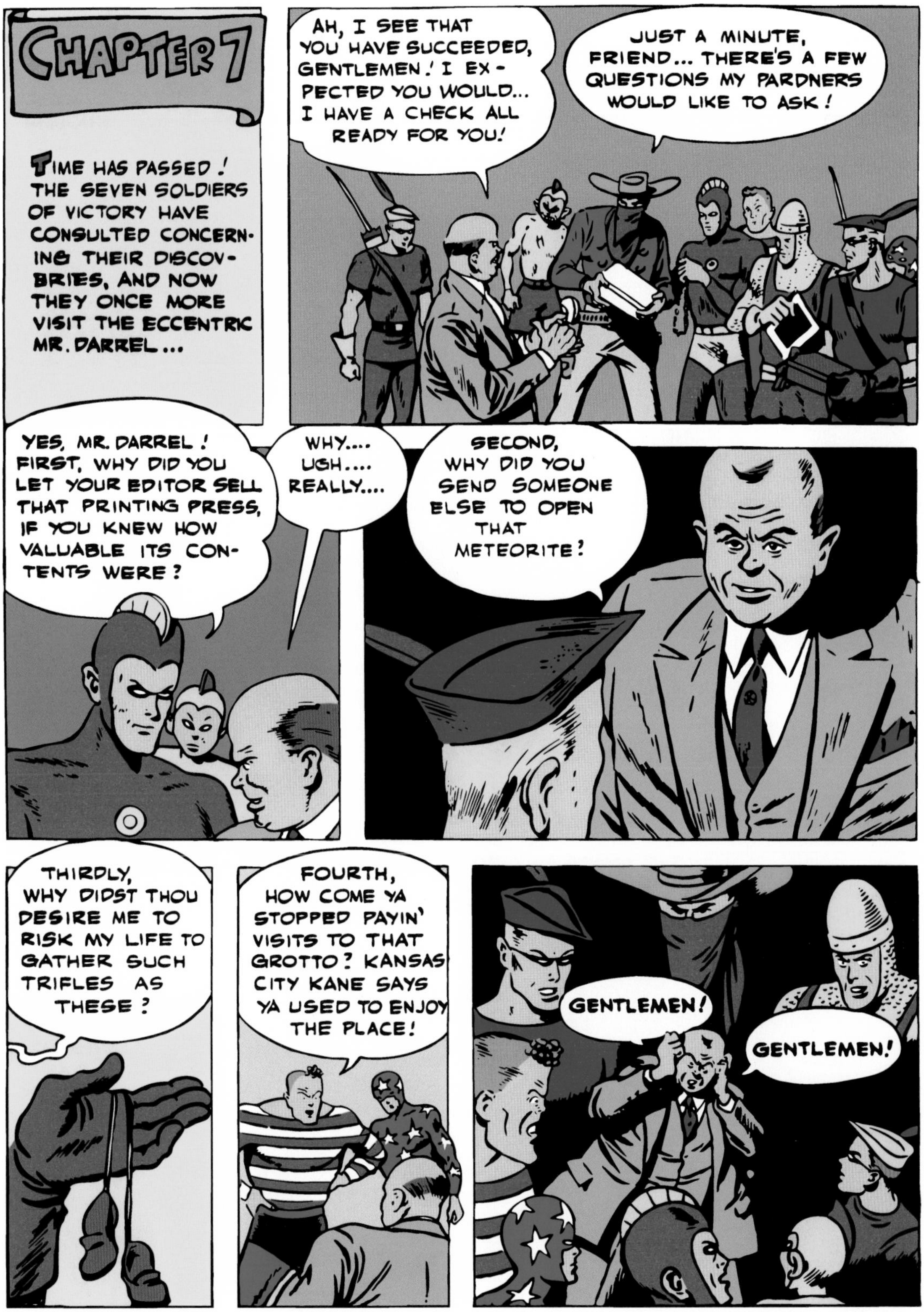
CHAPTER 7
TIME HAS PASSED! THE SEVEN SOLDIERS OF VICTORY HAVE CONSULTED CONCERNING THEIR DISCOVERIES, AND NOW THEY ONCE MORE VISIT THE ECCENTRIC MR. DARREL...
AH, I SEE THAT YOU HAVE SUCCEEDED, GENTLEMEN! I EXPECTED YOU WOULD... I HAVE A CHECK ALL READY FOR YOU!
JUST A MINUTE, FRIEND... THERE'S A FEW QUESTIONS MY PARDNERS WOULD LIKE TO ASK!
YES, MR. DARREL! FIRST, WHY DID YOU LET YOUR EDITOR SELL THAT PRINTING PRESS, IF YOU KNEW HOW VALUABLE ITS CONTENTS WERE?
WHY.... UGH.... REALLY....
SECOND, WHY DID YOU SEND SOMEONE ELSE TO OPEN THAT METEORITE?
THIRDLY, WHY DIDST THOU DESIRE ME TO RISK MY LIFE TO GATHER SUCH TRIFLES AS THESE?
FOURTH, HOW COME YA STOPPED PAYIN' VISITS TO THAT GROTTO? KANSAS CITY KANE SAYS YA USED TO ENJOY THE PLACE!
GENTLEMEN!
GENTLEMEN!

GENTLEMEN, YOU ASTONISH ME! I HAD EXPECTED A HAPPY, CAREFREE ATTITUDE! INSTEAD, YOU SEEM TO BE ACCUSING ME OF SOMETHING!..

YOU'RE RIGHT, VARMINT, WE **ARE** ACCUSIN' YUH! AND SEEIN' AS HOW YOU WON'T ANSWER OUR QUESTIONS, WE'LL ANSWER THEM FOR YOU!

FIRST, YOU WEREN'T INTERESTED IN THAT PRESS BECAUSE YOU **DIDN'T KNOW** HOW VALUABLE IT WAS!

YOU NOT CLEVER ENOUGH TO FIGURE OUT CLUE!

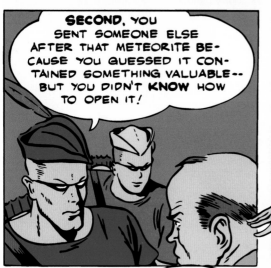

SECOND, YOU SENT SOMEONE ELSE AFTER THAT METEORITE BE- CAUSE YOU GUESSED IT CON- TAINED SOMETHING VALUABLE-- BUT YOU DIDN'T **KNOW** HOW TO OPEN IT!

THIRDLY, THOU DIDST BELIEVE THERE WERE **REAL** TREASURES, NOT THESE TRIFLES, WITHIN THE PYRAMID... BUT THOU COULDST NOT REACH THEM AND THEREFORE SENT ME!

AS FER THE LAST QUESTION... WHY DID MR. DARREL STOP COMIN' TO THE GROTTO...

THE ANSWER IS .... MR. DARREL **ISN'T** MR. DARREL!

IN OTHER WORDS, RAT, YOU TOOK THE REAL DARREL'S PLACE AND TRIED TO COLLECT WHAT BELONGED TO HIM! BUT THE JOB WAS TOO HARD AND DANGEROUS FOR YOU AND YOUR GANG... SO YOU PASSED IT ON TO **US!**

HMM, YOU'VE ACTUALLY GUESSED THE TRUTH! HOW- EVER THERE'S ALSO ANOTHER REASON...

I DID THINK OF HIRING OTHERS OUTSIDE MY OWN GANG TO DO WHAT I WANTED, BUT I COULDN'T TRUST THEIR HONESTY! I WAS AFRAID THEY WOULDN'T RETURN THE TREASURES TO ME AND THERE WAS TOO MUCH MONEY IN- VOLVED TO RISK LOSING!

②

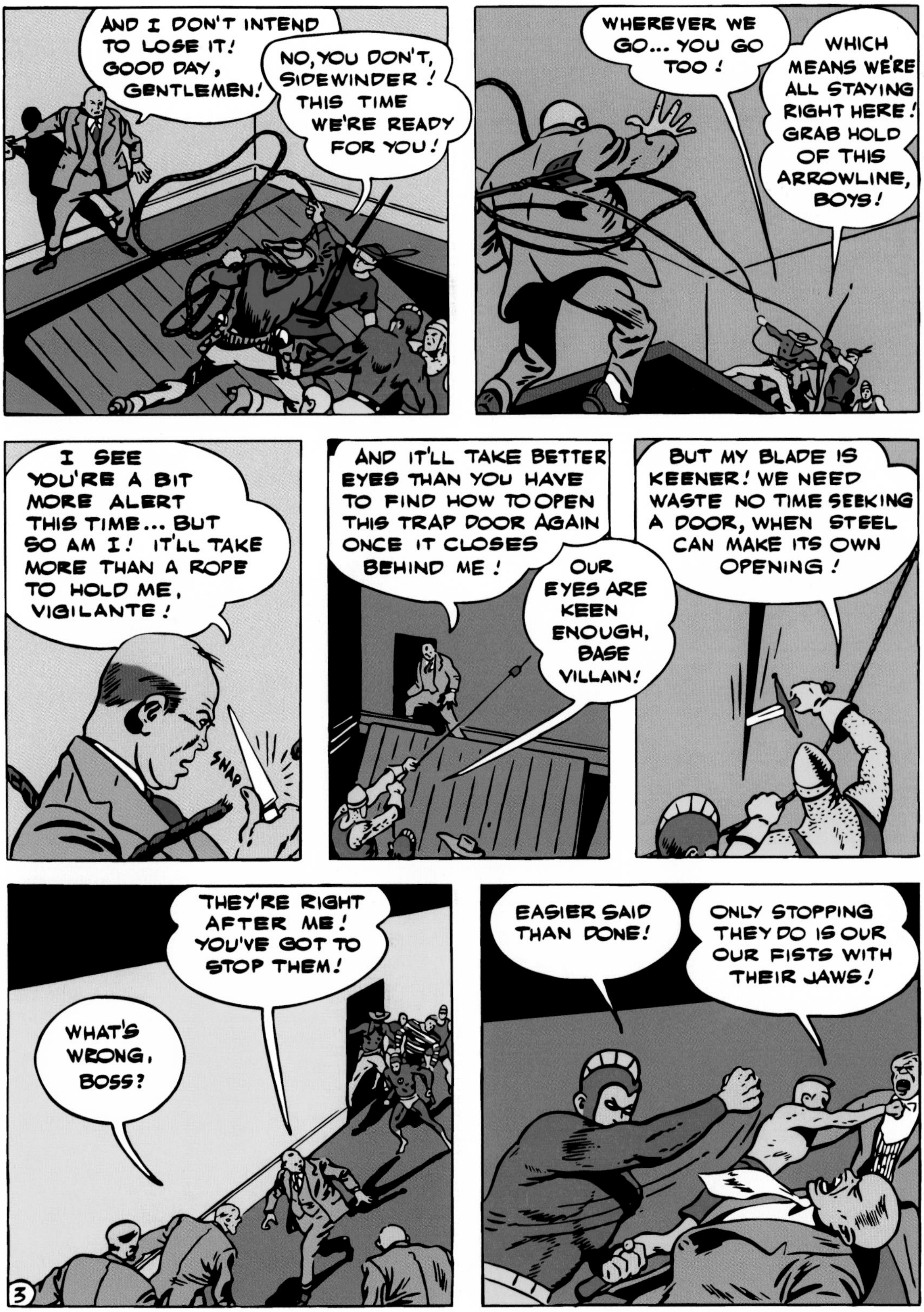
AND I DON'T INTEND TO LOSE IT! GOOD DAY, GENTLEMEN!
NO, YOU DON'T, SIDEWINDER! THIS TIME WE'RE READY FOR YOU!
WHEREVER WE GO... YOU GO TOO!
WHICH MEANS WE'RE ALL STAYING RIGHT HERE! GRAB HOLD OF THIS ARROWLINE, BOYS!
I SEE YOU'RE A BIT MORE ALERT THIS TIME... BUT SO AM I! IT'LL TAKE MORE THAN A ROPE TO HOLD ME, VIGILANTE!
SNAP
AND IT'LL TAKE BETTER EYES THAN YOU HAVE TO FIND HOW TO OPEN THIS TRAP DOOR AGAIN ONCE IT CLOSES BEHIND ME!
OUR EYES ARE KEEN ENOUGH, BASE VILLAIN!
BUT MY BLADE IS KEENER! WE NEED WASTE NO TIME SEEKING A DOOR, WHEN STEEL CAN MAKE ITS OWN OPENING!
THEY'RE RIGHT AFTER ME! YOU'VE GOT TO STOP THEM!
WHAT'S WRONG, BOSS?
3
EASIER SAID THAN DONE!
ONLY STOPPING THEY DO IS OUR OUR FISTS WITH THEIR JAWS!

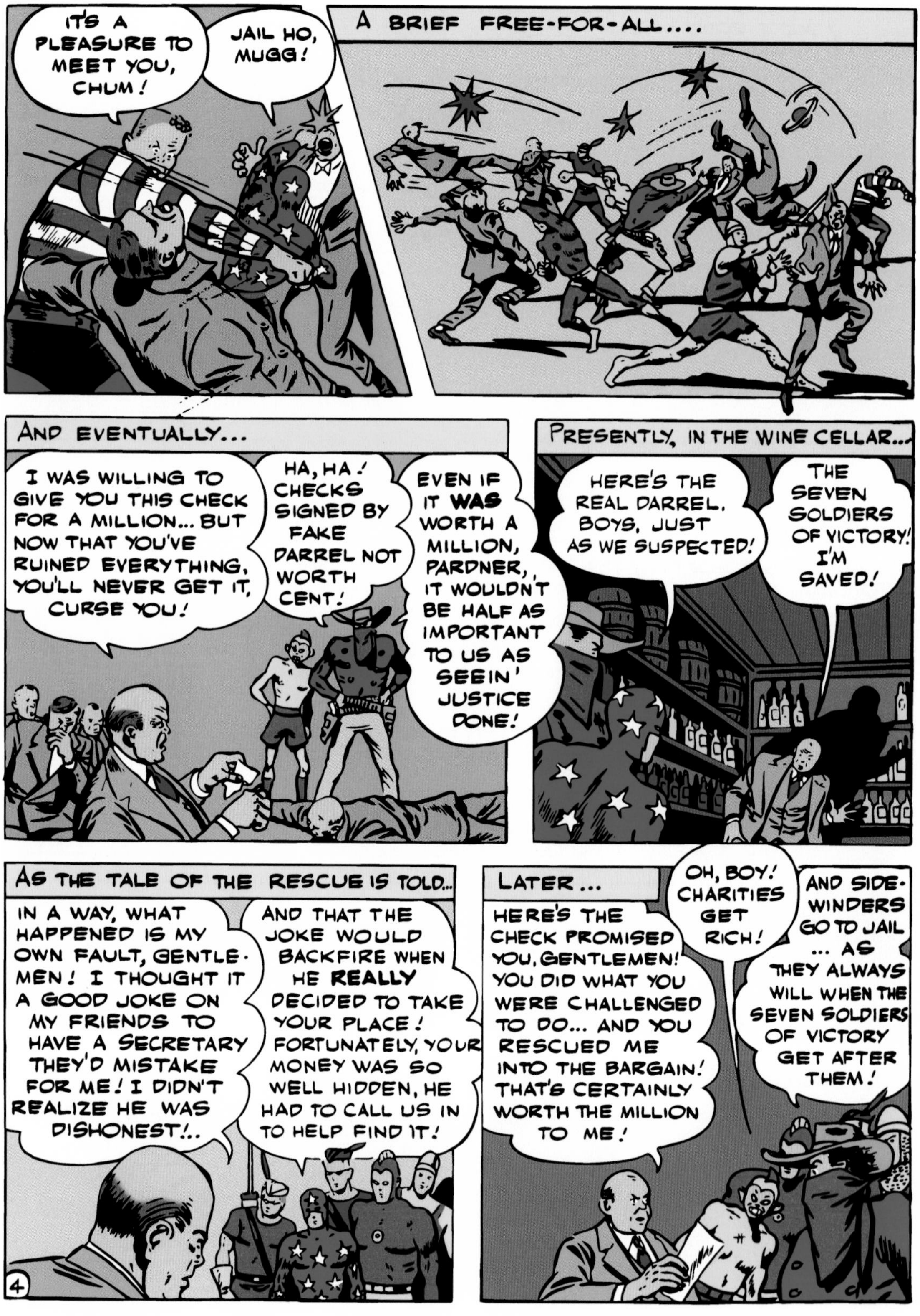
IT'S A PLEASURE TO MEET YOU, CHUM!
JAIL HO, MUGG!
A BRIEF FREE-FOR-ALL....
AND EVENTUALLY...
I WAS WILLING TO GIVE YOU THIS CHECK FOR A MILLION... BUT NOW THAT YOU'VE RUINED EVERYTHING, YOU'LL NEVER GET IT, CURSE YOU!
HA, HA! CHECKS SIGNED BY FAKE DARREL NOT WORTH CENT!
EVEN IF IT WAS WORTH A MILLION, PARDNER, IT WOULDN'T BE HALF AS IMPORTANT TO US AS SEEIN' JUSTICE DONE!
PRESENTLY, IN THE WINE CELLAR...
HERE'S THE REAL DARREL, BOYS, JUST AS WE SUSPECTED!
THE SEVEN SOLDIERS OF VICTORY! I'M SAVED!
AS THE TALE OF THE RESCUE IS TOLD...
IN A WAY, WHAT HAPPENED IS MY OWN FAULT, GENTLEMEN! I THOUGHT IT A GOOD JOKE ON MY FRIENDS TO HAVE A SECRETARY THEY'D MISTAKE FOR ME! I DIDN'T REALIZE HE WAS DISHONEST!..
AND THAT THE JOKE WOULD BACKFIRE WHEN HE REALLY DECIDED TO TAKE YOUR PLACE! FORTUNATELY, YOUR MONEY WAS SO WELL HIDDEN, HE HAD TO CALL US IN TO HELP FIND IT!
4
LATER...
HERE'S THE CHECK PROMISED YOU, GENTLEMEN! YOU DID WHAT YOU WERE CHALLENGED TO DO... AND YOU RESCUED ME INTO THE BARGAIN! THAT'S CERTAINLY WORTH THE MILLION TO ME!
OH, BOY! CHARITIES GET RICH!
AND SIDEWINDERS GO TO JAIL ... AS THEY ALWAYS WILL WHEN THE SEVEN SOLDIERS OF VICTORY GET AFTER THEM!

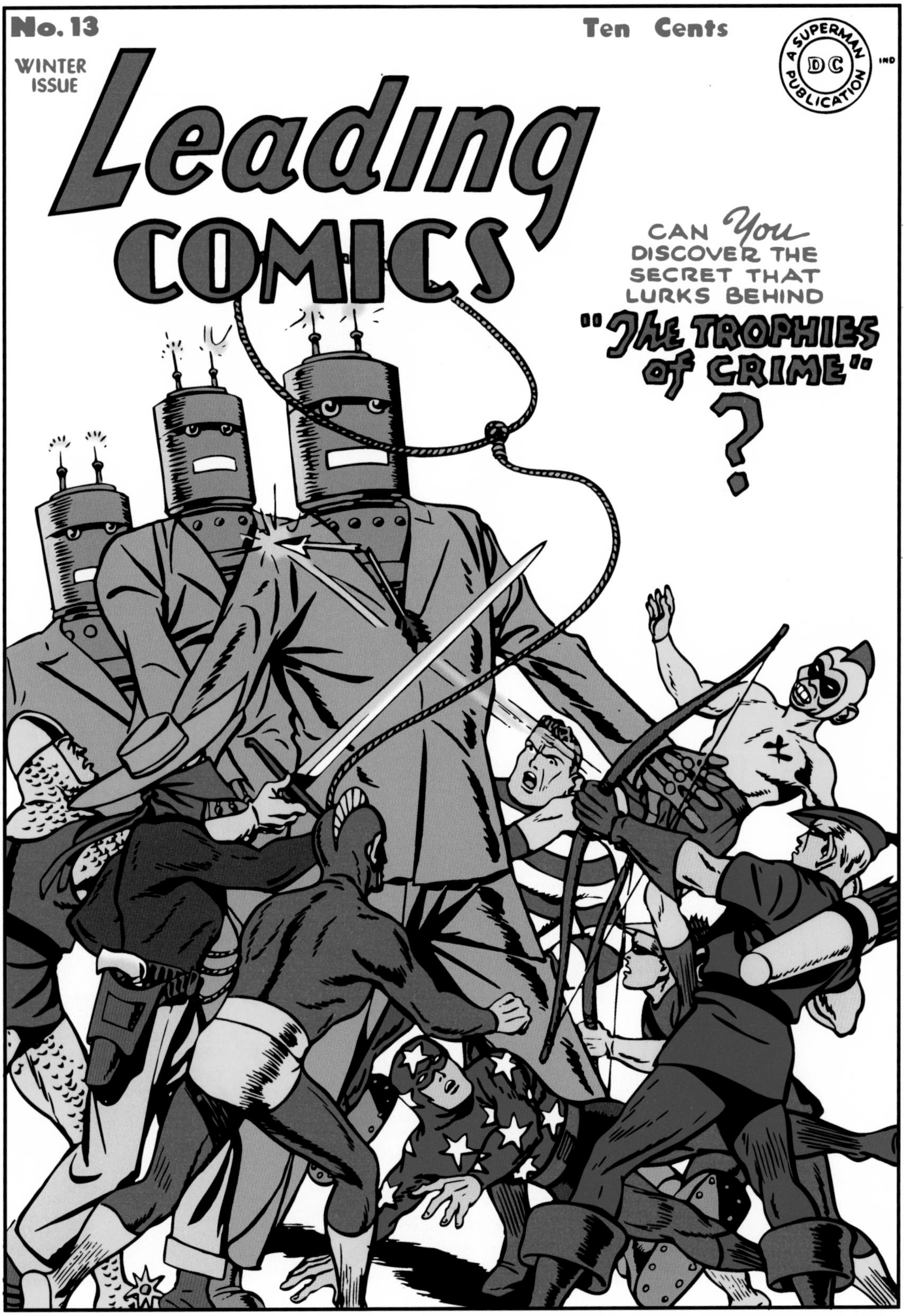
No. 13
Ten Cents
A SUPERMAN DC PUBLICATION
IND
WINTER ISSUE
Leading COMICS
CAN You DISCOVER THE SECRET THAT LURKS BEHIND "The TROPHIES of CRIME"?

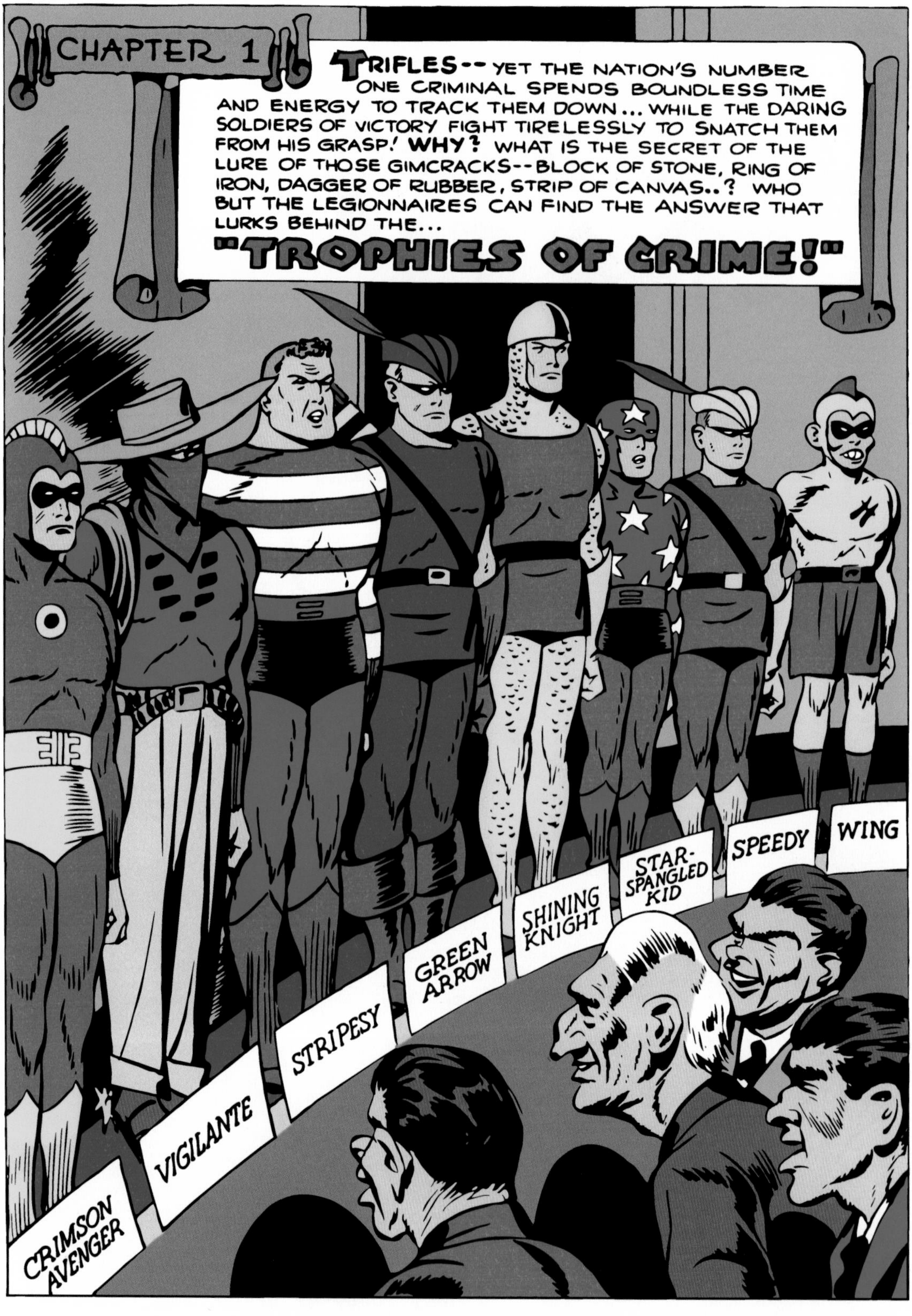
CHAPTER 1
TRIFLES-- YET THE NATION'S NUMBER ONE CRIMINAL SPENDS BOUNDLESS TIME AND ENERGY TO TRACK THEM DOWN... WHILE THE DARING SOLDIERS OF VICTORY FIGHT TIRELESSLY TO SNATCH THEM FROM HIS GRASP! WHY? WHAT IS THE SECRET OF THE LURE OF THOSE GIMCRACKS--BLOCK OF STONE, RING OF IRON, DAGGER OF RUBBER, STRIP OF CANVAS..? WHO BUT THE LEGIONNAIRES CAN FIND THE ANSWER THAT LURKS BEHIND THE...
"TROPHIES OF CRIME!"
CRIMSON AVENGER
VIGILANTE
STRIPESY
GREEN ARROW
SHINING KNIGHT
STAR-SPANGLED KID
SPEEDY
WING

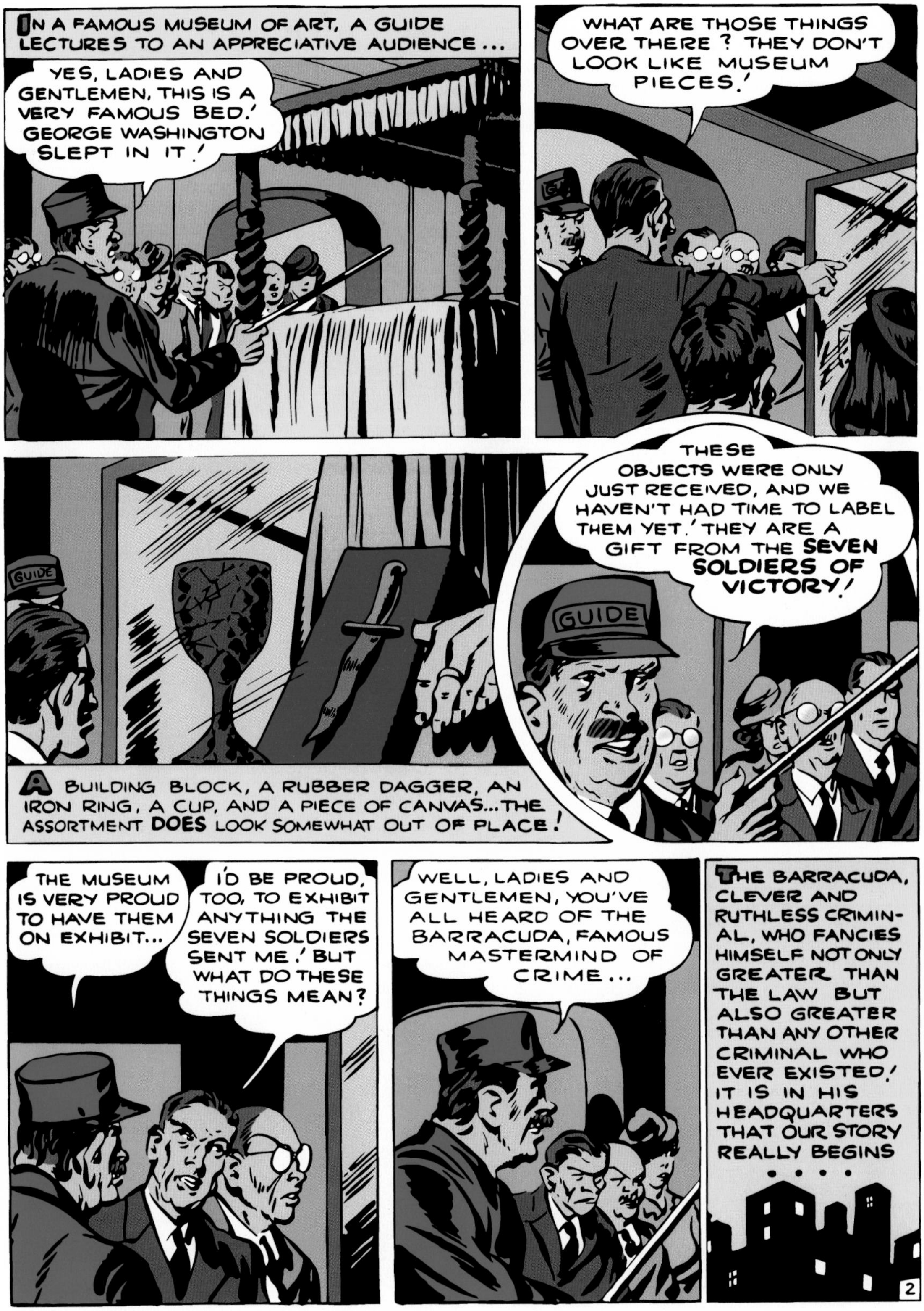
IN A FAMOUS MUSEUM OF ART, A GUIDE LECTURES TO AN APPRECIATIVE AUDIENCE...
YES, LADIES AND GENTLEMEN, THIS IS A VERY FAMOUS BED! GEORGE WASHINGTON SLEPT IN IT!
WHAT ARE THOSE THINGS OVER THERE? THEY DON'T LOOK LIKE MUSEUM PIECES!
GUIDE
GUIDE
A BUILDING BLOCK, A RUBBER DAGGER, AN IRON RING, A CUP, AND A PIECE OF CANVAS...THE ASSORTMENT DOES LOOK SOMEWHAT OUT OF PLACE!
THESE OBJECTS WERE ONLY JUST RECEIVED, AND WE HAVEN'T HAD TIME TO LABEL THEM YET! THEY ARE A GIFT FROM THE SEVEN SOLDIERS OF VICTORY!
GUIDE
THE MUSEUM IS VERY PROUD TO HAVE THEM ON EXHIBIT...
I'D BE PROUD, TOO, TO EXHIBIT ANYTHING THE SEVEN SOLDIERS SENT ME! BUT WHAT DO THESE THINGS MEAN?
WELL, LADIES AND GENTLEMEN, YOU'VE ALL HEARD OF THE BARRACUDA, FAMOUS MASTERMIND OF CRIME...
THE BARRACUDA, CLEVER AND RUTHLESS CRIMINAL, WHO FANCIES HIMSELF NOT ONLY GREATER THAN THE LAW BUT ALSO GREATER THAN ANY OTHER CRIMINAL WHO EVER EXISTED! IT IS IN HIS HEADQUARTERS THAT OUR STORY REALLY BEGINS....
2

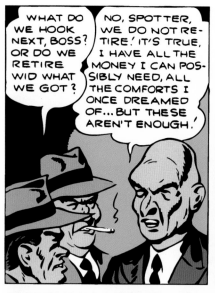

WHAT DO WE HOOK NEXT, BOSS? OR DO WE RETIRE WID WHAT WE GOT?

NO, SPOTTER, WE DO NOT RETIRE! IT'S TRUE, I HAVE ALL THE MONEY I CAN POSSIBLY NEED, ALL THE COMFORTS I ONCE DREAMED OF...BUT THESE AREN'T ENOUGH!

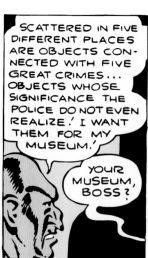

SCATTERED IN FIVE DIFFERENT PLACES ARE OBJECTS CONNECTED WITH FIVE GREAT CRIMES... OBJECTS WHOSE SIGNIFICANCE THE POLICE DO NOT EVEN REALIZE! I WANT THEM FOR MY MUSEUM.

YOUR MUSEUM, BOSS?

YES, SPOTTER, A MUSEUM OF CRIME SUCH AS THE WORLD HAS NEVER SEEN! IT WILL PUT SCOTLAND YARD OR THE NEW YORK POLICE DEPARTMENT TO SHAME! I'VE PREPARED MY PLANS... ALL I NEED DO IS SEND OUT ORDERS...

IT SO HAPPENS THAT AT THAT VERY MOMENT...

THE BARRACUDA DOESN'T KNOW WE'VE LEARNED WHERE HIS HIDEOUT IS... IF WE STRIKE PRONTO, HE'S A SKINNED RATTLER!

RIGHT, VIGILANTE! NO USE DELAYING... LET'S GO!

AND THE LEGIONNAIRES CONVERGE ON THE LONG-CONCEALED HIDEOUT...

AS THE FLYING LEGIONNAIRES DESCEND TO EARTH, THEY ARE JOINED BY THEIR COMRADES, THE WIZARD ARCHERS...

HERE COME THE GREEN ARROW AND SPEEDY, SHOT FROM THEIR CATAPULT! AND THE BARRACUDA DOESN'T EVEN KNOW WE'RE HERE!

BUT WHEN THE CRIME-SMASHERS PLUNGE FORWARD...

RRRIIIIINNNGGGG!

AAA...

BOP!

THE ALARM! WE'D BETTER STEP ON IT!

THOUGH STEEL GATES CLANG SHUT TO BAR THE WAY, THE SOLDIERS OF VICTORY DO NOT HESITATE.'

STEEL IS NO BARRIER TO MY MAGIC SWORD.' FORWARD, COMRADES!

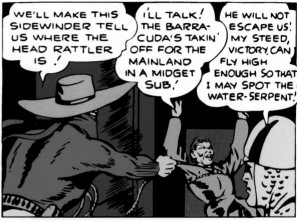

WE'LL MAKE THIS SIDEWINDER TELL US WHERE THE HEAD RATTLER IS.'

I'LL TALK! THE BARRACUDA'S TAKIN' OFF FOR THE MAINLAND IN A MIDGET SUB.'

HE WILL NOT ESCAPE US! MY STEED, VICTORY, CAN FLY HIGH ENOUGH SO THAT I MAY SPOT THE WATER-SERPENT!

AH, HERE HE IS.' NOW I WILL TEST MY BLADE UPON HIS HIDE!

I HAVE WOUNDED HIM MORTALLY... NOW THE RATS WITHIN SEEK TO FLEE THEIR DOOM.'

HELP... GLUG!

MOMENTS LATER...

HA, HA! THE BARRACUDA HAD AN IDEA YOU MIGHT SPOT THE SUB...SO HE HAD US FIRE HIM OUT OF A TORPEDO TUBE OFF TO ONE SIDE.'

SO THAT'S WHY THE OTHER RAT WAS WILLIN' TO TALK!

BUT THE BARRACUDA'S BEST LIEUTENANTS ARE GONE, TOO!' THEY COULDN'T ALL HAVE ESCAPED FROM A TORPEDO TUBE.'

MAYBE THESE PAPERS WILL HELP TO EXPLAIN!

THEY'RE INFORMATION AS TO THE WHEREABOUTS OF CERTAIN OBJECTS THE BARRACUDA WANTED FOR A CRIME MUSEUM... HE MUST HAVE SENT HIS MEN TO GET THEM BEFORE WE LANDED.'

THERE'S OUR LEAD, PARDNERS!' WE'LL HEAD FOR WHERE THEY HEAD.'

RIGHT.' I'LL READ OFF THE DIFFERENT OBJECTS, AND WE'LL DECIDE WHERE EACH OF US IS TO TAKE UP THE CHASE.'

A BUILDING BLOCK, A RUBBER DAGGER, AN IRON RING, A CUP, AND A PIECE OF CANVAS... WHAT ADVENTURES DO THEY PORTEND FOR THE DARING LEGIONNAIRES?

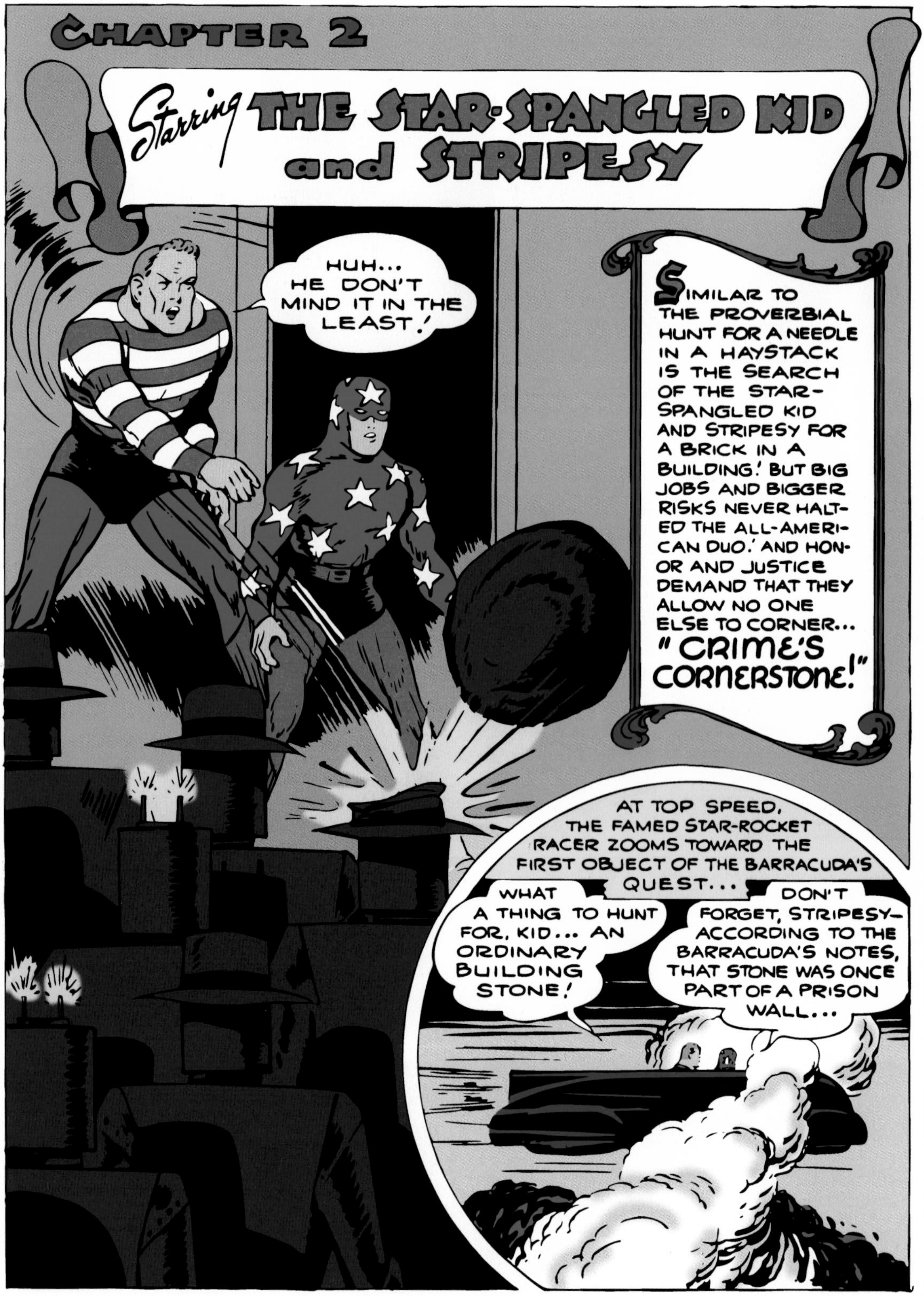
CHAPTER 2
Starring THE STAR-SPANGLED KID and STRIPESY
HUH... HE DON'T MIND IT IN THE LEAST!
SIMILAR TO THE PROVERBIAL HUNT FOR A NEEDLE IN A HAYSTACK IS THE SEARCH OF THE STAR-SPANGLED KID AND STRIPESY FOR A BRICK IN A BUILDING! BUT BIG JOBS AND BIGGER RISKS NEVER HALTED THE ALL-AMERICAN DUO! AND HONOR AND JUSTICE DEMAND THAT THEY ALLOW NO ONE ELSE TO CORNER... "CRIME'S CORNERSTONE!"
AT TOP SPEED, THE FAMED STAR-ROCKET RACER ZOOMS TOWARD THE FIRST OBJECT OF THE BARRACUDA'S QUEST...
WHAT A THING TO HUNT FOR, KID... AN ORDINARY BUILDING STONE!
DON'T FORGET, STRIPESY— ACCORDING TO THE BARRACUDA'S NOTES, THAT STONE WAS ONCE PART OF A PRISON WALL...

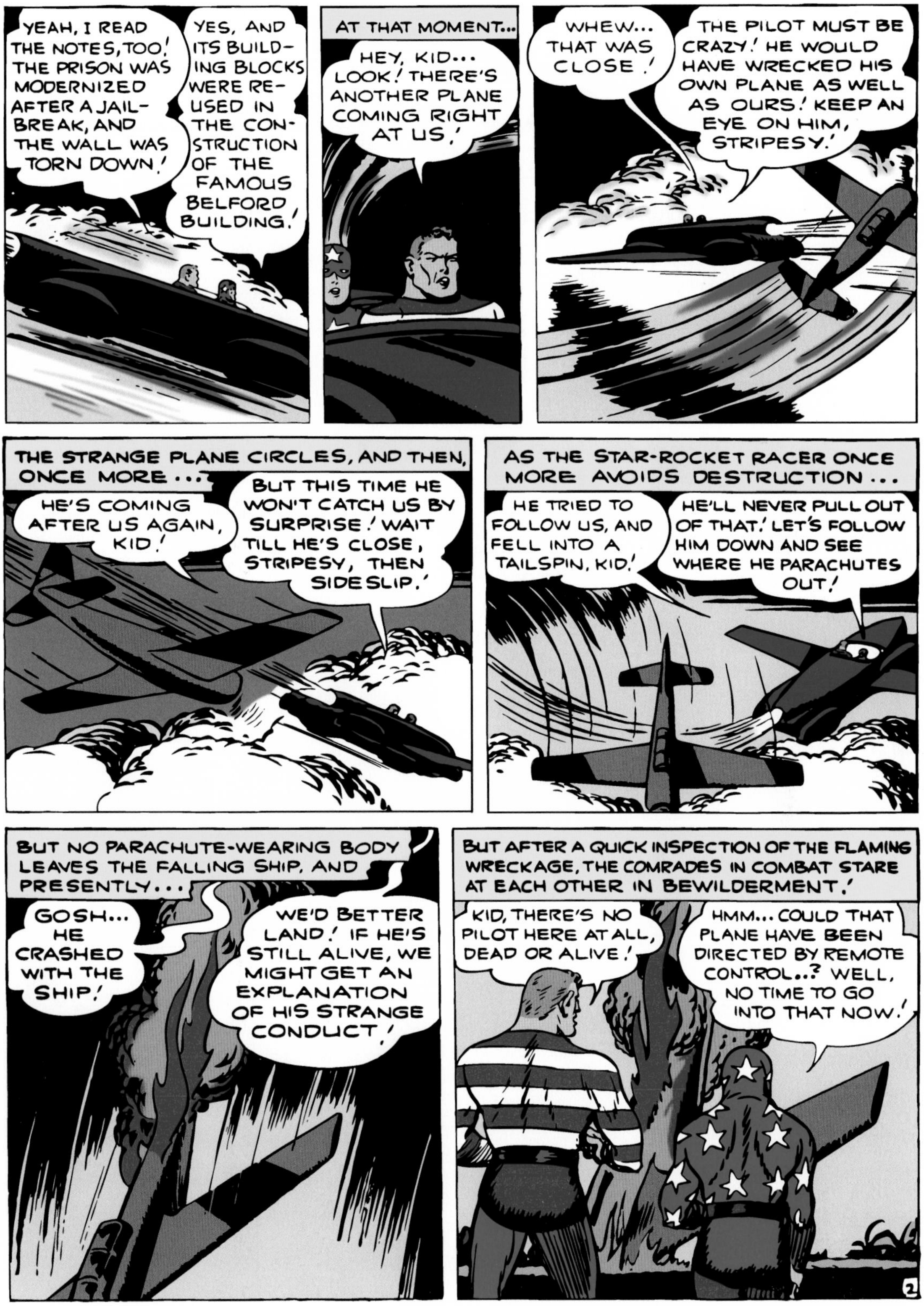
YEAH, I READ THE NOTES, TOO! THE PRISON WAS MODERNIZED AFTER A JAIL-BREAK, AND THE WALL WAS TORN DOWN!
YES, AND ITS BUILDING BLOCKS WERE RE-USED IN THE CONSTRUCTION OF THE FAMOUS BELFORD BUILDING!
AT THAT MOMENT...
HEY, KID... LOOK! THERE'S ANOTHER PLANE COMING RIGHT AT US!
WHEW... THAT WAS CLOSE!
THE PILOT MUST BE CRAZY! HE WOULD HAVE WRECKED HIS OWN PLANE AS WELL AS OURS! KEEP AN EYE ON HIM, STRIPESY!
THE STRANGE PLANE CIRCLES, AND THEN, ONCE MORE...
HE'S COMING AFTER US AGAIN, KID!
BUT THIS TIME HE WON'T CATCH US BY SURPRISE! WAIT TILL HE'S CLOSE, STRIPESY, THEN SIDESLIP!
AS THE STAR-ROCKET RACER ONCE MORE AVOIDS DESTRUCTION...
HE TRIED TO FOLLOW US, AND FELL INTO A TAILSPIN, KID!
HE'LL NEVER PULL OUT OF THAT! LET'S FOLLOW HIM DOWN AND SEE WHERE HE PARACHUTES OUT!
BUT NO PARACHUTE-WEARING BODY LEAVES THE FALLING SHIP, AND PRESENTLY...
GOSH... HE CRASHED WITH THE SHIP!
WE'D BETTER LAND! IF HE'S STILL ALIVE, WE MIGHT GET AN EXPLANATION OF HIS STRANGE CONDUCT!
BUT AFTER A QUICK INSPECTION OF THE FLAMING WRECKAGE, THE COMRADES IN COMBAT STARE AT EACH OTHER IN BEWILDERMENT!
KID, THERE'S NO PILOT HERE AT ALL, DEAD OR ALIVE!
HMM... COULD THAT PLANE HAVE BEEN DIRECTED BY REMOTE CONTROL..? WELL, NO TIME TO GO INTO THAT NOW!
2

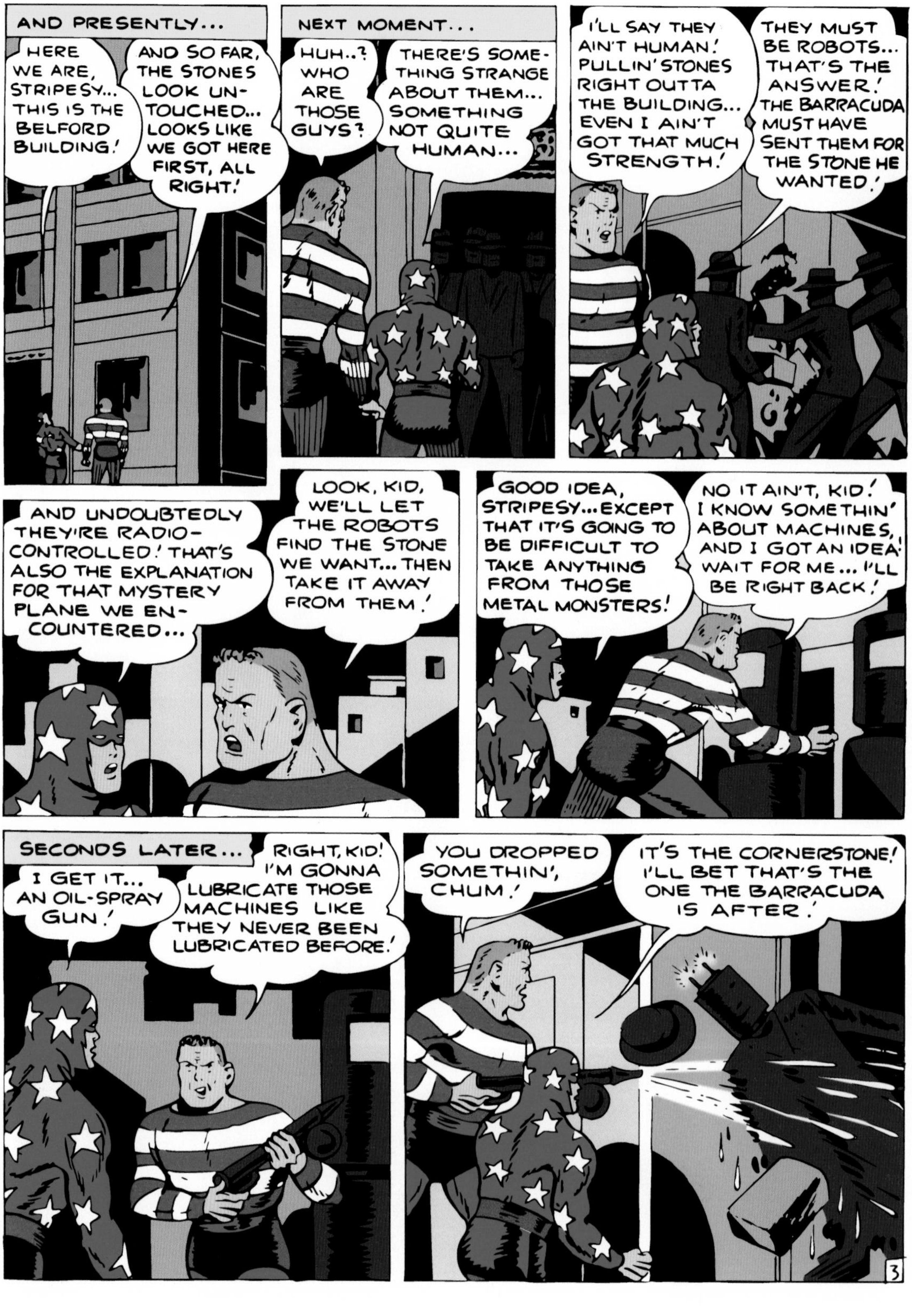
AND PRESENTLY...
HERE WE ARE, STRIPESY... THIS IS THE BELFORD BUILDING!
AND SO FAR, THE STONES LOOK UN-TOUCHED... LOOKS LIKE WE GOT HERE FIRST, ALL RIGHT!
NEXT MOMENT...
HUH..? WHO ARE THOSE GUYS?
THERE'S SOME-THING STRANGE ABOUT THEM... SOMETHING NOT QUITE HUMAN...
I'LL SAY THEY AIN'T HUMAN! PULLIN' STONES RIGHT OUTTA THE BUILDING... EVEN I AIN'T GOT THAT MUCH STRENGTH!
THEY MUST BE ROBOTS... THAT'S THE ANSWER! THE BARRACUDA MUST HAVE SENT THEM FOR THE STONE HE WANTED!
AND UNDOUBTEDLY THEY'RE RADIO-CONTROLLED! THAT'S ALSO THE EXPLANATION FOR THAT MYSTERY PLANE WE EN-COUNTERED...
LOOK, KID, WE'LL LET THE ROBOTS FIND THE STONE WE WANT... THEN TAKE IT AWAY FROM THEM!
GOOD IDEA, STRIPESY... EXCEPT THAT IT'S GOING TO BE DIFFICULT TO TAKE ANYTHING FROM THOSE METAL MONSTERS!
NO IT AIN'T, KID! I KNOW SOMETHIN' ABOUT MACHINES, AND I GOT AN IDEA! WAIT FOR ME... I'LL BE RIGHT BACK!
SECONDS LATER...
I GET IT... AN OIL-SPRAY GUN!
RIGHT, KID! I'M GONNA LUBRICATE THOSE MACHINES LIKE THEY NEVER BEEN LUBRICATED BEFORE!
YOU DROPPED SOMETHIN', CHUM!
IT'S THE CORNERSTONE! I'LL BET THAT'S THE ONE THE BARRACUDA IS AFTER!
3

BUT IN A DISTANT RE-TREAT THE BARRACUDA SITS WATCHING!

SO THE STAR-SPANGLED KID AND STRIPESY ARE TRYING TO INTERFERE, ARE THEY? I'LL TEACH THEM BETTER!

AND AN INSTANT LATER, AT THE BELFORD BUILDING...

WHA..? THEY'RE BURNIN' UP THE OIL!

AND THEY'RE TRYING TO BURN YOU, TOO! TIME TO RETREAT, STRIPESY!

HUH..? WHY RUN IN THERE, KID?

I'VE GOT AN IDEA HOW TO HANDLE THOSE FLAMING YOUTHS!

STORES

THIS DRY ICE IS WHAT I WANTED! IT'S SOLID CARBON DIOXIDE, AND VAPORIZES TO GIVE CARBON DIOXIDE GAS, WHICH PUTS OUT FIRES!

THEN...

HEY..!

HERE'S HOW YOU CAN GET BY THEM, KID! I'LL SLOW THEM UP!

AND NOW, STRIPESY, ALONE, COURA-GEOUSLY TACKLES THE METAL MEN!

I CAN'T HOIT THESE BABIES... BUT I CAN STOP THEM FROM FOL-LOWING THE KID!

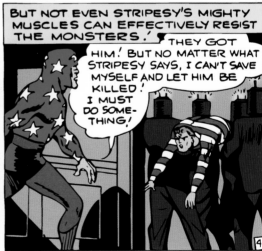

BUT NOT EVEN STRIPESY'S MIGHTY MUSCLES CAN EFFECTIVELY RESIST THE MONSTERS!

THEY GOT HIM! BUT NO MATTER WHAT STRIPESY SAYS, I CAN'T SAVE MYSELF AND LET HIM BE KILLED! I MUST DO SOME-THING!

4

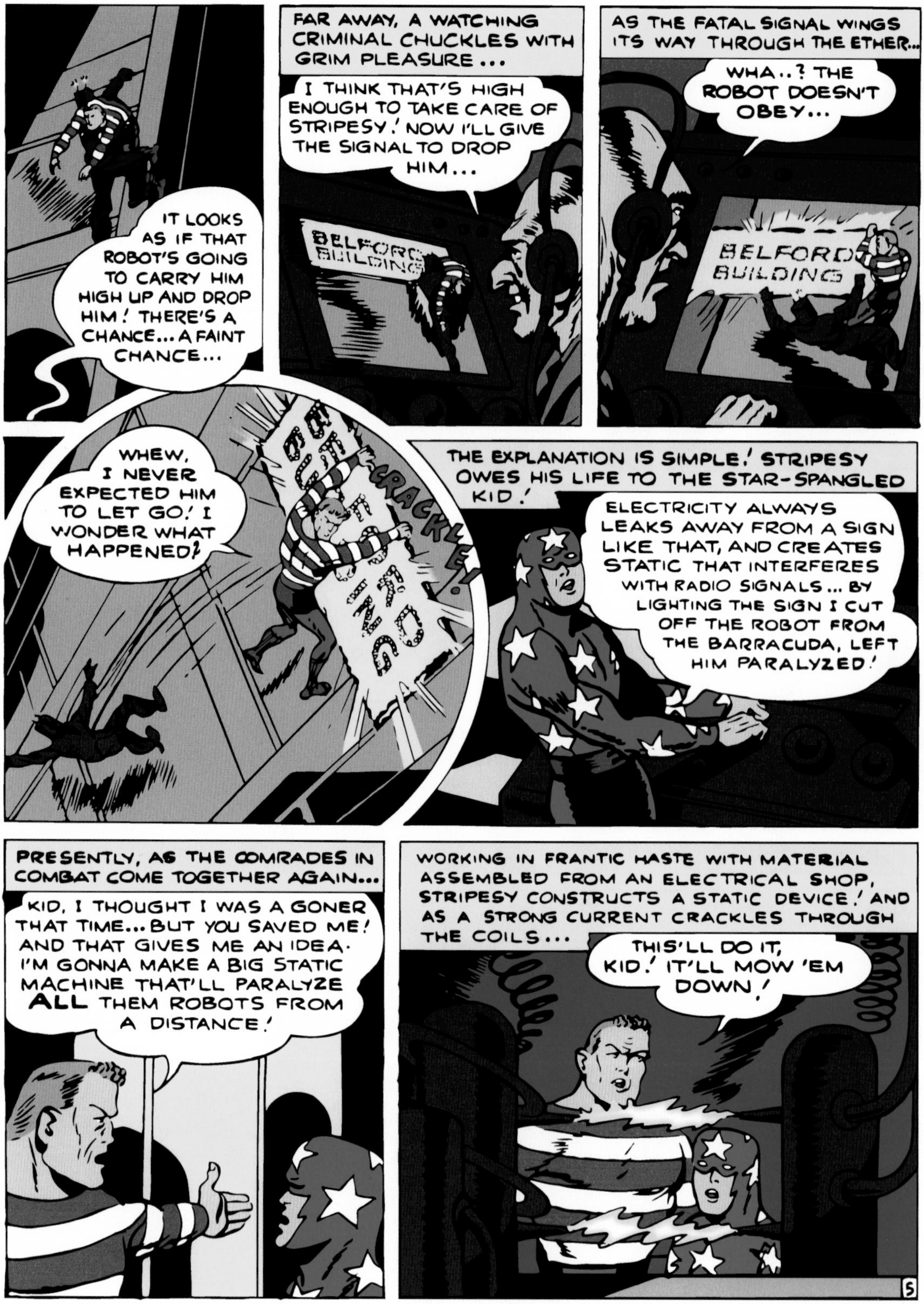
IT LOOKS AS IF THAT ROBOT'S GOING TO CARRY HIM HIGH UP AND DROP HIM! THERE'S A CHANCE... A FAINT CHANCE...
FAR AWAY, A WATCHING CRIMINAL CHUCKLES WITH GRIM PLEASURE...
I THINK THAT'S HIGH ENOUGH TO TAKE CARE OF STRIPESY! NOW I'LL GIVE THE SIGNAL TO DROP HIM...
AS THE FATAL SIGNAL WINGS ITS WAY THROUGH THE ETHER...
WHA..? THE ROBOT DOESN'T OBEY...
BELFORD BUILDING
WHEW, I NEVER EXPECTED HIM TO LET GO! I WONDER WHAT HAPPENED?
CRACKLE!
THE EXPLANATION IS SIMPLE! STRIPESY OWES HIS LIFE TO THE STAR-SPANGLED KID!
ELECTRICITY ALWAYS LEAKS AWAY FROM A SIGN LIKE THAT, AND CREATES STATIC THAT INTERFERES WITH RADIO SIGNALS... BY LIGHTING THE SIGN I CUT OFF THE ROBOT FROM THE BARRACUDA, LEFT HIM PARALYZED!
PRESENTLY, AS THE COMRADES IN COMBAT COME TOGETHER AGAIN...
KID, I THOUGHT I WAS A GONER THAT TIME... BUT YOU SAVED ME! AND THAT GIVES ME AN IDEA. I'M GONNA MAKE A BIG STATIC MACHINE THAT'LL PARALYZE ALL THEM ROBOTS FROM A DISTANCE!
WORKING IN FRANTIC HASTE WITH MATERIAL ASSEMBLED FROM AN ELECTRICAL SHOP, STRIPESY CONSTRUCTS A STATIC DEVICE! AND AS A STRONG CURRENT CRACKLES THROUGH THE COILS...
THIS'LL DO IT, KID! IT'LL MOW 'EM DOWN!
5

AND MOW 'EM DOWN, IT DOES!

QUICKLY ARRIVING ON THE SCENE...

THERE THEY ARE, KID... FINISHED FOR GOOD!

NOW TO GET THAT STOLEN CORNER- STONE!

HERE IT IS! WE'LL SEE WHAT MAKES IT SO UNUSUAL! IT FEELS A LITTLE LIGHT FOR ITS SIZE... I WONDER...

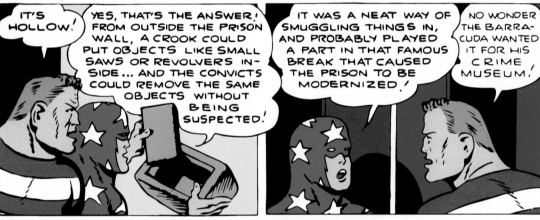

IT'S HOLLOW!

YES, THAT'S THE ANSWER! FROM OUTSIDE THE PRISON WALL, A CROOK COULD PUT OBJECTS LIKE SMALL SAWS OR REVOLVERS IN- SIDE... AND THE CONVICTS COULD REMOVE THE SAME OBJECTS WITHOUT BEING SUSPECTED!

IT WAS A NEAT WAY OF SMUGGLING THINGS IN, AND PROBABLY PLAYED A PART IN THAT FAMOUS BREAK THAT CAUSED THE PRISON TO BE MODERNIZED!

NO WONDER THE BARRA- CUDA WANTED IT FOR HIS CRIME MUSEUM!

WELL, WE'LL SEND HIM A SUBSTITUTE! WE'LL PUT AN ORDINARY BUILDING STONE IN THAT ROBOT'S CHEST, SO EVERYTHING WILL SEEM THE SAME AS BEFORE! THEN WE'LL CUT OFF THE STATIC MACHINE...

I GET IT, KID! THE ROBOTS WILL HEAD FOR THE BARRACUDA'S NEW HIDEOUT, AND LEAD US THERE! SWELL IDEA!

MEANWHILE...

AH, THIS CURSED STATIC IS CLEARING AT LAST! IN THE FUTURE, I'LL HAVE TO OPERATE THESE ROBOTS BY FREQUENCY MODULATION!

6

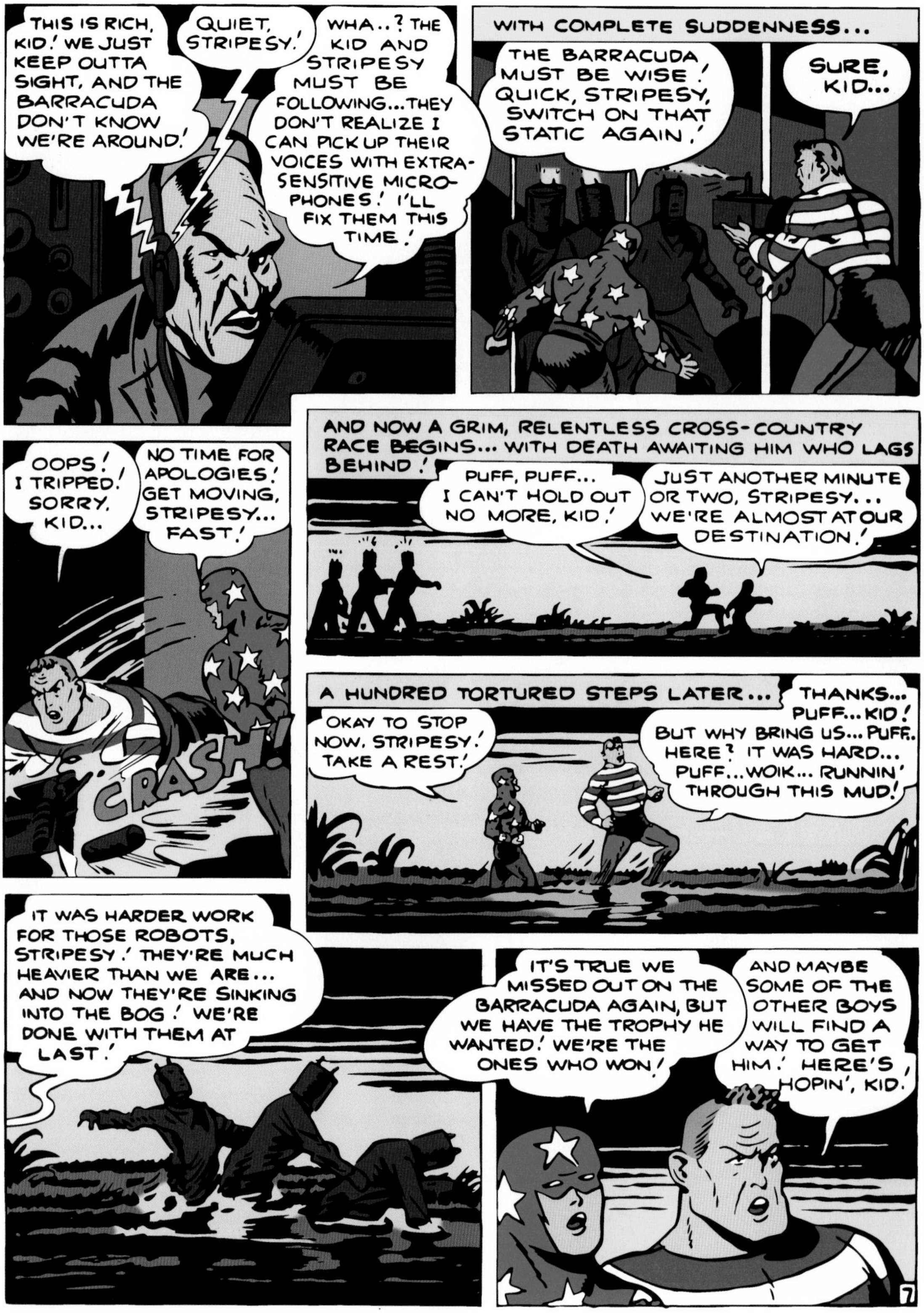
THIS IS RICH, KID! WE JUST KEEP OUTTA SIGHT, AND THE BARRACUDA DON'T KNOW WE'RE AROUND!
QUIET, STRIPESY!
WHA..? THE KID AND STRIPESY MUST BE FOLLOWING...THEY DON'T REALIZE I CAN PICK UP THEIR VOICES WITH EXTRA-SENSITIVE MICRO-PHONES! I'LL FIX THEM THIS TIME!
WITH COMPLETE SUDDENNESS...
THE BARRACUDA MUST BE WISE! QUICK, STRIPESY, SWITCH ON THAT STATIC AGAIN!
SURE, KID...
OOPS! I TRIPPED! SORRY, KID...
NO TIME FOR APOLOGIES! GET MOVING, STRIPESY... FAST!
CRASH!
AND NOW A GRIM, RELENTLESS CROSS-COUNTRY RACE BEGINS... WITH DEATH AWAITING HIM WHO LAGS BEHIND!
PUFF, PUFF... I CAN'T HOLD OUT NO MORE, KID!
JUST ANOTHER MINUTE OR TWO, STRIPESY... WE'RE ALMOST AT OUR DESTINATION!
A HUNDRED TORTURED STEPS LATER...
OKAY TO STOP NOW, STRIPESY! TAKE A REST!
THANKS... PUFF... KID! BUT WHY BRING US... PUFF... HERE? IT WAS HARD... PUFF... WOIK... RUNNIN' THROUGH THIS MUD!
IT WAS HARDER WORK FOR THOSE ROBOTS, STRIPESY! THEY'RE MUCH HEAVIER THAN WE ARE... AND NOW THEY'RE SINKING INTO THE BOG! WE'RE DONE WITH THEM AT LAST!
IT'S TRUE WE MISSED OUT ON THE BARRACUDA AGAIN, BUT WE HAVE THE TROPHY HE WANTED! WE'RE THE ONES WHO WON!
AND MAYBE SOME OF THE OTHER BOYS WILL FIND A WAY TO GET HIM! HERE'S HOPIN', KID.
7

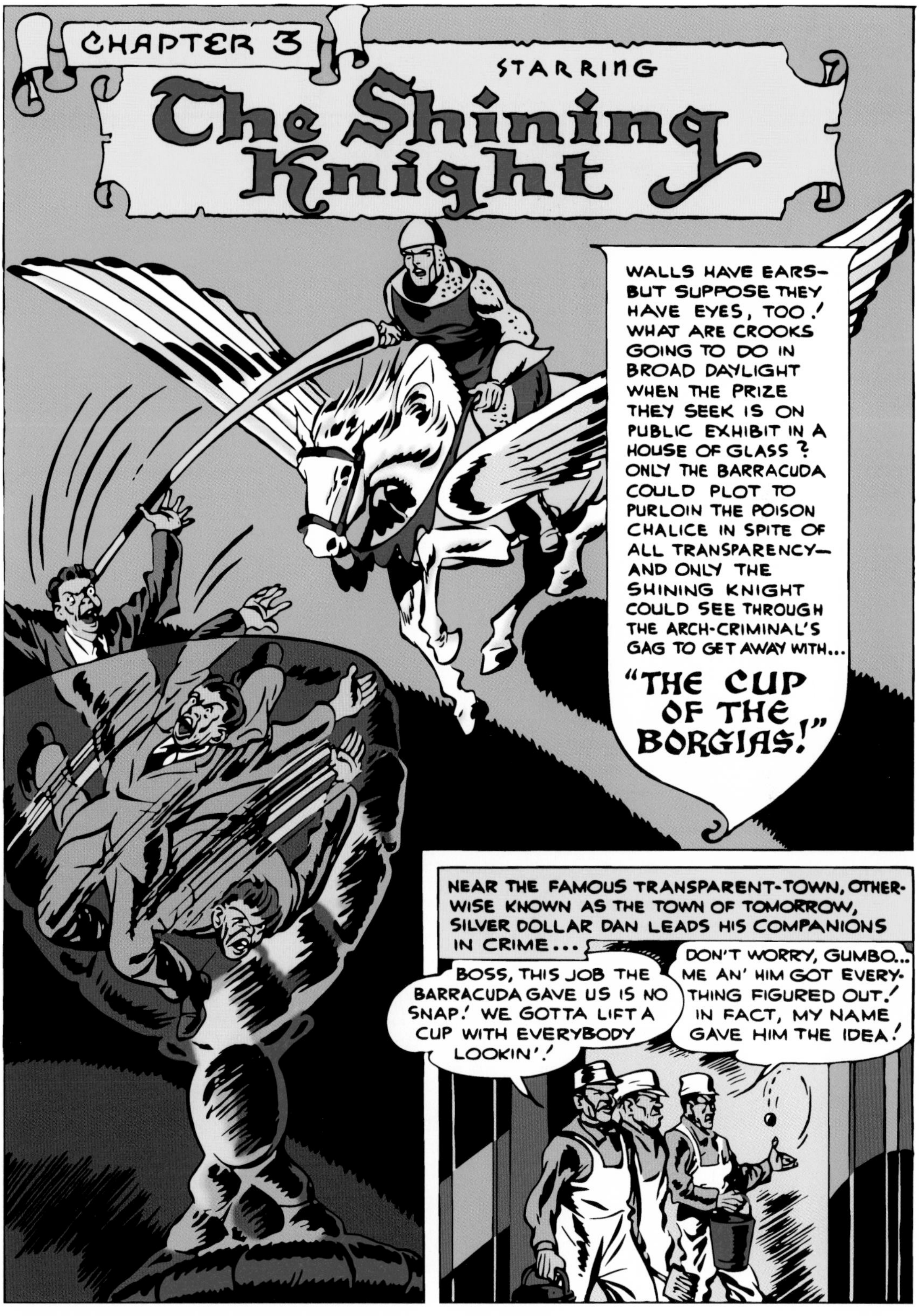
CHAPTER 3
STARRING
The Shining Knight
WALLS HAVE EARS- BUT SUPPOSE THEY HAVE EYES, TOO! WHAT ARE CROOKS GOING TO DO IN BROAD DAYLIGHT WHEN THE PRIZE THEY SEEK IS ON PUBLIC EXHIBIT IN A HOUSE OF GLASS? ONLY THE BARRACUDA COULD PLOT TO PURLOIN THE POISON CHALICE IN SPITE OF ALL TRANSPARENCY— AND ONLY THE SHINING KNIGHT COULD SEE THROUGH THE ARCH-CRIMINAL'S GAG TO GET AWAY WITH...
"THE CUP OF THE BORGIAS!"
NEAR THE FAMOUS TRANSPARENT-TOWN, OTHERWISE KNOWN AS THE TOWN OF TOMORROW, SILVER DOLLAR DAN LEADS HIS COMPANIONS IN CRIME...
BOSS, THIS JOB THE BARRACUDA GAVE US IS NO SNAP! WE GOTTA LIFT A CUP WITH EVERYBODY LOOKIN'!
DON'T WORRY, GUMBO... ME AN' HIM GOT EVERYTHING FIGURED OUT! IN FACT, MY NAME GAVE HIM THE IDEA!

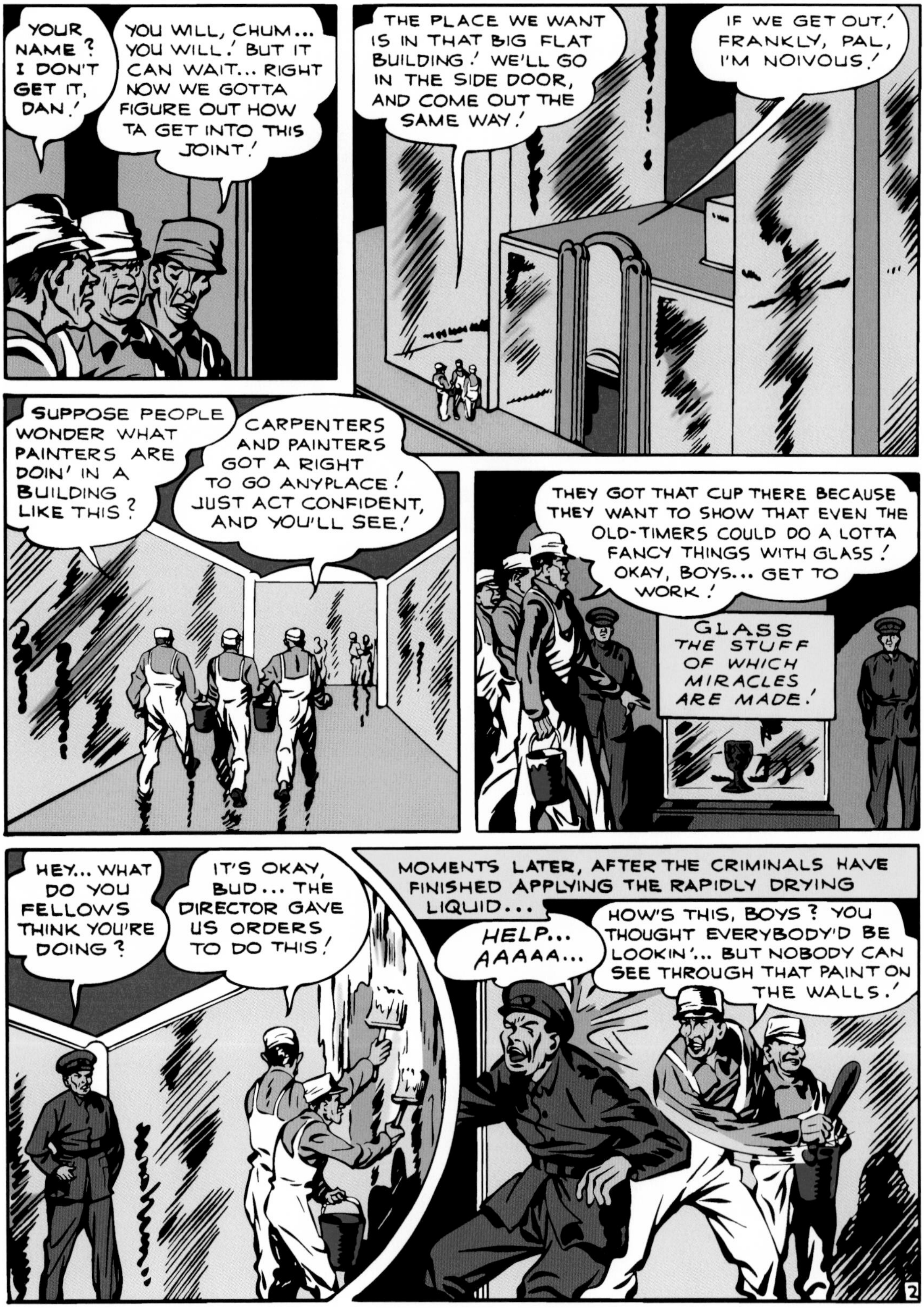
YOUR NAME? I DON'T GET IT, DAN!
YOU WILL, CHUM... YOU WILL! BUT IT CAN WAIT... RIGHT NOW WE GOTTA FIGURE OUT HOW TA GET INTO THIS JOINT!
THE PLACE WE WANT IS IN THAT BIG FLAT BUILDING! WE'LL GO IN THE SIDE DOOR, AND COME OUT THE SAME WAY!
IF WE GET OUT! FRANKLY, PAL, I'M NOIVOUS!
SUPPOSE PEOPLE WONDER WHAT PAINTERS ARE DOIN' IN A BUILDING LIKE THIS?
CARPENTERS AND PAINTERS GOT A RIGHT TO GO ANYPLACE! JUST ACT CONFIDENT, AND YOU'LL SEE!
THEY GOT THAT CUP THERE BECAUSE THEY WANT TO SHOW THAT EVEN THE OLD-TIMERS COULD DO A LOTTA FANCY THINGS WITH GLASS! OKAY, BOYS... GET TO WORK!
GLASS THE STUFF OF WHICH MIRACLES ARE MADE!
HEY... WHAT DO YOU FELLOWS THINK YOU'RE DOING?
IT'S OKAY, BUD... THE DIRECTOR GAVE US ORDERS TO DO THIS!
MOMENTS LATER, AFTER THE CRIMINALS HAVE FINISHED APPLYING THE RAPIDLY DRYING LIQUID...
HELP... AAAAA...
HOW'S THIS, BOYS? YOU THOUGHT EVERYBODY'D BE LOOKIN'... BUT NOBODY CAN SEE THROUGH THAT PAINT ON THE WALLS!
2

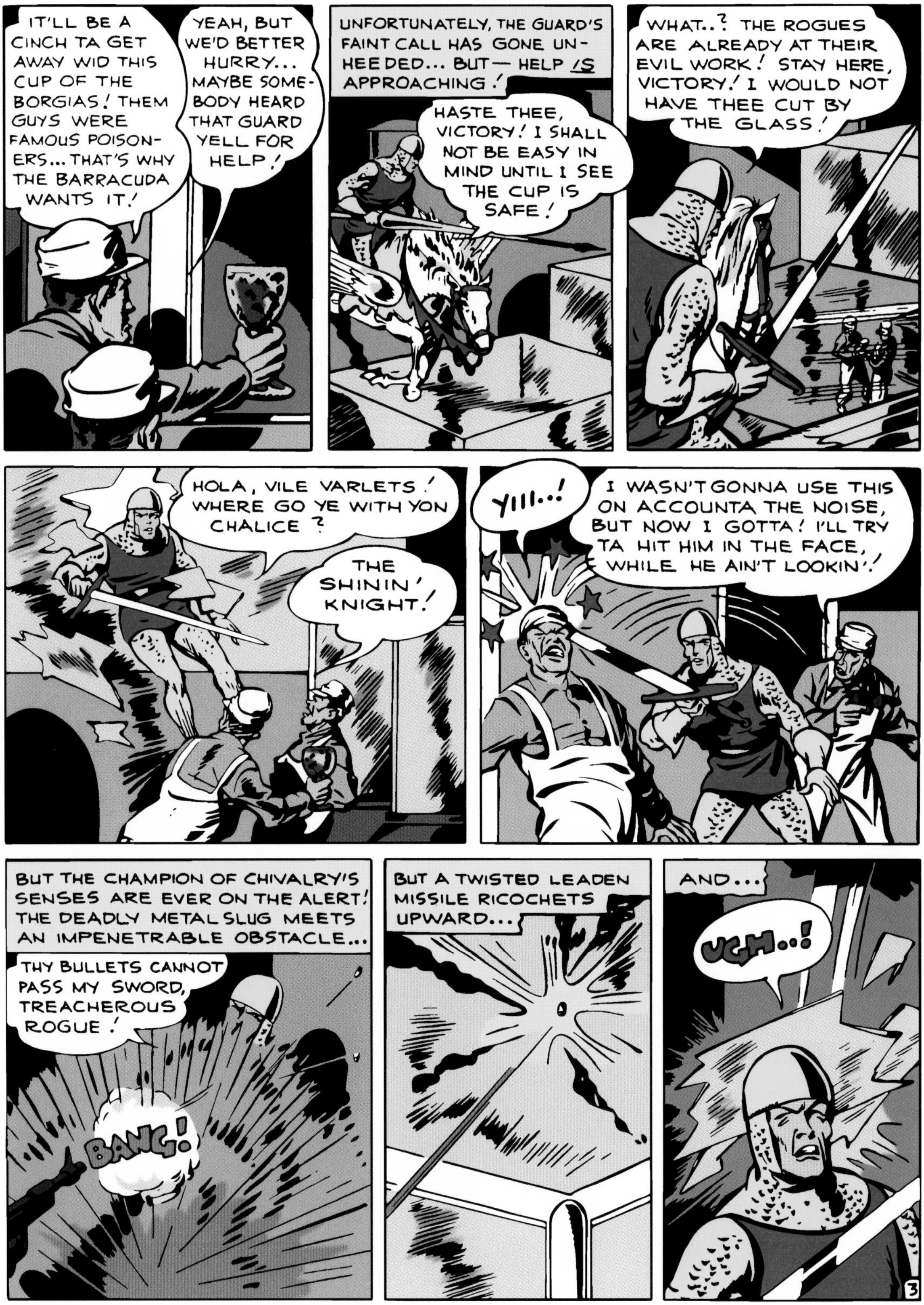
IT'LL BE A CINCH TA GET AWAY WID THIS CUP OF THE BORGIAS! THEM GUYS WERE FAMOUS POISONERS... THAT'S WHY THE BARRACUDA WANTS IT!
YEAH, BUT WE'D BETTER HURRY... MAYBE SOMEBODY HEARD THAT GUARD YELL FOR HELP!
UNFORTUNATELY, THE GUARD'S FAINT CALL HAS GONE UNHEEDED... BUT— HELP *IS* APPROACHING!
HASTE THEE, VICTORY! I SHALL NOT BE EASY IN MIND UNTIL I SEE THE CUP IS SAFE!
WHAT..? THE ROGUES ARE ALREADY AT THEIR EVIL WORK! STAY HERE, VICTORY! I WOULD NOT HAVE THEE CUT BY THE GLASS!
HOLA, VILE VARLETS! WHERE GO YE WITH YON CHALICE?
THE SHININ' KNIGHT!
YIII..!
I WASN'T GONNA USE THIS ON ACCOUNTA THE NOISE, BUT NOW I GOTTA! I'LL TRY TA HIT HIM IN THE FACE, WHILE HE AIN'T LOOKIN'!
BUT THE CHAMPION OF CHIVALRY'S SENSES ARE EVER ON THE ALERT! THE DEADLY METAL SLUG MEETS AN IMPENETRABLE OBSTACLE...
THY BULLETS CANNOT PASS MY SWORD, TREACHEROUS ROGUE!
BANG!
BUT A TWISTED LEADEN MISSILE RICOCHETS UPWARD...
AND...
UGH..!
3

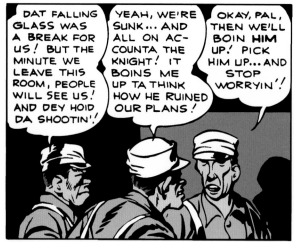

DAT FALLING GLASS WAS A BREAK FOR US! BUT THE MINUTE WE LEAVE THIS ROOM, PEOPLE WILL SEE US! AND DEY HOID DA SHOOTIN'!

YEAH, WE'RE SUNK... AND ALL ON ACCOUNTA THE KNIGHT! IT BOINS ME UP TA THINK HOW HE RUINED OUR PLANS!

OKAY, PAL, THEN WE'LL BOIN **HIM** UP! PICK HIM UP... AND STOP WORRYIN'!

MOMENTS LATER...

HEY, DAN... EVERYBODY CAN SEE YA DO THIS!

STOP WORRYIN', I SAID! JUST WATCH!

THIS SOICHLIGHT IS SUPPOSED TA LIGHT UP THE WHOLE PLACE! BUT THIS COLUMN CONCENTRATES THE RAYS... AND WILL THAT BOIN UP THE KNIGHT!

NOW, CHUMPS, IF YOU'RE STILL WORRIED, TAKE A LOOK AT THAT! THAT PAINT WE USED WAS **SILVER** PAINT! LIKE I TOLD YA, THE BARRACUDA GOT THE IDEA FROM MY NAME! AND WHEN YA PUT SILVER IN BACK OF GLASS...

YA GOT A MIRROR! SO THE GUARDS'LL GET ALL MIXED UP LOOKIN' FER US, ON ACCOUNTA THEM WALLS ARE ALL MIRRORS!

OKAY SO FAR! BUT WHAT HAPPENS WHEN WE TRY TA GET OUT?

YOU GUYS CAN'T FIGURE OUT NUTTIN'! PICK UP THAT CUP AND COME WID ME... I'LL SHOW YOU!

AS THE MAN OF YESTERDAY IS LEFT ALONE...

W-WHERE AM I? I BURN SO FIERCELY... MAYHAP THIS IS A FURNACE!

BUT AS FULL CONSCIOUSNESS ONCE MORE RETURNS, AND HE GRASPS THE SITUATION...

UGH... THESE ROPES ARE TIED TOO WELL TO LOOSEN! HAD I BUT A MOMENT'S RESPITE FROM THE FIERCENESS OF THE HEAT... HMM, MAYHAP THIS TABLE WILL HELP!

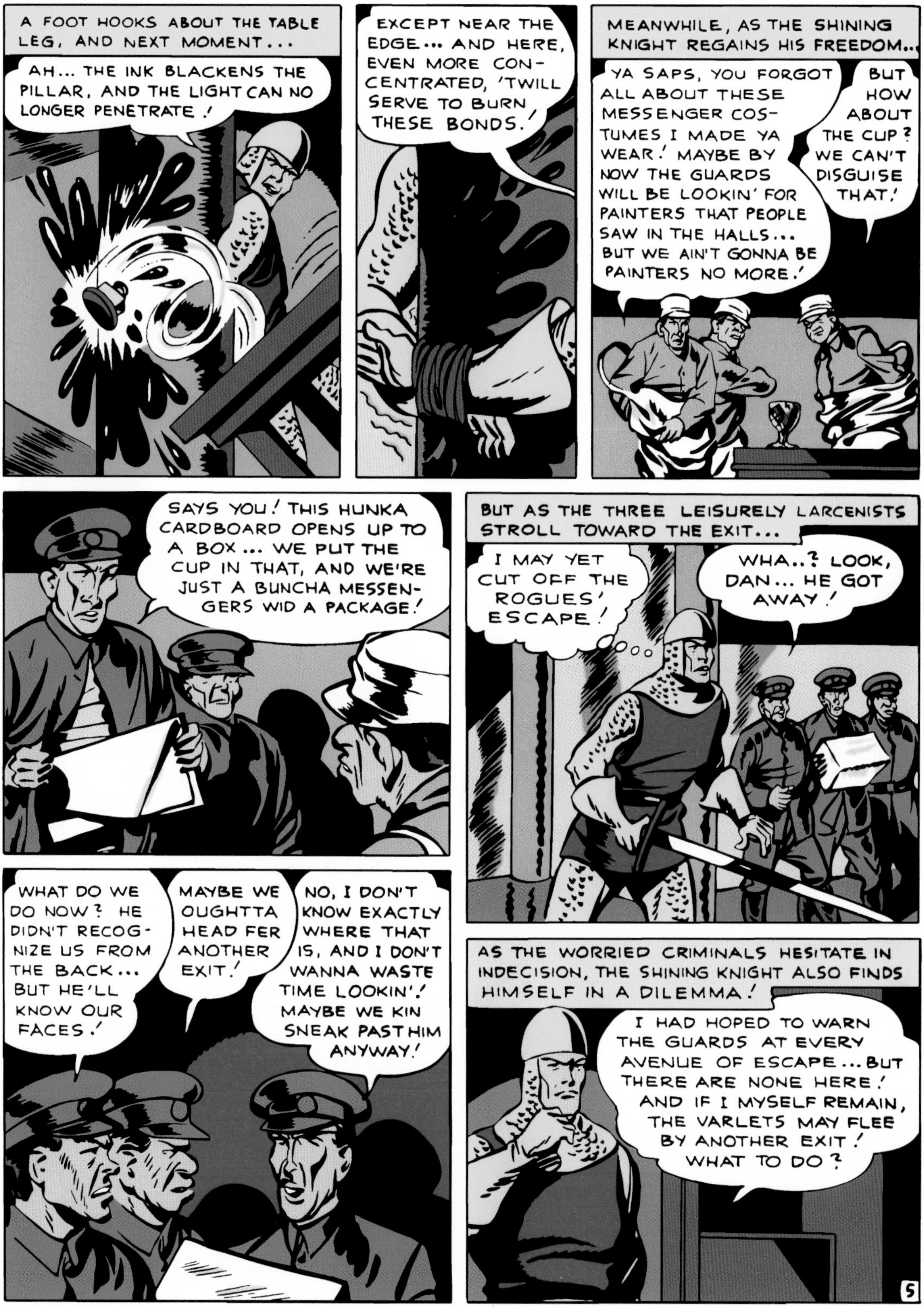
A FOOT HOOKS ABOUT THE TABLE LEG, AND NEXT MOMENT...
AH... THE INK BLACKENS THE PILLAR, AND THE LIGHT CAN NO LONGER PENETRATE!
EXCEPT NEAR THE EDGE... AND HERE, EVEN MORE CON-CENTRATED, 'TWILL SERVE TO BURN THESE BONDS!
MEANWHILE, AS THE SHINING KNIGHT REGAINS HIS FREEDOM...
YA SAPS, YOU FORGOT ALL ABOUT THESE MESSENGER COS-TUMES I MADE YA WEAR! MAYBE BY NOW THE GUARDS WILL BE LOOKIN' FOR PAINTERS THAT PEOPLE SAW IN THE HALLS... BUT WE AIN'T GONNA BE PAINTERS NO MORE!
BUT HOW ABOUT THE CUP? WE CAN'T DISGUISE THAT!
SAYS YOU! THIS HUNKA CARDBOARD OPENS UP TO A BOX... WE PUT THE CUP IN THAT, AND WE'RE JUST A BUNCHA MESSEN-GERS WID A PACKAGE!
BUT AS THE THREE LEISURELY LARCENISTS STROLL TOWARD THE EXIT...
I MAY YET CUT OFF THE ROGUES' ESCAPE!
WHA..? LOOK, DAN... HE GOT AWAY!
WHAT DO WE DO NOW? HE DIDN'T RECOG-NIZE US FROM THE BACK... BUT HE'LL KNOW OUR FACES!
MAYBE WE OUGHTTA HEAD FER ANOTHER EXIT!
NO, I DON'T KNOW EXACTLY WHERE THAT IS, AND I DON'T WANNA WASTE TIME LOOKIN'! MAYBE WE KIN SNEAK PAST HIM ANYWAY!
AS THE WORRIED CRIMINALS HESITATE IN INDECISION, THE SHINING KNIGHT ALSO FINDS HIMSELF IN A DILEMMA!
I HAD HOPED TO WARN THE GUARDS AT EVERY AVENUE OF ESCAPE... BUT THERE ARE NONE HERE! AND IF I MYSELF REMAIN, THE VARLETS MAY FLEE BY ANOTHER EXIT! WHAT TO DO?
5

AH, I HAVE IT! I MUST NOT STAY... BUT YET CAN I CONCEAL THIS PATH SO THAT THE VILLAINS NEVER FIND IT!

THUS, A MOMENT LATER, AS THE CRIMINALS TIMIDLY APPROACH ...

HE'S GOIN' AWAY AGAIN! NOW WE CAN SCRAM!

QUICK, GET TO THAT EXIT BEFORE HE CHANGES HIS MIND AND COMES BACK!

THE BANDITS HASTEN FORWARD... ONLY TO PAUSE IN BEWILDERMENT!

HEY, THIS AIN'T THE WAY OUT! WE MADE A MISTAKE... WE MUST BE NEAR THE MIDDLE OF THE BUILDING!

WE BETTER HEAD BACK FAST, DAN!

BUT MOMENTS LATER ...

WE'RE LOST... WE CAN'T GET OUT!

WE **GOTTA** GET OUT! KEEP ON LOOKIN'!

WHILE AT EACH OF THE OTHER EXITS...

'TIS A WORTHY JEST ON THE VILE ROGUES! I CONCEAL EACH EXIT WITH A MIRROR, CONFUSING THEM AS THEY SOUGHT TO CONFUSE OTHERS! NOW I WILL CALL THE GUARDS WITHOUT FEAR OF THEIR ESCAPING!

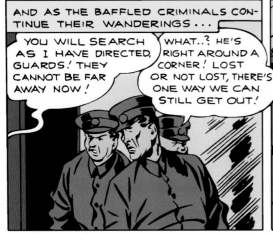

AND AS THE BAFFLED CRIMINALS CONTINUE THEIR WANDERINGS ...

YOU WILL SEARCH AS I HAVE DIRECTED, GUARDS! THEY CANNOT BE FAR AWAY NOW!

WHAT..? HE'S RIGHT AROUND A CORNER! LOST OR NOT LOST, THERE'S ONE WAY WE CAN STILL GET OUT!

THESE WALLS ARE GLASS... I'LL BREAK THROUGH EVERY ONE IN THE PLACE BEFORE I LET MYSELF GET CAUGHT!

CRASH!

6

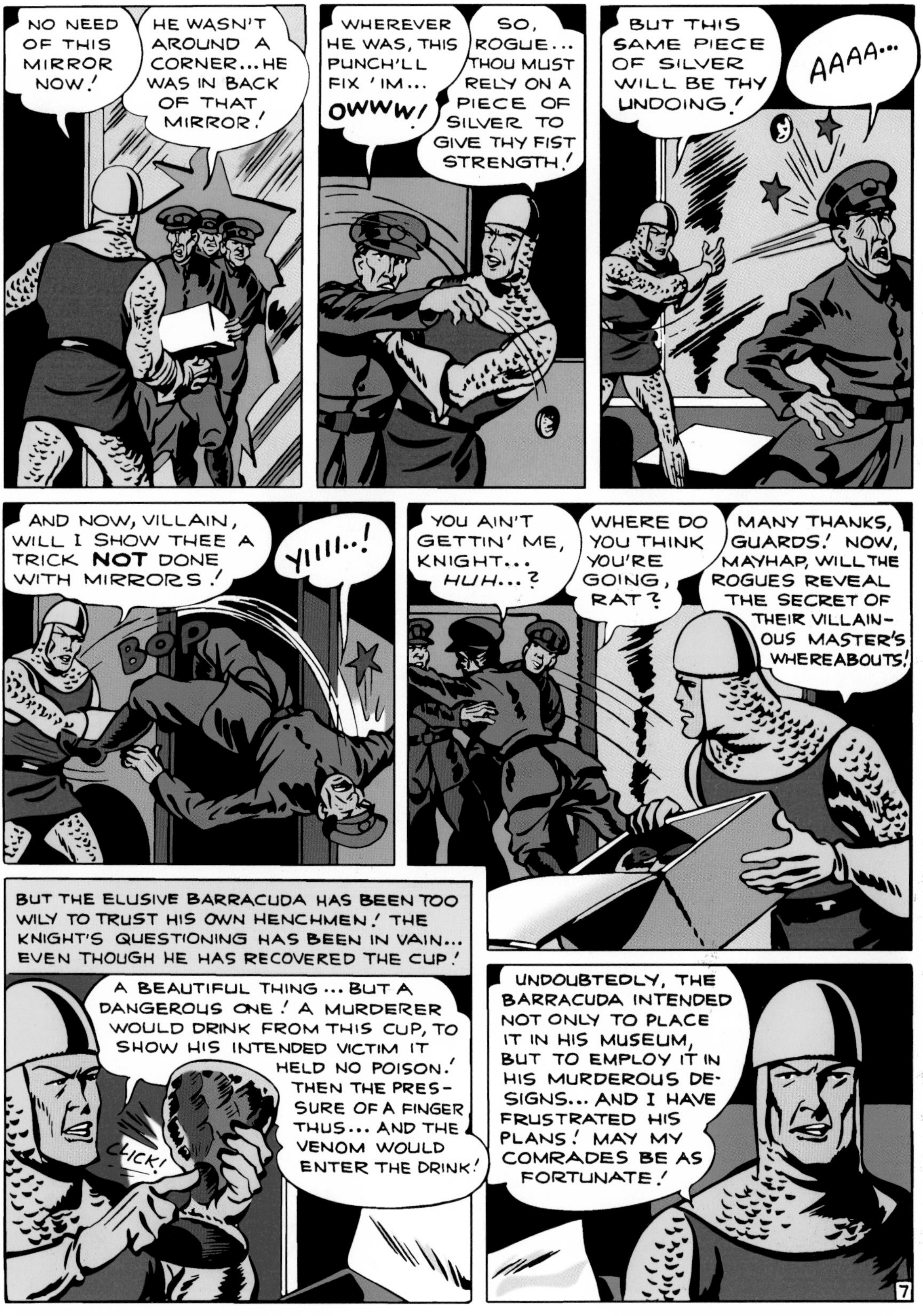
NO NEED OF THIS MIRROR NOW!
HE WASN'T AROUND A CORNER...HE WAS IN BACK OF THAT MIRROR!
WHEREVER HE WAS, THIS PUNCH'LL FIX 'IM... OWWW!
SO, ROGUE... THOU MUST RELY ON A PIECE OF SILVER TO GIVE THY FIST STRENGTH!
BUT THIS SAME PIECE OF SILVER WILL BE THY UNDOING!
AAAA...
AND NOW, VILLAIN, WILL I SHOW THEE A TRICK NOT DONE WITH MIRRORS!
YIIII..!
BOP
YOU AIN'T GETTIN' ME, KNIGHT... HUH...?
WHERE DO YOU THINK YOU'RE GOING, RAT?
MANY THANKS, GUARDS! NOW, MAYHAP, WILL THE ROGUES REVEAL THE SECRET OF THEIR VILLAINOUS MASTER'S WHEREABOUTS!
BUT THE ELUSIVE BARRACUDA HAS BEEN TOO WILY TO TRUST HIS OWN HENCHMEN! THE KNIGHT'S QUESTIONING HAS BEEN IN VAIN... EVEN THOUGH HE HAS RECOVERED THE CUP!
A BEAUTIFUL THING... BUT A DANGEROUS ONE! A MURDERER WOULD DRINK FROM THIS CUP, TO SHOW HIS INTENDED VICTIM IT HELD NO POISON! THEN THE PRESSURE OF A FINGER THUS... AND THE VENOM WOULD ENTER THE DRINK!
CLICK!
UNDOUBTEDLY, THE BARRACUDA INTENDED NOT ONLY TO PLACE IT IN HIS MUSEUM, BUT TO EMPLOY IT IN HIS MURDEROUS DESIGNS... AND I HAVE FRUSTRATED HIS PLANS! MAY MY COMRADES BE AS FORTUNATE!
7

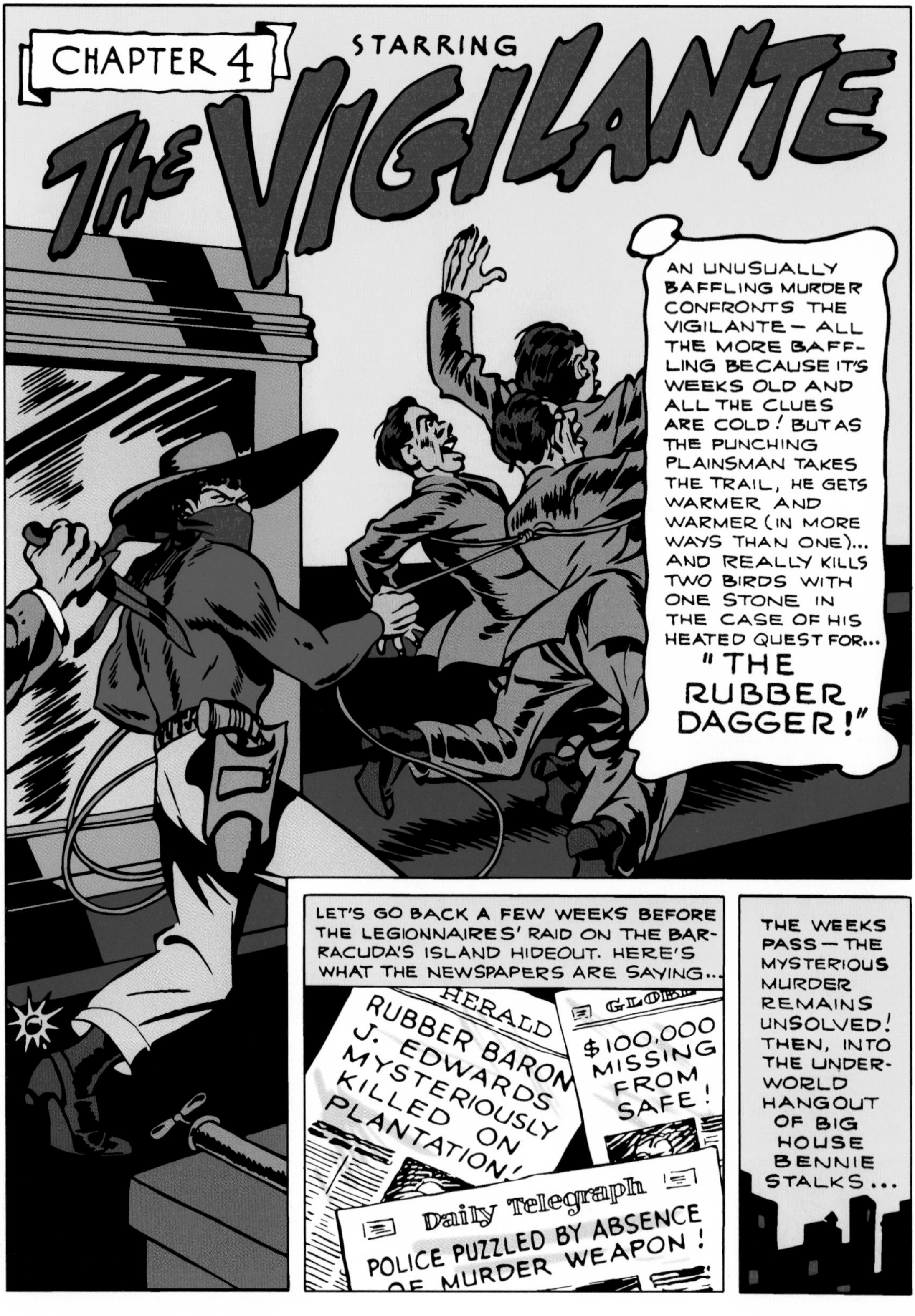
CHAPTER 4
STARRING
THE VIGILANTE
AN UNUSUALLY BAFFLING MURDER CONFRONTS THE VIGILANTE — ALL THE MORE BAFFLING BECAUSE IT'S WEEKS OLD AND ALL THE CLUES ARE COLD! BUT AS THE PUNCHING PLAINSMAN TAKES THE TRAIL, HE GETS WARMER AND WARMER (IN MORE WAYS THAN ONE)... AND REALLY KILLS TWO BIRDS WITH ONE STONE IN THE CASE OF HIS HEATED QUEST FOR...
"THE RUBBER DAGGER!"
LET'S GO BACK A FEW WEEKS BEFORE THE LEGIONNAIRES' RAID ON THE BARRACUDA'S ISLAND HIDEOUT. HERE'S WHAT THE NEWSPAPERS ARE SAYING...
HERALD
RUBBER BARON J. EDWARDS MYSTERIOUSLY KILLED ON PLANTATION!
$100,000 MISSING FROM SAFE!
Daily Telegraph
POLICE PUZZLED BY ABSENCE OF MURDER WEAPON!
THE WEEKS PASS — THE MYSTERIOUS MURDER REMAINS UNSOLVED! THEN, INTO THE UNDERWORLD HANGOUT OF BIG HOUSE BENNIE STALKS...

HUH..? THE **BARRACUDA!**... GOSH, DIS IS A HONOR!

I'M HERE ON BUSINESS, BENNIE!

I HAVE A JOB FOR YOU! I WANT YOU TO GO TO THE EDWARDS RUBBER PLANTATION AND OBTAIN THE MURDER WEAPON! YOU KNOW WHAT IT IS!

THEN, AS WE HAVE SEEN, THERE FOLLOWS THE RAID ON THE BARRACUDA'S HIDEOUT...THE BARRACUDA'S ESCAPE... THE DISCOVERY BY THE SEVEN SOLDIERS OF THE VARIOUS LEADS. THUS, BIG HOUSE BENNIE ISN'T THE ONLY UNEXPECTED VISITOR AT THE EDWARDS **RUBBER** PLANTATION! THE VIGILANTE IS ANOTHER!

THIS EDWARDS MUST HAVE BEEN A CLEVER HOMBRE, GROWIN' RUBBER TREES IN THE U.S.A.! WONDER IF HIS PARDNER, RUXBY, IS AS GOOD AS HE WAS?

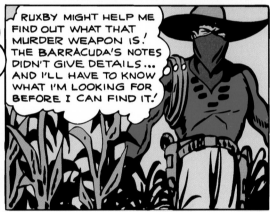

RUXBY MIGHT HELP ME FIND OUT WHAT THAT MURDER WEAPON IS! THE BARRACUDA'S NOTES DIDN'T GIVE DETAILS... AND I'LL HAVE TO KNOW WHAT I'M LOOKING FOR BEFORE I CAN FIND IT!

AS THE VIGILANTE APPROACHES THE MAIN BUILDING ON THE PLANTATION...

TAKE IT EASY, CHUMS... I AIN'T SHOOTIN' UNLESS YOU GUYS DON'T HAND OVER THAT RUBBER DAGGER I CAME FOR!

THE BARRACUDA'S MAN IS AHEAD OF ME! A **RUBBER DAGGER!** CAN THAT BE THE MURDER WEAPON?

I'LL PUZZLE IT OUT LATER! RIGHT NOW, I'VE GOT TO ROUND UP THESE COYOTES!

THE VIGILANTE!

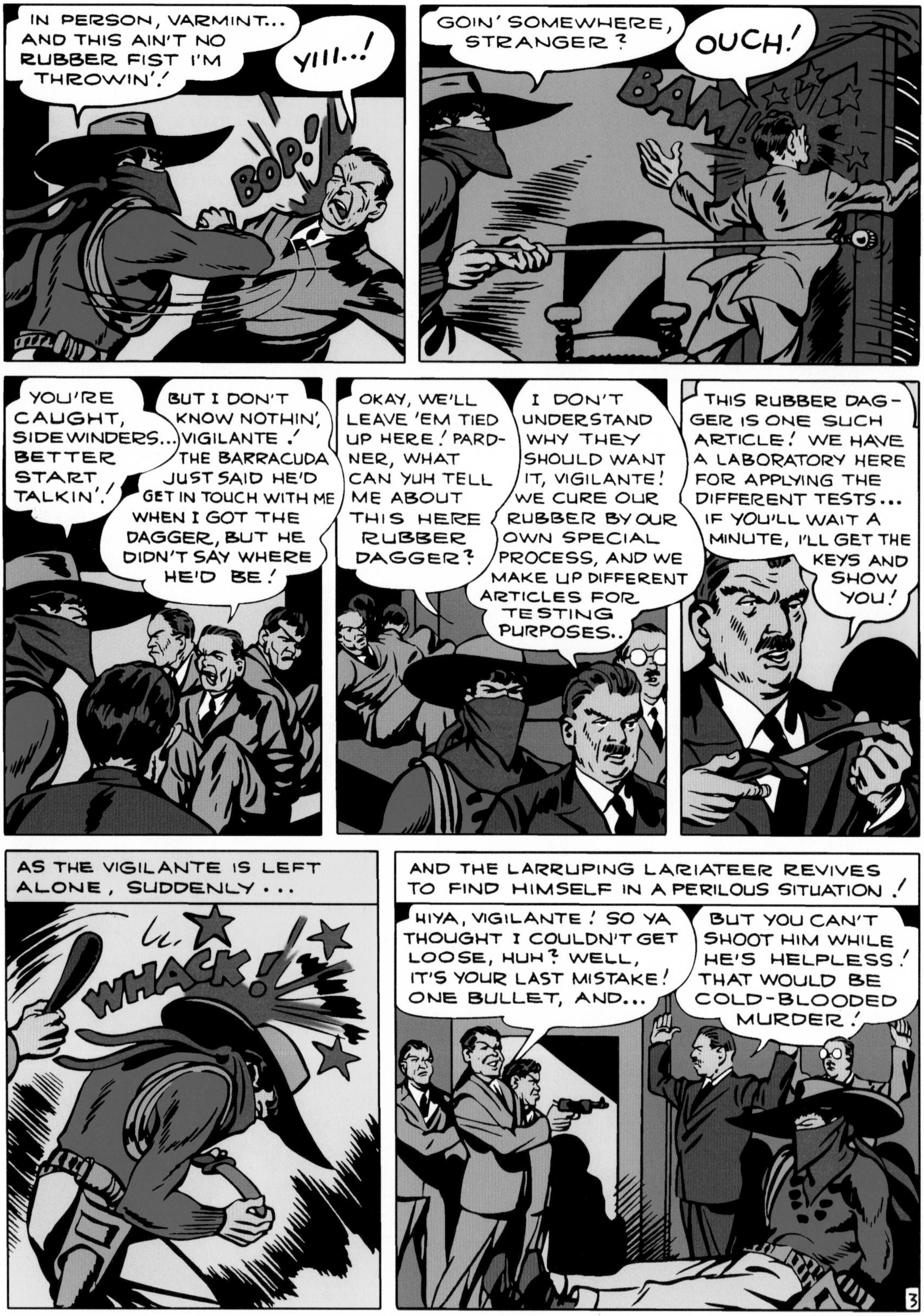
IN PERSON, VARMINT... AND THIS AIN'T NO RUBBER FIST I'M THROWIN'!
YIII...!
BOP!
GOIN' SOMEWHERE, STRANGER?
OUCH!
BAM!
YOU'RE CAUGHT, SIDEWINDERS... BETTER START TALKIN'!
BUT I DON'T KNOW NOTHIN', VIGILANTE! THE BARRACUDA JUST SAID HE'D GET IN TOUCH WITH ME WHEN I GOT THE DAGGER, BUT HE DIDN'T SAY WHERE HE'D BE!
OKAY, WE'LL LEAVE 'EM TIED UP HERE! PARDNER, WHAT CAN YUH TELL ME ABOUT THIS HERE RUBBER DAGGER?
I DON'T UNDERSTAND WHY THEY SHOULD WANT IT, VIGILANTE! WE CURE OUR RUBBER BY OUR OWN SPECIAL PROCESS, AND WE MAKE UP DIFFERENT ARTICLES FOR TESTING PURPOSES..
THIS RUBBER DAGGER IS ONE SUCH ARTICLE! WE HAVE A LABORATORY HERE FOR APPLYING THE DIFFERENT TESTS... IF YOU'LL WAIT A MINUTE, I'LL GET THE KEYS AND SHOW YOU!
AS THE VIGILANTE IS LEFT ALONE, SUDDENLY...
WHACK!
AND THE LARRUPING LARIATEER REVIVES TO FIND HIMSELF IN A PERILOUS SITUATION!
HIYA, VIGILANTE! SO YA THOUGHT I COULDN'T GET LOOSE, HUH? WELL, IT'S YOUR LAST MISTAKE! ONE BULLET, AND...
BUT YOU CAN'T SHOOT HIM WHILE HE'S HELPLESS! THAT WOULD BE COLD-BLOODED MURDER!
3

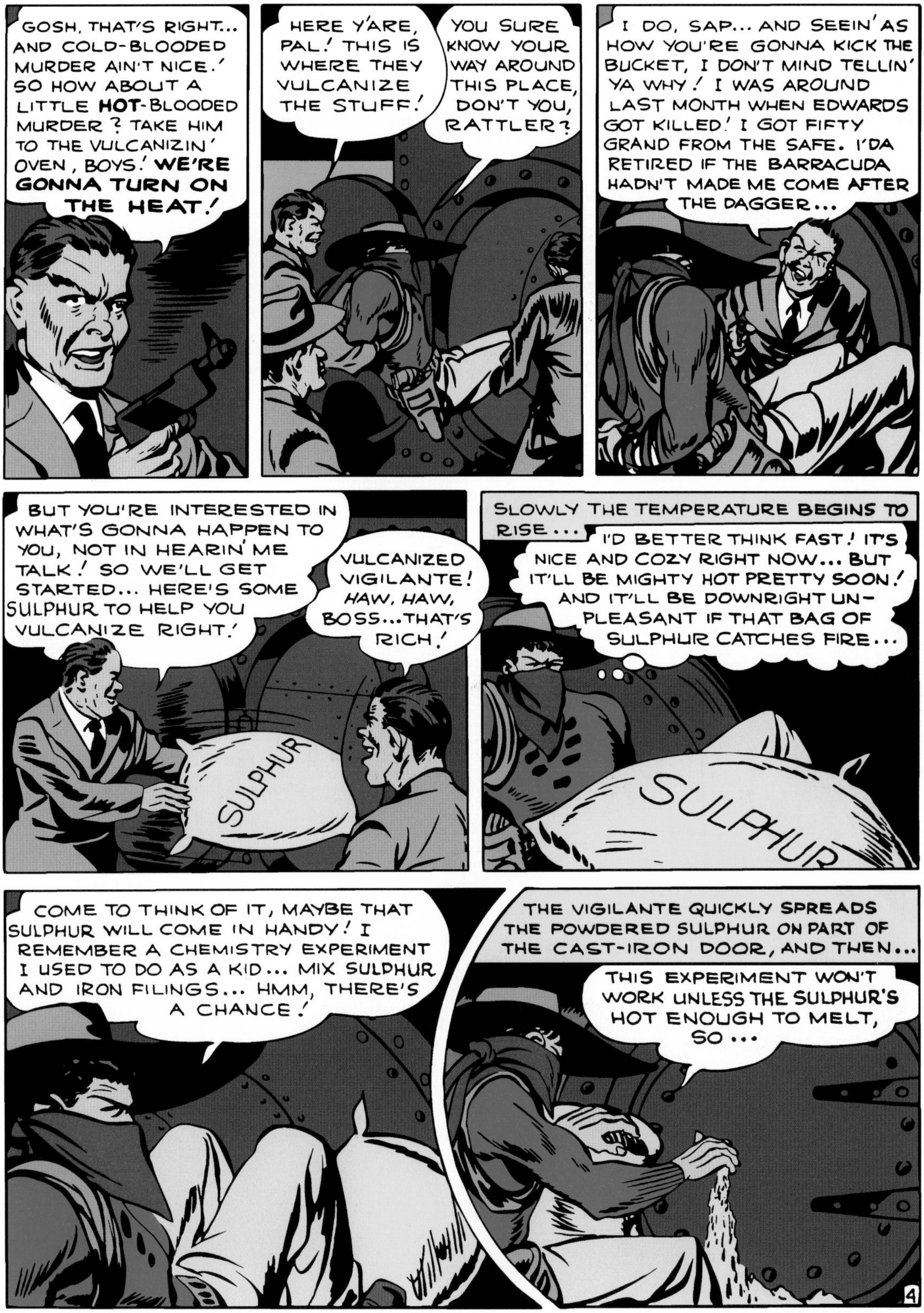
GOSH, THAT'S RIGHT... AND COLD-BLOODED MURDER AIN'T NICE! SO HOW ABOUT A LITTLE **HOT**-BLOODED MURDER? TAKE HIM TO THE VULCANIZIN' OVEN, BOYS! **WE'RE GONNA TURN ON THE HEAT!**
HERE Y'ARE, PAL! THIS IS WHERE THEY VULCANIZE THE STUFF!
YOU SURE KNOW YOUR WAY AROUND THIS PLACE, DON'T YOU, RATTLER?
I DO, SAP... AND SEEIN' AS HOW YOU'RE GONNA KICK THE BUCKET, I DON'T MIND TELLIN' YA WHY! I WAS AROUND LAST MONTH WHEN EDWARDS GOT KILLED! I GOT FIFTY GRAND FROM THE SAFE. I'DA RETIRED IF THE BARRACUDA HADN'T MADE ME COME AFTER THE DAGGER...
BUT YOU'RE INTERESTED IN WHAT'S GONNA HAPPEN TO YOU, NOT IN HEARIN' ME TALK! SO WE'LL GET STARTED... HERE'S SOME SULPHUR TO HELP YOU VULCANIZE RIGHT!
VULCANIZED VIGILANTE! *HAW, HAW,* BOSS...THAT'S RICH!
SULPHUR
SLOWLY THE TEMPERATURE BEGINS TO RISE...
I'D BETTER THINK FAST! IT'S NICE AND COZY RIGHT NOW... BUT IT'LL BE MIGHTY HOT PRETTY SOON! AND IT'LL BE DOWNRIGHT UN-PLEASANT IF THAT BAG OF SULPHUR CATCHES FIRE...
SULPHUR
COME TO THINK OF IT, MAYBE THAT SULPHUR WILL COME IN HANDY! I REMEMBER A CHEMISTRY EXPERIMENT I USED TO DO AS A KID... MIX SULPHUR AND IRON FILINGS... HMM, THERE'S A CHANCE!
THE VIGILANTE QUICKLY SPREADS THE POWDERED SULPHUR ON PART OF THE CAST-IRON DOOR, AND THEN...
THIS EXPERIMENT WON'T WORK UNLESS THE SULPHUR'S HOT ENOUGH TO MELT, SO...
4

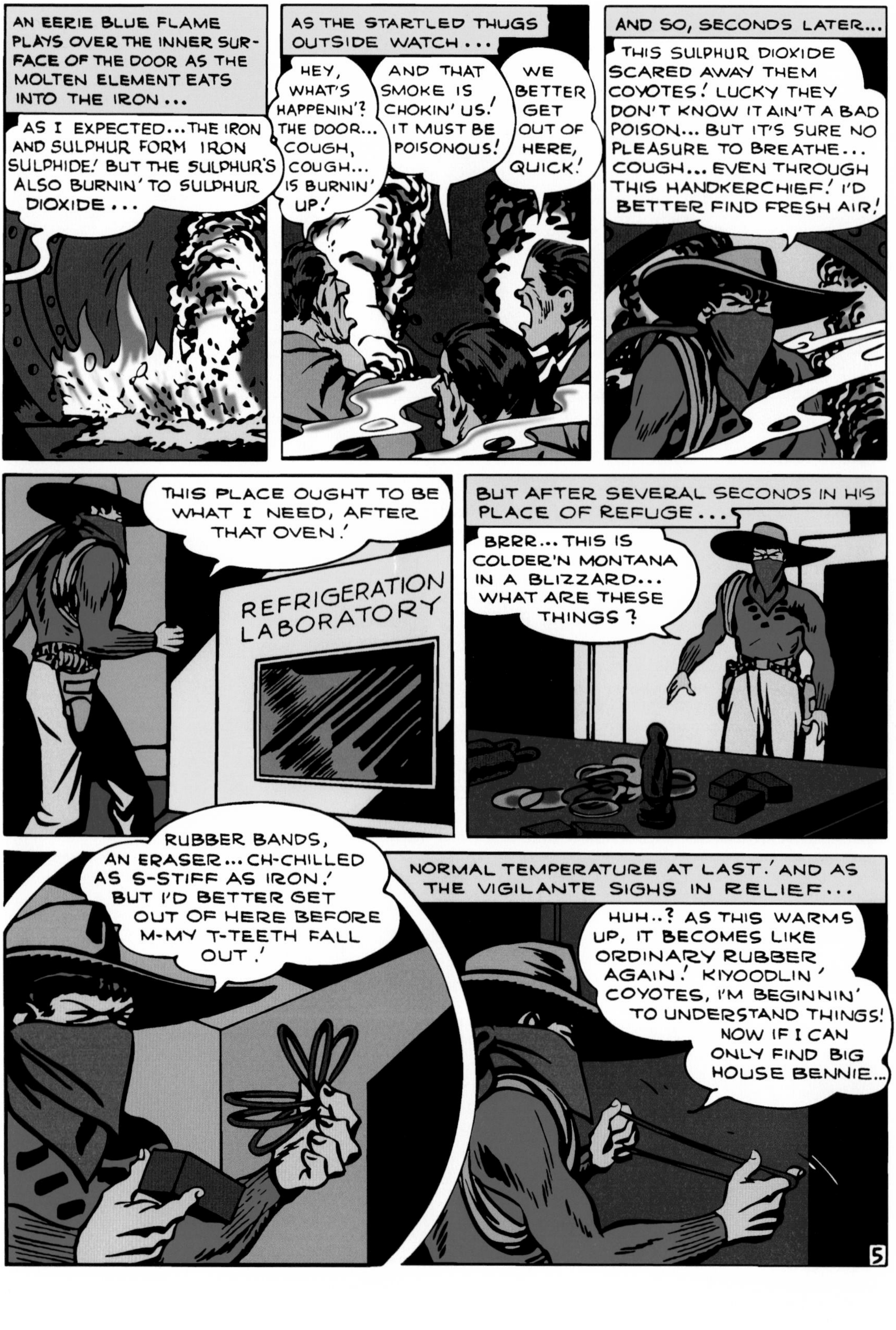
AN EERIE BLUE FLAME PLAYS OVER THE INNER SURFACE OF THE DOOR AS THE MOLTEN ELEMENT EATS INTO THE IRON...
AS I EXPECTED...THE IRON AND SULPHUR FORM IRON SULPHIDE! BUT THE SULPHUR'S ALSO BURNIN' TO SULPHUR DIOXIDE...
AS THE STARTLED THUGS OUTSIDE WATCH...
HEY, WHAT'S HAPPENIN'? THE DOOR... COUGH, COUGH... IS BURNIN' UP!
AND THAT SMOKE IS CHOKIN' US! IT MUST BE POISONOUS!
WE BETTER GET OUT OF HERE, QUICK!
AND SO, SECONDS LATER...
THIS SULPHUR DIOXIDE SCARED AWAY THEM COYOTES! LUCKY THEY DON'T KNOW IT AIN'T A BAD POISON... BUT IT'S SURE NO PLEASURE TO BREATHE... COUGH... EVEN THROUGH THIS HANDKERCHIEF! I'D BETTER FIND FRESH AIR!
THIS PLACE OUGHT TO BE WHAT I NEED, AFTER THAT OVEN!
REFRIGERATION LABORATORY
BUT AFTER SEVERAL SECONDS IN HIS PLACE OF REFUGE...
BRRR... THIS IS COLDER'N MONTANA IN A BLIZZARD... WHAT ARE THESE THINGS?
RUBBER BANDS, AN ERASER...CH-CHILLED AS S-STIFF AS IRON! BUT I'D BETTER GET OUT OF HERE BEFORE M-MY T-TEETH FALL OUT!
NORMAL TEMPERATURE AT LAST! AND AS THE VIGILANTE SIGHS IN RELIEF...
HUH..? AS THIS WARMS UP, IT BECOMES LIKE ORDINARY RUBBER AGAIN! KIYOODLIN' COYOTES, I'M BEGINNIN' TO UNDERSTAND THINGS! NOW IF I CAN ONLY FIND BIG HOUSE BENNIE...
5

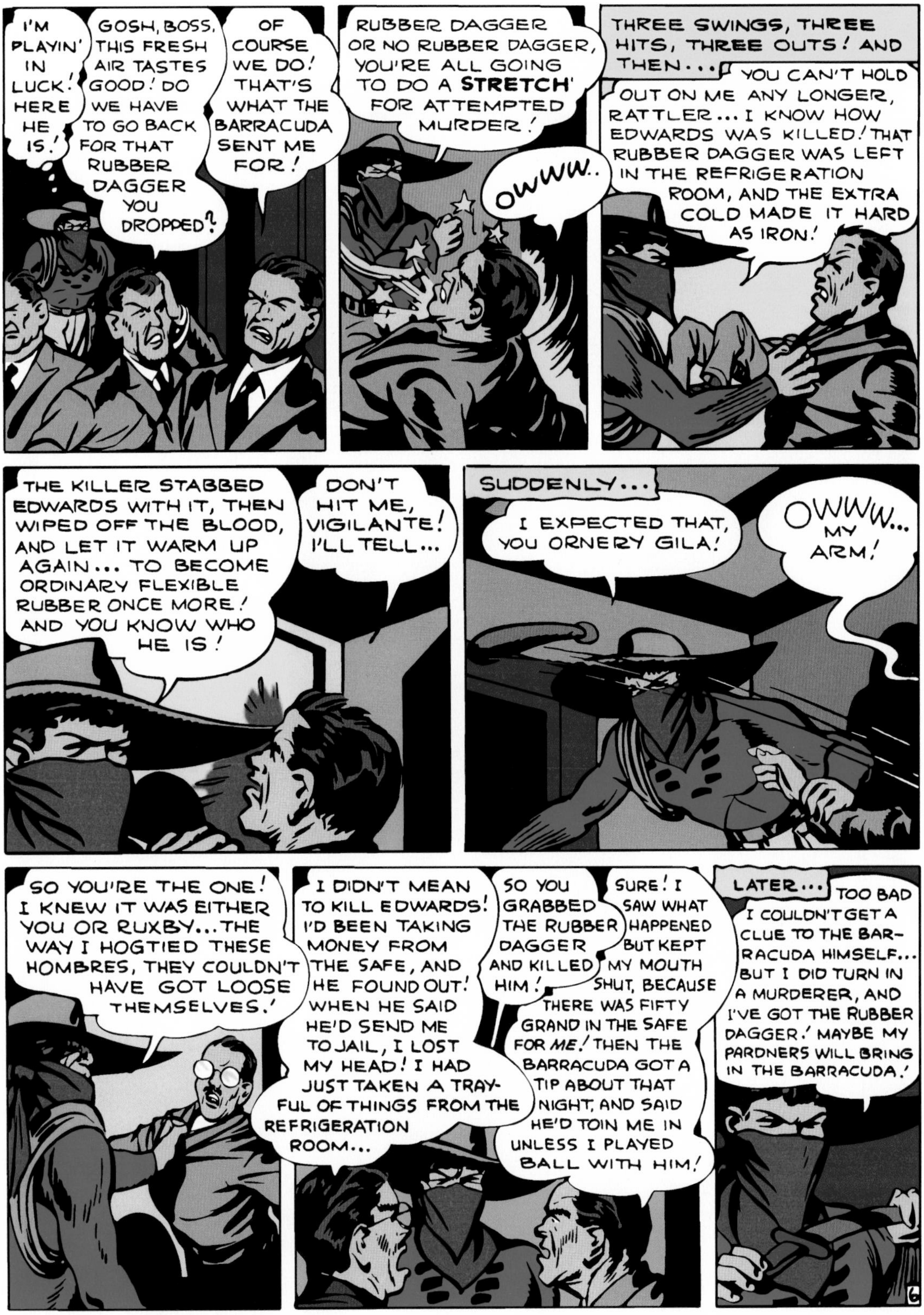
I'M PLAYIN' IN LUCK! HERE HE IS!
GOSH, BOSS, THIS FRESH AIR TASTES GOOD! DO WE HAVE TO GO BACK FOR THAT RUBBER DAGGER YOU DROPPED?
OF COURSE WE DO! THAT'S WHAT THE BARRACUDA SENT ME FOR!
RUBBER DAGGER OR NO RUBBER DAGGER, YOU'RE ALL GOING TO DO A STRETCH' FOR ATTEMPTED MURDER!
OWWW..
THREE SWINGS, THREE HITS, THREE OUTS! AND THEN...
YOU CAN'T HOLD OUT ON ME ANY LONGER, RATTLER... I KNOW HOW EDWARDS WAS KILLED! THAT RUBBER DAGGER WAS LEFT IN THE REFRIGERATION ROOM, AND THE EXTRA COLD MADE IT HARD AS IRON!
THE KILLER STABBED EDWARDS WITH IT, THEN WIPED OFF THE BLOOD, AND LET IT WARM UP AGAIN... TO BECOME ORDINARY FLEXIBLE RUBBER ONCE MORE! AND YOU KNOW WHO HE IS!
DON'T HIT ME, VIGILANTE! I'LL TELL...
SUDDENLY...
I EXPECTED THAT, YOU ORNERY GILA!
OWWW... MY ARM!
SO YOU'RE THE ONE! I KNEW IT WAS EITHER YOU OR RUXBY... THE WAY I HOGTIED THESE HOMBRES, THEY COULDN'T HAVE GOT LOOSE THEMSELVES!
I DIDN'T MEAN TO KILL EDWARDS! I'D BEEN TAKING MONEY FROM THE SAFE, AND HE FOUND OUT! WHEN HE SAID HE'D SEND ME TO JAIL, I LOST MY HEAD! I HAD JUST TAKEN A TRAY-FUL OF THINGS FROM THE REFRIGERATION ROOM...
SO YOU GRABBED THE RUBBER DAGGER AND KILLED HIM!
SURE! I SAW WHAT HAPPENED BUT KEPT MY MOUTH SHUT, BECAUSE THERE WAS FIFTY GRAND IN THE SAFE FOR ME! THEN THE BARRACUDA GOT A TIP ABOUT THAT NIGHT, AND SAID HE'D TOIN ME IN UNLESS I PLAYED BALL WITH HIM!
LATER...
TOO BAD I COULDN'T GET A CLUE TO THE BAR-RACUDA HIMSELF... BUT I DID TURN IN A MURDERER, AND I'VE GOT THE RUBBER DAGGER! MAYBE MY PARDNERS WILL BRING IN THE BARRACUDA!
6

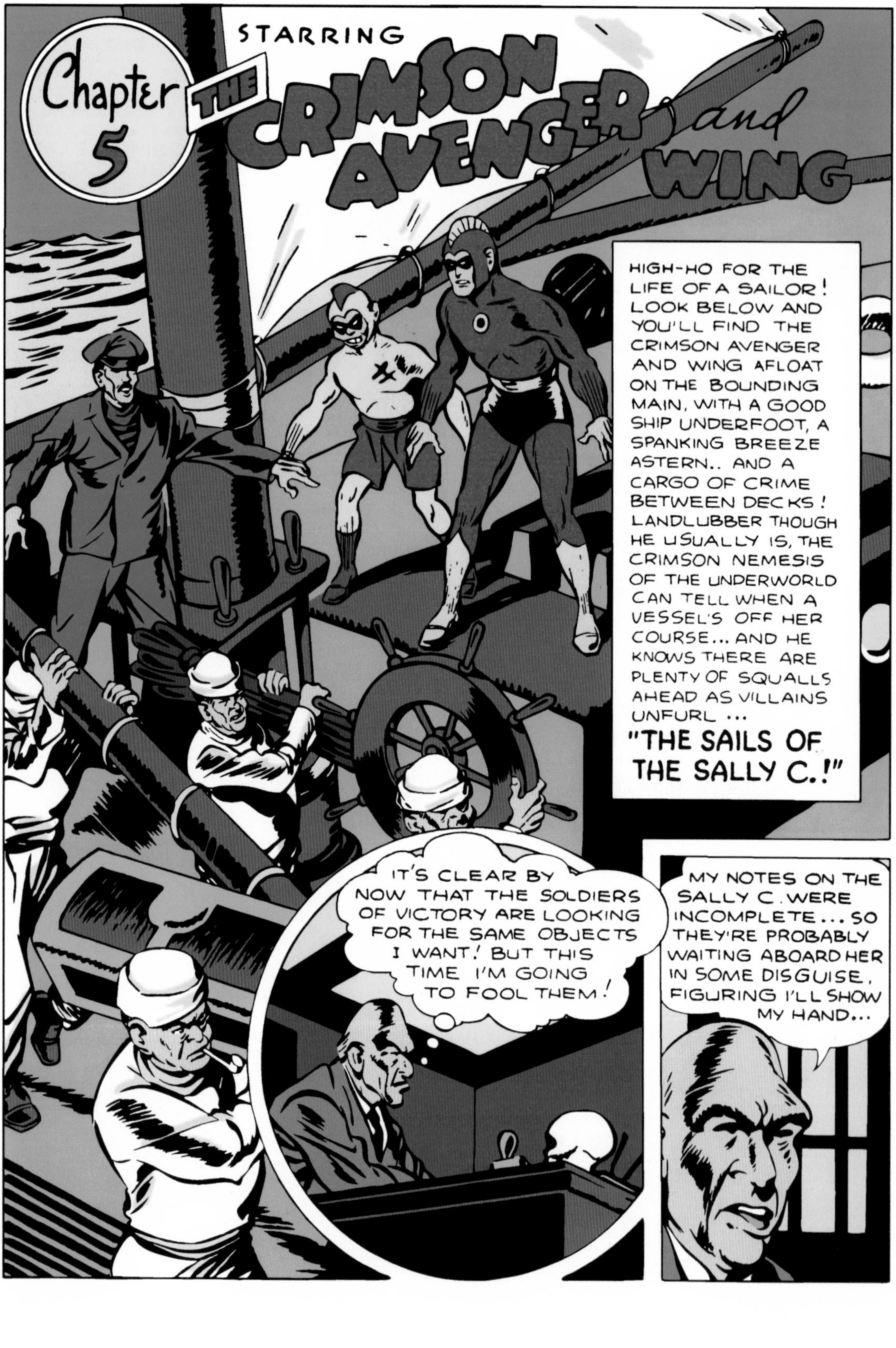
Chapter 5
STARRING
THE CRIMSON AVENGER and WING
HIGH-HO FOR THE LIFE OF A SAILOR! LOOK BELOW AND YOU'LL FIND THE CRIMSON AVENGER AND WING AFLOAT ON THE BOUNDING MAIN, WITH A GOOD SHIP UNDERFOOT, A SPANKING BREEZE ASTERN.. AND A CARGO OF CRIME BETWEEN DECKS! LANDLUBBER THOUGH HE USUALLY IS, THE CRIMSON NEMESIS OF THE UNDERWORLD CAN TELL WHEN A VESSEL'S OFF HER COURSE... AND HE KNOWS THERE ARE PLENTY OF SQUALLS AHEAD AS VILLAINS UNFURL ...
"THE SAILS OF THE SALLY C.!"
IT'S CLEAR BY NOW THAT THE SOLDIERS OF VICTORY ARE LOOKING FOR THE SAME OBJECTS I WANT! BUT THIS TIME I'M GOING TO FOOL THEM!
MY NOTES ON THE SALLY C. WERE INCOMPLETE... SO THEY'RE PROBABLY WAITING ABOARD HER IN SOME DISGUISE, FIGURING I'LL SHOW MY HAND...

WELL, I WON'T DISAPPOINT THEM! I'VE MADE PLANS TO SHOW IT... IN SUCH A WAY AS TO TELL THEM NOTHING AND LEAD TO THEIR CAPTURE AT THE SAME TIME!

THE SALLY C., ONE OF THE LAST OF THE WIND-JAMMERS... NIGH A HUNDRED YEARS OLD AND STILL AT WORK...

SALLY C.

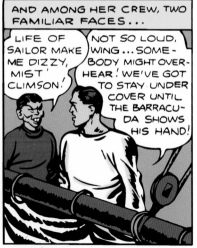

AND AMONG HER CREW, TWO FAMILIAR FACES...

LIFE OF SAILOR MAKE ME DIZZY, MIST' CLIMSON!

NOT SO LOUD, WING... SOMEBODY MIGHT OVERHEAR! WE'VE GOT TO STAY UNDER COVER UNTIL THE BARRACUDA SHOWS HIS HAND!

THE BARRACUDA'S NOTES TOLD US HE WANTED PART OF THIS SHIP... BUT WE DON'T KNOW WHICH PART, AND WE DON'T KNOW WHY— THOUGH IT'S PROBABLY CONNECTED WITH THE FAMOUS ESCAPE OF A CROOK CALLED HURRICANE SMITH...

WING REMEMBER! IN MIDDLE OF OCEAN POLICE LOOK ON THIS SHIP FOR SMITH, CAN'T FIND HIM, THINK HE JUMP OVERBOARD! TWO WEEKS LATER, SHIP LAND... AND SMITH RUN DOWN GANGPLANK!

AND NO ONE EVER DISCOVERED WHERE HE HID. BUT MAYBE, WITH THE BARRACUDA'S HELP, WE WILL!

THAT VERY EVENING...

THE BARRACUDA WOULD LIKE TO HAVE A SPOKE OF THAT WHEEL, CHUM... IF YOU DON'T MIND!

AAAAA...OOO

THE BARRACUDA STRIKE AT LAST, MIST' CLIMSON!

YES! INTO ACTION, WING!

2

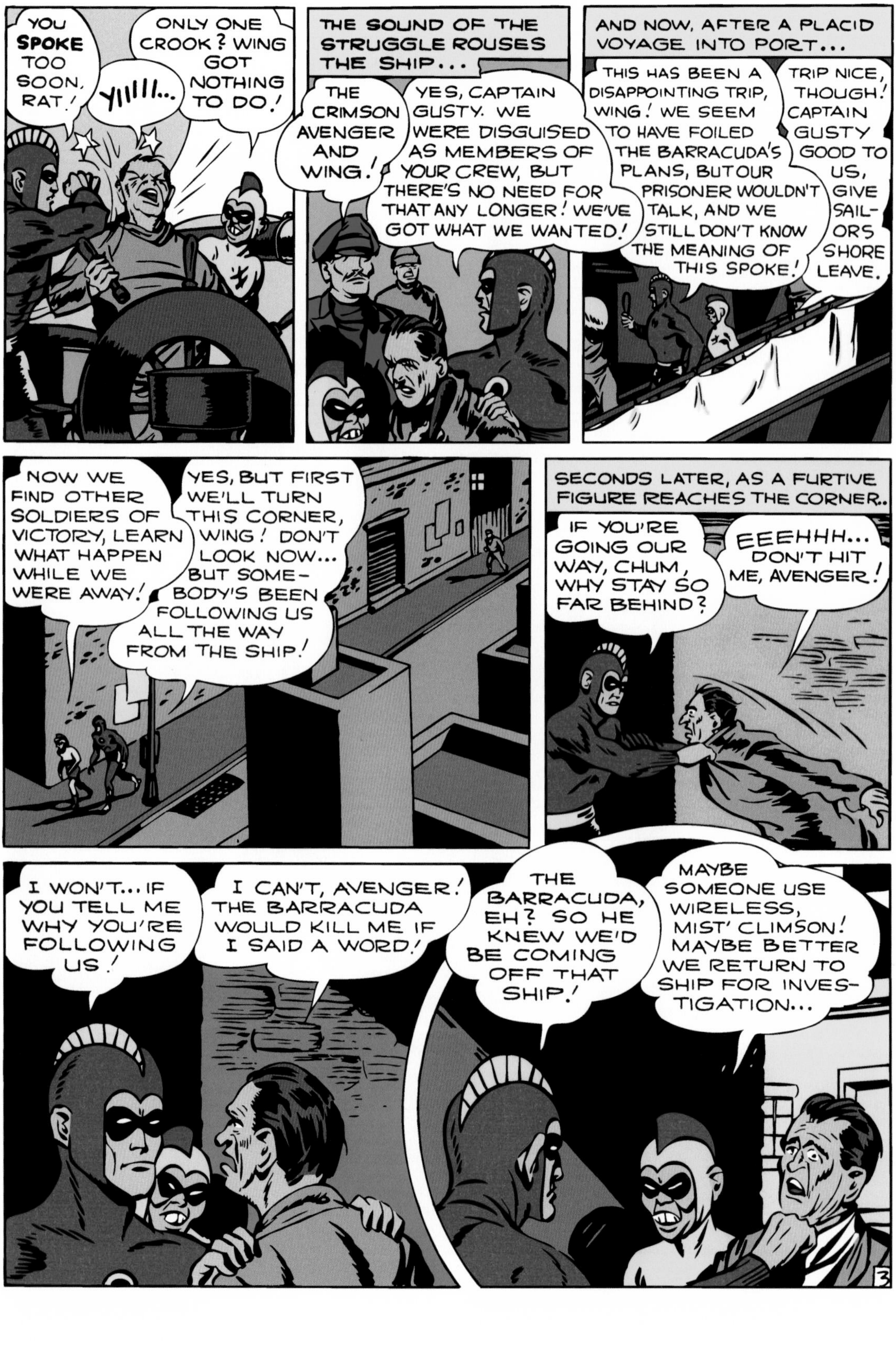
YOU SPOKE TOO SOON, RAT!
YIIIII...
ONLY ONE CROOK? WING GOT NOTHING TO DO!
THE SOUND OF THE STRUGGLE ROUSES THE SHIP...
THE CRIMSON AVENGER AND WING!
YES, CAPTAIN GUSTY. WE WERE DISGUISED AS MEMBERS OF YOUR CREW, BUT THERE'S NO NEED FOR THAT ANY LONGER! WE'VE GOT WHAT WE WANTED!
AND NOW, AFTER A PLACID VOYAGE INTO PORT...
THIS HAS BEEN A DISAPPOINTING TRIP, WING! WE SEEM TO HAVE FOILED THE BARRACUDA'S PLANS, BUT OUR PRISONER WOULDN'T TALK, AND WE STILL DON'T KNOW THE MEANING OF THIS SPOKE!
TRIP NICE, THOUGH! CAPTAIN GUSTY GOOD TO US, GIVE SAILORS SHORE LEAVE.
NOW WE FIND OTHER SOLDIERS OF VICTORY, LEARN WHAT HAPPEN WHILE WE WERE AWAY!
YES, BUT FIRST WE'LL TURN THIS CORNER, WING! DON'T LOOK NOW... BUT SOMEBODY'S BEEN FOLLOWING US ALL THE WAY FROM THE SHIP!
SECONDS LATER, AS A FURTIVE FIGURE REACHES THE CORNER..
IF YOU'RE GOING OUR WAY, CHUM, WHY STAY SO FAR BEHIND?
EEEHHH... DON'T HIT ME, AVENGER!
I WON'T... IF YOU TELL ME WHY YOU'RE FOLLOWING US!
I CAN'T, AVENGER! THE BARRACUDA WOULD KILL ME IF I SAID A WORD!
THE BARRACUDA, EH? SO HE KNEW WE'D BE COMING OFF THAT SHIP!
MAYBE SOMEONE USE WIRELESS, MIST' CLIMSON! MAYBE BETTER WE RETURN TO SHIP FOR INVESTIGATION...
3

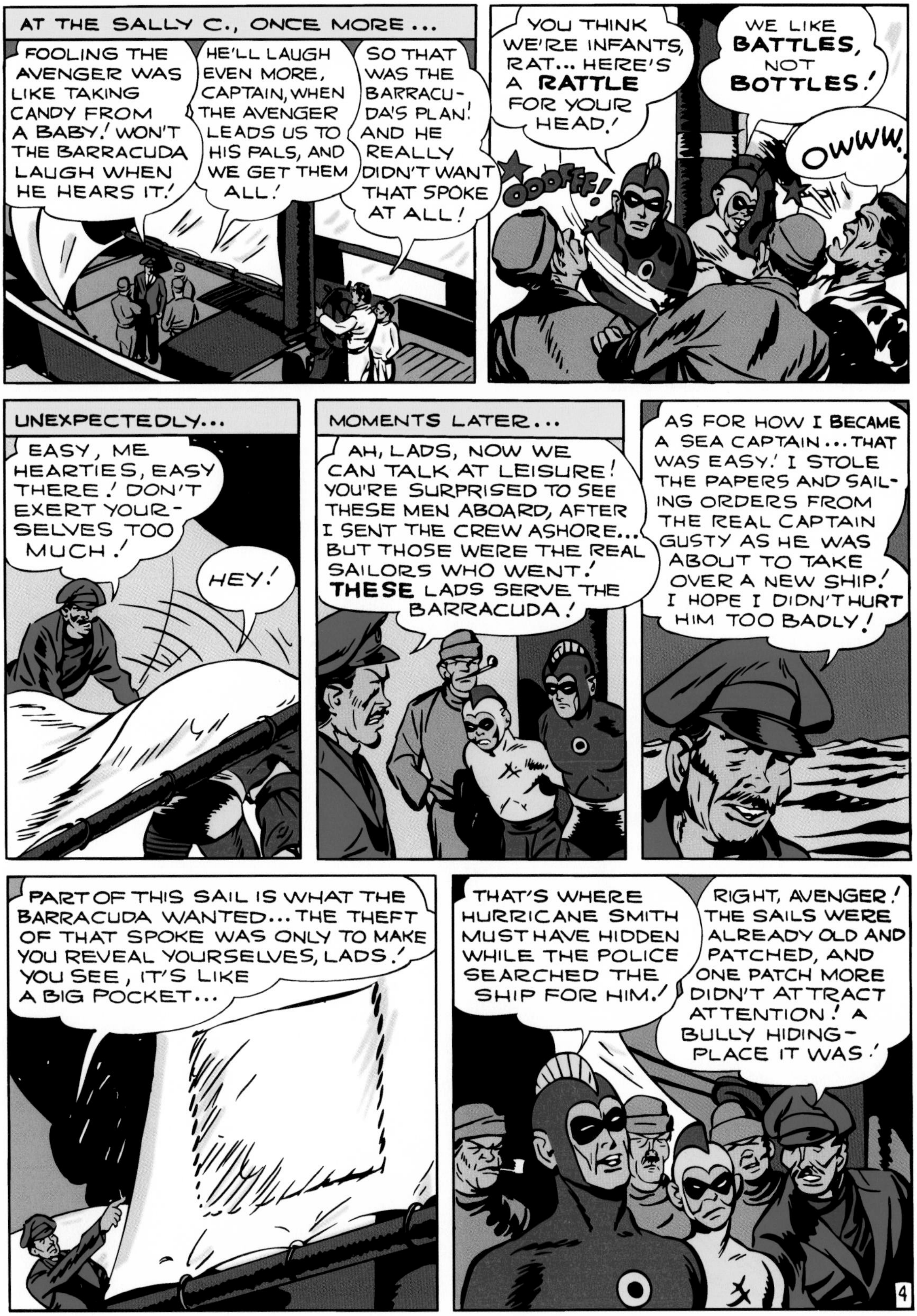
AT THE SALLY C., ONCE MORE...
FOOLING THE AVENGER WAS LIKE TAKING CANDY FROM A BABY! WON'T THE BARRACUDA LAUGH WHEN HE HEARS IT!
HE'LL LAUGH EVEN MORE, CAPTAIN, WHEN THE AVENGER LEADS US TO HIS PALS, AND WE GET THEM ALL!
SO THAT WAS THE BARRACUDA'S PLAN! AND HE REALLY DIDN'T WANT THAT SPOKE AT ALL!
YOU THINK WE'RE INFANTS, RAT... HERE'S A RATTLE FOR YOUR HEAD!
WE LIKE BATTLES, NOT BOTTLES!
OOOFFF!
OWWW!
UNEXPECTEDLY...
EASY, ME HEARTIES, EASY THERE! DON'T EXERT YOURSELVES TOO MUCH!
HEY!
MOMENTS LATER...
AH, LADS, NOW WE CAN TALK AT LEISURE! YOU'RE SURPRISED TO SEE THESE MEN ABOARD, AFTER I SENT THE CREW ASHORE... BUT THOSE WERE THE REAL SAILORS WHO WENT! THESE LADS SERVE THE BARRACUDA!
AS FOR HOW I BECAME A SEA CAPTAIN... THAT WAS EASY! I STOLE THE PAPERS AND SAILING ORDERS FROM THE REAL CAPTAIN GUSTY AS HE WAS ABOUT TO TAKE OVER A NEW SHIP! I HOPE I DIDN'T HURT HIM TOO BADLY!
PART OF THIS SAIL IS WHAT THE BARRACUDA WANTED... THE THEFT OF THAT SPOKE WAS ONLY TO MAKE YOU REVEAL YOURSELVES, LADS! YOU SEE, IT'S LIKE A BIG POCKET...
THAT'S WHERE HURRICANE SMITH MUST HAVE HIDDEN WHILE THE POLICE SEARCHED THE SHIP FOR HIM!
RIGHT, AVENGER! THE SAILS WERE ALREADY OLD AND PATCHED, AND ONE PATCH MORE DIDN'T ATTRACT ATTENTION! A BULLY HIDING-PLACE IT WAS!
4

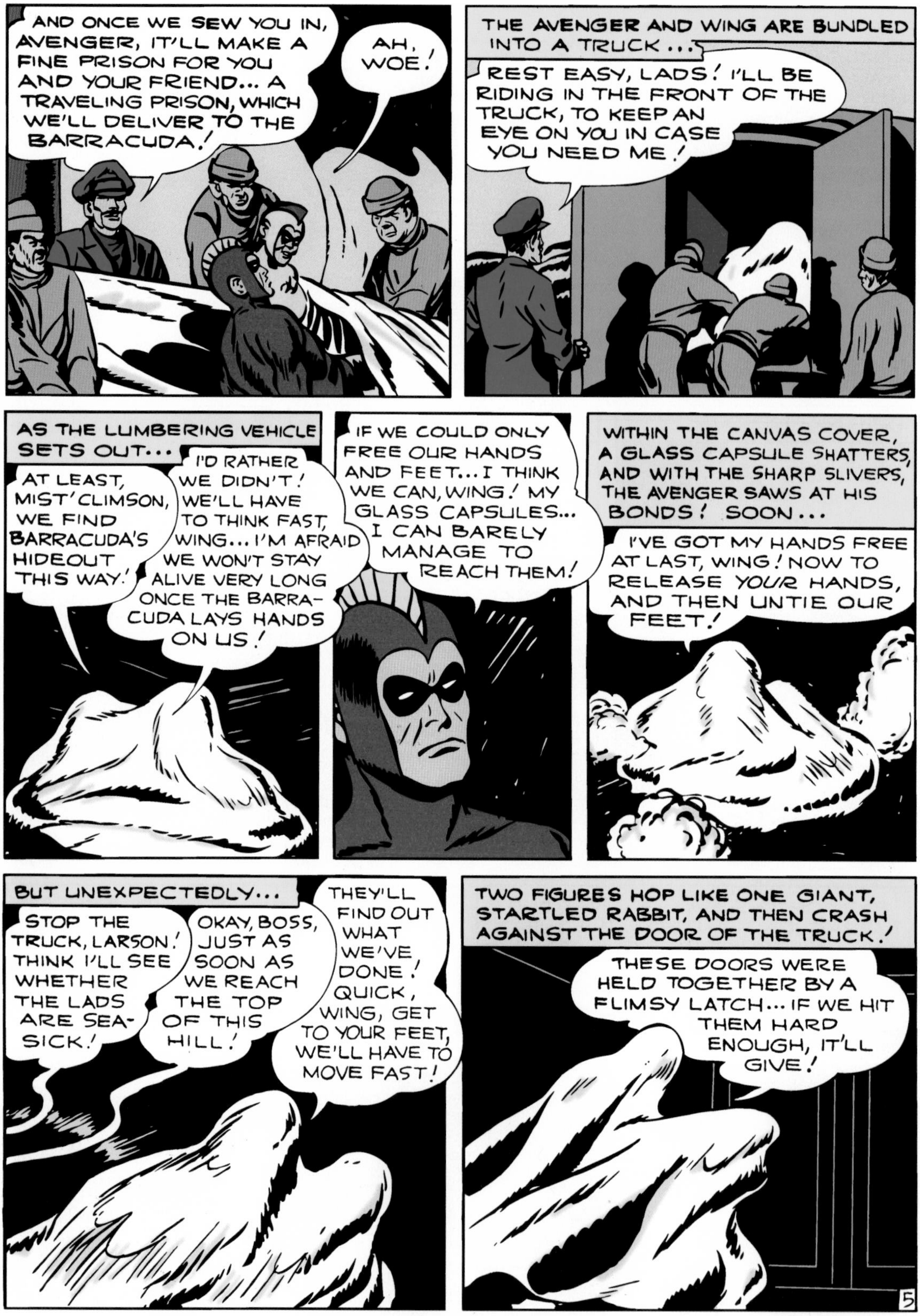
AND ONCE WE SEW YOU IN, AVENGER, IT'LL MAKE A FINE PRISON FOR YOU AND YOUR FRIEND... A TRAVELING PRISON, WHICH WE'LL DELIVER TO THE BARRACUDA!
AH, WOE!
THE AVENGER AND WING ARE BUNDLED INTO A TRUCK...
REST EASY, LADS! I'LL BE RIDING IN THE FRONT OF THE TRUCK, TO KEEP AN EYE ON YOU IN CASE YOU NEED ME!
AS THE LUMBERING VEHICLE SETS OUT...
AT LEAST, MIST' CLIMSON, WE FIND BARRACUDA'S HIDEOUT THIS WAY!
I'D RATHER WE DIDN'T! WE'LL HAVE TO THINK FAST, WING... I'M AFRAID WE WON'T STAY ALIVE VERY LONG ONCE THE BARRACUDA LAYS HANDS ON US!
IF WE COULD ONLY FREE OUR HANDS AND FEET... I THINK WE CAN, WING! MY GLASS CAPSULES... I CAN BARELY MANAGE TO REACH THEM!
WITHIN THE CANVAS COVER, A GLASS CAPSULE SHATTERS, AND WITH THE SHARP SLIVERS, THE AVENGER SAWS AT HIS BONDS! SOON...
I'VE GOT MY HANDS FREE AT LAST, WING! NOW TO RELEASE YOUR HANDS, AND THEN UNTIE OUR FEET!
BUT UNEXPECTEDLY...
STOP THE TRUCK, LARSON! THINK I'LL SEE WHETHER THE LADS ARE SEA-SICK!
OKAY, BOSS, JUST AS SOON AS WE REACH THE TOP OF THIS HILL!
THEY'LL FIND OUT WHAT WE'VE DONE! QUICK, WING, GET TO YOUR FEET, WE'LL HAVE TO MOVE FAST!
TWO FIGURES HOP LIKE ONE GIANT, STARTLED RABBIT, AND THEN CRASH AGAINST THE DOOR OF THE TRUCK!
THESE DOORS WERE HELD TOGETHER BY A FLIMSY LATCH... IF WE HIT THEM HARD ENOUGH, IT'LL GIVE!
5

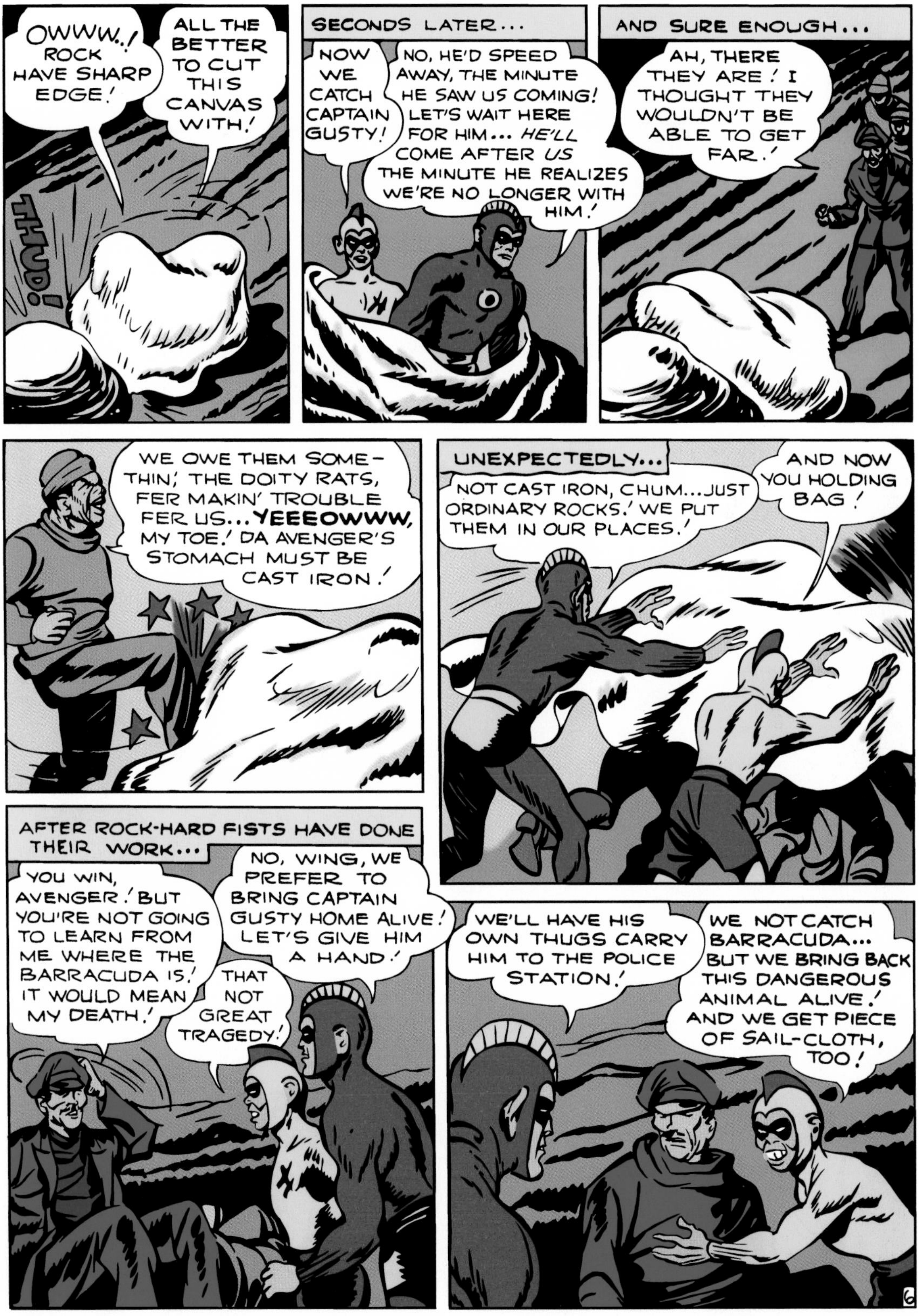
OWWW..! ROCK HAVE SHARP EDGE!
ALL THE BETTER TO CUT THIS CANVAS WITH!
THUD!
SECONDS LATER...
NOW WE CATCH CAPTAIN GUSTY!
NO, HE'D SPEED AWAY, THE MINUTE HE SAW US COMING! LET'S WAIT HERE FOR HIM... HE'LL COME AFTER US THE MINUTE HE REALIZES WE'RE NO LONGER WITH HIM!
AND SURE ENOUGH...
AH, THERE THEY ARE! I THOUGHT THEY WOULDN'T BE ABLE TO GET FAR!
WE OWE THEM SOME-THIN', THE DOITY RATS, FER MAKIN' TROUBLE FER US... YEEEOWWW, MY TOE! DA AVENGER'S STOMACH MUST BE CAST IRON!
UNEXPECTEDLY...
NOT CAST IRON, CHUM... JUST ORDINARY ROCKS! WE PUT THEM IN OUR PLACES!
AND NOW YOU HOLDING BAG!
AFTER ROCK-HARD FISTS HAVE DONE THEIR WORK...
YOU WIN, AVENGER! BUT YOU'RE NOT GOING TO LEARN FROM ME WHERE THE BARRACUDA IS! IT WOULD MEAN MY DEATH!
NO, WING, WE PREFER TO BRING CAPTAIN GUSTY HOME ALIVE! LET'S GIVE HIM A HAND!
THAT NOT GREAT TRAGEDY!
WE'LL HAVE HIS OWN THUGS CARRY HIM TO THE POLICE STATION!
WE NOT CATCH BARRACUDA... BUT WE BRING BACK THIS DANGEROUS ANIMAL ALIVE! AND WE GET PIECE OF SAIL-CLOTH, TOO!
6

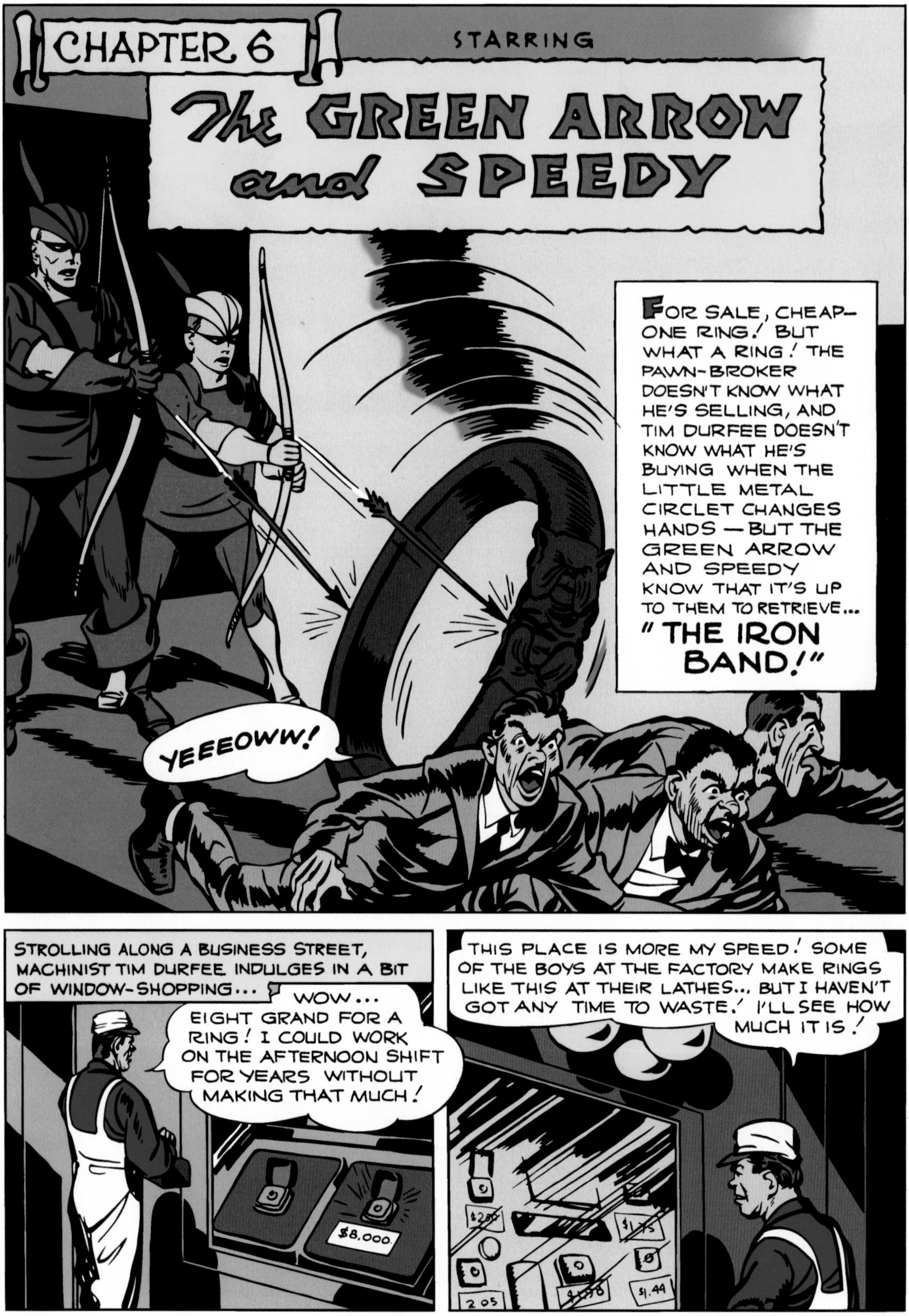

CHAPTER 6
STARRING
The GREEN ARROW and SPEEDY
FOR SALE, CHEAP-ONE RING! BUT WHAT A RING! THE PAWN-BROKER DOESN'T KNOW WHAT HE'S SELLING, AND TIM DURFEE DOESN'T KNOW WHAT HE'S BUYING WHEN THE LITTLE METAL CIRCLET CHANGES HANDS — BUT THE GREEN ARROW AND SPEEDY KNOW THAT IT'S UP TO THEM TO RETRIEVE... "THE IRON BAND!"
YEEEOWW!
STROLLING ALONG A BUSINESS STREET, MACHINIST TIM DURFEE INDULGES IN A BIT OF WINDOW-SHOPPING...
WOW... EIGHT GRAND FOR A RING! I COULD WORK ON THE AFTERNOON SHIFT FOR YEARS WITHOUT MAKING THAT MUCH!
$8,000
THIS PLACE IS MORE MY SPEED! SOME OF THE BOYS AT THE FACTORY MAKE RINGS LIKE THIS AT THEIR LATHES... BUT I HAVEN'T GOT ANY TIME TO WASTE! I'LL SEE HOW MUCH IT IS!
$1.44

A MOMENT LATER...

DIS IS THE PLACE, BOYS! NOW, NO ROUGH STUFF... DA BARRACUDA SAID TO JUST WALK IN AND BUY THE RING!

GOSH, STRETCH, IMAGINE US **BUYIN'** ANYTHING! IT'S AGAINST ME PRINCIPLES!

GOSH, I LIKE THIS BETTER BY THE MINUTE!

HUH... LOOK! WE'RE TOO LATE! DIS GUY'S ALREADY BOUGHT THE RING!

OKAY, STRETCH, IT'LL BE A CINCH TA TAKE IT AWAY FROM HIM!

NOT OUT HERE, WITH THE COPS WATCHIN', YA SAP! WE'LL DO LIKE THE BARRACUDA SAID... BUY IT!

JUST A MINUTE, PAL. I'LL GIVE YA A HUNNERD SMACKERS FER YOUR RING!

A HUNDRED..? WHO YOU TRYING TO KID?

WE'LL MAKE IT **TWO HUNNERD!**

I HAVEN'T ANY TIME TO WASTE ON WISE GUYS! I'VE GOT TO PUNCH A TIME CLOCK... AND THERE'S MY TROLLEY!

WE'LL GIVE YA **FIVE** HUNNERD, YA SAP!

WE OFFERED HIM TOO MUCH DOUGH... HE THOUGHT WE WERE KIDDIN'!

WE SHOULDA DONE LIKE I SAID, BOSS... TAKE IT AWAY FROM HIM!

OKAY, WE'LL DO THAT NOW! CALL A TAXI, BOYS... WE'LL FIND OUT WHAT FACTORY HE GOES TO.

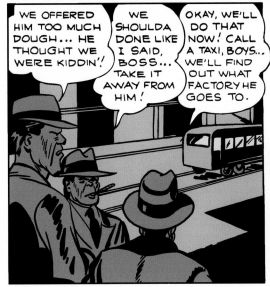

MEANWHILE, TWO NEWCOMERS JOIN THE SEARCH!

AN IRON RING? SORRY, GREEN ARROW... I SOLD THE ONLY ONE I HAD A FEW HOURS AGO! BUT IF YOU WANT ONE BADLY ENOUGH, THE MAN WHO HAS IT MIGHT RESELL IT! HE SAID HE WORKED IN A RADIO FACTORY...

THERE'S ONLY ONE RADIO FACTORY NEAR HERE! COME ON, SPEEDY, WE'LL GET HIS DESCRIPTION AND HURRY RIGHT OVER!

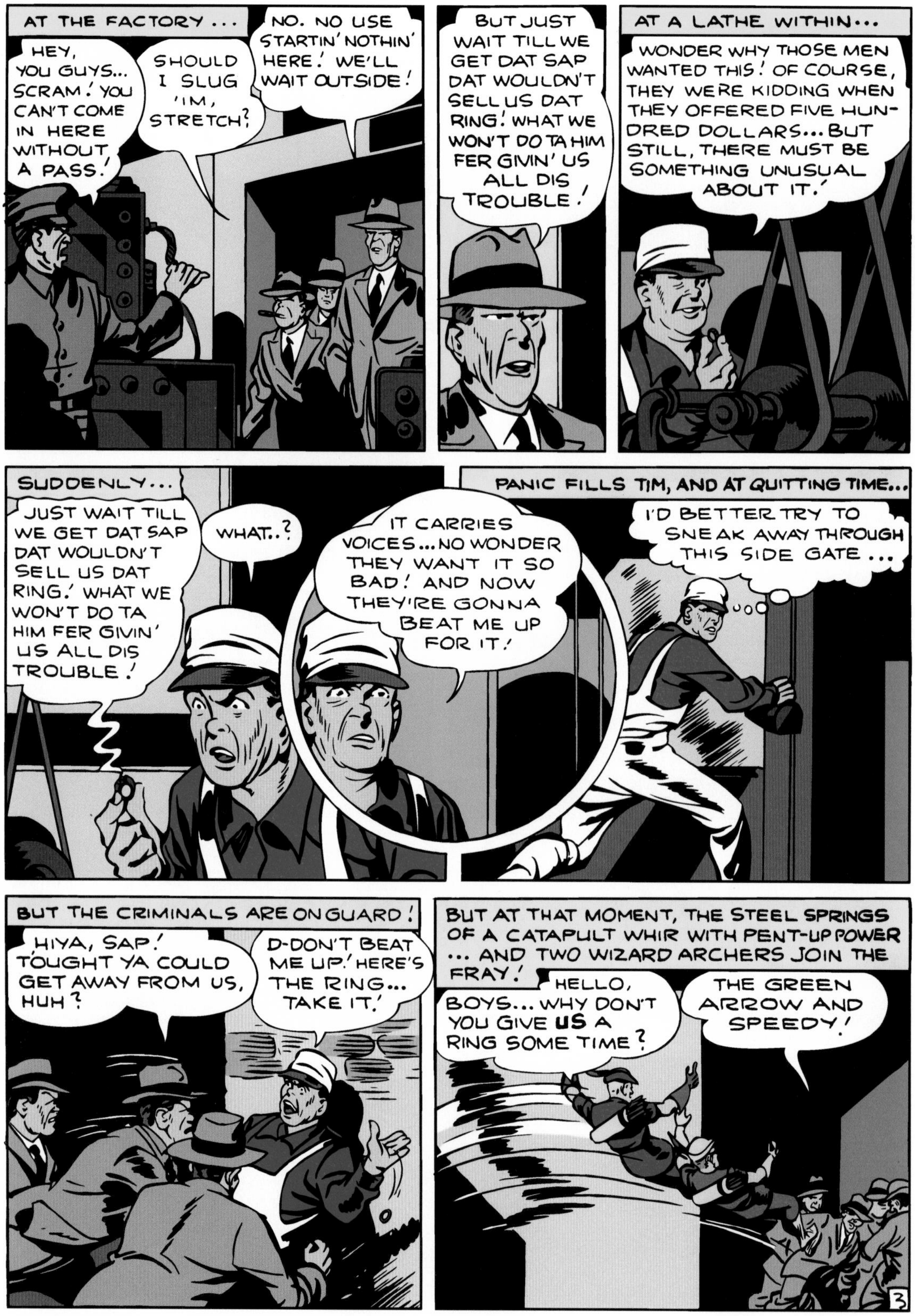
AT THE FACTORY ...
HEY, YOU GUYS... SCRAM! YOU CAN'T COME IN HERE WITHOUT A PASS!
SHOULD I SLUG 'IM, STRETCH?
NO. NO USE STARTIN' NOTHIN' HERE! WE'LL WAIT OUTSIDE!
BUT JUST WAIT TILL WE GET DAT SAP DAT WOULDN'T SELL US DAT RING! WHAT WE WON'T DO TA HIM FER GIVIN' US ALL DIS TROUBLE!
AT A LATHE WITHIN...
WONDER WHY THOSE MEN WANTED THIS! OF COURSE, THEY WERE KIDDING WHEN THEY OFFERED FIVE HUNDRED DOLLARS... BUT STILL, THERE MUST BE SOMETHING UNUSUAL ABOUT IT!
SUDDENLY...
JUST WAIT TILL WE GET DAT SAP DAT WOULDN'T SELL US DAT RING! WHAT WE WON'T DO TA HIM FER GIVIN' US ALL DIS TROUBLE!
WHAT..?
IT CARRIES VOICES... NO WONDER THEY WANT IT SO BAD! AND NOW THEY'RE GONNA BEAT ME UP FOR IT!
PANIC FILLS TIM, AND AT QUITTING TIME...
I'D BETTER TRY TO SNEAK AWAY THROUGH THIS SIDE GATE...
BUT THE CRIMINALS ARE ON GUARD!
HIYA, SAP! TOUGHT YA COULD GET AWAY FROM US, HUH?
D-DON'T BEAT ME UP! HERE'S THE RING... TAKE IT!
BUT AT THAT MOMENT, THE STEEL SPRINGS OF A CATAPULT WHIR WITH PENT-UP POWER ... AND TWO WIZARD ARCHERS JOIN THE FRAY!
HELLO, BOYS... WHY DON'T YOU GIVE US A RING SOME TIME?
THE GREEN ARROW AND SPEEDY!
3

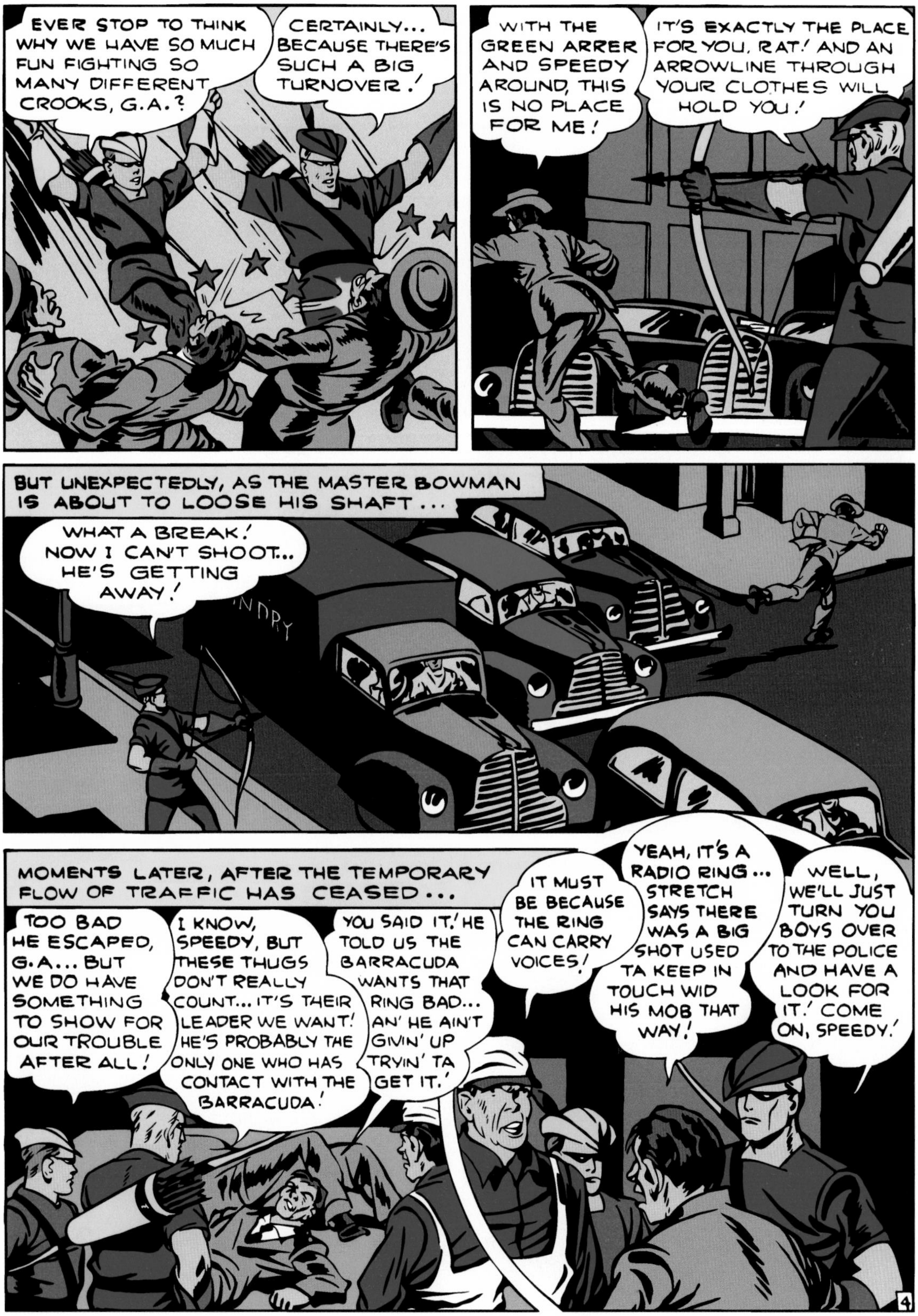
EVER STOP TO THINK WHY WE HAVE SO MUCH FUN FIGHTING SO MANY DIFFERENT CROOKS, G.A.?
CERTAINLY... BECAUSE THERE'S SUCH A BIG TURNOVER!
WITH THE GREEN ARRER AND SPEEDY AROUND, THIS IS NO PLACE FOR ME!
IT'S EXACTLY THE PLACE FOR YOU, RAT! AND AN ARROWLINE THROUGH YOUR CLOTHES WILL HOLD YOU!
BUT UNEXPECTEDLY, AS THE MASTER BOWMAN IS ABOUT TO LOOSE HIS SHAFT...
WHAT A BREAK! NOW I CAN'T SHOOT... HE'S GETTING AWAY!
MOMENTS LATER, AFTER THE TEMPORARY FLOW OF TRAFFIC HAS CEASED...
TOO BAD HE ESCAPED, G.A... BUT WE DO HAVE SOMETHING TO SHOW FOR OUR TROUBLE AFTER ALL!
I KNOW, SPEEDY, BUT THESE THUGS DON'T REALLY COUNT... IT'S THEIR LEADER WE WANT! HE'S PROBABLY THE ONLY ONE WHO HAS CONTACT WITH THE BARRACUDA!
YOU SAID IT! HE TOLD US THE BARRACUDA WANTS THAT RING BAD... AN' HE AIN'T GIVIN' UP TRYIN' TA GET IT.
IT MUST BE BECAUSE THE RING CAN CARRY VOICES!
YEAH, IT'S A RADIO RING... STRETCH SAYS THERE WAS A BIG SHOT USED TA KEEP IN TOUCH WID HIS MOB THAT WAY!
WELL, WE'LL JUST TURN YOU BOYS OVER TO THE POLICE AND HAVE A LOOK FOR IT! COME ON, SPEEDY!
4

BUT AFTER HOURS OF SEARCHING..

I CAN'T UNDER-STAND WHY WE CAN'T FIND IT, GREEN ARROW... I THREW IT RIGHT OUT THERE!

WELL, IT ISN'T THERE NOW! TOO BAD YOU DIDN'T KEEP YOUR EYES ON IT DUR-ING THE STRUGGLE!

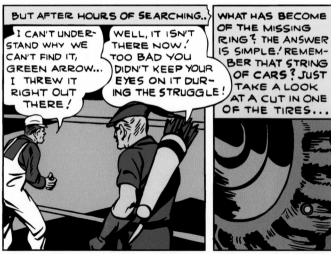

WHAT HAS BECOME OF THE MISSING RING? THE ANSWER IS SIMPLE! REMEM-BER THAT STRING OF CARS? JUST TAKE A LOOK AT A CUT IN ONE OF THE TIRES...

FOR A TIME, THE UNSUSPECTING DRIVER HAS NO REASON TO SUSPECT THAT ANYTHING UNUSUAL HAS HAP-PENED! BUT SOME MOMENTS LATER, AS THE CAR GOES OVER A BUMP..

GOSH, DRIVING ALONE IS MONOTONOUS! IF I ONLY HAD A RADIO SET...

O SOLE MIO...

YOU ARE MY SUNSHINE...

HUH..? ALL I GOTTA DO IS WISH FOR IT, AND I GOT IT! BUT WHERE IS IT?

QUICKLY APPLIED BREAKS BRING THE VEHICLE TO A QUICK STOP! BUT AS IT ROLLS OVER ANOTHER BUMP, THE MUSIC CEASES... AND A BADLY PUZZLED DRIVER STARES IN BEWILDERMENT!

IT STOPPED JUST AS SUDDENLY AS IT STARTED! AND THERE'S NO SIGN OF A RADIO ANY-PLACE!

N701

THE MIRACLES OF THE RING, HOWEVER, HAVE BUT BARELY BEGUN! ALMOST EVERY BUMP CAUSES A CHANGE IN PROGRAM... AND SOME TIME LATER...

SOUNDS LIKE DIS GUY'S WAGON PICKED UP THE RING! I'LL GET HOLD OF A COUPLA MORE BOYS AND INVESTIGATE!

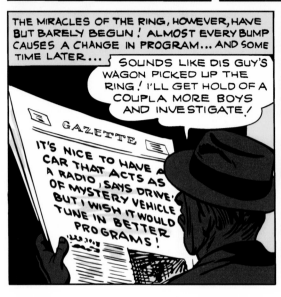

GAZETTE

IT'S NICE TO HAVE A CAR THAT ACTS AS A RADIO, SAYS DRIVE OF MYSTERY VEHICLE BUT I WISH IT WOULD TUNE IN BETTER PROGRAMS!

AND SO, THAT NIGHT...

THE CAR'S IN HERE! WE'LL TAKE IT FER A RIDE, AND THEN LOOK AT IT!

5

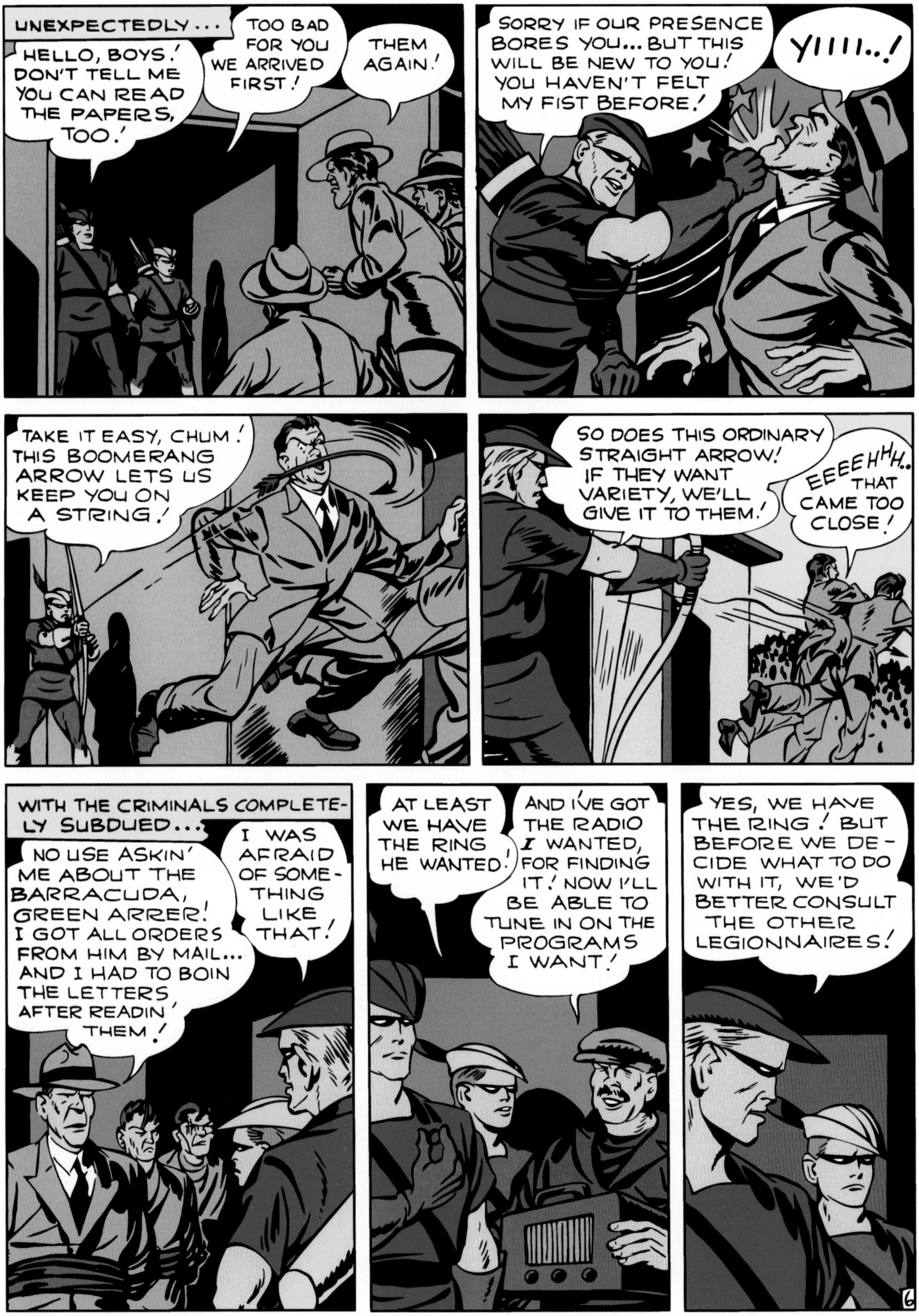
UNEXPECTEDLY...
HELLO, BOYS! DON'T TELL ME YOU CAN READ THE PAPERS, TOO!
TOO BAD FOR YOU WE ARRIVED FIRST!
THEM AGAIN!
SORRY IF OUR PRESENCE BORES YOU... BUT THIS WILL BE NEW TO YOU! YOU HAVEN'T FELT MY FIST BEFORE!
YIIII..!
TAKE IT EASY, CHUM! THIS BOOMERANG ARROW LETS US KEEP YOU ON A STRING!
SO DOES THIS ORDINARY STRAIGHT ARROW! IF THEY WANT VARIETY, WE'LL GIVE IT TO THEM!
EEEEHHH.. THAT CAME TOO CLOSE!
WITH THE CRIMINALS COMPLETELY SUBDUED...
NO USE ASKIN' ME ABOUT THE BARRACUDA, GREEN ARRER! I GOT ALL ORDERS FROM HIM BY MAIL... AND I HAD TO BOIN THE LETTERS AFTER READIN' THEM!
I WAS AFRAID OF SOMETHING LIKE THAT!
AT LEAST WE HAVE THE RING HE WANTED!
AND I'VE GOT THE RADIO I WANTED, FOR FINDING IT! NOW I'LL BE ABLE TO TUNE IN ON THE PROGRAMS I WANT!
YES, WE HAVE THE RING! BUT BEFORE WE DECIDE WHAT TO DO WITH IT, WE'D BETTER CONSULT THE OTHER LEGIONNAIRES!
6

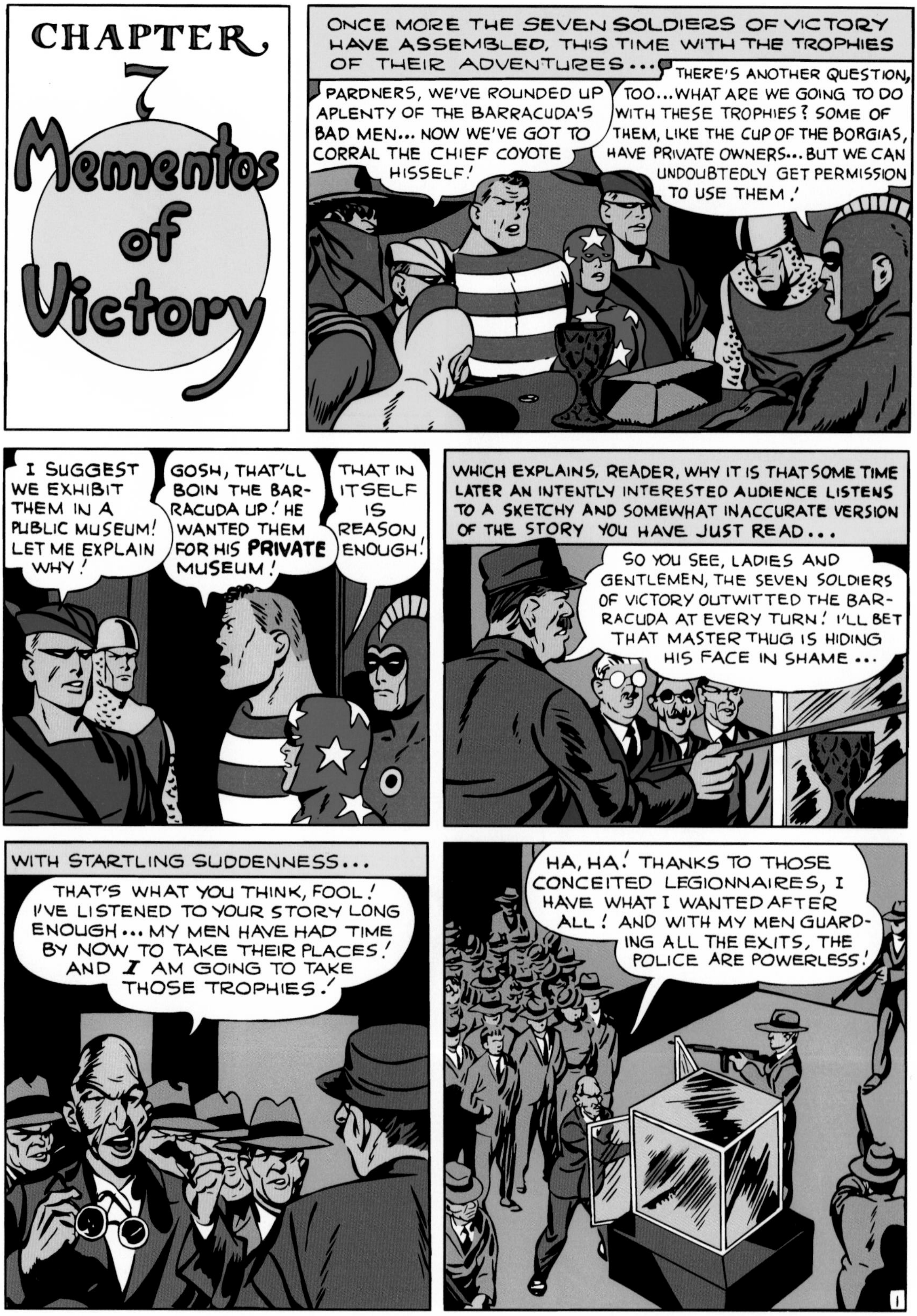
CHAPTER 7
Mementos of Victory
ONCE MORE THE SEVEN SOLDIERS OF VICTORY HAVE ASSEMBLED, THIS TIME WITH THE TROPHIES OF THEIR ADVENTURES...
PARDNERS, WE'VE ROUNDED UP APLENTY OF THE BARRACUDA'S BAD MEN... NOW WE'VE GOT TO CORRAL THE CHIEF COYOTE HISSELF!
THERE'S ANOTHER QUESTION, TOO...WHAT ARE WE GOING TO DO WITH THESE TROPHIES? SOME OF THEM, LIKE THE CUP OF THE BORGIAS, HAVE PRIVATE OWNERS... BUT WE CAN UNDOUBTEDLY GET PERMISSION TO USE THEM!
I SUGGEST WE EXHIBIT THEM IN A PUBLIC MUSEUM! LET ME EXPLAIN WHY!
GOSH, THAT'LL BOIN THE BARRACUDA UP! HE WANTED THEM FOR HIS PRIVATE MUSEUM!
THAT IN ITSELF IS REASON ENOUGH!
WHICH EXPLAINS, READER, WHY IT IS THAT SOME TIME LATER AN INTENTLY INTERESTED AUDIENCE LISTENS TO A SKETCHY AND SOMEWHAT INACCURATE VERSION OF THE STORY YOU HAVE JUST READ...
SO YOU SEE, LADIES AND GENTLEMEN, THE SEVEN SOLDIERS OF VICTORY OUTWITTED THE BARRACUDA AT EVERY TURN! I'LL BET THAT MASTER THUG IS HIDING HIS FACE IN SHAME...
WITH STARTLING SUDDENNESS...
THAT'S WHAT YOU THINK, FOOL! I'VE LISTENED TO YOUR STORY LONG ENOUGH... MY MEN HAVE HAD TIME BY NOW TO TAKE THEIR PLACES! AND I AM GOING TO TAKE THOSE TROPHIES!
HA, HA! THANKS TO THOSE CONCEITED LEGIONNAIRES, I HAVE WHAT I WANTED AFTER ALL! AND WITH MY MEN GUARDING ALL THE EXITS, THE POLICE ARE POWERLESS!
1

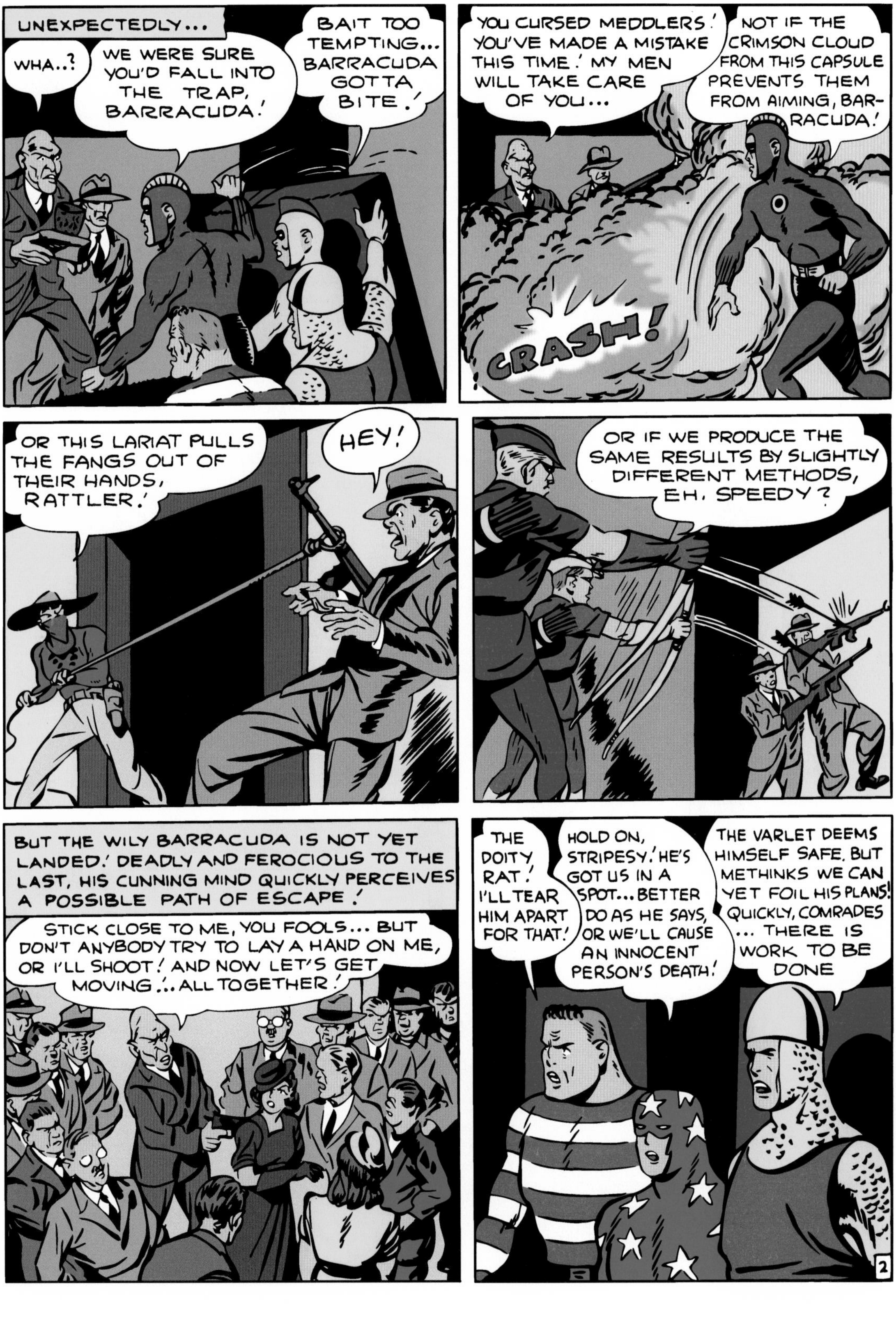
UNEXPECTEDLY...
WHA..?
WE WERE SURE YOU'D FALL INTO THE TRAP, BARRACUDA!
BAIT TOO TEMPTING... BARRACUDA GOTTA BITE!
YOU CURSED MEDDLERS! YOU'VE MADE A MISTAKE THIS TIME! MY MEN WILL TAKE CARE OF YOU...
NOT IF THE CRIMSON CLOUD FROM THIS CAPSULE PREVENTS THEM FROM AIMING, BAR-RACUDA!
CRASH!
OR THIS LARIAT PULLS THE FANGS OUT OF THEIR HANDS, RATTLER!
HEY!
OR IF WE PRODUCE THE SAME RESULTS BY SLIGHTLY DIFFERENT METHODS, EH, SPEEDY?
BUT THE WILY BARRACUDA IS NOT YET LANDED! DEADLY AND FEROCIOUS TO THE LAST, HIS CUNNING MIND QUICKLY PERCEIVES A POSSIBLE PATH OF ESCAPE!
STICK CLOSE TO ME, YOU FOOLS... BUT DON'T ANYBODY TRY TO LAY A HAND ON ME, OR I'LL SHOOT! AND NOW LET'S GET MOVING!.. ALL TOGETHER!
THE DOITY RAT! I'LL TEAR HIM APART FOR THAT!
HOLD ON, STRIPESY! HE'S GOT US IN A SPOT... BETTER DO AS HE SAYS, OR WE'LL CAUSE AN INNOCENT PERSON'S DEATH!
THE VARLET DEEMS HIMSELF SAFE, BUT METHINKS WE CAN YET FOIL HIS PLANS! QUICKLY, COMRADES... THERE IS WORK TO BE DONE
2

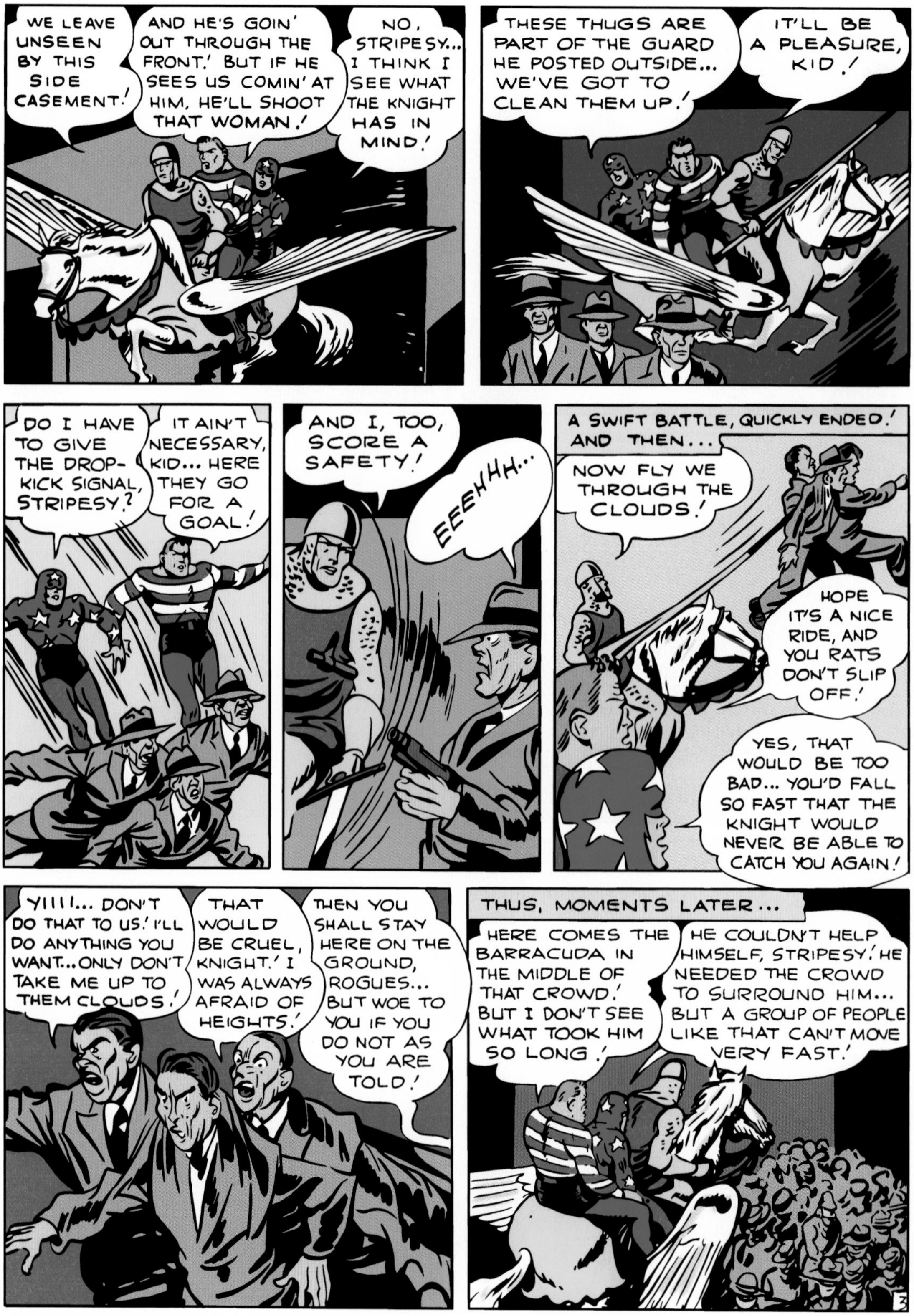
WE LEAVE UNSEEN BY THIS SIDE CASEMENT!
AND HE'S GOIN' OUT THROUGH THE FRONT! BUT IF HE SEES US COMIN' AT HIM, HE'LL SHOOT THAT WOMAN!
NO, STRIPESY... I THINK I SEE WHAT THE KNIGHT HAS IN MIND!
THESE THUGS ARE PART OF THE GUARD HE POSTED OUTSIDE... WE'VE GOT TO CLEAN THEM UP!
IT'LL BE A PLEASURE, KID!
DO I HAVE TO GIVE THE DROP-KICK SIGNAL, STRIPESY?
IT AIN'T NECESSARY, KID... HERE THEY GO FOR A GOAL!
AND I, TOO, SCORE A SAFETY!
EEEHHH...
A SWIFT BATTLE, QUICKLY ENDED! AND THEN...
NOW FLY WE THROUGH THE CLOUDS!
HOPE IT'S A NICE RIDE, AND YOU RATS DON'T SLIP OFF!
YES, THAT WOULD BE TOO BAD... YOU'D FALL SO FAST THAT THE KNIGHT WOULD NEVER BE ABLE TO CATCH YOU AGAIN!
YIIII... DON'T DO THAT TO US! I'LL DO ANYTHING YOU WANT... ONLY DON'T TAKE ME UP TO THEM CLOUDS!
THAT WOULD BE CRUEL, KNIGHT! I WAS ALWAYS AFRAID OF HEIGHTS!
THEN YOU SHALL STAY HERE ON THE GROUND, ROGUES... BUT WOE TO YOU IF YOU DO NOT AS YOU ARE TOLD!
THUS, MOMENTS LATER...
HERE COMES THE BARRACUDA IN THE MIDDLE OF THAT CROWD! BUT I DON'T SEE WHAT TOOK HIM SO LONG!
HE COULDN'T HELP HIMSELF, STRIPESY! HE NEEDED THE CROWD TO SURROUND HIM... BUT A GROUP OF PEOPLE LIKE THAT CAN'T MOVE VERY FAST!

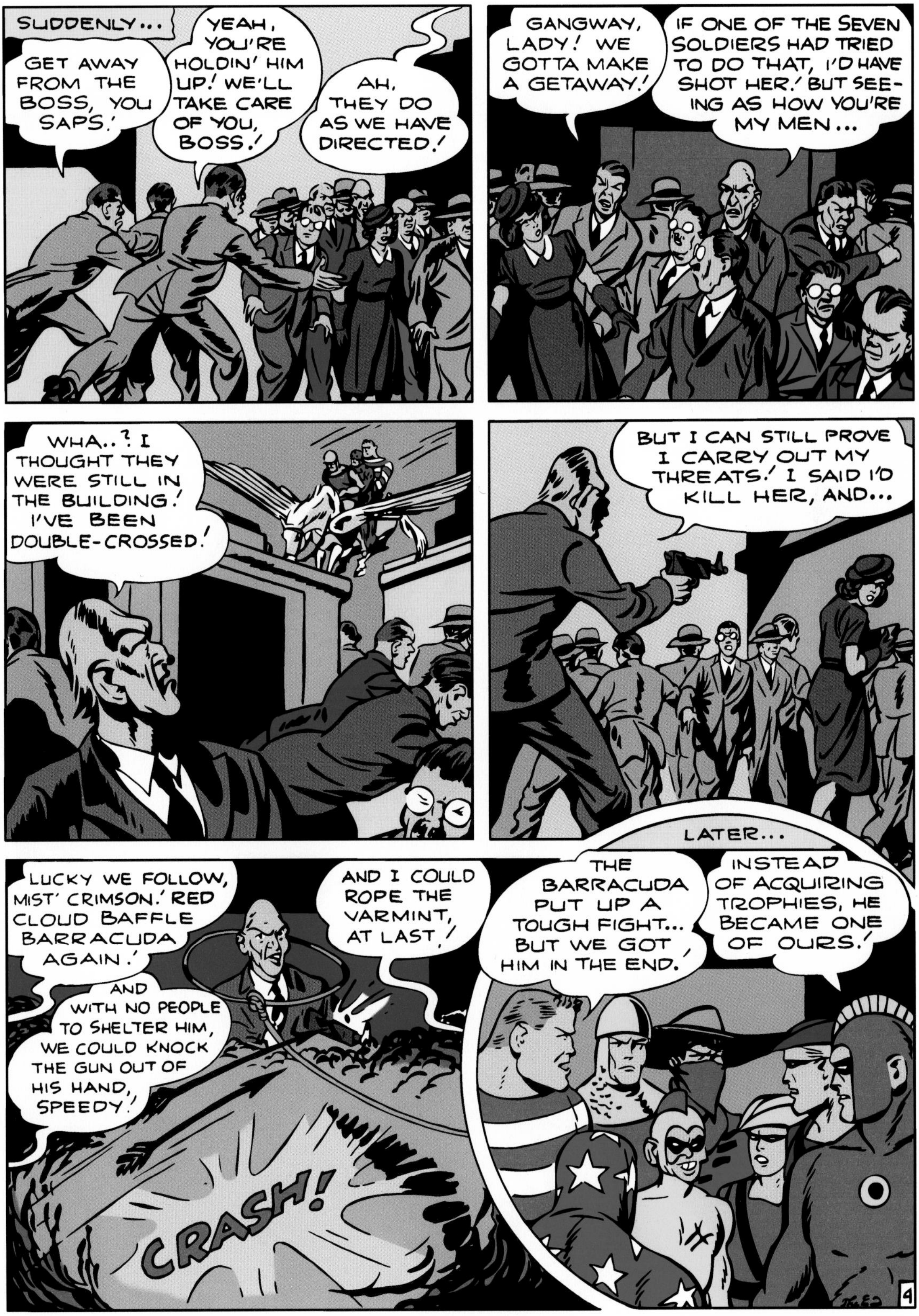
SUDDENLY...
GET AWAY FROM THE BOSS, YOU SAPS!
YEAH, YOU'RE HOLDIN' HIM UP! WE'LL TAKE CARE OF YOU, BOSS!
AH, THEY DO AS WE HAVE DIRECTED!
GANGWAY, LADY! WE GOTTA MAKE A GETAWAY!
IF ONE OF THE SEVEN SOLDIERS HAD TRIED TO DO THAT, I'D HAVE SHOT HER! BUT SEEING AS HOW YOU'RE MY MEN...
WHA..?! I THOUGHT THEY WERE STILL IN THE BUILDING! I'VE BEEN DOUBLE-CROSSED!
BUT I CAN STILL PROVE I CARRY OUT MY THREATS! I SAID I'D KILL HER, AND...
LUCKY WE FOLLOW, MIST' CRIMSON! RED CLOUD BAFFLE BARRACUDA AGAIN!
AND I COULD ROPE THE VARMINT, AT LAST!
AND WITH NO PEOPLE TO SHELTER HIM, WE COULD KNOCK THE GUN OUT OF HIS HAND, SPEEDY!
CRASH!
LATER...
THE BARRACUDA PUT UP A TOUGH FIGHT... BUT WE GOT HIM IN THE END.
INSTEAD OF ACQUIRING TROPHIES, HE BECAME ONE OF OURS!
4

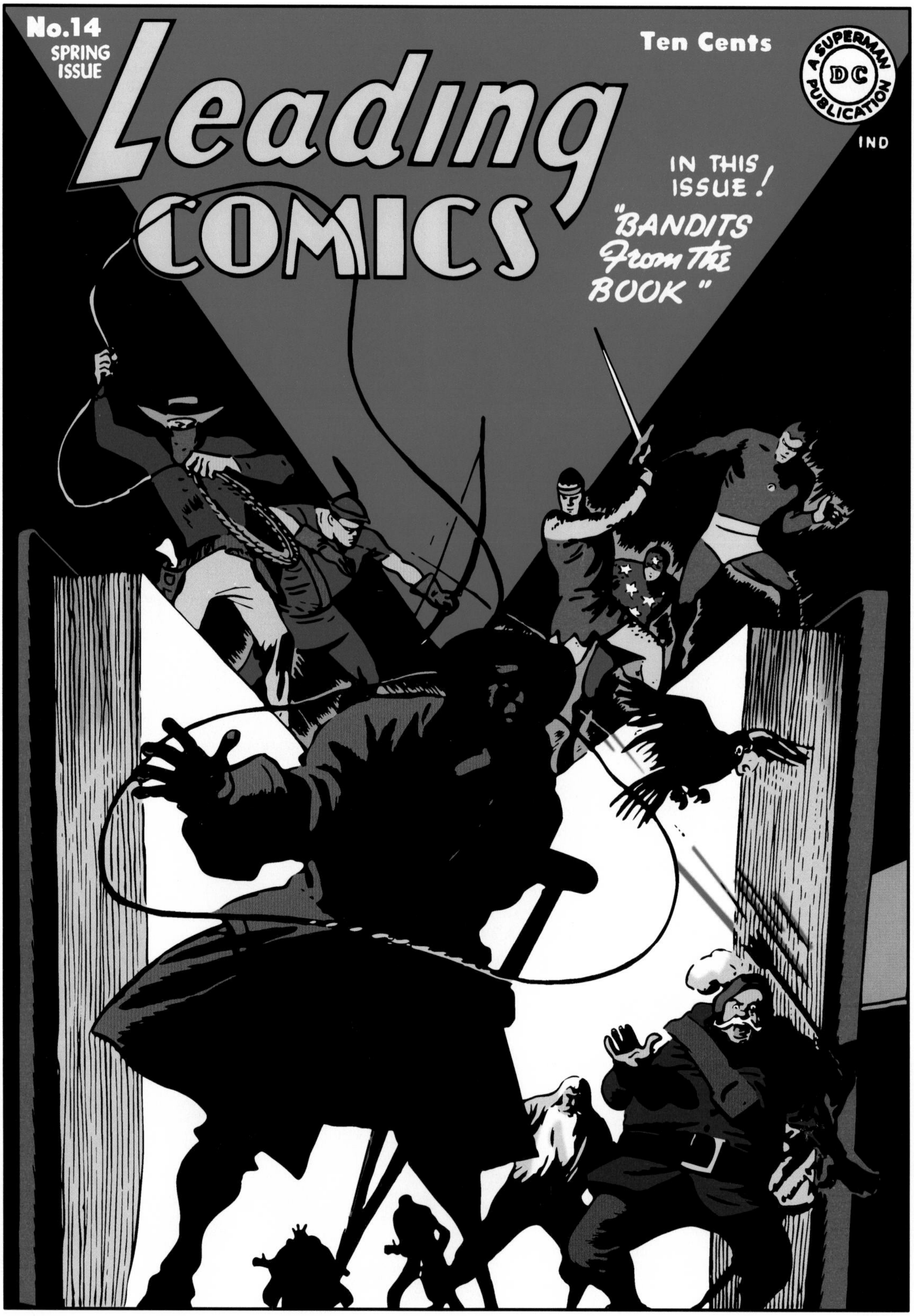
No.14
SPRING ISSUE
Leading
COMICS
Ten Cents
A SUPERMAN DC PUBLICATION
IND
IN THIS ISSUE!
"BANDITS From The BOOK"

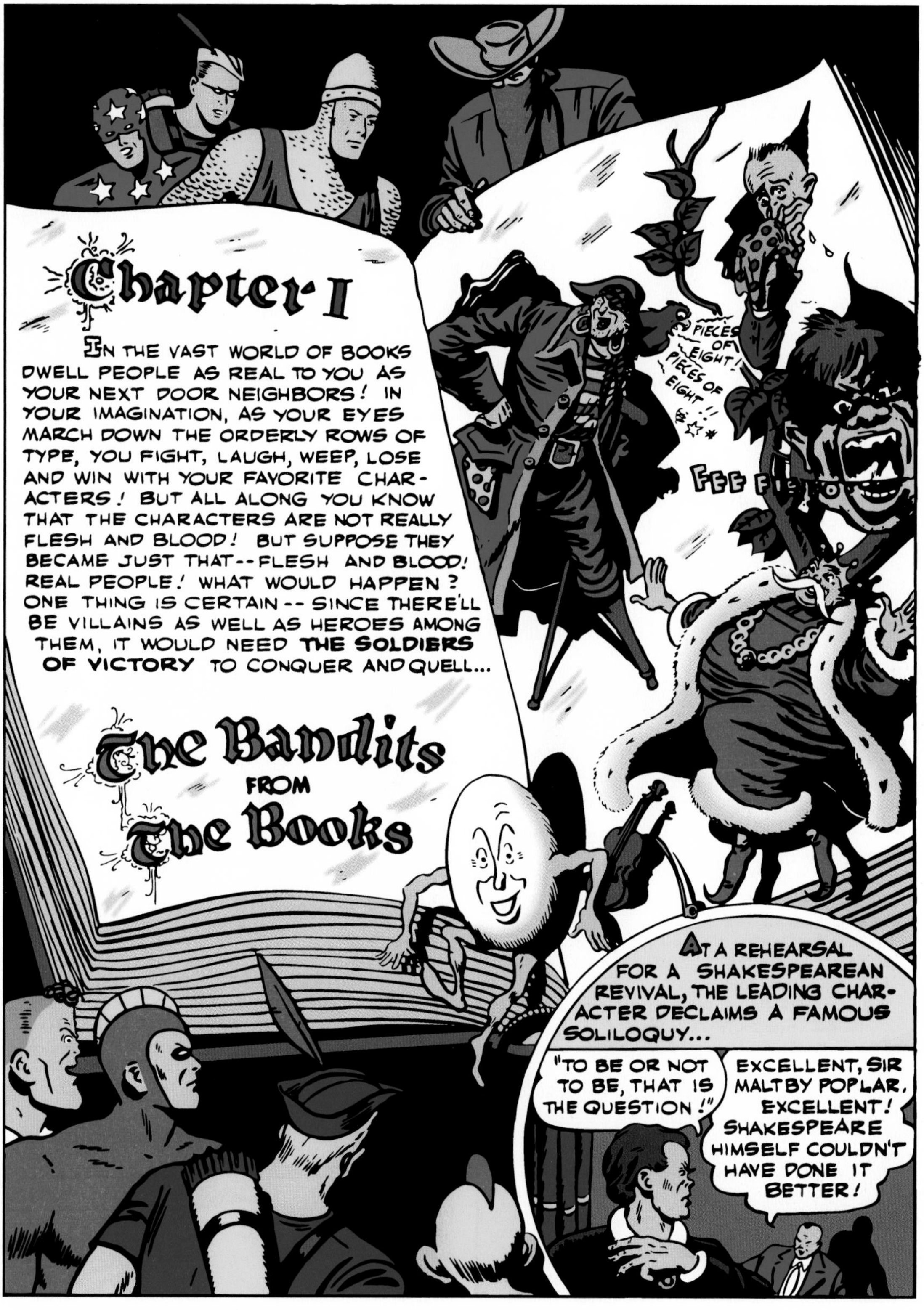
Chapter I
IN THE VAST WORLD OF BOOKS DWELL PEOPLE AS REAL TO YOU AS YOUR NEXT DOOR NEIGHBORS! IN YOUR IMAGINATION, AS YOUR EYES MARCH DOWN THE ORDERLY ROWS OF TYPE, YOU FIGHT, LAUGH, WEEP, LOSE AND WIN WITH YOUR FAVORITE CHARACTERS! BUT ALL ALONG YOU KNOW THAT THE CHARACTERS ARE NOT REALLY FLESH AND BLOOD! BUT SUPPOSE THEY BECAME JUST THAT--FLESH AND BLOOD! REAL PEOPLE! WHAT WOULD HAPPEN? ONE THING IS CERTAIN -- SINCE THERE'LL BE VILLAINS AS WELL AS HEROES AMONG THEM, IT WOULD NEED THE SOLDIERS OF VICTORY TO CONQUER AND QUELL...
The Bandits from The Books
PIECES OF EIGHT! PIECES OF EIGHT!!
FEE FI FO
AT A REHEARSAL FOR A SHAKESPEAREAN REVIVAL, THE LEADING CHARACTER DECLAIMS A FAMOUS SOLILOQUY...
"TO BE OR NOT TO BE, THAT IS THE QUESTION!"
EXCELLENT, SIR MALTBY POPLAR. EXCELLENT! SHAKESPEARE HIMSELF COULDN'T HAVE DONE IT BETTER!

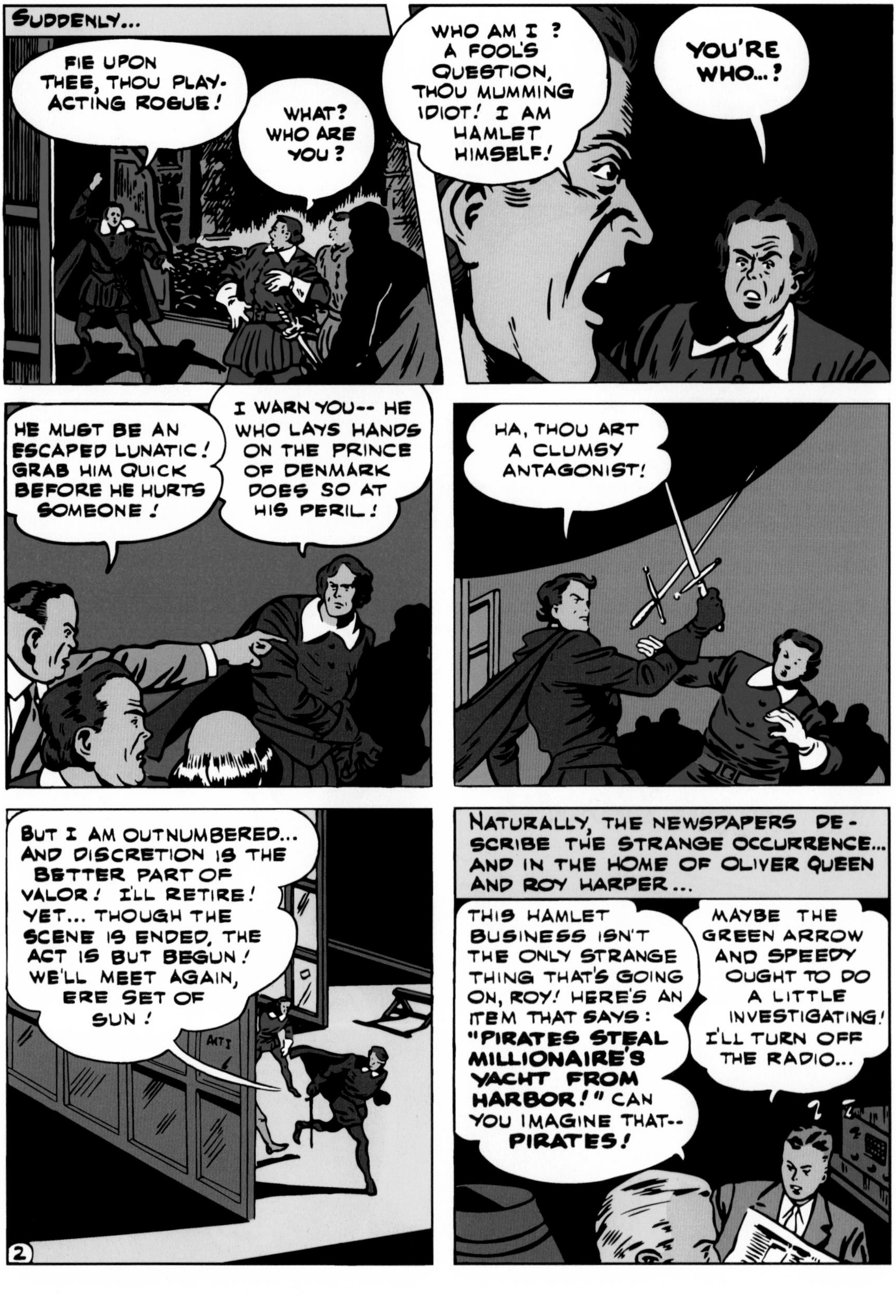
SUDDENLY...
FIE UPON THEE, THOU PLAY-ACTING ROGUE!
WHAT? WHO ARE YOU?
WHO AM I ? A FOOL'S QUESTION, THOU MUMMING IDIOT! I AM HAMLET HIMSELF!
YOU'RE WHO...?
HE MUST BE AN ESCAPED LUNATIC! GRAB HIM QUICK BEFORE HE HURTS SOMEONE!
I WARN YOU-- HE WHO LAYS HANDS ON THE PRINCE OF DENMARK DOES SO AT HIS PERIL!
HA, THOU ART A CLUMSY ANTAGONIST!
BUT I AM OUTNUMBERED... AND DISCRETION IS THE BETTER PART OF VALOR! I'LL RETIRE! YET... THOUGH THE SCENE IS ENDED, THE ACT IS BUT BEGUN! WE'LL MEET AGAIN, ERE SET OF SUN!
2
NATURALLY, THE NEWSPAPERS DE-SCRIBE THE STRANGE OCCURRENCE... AND IN THE HOME OF OLIVER QUEEN AND ROY HARPER...
THIS HAMLET BUSINESS ISN'T THE ONLY STRANGE THING THAT'S GOING ON, ROY! HERE'S AN ITEM THAT SAYS: "PIRATES STEAL MILLIONAIRE'S YACHT FROM HARBOR!" CAN YOU IMAGINE THAT-- PIRATES!
MAYBE THE GREEN ARROW AND SPEEDY OUGHT TO DO A LITTLE INVESTIGATING! I'LL TURN OFF THE RADIO...

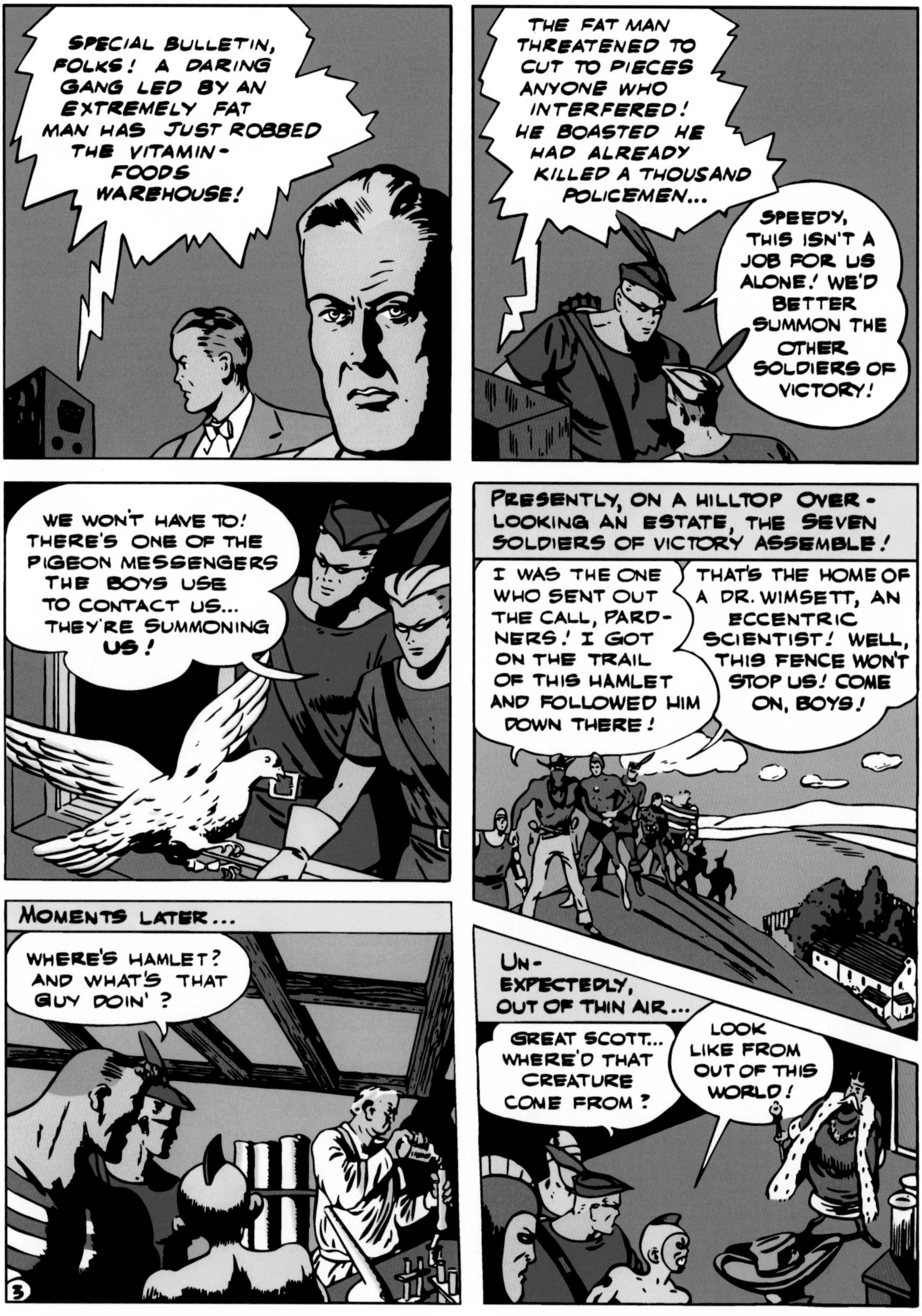
SPECIAL BULLETIN, FOLKS! A DARING GANG LED BY AN EXTREMELY FAT MAN HAS JUST ROBBED THE VITAMIN-FOODS WAREHOUSE!
THE FAT MAN THREATENED TO CUT TO PIECES ANYONE WHO INTERFERED! HE BOASTED HE HAD ALREADY KILLED A THOUSAND POLICEMEN...
SPEEDY, THIS ISN'T A JOB FOR US ALONE! WE'D BETTER SUMMON THE OTHER SOLDIERS OF VICTORY!
WE WON'T HAVE TO! THERE'S ONE OF THE PIGEON MESSENGERS THE BOYS USE TO CONTACT US... THEY'RE SUMMONING US!
PRESENTLY, ON A HILLTOP OVER-LOOKING AN ESTATE, THE SEVEN SOLDIERS OF VICTORY ASSEMBLE!
I WAS THE ONE WHO SENT OUT THE CALL, PARD-NERS! I GOT ON THE TRAIL OF THIS HAMLET AND FOLLOWED HIM DOWN THERE!
THAT'S THE HOME OF A DR. WIMSETT, AN ECCENTRIC SCIENTIST! WELL, THIS FENCE WON'T STOP US! COME ON, BOYS!
MOMENTS LATER...
WHERE'S HAMLET? AND WHAT'S THAT GUY DOIN'?
3
UN-EXPECTEDLY, OUT OF THIN AIR...
GREAT SCOTT... WHERE'D THAT CREATURE COME FROM?
LOOK LIKE FROM OUT OF THIS WORLD!

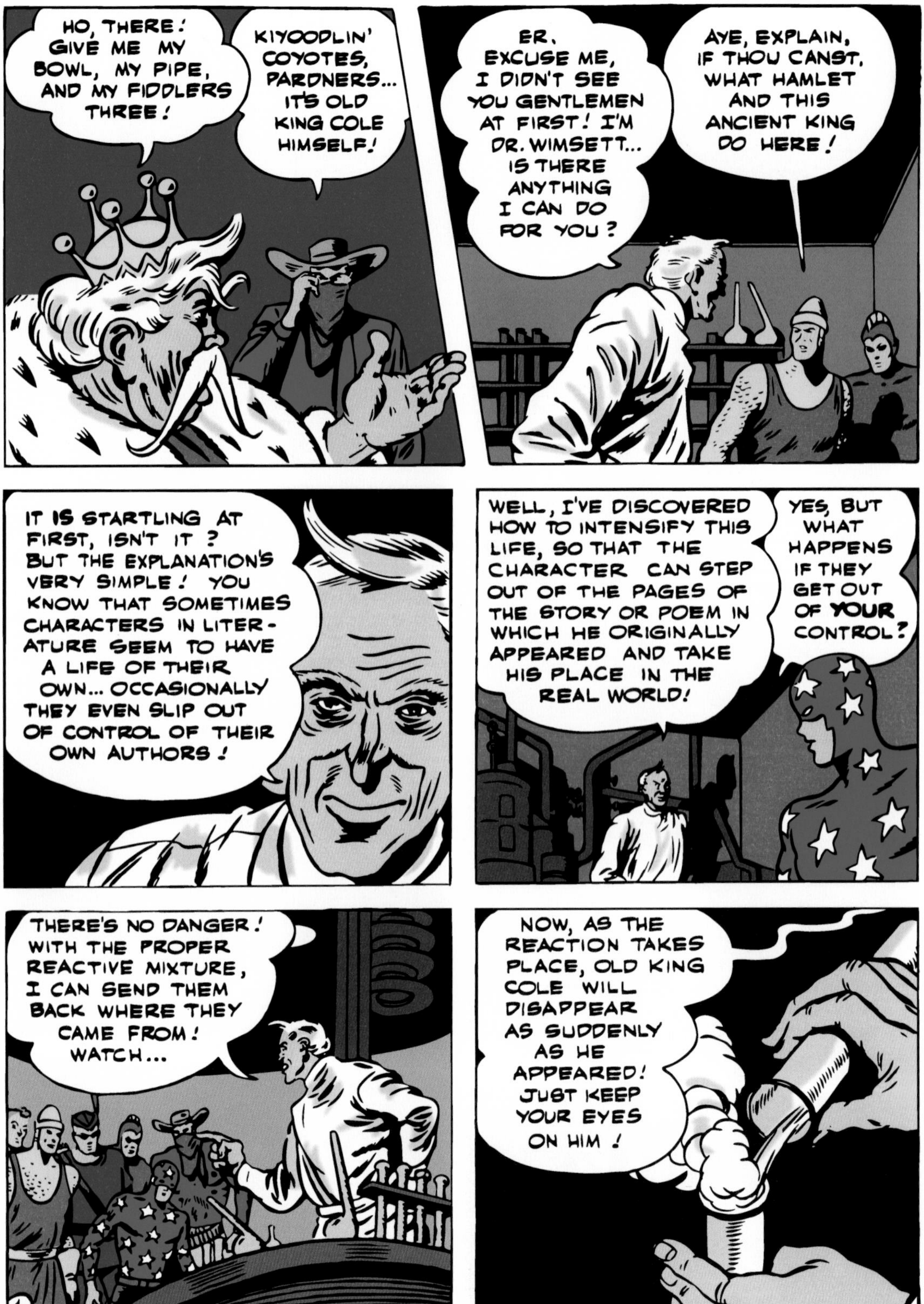
HO, THERE! GIVE ME MY BOWL, MY PIPE, AND MY FIDDLERS THREE!
KIYOODLIN' COYOTES, PARDNERS... IT'S OLD KING COLE HIMSELF!
ER. EXCUSE ME, I DIDN'T SEE YOU GENTLEMEN AT FIRST! I'M DR. WIMSETT... IS THERE ANYTHING I CAN DO FOR YOU?
AYE, EXPLAIN, IF THOU CANST, WHAT HAMLET AND THIS ANCIENT KING DO HERE!
IT IS STARTLING AT FIRST, ISN'T IT? BUT THE EXPLANATION'S VERY SIMPLE! YOU KNOW THAT SOMETIMES CHARACTERS IN LITER-ATURE SEEM TO HAVE A LIFE OF THEIR OWN... OCCASIONALLY THEY EVEN SLIP OUT OF CONTROL OF THEIR OWN AUTHORS!
WELL, I'VE DISCOVERED HOW TO INTENSIFY THIS LIFE, SO THAT THE CHARACTER CAN STEP OUT OF THE PAGES OF THE STORY OR POEM IN WHICH HE ORIGINALLY APPEARED AND TAKE HIS PLACE IN THE REAL WORLD!
YES, BUT WHAT HAPPENS IF THEY GET OUT OF YOUR CONTROL?
THERE'S NO DANGER! WITH THE PROPER REACTIVE MIXTURE, I CAN SEND THEM BACK WHERE THEY CAME FROM! WATCH...
4
NOW, AS THE REACTION TAKES PLACE, OLD KING COLE WILL DISAPPEAR AS SUDDENLY AS HE APPEARED! JUST KEEP YOUR EYES ON HIM!

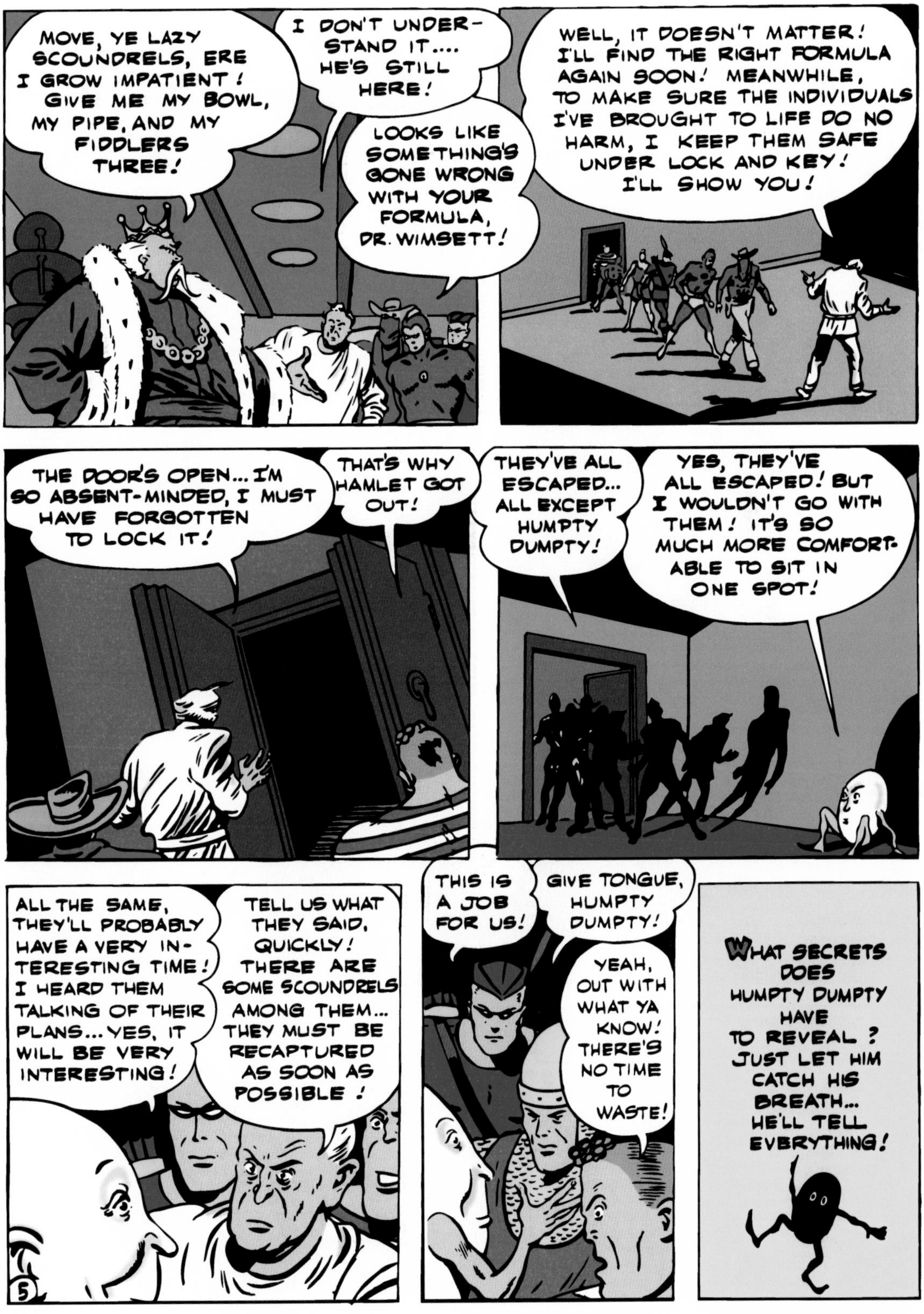
MOVE, YE LAZY SCOUNDRELS, ERE I GROW IMPATIENT! GIVE ME MY BOWL, MY PIPE, AND MY FIDDLERS THREE!
I DON'T UNDER-STAND IT.... HE'S STILL HERE!
LOOKS LIKE SOMETHING'S GONE WRONG WITH YOUR FORMULA, DR. WIMSETT!
WELL, IT DOESN'T MATTER! I'LL FIND THE RIGHT FORMULA AGAIN SOON! MEANWHILE, TO MAKE SURE THE INDIVIDUALS I'VE BROUGHT TO LIFE DO NO HARM, I KEEP THEM SAFE UNDER LOCK AND KEY! I'LL SHOW YOU!
THE DOOR'S OPEN... I'M SO ABSENT-MINDED, I MUST HAVE FORGOTTEN TO LOCK IT!
THAT'S WHY HAMLET GOT OUT!
THEY'VE ALL ESCAPED... ALL EXCEPT HUMPTY DUMPTY!
YES, THEY'VE ALL ESCAPED! BUT I WOULDN'T GO WITH THEM! IT'S SO MUCH MORE COMFORT-ABLE TO SIT IN ONE SPOT!
ALL THE SAME, THEY'LL PROBABLY HAVE A VERY IN-TERESTING TIME! I HEARD THEM TALKING OF THEIR PLANS... YES, IT WILL BE VERY INTERESTING!
TELL US WHAT THEY SAID, QUICKLY! THERE ARE SOME SCOUNDRELS AMONG THEM... THEY MUST BE RECAPTURED AS SOON AS POSSIBLE!
5
THIS IS A JOB FOR US!
GIVE TONGUE, HUMPTY DUMPTY!
YEAH, OUT WITH WHAT YA KNOW! THERE'S NO TIME TO WASTE!
WHAT SECRETS DOES HUMPTY DUMPTY HAVE TO REVEAL? JUST LET HIM CATCH HIS BREATH... HE'LL TELL EVERYTHING!

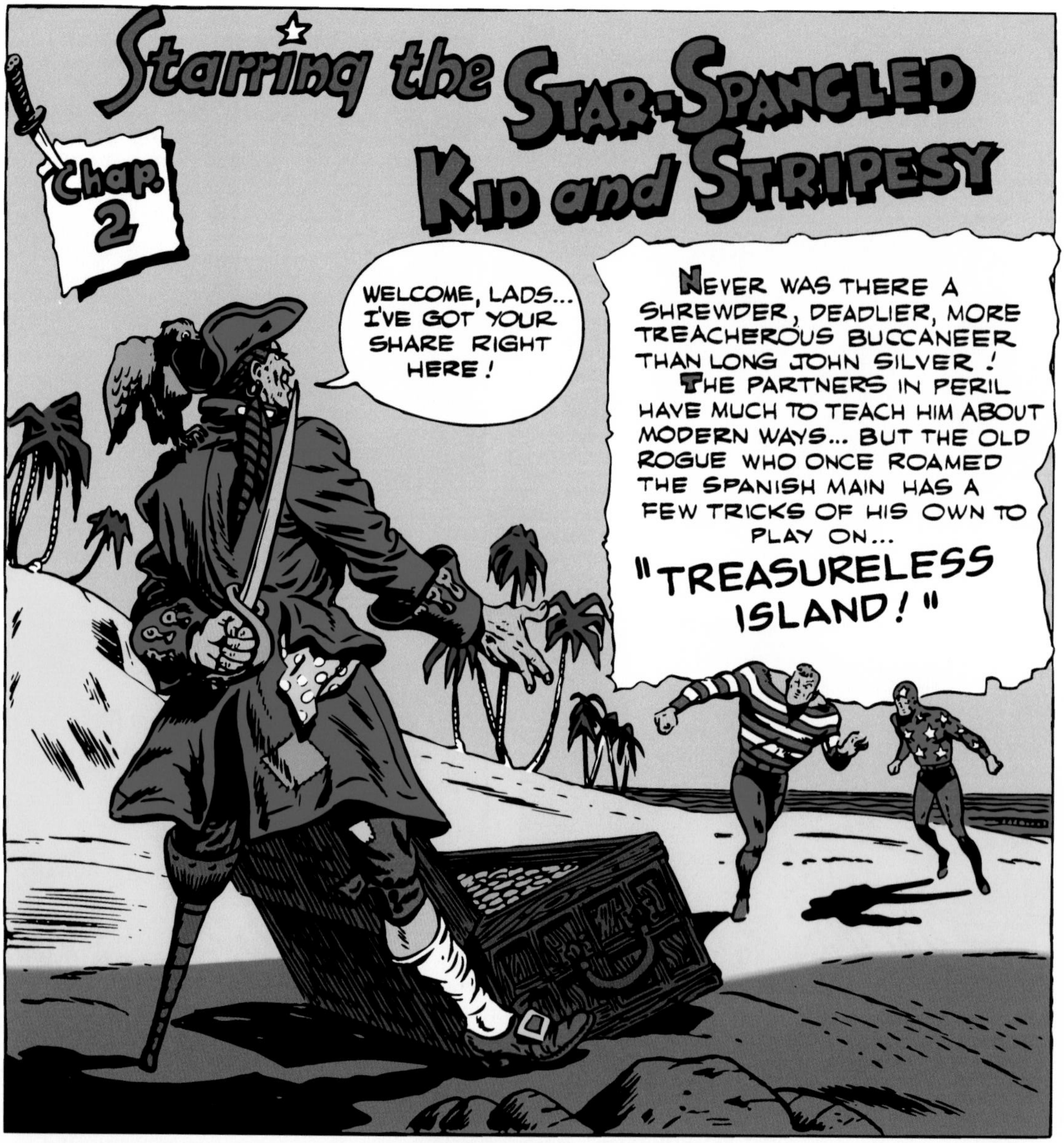
Starring the STAR-SPANGLED KID and STRIPESY
Chap. 2
WELCOME, LADS... I'VE GOT YOUR SHARE RIGHT HERE!
NEVER WAS THERE A SHREWDER, DEADLIER, MORE TREACHEROUS BUCCANEER THAN LONG JOHN SILVER! THE PARTNERS IN PERIL HAVE MUCH TO TEACH HIM ABOUT MODERN WAYS... BUT THE OLD ROGUE WHO ONCE ROAMED THE SPANISH MAIN HAS A FEW TRICKS OF HIS OWN TO PLAY ON...
"TREASURELESS ISLAND!"

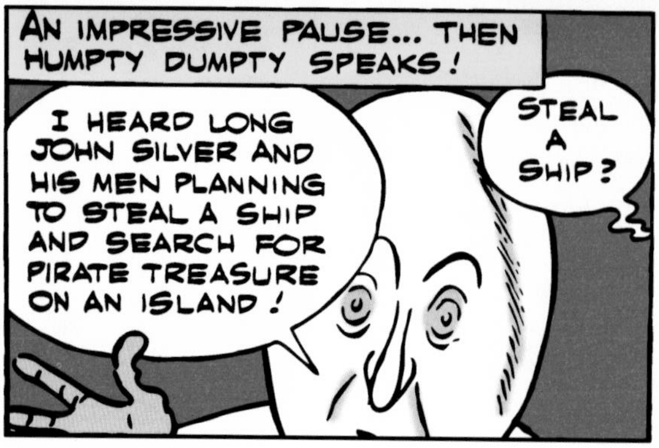
AN IMPRESSIVE PAUSE... THEN HUMPTY DUMPTY SPEAKS!
I HEARD LONG JOHN SILVER AND HIS MEN PLANNING TO STEAL A SHIP AND SEARCH FOR PIRATE TREASURE ON AN ISLAND!
STEAL A SHIP?

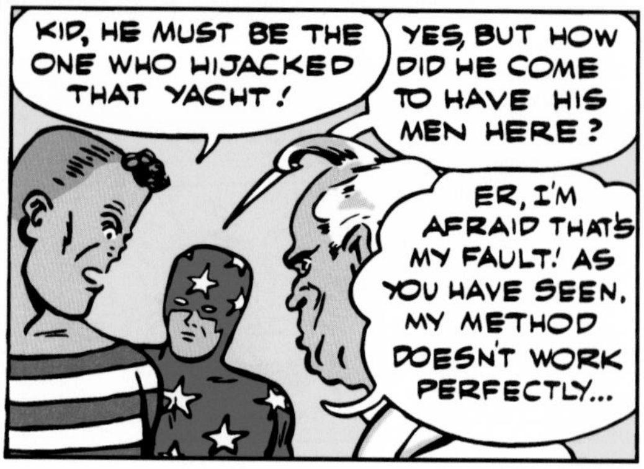
KID, HE MUST BE THE ONE WHO HIJACKED THAT YACHT!
YES, BUT HOW DID HE COME TO HAVE HIS MEN HERE?
ER, I'M AFRAID THAT'S MY FAULT! AS YOU HAVE SEEN, MY METHOD DOESN'T WORK PERFECTLY...

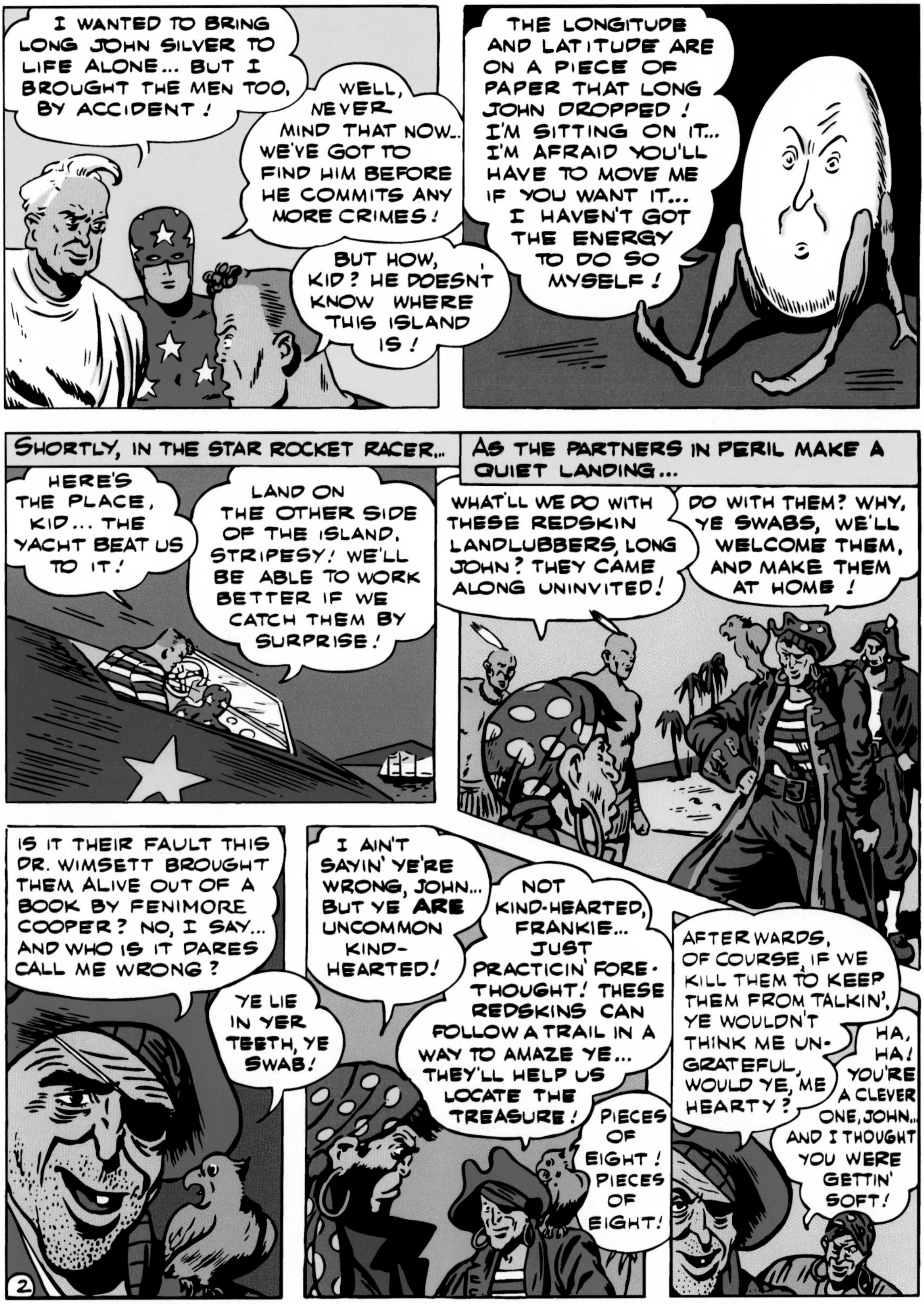
I WANTED TO BRING LONG JOHN SILVER TO LIFE ALONE... BUT I BROUGHT THE MEN TOO, BY ACCIDENT!
WELL, NEVER MIND THAT NOW... WE'VE GOT TO FIND HIM BEFORE HE COMMITS ANY MORE CRIMES!
BUT HOW, KID? HE DOESN'T KNOW WHERE THIS ISLAND IS!
THE LONGITUDE AND LATITUDE ARE ON A PIECE OF PAPER THAT LONG JOHN DROPPED! I'M SITTING ON IT... I'M AFRAID YOU'LL HAVE TO MOVE ME IF YOU WANT IT... I HAVEN'T GOT THE ENERGY TO DO SO MYSELF!
SHORTLY, IN THE STAR ROCKET RACER...
HERE'S THE PLACE, KID... THE YACHT BEAT US TO IT!
LAND ON THE OTHER SIDE OF THE ISLAND, STRIPESY! WE'LL BE ABLE TO WORK BETTER IF WE CATCH THEM BY SURPRISE!
AS THE PARTNERS IN PERIL MAKE A QUIET LANDING...
WHAT'LL WE DO WITH THESE REDSKIN LANDLUBBERS, LONG JOHN? THEY CAME ALONG UNINVITED!
DO WITH THEM? WHY, YE SWABS, WE'LL WELCOME THEM, AND MAKE THEM AT HOME!
IS IT THEIR FAULT THIS DR. WIMSETT BROUGHT THEM ALIVE OUT OF A BOOK BY FENIMORE COOPER? NO, I SAY... AND WHO IS IT DARES CALL ME WRONG?
YE LIE IN YER TEETH, YE SWAB!
2
I AIN'T SAYIN' YE'RE WRONG, JOHN... BUT YE ARE UNCOMMON KIND-HEARTED!
NOT KIND-HEARTED, FRANKIE... JUST PRACTICIN' FORE-THOUGHT! THESE REDSKINS CAN FOLLOW A TRAIL IN A WAY TO AMAZE YE... THEY'LL HELP US LOCATE THE TREASURE!
PIECES OF EIGHT! PIECES OF EIGHT!
AFTERWARDS, OF COURSE, IF WE KILL THEM TO KEEP THEM FROM TALKIN', YE WOULDN'T THINK ME UN-GRATEFUL, WOULD YE, ME HEARTY?
HA, HA! YOU'RE A CLEVER ONE, JOHN... AND I THOUGHT YOU WERE GETTIN' SOFT!

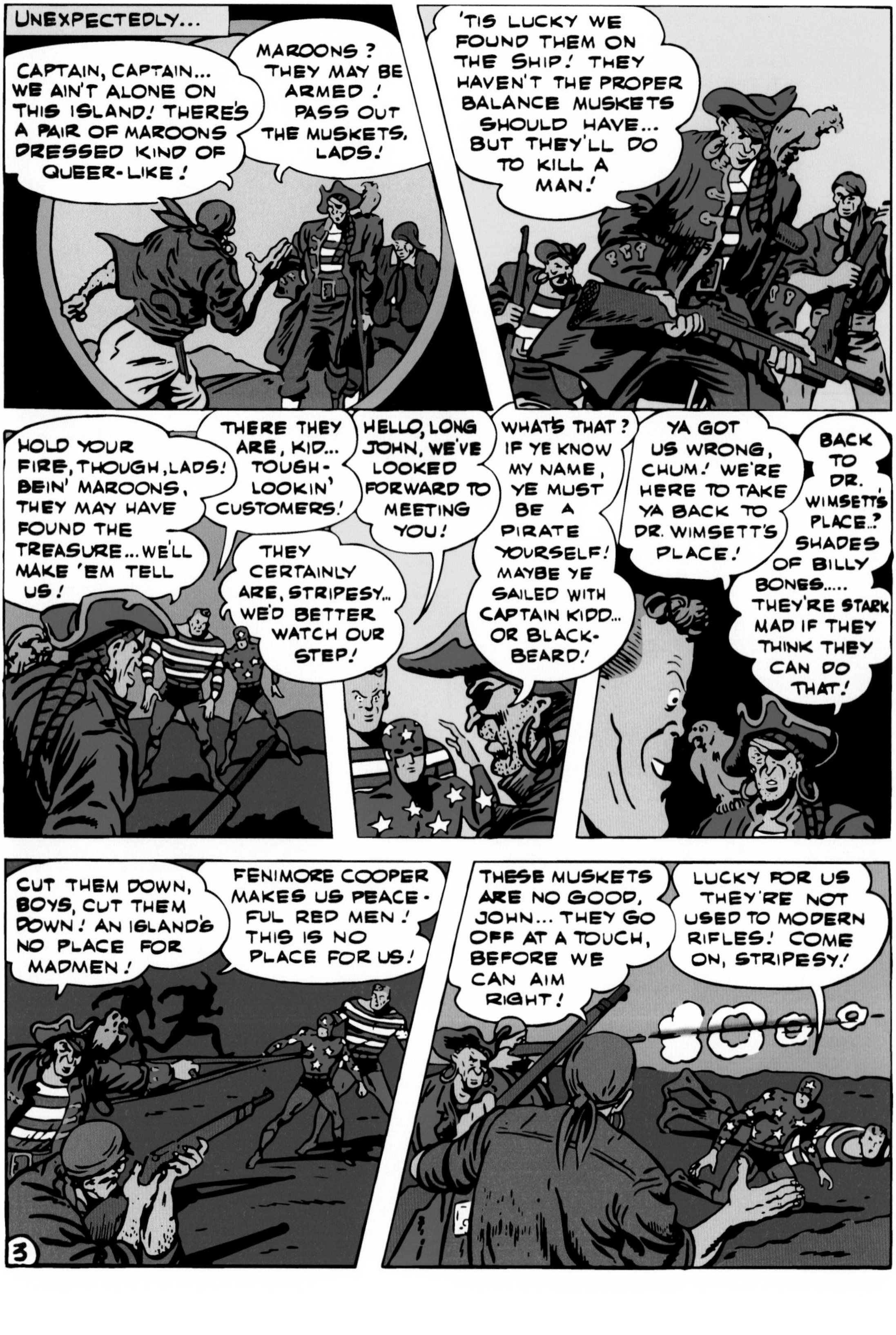
UNEXPECTEDLY...
CAPTAIN, CAPTAIN... WE AIN'T ALONE ON THIS ISLAND! THERE'S A PAIR OF MAROONS DRESSED KIND OF QUEER-LIKE!
MAROONS? THEY MAY BE ARMED! PASS OUT THE MUSKETS, LADS!
'TIS LUCKY WE FOUND THEM ON THE SHIP! THEY HAVEN'T THE PROPER BALANCE MUSKETS SHOULD HAVE... BUT THEY'LL DO TO KILL A MAN!
HOLD YOUR FIRE, THOUGH, LADS! BEIN' MAROONS, THEY MAY HAVE FOUND THE TREASURE... WE'LL MAKE 'EM TELL US!
THERE THEY ARE, KID... TOUGH-LOOKIN' CUSTOMERS!
THEY CERTAINLY ARE, STRIPESY... WE'D BETTER WATCH OUR STEP!
HELLO, LONG JOHN, WE'VE LOOKED FORWARD TO MEETING YOU!
WHAT'S THAT? IF YE KNOW MY NAME, YE MUST BE A PIRATE YOURSELF! MAYBE YE SAILED WITH CAPTAIN KIDD... OR BLACK-BEARD!
YA GOT US WRONG, CHUM! WE'RE HERE TO TAKE YA BACK TO DR. WIMSETT'S PLACE!
BACK TO DR. WIMSETT'S PLACE..? SHADES OF BILLY BONES..... THEY'RE STARK MAD IF THEY THINK THEY CAN DO THAT!
CUT THEM DOWN, BOYS, CUT THEM DOWN! AN ISLAND'S NO PLACE FOR MADMEN!
FENIMORE COOPER MAKES US PEACE-FUL RED MEN! THIS IS NO PLACE FOR US!
THESE MUSKETS ARE NO GOOD, JOHN... THEY GO OFF AT A TOUCH, BEFORE WE CAN AIM RIGHT!
LUCKY FOR US THEY'RE NOT USED TO MODERN RIFLES! COME ON, STRIPESY!
3

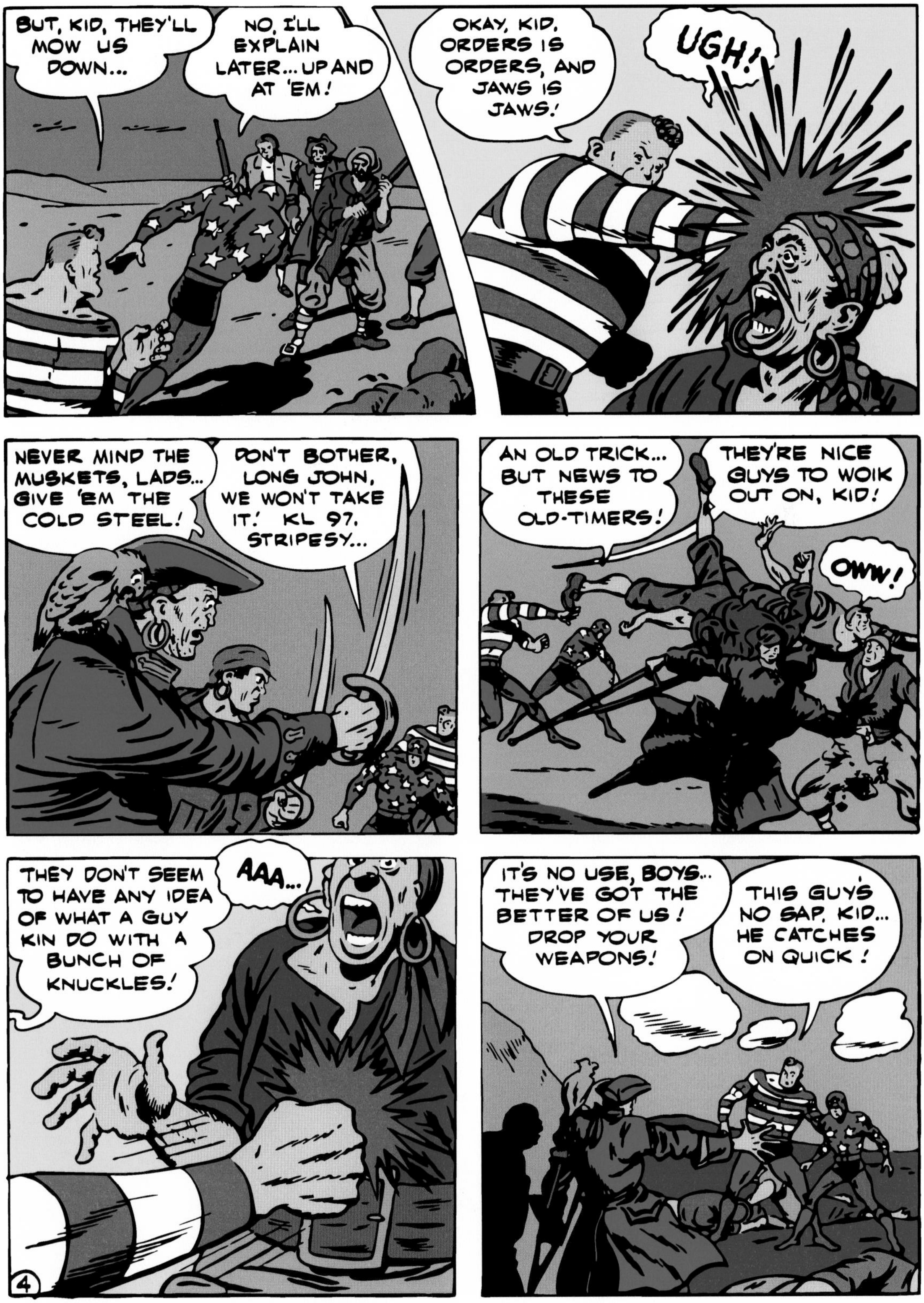
BUT, KID, THEY'LL MOW US DOWN...
NO, I'LL EXPLAIN LATER... UP AND AT 'EM!
OKAY, KID, ORDERS IS ORDERS, AND JAWS IS JAWS!
UGH!
NEVER MIND THE MUSKETS, LADS... GIVE 'EM THE COLD STEEL!
DON'T BOTHER, LONG JOHN, WE WON'T TAKE IT! KL 97, STRIPESY...
AN OLD TRICK... BUT NEWS TO THESE OLD-TIMERS!
THEY'RE NICE GUYS TO WOIK OUT ON, KID!
OWW!
THEY DON'T SEEM TO HAVE ANY IDEA OF WHAT A GUY KIN DO WITH A BUNCH OF KNUCKLES!
AAA...
4
IT'S NO USE, BOYS... THEY'VE GOT THE BETTER OF US! DROP YOUR WEAPONS!
THIS GUY'S NO SAP, KID... HE CATCHES ON QUICK!

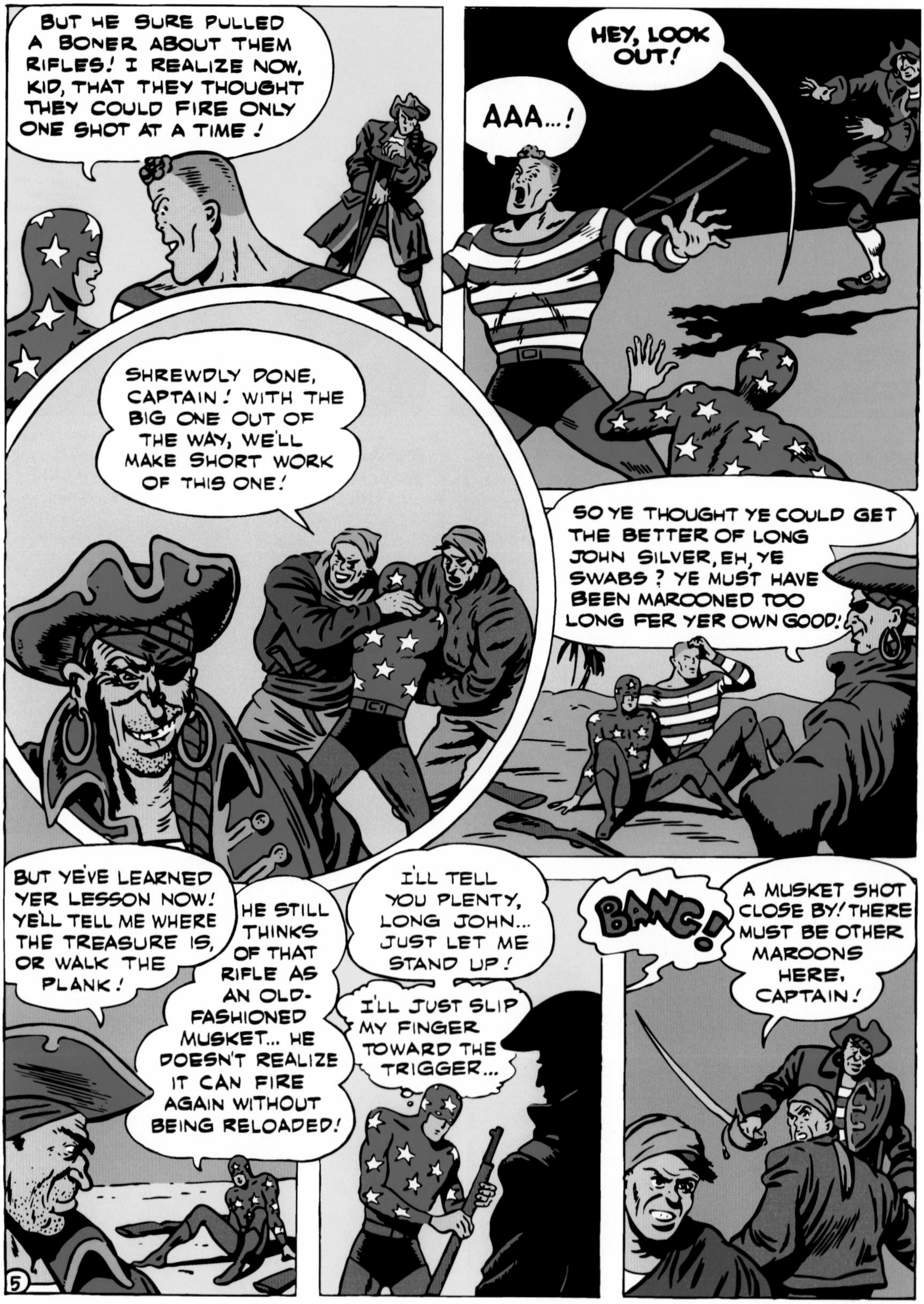
BUT HE SURE PULLED A BONER ABOUT THEM RIFLES! I REALIZE NOW, KID, THAT THEY THOUGHT THEY COULD FIRE ONLY ONE SHOT AT A TIME!
HEY, LOOK OUT!
AAA...!
SHREWDLY DONE, CAPTAIN! WITH THE BIG ONE OUT OF THE WAY, WE'LL MAKE SHORT WORK OF THIS ONE!
SO YE THOUGHT YE COULD GET THE BETTER OF LONG JOHN SILVER, EH, YE SWABS? YE MUST HAVE BEEN MAROONED TOO LONG FER YER OWN GOOD!
BUT YE'VE LEARNED YER LESSON NOW! YE'LL TELL ME WHERE THE TREASURE IS, OR WALK THE PLANK!
HE STILL THINKS OF THAT RIFLE AS AN OLD-FASHIONED MUSKET... HE DOESN'T REALIZE IT CAN FIRE AGAIN WITHOUT BEING RELOADED!
I'LL TELL YOU PLENTY, LONG JOHN... JUST LET ME STAND UP!
I'LL JUST SLIP MY FINGER TOWARD THE TRIGGER...
BANG!
A MUSKET SHOT CLOSE BY! THERE MUST BE OTHER MAROONS HERE, CAPTAIN!
5

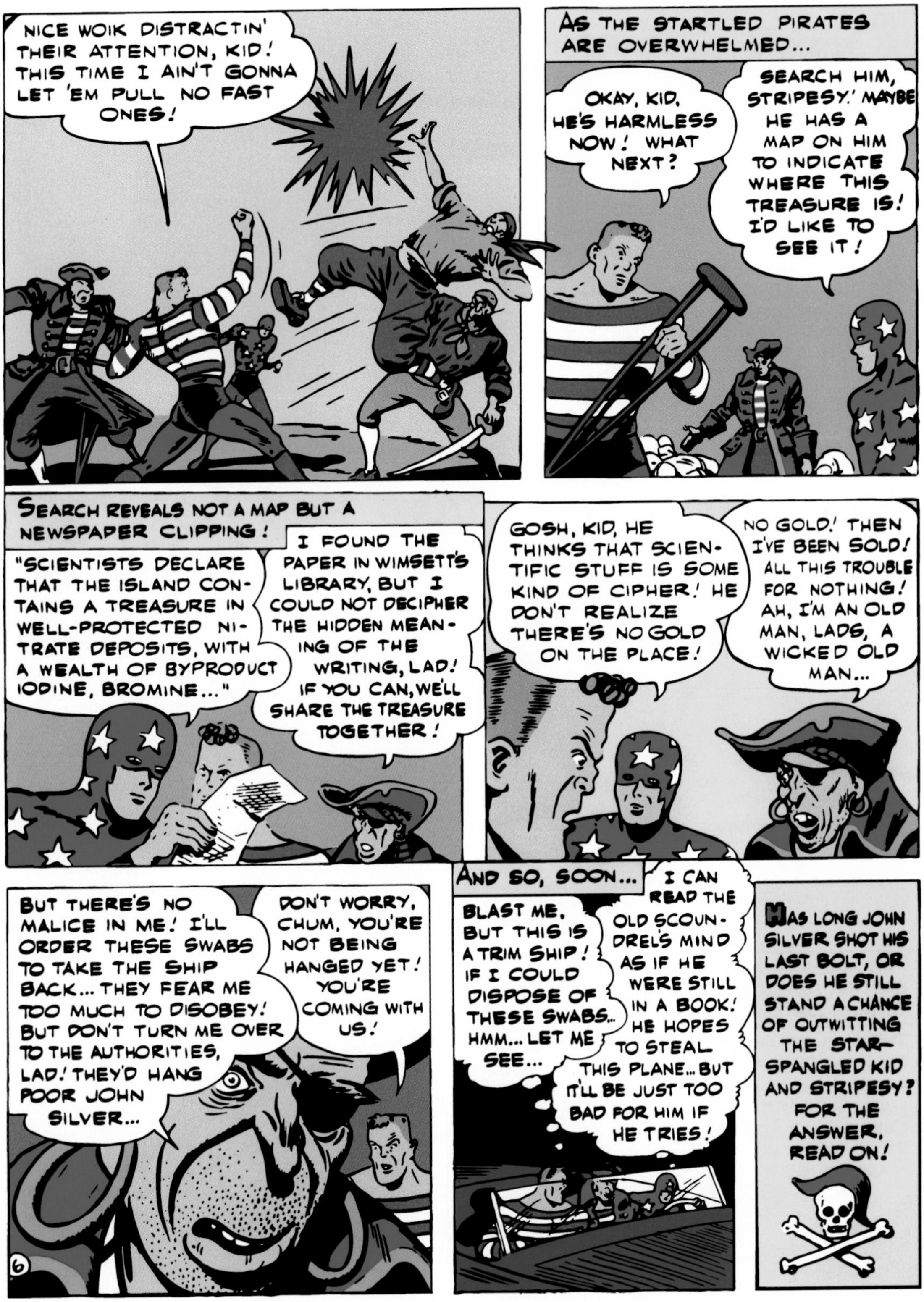
NICE WOIK DISTRACTIN' THEIR ATTENTION, KID! THIS TIME I AIN'T GONNA LET 'EM PULL NO FAST ONES!
AS THE STARTLED PIRATES ARE OVERWHELMED...
OKAY, KID, HE'S HARMLESS NOW! WHAT NEXT?
SEARCH HIM, STRIPESY! MAYBE HE HAS A MAP ON HIM TO INDICATE WHERE THIS TREASURE IS! I'D LIKE TO SEE IT!
SEARCH REVEALS NOT A MAP BUT A NEWSPAPER CLIPPING!
"SCIENTISTS DECLARE THAT THE ISLAND CONTAINS A TREASURE IN WELL-PROTECTED NITRATE DEPOSITS, WITH A WEALTH OF BYPRODUCT IODINE, BROMINE..."
I FOUND THE PAPER IN WIMSETT'S LIBRARY, BUT I COULD NOT DECIPHER THE HIDDEN MEANING OF THE WRITING, LAD! IF YOU CAN, WE'LL SHARE THE TREASURE TOGETHER!
GOSH, KID, HE THINKS THAT SCIENTIFIC STUFF IS SOME KIND OF CIPHER! HE DON'T REALIZE THERE'S NO GOLD ON THE PLACE!
NO GOLD! THEN I'VE BEEN SOLD! ALL THIS TROUBLE FOR NOTHING! AH, I'M AN OLD MAN, LADS, A WICKED OLD MAN...
BUT THERE'S NO MALICE IN ME! I'LL ORDER THESE SWABS TO TAKE THE SHIP BACK... THEY FEAR ME TOO MUCH TO DISOBEY! BUT DON'T TURN ME OVER TO THE AUTHORITIES, LAD! THEY'D HANG POOR JOHN SILVER...
DON'T WORRY, CHUM, YOU'RE NOT BEING HANGED YET! YOU'RE COMING WITH US!
6
AND SO, SOON...
BLAST ME, BUT THIS IS A TRIM SHIP! IF I COULD DISPOSE OF THESE SWABS... HMM... LET ME SEE...
I CAN READ THE OLD SCOUNDREL'S MIND AS IF HE WERE STILL IN A BOOK! HE HOPES TO STEAL THIS PLANE... BUT IT'LL BE JUST TOO BAD FOR HIM IF HE TRIES!
HAS LONG JOHN SILVER SHOT HIS LAST BOLT, OR DOES HE STILL STAND A CHANCE OF OUTWITTING THE STAR-SPANGLED KID AND STRIPESY? FOR THE ANSWER, READ ON!

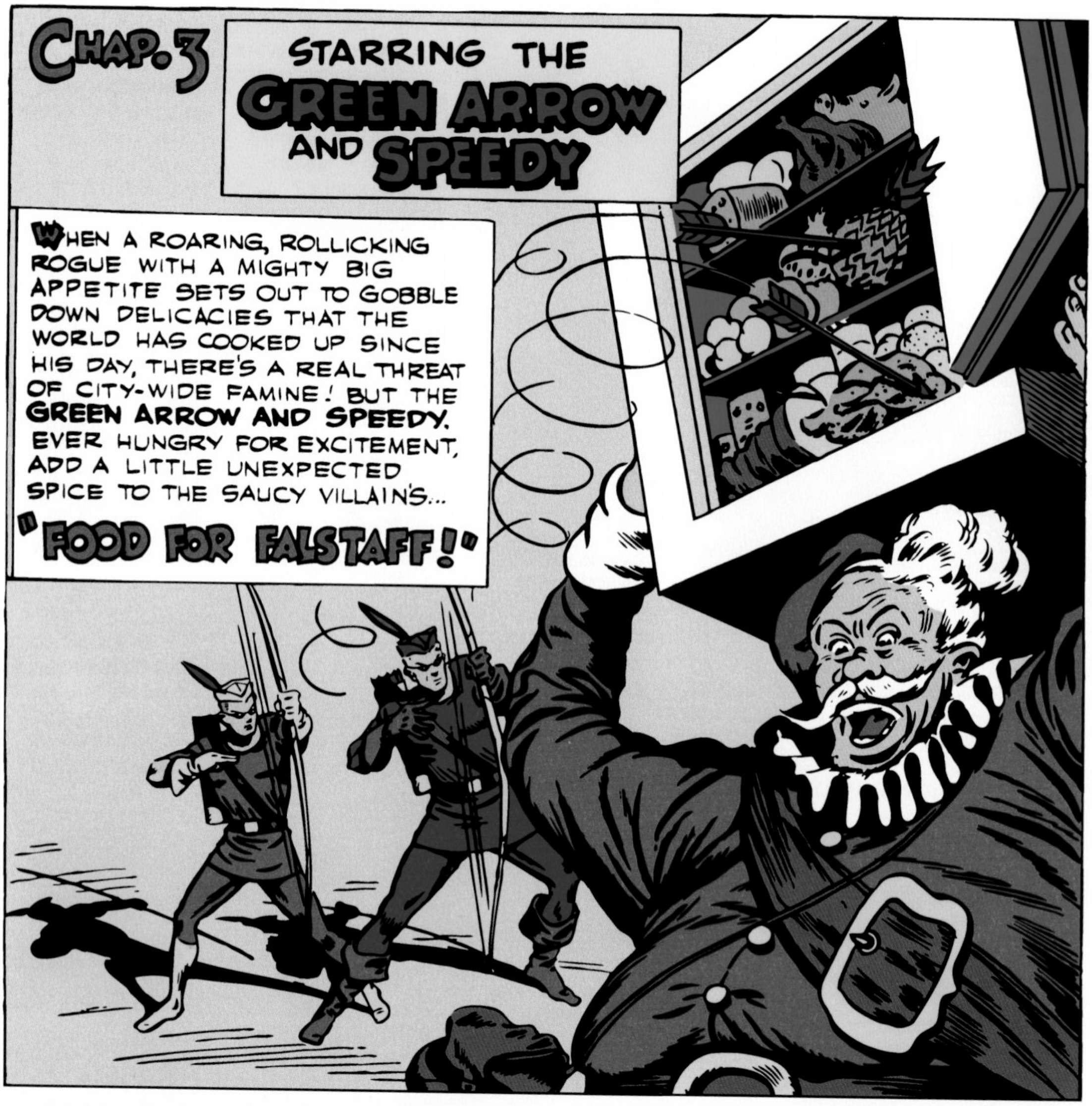
CHAP. 3
STARRING THE GREEN ARROW AND SPEEDY
WHEN A ROARING, ROLLICKING ROGUE WITH A MIGHTY BIG APPETITE SETS OUT TO GOBBLE DOWN DELICACIES THAT THE WORLD HAS COOKED UP SINCE HIS DAY, THERE'S A REAL THREAT OF CITY-WIDE FAMINE! BUT THE GREEN ARROW AND SPEEDY, EVER HUNGRY FOR EXCITEMENT, ADD A LITTLE UNEXPECTED SPICE TO THE SAUCY VILLAIN'S...
"FOOD FOR FALSTAFF!"

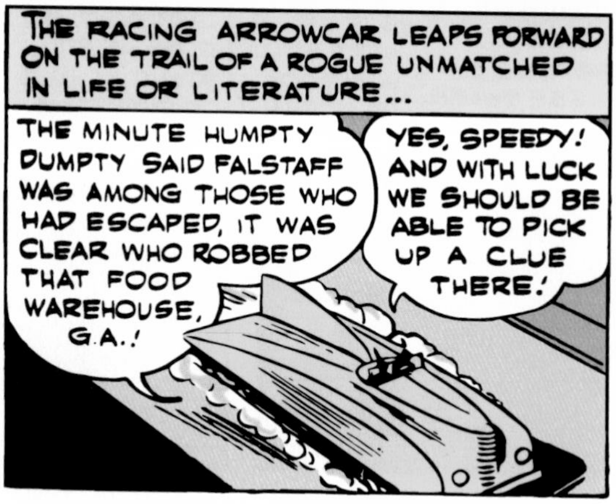
THE RACING ARROWCAR LEAPS FORWARD ON THE TRAIL OF A ROGUE UNMATCHED IN LIFE OR LITERATURE...
THE MINUTE HUMPTY DUMPTY SAID FALSTAFF WAS AMONG THOSE WHO HAD ESCAPED, IT WAS CLEAR WHO ROBBED THAT FOOD WAREHOUSE, G.A.!
YES, SPEEDY! AND WITH LUCK WE SHOULD BE ABLE TO PICK UP A CLUE THERE!

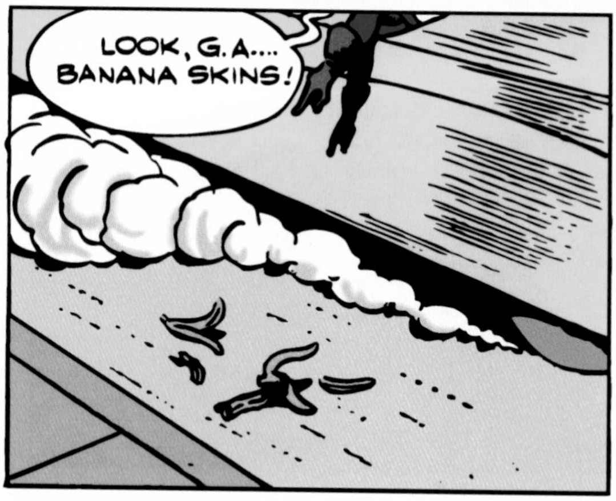
LOOK, G.A.... BANANA SKINS!

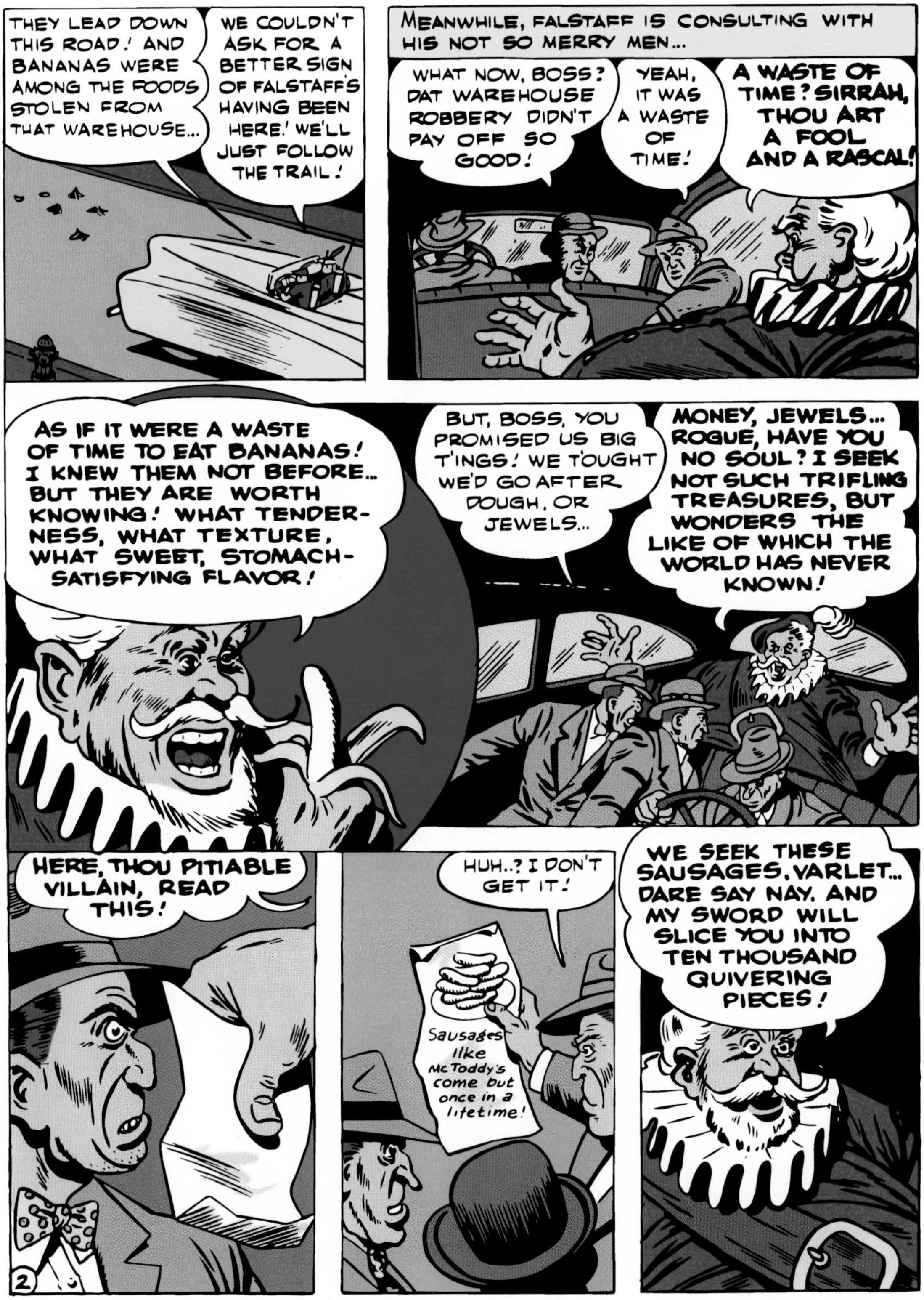
THEY LEAD DOWN THIS ROAD! AND BANANAS WERE AMONG THE FOODS STOLEN FROM THAT WAREHOUSE...
WE COULDN'T ASK FOR A BETTER SIGN OF FALSTAFF'S HAVING BEEN HERE! WE'LL JUST FOLLOW THE TRAIL!
MEANWHILE, FALSTAFF IS CONSULTING WITH HIS NOT SO MERRY MEN...
WHAT NOW, BOSS? DAT WAREHOUSE ROBBERY DIDN'T PAY OFF SO GOOD!
YEAH, IT WAS A WASTE OF TIME!
A WASTE OF TIME? SIRRAH, THOU ART A FOOL AND A RASCAL!
AS IF IT WERE A WASTE OF TIME TO EAT BANANAS! I KNEW THEM NOT BEFORE... BUT THEY ARE WORTH KNOWING! WHAT TENDERNESS, WHAT TEXTURE, WHAT SWEET, STOMACH-SATISFYING FLAVOR!
BUT, BOSS, YOU PROMISED US BIG T'INGS! WE T'OUGHT WE'D GO AFTER DOUGH, OR JEWELS...
MONEY, JEWELS... ROGUE, HAVE YOU NO SOUL? I SEEK NOT SUCH TRIFLING TREASURES, BUT WONDERS THE LIKE OF WHICH THE WORLD HAS NEVER KNOWN!
HERE, THOU PITIABLE VILLAIN, READ THIS!
HUH..? I DON'T GET IT!
Sausages like McToddy's come but once in a lifetime!
WE SEEK THESE SAUSAGES, VARLET... DARE SAY NAY, AND MY SWORD WILL SLICE YOU INTO TEN THOUSAND QUIVERING PIECES!
2

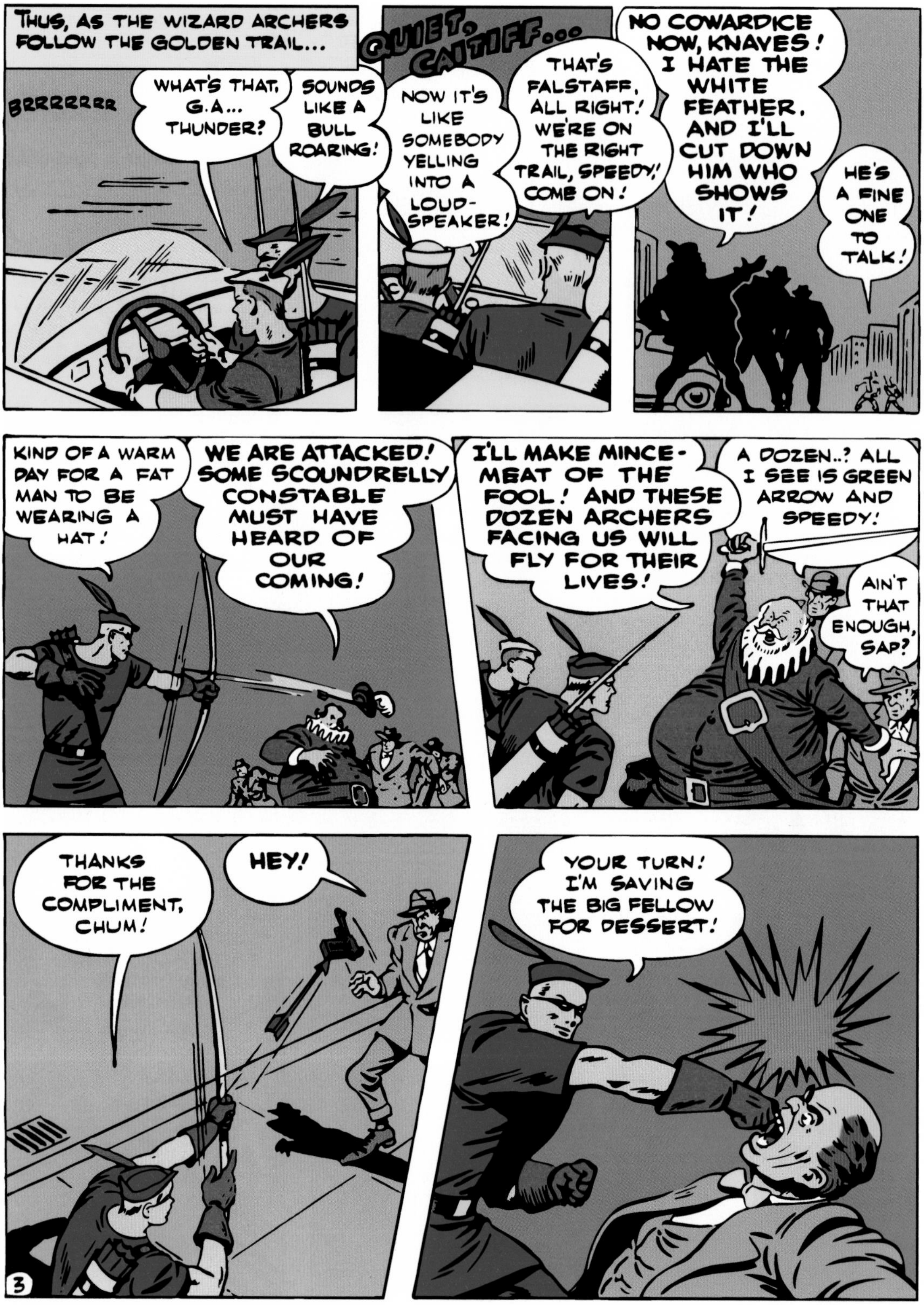
THUS, AS THE WIZARD ARCHERS FOLLOW THE GOLDEN TRAIL...
BRRRRRRRR
WHAT'S THAT, G.A... THUNDER?
SOUNDS LIKE A BULL ROARING!
QUIET, CAITIFF...
NOW IT'S LIKE SOMEBODY YELLING INTO A LOUD-SPEAKER!
THAT'S FALSTAFF, ALL RIGHT! WE'RE ON THE RIGHT TRAIL, SPEEDY! COME ON!
NO COWARDICE NOW, KNAVES! I HATE THE WHITE FEATHER. AND I'LL CUT DOWN HIM WHO SHOWS IT!
HE'S A FINE ONE TO TALK!
KIND OF A WARM DAY FOR A FAT MAN TO BE WEARING A HAT!
WE ARE ATTACKED! SOME SCOUNDRELLY CONSTABLE MUST HAVE HEARD OF OUR COMING!
I'LL MAKE MINCE-MEAT OF THE FOOL! AND THESE DOZEN ARCHERS FACING US WILL FLY FOR THEIR LIVES!
A DOZEN..? ALL I SEE IS GREEN ARROW AND SPEEDY!
AIN'T THAT ENOUGH, SAP?
THANKS FOR THE COMPLIMENT, CHUM!
HEY!
YOUR TURN! I'M SAVING THE BIG FELLOW FOR DESSERT!
3

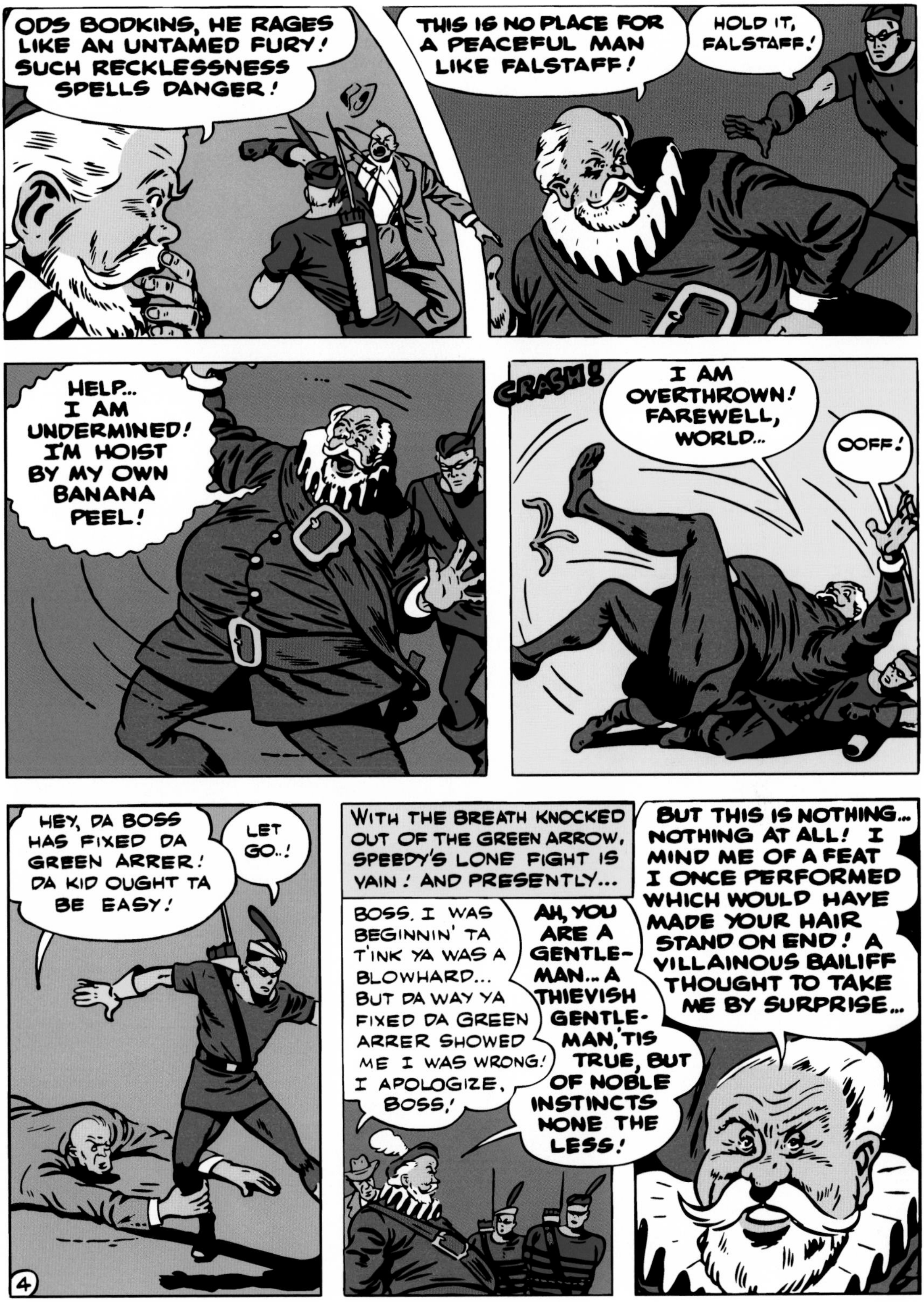
ODS BODKINS, HE RAGES LIKE AN UNTAMED FURY! SUCH RECKLESSNESS SPELLS DANGER!
THIS IS NO PLACE FOR A PEACEFUL MAN LIKE FALSTAFF!
HOLD IT, FALSTAFF!
HELP... I AM UNDERMINED! I'M HOIST BY MY OWN BANANA PEEL!
CRASH!
I AM OVERTHROWN! FAREWELL, WORLD...
OOFF!
HEY, DA BOSS HAS FIXED DA GREEN ARRER! DA KID OUGHT TA BE EASY!
LET GO..!
4
WITH THE BREATH KNOCKED OUT OF THE GREEN ARROW, SPEEDY'S LONE FIGHT IS VAIN! AND PRESENTLY...
BOSS, I WAS BEGINNIN' TA T'INK YA WAS A BLOWHARD... BUT DA WAY YA FIXED DA GREEN ARRER SHOWED ME I WAS WRONG! I APOLOGIZE, BOSS!
AH, YOU ARE A GENTLEMAN... A THIEVISH GENTLEMAN, 'TIS TRUE, BUT OF NOBLE INSTINCTS NONE THE LESS!
BUT THIS IS NOTHING... NOTHING AT ALL! I MIND ME OF A FEAT I ONCE PERFORMED WHICH WOULD HAVE MADE YOUR HAIR STAND ON END! A VILLAINOUS BAILIFF THOUGHT TO TAKE ME BY SURPRISE...

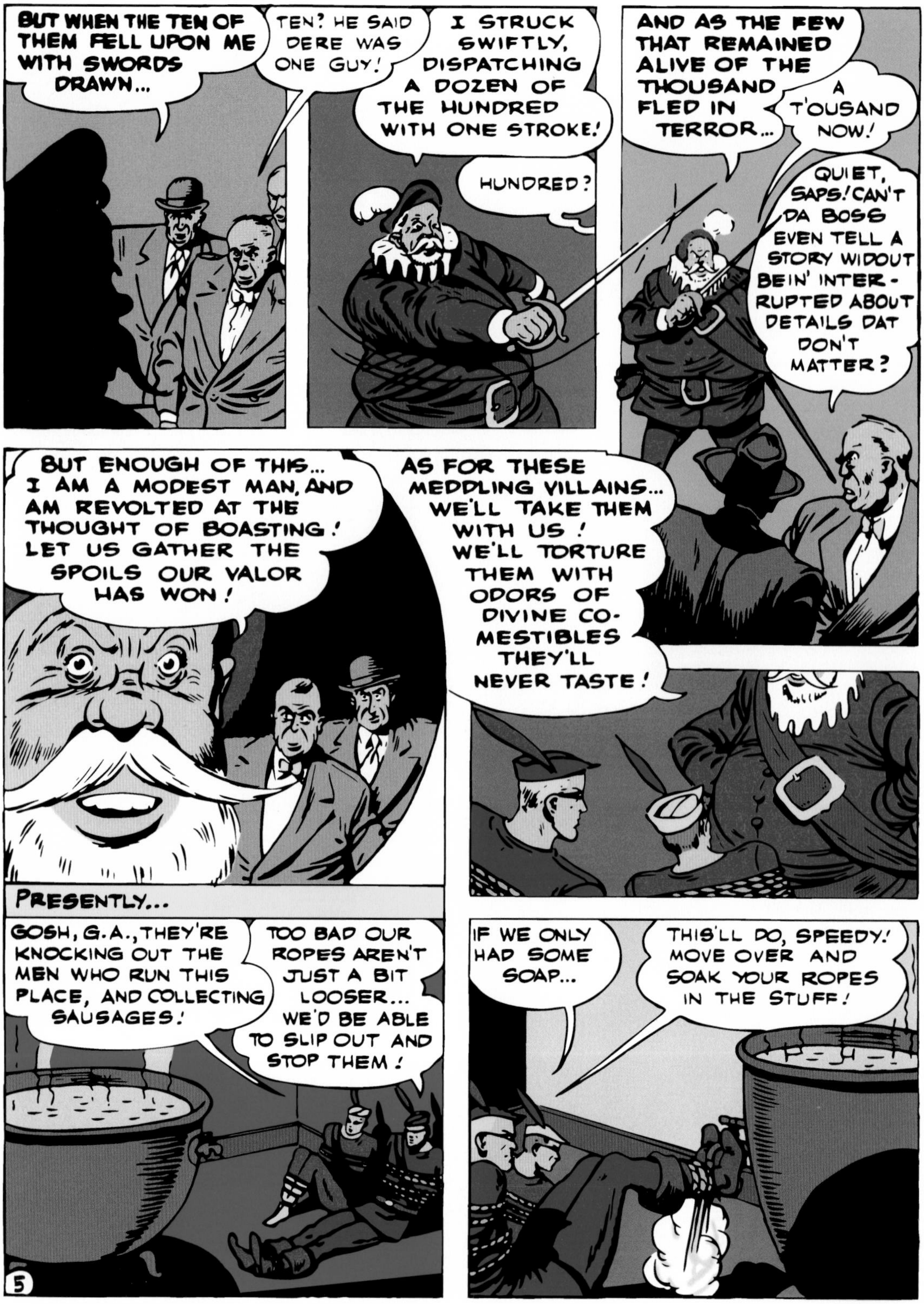
BUT WHEN THE TEN OF THEM FELL UPON ME WITH SWORDS DRAWN...
TEN? HE SAID DERE WAS ONE GUY!
I STRUCK SWIFTLY, DISPATCHING A DOZEN OF THE HUNDRED WITH ONE STROKE!
HUNDRED?
AND AS THE FEW THAT REMAINED ALIVE OF THE THOUSAND FLED IN TERROR...
A T'OUSAND NOW!
QUIET, SAPS! CAN'T DA BOSS EVEN TELL A STORY WIDOUT BEIN' INTER-RUPTED ABOUT DETAILS DAT DON'T MATTER?
BUT ENOUGH OF THIS... I AM A MODEST MAN, AND AM REVOLTED AT THE THOUGHT OF BOASTING! LET US GATHER THE SPOILS OUR VALOR HAS WON!
AS FOR THESE MEDDLING VILLAINS... WE'LL TAKE THEM WITH US! WE'LL TORTURE THEM WITH ODORS OF DIVINE CO-MESTIBLES THEY'LL NEVER TASTE!
PRESENTLY...
GOSH, G.A., THEY'RE KNOCKING OUT THE MEN WHO RUN THIS PLACE, AND COLLECTING SAUSAGES!
TOO BAD OUR ROPES AREN'T JUST A BIT LOOSER... WE'D BE ABLE TO SLIP OUT AND STOP THEM!
5
IF WE ONLY HAD SOME SOAP...
THIS'LL DO, SPEEDY! MOVE OVER AND SOAK YOUR ROPES IN THE STUFF!

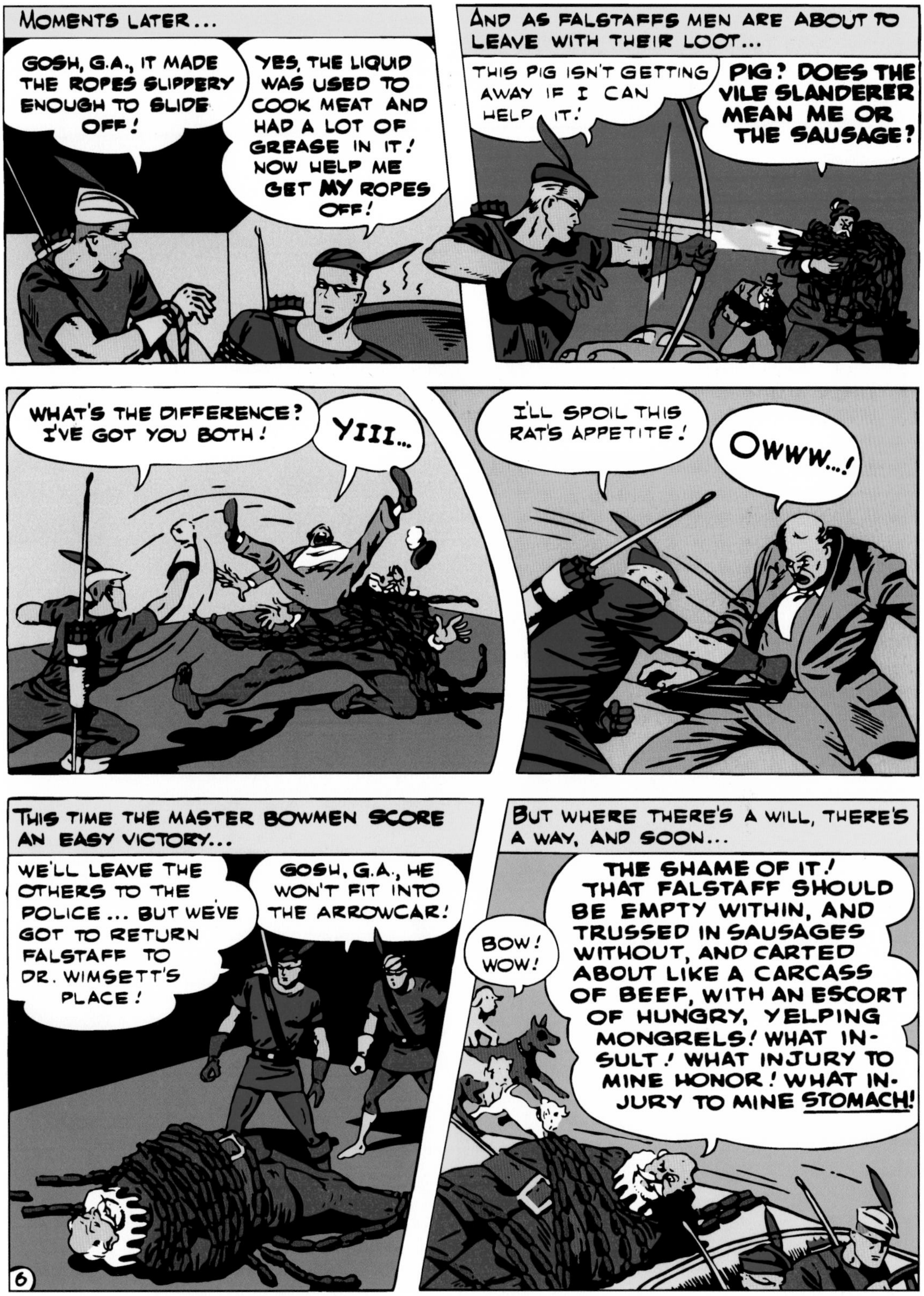
MOMENTS LATER...
GOSH, G.A., IT MADE THE ROPES SLIPPERY ENOUGH TO SLIDE OFF!
YES, THE LIQUID WAS USED TO COOK MEAT AND HAD A LOT OF GREASE IN IT! NOW HELP ME GET MY ROPES OFF!
AND AS FALSTAFFS MEN ARE ABOUT TO LEAVE WITH THEIR LOOT...
THIS PIG ISN'T GETTING AWAY IF I CAN HELP IT!
PIG? DOES THE VILE SLANDERER MEAN ME OR THE SAUSAGE?
WHAT'S THE DIFFERENCE? I'VE GOT YOU BOTH!
YIII...
I'LL SPOIL THIS RAT'S APPETITE!
OWWW...!
THIS TIME THE MASTER BOWMEN SCORE AN EASY VICTORY...
WE'LL LEAVE THE OTHERS TO THE POLICE... BUT WE'VE GOT TO RETURN FALSTAFF TO DR. WIMSETT'S PLACE!
GOSH, G.A., HE WON'T FIT INTO THE ARROWCAR!
6
BUT WHERE THERE'S A WILL, THERE'S A WAY, AND SOON...
BOW! WOW!
THE SHAME OF IT! THAT FALSTAFF SHOULD BE EMPTY WITHIN, AND TRUSSED IN SAUSAGES WITHOUT, AND CARTED ABOUT LIKE A CARCASS OF BEEF, WITH AN ESCORT OF HUNGRY, YELPING MONGRELS! WHAT IN-SULT! WHAT INJURY TO MINE HONOR! WHAT IN-JURY TO MINE STOMACH!

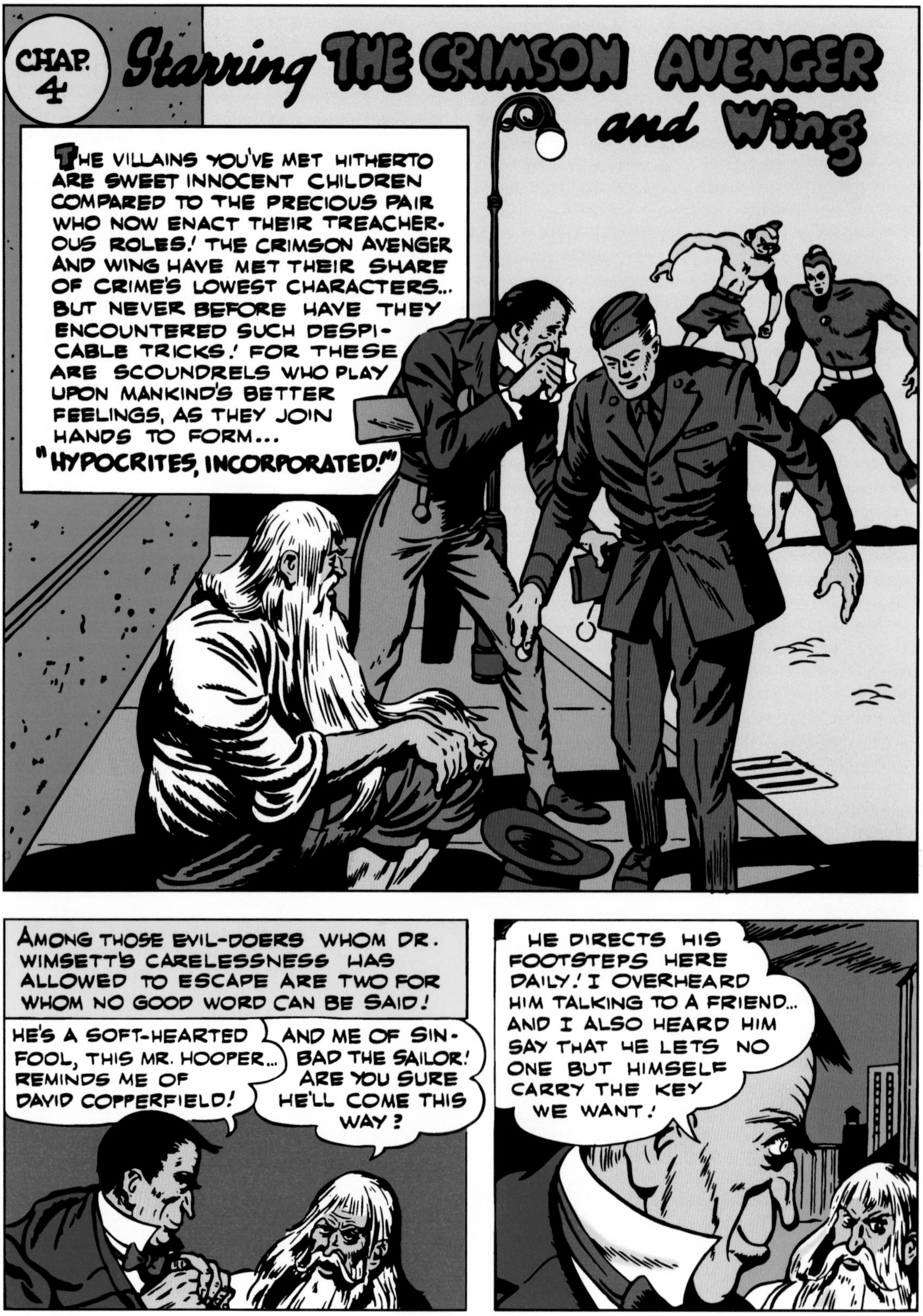
CHAP. 4
Starring THE CRIMSON AVENGER and Wing
THE VILLAINS YOU'VE MET HITHERTO ARE SWEET INNOCENT CHILDREN COMPARED TO THE PRECIOUS PAIR WHO NOW ENACT THEIR TREACHEROUS ROLES! THE CRIMSON AVENGER AND WING HAVE MET THEIR SHARE OF CRIME'S LOWEST CHARACTERS... BUT NEVER BEFORE HAVE THEY ENCOUNTERED SUCH DESPICABLE TRICKS! FOR THESE ARE SCOUNDRELS WHO PLAY UPON MANKIND'S BETTER FEELINGS, AS THEY JOIN HANDS TO FORM...
"HYPOCRITES, INCORPORATED!"
AMONG THOSE EVIL-DOERS WHOM DR. WIMSETT'S CARELESSNESS HAS ALLOWED TO ESCAPE ARE TWO FOR WHOM NO GOOD WORD CAN BE SAID!
HE'S A SOFT-HEARTED FOOL, THIS MR. HOOPER... REMINDS ME OF DAVID COPPERFIELD!
AND ME OF SINBAD THE SAILOR! ARE YOU SURE HE'LL COME THIS WAY?
HE DIRECTS HIS FOOTSTEPS HERE DAILY! I OVERHEARD HIM TALKING TO A FRIEND... AND I ALSO HEARD HIM SAY THAT HE LETS NO ONE BUT HIMSELF CARRY THE KEY WE WANT!

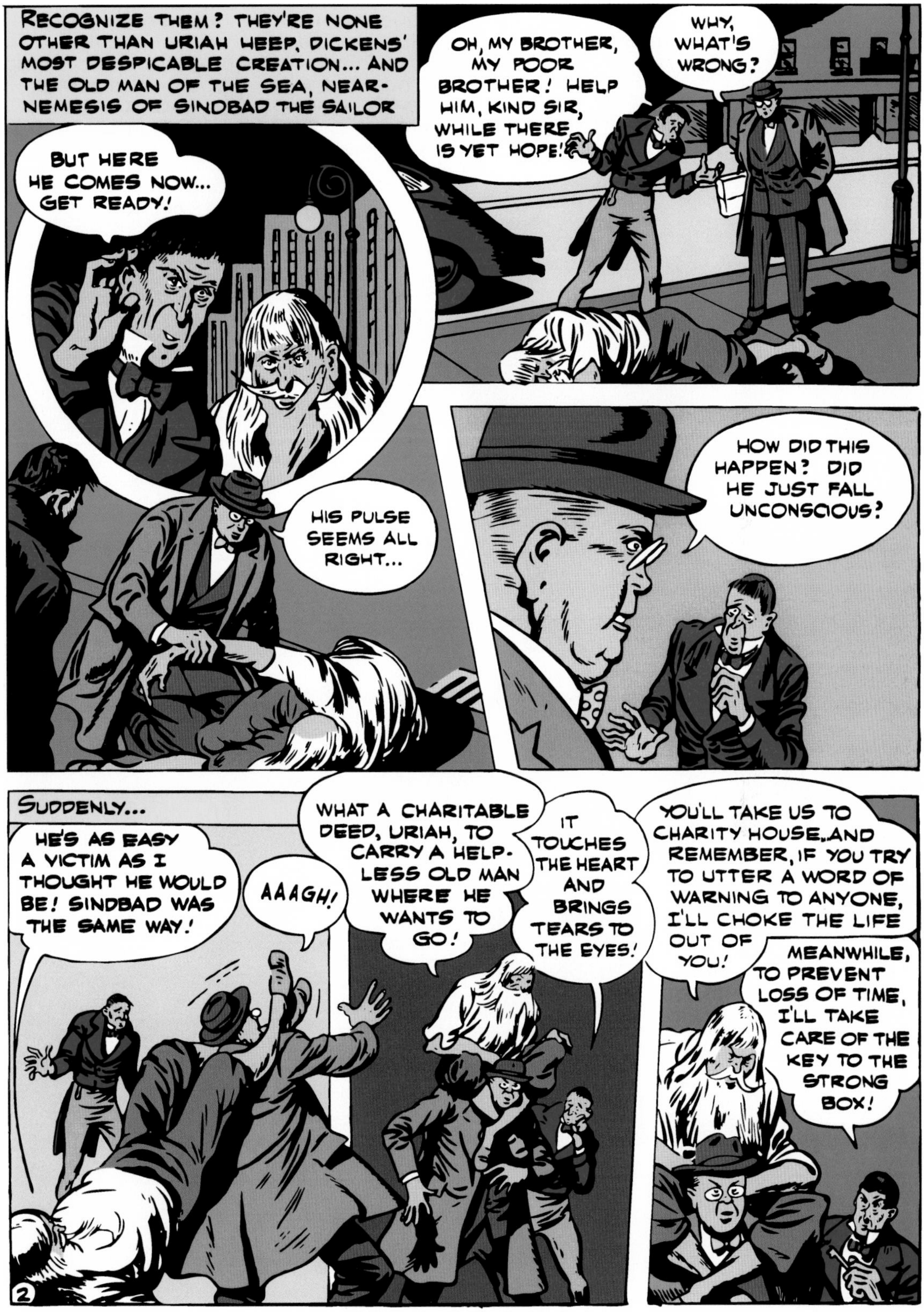
RECOGNIZE THEM? THEY'RE NONE OTHER THAN URIAH HEEP, DICKENS' MOST DESPICABLE CREATION... AND THE OLD MAN OF THE SEA, NEAR-NEMESIS OF SINDBAD THE SAILOR
BUT HERE HE COMES NOW... GET READY!
OH, MY BROTHER, MY POOR BROTHER! HELP HIM, KIND SIR, WHILE THERE IS YET HOPE!
WHY, WHAT'S WRONG?
HIS PULSE SEEMS ALL RIGHT...
HOW DID THIS HAPPEN? DID HE JUST FALL UNCONSCIOUS?
SUDDENLY...
HE'S AS EASY A VICTIM AS I THOUGHT HE WOULD BE! SINDBAD WAS THE SAME WAY!
AAAGH!
WHAT A CHARITABLE DEED, URIAH, TO CARRY A HELPLESS OLD MAN WHERE HE WANTS TO GO!
IT TOUCHES THE HEART AND BRINGS TEARS TO THE EYES!
YOU'LL TAKE US TO CHARITY HOUSE..AND REMEMBER, IF YOU TRY TO UTTER A WORD OF WARNING TO ANYONE, I'LL CHOKE THE LIFE OUT OF YOU!
MEANWHILE, TO PREVENT LOSS OF TIME, I'LL TAKE CARE OF THE KEY TO THE STRONG BOX!
2

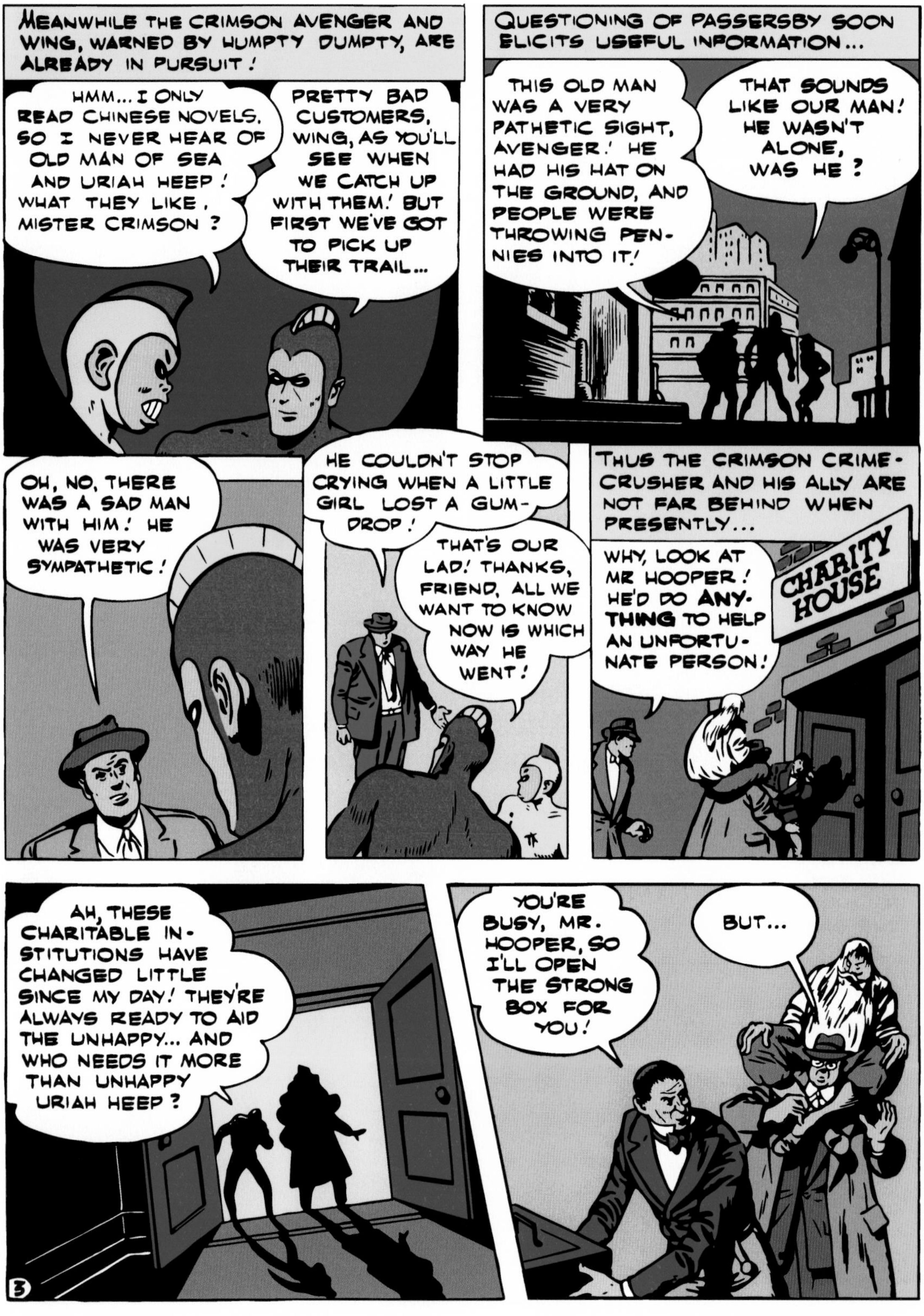
MEANWHILE THE CRIMSON AVENGER AND WING, WARNED BY HUMPTY DUMPTY, ARE ALREADY IN PURSUIT!
HMM... I ONLY READ CHINESE NOVELS, SO I NEVER HEAR OF OLD MAN OF SEA AND URIAH HEEP! WHAT THEY LIKE, MISTER CRIMSON?
PRETTY BAD CUSTOMERS, WING, AS YOU'LL SEE WHEN WE CATCH UP WITH THEM! BUT FIRST WE'VE GOT TO PICK UP THEIR TRAIL...
QUESTIONING OF PASSERSBY SOON ELICITS USEFUL INFORMATION...
THIS OLD MAN WAS A VERY PATHETIC SIGHT, AVENGER! HE HAD HIS HAT ON THE GROUND, AND PEOPLE WERE THROWING PENNIES INTO IT!
THAT SOUNDS LIKE OUR MAN! HE WASN'T ALONE, WAS HE?
OH, NO, THERE WAS A SAD MAN WITH HIM! HE WAS VERY SYMPATHETIC!
HE COULDN'T STOP CRYING WHEN A LITTLE GIRL LOST A GUM-DROP!
THAT'S OUR LAD! THANKS, FRIEND, ALL WE WANT TO KNOW NOW IS WHICH WAY HE WENT!
THUS THE CRIMSON CRIME-CRUSHER AND HIS ALLY ARE NOT FAR BEHIND WHEN PRESENTLY...
WHY, LOOK AT MR HOOPER! HE'D DO ANYTHING TO HELP AN UNFORTUNATE PERSON!
CHARITY HOUSE
AH, THESE CHARITABLE INSTITUTIONS HAVE CHANGED LITTLE SINCE MY DAY! THEY'RE ALWAYS READY TO AID THE UNHAPPY... AND WHO NEEDS IT MORE THAN UNHAPPY URIAH HEEP?
3
YOU'RE BUSY, MR. HOOPER, SO I'LL OPEN THE STRONG BOX FOR YOU!
BUT...

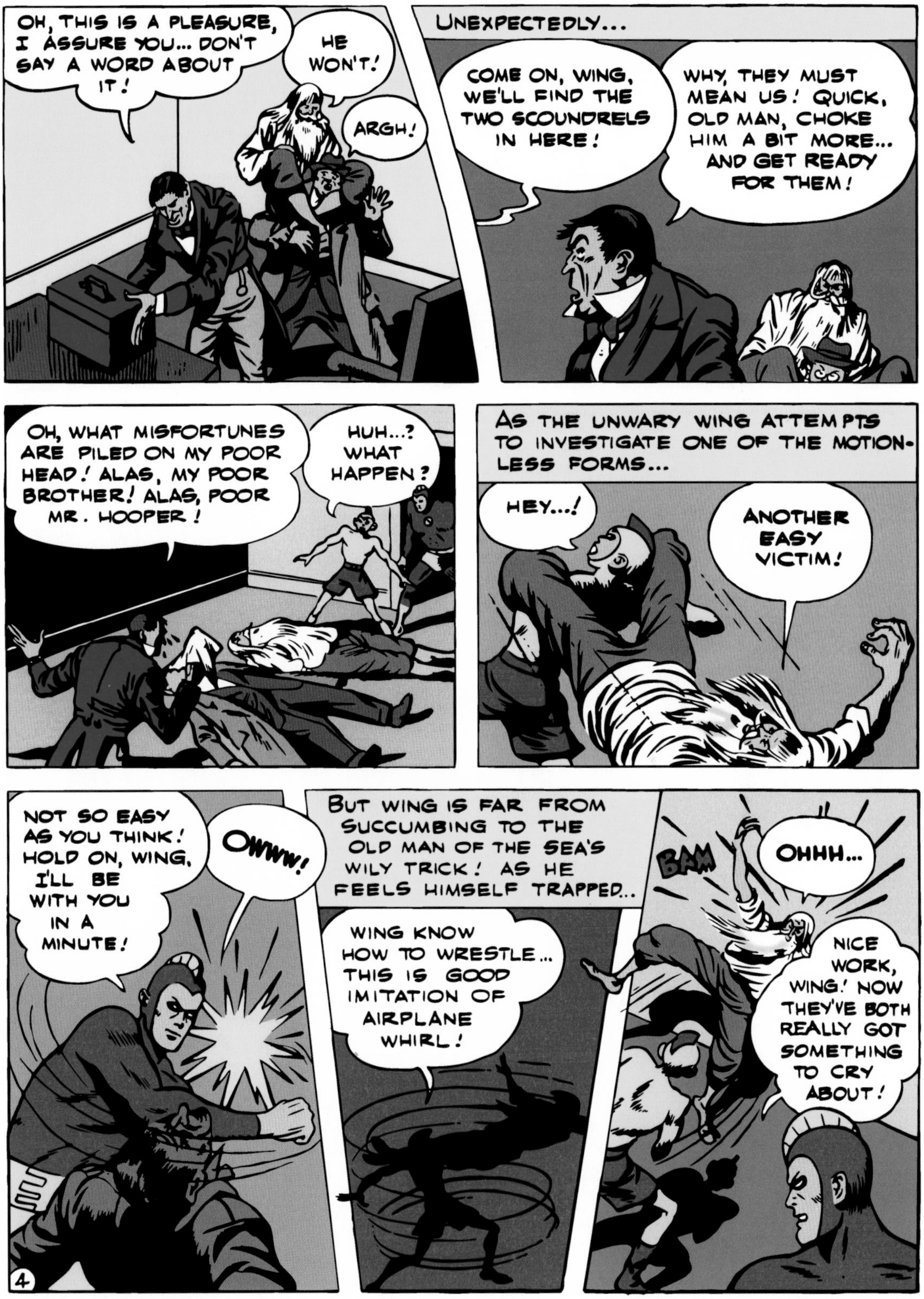
OH, THIS IS A PLEASURE, I ASSURE YOU... DON'T SAY A WORD ABOUT IT!
HE WON'T!
ARGH!
UNEXPECTEDLY...
COME ON, WING, WE'LL FIND THE TWO SCOUNDRELS IN HERE!
WHY, THEY MUST MEAN US! QUICK, OLD MAN, CHOKE HIM A BIT MORE... AND GET READY FOR THEM!
OH, WHAT MISFORTUNES ARE PILED ON MY POOR HEAD! ALAS, MY POOR BROTHER! ALAS, POOR MR. HOOPER!
HUH...? WHAT HAPPEN?
AS THE UNWARY WING ATTEMPTS TO INVESTIGATE ONE OF THE MOTIONLESS FORMS...
HEY...!
ANOTHER EASY VICTIM!
NOT SO EASY AS YOU THINK! HOLD ON, WING, I'LL BE WITH YOU IN A MINUTE!
OWWW!
BUT WING IS FAR FROM SUCCUMBING TO THE OLD MAN OF THE SEA'S WILY TRICK! AS HE FEELS HIMSELF TRAPPED...
WING KNOW HOW TO WRESTLE... THIS IS GOOD IMITATION OF AIRPLANE WHIRL!
BAM
OHHH...
NICE WORK, WING! NOW THEY'VE BOTH REALLY GOT SOMETHING TO CRY ABOUT!
4

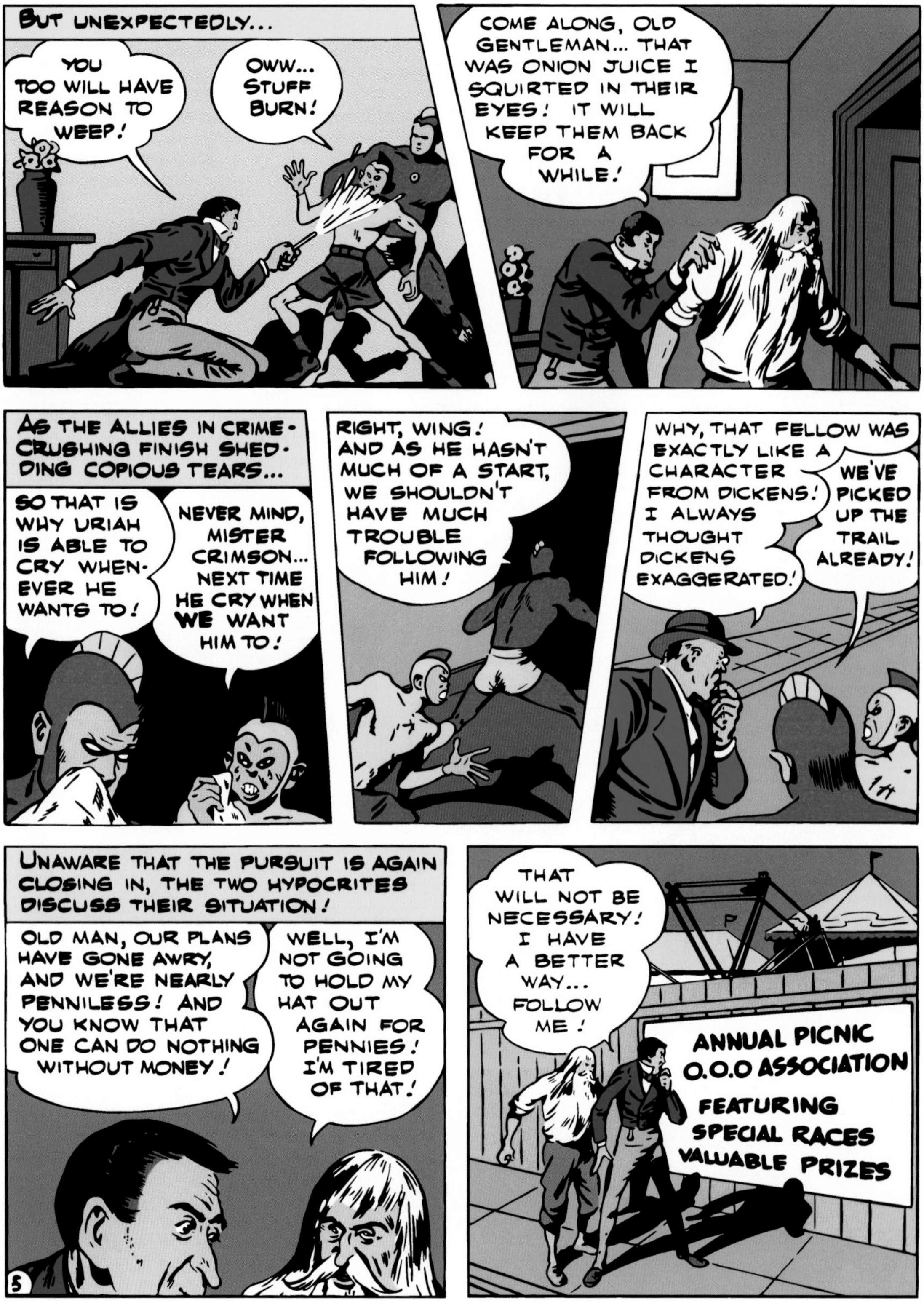
BUT UNEXPECTEDLY...
YOU TOO WILL HAVE REASON TO WEEP!
OWW... STUFF BURN!
COME ALONG, OLD GENTLEMAN... THAT WAS ONION JUICE I SQUIRTED IN THEIR EYES! IT WILL KEEP THEM BACK FOR A WHILE!
AS THE ALLIES IN CRIME-CRUSHING FINISH SHED-DING COPIOUS TEARS...
SO THAT IS WHY URIAH IS ABLE TO CRY WHEN-EVER HE WANTS TO!
NEVER MIND, MISTER CRIMSON... NEXT TIME HE CRY WHEN WE WANT HIM TO!
RIGHT, WING! AND AS HE HASN'T MUCH OF A START, WE SHOULDN'T HAVE MUCH TROUBLE FOLLOWING HIM!
WHY, THAT FELLOW WAS EXACTLY LIKE A CHARACTER FROM DICKENS! I ALWAYS THOUGHT DICKENS EXAGGERATED!
WE'VE PICKED UP THE TRAIL ALREADY!
UNAWARE THAT THE PURSUIT IS AGAIN CLOSING IN, THE TWO HYPOCRITES DISCUSS THEIR SITUATION!
OLD MAN, OUR PLANS HAVE GONE AWRY, AND WE'RE NEARLY PENNILESS! AND YOU KNOW THAT ONE CAN DO NOTHING WITHOUT MONEY!
WELL, I'M NOT GOING TO HOLD MY HAT OUT AGAIN FOR PENNIES! I'M TIRED OF THAT!
5
THAT WILL NOT BE NECESSARY! I HAVE A BETTER WAY... FOLLOW ME!
ANNUAL PICNIC O.O.O ASSOCIATION
FEATURING SPECIAL RACES VALUABLE PRIZES

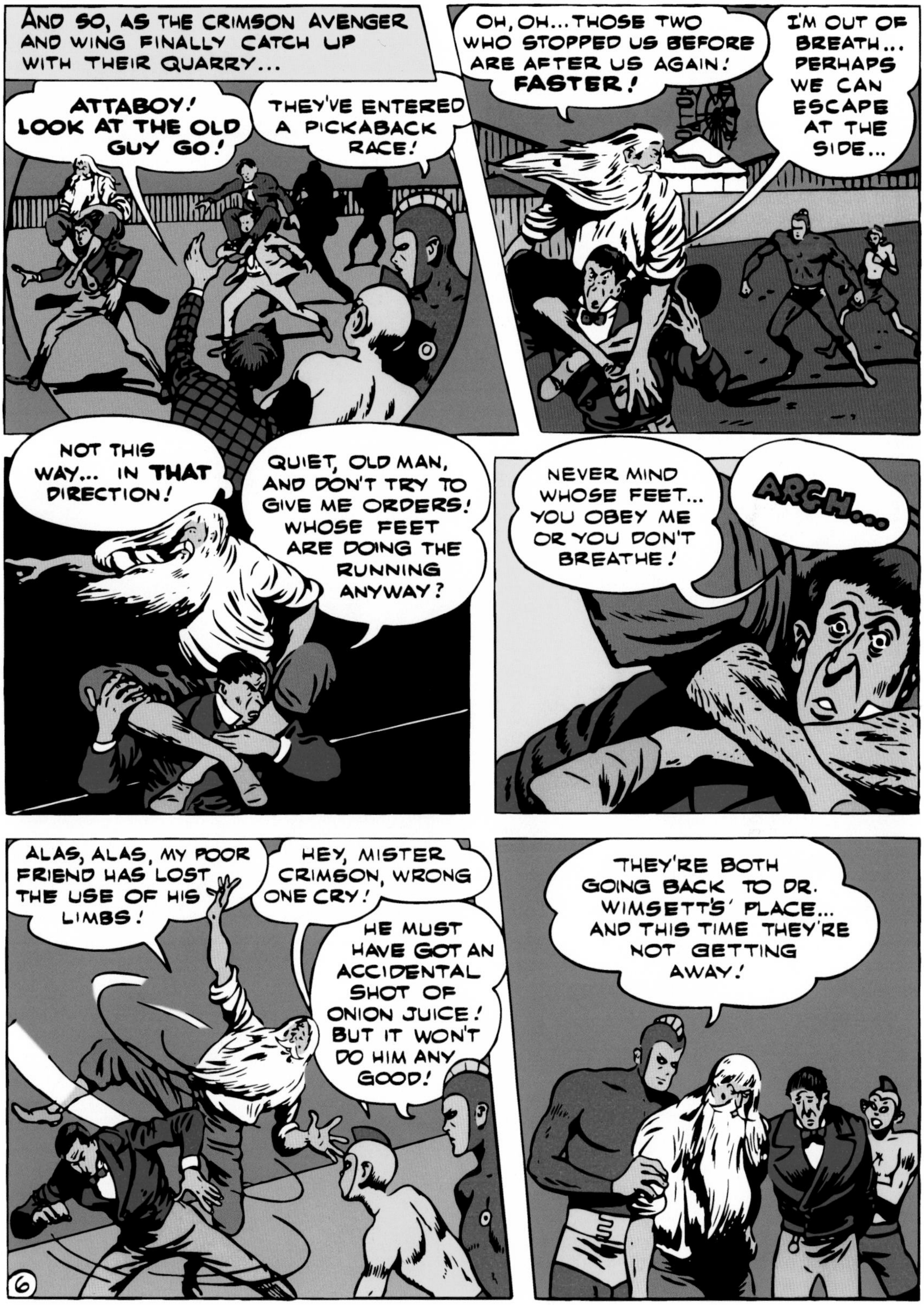
AND SO, AS THE CRIMSON AVENGER AND WING FINALLY CATCH UP WITH THEIR QUARRY...
ATTABOY! LOOK AT THE OLD GUY GO!
THEY'VE ENTERED A PICKABACK RACE!
OH, OH... THOSE TWO WHO STOPPED US BEFORE ARE AFTER US AGAIN! FASTER!
I'M OUT OF BREATH... PERHAPS WE CAN ESCAPE AT THE SIDE...
NOT THIS WAY... IN THAT DIRECTION!
QUIET, OLD MAN, AND DON'T TRY TO GIVE ME ORDERS! WHOSE FEET ARE DOING THE RUNNING ANYWAY?
NEVER MIND WHOSE FEET... YOU OBEY ME OR YOU DON'T BREATHE!
ARGH...
ALAS, ALAS, MY POOR FRIEND HAS LOST THE USE OF HIS LIMBS!
HEY, MISTER CRIMSON, WRONG ONE CRY!
HE MUST HAVE GOT AN ACCIDENTAL SHOT OF ONION JUICE! BUT IT WON'T DO HIM ANY GOOD!
6
THEY'RE BOTH GOING BACK TO DR. WIMSETT'S PLACE... AND THIS TIME THEY'RE NOT GETTING AWAY!

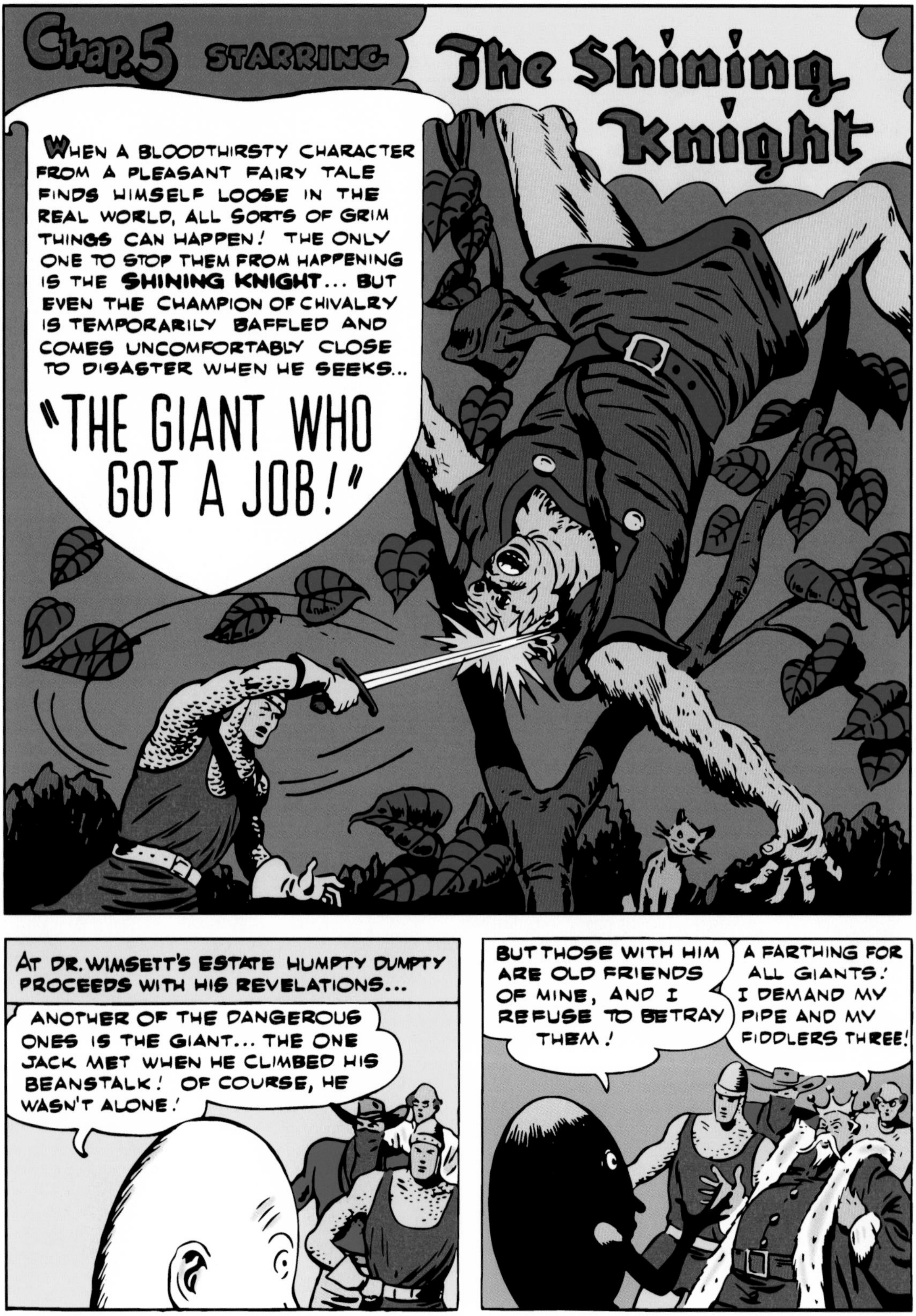
Chap. 5 STARRING The Shining Knight
WHEN A BLOODTHIRSTY CHARACTER FROM A PLEASANT FAIRY TALE FINDS HIMSELF LOOSE IN THE REAL WORLD, ALL SORTS OF GRIM THINGS CAN HAPPEN! THE ONLY ONE TO STOP THEM FROM HAPPENING IS THE SHINING KNIGHT... BUT EVEN THE CHAMPION OF CHIVALRY IS TEMPORARILY BAFFLED AND COMES UNCOMFORTABLY CLOSE TO DISASTER WHEN HE SEEKS...
"THE GIANT WHO GOT A JOB!"
AT DR. WIMSETT'S ESTATE HUMPTY DUMPTY PROCEEDS WITH HIS REVELATIONS...
ANOTHER OF THE DANGEROUS ONES IS THE GIANT... THE ONE JACK MET WHEN HE CLIMBED HIS BEANSTALK! OF COURSE, HE WASN'T ALONE!
BUT THOSE WITH HIM ARE OLD FRIENDS OF MINE, AND I REFUSE TO BETRAY THEM!
A FARTHING FOR ALL GIANTS! I DEMAND MY PIPE AND MY FIDDLERS THREE!

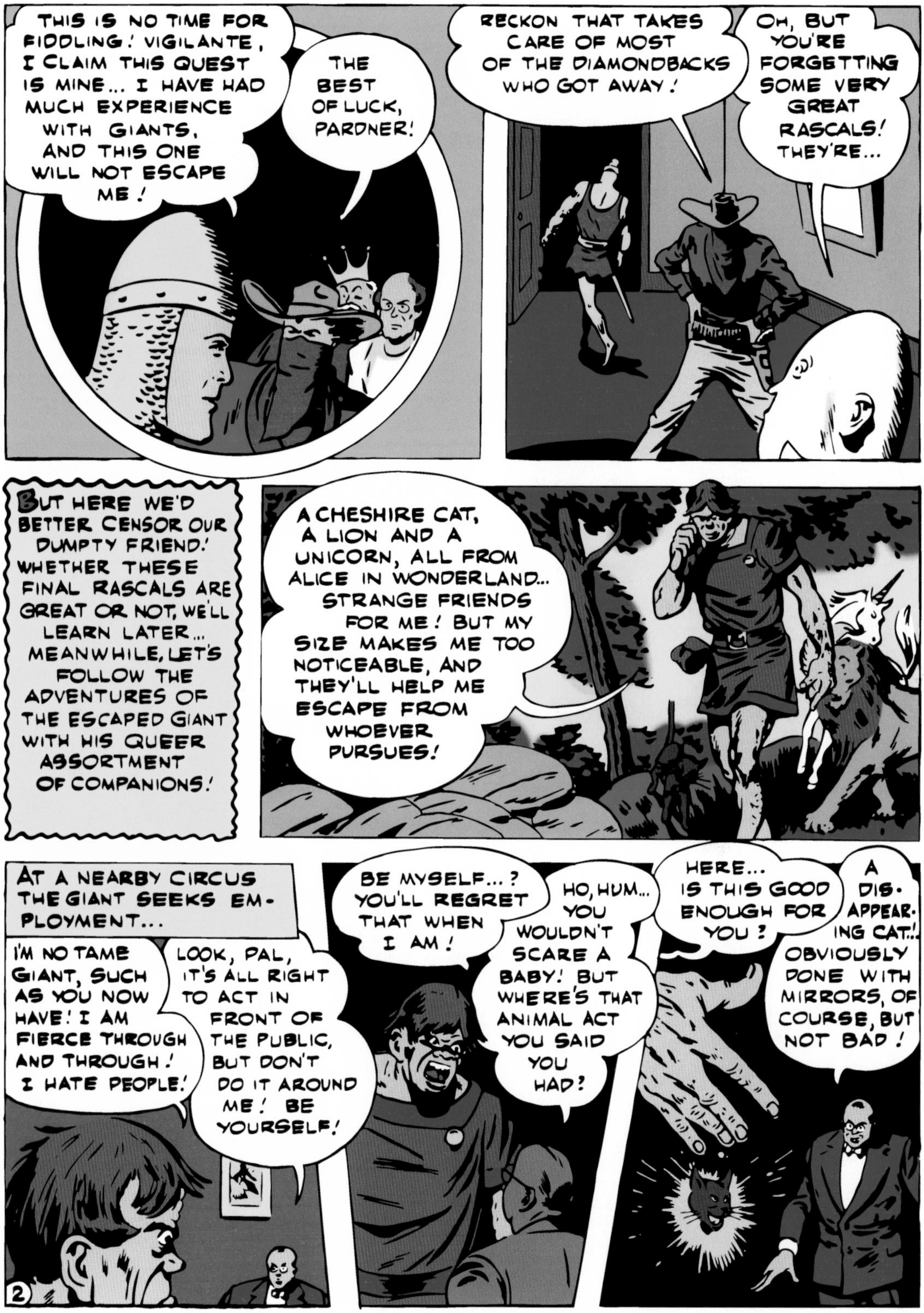
THIS IS NO TIME FOR FIDDLING! VIGILANTE, I CLAIM THIS QUEST IS MINE... I HAVE HAD MUCH EXPERIENCE WITH GIANTS, AND THIS ONE WILL NOT ESCAPE ME!
THE BEST OF LUCK, PARDNER!
RECKON THAT TAKES CARE OF MOST OF THE DIAMONDBACKS WHO GOT AWAY!
OH, BUT YOU'RE FORGETTING SOME VERY GREAT RASCALS! THEY'RE...
BUT HERE WE'D BETTER CENSOR OUR DUMPTY FRIEND! WHETHER THESE FINAL RASCALS ARE GREAT OR NOT, WE'LL LEARN LATER... MEANWHILE, LET'S FOLLOW THE ADVENTURES OF THE ESCAPED GIANT WITH HIS QUEER ASSORTMENT OF COMPANIONS!
A CHESHIRE CAT, A LION AND A UNICORN, ALL FROM ALICE IN WONDERLAND... STRANGE FRIENDS FOR ME! BUT MY SIZE MAKES ME TOO NOTICEABLE, AND THEY'LL HELP ME ESCAPE FROM WHOEVER PURSUES!
AT A NEARBY CIRCUS THE GIANT SEEKS EMPLOYMENT...
I'M NO TAME GIANT, SUCH AS YOU NOW HAVE! I AM FIERCE THROUGH AND THROUGH! I HATE PEOPLE!
LOOK, PAL, IT'S ALL RIGHT TO ACT IN FRONT OF THE PUBLIC, BUT DON'T DO IT AROUND ME! BE YOURSELF!
2
BE MYSELF...? YOU'LL REGRET THAT WHEN I AM!
HO, HUM... YOU WOULDN'T SCARE A BABY! BUT WHERE'S THAT ANIMAL ACT YOU SAID YOU HAD?
HERE... IS THIS GOOD ENOUGH FOR YOU?
A DISAPPEARING CAT!.. OBVIOUSLY DONE WITH MIRRORS, OF COURSE, BUT NOT BAD!

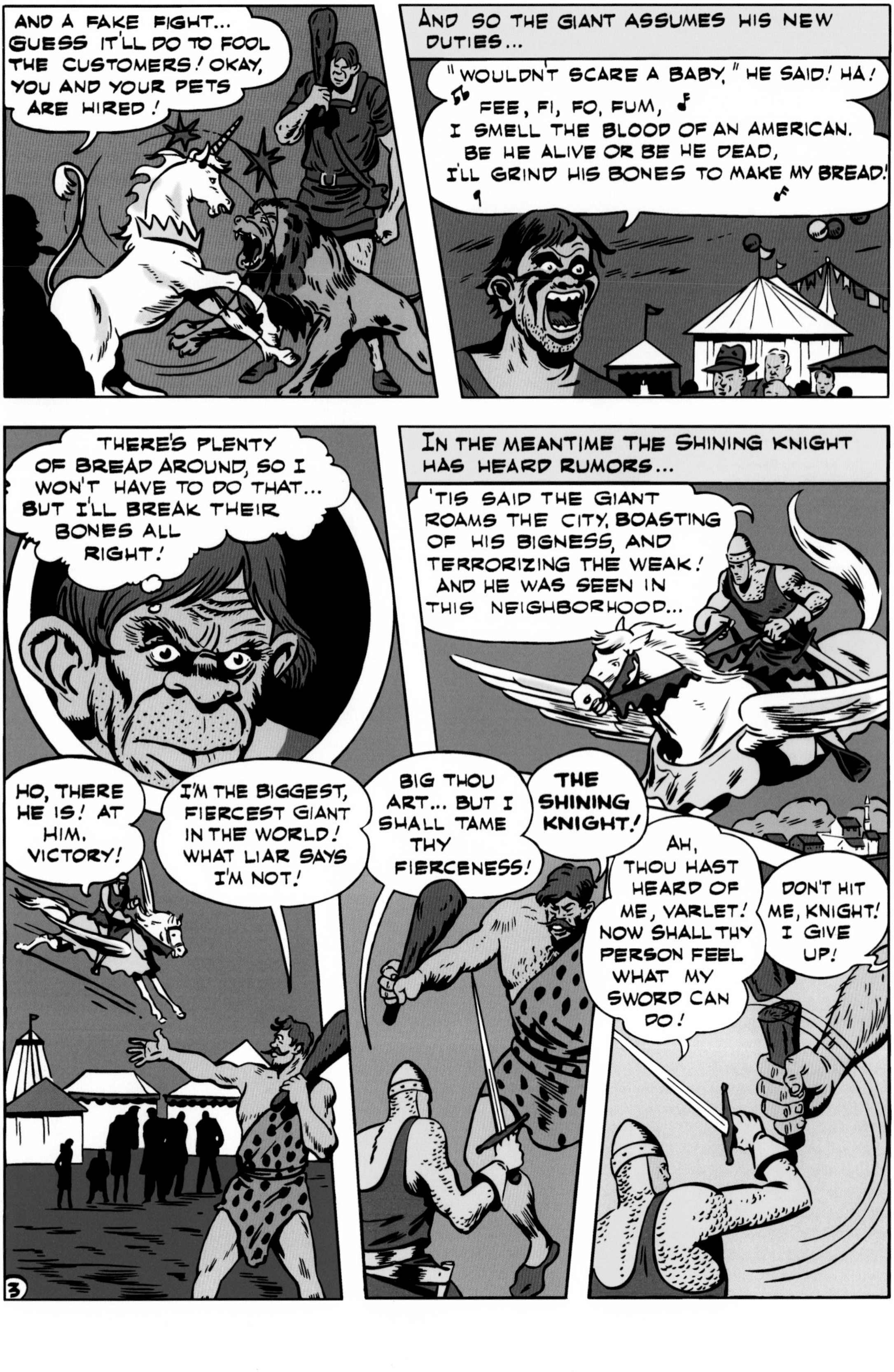
AND A FAKE FIGHT... GUESS IT'LL DO TO FOOL THE CUSTOMERS! OKAY, YOU AND YOUR PETS ARE HIRED!
AND SO THE GIANT ASSUMES HIS NEW DUTIES...
"WOULDN'T SCARE A BABY," HE SAID! HA! FEE, FI, FO, FUM, I SMELL THE BLOOD OF AN AMERICAN. BE HE ALIVE OR BE HE DEAD, I'LL GRIND HIS BONES TO MAKE MY BREAD!
THERE'S PLENTY OF BREAD AROUND, SO I WON'T HAVE TO DO THAT... BUT I'LL BREAK THEIR BONES ALL RIGHT!
IN THE MEANTIME THE SHINING KNIGHT HAS HEARD RUMORS...
'TIS SAID THE GIANT ROAMS THE CITY, BOASTING OF HIS BIGNESS, AND TERRORIZING THE WEAK! AND HE WAS SEEN IN THIS NEIGHBORHOOD...
HO, THERE HE IS! AT HIM, VICTORY!
I'M THE BIGGEST, FIERCEST GIANT IN THE WORLD! WHAT LIAR SAYS I'M NOT!
BIG THOU ART... BUT I SHALL TAME THY FIERCENESS!
THE SHINING KNIGHT!
AH, THOU HAST HEARD OF ME, VARLET! NOW SHALL THY PERSON FEEL WHAT MY SWORD CAN DO!
DON'T HIT ME, KNIGHT! I GIVE UP!
3

I'M NOT REALLY FIERCE! I JUST LIKE TO SCARE PEOPLE!

BY MY HALIDOME, THIS IS PASSING STRANGE! SO GREAT A GIANT TO YIELD HIM AT THE FIRST BLOW! WHAT CAN THE REASON BE?

THE ANSWER'S SIMPLE, IF ONLY SIR JUSTIN KNEW! HE HAS CONQUERED THE OLD CIRCUS GIANT DISCHARGED AFTER THE NEW ONE WAS HIRED! AND AS HIS VANQUISHED FOE IS TAKEN INTO CUSTODY...

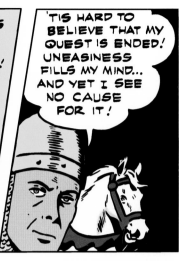

'TIS HARD TO BELIEVE THAT MY QUEST IS ENDED! UNEASINESS FILLS MY MIND... AND YET I SEE NO CAUSE FOR IT!

A VANISHING CAT? HUMPTY DUMPTY TALKED OF FRIENDS OF HIS...

GREATEST SHOW ON EARTH! FEATURES THE REMARKABLE AND STUPENDOUS FEAT OF THE VANISHING FELINE!

I HAVE IT... THE CHESHIRE CAT! AND IF THAT IS IN THE CIRCUS, THEN PERHAPS THE REAL GIANT, TOO... AH, VICTORY, MAYHAP OUR QUEST IS JUST BEGINNING!

UNDER THE BIG TOP...

WHY, YES, KNIGHT, I DID RECENTLY HIRE A NEW GIANT! YOU'LL FIND HIM IN ONE OF THE NEW TENTS!

I'LL SEEK HIM AT ONCE!

4

FEE, FI, FO, FUM, I SMELL THE BLOOD OF AN ENGLISHMAN...

AH, THIS IS THE VILLAIN!

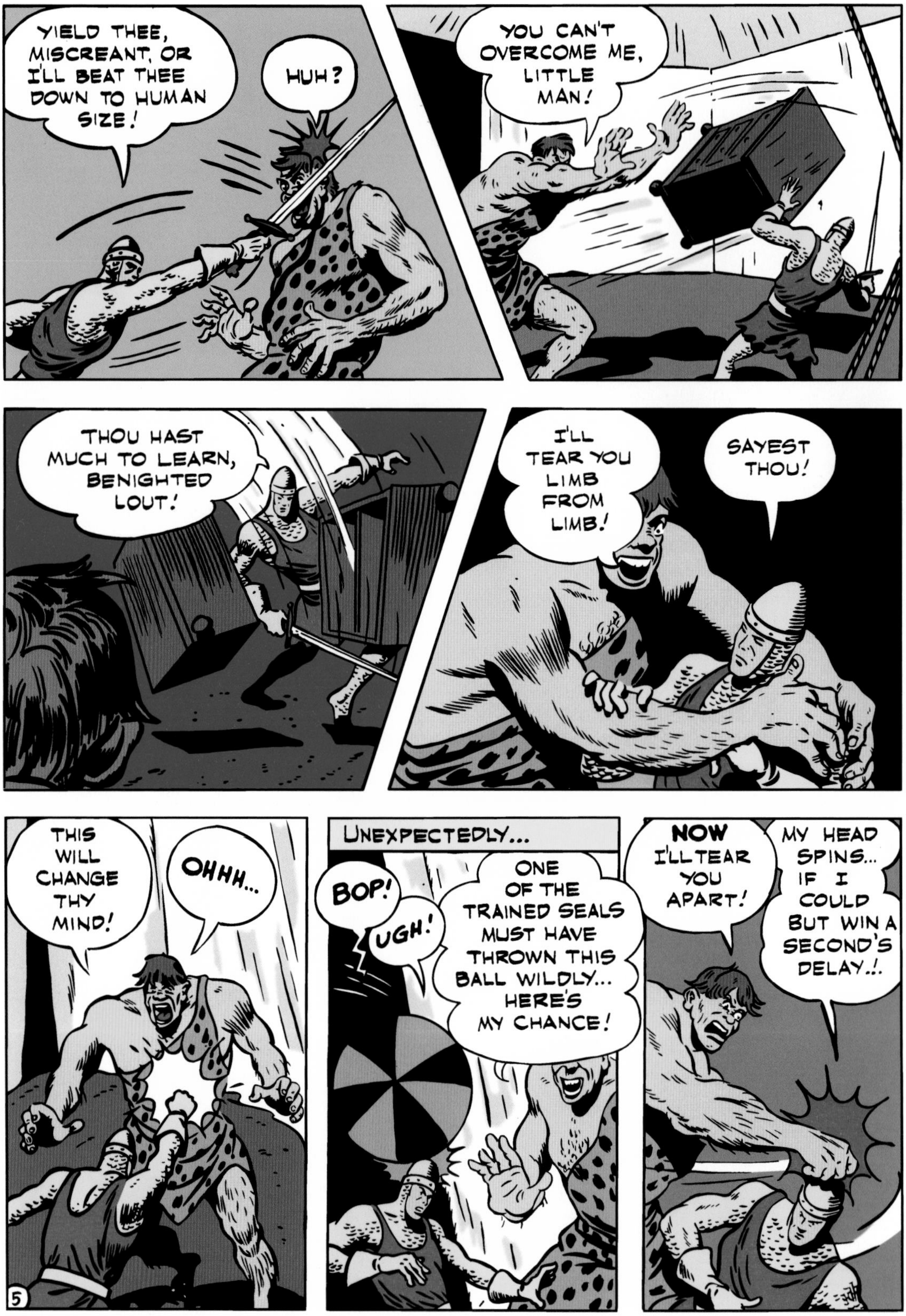
YIELD THEE, MISCREANT, OR I'LL BEAT THEE DOWN TO HUMAN SIZE!
HUH?
YOU CAN'T OVERCOME ME, LITTLE MAN!
THOU HAST MUCH TO LEARN, BENIGHTED LOUT!
I'LL TEAR YOU LIMB FROM LIMB!
SAYEST THOU!
THIS WILL CHANGE THY MIND!
OHHH...
5
UNEXPECTEDLY...
BOP!
UGH!
ONE OF THE TRAINED SEALS MUST HAVE THROWN THIS BALL WILDLY... HERE'S MY CHANCE!
NOW I'LL TEAR YOU APART!
MY HEAD SPINS... IF I COULD BUT WIN A SECOND'S DELAY..!.

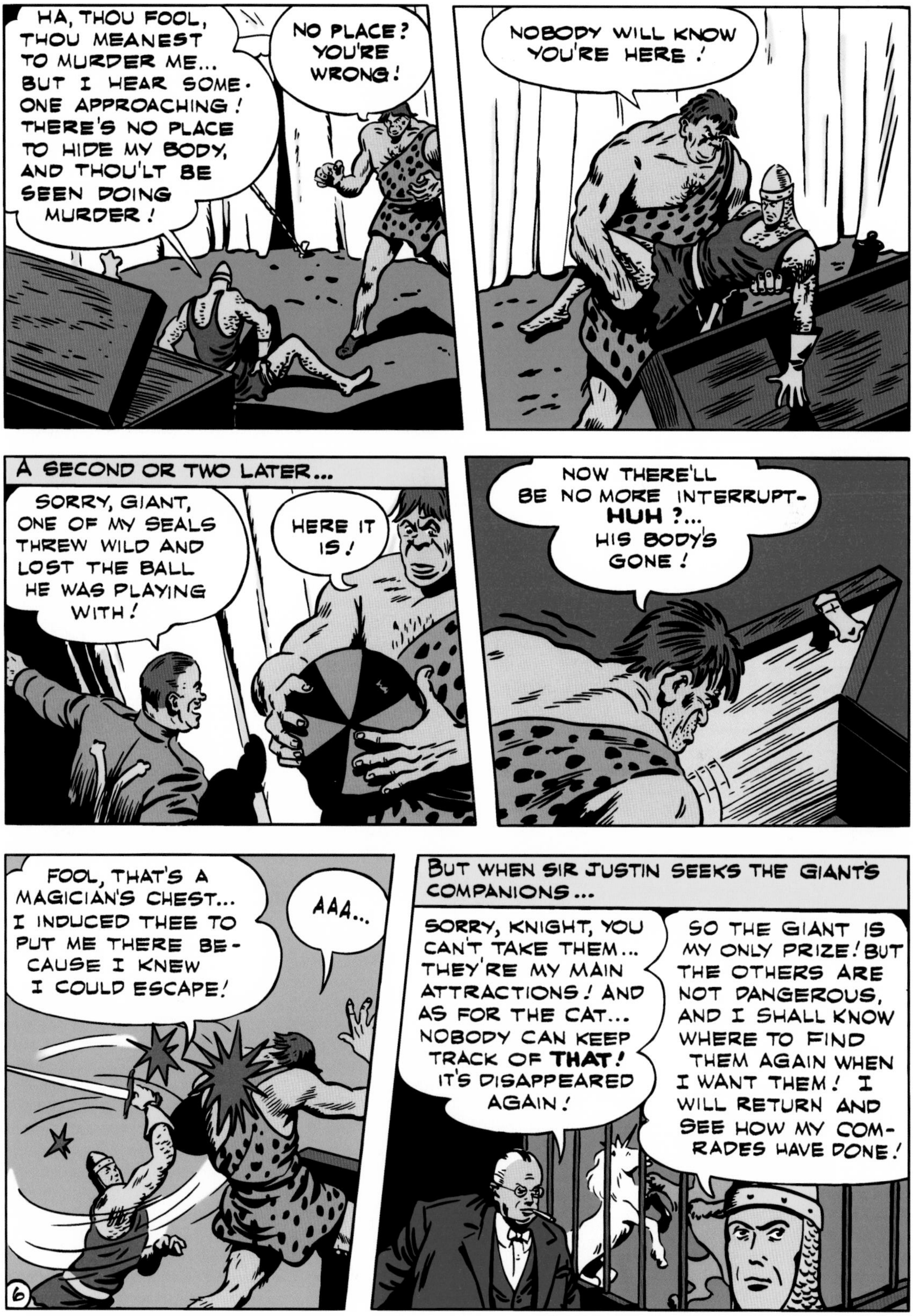
HA, THOU FOOL, THOU MEANEST TO MURDER ME... BUT I HEAR SOME-ONE APPROACHING! THERE'S NO PLACE TO HIDE MY BODY, AND THOU'LT BE SEEN DOING MURDER!
NO PLACE? YOU'RE WRONG!
NOBODY WILL KNOW YOU'RE HERE!
A SECOND OR TWO LATER...
SORRY, GIANT, ONE OF MY SEALS THREW WILD AND LOST THE BALL HE WAS PLAYING WITH!
HERE IT IS!
NOW THERE'LL BE NO MORE INTERRUPT- **HUH** ?... HIS BODY'S GONE!
FOOL, THAT'S A MAGICIAN'S CHEST... I INDUCED THEE TO PUT ME THERE BE-CAUSE I KNEW I COULD ESCAPE!
AAA...
6
BUT WHEN SIR JUSTIN SEEKS THE GIANT'S COMPANIONS...
SORRY, KNIGHT, YOU CAN'T TAKE THEM... THEY'RE MY MAIN ATTRACTIONS! AND AS FOR THE CAT... NOBODY CAN KEEP TRACK OF **THAT**! IT'S DISAPPEARED AGAIN!
SO THE GIANT IS MY ONLY PRIZE! BUT THE OTHERS ARE NOT DANGEROUS, AND I SHALL KNOW WHERE TO FIND THEM AGAIN WHEN I WANT THEM! I WILL RETURN AND SEE HOW MY COM-RADES HAVE DONE!

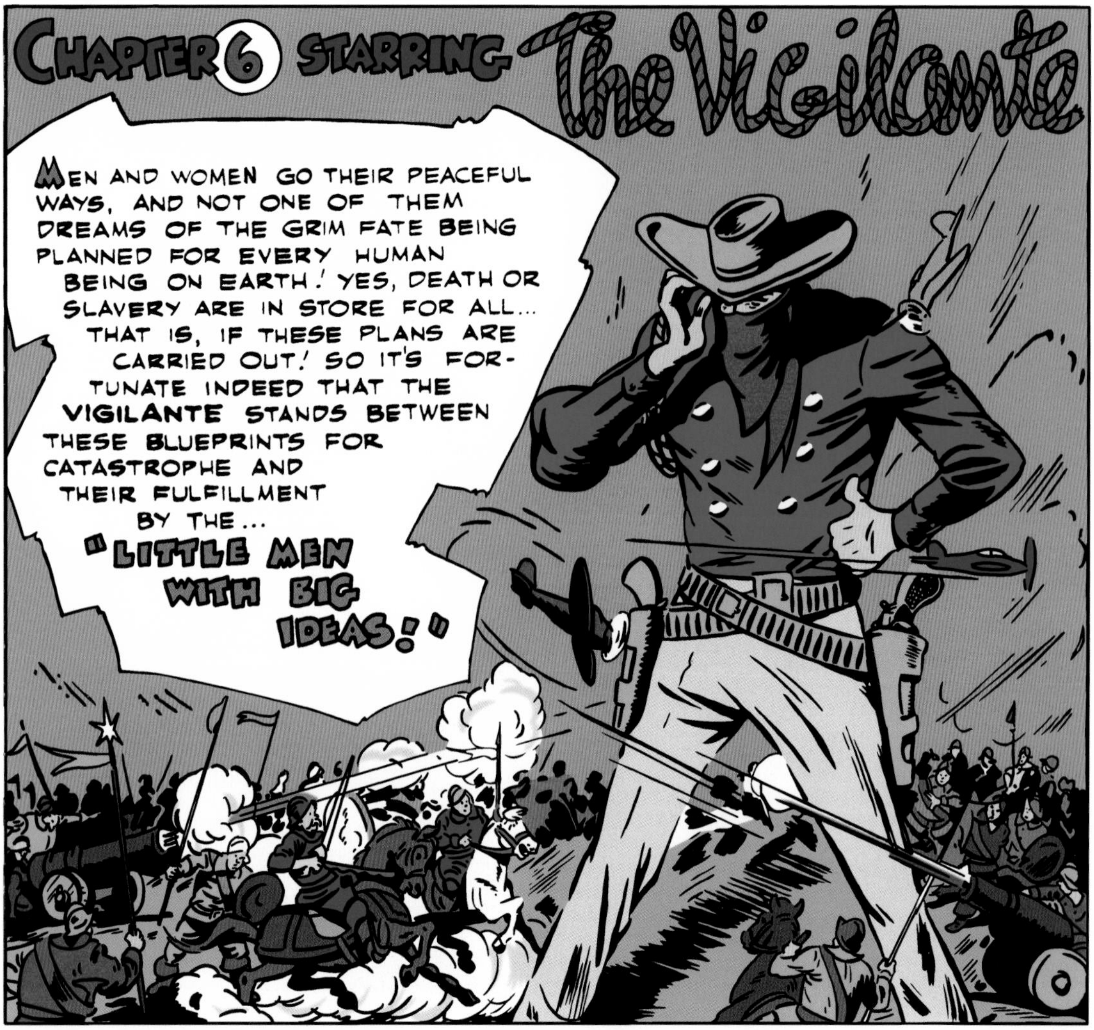
CHAPTER 6 STARRING
The Vigilante
MEN AND WOMEN GO THEIR PEACEFUL WAYS, AND NOT ONE OF THEM DREAMS OF THE GRIM FATE BEING PLANNED FOR EVERY HUMAN BEING ON EARTH! YES, DEATH OR SLAVERY ARE IN STORE FOR ALL... THAT IS, IF THESE PLANS ARE CARRIED OUT! SO IT'S FORTUNATE INDEED THAT THE VIGILANTE STANDS BETWEEN THESE BLUEPRINTS FOR CATASTROPHE AND THEIR FULFILLMENT BY THE...
"LITTLE MEN WITH BIG IDEAS!"

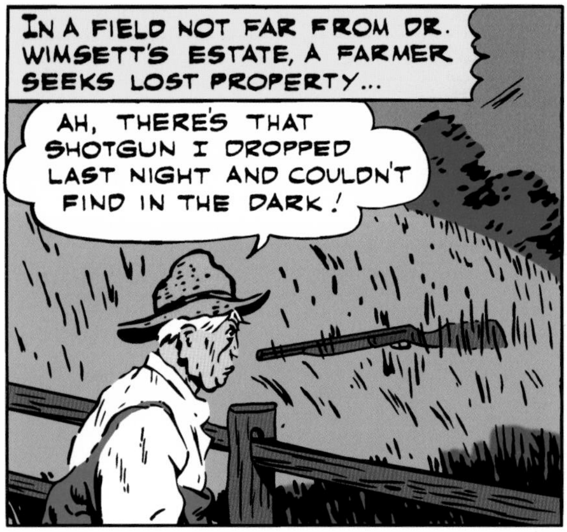
IN A FIELD NOT FAR FROM DR. WIMSETT'S ESTATE, A FARMER SEEKS LOST PROPERTY...
AH, THERE'S THAT SHOTGUN I DROPPED LAST NIGHT AND COULDN'T FIND IN THE DARK!

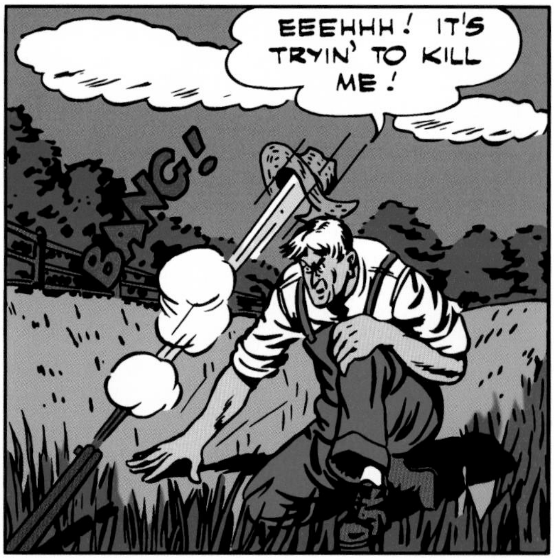
EEEHHH! IT'S TRYIN' TO KILL ME!
BANG!

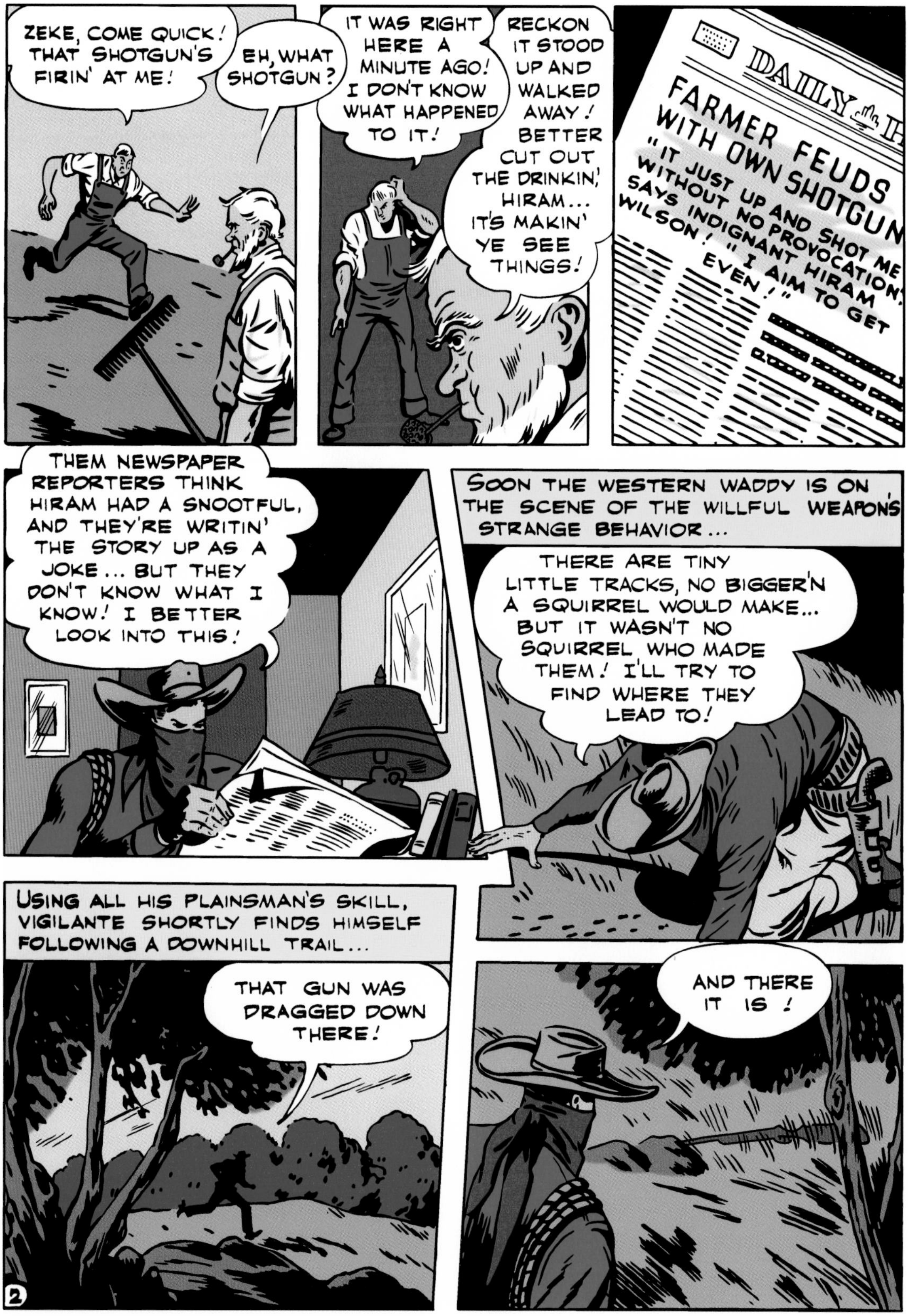
ZEKE, COME QUICK! THAT SHOTGUN'S FIRIN' AT ME!
EH, WHAT SHOTGUN?
IT WAS RIGHT HERE A MINUTE AGO! I DON'T KNOW WHAT HAPPENED TO IT!
RECKON IT STOOD UP AND WALKED AWAY! BETTER CUT OUT THE DRINKIN', HIRAM... IT'S MAKIN' YE SEE THINGS!
DAILY
FARMER FEUDS WITH OWN SHOTGUN
"IT JUST UP AND SHOT ME WITHOUT NO PROVOCATION," SAYS INDIGNANT HIRAM WILSON! "I AIM TO GET EVEN!"
THEM NEWSPAPER REPORTERS THINK HIRAM HAD A SNOOTFUL, AND THEY'RE WRITIN' THE STORY UP AS A JOKE... BUT THEY DON'T KNOW WHAT I KNOW! I BETTER LOOK INTO THIS!
SOON THE WESTERN WADDY IS ON THE SCENE OF THE WILLFUL WEAPON'S STRANGE BEHAVIOR...
THERE ARE TINY LITTLE TRACKS, NO BIGGER'N A SQUIRREL WOULD MAKE... BUT IT WASN'T NO SQUIRREL WHO MADE THEM! I'LL TRY TO FIND WHERE THEY LEAD TO!
USING ALL HIS PLAINSMAN'S SKILL, VIGILANTE SHORTLY FINDS HIMSELF FOLLOWING A DOWNHILL TRAIL...
THAT GUN WAS DRAGGED DOWN THERE!
AND THERE IT IS!
2

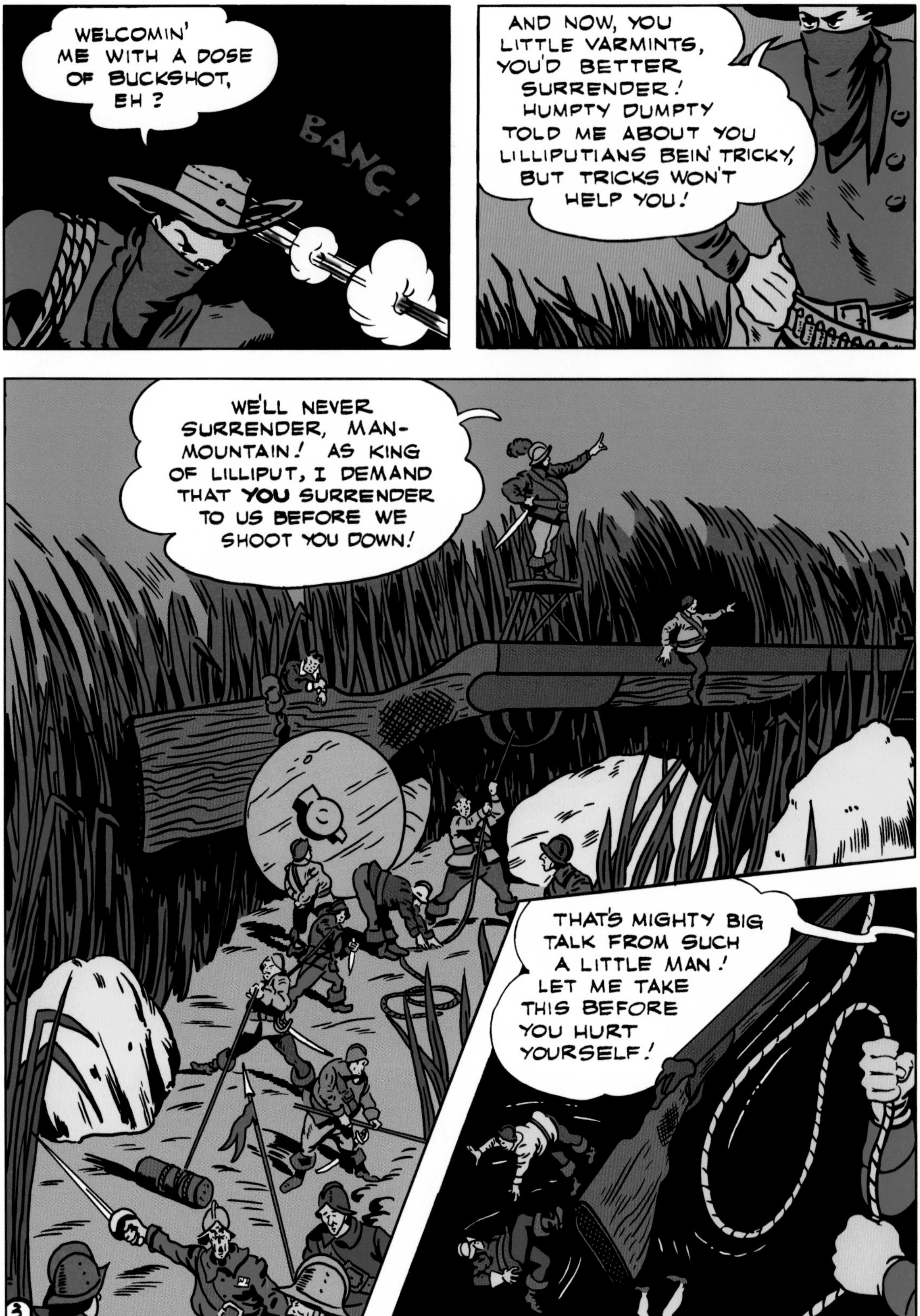
WELCOMIN' ME WITH A DOSE OF BUCKSHOT, EH ?
BANG !
AND NOW, YOU LITTLE VARMINTS, YOU'D BETTER SURRENDER! HUMPTY DUMPTY TOLD ME ABOUT YOU LILLIPUTIANS BEIN' TRICKY, BUT TRICKS WON'T HELP YOU!
WE'LL NEVER SURRENDER, MAN-MOUNTAIN! AS KING OF LILLIPUT, I DEMAND THAT **YOU** SURRENDER TO US BEFORE WE SHOOT YOU DOWN!
THAT'S MIGHTY BIG TALK FROM SUCH A LITTLE MAN! LET ME TAKE THIS BEFORE YOU HURT YOURSELF!
3

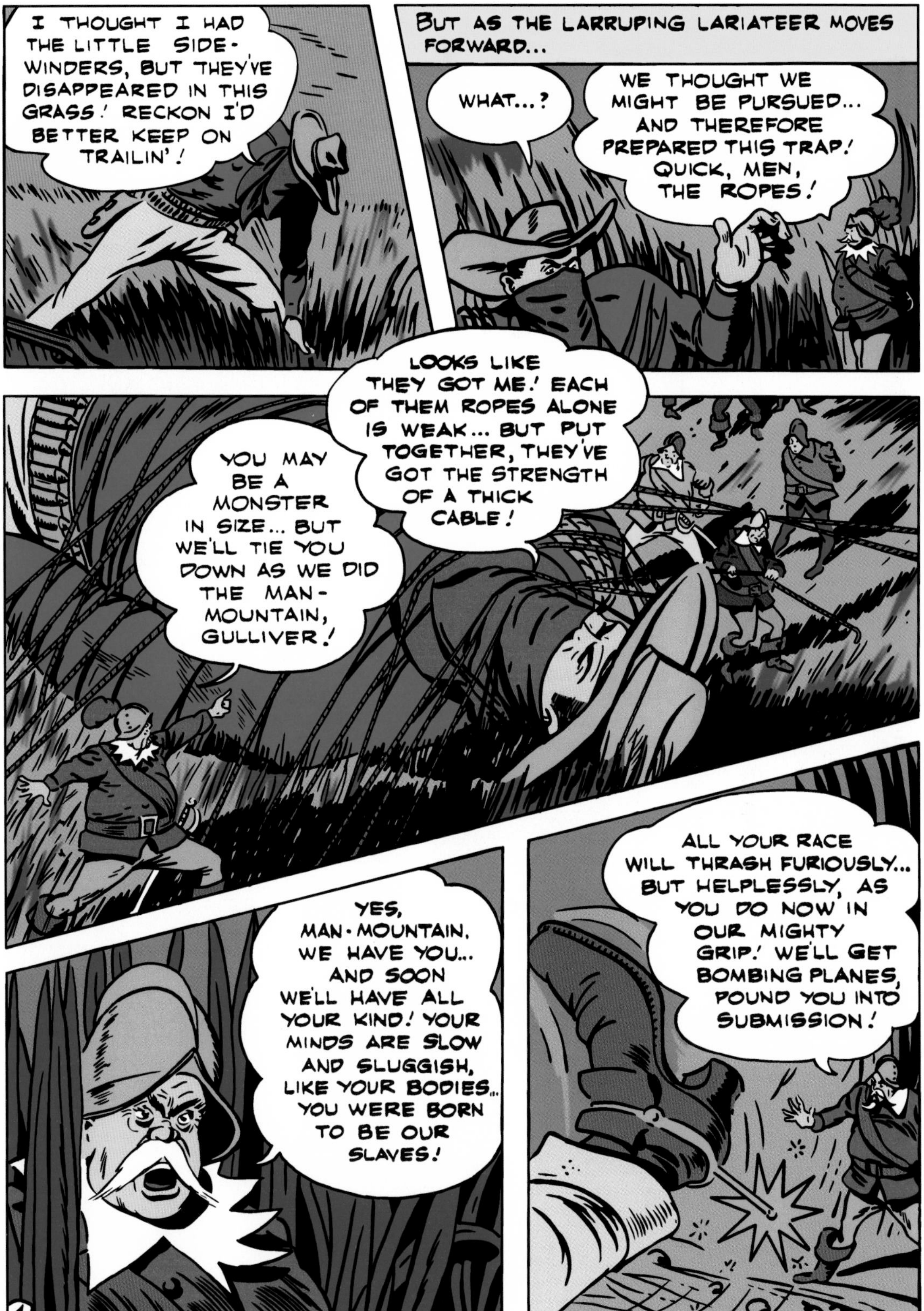
I THOUGHT I HAD THE LITTLE SIDE-WINDERS, BUT THEY'VE DISAPPEARED IN THIS GRASS! RECKON I'D BETTER KEEP ON TRAILIN'!
BUT AS THE LARRUPING LARIATEER MOVES FORWARD...
WHAT...?
WE THOUGHT WE MIGHT BE PURSUED... AND THEREFORE PREPARED THIS TRAP! QUICK, MEN, THE ROPES!
YOU MAY BE A MONSTER IN SIZE... BUT WE'LL TIE YOU DOWN AS WE DID THE MAN-MOUNTAIN, GULLIVER!
LOOKS LIKE THEY GOT ME! EACH OF THEM ROPES ALONE IS WEAK... BUT PUT TOGETHER, THEY'VE GOT THE STRENGTH OF A THICK CABLE!
YES, MAN-MOUNTAIN, WE HAVE YOU... AND SOON WE'LL HAVE ALL YOUR KIND! YOUR MINDS ARE SLOW AND SLUGGISH, LIKE YOUR BODIES... YOU WERE BORN TO BE OUR SLAVES!
ALL YOUR RACE WILL THRASH FURIOUSLY... BUT HELPLESSLY, AS YOU DO NOW IN OUR MIGHTY GRIP! WE'LL GET BOMBING PLANES, POUND YOU INTO SUBMISSION!
4

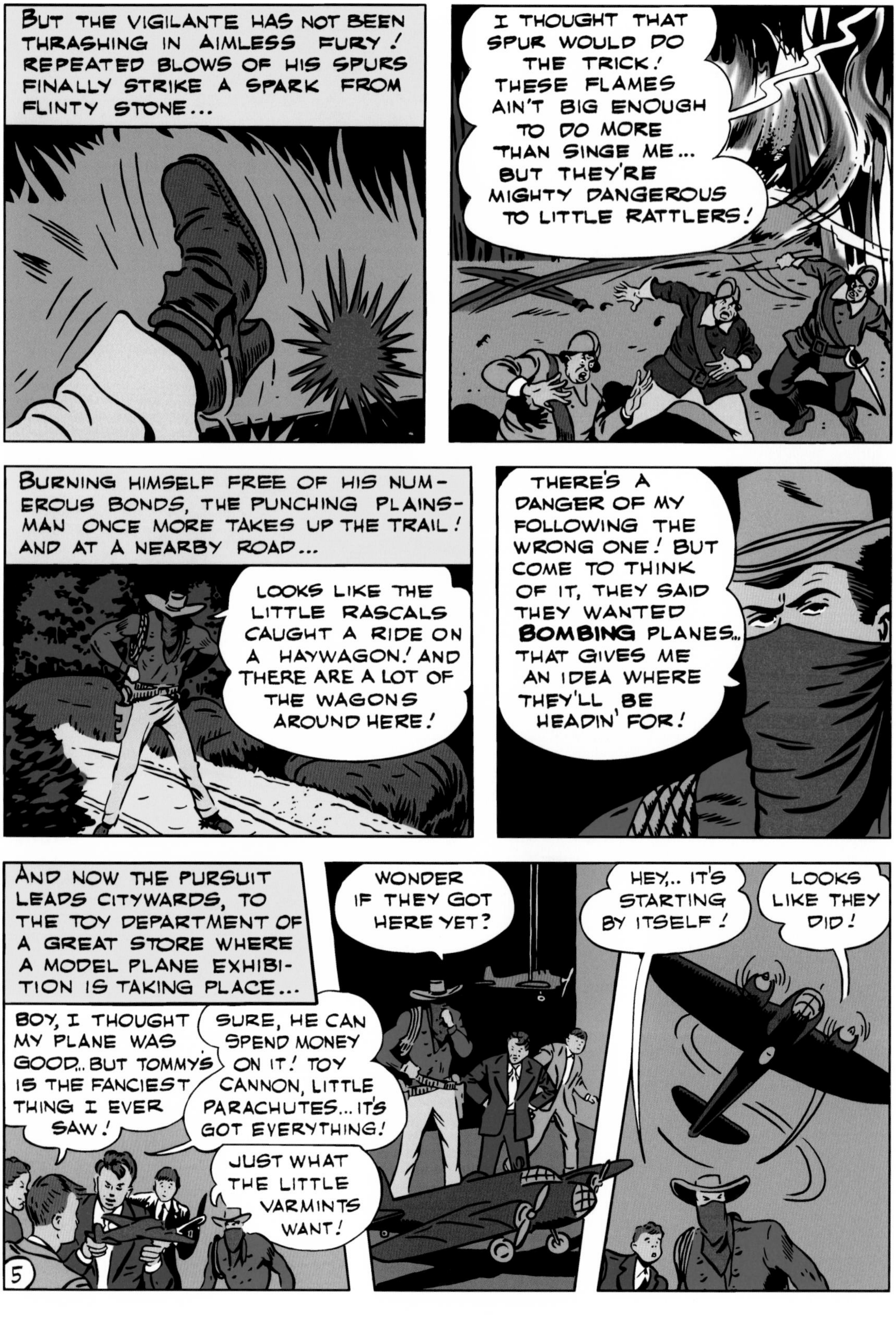
BUT THE VIGILANTE HAS NOT BEEN THRASHING IN AIMLESS FURY! REPEATED BLOWS OF HIS SPURS FINALLY STRIKE A SPARK FROM FLINTY STONE...
I THOUGHT THAT SPUR WOULD DO THE TRICK! THESE FLAMES AIN'T BIG ENOUGH TO DO MORE THAN SINGE ME... BUT THEY'RE MIGHTY DANGEROUS TO LITTLE RATTLERS!
BURNING HIMSELF FREE OF HIS NUMEROUS BONDS, THE PUNCHING PLAINSMAN ONCE MORE TAKES UP THE TRAIL! AND AT A NEARBY ROAD...
LOOKS LIKE THE LITTLE RASCALS CAUGHT A RIDE ON A HAYWAGON! AND THERE ARE A LOT OF THE WAGONS AROUND HERE!
THERE'S A DANGER OF MY FOLLOWING THE WRONG ONE! BUT COME TO THINK OF IT, THEY SAID THEY WANTED BOMBING PLANES... THAT GIVES ME AN IDEA WHERE THEY'LL BE HEADIN' FOR!
AND NOW THE PURSUIT LEADS CITYWARDS, TO THE TOY DEPARTMENT OF A GREAT STORE WHERE A MODEL PLANE EXHIBITION IS TAKING PLACE...
BOY, I THOUGHT MY PLANE WAS GOOD... BUT TOMMY'S IS THE FANCIEST THING I EVER SAW!
SURE, HE CAN SPEND MONEY ON IT! TOY CANNON, LITTLE PARACHUTES... IT'S GOT EVERYTHING!
JUST WHAT THE LITTLE VARMINTS WANT!
5
WONDER IF THEY GOT HERE YET?
HEY,.. IT'S STARTING BY ITSELF!
LOOKS LIKE THEY DID!

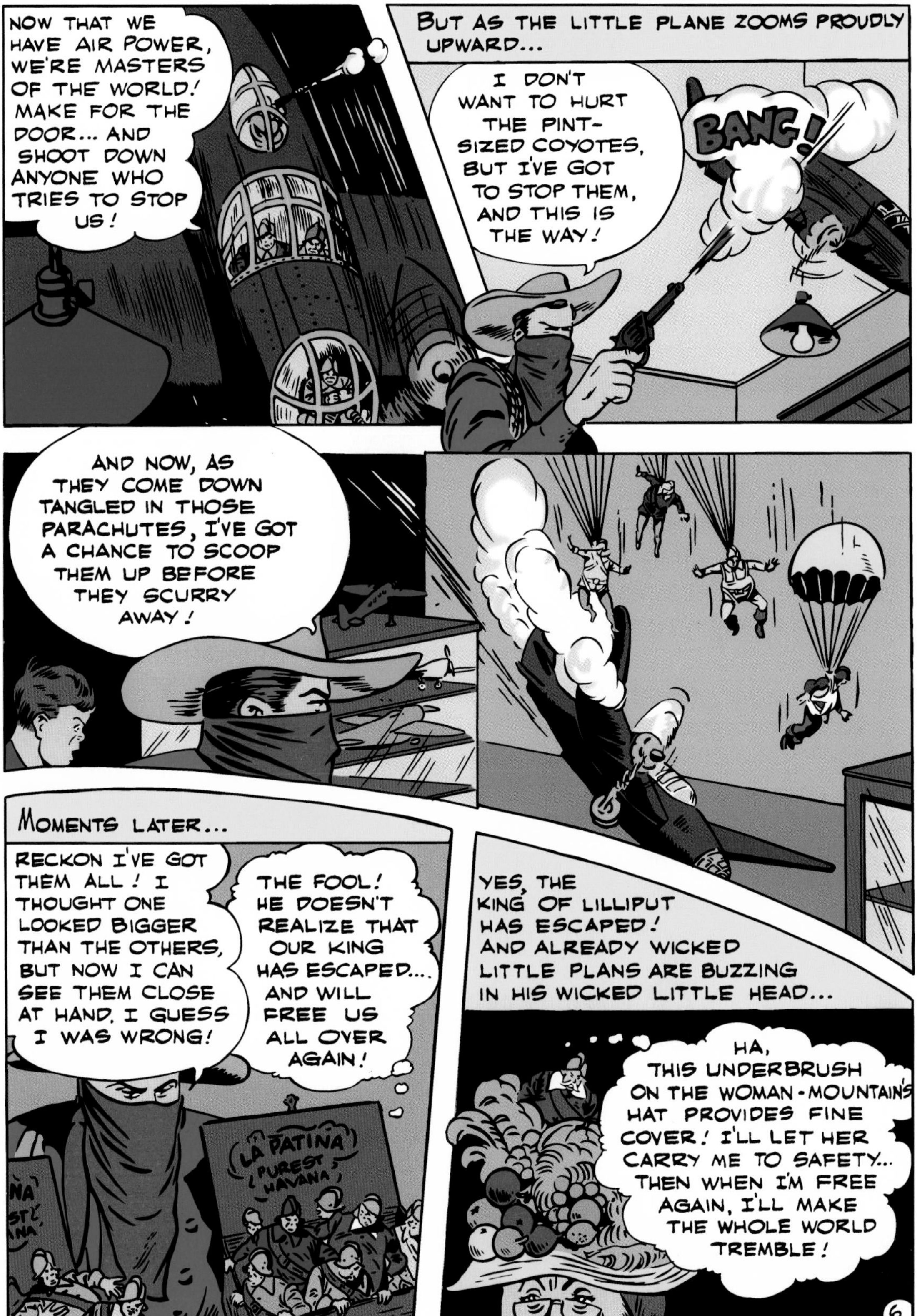
NOW THAT WE HAVE AIR POWER, WE'RE MASTERS OF THE WORLD! MAKE FOR THE DOOR... AND SHOOT DOWN ANYONE WHO TRIES TO STOP US!
BUT AS THE LITTLE PLANE ZOOMS PROUDLY UPWARD...
I DON'T WANT TO HURT THE PINT-SIZED COYOTES, BUT I'VE GOT TO STOP THEM, AND THIS IS THE WAY!
BANG!
AND NOW, AS THEY COME DOWN TANGLED IN THOSE PARACHUTES, I'VE GOT A CHANCE TO SCOOP THEM UP BEFORE THEY SCURRY AWAY!
MOMENTS LATER...
RECKON I'VE GOT THEM ALL! I THOUGHT ONE LOOKED BIGGER THAN THE OTHERS, BUT NOW I CAN SEE THEM CLOSE AT HAND, I GUESS I WAS WRONG!
THE FOOL! HE DOESN'T REALIZE THAT OUR KING HAS ESCAPED... AND WILL FREE US ALL OVER AGAIN!
LA PATINA PUREST HAVANA
YES, THE KING OF LILLIPUT HAS ESCAPED! AND ALREADY WICKED LITTLE PLANS ARE BUZZING IN HIS WICKED LITTLE HEAD...
HA, THIS UNDERBRUSH ON THE WOMAN-MOUNTAIN'S HAT PROVIDES FINE COVER! I'LL LET HER CARRY ME TO SAFETY... THEN WHEN I'M FREE AGAIN, I'LL MAKE THE WHOLE WORLD TREMBLE!
6

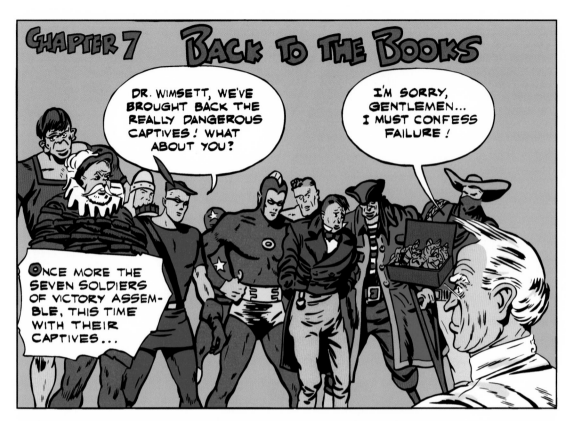

CHAPTER 7 BACK TO THE BOOKS

DR. WIMSETT, WE'VE BROUGHT BACK THE REALLY DANGEROUS CAPTIVES! WHAT ABOUT YOU?

I'M SORRY, GENTLEMEN... I MUST CONFESS FAILURE!

ONCE MORE THE SEVEN SOLDIERS OF VICTORY ASSEMBLE, THIS TIME WITH THEIR CAPTIVES...

I STILL DON'T KNOW WHAT'S GONE WRONG! I HAVE NO TROUBLE AT ALL IN BRINGING CHARACTERS OUT OF BOOKS...

FOR THE LAST TIME... DO I GET MY PIPE, MY BOWL, AND MY FIDDLERS THREE?

ALL RIGHT, KING COLE -- IN JUST A MINUTE!

AT LAST! LIGHT MY PIPE, GIVE ME MY BOWL, AND START PLAYING!

YOU SEE? BRINGING THEM HERE'S EASY AS PIE... BUT I CAN'T SEND THEM BACK!

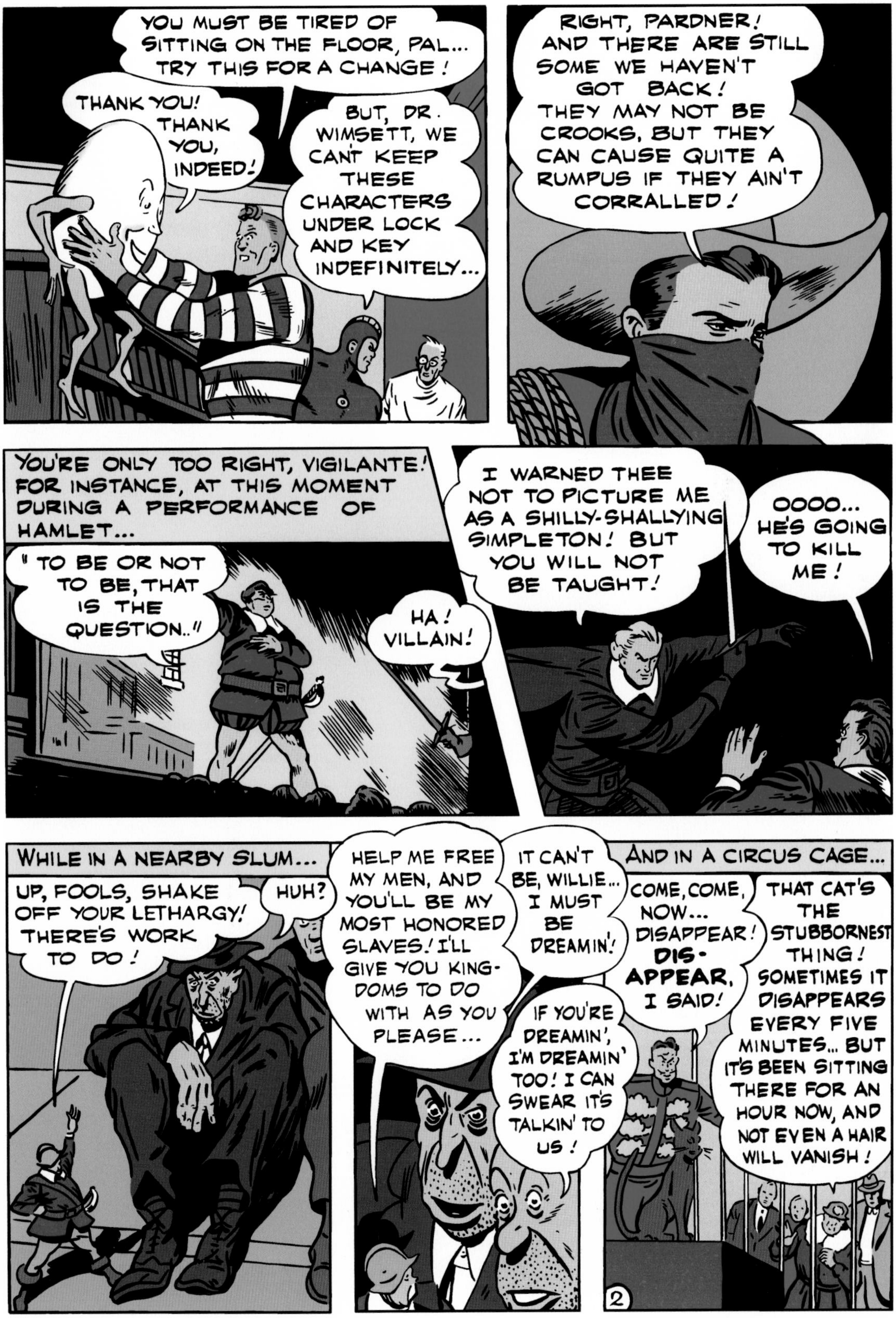
YOU MUST BE TIRED OF SITTING ON THE FLOOR, PAL... TRY THIS FOR A CHANGE!
THANK YOU! THANK YOU, INDEED!
BUT, DR. WIMSETT, WE CAN'T KEEP THESE CHARACTERS UNDER LOCK AND KEY INDEFINITELY...
RIGHT, PARDNER! AND THERE ARE STILL SOME WE HAVEN'T GOT BACK! THEY MAY NOT BE CROOKS, BUT THEY CAN CAUSE QUITE A RUMPUS IF THEY AIN'T CORRALLED!
YOU'RE ONLY TOO RIGHT, VIGILANTE! FOR INSTANCE, AT THIS MOMENT DURING A PERFORMANCE OF HAMLET...
"TO BE OR NOT TO BE, THAT IS THE QUESTION.."
HA! VILLAIN!
I WARNED THEE NOT TO PICTURE ME AS A SHILLY-SHALLYING SIMPLETON! BUT YOU WILL NOT BE TAUGHT!
OOOO... HE'S GOING TO KILL ME!
WHILE IN A NEARBY SLUM...
UP, FOOLS, SHAKE OFF YOUR LETHARGY! THERE'S WORK TO DO!
HUH?
HELP ME FREE MY MEN, AND YOU'LL BE MY MOST HONORED SLAVES! I'LL GIVE YOU KING-DOMS TO DO WITH AS YOU PLEASE...
IT CAN'T BE, WILLIE... I MUST BE DREAMIN'!
IF YOU'RE DREAMIN', I'M DREAMIN' TOO! I CAN SWEAR IT'S TALKIN' TO US!
AND IN A CIRCUS CAGE...
COME, COME, NOW... DISAPPEAR! DIS-APPEAR, I SAID!
THAT CAT'S THE STUBBORNEST THING! SOMETIMES IT DISAPPEARS EVERY FIVE MINUTES... BUT IT'S BEEN SITTING THERE FOR AN HOUR NOW, AND NOT EVEN A HAIR WILL VANISH!
2

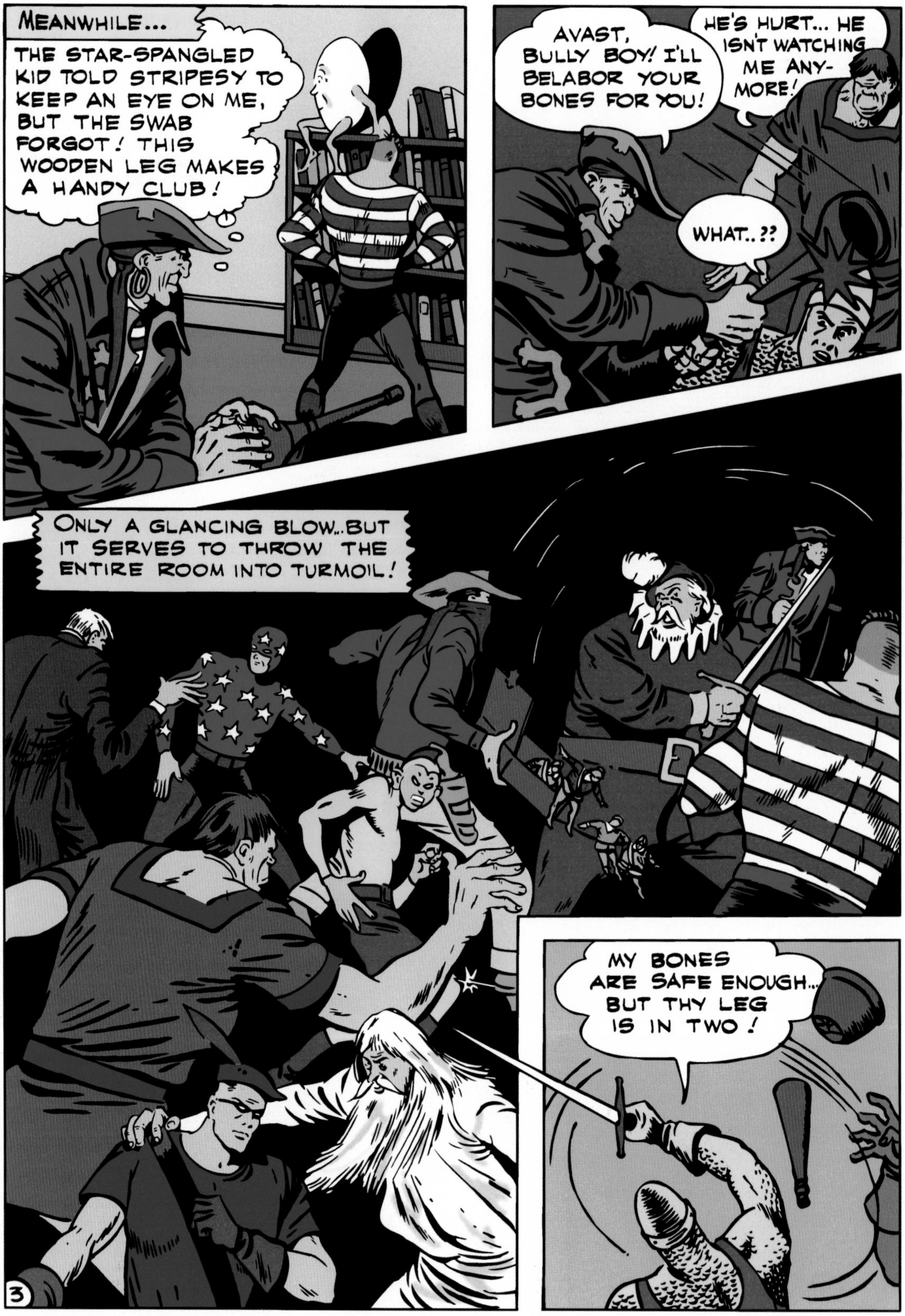
MEANWHILE...
THE STAR-SPANGLED KID TOLD STRIPESY TO KEEP AN EYE ON ME, BUT THE SWAB FORGOT! THIS WOODEN LEG MAKES A HANDY CLUB!
AVAST, BULLY BOY! I'LL BELABOR YOUR BONES FOR YOU!
HE'S HURT... HE ISN'T WATCHING ME ANY-MORE!
WHAT..??
ONLY A GLANCING BLOW...BUT IT SERVES TO THROW THE ENTIRE ROOM INTO TURMOIL!
MY BONES ARE SAFE ENOUGH... BUT THY LEG IS IN TWO!
3

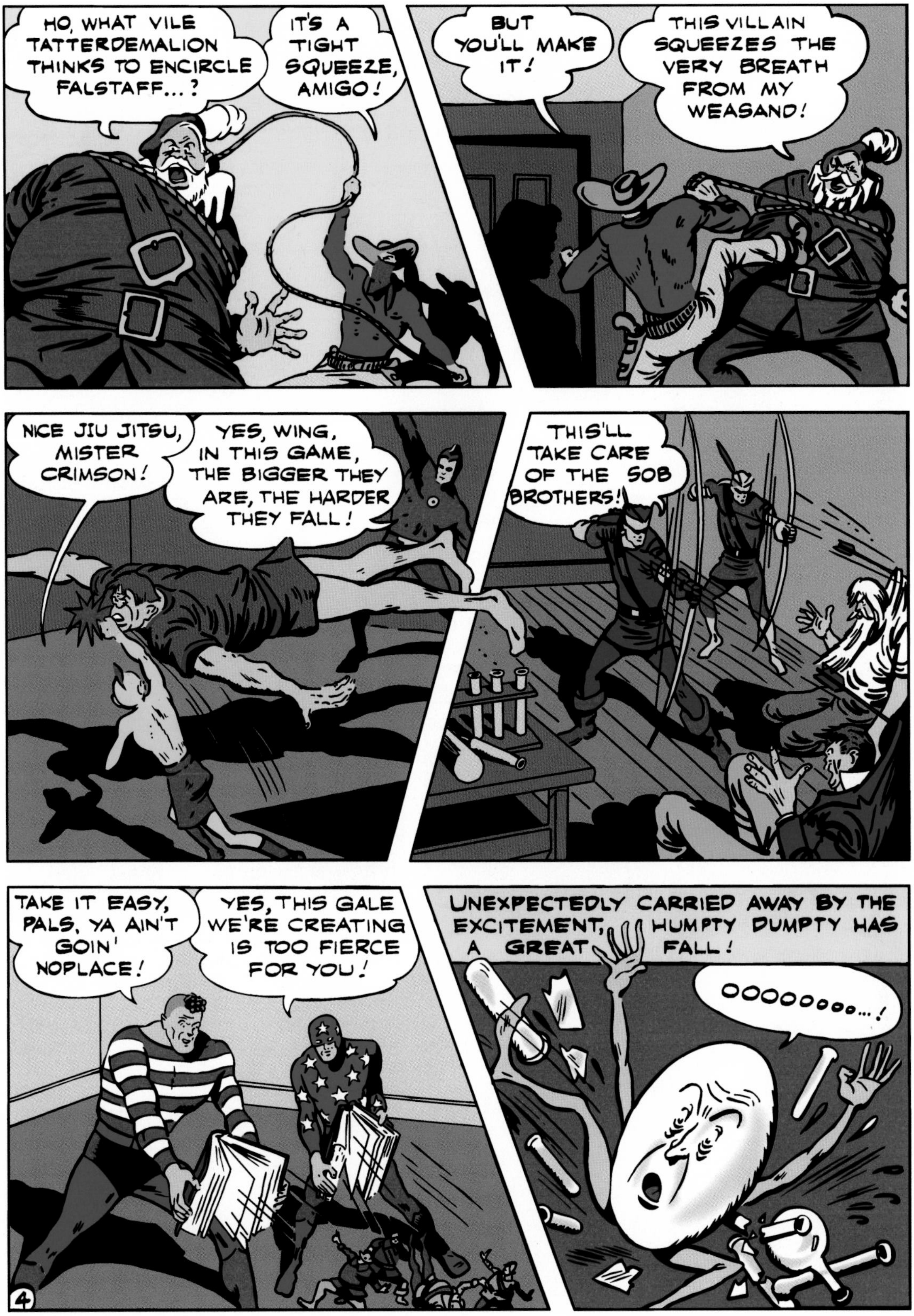
HO, WHAT VILE TATTERDEMALION THINKS TO ENCIRCLE FALSTAFF...?
IT'S A TIGHT SQUEEZE, AMIGO!
BUT YOU'LL MAKE IT!
THIS VILLAIN SQUEEZES THE VERY BREATH FROM MY WEASAND!
NICE JIU JITSU, MISTER CRIMSON!
YES, WING, IN THIS GAME, THE BIGGER THEY ARE, THE HARDER THEY FALL!
THIS'LL TAKE CARE OF THE SOB BROTHERS!
TAKE IT EASY, PALS, YA AIN'T GOIN' NOPLACE!
YES, THIS GALE WE'RE CREATING IS TOO FIERCE FOR YOU!
4
UNEXPECTEDLY CARRIED AWAY BY THE EXCITEMENT, HUMPTY DUMPTY HAS A GREAT FALL!
OOOOOOOO...!

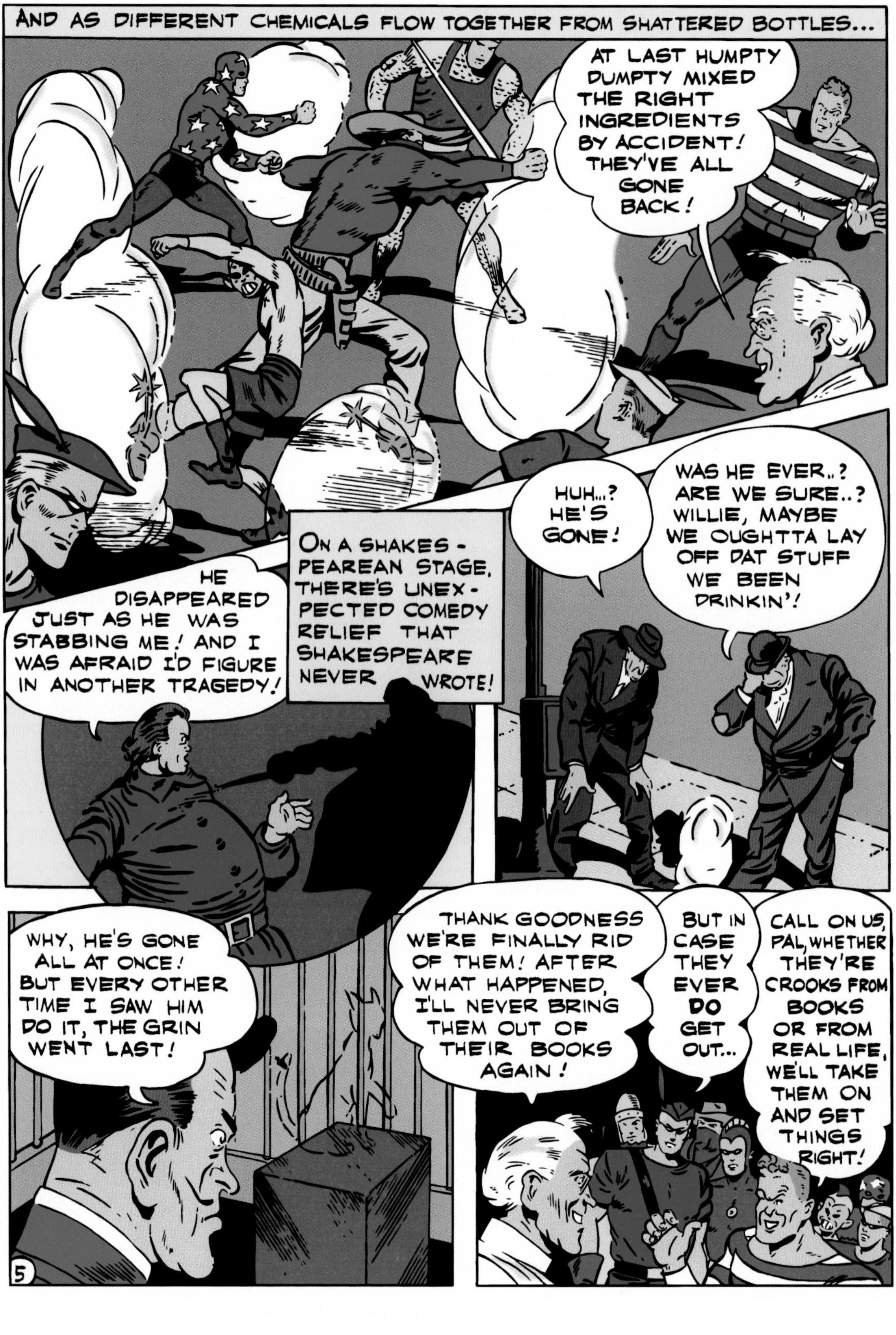
AND AS DIFFERENT CHEMICALS FLOW TOGETHER FROM SHATTERED BOTTLES...
AT LAST HUMPTY DUMPTY MIXED THE RIGHT INGREDIENTS BY ACCIDENT! THEY'VE ALL GONE BACK!
ON A SHAKES-PEAREAN STAGE, THERE'S UNEX-PECTED COMEDY RELIEF THAT SHAKESPEARE NEVER WROTE!
HE DISAPPEARED JUST AS HE WAS STABBING ME! AND I WAS AFRAID I'D FIGURE IN ANOTHER TRAGEDY!
HUH...? HE'S GONE!
WAS HE EVER..? ARE WE SURE..? WILLIE, MAYBE WE OUGHTTA LAY OFF DAT STUFF WE BEEN DRINKIN'!
WHY, HE'S GONE ALL AT ONCE! BUT EVERY OTHER TIME I SAW HIM DO IT, THE GRIN WENT LAST!
5
THANK GOODNESS WE'RE FINALLY RID OF THEM! AFTER WHAT HAPPENED, I'LL NEVER BRING THEM OUT OF THEIR BOOKS AGAIN!
BUT IN CASE THEY EVER DO GET OUT...
CALL ON US, PAL, WHETHER THEY'RE CROOKS FROM BOOKS OR FROM REAL LIFE, WE'LL TAKE THEM ON AND SET THINGS RIGHT!

THE WORLD OF MAGIC
Joe Samachson's script for LEADING COMICS #15

P. 6

1. Scene: Vig, normal again, facing normal gnomes.

Vig: You see what I can do, muchachos, so ~~don't~~ better

               not rile me.

Gnome: We'll be careful, stranger. We won't fight with

               you any more...only with each other.
                                    and
2. Scene: Vig ~~facing normal~~ gnomes.

Vig: You won't do that neither, amigos...I've found a
                               your
               way to settle ~~the~~ argument. ~~Then you're right~~
               Ah, you've decided that
Gnome (Littlehead): We're right, of course.
                    he's decided that
Bighead: No, we're right.
                  ^
3. Scene: Vig, facing startled gnomes.
                                                     speakin'
Vig: Both of you are right. But instead of ~~saying~~
                                                      ^
               your remarks, you gotta sing them.

Bunch of gnomes: Sing them?

4. Caption: ~~reading~~ The Vigilante's new music students are

               hardly the type ~~likely~~ to make a success in opera,

               but soon, under his expert instruction...
                                      conducting with baton.
Scene: Littleheads singing. Vig ~~leading them~~
                                         ^
Littleheads: A straight line is...

5. Scene: Bigheads singing, Vig turned to conduct them also.

Bigheads: The shortest distance between two points is...
Littleheads: The shortest distance between two points.
6. Scene: Vig conducting ~~Littleheads again~~ all.

Bigheads: A straight line. The shortest distance between two points is

Littleheads: A straight line is the shortest distance between two points.

Vig: Perfect. This round can keep goin' forever...and

               you'll both be right.

Although the adventure chronicled in LEADING COMICS #14 proved to be the final Seven Soldiers story published during the Golden Age, writer Joe Samachson had already finished his script for issue #15 by the time the decision was made to switch the title's content to funny animal comics. His original manuscript (a sample page of which is reproduced above) went into a drawer, where it remained until assistant editor Paul Levitz rediscovered it in 1974. After being updated, the story ran in 1975 as a serialized back-up feature in ADVENTURE COMICS #438-443, edited by Joe Orlando and illustrated by Dick Dillin, Tex Blaisdell, Howard Chaykin, Lee Elias, Mike Grell, Ernie Chua, José Luis García-López and Mike Royer. Now, as a unique coda to the original run of the Law's Legionnaires, DC is proud to present the full text of Samachson's script for this lost issue of LEADING COMICS, complete and unabridged.

LEADING COMICS

LEGEND: The Soldiers of Victory have experienced adventures as strange and unbelievable as human beings ever had... but never before have they even dreamed of such fantastic and bewildering events as follows their meeting with Willie Wisher. For Willie has the unique gift of being able to make anything he wishes come true: and what he wishes up for the Legionnaires is almost beyond imagination in our ordinary world, although it's merely commonplace in the...
"LAND OF MAGIC!"

SPLASH PANEL: Willie, wearing a magician's dunce-cap cocked on his head at a jaunty angle, is stirring a great pot, in which our different heroes can be seen, much smaller than Willie. He is dumping into the pot from a ladle some of the characters that will appear later... animals in the style of animal comics, gnomish-looking creatures, the magician of Chapter II, etc.

P. 2

1. **Caption:** Before a distinguished audience, a new film is about to have its first showing.

Scene: John Shoman, movie producer type, standing before movie screen, facing audience vaguely seen in front of him.

Shoman: Ladies and Gentlemen, you are about to witness the most sensational, colossal newsreel epic ever filmed! This masterpiece of the silver screen depicts the adventures of the famous Soldiers of Victory...

2. **Scene:** Several members of audience whispering to each other.

Man: So that's John Shoman? Never heard his name before. Who is he?

Second Man: Oh, Shoman's a rich man who's made a hobby of helping charities. Besides that, he's been trying to produce movies for years. Never got anyplace though.

3. These two guys, closer shot.

First Man: Well, he's got something this time... any picture showing the Soldiers of Victory is sure to be a hit.

Second Man: Yes. I wonder why they let him photograph their adventures.

4. These two guys seen only as silhouettes, against movie screen up front.

First Man: Maybe we'll find out... shhh, it's starting.

5. **Scene:** The screen. The following caption as screen subtitle: "In response to a summons that brooks no delay, the Soldiers of Victory have assembled at an undisclosed meeting place... "

6. **Scene:** As if seen on a screen, in black & white. All heroes together. Vig facing others.

Vig: Well, pardners, here we are. Who sent them carrier pigeons with the message?

Stripesy: Carrier pigeons? You got it wrong, Vig. The Kid and me just got a telegram.

P. 3

1. **Scene:** Avenger and Wing. No longer black & white. Ordinary comic style.

Avenger: Seems to be a slight mix-up here. I read about the meeting in the Personal ad column.

2. **Scene:** G.A. and Speedy.

G.A.: Mix-up is no word for it. We got the summons when a plane did some sky-writing.

3. **Scene:** Shining Knight and Victory.

Shining Knight: By my halidome, this is passing strange. <u>My</u> message was straight from the horse's mouth... my steed, Victory, held the note between his teeth.

4. **Scene:** Heroes baffled and bewildered.

Kid: Boys, there's something so wrong it's got me worried. If none of us sent the messages, who did? And how did he know where to reach us?

5. **Scene:** All swinging around to face Willie Wisher, a good-natured little man with a little spit-curl in the middle of his forehead.

Willie: Excuse me, gentlemen, I am Willie Wisher... I sent the messages.

Stripesy: Huh... ? You?

6. **Scene:** Willie holding up his hand to quiet them.

Willie: Of course... I simply <u>wished</u> you to have them. You see, I can make anything at all come true just by wishing for it.

P. 4

1. **Scene:** Heroes all guffawing as they face Willie.

Wing: Ho, ho. Little man must have good sense of humor.

Speedy: He'd be a riot on the stage.

Willie: I know you don't believe me... but you will soon, when you have your wonderful adventures. Now, to make sure we have a record of them...

1. **Scene:** Willie alone, very thoughtful.

Willie: I wish... I wish for John Shoman and some newsreel cameramen.

3. **Scene:** Heroes staring at Willie and five newsreel cameramen who have suddenly popped into existence.

Sound: Pop!

G.A.: Huh..? What..?

Vig: It can't be! My eyes are goin' back on me!

4. **Scene:** Willie, very thoughtful, as the others stare.

Willie: Ah, now you're beginning to believe. Now, where shall I send you? Let me see... how about the Land of Magic?

Kid: Land of Magic? There's no such place.

5. **Scene:** Close-up of Willie.

Willie: Is that so? I just wish you were there... you'd find out! Yes, I wish you were there!

6. **Scene:** Heroes and newsreel men, small, shown flying through the air over river, spreading out, but heading in the same general direction.

Stripesy: Yiii... what's happenin' to us? Where are we headin' for?

7. **Scene:** Screen subtitle again.

Subtitle: Where are you heading for? The Land of Magic, of course! It's such a land as you have never even remotely imagined... wait till you see it!

CHAPTER II

STARRING THE SHINING KNIGHT

LEGEND: Suppose you had to fight an opponent who could anticipate your every move. He knows how you feel and what you think... because he thinks and feels exactly the same way himself. He's just as strong as you are, just as clever, just as quick... and he has a few friends to help him, which you have not. You'd be in a spot, huh? Well, that's exactly the spot the Shining Knight is in when he tangles with a magician, and the wily wizard sets...
"KNIGHT AFTER KNIGHT!"

SPLASH PANEL: The Knight is dueling with his own image as seen in a large mirror, the sword coming out of the mirror to clash against his own sword. Surlin, the magician, is standing by, grinning.

1. **Caption:** The champion of chivalry and Victory come to earth to find a familiar touch to unfamiliar surroundings.

Scene: Knight and Victory landing, close but separate. There's a castle off to one side.

Knight: Hola, Victory, seest what I see? 'Tis a castle... such a castle as abounded in the days of King Arthur.

2. **Scene:** Knight and Vic watching as a couple of men in strange costumes pass by. They wear what seem to be clown costumes with short pants.

First Man: Beware, friend. Let us not pass too close to the castle of the magician, Surlin.

Second Man: Yes. He has captured the Princess of Twin Oaks, and he means to keep her, so he is suspicious of strangers.

P. 2

1. **Scene:** Knight and Victory.

Knight: Didst hear, Victory? An evil magician holds a fair maiden in duress vile! 'Tis as in the days of the Round Table.

2. **Scene:** Knight on Victory flying toward castle.

Knight: But we shall rescue the maiden or die in the attempt. Spare not thy wings, brave steed.

3. **Scene:** Knight on Victory flying in through window to see magician, more or less like Merlin, and his thugs, dressed much as

passersby were.

Knight: Ah, there he is!

Magician: The Shining Knight! I have heard of him!

4. Scene: Magician starting magic gestures. Knight dismounted, coming at him.

Magician: But my magic will deprive him of his strength...

Knight: He may be dangerous. Wait without, Victory, while I dispose of the villain.

5. Scene: Knight socking magician, who goes flying.

Knight: Ah, 'tis my strength will deprive him of his magic.

Magician: Yiiii... !

6. Scene: Knight using his sword to cut through bunch of swords held by thugs who come at him.

Knight: As for these rogues, I will shorten their swords with my own enchanted weapon.

Thug: Owww..!

7. Scene: Knight knocking what's left of sword out of hand of one thug, so that hilt hits other thug on jaw.

Knight: And they shall taste defeat to the hilt.

Thug: Eeeehhh...

P. 3

1. Caption: But as the man of yesterday steps back to avoid a missile...

Scene: Knight stepping to one side to avoid a dagger thrown at him, at the same time cutting dagger in two with his sword.

Knight: I fear neither swords nor daggers, villains...

2. Scene: Knight stepping in front of mirror to see his image.

Knight: But who..?

3. Scene: Knight staring at his image, which stares back.

Knight: Ha, 'tis only mine own image. For a moment, so clear it was, I thought 'twas another Knight.

4. Scene: Image stepping out of mirror to confront Knight.

New Knight: Thou art right, Shining Knight... and also wrong. I am indeed thy image... but that does not prevent me from stepping out of this magic mirror!

Knight: Wha..?

5. Scene: Both Knights holding swords up, ready to clash.

New Knight: And as the mirror belongs to Surlin, I do too! So — On guard!

Knight: Nay, this cannot be!

6. Scene: Knights dueling.

New Knight: It is! Thou wilt doubt no more when my sword cuts through thy coat of mail.

Knight: That will never be. Lay on, Knight, thou shalt soon have thy fill.

P. 4

1. Caption: But with each swordsman the exact duplicate of the other, never were opponents so evenly matched! Blade clashes on blade, and as the moments go by, with no advantage to either man...

Scene: The two Knights dueling.

New Knight: By my troth, I never thought to meet my equal with the sword! But I have met him today.

Knight: Aye, and so have I. My arm tires...

2. Scene: Thugs tackling real Knight, downing him. Surlin watching.

Thug: That's what we were waiting for, Knight.

Surlin: Aye, now he cannot fight back. Thanks, Knight of the Mirror.

3. Scene: Knight held by thugs.

Knight (bubble): Now will the magician slay me... unless I think fast. But what can I do?

4. Scene: Knight held by thugs, nodding toward his opponent.

Knight (bubble): Ah, I have it.

Knight: Let go of me, scurvy knaves! Thou hast mistaken me for the other Knight... <u>he</u> is your enemy!

Thug: The other one?

5. **Scene:** Thugs still holding Knight, facing Surlin.

Thug: Which one have we, Surlin, the real Knight or the one from the mirror?

Surlin: Hmm, I myself cannot tell them apart. Best to take no chances...

6. **Scene:** Surlin pointing to other Knight, thugs plunging at latter.

Surlin: Seize him too!

Knight: Why, thou scurvy magician..!

Thug: Save your breath, Knight, you'll need it.

7. **Caption:** Presently...

Scene: Both Knights sitting on ground, hands tied behind them, as Surlin leaves them. Feet tied together.

Surlin: Later, I shall find a way to decide which is which... meanwhile, both will be safe here.

P. 5

1. **Scene:** Knight staring at his bonds, twisting around to look at them.

Knight: The rogues have bound me well... try as I will, I cannot cut the ropes with my sword.

2. **Scene:** Knight inching along floor toward the mirror. He pushes himself backward using his bound feet.

Knight: But I have a plan. First must I reach the magic mirror.

3. **Scene:** Knight is in front of mirror, with his back to it. His reflection in it as before.

Knight: The blade in the mirror is as sharp as mine...

4. **Scene:** Knight rubbing ropes against the blade of sword in mirror near hilt, where it sticks out of scabbard.

Knight: And that blade I _can_ reach.

5. **Scene:** Knight standing up, ropes falling from him.

Knight: Ah, I have outwitted the magician with his own mirror.

6. **Scene:** The other Knight running toward Knight, sword drawn.

Knight: What? Thou too art free?

New Knight: Aye, I was not tied as tightly as thou. Now, with none to interfere, shall we see who is master.

7. **Caption:** But as sword clangs against sword...

Scene: Knights dueling again, thugs running in once more.

Thug: They both got loose!

Second Thug: And this time we have no idea which is which! We'd better get them both again!

P. 6

1. **Caption:** But there is someone who _does_ have an idea. Suddenly...

Scene: Both Knights looking up to see Victory flying in through window.

Knight: Victory! Thou must have grown tired waiting!

2. **Scene:** Victory knocking over thugs with wing as they go after real Knight. Real Knight knocking sword out of other's hand.

Victory: Thanks, brave steed. Thou, at least, knowest me.

3. **Caption:** And as Victory's aid tips the scale of battle...

Scene: Thugs on floor, Knight with sword out facing magician.

Knight: Now, thou magicking rogue, either release the Princess of Twin Oaks or thy life will pay the forfeit.

Magician: The Princess..? You don't understand, Knight... let me show you!

4. **Scene:** Magician indicating prize sow in pigpen as Knight stares.

Magician: _There_ is the Princess of Twin Oaks... a prize sow. Her owner promised to sell her to me, then changed his mind, so I took her by force.

Knight: And I thought to find a damsel in distress! Well, at any rate, thou must return her to her owner.

5. **Caption:** And as the magician promises to do no further harm...

Scene: Knight and Victory watching other Knight about to return to mirror.

New Knight: Thou hast been a chivalrous opponent, Knight. So, before I return whence I came, this word of advice. Thou too canst use the mirror... step into it, and thou goest where thou wilt.

Knight: Thanks, Knight.

6. **Scene:** Knight and Victory watching other knight step into mirror.

Knight: I fear lest some misfortune has happened to my comrades. And there is only one man who knows where they have all gone.

7. **Scene:** Knight on Victory riding into mirror.

Knight: So 'tis back to Willie Wisher for us, Victory. And woe betide him if they have come to harm!

CHAPTER III

STARRING THE STAR-SPANGLED KID AND STRIPESY

LEGEND: In a country where anything can happen... you should see what happens to a dog! It happens also to cats, sheep, and other once-friendly creatures, who run wild for lack of proper training. And the result is that the Star-Spangled Kid and Stripesy have some wild adventures ahead of them when they run into the...
"DEAD END ANIMALS!"

SPLASH PANEL: Kid and Stripesy are crouching, all set to leap at a group of the animals, who have cigarettes drooping in typical dead-end style from their mouths. The kangaroo is reaching stealthily into his pouch, pulling out a gun.

Caption: A three-point landing brings the Star-Spangled Kid and Stripesy to their journey's end.

Scene: Kid and Stripesy coming to earth, sitting down.

Sound: Bump!

Stripesy: Owww..!

Kid: I wish Willie had wished us an easier landing!

2. **Scene:** Kid and Stripesy standing up, looking around.

Sound from side: GRRRRR..! Wow! Yiii..! Help!

Stripesy: Never mind that, Kid... he wished us into a place where somethin's happenin'. We couldn't ask for anything more.

Kid: Right, Stripesy, let's go.

P. 2

1. **Scene:** Kid and Stripesy running into building marked LEO'S PAL CLUB.

Sounds: Same as before, but louder.

Kid: This is the place.

Stripesy: Sounds like a free-for-all.

2. **Scene:** Kid and Stripesy have entered to see animals engaged in free-for-all. There are cats, dogs, black sheep, a bear, a kangaroo, a goose, etc. All drawn with clothes, as in style of animal comics. This is a big scene, and off to one side is a lion, moaning and wringing his hands.

Sounds: As before, but louder.

Lion: Oh, dear, oh, dear, what shall I do?

Stripesy: Kid, do you see what I do?

Kid: What are they... man or beast?

3. **Scene:** Animals have stopped, are staring at Kid and Stripesy.

Black Sheep: Who are dose funny-lookin' guys buttin' in?

Goose: I dunno, Shep... but if dey're lookin' for trouble, dis is da place ta find it!

4. **Scene:** Kangaroo has leaped feet first toward Stripesy, the black sheep laughing.

Sheep: Attaboy, Pockets... kick deir brains out.

Kid: We've got somethin' to say about that, chum. K47, Stripesy...

Stripesy: Got it, Kid.

5. **Scene:** Stripesy has ducked, at the same time sticking one hand up to grab kangaroo's foot, as latter sails over him.

Stripesy: End of the line, my high-stepping friend.

P. 3

1. **Scene:** Kid has grabbed kangaroo's head, Stripesy his feet. They're beginning to swing him.

Kid: Nice work. Now to build up steam...

2. **Scene:** They've tossed the kangaroo into the middle of the other animals, causing big commotion.

Kid: And send you back where you came from.

Animal Sounds: Yiiii..! Grrr..! Wow..!

3. **Scene:** Stripesy tossing chair into middle of animals.

Stripesy: Here's something else to keep you busy.

Animal Sounds: Grrr..! Wow..!

4. **Caption:** Unexpectedly...

Scene: The chair sailing back, hitting Stripesy on head. Kid watching.

Stripesy: Argh...

Kid: Huh..? Who threw that?

5. **Scene:** Animals overwhelming Kid.

Sheep: You'll never know, sap. I'm gonna pull da wool over your eyes.

Kangaroo: Yeah, and you're goin' out like a light.

6. **Caption:** Out like a light it is! And some time later, when the comrades in combat awaken...

Scene: Kid and Stripesy sitting up, hands tied behind back.

Stripesy: Owww, my head hurts so much, I don't know whether I had a nightmare or we were really fightin' with a bunch of animals.

Kid: If it was a nightmare, Stripesy, I'm in it with you... my hands are tied too.

P. 4

1. **Scene:** Lion facing them.

Lion: Don't worry, I'll untie you. I'm so ashamed of the way the boys behaved... so ashamed. I try to teach them to be useful members of society, but it's no use.

2. **Scene:** Lion alone, looking mournful.

Lion: They're wild, very wild... and the wildest of them all is that black sheep. He's always leading the others astray.

3. **Scene:** Lion staring at ropes, preparing to untie them.

Stripesy: Never mind the sob story now, pal. Untie us first, and then talk.

Lion: Don't be offended, I was just trying to figure out how to start.

Balloon from side, very small letters: Is that so?

4. **Scene:** Lion terrified, looking off to side. We don't see what he sees.

Balloon as before: Get away from dem ropes before I knock yer teeth down yer t'roat!

Lion: Yiii... don't hit me, don't hit me! I'll do anything you say!

5. **Scene:** We see a little mouse swaggering toward lion while startled heroes look on.

Kid: Why, it's a mouse!

Mouse: Yeah, and it's lucky da boys left me ta keep an eye on t'ings. I'm tough, see? I don't take nuttin' from nobody. So ya better not start anyt'ing.

Lion: S-sure, Mousey, I don't want to start anything.

6. **Scene:** Kid staring at mouse.

Kid (bubble): Hmm, this mouse may be as tough as he seems, but I'll bet he has his weak spot. And I think I can find it.

7. **Scene:** Kid talking to mouse.

Kid: So you think you're sitting pretty, huh? Well, Mousey, you're only a sap... the biggest sap I ever saw. If you only knew!

Mouse: Me, a sap? Listen, chum, I told ya I don't take dat from nobody.

P. 5

1. **Scene:** Mouse close to Kid and Stripesy.

Kid: That's what you think. Don't you realize what's happening?

Stripesy: Why, you're being played for the biggest sap in the world. (Don't know what the Kid's game is, but it won't hurt to help him on.)

Mouse: Me?

2. **Scene:** Kid and mouse.

Kid: Sure, <u>you</u>. Don't you know you can't trust cats? Well, those seemingly friendly felines in your own gang are preparing the sweetest double-cross you ever saw. They're...

Mouse: Go on, go on, don't keep me in suspense.

3. **Scene:** Kid alone, very airy.

Kid: They're... Oh, what's the use of telling you? You wouldn't believe it. Just wait till it happens to you, that's all. And you thought they were your pals.

4. **Scene:** The others watching enraged mouse.

Mouse: The dirty rats... I mean, cats... so they're tryin' to pull a fast one, huh? I never did trust them guys... they slink too much.

5. **Scene:** Mouse scurrying toward door as others watch.

Kid: They're clever. They got you out of the way by having you watch us, so they could cook up their dirty work.

Mouse: Yeah? Well, it ain't gonna woik. I'm keeping an eye on them rats... I mean, cats.

6. **Scene:** Lion untying them.

Stripesy: Nice work, Kid.

Lion: Yes, I'm so glad you got rid of him. He simply terrifies me.

7. **Caption:** As the partners in peril are released... well, prepare yourself for a shock. For the chances are that you won't believe your eyes any more than they did.

Scene: Kid and Stripesy watching chair move.

Chair: I'm in the wrong place. I belong over on the other side.

Stripesy: Kid, that chair! He... it... talked!

Kid: And walked!

P. 6

1. **Scene:** They and lion staring at chair.

Lion: Oh, I thought you knew. In this country, all sorts of things you consider lifeless can move. Usually, they don't though, because they're lazy.

Chair: No, we're not lazy. We're just peaceful, that's all.

2. **Scene:** Chair facing Kid and Stripesy.

Chair: But when this big bum with the stripes threw me around, I wouldn't stand for it. So naturally, I came right back and hit him.

Stripesy: So that's the way it happened. And I thought someone threw you at me.

3. **Scene:** Baseball crashing through window, as they watch.

Sound: Crash!

Balloon from outside: Yippeee! Shep hit a home run!

Kid: It's those animals... they're outside playing baseball.

Lion: Yes, they play all the time. I don't mind their having a good time... but they should do <u>some</u> work.

4. **Scene:** Kid facing Stripesy and Lion.

Kid: Well, I think I know how to reform them. Come on, Stripesy.

5. **Scene:** Outside, Kid and Stripesy. They're watching animals play baseball. Kangaroo is umpire. Sheep batting.

Kangaroo: Strike t'ree, yer out.

Sheep: Why, ya doity bum!

Stripesy: What's up, Kid?

Kid: They're busy with their game, so I can use my skill as a pickpocket... in reverse.

6. **Scene:** Kid slipping torch and matches into kangaroo's pouch, reaching out from behind a bench to do so. Kangaroo too busy to notice.

Kangaroo: Ball two!

Balloon from side: Why, dat umpire's blind.

Kid (bubble): What a surprise when he finds this torch and these matches in his pouch.

P. 7

1. **Caption:** And then...

Scene: Kid throwing lighted torch into Pal

club, through window, Stripesy watching.

Kid: Get ready to fade to one side, Stripesy. This torch will make them hopping mad.

2. **Caption:** The Star-Spangled Kid is right. A second later...

Scene: Chairs, table, desk, sailing through window.

Table: Lucky I put that torch out. Why, there might have been a terrible conflagration.

Desk: Fun is fun, but trying to set us on fire is too much.

3. **Scene:** Furniture staring at torch in pouch of kangaroo.

Chair: A torch! There's the guy that did it.

Table: We'll teach him not to do it again. Com on, boys.

4. **Scene:** Table sailing into kangaroo. Chair knocking over sheep.

Table: Trying to burn us up, huh?

Kangaroo: Hey..!

Sheep: Eeeehhh..!

5. **Caption:** Baseballs and bats join the fray!

Scene: Fight scene, with chairs knocking animals around, baseballs bouncing off them, bats hitting them over head.

Bat: Yippee! This is more fun than playing the same game day after day.

Animal: Yiii..!

6. **Caption:** And presently...

Scene: Table and chair staring at knocked-down animals.

Table: Had enough, huh? Well, this is just the beginning.

Chair: Yes, from now on you guys better be good, or else!!!

7. **Caption:** A happy lion expresses his gratitude.

Scene: In water, Kid and Stripesy mounted on whale, lion waving good-bye from shore with handkerchief.

Lion: Thanks ever so much for helping reform

those naughty boys. They won't cause any more trouble now.

Kid: Thank you for supplying your whale friend to take us home.

Stripesy: Yes, we wanna get back fast and see what happened to the others. So long, Leo!

CHAPTER IV

STARRING THE GREEN ARROW AND SPEEDY

LEGEND: Heavenly days are here for the Green Arrow and Speedy as they run into the looniest, most unearthly argument ever heard. And when comets and planets leave their orbits to play a part in settling it, the wizard archers have tough sledding against stellar opposition in...
"FATHER TIME'S INN!"

SPLASH PANEL: The Full Moon and First Quarter Moon each have hold of Speedy's hand, are flying with him through sky. Sun and Saturn have hold of G.A. similarly. Father Time is leafing through a HEAVENLY TIME-TABLE, saying in a puzzled way: "Hmm, I can't find those fellows listed here."

1. **Caption:** Arriving in a strange new land, the wizard archers find unexpected hospitality.

Scene: G.A. and Speedy staring at inn. Sign: "FATHER TIME'S INN... ROOMS BY THE YEAR OR CENTURY."

Speedy: Gosh, G.A., wonder what kind of boarders stay for a century.

G.A.: Let's go in and find out, Speedy. An inn is always a good place to pick up information.

2. **Scene:** They're walking inside to see Father Time, with his scythe, and an hour glass beside him.

Speedy: Father Time himself!

G.A.: Yes, and look at the boarders!

P. 2

1. **Scene:** G.A. and Speedy small at side of big scene, in which Father Time faces a First-Quarter Moon, the Sun, Stars, Comets, Planets (including Saturn, with rings).

G.A.: All the heavenly bodies!

Speedy: Yes, and they seem to be having an argument.

2. **Scene:** G.A. and Speedy watching as First-Quarter Moon and Full Moon argue with Father Time.

First-Quarter: Father Time, you've got to admit that I'm the best First-Quarter Moon you ever had.

Time: Yes, I know that, but...

3. **Scene:** First-Quarter, indignant.

First-Quarter: Never mind the <u>buts</u>. Here I get all polished up, so that I'll look nice in the sky, and what happens?

4. **Scene:** First-Quarter pointing at Sun, who looks a little ashamed of himself.

First-Quarter: Just when I come out and make a bow... the Sun has to hide in back of the earth and eclipse me!

Sun: Gosh, I couldn't help it. Astronomers figured out it was time for an eclipse, and I gotta do what they say, don't I?

5. **Scene:** First-Quarter and Full Moon facing Time. G.A. and Speedy at side.

First-Quarter: Well, the least you can do is let me go on again. Full Moon here is willing to let me take his place for one night.

Full Moon: Sure, I won't mind taking a shift off.

Father Time: Now, just a minute, boys, just a minute.

P. 3

1. **Scene:** Father Time facing indignant First-Quarter.

Time: I don't like to be a killjoy... but it can't be done. Rules is rules around here, and they can't be changed.

First-Quarter: That's what <u>you</u> think, Father Time.

2. **Scene:** First-Quarter drawing back arm, winding up to throw a punch.

First-Quarter: There's a rule that you can't kill time around here, but I'll show you...

3. **Scene:** First-Quarter has drawn arm back too far, knocked Saturn's rings awry.

Saturn: Hey, watch what you're doing, Moony, or I'll push your face in.

First-Quarter: Huh..? Listen, Saturn, I can fight rings around you... wanna see me do it?

4. **Caption:** Tempers are running high, and in just a second or two...

Scene: Many of heavenly bodies in free-for-all, our heroes watching.

Speedy: Gosh, G.A., they're sure quick-tempered.

G.A.: Yes, I'm afraid somebody might get hurt.

5. **Scene:** Comet has flown through air to knock G.A. off his feet.

G.A.: Owww... I should have known it would be the innocent bystander!

6. **Scene:** Speedy has picked up star, is throwing him into middle of crowd.

Speedy: Let's see what a shooting star will do to quiet them down.

G.A.: Keep cool, Speedy, keep cool.

P. 4

1. **Scene:** Time lifting scythe as if about to use it. G.A. alarmed and Speedy alarmed.

Speedy: Keep cool? Why, even Time is losing his head. He's going to cut somebody down.

G.A.: I'd better stop him.

2. **Scene:** G.A. shooting arrow to knock scythe out of Time's hand.

G.A.: Drop that, Father Time.

Time: Huh..?

3. **Scene:** Time staring at them, as do all the others.

Time: Why, I hadn't noticed. Look, boys... strangers. What are they doing here?

Comet: I don't know... I thought they were friends of yours.

4. **Scene:** Time pointing at them, others rushing toward them.

Time: Time is everybody's friend... and enemy at the same time. Get them!

5. **Scene:** Mars and Mercury sail into two heroes, knocking them off their feet.

Note to colorist: Be sure Mars colored red.

G.A.: Mars and Mercury in conjunction... owww!

6. **Caption**: Presently...

Scene: Time and others staring down at G.A. and Speedy.

Time: Two Archers! Well, I already have an Archer in the Zodiac, but two are always better than one.

7. **Caption**: "Think I'll put them up in the sky in his place. They'll make a wonderful new constellation."

Scene: Up in sky, we have outlines of G.A. and Speedy. Stars in their bodies more or less trace outlines, as is usually done with Great Bear, etc.

P. 5

1. **Scene**: Father Time laughing as he waves them aside.

Time: However, I haven't got time to take care of them now, so I'll wait till later. A joke on me, eh what? Father Time with no time to spare!

2. **Scene**: G.A. and Speedy together. Time in background.

Speedy: G.A., I'm beginning to think that Father Time's a whack.

G.A.: Yes, it's well known that time produces the craziest changes. But what's going to happen to us is no joke.

3. **Scene**: G.A. and Speedy.

Speedy: And the worst is, that with all those guys hanging around, there's nothing that we can do about it.

G.A.: Maybe there is, Speedy. Time is busy, and the others aren't paying attention to us...

4. **Scene**: G.A. stretching his feet out to grab hourglass between them, turn it upside down.

G.A.: So I can turn Time's hourglass upside down without being noticed.

Speedy: Huh..? What good will that do?

5. **Caption**: What good? When the sands of time run backward, strange things happen!

Scene: Speedy and G.A. staring at their ropes,

which are untying themselves.

Speedy: Look, G.A. ... our ropes are untying themselves!

G.A.: Yes, I figured that would happen!

6. **Scene**: G.A. and Speedy rising to their feet, shaking off ropes, to watch Time and First-Quarter arguing again.

G.A.: And with Time reversed... Father Time and First-Quarter Moon are back at the beginning of their argument again.

7. **Scene**: G.A. and Speedy watching Time turn hour glass back again.

Time: Say, who turned this upside down?

Speedy: Oh, oh, he's wise!

G.A.: And we're in for more trouble.

P. 6

1. **Scene**: Some of constellations of Zodiac running in. These include the Archer, The Crab, Scorpion, Twins, etc., and any more that can be got in. They should be shown as G.A. and Speedy were before — in outline, with stars over different parts of them. If you want to be authentic, you can take a look in the Encyclopedia or dictionary and see how stars are distributed, but there's no real need of that. G.A. and Speedy watching.

Speedy: Trouble is no word for it. Here come some constellations right out of the sky.

2. **Scene**: Archer shooting starry arrows at G.A. and Speedy.

Archer: So you want to take my place, do you?

3. **Scene**: G.A. hitting one starry arrow with his own arrow, Speedy hitting another, stars flying in all directions.

G.A.: No, chum, I don't... I'm satisfied with my own place in the sun.

4. **Scene**: Father Time alarmed as he sees stars being knocked out of Crab as G.A. socks it.

G.A.: I'm not crabbing in the least.

Time: Stop! You'll knock the stars out of place and ruin all the constellations.

5. **Scene**: G.A. and Speedy facing Time, First-Quarter Moon near them.

G.A.: I certainly wouldn't want to do that. But, Father Time, why not settle this quarrel once and for all? I've got an idea...

6. **Scene:** G.A. putting First-Quarter Moon and Last-Quarter together. Speedy and G.A. watching.

G.A.: Why not let First-Quarter and Last-Quarter together take Full Moon's place? All First-Quarter's friends will know about it and be proud of him... but nobody on earth will suspect, especially if clouds drift past the middle.

Time: A wonderful idea, my friend. Now, how can I reward you for that?

7. **Caption:** How? Well, presently...

Scene: G.A. and Speedy rushing through sky on a comet.

Speedy: Nice of Father Time to send us home on this comet, isn't it, G.A.?

G.A.: Sure is, Speedy. I'll bet none of the other boys gets transportation like this.

CHAPTER V

STARRING THE CRIMSON AVENGER AND WING

LEGEND: 'Mid pleasures and palaces, the Crimson Avenger and Wing roam, suffering from growing pains... until they find a royal welcome. But they experience royal treachery as well, when a small-minded monarch tries to frustrate their big-hearted plans. And their situation is desperate, as rulers make their own rules, and...
"KINGS MAKE A FULL HOUSE!"

SPLASH PANEL: Adelbert, as giant, has been holding small Wing and Avenger in his hand close to his face. They're leaping up at him, one to bop him on the nose, the other on the jaw.

1. **Caption:** A distant palace beckons to the Crimson Avenger and Wing.

Scene: Avenger and Wing staring at palace seen in distance.

Wing: This Land of Magic not so bad, Mist' Crimson. Look like nice place.

Avenger: A little fancy for people like us, Wing, but we'll see what goes on there.

2. **Scene:** The two of them coming to very narrow stream.

Wing: Oh, oh, must cross river.

Avenger: It looks shallow. We'll hardly get our feet wet.

P. 2

1. **Scene:** Wing bending down to drink from river. Avenger watching.

Wing: Wing not worried about wet feet. Feel thirsty, wet whistle.

2. **Caption:** Unexpectedly...

Scene: Avenger staring up at Wing, who has grown to twice former size.

Avenger: Huh..? You've shot up to twice your former size!

Wing: And still growing! Always knew I be big man some day!

3. **Scene:** Wing, now about five times Avenger's size, has picked up Avenger, stepped across stream.

Avenger: Well, I'm not drinking that water until I know how to reverse the action. I don't want to be a giant for the rest of my life.

Wing: Wing not worried. Nice to be big... not even get feet wet as expected.

4. **Scene:** They're approaching another little river.

Avenger: Maybe, but I'd rather try what looks like non-magic water. Think I'll have a drink <u>here</u>.

5. **Scene:** Avenger getting smaller. He's about twice height of blades of grass. We see Wing's giant feet.

Avenger: Hey, it's making me <u>shrink</u>!

Wing: Be careful, Mist' Crimson, you get lost in grass!

6. **Caption:** Careful experiments with water from the two streams follow, and presently...

Scene: Giants, they stride over trees toward palace. Each carries bottle full of water.

Avenger: With Growing Water and Shrinking Water in these two bottles, we can control our size as we please.

Wing: Only must watch where we step, not knock over trees.

7. **Scene:** They rush toward palace, whose walls seem to be falling down.

Sound: BOOM!

Wing: Look, Mist' Crimson, palace walls start to fall.

Avenger: Maybe we can save it. Hurry, Wing!

P. 3

1. **Scene:** Wing wrapping his arms around palace to keep walls from falling, Avenger dragging bunch of uprooted trees.
Wing: I got 'em! And if they no fall, they no break.

Avenger: Swell... hold it.

2. **Scene:** Avenger propping up walls with trees.

Avenger: These trees will keep them in place temporarily.

Wing: We pretty good, Mist' Crimson... bet Superman be jealous if he know.

3. **Scene:** King Mistybrain, normal size, running toward giant Wing and Avenger.

Mistybrain: Oh, oh, why did you do it? Why did you save my palace?

Wing: Sound like somebody talking to us.

Avenger: Kind of far away, though. We'd better shrink to normal size to carry on a conversation.

4. **Caption:** A sip of the proper fluid, and then...

Scene: Normal-sized Avenger and Wing facing Mistybrain.

Mistybrain: I'm King Mistybrain, and I've got a right to dynamite and destroy my own palace if I want to.

Avenger: Your own palace?

Wing: He weak in head, Mist' Crimson.

5. **Scene:** Mistybrain tearing hair out.

Mistybrain: I am not weak in the head. But I've got relatives visiting me... they've been here for weeks and they won't go home. And this is the only way I knew of to get rid of them.

6. **Scene:** Wing and Avenger, Misty in middle.

Wing: Very silly. Why not tell them go home?

Misty: Because they're all kings like myself... and you can't tell a king to leave. It simply isn't done.

Avenger: He's right, Wing. Once a king gets his hands on something, he never lets go. And you can't order him to do it. You have to pry him loose.

7. **Scene:** Avenger talking to Misty, Wing at side.

Avenger: But don't worry, King, we've known what it is to have relatives staying too long ourselves... we'll help you.
P. 4

1. **Caption:** Unknown to the Crimson Avenger, however, his conversation with King Mistybrain has been overheard by His Majesty, Adelbert the Addled...

Scene: Adelbert, a villain with a long white beard, crown on his head tilted to one side, pacing up and down.

Adelbert: So they want to get rid of us, do they? Well, as the oldest king here, it's my job to stop them.

2. **Scene:** Close-up of Adelbert.

Adelbert: Those giants shrank to normal size when they took a sip from one of those bottles... hmm, I think I know what to do.

3. **Caption:** Adelbert is an old hand at plotting evil. And that evening, as Mistybrain assembles his guests for what he hopes will be their last meal...

Scene: Misty, Avenger, and Wing at head of table, facing very long table surrounded by kings.

Misty: Fellow Majesties, I have the honor to present the Crimson Avenger, who will... who will tell you... who has a message for you.

4. **Scene:** Adelbert springing up, glass in hand.

Adelbert: We shall be pleased to welcome your guests, Misty, old Majesty. But first, a toast... to you, our host!

5. **Scene:** Avenger and Wing drinking, glasses tilted back. Adelbert, who has already drunk, watching them slyly.

Adel: That's it! Drink up, everybody!

6. **Caption:** Unexpectedly...

Scene: Avenger and Wing shrinking. Adelbert staring down at them.

Wing: Mist' Crimson, we get small again!

Adelbert: Ho, ho... I spiked your drink with plenty of your own Shrinking Water.

7. **Scene:** Adelbert has put them on banquet table, is jeering at them. They're now about a couple of inches high.

Adelbert: And now, what have you to say for yourselves before I squash you like the bugs you are?

Wing: Ah, woe, look like we in soup.

Avenger: Not quite, Wing...

P. 5

1. **Scene:** Both of them leaping toward big salad bowl. This contains radishes, lettuce, tomatoes, green pepper, watercress, and anything else you want to put in.

Avenger: We're in the salad. It'll make a wonderful hiding place.

2. **Scene:** Adelbert, his face close to salad bowl, is removing several leaves of lettuce. Heroes escaping around radish.

Adelbert: So they think they'll escape me, do they? I'll show them...

3. **Scene:** Wing and Avenger have appeared on tomato half, each tossing a scallion into Adelbert's face.

Avenger: That's what you think. Scallions to you, King Adelbert!

4. **Scene:** Adelbert getting slice of tomato in eye, from salad bowl, heroes invisible.

Balloon from salad bowl: Here's a beauty treatment for your eye, tomatonose!

5. **Scene:** Adelbert, roaring.

Adelbert: The dirty little commoners! Bring me the mayonnaise... I'll eat the whole salad, and they'll have no place to hide.

6. **Scene:** Wing and Avenger have leaped to edge of bowl nearest Adelbert, tipping whole bowlful of salad into his face, including dish of mayonnaise which vegetable knocks out of his hand.

Avenger: Take the salad... we don't want it any more.

Adel: Yiii...

P. 6

1. **Scene:** Avenger and Wing hopping down from table, Adelbert some distance behind them.

Avenger: Quick, Wing, we've got to get to our Growing Water before he recovers his wits.

2. **Scene:** They've sprung toward bottle, which is open on desk. Big hand closing in on them from behind.

Avenger: There's no time to drink here... dive into the bottle.

3. **Scene:** Wing already in bottle, Avenger diving in. Wing growing inside bottle.

Wing: Glub!

4. **Caption:** The next moment...

Scene: They've grown so much they're breaking bottle apart. Adelbert looking on.

Sound: Crack!

Adel: They're growing so fast they're breaking the bottle!

Avenger: Sure! Just blink... then look at us.

5. **Scene:** They're giants; Adelbert and other kings, small compared to them, turning and running in terror.

Adel: Yiii... they're giants!

Avenger: After them, Wing. Bet they've never done an honest day's work in their life... but we'll change that. We'll find them all jobs.

6. **Scene:** Giant Wing and Avenger watching all kings scurry away so fast they can hardly see them for the dust.

Sound: Woosh!

Wing: Mist' Crimson, they run so fast we can hardly see.

Avenger: Yes, Wing, I know that any mention of hard work would send them scurrying home.

7. **Scene:** The two of them, as giants, striding over tiny railroad train that looks like toy.

Wing: But we no help King Mistybrain. He so scared by word "job," he run away too!

Avenger: Too bad. Guess the only thing for us to do is return home. It won't take us long, as giants... and when we get there, we can use our last bit of Shrinking Water to reach normal size again.

CHAPTER VI

STARRING THE VIGILANTE

LEGEND: The startled Vigilante turns up on a bristling battlefield to take an unwilling part in the weirdest of wars. And he very soon learns that things are not what they seem... and that his danger's all the greater because he didn't choose sides, and remained right in the middle of...
"GNOME MAN'S LAND!"

SPLASH PANEL: The Vigilante is in the middle, with his guns drawn, and a tense expression on his face, the guns pointing to right and left. Coming at him from one side is one group of queer distorted gnomes. From the other side, the other group.

1. **Caption**: It's a wonderful landing place the Vigilante finds in the Land of Magic... now he know how an umpire feels.

Scene: A single panel taking place of the usual two panels on this page. Vig is in the middle of battlefield. On each side is an army of gnomes. One group with large heads and small bodies, the other with small heads and large bodies. They're both armed with pikes, and wear strange helmets.

Balloon from one side: Ready for the battle to begin?

Vig: Kiyoodlin' coyotes, I <u>would</u> pick a battlefield to sit down in!

Balloon from other side: Wait a minute... what's that stranger doing there?

P. 2

1. **Scene**: A gnome general from either side approaching Vig.

First general: I never saw anything like him before, General Widdle.

Second general: Neither did I, General Tiddle.

2. **Scene**: Two generals and Vig.

Vig: Excuse me, amigos... I didn't mean to interrupt. I didn't even know any hombres like

you were fighting a war.

General: You didn't? Why, this is a very important war.

3. **Scene**: Two generals facing each other, Vig slightly at side, pushing his hat back in bewilderment.

General: We're fighting for a principle. We Littleheads firmly believe that A STRAIGHT LINE IS THE SHORTEST DISTANCE BETWEEN TWO POINTS.

Other general: And we Bigheads insist that: THE SHORTEST DISTANCE BETWEEN TWO POINTS IS A STRAIGHT LINE.

Vig: Huh..?

4. **Scene**: Vig facing both of them.

Vig: But you're both sayin' the same thing!

Little head general: Oh, no.

5. **Scene**: Littlehead and Bighead both turning away.

Littlehead: We're right... <u>they've</u> got it backwards.

Bighead: They're the ones who've got it backwards... and we'll prove it right now.

Vig: Sounds loco to me.

6. **Caption**: And as a still baffled Vigilante tries to make head or tail of this strange controversy...

Scene: Very big, distorted-looking dwarfs, very ugly, and looking like animals, coming across the battlefield at him.

Vig: Great Gila monsters, what's that?

P. 3

1. **Scene**: Vig has roped his first monster.

Vig: Better rope it first and find out what it is afterward.

2. **Scene**: Monster has shrunk in part where rope has it, just slipped out.

Vig: What..? It just stepped right out of the rope.

3. **Scene**: Vig pulling gun.

Vig: But maybe a bullet'll stop it.

4. **Scene**: Bullet shooting past monster, which is now about as thin as a broomstick.

Sound of bullet: Crack!

Vig: Well, I'll be dingbusted! There's hardly anything to shoot at!

5. **Caption**: All along the battlefront the strange creatures make their appearance, and suddenly...

Scene: Vig is small figure. A line of monsters, not all alike, approaching from each side.

Balloon from each line of monsters: Boo!

Vig: I'm hearin' things! Sounds like...

6. **Scene**: Vig staring at one group of monsters.

Monsters: Shucks! They didn't scare at all.

Vig: They are... they're tryin' to scare each other! That's the only kind of fightin' they're doin'!

P. 4

1. **Scene**: Monsters piling on Vig.

Monsters: Except with you, stranger. You tried to use weapons... that isn't allowed!

2. **Scene**: One monster has lengthened out, coiled around Vig, pinning arms to side. Another has wrapped self around his legs, so that he can't walk. A third wrapping arms around his throat.

Monster with arms around throat: So you'd better go with us and leave this battlefield, or you'll get hurt.

Vig: Ugh... the varmints got me.

3. **Caption**: Shortly, the western waddy finds himself in an underground dungeon.

Scene: Vig in dungeon, looking out through barred window.

Vig: Never seen anything like the way them coyotes can change their shapes. Wish I could do that.

4. **Scene**: Vig turning away from window.

Vig: They wouldn't have taken me so easy. I'd have just stretched out my arms a couple of yards...

5. **Scene**: Vig stretching out arm a couple of yards.

Vig: Huh..? Kiyoodlin' coyotes... I can do it!

6. **Scene**: Close-up of Vig.

Vig: Reckon there's somethin' about this place that lets people change their shapes. And I didn't even realize it.

7. **Scene**: Vig lengthening out, becoming very thin.

Vig: That kinda simplifies things. I'll just thin out a mite...

P. 5

1. **Scene**: On other side of door, Vig is coming through keyhole. Part of his body already through has broadened out again, but from about waist down, he's thin enough to go through keyhole.

Vig: ... And slip through the keyhole. Bein' able to change shape makes escapin' a pleasure.

2. **Scene**: Vig back to natural shape, watching distant armies still trying to scare each other.

Vig: Now to take care of them funny-lookin' hombres, and settle this loco quarrel.

3. **Scene**: Vig's head remains same, but his body is beginning to broaden.

Vig: Lariats and six-shooters ain't much good against them... but I reckon I know somethin' that is.

4. **Caption**: Presently, the most horrible monster ever seen in the land of gnomes makes a dramatic appearance.

Scene: Right in middle of battlefield has appeared a monster about size of horse. This is nothing but an ordinary house-fly, magnified, with Vig's head. (See Ency. under House-fly, big plate.) Two armies of startled gnomes, themselves somewhat distorted, staring at it.

Vig: BOOOO..!

Gnomes: Yiii..!

5. **Scene**: Downward shot showing Vig-monster in middle, gnomes running away on all sides.

Gnome: We give up! Please, change back!

Second Gnome: We can't stay in the same

country with a monster like <u>that</u>!

Vig (bubble): I'm just taking the shape of an ordinary house-fly magnified... but it looks worse than any dragon.

P. 6

1. **Scene:** Vig, normal again, facing normal gnomes.

Vig: You see what I can do, muchachos, so better not rile me.

Gnome: We'll be careful, stranger. We won't fight with you any more... only with each other.

2. **Scene:** Vig and gnomes.

Vig: You won't do that neither, amigos... I've found a way to settle your argument.

Gnome (Littlehead): Ah, you've decided that we're right, of course.

Bighead: No, he's decided that <u>we're</u> right.

3. **Scene:** Vig, facing startled gnomes.

Vig: <u>Both</u> of you are right. But instead of speakin' your remarks, you gotta sing them.

Bunch of gnomes: Sing them?

4. **Caption:** The Vigilante's new music students are hardly the type to make a success in opera, but soon, under his expert instruction...

Scene: Littleheads singing. Vig conducting with baton.

Littleheads: A straight line is...

5. **Scene:** Bigheads are singing, Vig turned to conduct them also.

Littleheads: The shortest distance between two points.

Bigheads: The shortest distance between two points is...

6. **Scene:** Vig conducting all.

Bigheads: A straight line. The shortest distance between two points is...

Littleheads: A straight line is the shortest distance between two points.

Vig: Perfect. This round can keep goin' forever... and you'll both be right.

7. **Caption:** With the great quarrel settled, the Vigilante heads for home, taking a shortcut through the ground itself.

Scene: Vig is slipping through ground, using his new-found power to stretch out and slip through cracks, etc.

Vig: Bein' able to thin out and slip between cracks in the ground makes gettin' home simple. Hope the rest of the boys are there to meet me.

CHAPTER VII

WILLIE'S LAST WISH

1. **Caption:** Returned from their exile in the Land of Magic, the Soldiers of Victory once more confront Willie Wisher.

Scene: Heroes confronting Willie.

Kid: Now, Mr. Wisher, it's time we settled things. You seem to have a dangerous gift.

Vigilante: And you sure raise a mighty rumpus with it.

Willie: Oh, that's nothing to what I could do if I tried.

2. **Scene:** Willie.

Willie: I wish... I wish there were a great big steel wall between us, so that you couldn't bother me.

3. **Scene:** Sideview, showing wall between them, as per Willie's wish.

Willie: Now, what are you going to do about that?

Knight: The answer is nigh as easy as wishing.

4. **Scene:** Knight has slashed through steel wall with his sword, chopping it up into several pieces.

Knight: My enchanted blade will cut through any steel.

Willie: Hmm, not bad. But I wish I knew what you'd do if I wished up a bunch of gorillas to protect me.

P. 2

1. **Scene:** About half a dozen gorillas confronting heroes.

Willie: They're vicious beasts... don't you think you'd better run?

Avenger: Not yet, pal.

2. **Caption:** The Crimson Avenger shatters a tiny glass capsule, and a crimson cloud arises...

Scene: Gorillas in middle of crimson cloud, Avenger at side.

Avenger: What they can't see, they can't hurt.

3. **Scene:** Vig's lasso circling around a couple of gorillas.

Vig: Which makes them so mad, they're fit to be tied... so I reckon I'll do that.

4. **Scene:** Willie in pose of deep thought, gorillas vanishing.

Willie: That was easy for you too. But let me see... suppose I wished up some more intelligent bodyguards... professional thugs?

5. **Scene:** Bunch of thugs plunging at heroes.

Stripesy: Gosh, Kid, look what's here. Don't they make you feel at home?

Kid: They sure do, Stripesy. Signals R 76...

6. **Scene:** Stripesy has thrown Kid head first into thug's stomach.

Kid: The old battering ram breaches their lines.

Thug: Yiii..!

P. 3

1. **Scene:** Kid and Stripesy each holding thug by feet,. Swinging them around to knock down other thugs.

Stripesy: And this finishes them. I could do this with my eyes closed, Kid.

Kid: Better close _their_ eyes, Stripesy... it makes the trick safer.

2. **Caption:** Seconds later, with the thugs vanquished...

Scene: Willie riding on a broomstick away from them.

Willie: You boys are pretty good. I think I'll leave and decide later what to do with you.

3. **Scene:** G.A. and Speedy shooting arrowlines at broomstick.

G.A.: No, you don't, Willie... we can decide

right now.

4. **Scene:** Arrows have sunk into broomstick. G.A. and Speedy have tugged on arrowlines to pull broomstick out from under.

G.A.: Better get a horse!

Speedy: Hope you don't land with too much of a bump.

Willie: Thanks, but don't worry. I wish...

5. **Scene:** Willie landing on an enormous pillow.

Willie: For a big pillow.

Speedy: Gosh, that appeared just in the nick of time.

6. **Scene:** Willie facing them, a pleased smile on his face.

Willie: Oh, I've learned to wish fast. Let me see now, what shall I think of to plague you next?

7. **Scene:** Avenger facing Willie.

Avenger: Wait a minute, Willie... before you go to any more trouble, suppose we Legionnaires talk this over.

Willie: Go ahead. No matter what you cook up, you won't be able to get the better of me.

P. 4

1. **Scene:** Avenger facing other heroes.

Avenger: Boys, he's right. If we keep on like this, we'll never get the better of Willie. He's just playing with us.

G.A.: Yes, and when he gets tired playing, he'll wish us thousands of miles away, as he did before.

Kid: We've got to use brains instead of brawn.

2. **Caption:** And so, brains are racked to the limit, and soon...

Scene: Avenger, Wing, Vig facing Willie.

Avenger: Willie, the more we think about you, the more impressed we are. Your powers are simply terrific.

Vig: You can do a lot of good and a lot of harm.

Wing: Without you even know.

Willie: Harm? I don't mean any harm.

3. **Scene:** Kid, Speedy, Knight facing him.

Speedy: But you must have done plenty of it. Suppose you just wish for some money. At once it's in front of you.

Kid: But where did it come from? Maybe from a poor man who needed it to pay off a mortgage.

Knight: Or mayhap from a widow supporting her needy brood.

Willie: Gee, I never thought of that.

4. **Scene:** G.A. and Stripesy facing Willie.

G.A.: Yes, Willie, we know your intentions were never bad... but it's men like you who do the most damage.

Stripesy: When I think how many people you must have hurt without meanin' to... I feel like bustin' out cryin'. Boo hoo!

Willie: Boo hoo! Oh, you make me feel so awful!

5. **Scene:** Willie with flood of tears coming from him.

Willie: I wish I had never been born!

6. **Scene:** All heroes staring at where Willie was.

Sound: Pop!

Stripesy: Gosh, he disappeared... just like we figured he would.

G.A.: Yes, he wished he had never been born, and so it's as if he never had. In fact, it's as if he had never existed... and we never had those adventures he sent us on!

7. **Scene:** Back to the screen again. There is a subtitle, THE END. Shoman is silhouetted in front of the screen.

Shoman: And so, ladies and gentlemen, we conclude our program. I thank you.

P. 5

1. **Scene:** All heroes rising together from front row to confront Shoman.

Balloon from all: Just a minute, Mr. Shoman.

Shoman: The Soldiers of Victory themselves! Why, I didn't know you were in the audience...

2. **Scene:** Shoman sweating and wiping brow.

Shoman: This is a terrible... I mean, this is a terribly great honor. A pleasure, I assure you. Come up on the stage, gentlemen, where the audience can see you.

3. **Scene:** On stage, sweating Shoman facing heroes.

Shoman: Pssst... just a word in private. I, er... you see, I'm showing this picture for charity, and I plan to show it again and raise a great deal of money. So, please don't ruin things!

4. **Scene:** Shoman facing audience. One or two heroes at side.

Balloons from audience: It's a fake! It never happened! You made it in a studio!

Shoman: They already doubt that it's authentic... please don't encourage their suspicions.

Avenger: We won't lie to them, Mr. Shoman... that's against our principles.

G.A.: But you've given them a good show, so we'll give you a break.

5. **Scene:** Kid facing audience. Vig at side.

Kid: Folks, this is the most wonderful newsreel ever made. Wouldn't it be swell if all it shows had really happened?

Vig: It sure would. And one thing you can be sure of, pardners...

6. **Scene:** Heroes together, facing dimly seen audience.

Heroes: Wrong is righted and justice done wherever we are... right here or in the Land of Magic! You believe that, don't you?

Audience: Sure, we believe it! Hurray for John Shoman!

Second Balloon: And for the Soldiers of Victory!

ARTURO CAZENEUVE

Born in 1919 in Argentina, Arturo Cazeneuve and his older brother Luis moved to the United States in 1939 to work in the burgeoning American comics industry. A contributor to the Eisner & Iger shop, he also shared a studio with his brother Luis and fellow artist Pierce Rice through the early 1940s, providing artwork for the Harvey and Fox features Black Cat, the Flame, Blockbuster Barton and the Lynx as well as such DC features as the Seven Soldiers of Victory, the Newsboy Legion and the Guardian. From 1945 through 1948 Cazeneuve was an illustrator for the U.S. Army newspaper *Stars and Stripes*, and from 1970 through 1983 he served as an illustrator and assistant art editor for *Time* magazine's overseas edition. He passed away in 1992.

LUIS CAZENEUVE

Born in Argentina in 1908, Luis Cazeneuve emigrated to the United States in 1939 with his younger brother Arturo to find work in the American comics field. Already an accomplished cartoonist in his native country, Cazeneuve had illustrated the adventure strips *Quique, el Niño Pirata* (*Quique, the Pirate Boy*) *Aventuras de Caza del Pibe Palito* (*Pibe Palito's Hunting Adventures*) *and Aventuras de dos Argentinos en un País Salvaje* (*Adventures of Two Argentines in a Wild Country*) before moving north. Working for both the Eisner & Iger shop and his studio partnership with Arturo and Pierce Rice, Cazeneuve contributed to a wide variety of features in the 1940s, including the Blue Beetle, Banshee and the Green Mask for Fox; the Boy Heroes, Dr. Miracle and the Phantom Sphinx for Harvey; the Red Raven, Jack Frost and Captain America for Timely/Marvel; and Aquaman, the Boy Commandos and all of the members of the Seven Soldiers of Victory for DC. Cazeneuve left the industry in 1949, and died in New York City in 1977.

JOE SAMACHSON

Joe Samachson was born on October 13, 1906 in Trenton, New Jersey. He earned a doctorate in chemistry and became a biochemist, and as a writer he translated a number of scientific papers as well as writing books on theater and ballet with his wife Dorothy. His science fiction work, written under the pseudonym William Morrison, includes two novels serialized in *Startling Stories* and several Captain Future novels written around 1942. Later that same year he began working for DC, where he wrote for such characters as Batman, Airwave, Robotman, the Star-Spangled Kid and the Seven Soldiers of Victory, as well as a string of science fiction stories between 1955 and 1956 for STRANGE ADVENTURES and MYSTERY IN SPACE. Samachson died in 1980.

JON SMALL

Born in England and educated at St. Martin's School of Art, Jon Small drew the U.K.-published adventures of *The Lone Ranger* from 1930 until 1939, when he moved to the United States to work in the American comic book field. After illustrating for Feature, Street & Smith and Fawcett (where he was the original artist for Bulletman, one of the first of the comic book super-heroes), he began working for DC in 1943, inking covers and drawing such features as the Star-Spangled Kid, the Crimson Avenger and Vigilante. Though he returned to England in 1955, Small continued working in comics both in the U.S. and the U.K., contributing work to Dell and a variety of British publishers throughout the 1950s. He passed away in 1966.

Some biographical material provided by Craig Delich.